Managing Knowledge, Absorptive Capacity and Innovation

Series on Technology Management

Series Editor: J. Tidd (*University of Sussex, UK*) ISSN 0219-9823

The Technology Management Series is dedicated to the advancement of academic research and management practice in the field of technology and innovation management. The series features titles which adopt an interdisciplinary, multifunctional approach to the management of technology and innovation, and includes work which seeks to integrate the management of technological, market and organisational innovation. All titles are based on original empirical research, and includes research monographs and multiauthor edited works. The focus throughout is on the management of technology and innovation at the level of the organisation or firm, rather than on the analysis of sectoral trends or national policy.

Published

Vol. 37 *Managing Knowledge, Absorptive Capacity and Innovation*
by Joseph Tidd (University of Sussex, UK)

Vol. 36 *Digital Disruptive Innovation*
edited by Joe Tidd (University of Sussex, UK)

Vol. 35 *Developing Holistic Strategic Management in the Advanced ICT Era*
by Mitsuru Kodama (Nihon University, Japan)

Vol. 34 *Managing Innovation: Internationalization of Innovation*
edited by Alexander Brem (Friedrich-Alexander-Universität Erlangen-Nürnberg, Germany & University of Southern Denmark, Denmark), Joe Tidd (University of Sussex, UK) & Tugrul Daim (Portland State University, USA)

Vol. 33 *Managing Innovation: What Do We Know About Innovation Success Factors?*
edited by Alexander Brem (Friedrich-Alexander-Universität Erlangen-Nürnberg, Germany & University of Southern Denmark, Denmark), Joe Tidd (University of Sussex, UK) & Tugrul Daim (Portland State University, USA)

Vol. 32 *Managing Innovation: Understanding and Motivating Crowds*
edited by Alexander Brem (Friedrich-Alexander-Universität Erlangen-Nürnberg, Germany & University of Southern Denmark, Denmark), Joe Tidd (University of Sussex, UK) & Tugrul Daim (Portland State University, USA)

Vol. 31 *Innovation Heroes: Understanding Customers as a Valuable Innovation Resource*
by Fiona Schweitzer (Grenoble École de Management, France & University of Applied Sciences Upper Austria, Austria) & Joe Tidd (University of Sussex, UK)

Vol. 30 *Innovation Discovery: Network Analysis of Research and Invention Activity for Technology Management*
edited by Tugrul Daim (Portland State University, USA) & Alan Pilkington (University of Westminster, UK)

More information on this series can also be found at http://www.worldscientific.com/series/stm

(Continued at the end of the book)

SERIES ON TECHNOLOGY MANAGEMENT – VOL. 37

Managing Knowledge, Absorptive Capacity and Innovation

Editor

Joe Tidd

Science Policy Research Unit (SPRU)
University of Sussex, UK

World Scientific

NEW JERSEY • LONDON • SINGAPORE • BEIJING • SHANGHAI • HONG KONG • TAIPEI • CHENNAI • TOKYO

Published by

World Scientific Publishing Europe Ltd.
57 Shelton Street, Covent Garden, London WC2H 9HE
Head office: 5 Toh Tuck Link, Singapore 596224
USA office: 27 Warren Street, Suite 401-402, Hackensack, NJ 07601

Library of Congress Cataloging-in-Publication Data
Names: Tidd, Joseph, 1960– editor.
Title: Managing knowledge, absorptive capacity and innovation / [edited by] Joseph Tidd, University of Sussex, UK.
Description: USA : World Scientific, 2021. | Series: Series on technology management, 0219-9823 ; Vol. 37 | Includes bibliographical references.
Identifiers: LCCN 2021009491 | ISBN 9781800610309 (hardcover) | ISBN 9781800610316 (ebook) | ISBN 9781800610323 (ebook other)
Subjects: LCSH: Knowledge management. | Organizational learning. | Technological innovations--Management.
Classification: LCC HD30.2 .M36454 2021 | DDC 658.4/038--dc23
LC record available at https://lccn.loc.gov/2021009491

British Library Cataloguing-in-Publication Data
A catalogue record for this book is available from the British Library.

For any available supplementary material, please visit
https://www.worldscientific.com/worldscibooks/10.1142/Q0303#t=suppl

Desk Editors: Priyanka Murugan/Natalie Wee/Karimah Samsudin

Typeset by Stallion Press
Email: enquiries@stallionpress.com

About the Author

Joe Tidd is Professor of technology and innovation management at the Science Policy Research Unit (SPRU), visiting Professor at University College London and was previously at Imperial College, Copenhagen Business School and Rotterdam School of Management. He was policy adviser to the CBI (Confederation of British Industry), presented expert evidence to three Select Committee Enquiries at the House of Commons and Lords and was the only academic member of the UK Government Innovation Review. He worked on the program at the Massachusetts Institute of Technology (MIT) that identified Lean Production, with global consultants Arthur D. Little, CAP Gemini and McKinsey, and the international agencies UNESCO in Africa and WHO in Asia. He has written nine books and more than 90 papers, including *Managing Innovation* (7th edition, 2020, with John Bessant), has 25,000 research citations (Google Scholar) and is Managing Editor of the *International Journal of Innovation Management.*

Contents

Introduction

Joe Tidd

Organizations can acquire knowledge by experience, experimentation or acquisition (Tidd and Bessant, 2020). Of these, learning from experience appears to be the least effective. In practice, organizations do not easily translate experience into knowledge. Moreover, learning may be unintentional and so unexploited, or it may not result in improvement or innovation. Organizations can incorrectly learn, and they can learn practices which are ineffective or harmful, such as popular but unproven or inappropriate "best-practices" (Tidd, 2021; Tidd and Bessant, 2018; Tidd and Thuriaux-Alemán, 2016).

Experimentation is a more systematic approach to learning. It is a central feature of formal R&D activities, market research and some organizational alliances and networks. When undertaken with intent, a strategy of learning through incremental trial and error acknowledges the complexities of existing technologies and markets, as well as the uncertainties associated with technology and market change and in forecasting the future. The use of alliances for learning is less common and requires an intent to use them as an opportunity for learning, a receptivity to external know-how and partners of sufficient transparency. Whether the acquisition of know-how results in organizational learning depends on the rationale for the acquisition and the process of acquisition and transfer. For example, the cumulative effect of outsourcing various technologies based on the comparative transaction costs may limit future technological options and reduce competitiveness in the long term.

A more active approach to the acquisition of knowledge involves identifying sources in the internal and external environments of the organization. Exploiting internal knowledge is the focus of the field of Knowledge Management, whereas external knowledge is central to Open Innovation. Open Innovation proposes that organizations should acquire valuable resources from other organizations and share internal resources for new product/service development, but the question of in what circumstances and how a firm sources external knowledge, shares internal knowledge and — above all — combines these activities to create innovations is less clear. The research on Open Innovation has focused on the sources of external, or inbound, knowledge — such as suppliers, customers or partners, and well as the search mechanisms to help identify these sources, but it has relatively little to say about how organizations subsequently internalize, adapt and apply such knowledge. The aim of this book is to explore how the classic notion of absorptive capacity (Cohen and Levinthal, 1990) can help to explain how organizations translate external knowledge into innovation.

An important challenge in Open Innovation is the capability to absorb and exploit external inbound knowledge, and how internal R&D may facilitate or hinder this (Tidd and Trewhella, 1997). Conventionally, internal R&D expenditure is used as a proxy for absorptive capacity, but in the context of Open Innovation, this can be problematic. Internal R&D may also constrain present and future absorption, and restrict exploitation for a number of reasons, e.g. degree of development, structural, geographical or relevance to existing business units and markets. Conversely, external sources of innovation can be difficult to identify, evaluate and absorb, but may be more codified, as by definition they are available in the market, and more fully developed to demonstrate commercial potential.

We argue that two key issues may have undermined research and practice. Firstly, in open innovation research and practice, much of the focus has been on how organizations search for potential inbound innovation (Schweitzer *et al.*, 2011), and the extent to which inbound innovation complements or substitutes for internal

R&D (Denicolai *et al.*, 2014, 2016). However, although internal R&D and technology sourcing may show some complementarities, they remain two inherently different activities. There has been relatively little research on the subsequent challenges of absorbing and exploiting inbound knowledge. We therefore contribute to a shift in the debate from potentially misleading general prescriptions, and in this book provide conceptual and empirical insights into the challenges of absorbing and exploiting inbound external sources of innovation.

Managing Knowledge and Learning

Clearly, individuals do learn within the context of organizations. This context affects their learning, which, in turn, may affect the performance of the organization. However, individuals and organizations are very different entities, and there is no reason why organizational learning should be conceptually or empirically the same as learning by individuals or individuals learning within organizations. Existing theory and research on organizational learning has been dominated by a weak metaphor of human learning and cognitive development, but such simplistic and inappropriate anthropomorphizing of organizational characteristics has contributed to confused research and misleading conclusions.

Knowledge can be embodied in people, organizational culture, routines and tools, technologies, processes and systems. Organizations consist of a variety of individuals, groups and functions with different cultures, goals and frames of reference. Knowledge management consists of identifying and sharing knowledge across these disparate entities. There is a range of integrating mechanisms that can help to do this. In their influential book, Nonaka and Takeuchi (1995) argue that the conversion of tacit to explicit knowledge is a critical mechanism underlying the link between individual and organizational knowledge. They argue that all new knowledge originates with an individual, but that through a process of dialogue, discussion, experience sharing and observation, such knowledge is amplified at the group and organizational levels. This creates an expanding community of interaction, or knowledge network, which crosses intra- and interorganizational levels and boundaries. Such knowledge networks are a means to accumulate knowledge from outside the organization, share it widely within the organization and store it for future use.

Knowledge sharing and distribution is the process by which information from different sources is shared and, therefore, leads to new knowledge or understanding. Greater organizational learning occurs when more of an organization's components obtain new knowledge and recognize it as being of potential use. Tacit knowledge is not easily imitated by competitors because it is not fully encoded, but for the same reasons it may not be fully visible to all members of an organization. As a result, organizational units with potentially synergistic information may not be aware of where such information could be applied. The speed and extent to which knowledge is shared between members of an organization are likely to be a function of how codified the knowledge is.

This process of conversion and connection is underpinned by communities of practice. A community of practice is a group of people related by a shared task, process or the need to solve a problem, rather than by formal structural or functional relationships. Through practice, a group within which knowledge is shared becomes a community of practice through a common understanding of what it does, how to do it and how it relates to other communities of practice.

Within communities of practice, people share tacit knowledge and learn through experimentation. Therefore, the formation and maintenance of such communities represents an important link between individual and organizational learning. These communities naturally emerge around local work practice and so tend to reinforce functional or professional silos, but also can extend to wider, dispersed networks of similar practitioners.

The existence of communities of practice facilitates the sharing of knowledge within a community, due to both the sense of collective identity and the existence of a significant common knowledge base. However, the sharing of knowledge between communities is much more problematic due to the lack of both these elements. Thus, the dynamics of knowledge sharing within and between communities of practice are likely to be very different, with the sharing of knowledge between communities typically being much more complex, difficult and problematic.

Many factors can prevent the sharing of knowledge between communities of practice, such as the distinctiveness of different knowledge bases and lack of common knowledge, goals, assumptions and interpretative frameworks. These differences significantly increase the difficulty not just of sharing knowledge between communities but appreciating the knowledge of another community.

For example, cross-functional team working can help to promote this intercommunal exchange. Functional diversity tends to extend the range of knowledge available and increase the number of options considered, but can also have a negative effect on group cohesiveness and the cost of projects and efficiency of decision-making. However, a major benefit of cross-functional team working is the access it provides to the bodies of knowledge that are external to the team. In general, a high frequency of knowledge sharing outside of a group is associated with improved technical and project performance, as gatekeeper individuals pick up and import vital signals and knowledge. In particular, cross-functional composition in teams is argued to permit access to disciplinary knowledge outside. Therefore, cross-functional team working is a critical way of promoting the exchange of knowledge and practice across disciplines and communities.

Absorptive Capacity and Open Innovation

Arguably, much of the work on knowledge management focuses on the sources, storage and sharing of knowledge within the organization, whereas Open Innovation is more concerned with exploiting external sources. However, this simple dichotomy between open and closed approaches is unhelpful and not realistic (Tidd, 2013).

Much of this research focuses on the external sources of knowledge, such as suppliers (Brem and Tidd, 2012) or customers (Schweitzer and Tidd, 2018), and how to search for these. Searching consists of identifying relevant sources, filtering and evaluating potential opportunities from outside the organization, including related and emerging technologies, new market and services, which can be exploited by applying or combining with existing competencies. Opportunity recognition, which is a precursor to entrepreneurial behaviour, is often associated with a flash of genius, but in practice, is probably more often the result of a laborious process of environmental scanning. External scanning can be conducted at various levels. It can be an operational initiative with market- or technology-focused managers becoming more conscious of new developments within their own environments or a top-driven initiative where venture managers or professional capital firms are used to monitor and invest in potential opportunities.

More recent research has begun to explore the influences of inbound open innovation on outcomes and performance. Schweitzer *et al.* (2011) found Open Innovation in general to have a positive influence on performance in dynamic settings, and that customers are central when market dynamics are high, but suppliers are more important in technologically challenging environments. Significantly, inbound knowledge from other sectors is found to be effective irrespective of the setting, which is consistent with the notion of complementary assets. Returns from Open Innovation are greatest when firms maintain their internal research capacity, and advocate strong cross-functional collaboration. Cruz-González *et al.* (2014) found that search breadth was positively associated with performance in more mature sectors, but harms performance in technologically dynamic environments. Denicolai *et al.* (2014, 2016) show that the balance between internal and external knowledge is critical to innovation, and that this relationship changes over time.

Such studies highlight that interaction between internal and external knowledge is closely associated with the dynamic capabilities of an organization, and its ability to accumulate and renew knowledge over time (Tidd, 2012). Therefore, the simple dichotomy between open and closed approaches is unhelpful and not realistic (Tidd, 2013). In particular, we need to better understand the interactions between internal and external knowledge, and how these influence innovation outcomes under different conditions (Tidd, 2002). This provides an opportunity to combine contemporary interests in Open Innovation with the classic notion of absorptive capacity (Cohen and Levinthal, 1990), to better understand how organizations can manage the absorption and exploitation of inbound external sources of knowledge in order to innovate.

References

Brem, A. and J. Tidd (2012). *Perspectives on Supplier Innovation: Theories, Concepts and Empirical Insights on Open Innovation and the Integration of Suppliers.* Imperial College Press, London.

Cohen, W.M. and D.A. Levinthal (1990). Absorptive capacity: A new perspective on learning and innovation, *Administrative Science Quarterly*, 35(1), 128–152.

Cruz-González, J., P. López-Sáez, J. EmilioNavas-López and M. Delgado-Verde, M. (2014). Open search strategies and firm performance: The different moderating role of technological environmental dynamism, *Technovation*, 35(1), 32–45.

Denicolai, S., M. Ramirez and J. Tidd (2014). Creating and capturing value from external knowledge: the moderating role of knowledge intensity, *R&D Management*, 44 (3), 248–264.

Denicolai, S., M. Ramirez and J. Tidd (2016). Overcoming the false dichotomy between internal R&D and external knowledge acquisition: Absorptive capacity dynamics over time, *Technological Forecasting and Social Change*, 104(1), 57–65.

Nonaka, I. and K. Takeuchi (1995). *The Knowledge Creating Company.* Oxford University Press, Oxford.

Schweitzer, F.M., O. Gassmann and K. Gaubinger (2011). Open innovation and its ability to embrace turbulent environments, *International Journal of Innovation Management*, 15(6), 1191–1208.

Schweitzer, F.M. and J. Tidd (2018). *Innovation Heroes: Understanding Customers as a Valuable Innovation Resource.* World Scientific, London.

Tidd, J. (2002). Innovation management in context: environment, organization and performance, *International Journal of Management Reviews*, 3(3), 169–183.

Tidd, J. (2012). *From Knowledge Management to Strategic Competence* (3rd Edition). Imperial College Press, London.

Tidd, J. (2013). *Open Innovation Research, Management and Practice.* Imperial College Press, London.

Tidd, J. (2021). A review and critical assessment of the ISO56002 innovation management systems standard: Evidence and limitations, *International Journal of Innovation Management*, 25(1). https://doi.org/10.1142/S1363919621500493.

Tidd, J. and J. Bessant (2018). Innovation management challenges: From fads to fundamentals, *International Journal of Innovation Management*, 22(5), 1840007.

Tidd, J. and J. Bessant (2020). *Managing Innovation: Integrating Technological, Market and Organizational Change* (7th Edition). Wiley, New York.

Tidd, J. and B. Thuriaux-Alemán (2016). Innovation management practices: Cross-sectorial adoption, variation and effectiveness, *R&D Management*, 46(3), 1024–1043.

Tidd, J. and M. Trewhella (1997). Organizational and technological antecedents for knowledge acquisition and learning, *R&D Management*, 27(4), 359–375.

Section 1

Knowledge Management

Chapter 1

EFFECTS OF EMPLOYEE CREATIVE PROBLEM-SOLVING ON INNOVATION OUTCOMES AND NON-FINANCIAL PERFORMANCE: THE MODERATING ROLE OF CULTURE AND COMMUNICATION[†]

NOUFOU OUEDRAOGO

School of Business, MacEwan University
Edmonton, Canada

MOHAMMED LAID OUAKOUAK*

College of Business Administration
Gulf University for Science & Technology, Mishref, Kuwait
ouakouak.m@gust.edu.kw

TAREK SALEM

School of Business, MacEwan University
Edmonton, Canada

Published 8 October 2019

The purpose of this paper is to investigate the effects of employees' creative problem-solving on organisations' innovation outcomes, as well as the effects of innovation outcomes on organisations non-financial performance. Based on a sample of 320 participants from diverse organisations, using structural equation modelling techniques, we find that creative problem-solving does not have any effect on innovation outcomes, except with the moderating influence of an innovative culture or communication. We also find that innovation outcomes have a positive relationship with non-financial performance. We make theoretical contributions into the antecedents of innovation outcomes, while offering several practical insights for leading creative employees and managing innovation.

Keywords: Innovative culture; creative problem-solving; innovation outcome; non-financial performance; size; purpose.

*Corresponding author.

[†]This article originally appeared in *International Journal of Innovation Management*, **24** 2050069-1-28

Introduction

Innovation is a key ingredient for the long-term success and even survival of contemporary organisations. Defined as the "successful implementation of creative ideas within an organisation" (Amabile and Pratt, 2016, p. 158), innovation has attracted the attention of both scholars and practitioners over the last three decades (Schippers *et al.*, 2015), and organisations have increasingly become acutely aware of its role in sustaining a competitive advantage and organisational effectiveness (Li *et al.*, 2018). The need for innovation will certainly remain high over the years to come, given that organisations operate in increasingly volatile and complex market environments, characterised by rapid technological changes combined with fierce global competition.

Research on innovation so far has focused on the factors that enable it (Orfila-Sintes and Mattsson, 2009; Yoshida *et al.*, 2014), the obstacles that hinder it (Birgit *et al.*, 2018) and its importance in building a competitive advantage (Li *et al.*, 2018) and facilitating effective organisational performance (Anderson *et al.*, 2014).

Innovation and creativity are sometimes used interchangeably (Baer, 2012). Being two components of the same process (Sarooghi *et al.*, 2015), they certainly feed into one another (Amabile and Pratt, 2016). However, they are two distinct concepts in that creativity, which refers to the production of novel and useful ideas (Amabile and Pratt, 2016), representing the "fuzzy front end" of innovation (Koen *et al.*, 2002). In other words, creativity is only one part of innovation, which requires first and foremost creative individuals, among other conditions, in order to be realised. Indeed, while innovation is typically analysed at the organisational level, creativity is commonly examined at the individual or team level (Amabile and Pratt, 2016).

Research shows that creativity is also increasingly important not only for innovation, but also for organisational effectiveness and prosperity (Shalley *et al.*, 2009; Liu *et al.*, 2012). Beyond these studies, the positive influence of creativity on innovation is well supported in the literature (Hirst *et al.*, 2009). For instance, Bharadwaj and Menon (2000) noted that creative employees provide their organisations with significant input necessary for the development of new products or services. Given the importance of creativity, most organisations constantly seek ways to promote it (Jiang and Gu, 2015). However, the conversion of creative ideas into innovation has long been a challenge for organisations (Sarooghi *et al.*, 2015). For instance, there is still a knowledge gap on how employees' creative problem-solving influences innovation outcomes and non-financial performance, which we endeavour to address in this study. Creative problem-solving is one of the components of adaptive performance (Pulakos *et al.*, 2000), which is defined as an employee's ability to adapt to dynamic work situations by adjusting personal behaviours to fit new requirements (Hesketh and Neal, 1999). The other components of adaptive performance include coping with uncertainty; handling emergencies or crisis situations; handling stress; learning new tasks, technologies and procedures and exhibiting interpersonal, cultural and physical adaptability (Pulakos *et al.*, 2000).

Creative problem-solving encourages whole-brain, iterative thinking and is more productive when done in teams (Lumsdaine and Lumsdaine, 1994). It challenges conventional thinking and enables individuals and teams to look at situations from different and new perspectives. As such, it can offer a new explanation for innovation dynamics and organisational non-financial performance.

Hence, the purpose of this study is twofold: (1) to investigate the effects of creative problem-solving on innovation outcomes and (2) to investigate the effects of innovation outcomes on non-financial performance.

Although various empirical studies point to a positive relationship between employee creativity and organisational innovation outcomes, it is still unclear how and under what conditions creative problem-solving impacts innovation outcomes. The relationship between creativity and innovation is not systematic; a study by Sarooghi *et al.* (2015) suggested that the process of converting creative ideas into innovative outcomes is affected by several internal and external factors. We, therefore, investigate the possible moderating roles of innovative culture and organisational communication on the creativity–innovation relationship. According to Tushman and O'Reilly (1997), culture is a critical element in innovation management. Organisational communication is another key element in the innovation process, as reported in the literature (e.g., Garcia *et al.*, 2014; Lewis, 2007). In particular, the process of turning creative ideas into innovative products requires effective communication (Adams *et al.*, 2006; Lewis *et al.*, 2001). Communication within the organisation also enhances trust and commitment among organisational members, which are important ingredients for the implementation of innovation processes (Byrne and LeMay, 2006).

Despite numerous empirical studies on the subject, the relationship between innovation and organisational performance remains uncertain (Bowen *et al.*, 2010), although Damanpour and Schneider (2006) noted that innovation is generally seen as a critical driver of organisational performance. Eze (2018) also observed that most related studies have employed financial performance measures; as such, the effect of innovation on non-financial performance appears not to have been fully explored. Indeed, researchers have extensively explored the influence of innovation on financial performance, showing, for instance, its effect on sales (Cassiman and Veugelers, 2006) and profitability (Jansen *et al.*, 2006). However, organisational performance is a broad concept that goes beyond financial accomplishments for two reasons. First, not all organisations measure their success by their financial performance. For example, non-profit organisations may not find financial indicators relevant. Secondly, even for-profit organisations should also consider non-financial measures because financial assessments provide only a limited perspective of an organisation's performance and do not indicate its ability to sustain long-term success (Kaplan and Norton, 2007). In addition, innovation is a tool for improving short-term financial performance; it is also a survival kit (Burisch and Wohlgemuth, 2016). Innovation should, therefore, also serve the organisation over the long run by meeting performance indicators pertaining to important stakeholders, such as customers, employees and shareholders. Thus, this research tests the influence of innovation outcomes on non-financial performance as well.

The rest of the paper is organised as follows. First, we review the extent literature on creative problem-solving and its possible influence on innovation outcomes and non-financial performance. In so doing, we provide the theoretical underpinnings of our hypotheses. Then, we present our methods of data collection and analysis, followed by our findings. Finally, we discuss our results and highlight our contributions to theory and practice, while suggesting future research directions.

Literature and Hypotheses

Influence of creative problem-solving on innovation outcomes

Creativity is an individual's ability to devise new approaches and find solutions to tackle complex or unknown problems (Charbonnier-Voirin and Roussel, 2012). As such, organisations increasingly encourage individual creativity because it is an important source of innovation and competitive advantage (Zhang and Bartol, 2010). For instance, based on a meta-analysis, Sarooghi *et al.* (2015) found strong positive relationships between individual creativity and individual innovation. Likewise, a study by Naranjo-Valencia *et al.* (2017) concluded that the more innovative the employee behaviour, the more radical the innovation will be. In fact, for innovation to take place in an organisation, employees should seek opportunities, generate and evaluate ideas and finally develop plans for implementing those ideas (Abstein and Spieth, 2014). Creative employees thus provide an organisation with the input needed for subsequent development of new products and services (Bharadwaj and Menon, 2000) such that enhancing employee creativity results in more innovation for the organisation (Çokpekin and Knudsen, 2012; Sarooghi *et al.*, 2015). In general, the literature assumes that innovation requires employees to exhibit innovative behaviours (Abstein and Spieth, 2014;

Griffin *et al.*, 2009) and to be creative (Amabile and Pratt, 2016). Considering these findings, we predict that employee creative problem-solving leads to innovation outcomes for the organisation. Accordingly, we hypothesise the following:

H1: *Creative problem-solving is positively related to innovation outcomes.*

The moderating effect of an innovative culture on the relationship between creative problem-solving and innovation outcomes

Organisational culture generally refers to values communicated through norms, artefacts and observed behavioural patterns (Homburg and Pflesser, 2000). Colloquially defined as "the way we do things around here" (Lundy and Cowling, 1996, p. 168), organisational culture touches deeper levels of basic shared values, assumptions and beliefs (Martín-de Castro *et al.*, 2013). An organisation's culture strongly influences employees' behaviours and does so beyond formal control systems, procedures and authority (Hogan and Coote, 2014). As such, it acts as a control on employees' behaviour (Büschgens *et al.*, 2013). In fact, once the culture is engrained and embedded in an organisation, it even shapes the style of leadership (Dastmalchian *et al.*, 2000). A good understanding of an organisation's culture, therefore, provides insight into why some employees act and behave a certain way and why certain outcomes are achieved. Not only is organisational culture a key variable in the success or failure of an organisation (Detert *et al.*, 2000), it is also a moderator in the achievement of better business performance (Hsu and Fang, 2009). Specifically, culture moderates the relationship between creativity and innovation (Sarooghi *et al.*, 2015).

Given that organisational culture is a multi-dimensional concept (Martins and Terblanche, 2003), we focus this study on innovative culture. The latter is an organisation's orientation or inclination towards experimenting with ideas, alternatives and approaches by exploring new resources, challenging and possibly breaking existing norms and creating new products to improve its performance (Ireland *et al.*, 2006). In other words, when an organisation's culture tolerates risk, supports personal growth and development and encourages employees to exhibit their innovation potential, that culture may be labelled innovative (Menzel *et al.*, 2007).

An innovative culture, thus, indirectly influences employee behaviour (Martins and Terblanche, 2003) and enables leaders to deliberately act to stimulate idea generation and application (De Jong and Den Hartog, 2007). Therefore, an innovative culture is essential for organisational innovation (Škerlavaj *et al.*, 2010), which complements rational managerial tools (Martins and Terblanche, 2003).

Notwithstanding the importance of culture for innovation in general, studies on the specific influence of innovative culture on the relationship between creative problem-solving and innovative outcomes are still warranted. Although the componential theory of innovation (Amabile and Pratt, 2016) hinted at a possible relationship, no empirical support was provided.

In fact, some aspects of organisational culture may prevent creative problem-solving from turning into innovation for an organisation. For instance, contrary to low power distance cultures that positively impact innovation (Çakar and Ertürk, 2010), high power distance organisations tend to have strict rules and procedure-based control systems that may inhibit employee creativity and inventiveness (Herbig and Dunphy, 1998). Likewise, avoidance of uncertainty is negatively related to innovativeness (Thomas and Mueller, 2000).

Conversely, employees exhibit more innovative behaviour when they perceive their supervisors as supporting such behaviour (Jansen *et al.*, 2006). Along the same lines, Litchfield *et al.* (2015) reported that the positive relationship between individual creativity and organisational innovation is strengthened by a highly creative team environment. Therefore, we contend that the extent to which individual creative problem-solving results in innovation depends on how innovation-friendly the culture is.

H2: *Innovative culture moderates the relationship between creative problem-solving and innovation outcomes.*

The moderating effect of organisational communication on the relationship between creative problem-solving and innovation outcomes

Broadly defined, communication is "the process of transferring information and meaning between senders and receivers, using one or more written, oral, visual, or electronic channels" (Bovée and Thill, 2010, p. 4). Organisational communication entails the transmission of ideas and ideally involves some form of feedback to ensure achievement of organisational goals (Popa, 2016). The importance of organisational communication in the innovation process hardly needs justification. Risk and complexity are characteristics of innovation, and communication channels are pivotal in the successful implementation of innovation (Fidler and Johnson, 1984). Indeed, intense interaction and communication are typically required for innovation. Thus, one would expect that the extent to which individual creative problem-solving leads to innovation outcomes for an organisation depends on effective communication, which the extent literature hints. For instance, Ebadi and Utterback (1984) noted that both individual and organisational level communication positively relates to technological innovation. Effective internal communication is also a critical success factor for innovation in the financial service industry (Lievens *et al.*, 1999). Beyond the realm of innovation, communication is also a predictor of employee satisfaction and performance (Goris, 2007) and contributes to employees' favourable behaviours towards change, leading to positive organisational change results (Saruhan, 2014). Studies also show that communication moderates the relationship between employees' satisfaction with their pay and their performance (Pettit *et al.*, 1997) and mediates the relationship between organisational culture and performance (Garnett *et al.*, 2008).

Given the empirical evidence that communication acts as a predictor, a mediator or a moderator in the attainment of positive organisational outcomes, we hypothesise the following:

H3: *Organisational communication moderates the relationship between creative problem-solving and innovation outcomes such that highly effective organisational communication leads to greater innovation outcomes.*

Influence of innovation outcomes on organisational performance

Given that innovation reshapes the competitive landscape and creates new market opportunities, its relationship with an organisation's financial performance should be positive. Although innovation is associated with increased employee dissatisfaction, unwarranted changes and higher exposure to market risks (Simpson *et al.*, 2006), it has increasingly become an important source of organisational performance, success and long-term survival (Anderson *et al.*, 2014). For instance, Jiménez-Jiménez and Sanz-Valle (2011) reported a positive relationship between innovation and performance and noted that most findings on the topic reflected the same conclusion. Additionally, Gavrea *et al.* (2011) reported that innovation is a key predictor of organisational performance, whereas Laforet (2013) concluded that innovation improves company profit margins. Likewise, based on a study of 144 Spanish industrial firms, Camisón and Villar-López (2014) found that organisational innovation enhances technological innovation capabilities. Furthermore, Gunday *et al.* (2011) reported positive effects of organisational, process, product and marketing innovations on the performance of manufacturing companies. Walker (2004) reported that innovation positively affects an organisation's corporate performance by improving its market position and competitive advantage. In addition, a study by Gunday *et al.* (2011) found positive effects of innovation on both financial and non-financial performance. However, because innovation has often been studied in the context of for-profit organisations (Hull and Lio, 2006), most research investigates its impact on financial performance. As a result, there is

N. Ouedraogo, M. L. Ouakouak & T. Salem

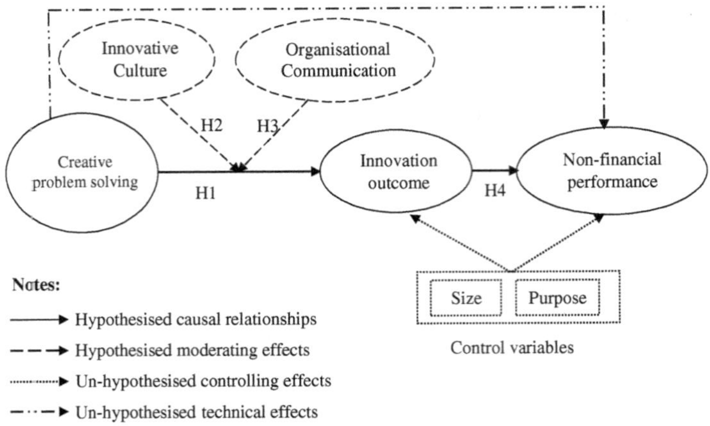

Fig. 1. Research model.

limited research evidence documenting innovation's effect on non-financial performance. Considering these research findings, we hypothesise the following:

H4: *Innovation outcomes positively affect organisational non-financial performance.*

Figure 1 depicts the hypothesised relationships.

Research Methodology

Sample and data collection

This study is part of a larger research project investigating the factors that contribute to change success and innovation outcomes in organisations. To gather data from participants, we created and uploaded a survey questionnaire on www.surveymonkey.com, a website specialising in online data collection. Our participant pool consisted of our LinkedIn professional contacts of individuals whose positions or profiles met key terms, such as manager, consultant, executive, director, leader and facilitator. This ensured that respondents had experience dealing with organisational change and innovation so that they could provide meaningful responses to the survey questions.

We sent a message to everyone in the participant pool, inviting them to participate in the study by completing the survey. Two weeks later, we sent a reminder to those who did not reply to the first message.

Out of a total 1761 prospective respondents contacted, we received 402 responses, of which 320 were complete and included in this study, resulting in an 18% usable response rate.

Over 80% of the respondents held managerial positions (25% as top executives, 49% as middle managers and 6.9% as supervisors). The tertiary sector was the most represented, with 75.9% of respondents. Sixty percent of the respondents worked in large organisations of more than 250 employees. A clear majority (70%) worked at for-profit organisations. Almost half of the respondents had been working at their current organisations for one to five years. The respondents were also predominantly male (60%). Table 1 provides a summary of the characteristics of sample population.

Measures

We extracted most measures from previously published studies to ensure validity and reliability of the scales. All variables were assessed on a five-point Likert scale, ranging from 1 = strongly disagree to 5 = strongly agree.

Table 1. Data description of the sample.

	Characteristics	%
Rank	Top executives	25.20
	Middle managers	49.10
	Supervisors	6.90
	Non-managerial employees	18.80
Age	Less than 34 years old	17.20
	Between 34 and 49 years old	48.40
	Over 49 years old	34.40
Sector	Tertiary sector	75.90
	Secondary sector	11.60
	Primary sector	12.50
Organisation size	Small and medium enterprises (SME) (1–249 employees)	39.40
	Large enterprises (more than 250 employees)	60.60
Tenure	Less than one year	16.6
	1–5 years	46.6
	6–10 years	0.9
	10–15 years	16.3
	16 years or more	9.4
		10.3
Purpose	For-profit businesses	70.00
	Non-profit organisations	30.00
Gender	Males	59.70
	Females	40.10

Creative problem-solving was measured using a scale developed by Charbonnier-Voirin and Roussel (2012) comprising the following items: (1) "I do not hesitate to go against established ideas in order to propose innovative solutions," (2) "Within my department, people rely on me to suggest new solutions," and (3) "I use various sources of information to come up with innovative solutions."

Innovation outcome. This construct was assessed by asking participants to give their perceptions of their organisation's innovation outcomes over the previous two years using a four-item scale. The first two items — "My organisation has improved its products (goods or services) designs or offerings" and "My organisation has reduced the time to develop new products" — were adapted from Camisón and Villar-López (2014). The last two items — "My organisation has increased the rate of introduction of new products to the market" and "My organisation has increased the percentage of revenue generated from the new products" — were adapted from Bolívar-Ramos *et al.* (2012).

Organisational performance can be measured through financial or non-financial indicators (Ong and Teh, 2009). Contrary to several previous studies that focused on financial indicators, this study used non-financial measurements adapted from Ouakouak and Ouedraogo (2013). For this category, participants were asked to compare their organisations' customer satisfaction, employee satisfaction, other stakeholder satisfaction and ability to retain their best employees with those of their immediate competitors.

Organisational culture. We used a five-item scale developed by Judge and Douglas (2009) to measure organisational culture. This scale includes the following items: (1) "My organisation values innovation," (2) "My organisation values change," (3) "My organisation attracts and retains creative people," (4) "My organisation provides resources to experiment with new ideas" and (5) "My organisation allows people to take risks and to occasionally fail."

Organisational communication. Based on the literature, we developed the following four-item scale to measure organisational communication: (1) "In my organisation, information flows effectively all the way from top executives to the front-line employees," (2) "In my organisation, information flows effectively all the way from the front-line employees to top executives," (3) "In my organisation, information flows effectively in a timely manner" and (4) "In my organisation, information flows effectively across organisational units."

Control variables. We controlled for the effects of *organisation size* and *purpose* on innovation outcomes and organisational performance.

Size: As reported by Damanpour (1992), organisation size positively relates to innovation, and this relationship is stronger in manufacturing and for-profit organisations compared with service and non-profit ones. More recently, a study by Yu and Lee (2017) of 542 Korean companies reported a positive impact of organisation size on innovative performance, and Sarooghi *et al.* (2015) also found that the relationship between creativity and innovation is stronger for large organisations. However, not all research points to the same results. For instance, Laforet (2013) reported that compared with large organisations, innovation impacts small companies to a greater extent.

Compared with small organisations that tend to be more flexible, large organisations are typically rigid and more formalised and may prove less innovative. Although large organisations are good at exploiting an innovation to its full potential, they are not necessarily quick to recognise and seize innovative ideas. This probably explains why they often acquire small innovative companies.

Size also affects firm performance. For example, Bourlakis *et al.* (2014) found that small firms are top performers in terms of sustainability. Babalola (2013) also reported that firm size, measured in terms of total assets and total sales, affects the profitability of manufacturing firms.

Purpose: We investigated whether organisation purpose has a control effect on the organisation's innovation output or non-financial performance. Whether an organisation pursues profit as its main purpose or not would affect the importance it gives to non-financial performance. For-profit and non-profit organisations present differences in many respects. For example, non-profit organisations are perceived are warmer, whereas for-profit companies are perceived as more competent (Aaker *et al.*, 2010). In a comparative study, Nowy *et al.* (2015) also reported that for-profit sport organisations outperform their non-profit counterparts on financial dimensions. This implies that the legal form of an organisation has implications in terms of the amount of resources available, for example, for new innovative projects.

Therefore, we included both size and purpose to control our results. Organisation size was measured using a scale comprising six intervals indicating the number of employees (**1** = 1–9; **2** = 10–49; **3** = 50–99; **4** = 100–249; **5**= 250–499; **6** = 500 and more). We divided this variable into two groups: 1 = less than 250 employees (small and medium enterprises) and 2 = more than 250 employees (large enterprises). Organisation purpose was reported using a binary variable (for-profit business = 1; non-profit organisation = 2).

Methods of data analysis

We used three statistical packages to analyse the data. First, we used SPSS software to compute the descriptive statistics (means, standard deviations), correlations between constructs, and Cronbach's alpha and the principal component analysis (PCA). Secondly, we used SmartPLS to compute the composite reliability (CR) and average variance extracted (AVE). Thirdly, we used AMOS to run a confirmatory factor analysis (CFA) and to test the causal relationships.

Data Analysis and Results

The data analysis was conducted using a two-stage methodology consisting of assessing the reliability and validity of all scales and then examining the structural relationships.

Reliability and validity of the constructs

We assessed the reliability and validity of the constructs using several statistical indices.

Reliability assessment

The reliability of the constructs was assessed using three indicators: Cronbach's alpha, CR and PCA with Varimax rotation. As shown in Table 3, the Cronbach's alpha value for each construct was above the recommended minimum value of 0.70, and all CR values were greater than the recommended minimum threshold of 0.7. The PCA with Varimax rotation resulted in five factors that explained 66.969% of the total variance. The results of the PCA showed that all items loaded significantly only on their respective constructs with a minimum load of 0.624, which was well above the recommended minimum value of 0.60 (Bagozzi and Yi, 1988), supporting the unidimensionality of all the factors (Table 2). Accordingly, the constructs in our research were sufficiently reliable.

We also ran a CFA to check if the items represented the latent constructs. To assess the CFA model fit, we applied the following statistical indices: goodness-of-fit index (GFI) greater than 0.80, comparative fit index (CFI) greater than 0.90, normed incremental fit index (NFI) greater than 0.90, ratio of chi-square to the degrees of freedom (χ^2/df) less than 3.0 and root mean square of approximation (RMSEA) less than 0.08 (Hair *et al.*, 2006; McKnight *et al.*, 2002).

The estimation of the CFA model produced the following statistical indices: GFI $= 0.917$; CFI $= 0.944$; NFI $= 0.908$; $\chi^2/df = 2.332$ and RMSEA $= 0.065$, all of which support a good model fit (see Appendix A for the recommended thresholds). As depicted in Table 3, all standardised factor loadings were greater than 0.60 and statistically significant ($p < 0.001$), except for the INN-BEH1 indicator. We kept this item in our analysis due to its significant loading.

Table 2. Factor loadings and cross-loadings.

Indicators	Factor 1	Factor 2	Factor 3	Factor 4	Factor 5
INN-BEH1	0.033	0.191	0.031	−0.050	**0.670**
INN-BEH2	0.067	−0.097	−0.112	0.087	**0.785**
INN-BEH3	0.018	−0.034	0.056	0.029	**0.820**
INN-OUT1	0.342	0.198	0.199	**0.660**	0.095
INN-OUT2	0.226	0.261	0.093	**0.652**	−0.071
INN-OUT3	0.189	0.122	0.152	**0.827**	0.043
INN-OUT4	0.101	0.107	0.181	**0.809**	0.035
NFI-PER1	0.185	0.156	**0.776**	0.153	−0.009
NFI-PER2	0.242	0.319	**0.785**	0.171	0.010
NFI-PER3	0.184	0.222	**0.787**	0.208	0.040
NFI-PER4	0.389	0.289	**0.671**	0.146	−0.094
INN-CUL1	**0.770**	0.137	0.153	0.241	0.010
INN-CUL2	**0.759**	0.087	0.228	0.162	0.063
INN-CUL3	**0.624**	0.263	0.337	0.264	−0.050
INN-CUL4	**0.731**	0.295	0.188	0.231	0.078
INN-CUL5	**0.695**	0.364	0.165	0.095	0.103
ORG-COM1	0.312	**0.802**	0.189	0.152	0.004
ORG-COM2	0.307	**0.761**	0.239	0.192	0.046
ORG-COM3	0.198	**0.785**	0.315	0.224	0.045
ORG-COM4	0.147	**0.818**	0.234	0.186	0.011

Assessment of convergent and discriminant validity

Convergent validity was assessed using three criteria as recommended by Hair *et al.* (2006). First, the CR values should be greater than 0.8. Secondly, the AVE should be above 0.5. As shown in Table 2, all CR values were greater than 0.8, and all AVE values were greater than 0.5. Thirdly, standardised factor loadings should be above 0.6. As shown in Table 3, this condition was met for all constructs, except for INN-BEH1.

Discriminant validity was assessed using the approach from Fornell and Larcker (1981), which consists of comparing the AVE of the constructs with the squared correlation of all possible pairs of constructs. As shown in Table 4, the AVE value of each construct was greater than the squared correlations between that construct and all other constructs. Therefore, the condition of discriminant validity was met.

Furthermore, common method bias (Podsakoff *et al.*, 2003) was assessed using Harman's one-factor test in SPSS. All indicators of the study constructs were entered into a single-factor analysis. The results showed that the single factor explained only 38.457% of the total variance, which is well below the 50%

Table 3. Results of the reliability, convergent validity and confirmatory factor analysis (CFA).

Constructs/indicators	Standardised factor loadings
Creative problem solving $\alpha = 0.619$ C.R. $= 0.795$ AVE $= 0.566$	
INN-BEH1	0.441
INN-BEH2	0.681
INN-BEH3	0.735
Innovation outcome $\alpha = 0.820$ C.R. $= 0.881$ AVE $= 0.651$	
INN-OUT1	0.756
INN-OUT2	0.657
INN-OUT3	0.793
INN-OUT4	0.722
Non-financial performance $\alpha = 0.872$ C.R. $= 0.913$ AVE $= 0.724$	
NFI-PER1	0.707
NFI-PER2	0.886
NFI-PER3	0.781
NFI-PER4	0.816
Innovative culture $\alpha = 0.869$ C.R. $= 0.897$ AVE $= 0.638$	
INN-CUL1	0.726
INN-CUL2	0.697
INN-CUL3	0.763
INN-CUL4	0.831
INN-CUL5	0.762
Organisational communication $\alpha = 0.912$ C.R. $= 0.938$ AVE $= 0.789$	
ORG-COM1	0.862
ORG-COM2	0.839
ORG-COM3	0.869
ORG-COM4	0.831

Table 4. Discriminant validity of the constructs.

Constructs	Innovative culture	Creative problem solving	Innovation outcome	Non-financial performance	Organisational communication
Creative problem solving	**0.566**				
Innovation outcome	0.006	**0.651**			
Non-financial performance	0.001	0.245	**0.724**		
Innovative culture	0.012	0.323	0.388	**0.638**	
Organisational communication	0.007	0.129	0.227	0.223	**0.789**

*The values in the diagonal represent the AVE and the other values are the squares of the inter-construct correlations.

Table 5. Means, standard deviations and correlations among the study variables.

No.	Constructs	Mean	S.D.	1	2	3	4	5	6	7
1	Organisational size	1.606	0.489	1	0.151**	−0.182**	−0.097	−0.210**	−0.103	−0.207**
2	Purpose	1.300	0.459		1	0.043	−0.192**	−0.151**	−0.153**	−0.200**
3	Creative problem solving	4.137	0.563			1	0.077	0.003	0.109	0.083
4	Innovation outcome	3.495	0.780				1	0.495**	0.568**	0.359**
5	Non-financial performance	3.521	0.856					1	0.623**	0.477**
6	Innovative culture	3.610	0.845						1	0.472**
7	Organisational communication	1.440	0.498							1

**Correlation is significant at the 0.01 level (two-tailed).

recommended maximum threshold. Therefore, the common method bias was not an issue in this study. The descriptive statistics and the correlation coefficients are shown in Table 5.

Tests of hypotheses

To test the hypothesised relationships, we used structural equation modelling (SEM) in AMOS.

Direct relationships analysis

Model 1. We ran Model 1 to test the direct relationships (creative problem-solving and innovation outcomes, innovation outcomes and organisational performance, creative problem-solving and organisational performance), and the controlling effects of organisational size and purpose on innovation outcomes and organisational performance.

The SEM results showed that the theoretical model had a good fit to the data (GFI = 0.948, CFI = 0.960, NFI = 0.921, $\chi^2/df = 1.914$ and RMSEA = 0.054). Figure 2 depicts the results of the first SEM model estimation. The path coefficients are the standardised beta coefficients, and the values between parentheses reflect the t-values.

Hypothesis (H1) predicting a positive effect of creative problem-solving on innovation outcomes was not supported ($\beta = 0.107$; $p = 0.142$). Hypothesis (H4), which proposed that innovation outcomes have a positive impact on organisational non-financial performance, was supported ($\beta = 0.552$; $p = 0.000$). Furthermore,

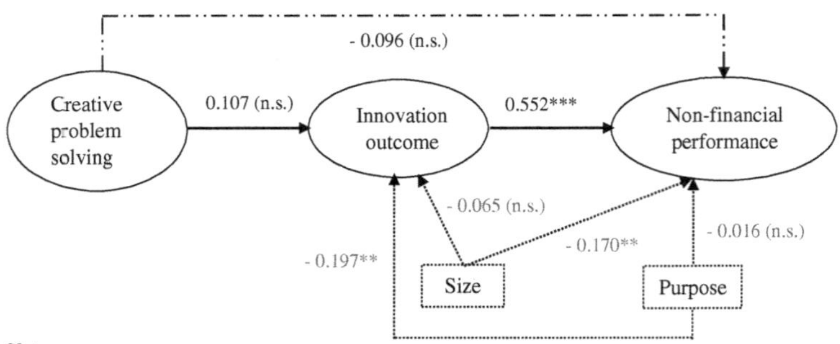

Notes:
** p < 0.01
*** p < 0.001
n.s.: non-significant

Fig. 2. Estimated research model (*Model* 1).

we technically tested the direct relationship between creative problem-solving and non-financial performance and found a non-significant relationship ($\beta = -0.096$; $p = 0.127$).

The estimation of Model 1 also showed that organisational size had a significant controlling effect on non-financial performance ($\beta = -0.170$; $p = 0.001$), but not on innovation outcomes ($\beta = -0.065$; $p = 0.278$). Furthermore, purpose had a significant controlling effect on innovation outcomes ($\beta = -0.197$; $p = 0.001$), but not on non-financial performance ($\beta = -0.016$; $p = 0.762$).

Moderation effects analysis (Models 2 and 3)

Model 2 is a multi-group moderation to test the effect of innovative culture on the relationship between creative problem-solving and innovation outcomes. To run this model, we dichotomised our sample into two groups using the median (3.70). This resulted in 160 responses for group 1 (low innovative culture) and 160 responses for group 2 (high innovative culture).

The estimation of this model provided the following indices: $\chi^2/df = 1.384$, CFI = 0.957, GFI = 0.928, NFI = 0.864 and RMSEA = 0.035. All fit indices were above the recommended minimum threshold, except for NFI. Therefore, the model showed an acceptable fit to the data.

The results of Model 2 revealed that Hypothesis (H2) predicting that innovative culture moderates the relationship between creative problem-solving and innovation outcomes was supported. As shown in Table 6, this relationship was significant when innovative culture was high ($\beta = 0.229$, $p = 0.034$) and insignificant otherwise ($\beta = -0.110$, $p = 0.319$).

Model 3 is also a multi-group moderation to examine the influence of organisational communication on the relationship between creative problem-solving and innovation outcomes. The same approach was used as for Model 2: we divided the sample into two groups using the median (3.25). This resulted in group 1 (low organisational communication) with 178 responses and group 2 (high organisational communication) with 142 responses.

Table 6. Results of the moderation effect of innovative culture (*Model* 2).

Hypothesis	Path specified	Innovative culture	Coefficient (β)	p-value
H2	Creative problem solving —	Low	−0.110	0.319
	Innovation outcome	High	0.229*	0.034

Note: $^*p < 0.05$.

N. Ouedraogo, M. L. Ouakouak & T. Salem

Table 7. Results of the moderation effect of organisational communication (*Model 3*).

Hypothesis	Path specified	Organisational communication	Coefficient (β)	p-value
H3	Creative problem solving—Innovation outcome	Low	−0.078	0.451
		High	0.343**	0.007

Note: **$p < 0.01$.

The estimation provided the following statistical indices: $\chi^2/df = 1.516$, CFI = 0.946, GFI = 0.921, NFI = 0.861 and RMSEA = 0.040, which were all above the recommended minimum thresholds, except for the NFI. Overall, these results indicated a good fit to the data.

The Model 2 results showed that creative problem-solving did not have a significant effect on innovation outcomes for organisations with a low level of organisational communication ($\beta = -0.078$, $p = 0.451$), but did have a significant effect for those with a high level of organisational communication ($\beta = 0.343$, $p = 0.007$). Thus, Hypothesis (H3) predicting a moderating effect of organisational communication on the creative problem-solving–innovation outcome relationship was supported (Table 7).

Discussion and Implications

Summary

Given that innovation is a key element for an organisation's performance and even survival, it is important to uncover its enabling factors. Therefore, this study investigated the effects of employee creative problem-solving on innovation outcomes and the effects of the latter on non-financial performance.

Based on a sample of 320 participants from diverse organisations, and using structural equation modelling techniques, we found that creative problem-solving does not have any positive effect on innovation outcomes.

However, our results indicate that an innovative culture moderates the relationship between creative problem-solving and innovation outcomes such that this relationship is significant when innovation culture is high. Likewise, our results further indicate that organisational communication moderates the creative problem-solving and innovation outcomes relationship such that the relationship is significant when the communication level is high. Furthermore, the findings illustrate that innovation outcomes are positively related to organisational non-financial performance. Finally, according to our study, size has a controlling effect on non-financial performance such that higher size relates to lower non-financial performance. Our study contributes to the extent literature on innovation and organisational performance and provides several insights for managing innovation.

Contributions to theory

First, we contribute to the literature on innovation by showing that creative problem-solving has no significant effect on innovation outcomes without the positive influence of innovative culture or effective communication. Creative problem-solving has been addressed in academic studies from the perspective of designing training programs to develop this skill (Proctor, 2014), including teaching creative problem-solving using a different paradigm (Morton, 1997) and designing interactive environments that support creative problem-solving (Hilliges *et al.*, 2007). Research has also investigated the brain activity and the thinking processes that take place during creative problem-solving (Lumsdaine and Lumsdaine, 1994), as well as the affective and emotional states that favour creative problem-solving (Isen, 1999). However, the literature is limited on how creative problem-solving contributes to innovation outcomes for the entire organisation. Therefore, this study contributes to closing this knowledge gap.

A second contribution of this research pertains to the role of culture and communication on innovation. The finding that the relationship between employee creative problem-solving and innovation outcomes is moderated by organisational communication and innovative culture suggests that an employee creative problem-solving behaviour can only have a very limited effect in the absence of the right organisational context and conditions. Creative problem-solving is risky, and one would not engage in it unless the culture is favourable. Moreover, effective communication allows employees to know what the organisation is aiming for in terms of innovation and to channel their creative problem-solving skills to that end. Innovation is a collective exercise that requires not only creative problem-solving, but also the right environment for such behaviour to flourish and come to fruition, so even if employees individually engage in creative problem-solving in an organisation, these efforts would not lead to meaningful innovation outcomes without the right culture and communication. It is even possible that creative problem solving — which involves suggesting new solutions to problems, going against established ideas and using various sources of information to come up with innovative solutions — could lead to negative outcomes if the right culture and communication are not in place.

Researchers such as Chandler *et al.* (2000) have investigated the determinants and consequences of innovative culture and found that it is enhanced by supervisory support and the right reward system. The same authors also found that innovative culture has no direct impact on firm performance, although it helps enhance firm earnings in a dynamic market environment. Our findings complement this line of research and enrich the theoretical understanding of innovation dynamics in organisations.

Thirdly, we contribute to the literature by showing that innovation outcomes positively affect organisational non-financial performance. In a very unpredictable market environment, organisations not only need to achieve good financial performance in the present, but they also need to develop the capabilities to sustain their long-term prosperity and even survival. The non-financial performance measures in this study are leading indicators in this regard. Research has extensively explored the influence of innovation on financial performance (Cassiman and Veugelers, 2006), but our study is among the few to provide empirical evidence on the effect of innovation outcomes on non-financial performance.

Fourth, our control variables provide insightful results on the effects of size on innovation and non-financial performance. We observe that small-sized organisations enjoy better non-financial performance. Although size has a positive effect on profitability (Babalola, 2013), it has a negative effect on non-financial performance as per our study results. In line with these findings, Bourlakis *et al.* (2014) also reported that small firms are top performers on another dimension of non-financial performance, namely, sustainability.

Contributions to practice

Our findings provide several practical insights for managing innovation.

First, the finding that creative problem-solving affects innovation outcomes and non-financial performance when innovative culture is high speaks to the importance of the latter.

It is not enough for managers to hire and retain creative and smart people. They also need to create a culture that values and promotes innovation throughout the organisation and provides resources employees need in order to take risks and experiment with new ideas. An innovative culture should also allow open discussions around ideas and, to some extent, allow employees to defy rules and policies that do not make sense (Sutton, 2001). Hiring employees who exhibit creative problem-solving is certainly a good start, but innovation requires more.

Secondly, managers need to emphasise the importance of effective organisational communication as well, because the relationship between creative problem-solving and innovation outcomes is positively influenced by it. Effective organisational communication contributes to facilitating change successfully (Kotter, 2012), enhancing employee perceived job satisfaction and performance

(Giri and Kumar, 2010) and motivating employees (Rajhans, 2012). Showing again the positive influence of communication, our study implies that managers should consider creative problem-solving and effective communication in tandem.

Thirdly, the finding that small organisations enjoy better non-financial performance implies that managers of large organisations who want to increase this aspect of their performance should look into the characteristics of small organisations that perform better on this measure and then create conditions within their large organisations to achieve the same results. We believe that organic and flexible structures, deep understanding of employees' needs, family-like cultures and proximities between employees and top executives are among the characteristics of small organisations that help them achieve better non-financial performance.

Limitations and Future Research Directions

Although our study makes several contributions to theory and practice as presented above, it nonetheless presents some limitations and opens avenues for research.

We used organisational non-financial performance as a dependent variable. The items of this construct act as performance enablers that give an indication of an organisation's ability to achieve future performance. As Kaplan and Norton (2007) explained, measuring an organisation's performance based solely on financial indicators is restrictive and may even be misleading. We, therefore, approached performance in comparative terms and from the non-financial perspective. Our approach is appropriate when considering for-profit and non-profit organisations of different sectors, but it also presents a limitation, since it does not assess current financial performance of for-profit companies. Future studies should extend the performance measurement to include both financial and non-financial indicators.

Also, we adopted a quantitative method, which worked well for testing the hypothesised relationships. However, for a topic as complex as innovation, there would be many other variables to consider. For instance, leadership style, internal resource availability, external market environment and innovation ecosystems in general can affect innovation. Future studies involving qualitative methodologies should consider these variables and delve into the intricacies of innovation in different organisational contexts.

Another limitation of our study is that we focused on solving problems creatively, which is only one component of adaptative performance (Pulakos *et al.*, 2000). Other studies should address the other components of this multi-faceted construct. For example, one would assume that dealing with uncertainty and showing adaptability is important for organisational change success, whereas learning new tasks, new technologies and procedures would be important for innovation. Therefore, more research is needed to understand the role of the other components of adaptive performance on organisational outcomes.

Likewise, this study dealt with creative problem-solving, a concept close to creativity. While creativity is the ability to come up with original ideas, creative problem-solving goes a step farther in that it consists of thinking and acting innovatively. Further research should endeavour to clarify the relationship between creativity and creative problem-solving.

Finally, we only tested the influence of communication and innovative culture as moderators. Future research should investigate these two variables as direct predictors of innovation outcomes and as indirect antecedents of innovation through other factors. For instance, a study on the cumulative effect of creative problem-solving, organisational communication and culture on innovation outcomes in the context of small- and medium-sized organisations versus large organisations would contribute to expanding our understanding of these important organisational issues.

References

Aaker, J, KD Vohs and C Mogilner (2010). Nonprofits are seen as warm and for-profits as competent: Firm stereotypes matter. *Journal of Consumer Research*, 37(2), 224–237.

Abstein, A and P Spieth (2014). Exploring HRM meta-features that foster employees' innovative work behaviour in times of increasing work–life conflict. *Creativity and Innovation Management*, 23(2), 211–225.

Adams, R, J Bessant and R Phelps (2006). Innovation management measurement: A review. *International Journal of Management Reviews*, 8(1), 21–47.

Amabile, TM and MG Pratt (2016). The dynamic componential model of creativity and innovation in organizations: Making progress, making meaning. *Research in Organizational Behavior*, 36, 157–183.

Anderson, N, K Potočnik and J Zhou (2014). Innovation and creativity in organizations: A state-of-the-science review, prospective commentary, and guiding framework. *Journal of Management*, 40(5), 1297–1333.

Babalola, YA (2013). The effect of firm size on firms profitability in Nigeria. *Journal of Economics and Sustainable Development*, 4(5), 90–94.

Baer, M (2012). Putting creativity to work: The implementation of creative ideas in organizations. *Academy of Management Journal*, 55(5), 1102–1119.

Bagozzi, RP and Y Yi (1988). On the evaluation of structural equation models. *Journal of the Academy of Marketing Science*, 16(1), 74–94.

Bharadwaj, S and A Menon (2000). Making innovation happen in organizations: Individual creativity mechanisms, organizational creativity mechanisms or both? *Journal of Product Innovation Management: An International Publication of the Product Development and Management Association*, 17(6), 424–434.

Birgit, P, P Mike and C Chung-Shing (2018). Needs, drivers and barriers of innovation: The case of an alpine community model destination. *Tourism Management Perspectives*, 25, 53–63.

Bolívar-Ramos, MT, VJ García-Morales and E García-Sánchez (2012). Technological distinctive competencies and organizational learning: Effects on organizational innovation to improve firm performance. *Journal of Engineering and Technology Management*, 29(3), 331–357.

Bourlakis, M, G Maglaras, E Aktas, D Gallear and C Fotopoulos (2014). Firm size and sustainable performance in food supply chains: Insights from Greek SMEs. *International Journal of Production Economics*, 152, 112–130.

Bovée, CL and JV Thill (2010). *Business Communication Today*, 10th edn. Upper Saddle River, NJ: Prentice Hall.

Bowen, FE, M Rostami and P Steel (2010). Timing is everything: A meta-analysis of the relationships between organizational performance and innovation. *Journal of Business Research*, 63(11), 1179–1185.

Burisch, R and V Wohlgemuth (2016). Blind spots of dynamic capabilities: A systems theoretic perspective. *Journal of Innovation and Knowledge*, 1(2), 109–116.

Büschgens, T, A Bausch and DB Balkin (2013). Organizational culture and innovation: A meta-analytic review. *Journal of Product Innovation Management*, 30(4), 763–781.

Byrne, ZS and E LeMay (2006). Different media for organizational communication: Perceptions of quality and satisfaction. *Journal of Business and Psychology*, 21, 149–173.

Çakar, ND and A Ertürk (2010). Comparing innovation capability of small and medium-sized enterprises: Examining the effects of organizational culture and empowerment. *Journal of Small Business Management*, 48(3), 325–359.

Camisón, C and A Villar-López (2014). Organizational innovation as an enabler of technological innovation capabilities and firm performance. *Journal of Business Research*, 67(1), 2891–2902.

Cassiman, B and R Veugelers (2006). In search of complementarity in innovation strategy: Internal R&D and external knowledge acquisition. *Management Science*, 52(1), 68–82.

Chandler, GN, C Keller and DW Lyon (2000). Unraveling the determinants and consequences of an innovation-supportive organizational culture. *Entrepreneurship Theory and Practice*, 25(1), 59–76.

Charbonnier-Voirin, A and P Roussel (2012). Adaptive performance: A new scale to measure individual performance in organizations. *Canadian Journal of Administrative Sciences/Revue Canadienne des Sciences de l'Administration*, 29(3), 280–293.

Çokpekin, Ö and MP Knudsen, (2012). Does organizing for creativity really lead to innovation? *Creativity and Innovation Management*, 21(3), 304–314.

Damanpour, F (1992). Organizational size and innovation. *Organization Studies*, 13(3), 375–402.

Damanpour, F and M Schneider (2006). Phases of the adoption of innovation in organizations: Effects of environment, organization and top managers. *British Journal of Management*, 17(3), 215–236.

Dastmalchian, A, S Lee and I Ng (2000). The interplay between organizational and national cultures: A comparison of organizational practices in Canada and South Korea using CVF. *International Journal of HRM*, 23(2), 95–98.

De Jong, JP and DN Den Hartog (2007). How leaders influence employees' innovative behaviour. *European Journal of Innovation Management*, 10(1), 41–64.

Detert, JR, RG Schroeder and JJ Mauriel (2000). A framework for linking culture and improvement initiatives in organizations. *Academy of Management Review*, 25(4), 850–863.

Ebadi, YM and JM Utterback (1984). The effects of communication on technological innovation. *Management Science*, 30(5), 572–585.

Eze, BU (2018). Corporate entrepreneurship and manufacturing firms' performance. *EMAJ: Emerging Markets Journal*, 8(1), 12–17.

Fidler, LA and JD Johnson (1984). Communication and innovation implementation. *Academy of Management Review*, 9(4), 704–711.

Fornell, C and DF Larcker (1981). Evaluating structural equation models with unobservable variables and measurement error, *Journal of Marketing Research*, 18(1), 39–50.

Garcia, AJ, S Mollaoglu-Korkmaz and VD Miller (2014). Progress loops in interorganizational project teams: An IPD case. In *Construction Research Congress 2014: Construction in a Global Network*, pp. 2011–2020.

Garnett, JL, J Marlowe and SK Pandey (2008). Penetrating the performance predicament: Communication as a mediator or moderator of organizational culture's impact on public organizational performance. *Public Administration Review*, 68(2), 266–281.

Gavrea, C, L Ilies and R Stegerean (2011). Determinants of organizational performance: The case of Romania. *Management and Marketing*, 6(2), 285–300.

Giri, VN and BP Kumar (2010). Assessing the impact of organizational communication on job satisfaction and job performance. *Psychological Studies*, 55(2), 137–143.

Goris, JR (2007). Effects of satisfaction with communication on the relationship between individual-job congruence and job performance/satisfaction. *Journal of Management Development*, 26(8), 737–752.

Griffin, A, RL Price, MM Maloney, BA Vojak and EW Sim (2009). Voices from the field: How exceptional electronic industrial innovators innovate. *Journal of Product Innovation Management*, 26(2), 222–240.

Gunday, G, G Ulusoy, K Kilic and L Alpkan (2011). Effects of innovation types on firm performance. *International Journal of Production Economics*, 133(2), 662–676.

Hair, JF, WC Babin, BJ Babin, RE Anderson and RL Tatham (2006). *Multivariate Data Analysis*, 6th edn. Englewood Cliffs, NJ: Prentice Hall.

Herbig, P and S Dunphy (1998). Culture and innovation. *Cross Cultural Management: An International Journal*, 5(4), 13–21.

Hesketh, B and A Neal (1999). Technology and performance. In *The Changing Nature of Performance: Implications for Staffing, Motivation and Development*, DR Ilgen and DP Pulakos (eds.), pp. 21–55. San Francisco: Jossey-Bass.

Hilliges, O, L Terrenghi, S Boring, D Kim, H Richter and A Butz (2007, June). Designing for collaborative creative problem solving. *Proceedings of the 6th ACM SIGCHI Conference on Creativity and Cognition*, pp. 137–146.

Hirst, G, D Van Knippenberg and J Zhou (2009). A cross-level perspective on employee creativity: Goal orientation, team learning behavior, and individual creativity. *Academy of Management Journal*, 52(2), 280–293.

Hogan, SJ and LV Coote (2014). Organizational culture, innovation, and performance: A test of Schein's model. *Journal of Business Research*, 67(8), 1609–1621.

Homburg, C and C Pflesser (2000). A multiple-layer model of market-oriented organizational culture: Measurement issues and performance outcomes. *Journal of Marketing Research*, 37(4), 449–462.

Hsu, YH and W Fang (2009). Intellectual capital and new product development performance: The mediating role of organizational learning capability. *Technological Forecasting and Social Change*, 76(5), 664–677.

Hull, CE and BH Lio (2006). Innovation in non-profit and for-profit organizations: Visionary, strategic, and financial considerations. *Journal of Change Management*, 6(1), 53–65.

Ireland, RD, DF Kuratko and MH Morris (2006). A health audit for corporate entrepreneurship: Innovation at all levels: Part I. *Journal of Business Strategy*, 27(1), 10–17.

Isen, AM (1999). On the relationship between affect and creative problem solving. *Affect, Creative Experience, and Psychological Adjustment*, 3, 17.

Jansen, JJ, FA Van Den Bosch and HW Volberda (2006). Exploratory innovation, exploitative innovation, and performance: Effects of organizational antecedents and environmental moderators. *Management Science*, 52(11), 1661–1674.

Jiang, W and Q Gu (2015). A moderated mediation examination of proactive personality on employee creativity: A person-environment fit perspective. *Journal of Organizational Change Management*, 28(3), 393–410.

Jiménez-Jiménez, D and R Sanz-Valle (2011). Innovation, organizational learning, and performance. *Journal of Business Research*, 64(4), 408–417.

Judge, W and T Douglas (2009). Organizational change capacity: The systematic development of a scale. *Journal of Organizational Change Management*, 22(6), 635–649.

Kaplan, RS and DP Norton (2007). Using the balanced scorecard as a strategic management system. *Harvard Business Review*, 85(7–8), 150–160.

Koen, PA, GM Ajamian, S Boyce, A Clamen, E Fisher, S Fountoulakis, … R Seibert (2002). *Fuzzy Front End: Effective Methods, Tools, and Techniques*. New York, NY: Wiley.

Kotter, JP (2012). *Leading Change*. Boston, MA: Harvard Business Press.

Laforet, S (2013). Organizational innovation outcome in SMEs: Effects of age, size, and sector. *Journal of World Business*, 48(4), 490–502.

Lewis, LK (2007). An organizational stakeholder model of change implementation communication. *Communication Theory*, 17(2), 176–204.

Lewis, LR, SA Hamel and BR Richardson (2001). Communicating change to nonprofit stakeholders: Models and predictors of implementers' approaches. *Management Communication Quarterly*, 15(1), 5–41.

Li, Y, M Wang, DD Van Jaarsveld, GK Lee and DG Ma (2018). From employee-experienced high-involvement work system to innovation: An emergence-based human resource management framework. *Academy of Management Journal*, 61(5), 2000–2019.

Lievens, A, RK Moenaert and RS Jegers (1999). Linking communication to innovation success in the financial services industry: A case study analysis. *International Journal of Service Industry Management*, 10(1), 23–48.

Litchfield, RC, CM Ford and RJ Gentry (2015). Linking individual creativity to organizational innovation. *The Journal of Creative Behavior*, 49(4), 279–294.

Liu, D, H Liao and R Loi (2012). The dark side of leadership: A three-level investigation of the cascading effect of abusive supervision on employee creativity. *Academy of Management Journal*, 55(5), 1187–1212.

Lumsdaine, E and M Lumsdaine (1994). Creative problem solving. *IEEE Potentials*, 13(5), 4–9.

Lundy, O and AG Cowling (1996). *Strategic Human Resource Management*. Boston: International Thomson Business Press.

Martín-de Castro, G, M Delgado-Verde, JE Navas-López and J Cruz-González (2013). The moderating role of innovation culture in the relationship between knowledge assets and product innovation. *Technological Forecasting and Social Change*, 80(2), 351–363.

Martins, EC and F Terblanche (2003). Building organisational culture that stimulates creativity and innovation. *European Journal of Innovation Management*, 6(1), 64–74.

McKnight, DH, V Choudhury and C Kacmar (2002). Developing and validating trust measures for e-commerce: An integrative typology. *Information Systems Research*, 13(3), 334–359.

Menzel, HC, I Aaltio and JM Ulijn (2007). On the way to creativity: Engineers as intrapreneurs in organizations. *Technovation*, 27(12), 732–743.

Morton, L (1997). Teaching creative problem solving: A paradigmatic approach. *California Western Law Review*, 34, 375.

Naranjo-Valencia, JC, D Jimenez-Jimenez and R Sanz-Valle (2017). Organizational culture and radical innovation: Does innovative behavior mediate this relationship? *Creativity and Innovation Management*, 26(4), 407–417.

Nowy, T, P Wicker, S Feiler and C Breuer (2015). Organizational performance of nonprofit and for-profit sport organizations. *European Sport Management Quarterly*, 15(2), 155–175.

Ong, TS and BH Teh (2009). The use of financial and non-financial performance measures in the Malaysian manufacturing companies. *Journal of Accounting Research*, 8, 23–30.

Orfila-Sintes, F and J Mattsson (2009). Innovation behaviour in the hotel industry. *Omega*, 37(2), 380–394.

Ouakouak, ML and N Ouedraogo (2013). The mediating role of employee strategic alignment in the relationship between rational strategic planning and firm performance: A European study. *Canadian Journal of Administrative Sciences/Revue Canadienne des Sciences de l'Administration*, 30(3), 143–158.

Pettit, JD Jr, JR Goris and BC Vaught (1997). An examination of organizational communication as a moderator of the relationship between job performance and job satisfaction. *The Journal of Business Communication*, 34(1), 81–98.

Podsakoff, PM, SB MacKenzie, JY Lee and NP Podsakoff (2003). Common method biases in behavioral research: A critical review of the literature and recommended remedies. *Journal of Applied Psychology*, 88(5), 879.

Popa, BM (2016). Communicating for success. *Journal of Defense Resources Management*, 7(2), 79–84.

Proctor, T (2014). *Creative Problem Solving for Managers: Developing Skills for Decision Making and Innovation*. New York: Routledge.

Pulakos, ED, S Arad, MA Donovan and KE Plamondon (2000). Adaptability in the workplace: Development of a taxonomy of adaptive performance. *Journal of Applied Psychology*, 85(4), 612.

Rajhans, K (2012). Effective organizational communication: A key to employee motivation and performance. *Interscience Management Review*, 2(2), 81–85.

Sarooghi, H, D Libaers and A Burkemper (2015). Examining the relationship between creativity and innovation: A meta-analysis of organizational, cultural, and environmental factors. *Journal of Business Venturing*, 30(5), 714–731.

Saruhan, N (2014). The role of corporate communication and perception of justice during organizational change process. *Business and Economics Research Journal*, 5(4), 143–166.

Schippers, MC, MA West and JF Dawson (2015). Team reflexivity and innovation: The moderating role of team context. *Journal of Management*, 41(3), 769–788.

Shalley, CE, LL Gilson and TC Blum (2009). Interactive effects of growth need strength, work context, and job complexity on self-reported creative performance. *Academy of Management Journal*, 52(3), 489–505.

Simpson, PM, JA Siguaw and CA Enz (2006). Innovation orientation outcome: The good and the bad. *Journal of Business Research*, 59(10–11), 1133–1141.

Škerlavaj, M, JH Song and Y Lee (2010). Organizational learning culture, innovative culture and innovations in South Korean firms. *Expert Systems with Applications*, 37(9), 6390–6403.

Sutton, RI (2001). The weird rules of creativity. *Harvard Business Review*, 79(8), 94–103.

Thomas, AS and SL Mueller (2000). A case for comparative entrepreneurship: Assessing the relevance of culture. *Journal of International Business Studies*, 31(2), 287–301.

Tushman, ML and CA O'Reilly II (1997). *Winning Through Innovation: A Practical Guide to Leading Organizational Change and Renewal*. Boston, MA: Harvard Business Press.

Walker, RM (2004). Innovation and organisational performance: Evidence and a research agenda. *Advanced Institute of Management Research Paper* (002).

Yoshida, DT, S Sendjaya, G Hirst and B Cooper (2014). Does servant leadership foster creativity and innovation? A multi-level mediation study of identification and prototypicality. *Journal of Business Research*, 67(7), 1395–1404.

Yu, GJ and J Lee (2017). When should a firm collaborate with research organizations for innovation performance? The moderating role of innovation orientation, size, and age. *The Journal of Technology Transfer*, 42(6), 1451–1465.

Zhang, X and KM Bartol (2010). The influence of creative process engagement on employee creative performance and overall job performance: A curvilinear assessment. *Journal of Applied Psychology*, 95(5), 862.

Chapter 2

DO EMPLOYEE RESILIENCE, FOCUS ON OPPORTUNITY, AND WORK-RELATED CURIOSITY PREDICT INNOVATIVE WORK BEHAVIOUR? THE MEDIATING ROLE OF CAREER ADAPTABILITY†

RAWAN ABUKHAIT[*,§], SHAKER BANI-MELHEM[†,¶] and
FARIDAHWATI MOHD SHAMSUDIN[‡,||]

[*]*Department of Management*
College of Business Administration
Ajman University, United Arab Emirates
[†]*Department of Management*
College of Business Administration
University of Sharjah, United Arab Emirates
[‡]*School of Business Administration*
Al Akhawayn University in Ifrane, Morocco
[§]*r.abukhait@ajman.ac.ae*
[¶]*ssaleh@sharjah.ac.ae*
[||]*f.mohdshamsudin@aui.ma*

Published 8 October 2019

Scholars suggest that only certain personality traits can easily adapt and react positively to organisational changes and consequently to innovative behaviour. Hence, in this study, we drew upon career construction theory to develop a hypothetical model examining how certain personality traits (i.e., curiosity, focus on opportunity, and resilience) are likely to influence career adaptability and consequently innovative behaviour. To test the model, we used two-wave longitudinal data focusing on 313 frontline employees operating in a random sample of five-star hotels in Dubai. Using Smart-PLS.3, we revealed that employees with a high level of curiosity, focus on opportunity, and resilience tend to increase the likelihood of their career adaptability significantly. In other words, employees with such work-related personality are more likely to adapt to organisational changes and fit different organisational environments. Furthermore, the result of the study found that career adaptability significantly mediated the relationship between these personality traits

[§]Corresponding author.

†This article originally appeared in *International Journal of Innovation Management*, **24** 2050070-1-30 © 2020 World Scientific Publishing Europe Ltd.

and innovative behaviour. The findings have significant implications for both theory and practice. They may also be contextual. These implications are discussed.

Keywords: Innovative behaviours; career adaptability; work-related curiosity; resilience; focus on opportunity.

Introduction

The marked changes over the last decades in how work is organised are reflected in increased global competition, job restructuring, and flatter organisational hierarchies. Consequently, it is necessary for workers in different types of jobs and at all levels in organisations to practice more innovative behaviour including in those positions where traditionally initiative and innovation was not required. It has been widely reported that innovative employee behaviour — non-routine suggestions and actions in response to workplace challenges — is a significant contributor to organisational performance (Pham *et al.*, 2016; Naranjo-Valencia *et al.*, 2016; Shanker *et al.*, 2017). Research on innovative work practice across the service sector remains, however, scarce (Abukhait *et al.*, 2018; Kim and Koo, 2017), and even more limited, in theoretical and empirical scope, for the tourism industry. This is attributable not only to a lack of available data, but also to conceptual difficulties related to specialised tourist services and activities and hotel chains. Therefore, determining the facilitating conditions of innovative employee behaviour in the hotel sector remains a justifiable research subject.

The current research seeks to supplement the literature by focusing on the role of personality as an important individual difference not previously considered in studies of innovative employee behaviour. Most studies that have highlighted personality as a facilitating condition of innovative behaviour have taken the Big Five model (Woods *et al.*, 2018) as their theoretical basis. Chen *et al.* (2010), for example, found that agreeableness, extraversion, and openness traits could reasonably explain an individual's innovative work behaviour. Madrid *et al.* (2014) showed that, among other personality traits, only openness was positively associated with innovative behaviour. Conversely, negative correlations between conscientiousness and devising novel solutions to problems have been found (Feist, 1998; Niu, 2014; Raja and Johns, 2010). Strict adherence to the Big Five model, it has been felt for some time, is probably no longer appropriate to the field of I–O psychology (Borman, 2004, p. 267). In their review of the Big Five model, Hough *et al.* (2015) noted several criticisms of the model, one of which is that the model "is missing many personality traits shown to be important in work settings (or may be important in the future)" (p. 188). Drawing from positive psychology that emphasises happiness, well-being, and positivity for human development and improvement (Seligman, 2002), we specifically proposed the personality traits of work-related curiosity, focus on opportunity, and resilience, because they have been found to affect behaviour and attitudes (Avey *et al.*, 2010). These traits reflect the strengths of individuals to cope with organisational change by broadening their outlook, encourage open decision making and provide the energy and vitality during the coping process (Avey *et al.*, 2008). Furthermore, past studies have demonstrated a significant effect of these psychological characteristics on creative performance and innovation (Abbas and Raja, 2015; Gupta and Singh, 2014; Sweetman *et al.*, 2011).

Since associations between personality traits and individual behaviours and outcomes resemble "black box" data (Kim *et al.*, 2007; Giebels *et al.*, 2016), to clarify these links it is proposed that career adaptability mediates the relationship between trait and innovative behaviour (George and Zhou, 2001; Sung and Choi, 2009; Williams, 2004). Career adaptability for employees has become essential in increasingly insecure work environments than knowledge content (Wagner, 2014), and it has been observed that personality has a strong influence on career adaptability. However, surprisingly a few studies of adaptability and uncertainty in change situations have been made (Cullen *et al.*, 2014; Rudolph *et al.*, 2017) notwithstanding practitioner interest in how individual personality variables affect workers' attitudes and performance. In the limited existing research, the findings of personality traits and adaptability have been discrepant (Huang *et al.*, 2014; Li *et al.*, 2015; Nilforooshan and Salimi, 2016). This paper's contribution to the literature lies in its deriving personality variables theoretically to examine their capacity as predictors of adaptive performance. Organisations may be enabled to accurately identify individuals most likely to demonstrate adaptive abilities through their recruitment and management practices (Safavi *et al.*, 2018).

The general cognitive ability has been observed in research to date to be a positive predictor of adaptive performance (e.g., Huang *et al.*, 2013; Ohme and Zacher, 2015; Pulakos *et al.*, 2000). Further, Jundt *et al.* (2015) and Neal *et al.* (2012) noted that the mechanisms of personality's effect on career adaptability, or future work self, were still little understood, as were additive or interactive effects of different personality factors on outcome variables. Moreover, there are few explicit comparisons of the effects of individual differences across a range of situations where adaptive career performance was important (Jundt *et al.*, 2015). Comparing within- and between-person variance in adaptive performance would allow a better understanding of individual differences in career adaptability.

The current study involved a large, representative sample of frontline employees working in the hotel industry geographically located in Dubai, United Arab Emirates. The development of the UAE's tourism industry has received strong support in the state's push for economic reform (Anwar and Sohail, 2004;

Bagaeen, 2015; Singh and Prashar, 2013). As one of the world's most visited nations, the UAE has benefited enormously from tourism (Karatepe and Tizabi, 2011), and to accommodate the increase in tourist numbers, the government has prioritised this sector for infrastructure development (construction of hotels, roads, airports (Akoum, 2008). Quality of service as measured by customer satisfaction is also important: hotels providing higher quality service have higher performance standards, confirmed by satisfied customers (Stock *et al.*, 2017; Tarofder *et al.*, 2017). Thus, it is useful to assess why hotel businesses thrive or fail, and why their levels of performance might fluctuate (Wang *et al.*, 2012). It is also important to determine the influence of employee innovation on these organisational outcomes. The innovative trend in the hospitality industry is manifested through the ability to generate a diverse range of initiatives (Zaitseva, 2013). When customers have agreeable experiences, their brand loyalty is strengthened (Li and Green, 2011).

To address the gaps in the current literature, this paper first presents a review of the relevant literature on innovative work behaviour and purported drivers, followed by the proposed research model and hypotheses development. The study's methodology, data analysis, and discussion of the results are then provided before the conclusion outlining the limitations of this research, implications for theory and practice, and recommendations for further investigation.

Literature Review

Career adaptability and innovative work behaviour

Currently, the capacity of employees to adapt to change in a world of fragmented, insecure and cross-border careers and negotiate one's own vocational development has become a topic of heightened interest (Biemann *et al.*, 2012; Zacher, 2014; Zacher *et al.*, 2015). The construct field for adaptive performance has been, to date, articulated only by Pulakos *et al.*'s (2000) work. Adaptive performance is competence in altering one's behaviour in response to the demands of change in the working environment. In this regard, career adaptability is defined as "the way an individual views his or her capacity to cope with and capitalise on change in the future, level of comfort with new work responsibilities, and ability to recover when unforeseen events alter career plans" (Rottinghaus *et al.*, 2005, p. 11).

This study proposed that individual adaptability correlates positively with innovative behaviour based on the adaptive job performance theory. This theoretical framework, conceived by Pulakos *et al.* (2012), states that adaptability can be unpacked under an eight-aspect demonstrable taxonomy: creative problem-solving; dealing with uncertainty in the work context; new task learning, technology, and procedures; interpersonal adaptability; cultural adaptability; physically-oriented adaptability; dealing with work stress; and handling emergencies or crises (p. 301).

Adaptive performance is related to creative problem-solving in the sense that flexibility is an advantage in situations of uncertainty or unpredictability. While how easily and well people deal with uncertainty may be related to their approach to problem-solving, the two are conceptually distinct and are thus treated as different components of career adaptability in this study. Although Collie and Martin (2016) pointed to some overlap between innovative behaviour and adaptability — both involve adjusting or modifying thoughts, behaviours, or actions — a salient difference is that adaptability connotes the unexpected and spontaneous whereas innovative behaviour requires planning, and its main aim is to improve performance. Employees with good adaptive performance can more effectively deal with work-context uncertainty arising, for example, from organisational restructuring, a change in priorities, or restricted resource availability. Good adaptors also can devise solutions and non-routine approaches to ambiguous, atypical, or compound problems.

Adaptability signals the ability to respond or adjust positively to a situation that may be novel, uncertain, or potentially stressful (Asamsama *et al.*, 2011; Burns and Martin, 2014; Martin *et al.*, 2013). Ngo and Loi (2008) and Roehling *et al.* (2000) explained that adaptable employee behaviour benefits an organisation by helping it adapt to an environment of changing job role requirements and become more agile in responses to external change. Since the inception of continuous technological advances that have forced the evolution of various occupations, employees have been pressured to respond effectively to change by adapting and tolerating uncertainty. Thus, it was predicted that employee adaptability will positively impact innovative work behaviour.

H1: *Career adaptability is a positive and significant correlative of innovative work behaviour.*

Employee resilience and career adaptability

There is a consensus in recent scholarship that resilient employees contribute critically to the organisation's capacity for not only survival but continuous development amid fierce competition, financial downturns, and uncertainty (Kuntz *et al.*, 2016; Linnenluecke, 2017; Southwick *et al.*, 2014).

Resilience research has been limited mainly to areas of clinical and positive psychology; some researchers have noted that resilience may also have application as one strategy that might facilitate labor market adaptability (e.g., Bimrose and Hearne, 2012; Buyukgoze-Kavas, 2016; Fleig-Palmer *et al.*, 2009). Luthans

(2002) defined the concept of resilience in an employment context as "the developable capacity to rebound or bounce back from adversity, conflict, and failure or even positive events, progress, and increased responsibility" (p. 702). Resilience is considered an aspect of personality, one among certain other traits that influence both [an employee's] attitude toward organisational change and coping with stress from organisational change (Seibert *et al.*, 2016), making it worthy of investigation.

In their study investigating resilience and career adaptability, Bimrose and Hearne (2012) found that resilience emerged as a crucial variable in overcoming individual and structural hurdles. Wanberg and Banas (2000) and Kantur and İşeri-Say (2012) found more resilient employees were those who were also better at coping with organisational change. It was previously reported that resilient employees might be valuable to the organisation because of their propensity to use an adverse experience to subsequently perform better (Hind *et al.*, 1996). Resilience developed and demonstrated in a certain situation leads to better preparation for upcoming events (Egeland *et al.*, 1993). Resilient individuals are more likely "to pursue novel, creative, and unscripted paths of thought and action" (Tugade and Fredrickson, 2004, p. 331). Such definition suggests that resilience is an enduring characteristic individuals have, which are developed over time as a result of life experiences and age and based on which they have the ability to respond to the environment (Roberts, 2018). There is a positive relationship between a high level of resilience and adaptability to change (Waugh *et al.*, 2011).

Thus, we speculated that a resilient employee might cope better with adverse and stressful situations and adapt more easily in a changing environment. The theory of cognitive flexibility has it that cognitive flexibility is inherent to a person's sentience in any given situation, and that there are alternatives available, such as the alacrity with which adaptation is made, and recognising resilience as a virtue of self (Malachowski *et al.*, 2012). Individuals who are able to perceive a situation with flexibility are more likely able to adapt to it. Cognitive flexibility is apparent only when a person recognises the need and is willing to be flexible. Since resilience encompasses adaptation, improvisation, and flexibility in situations characterised by change and uncertainty (Youssef and Luthans, 2007), we, therefore, proposed its positive correlation with career adaptability.

H2: *Employee resilience is positively and significantly related to career adaptability.*

Work-related curiosity and career adaptability

Curiosity is a personality construct that may be loosely defined as a desire to seek knowledge, resolve uncertainty, engage in continuous learning, and solve problems (Arnone *et al.*, 2011; Mussel, 2013; Peterson and Seligman, 2004). Mussel

(2013) noted that employee curiosity, which has become an important topic likely to become more important in the future, has nonetheless been neglected in organisational research. Kashdan *et al.* (2004) stated that curiosity is a "positive emotional-motivational system associated with the recognition, pursuit, and self-regulation of novel and challenging opportunities" (p. 291). Curiosity is regarded as a positive and desirable personality trait that fuels internal motivation and can significantly aid insight and understanding of how people engage in adaptive performance.

This study aimed to explore the relationship between curiosity and adaptability constructs because the relationship between them is unclear in the literature. Curiosity has been shown to be associated with a number of positive outcomes (Peterson and Seligman, 2004; Powell *et al.*, 2016). Mussel (2013) found curiosity could predict job performance and work-related outcomes. Curiosity and the exploratory behaviour it prompts is crucial in human development because it assists in the flexible adaptation to changing environmental conditions and implies development towards different ways of interacting and more effectively solving problems (Voss and Keller, 1983; Zacher, 2014). Normal patterns of cognitive development in adults are facilitated by the experience acquired as a result of curiosity and exploratory behaviour (Giambra *et al.*, 1992). The desire to seek information and knowledge has often been nominated as an important motivator of human actions throughout life (Loewenstein, 1994).

Here, it is proposed that curiosity prompts people's adaptability to workplace change. This is informed by Berlyne's (1960) optimal stimulation theory of exploratory behaviour which conceptualises curiosity as an intrinsic drive to reduce uncertainty. While organisms seek to sustain a personally optimal level of interaction with the environment, uncertainty can cause arousal. Curiosity drives organisms to seek out stimuli that reduce uncertainty, thus decreasing anxiety or vigilance to preferred levels. Therefore, employee curiosity prompts the gathering of occupational data and self-knowledge that determines the ability to fit the organisation environment. Openness to new experiences is the exploratory urge that may lead to the subsequent identification of career opportunities. Pulakos *et al.* (2000) illustrated that curious people perceive change and novel situations to be less stressful than do incurious individuals, and therefore they adapt more quickly. Accordingly, we hypothesised that curiosity is positively related to adaptability.

H3: *Work-related curiosity is positively and significantly related to career adaptability.*

Focus on opportunities and career adaptability

Focus on opportunities is a concept originally developed by developmental psychology (Zhou *et al.*, 2016). Focus on opportunities can be defined as the degree of which people believe that they have plans, goals, and possibilities in their future at work (Zacher and Frese, 2009, 2011). People who are highly focused on opportunities are those who are optimistic that they will be able to achieve their goals and plans based on the assessment of their past work experiences (Zacher and Frese, 2009, 2011). Its utility in the work context has been validated in various studies (Gielnik *et al.*, 2017; Schmitt *et al.*, 2013). In particular, having a focus on opportunity is argued to be an important trait for successful entrepreneurs (Pendergast, 2003). Focus on opportunity has been shown to positively influence current workplace motivation (Zacher and Frese, 2011). However, the role of focus on opportunities in adaptable performance has not, so far, been investigated. Foo *et al.* (2009) indicated that entrepreneurs' flexible focus on future opportunities predicted increased present effort beyond the requirement, and Schmitt *et al.* (2013) found a positive correlation of future focus with daily work engagement. While Zacher and Frese (2009) reported a negative correlation with age, job complexity was positively related to focus on opportunities where older employees with higher job complexity maintained a focus on work-related opportunities.

This study proposed that focus on opportunities is a source of motivation and energy for employees in their adaptation to a changing environment. The theoretical basis for this assumption is a social cognitive theoretical framework with a future-oriented dimension which motivation, and the motivational power of optimism about the future, is central (Aspinwall, 2005; Oettingen and Mayer, 2002). For employees, focusing on opportunities includes thinking positively about their personal work future, envisaging career possibilities, and planning and pursuing goals (Zacher and Frese, 2009, 2011). Employees who focus on opportunities may be more motivated to devote more efforts to their job since the anticipated value of their opportunities and future goals are higher (Karniol and Ross, 1996). Therefore, those with a higher-level focus give more attention and energy to work-related goals and are more likely to derive meaning from their work, which increases their ability to adapt to current and anticipated career changes and challenges. Thus, employees who focus on opportunities are equipped with a motivational resource that aids their adaptability to environmental changes.

H4: *Focus on opportunities is positively and significantly related to career adaptability.*

Career adaptability as a mediator

Individual career adaptability is proposed in this study to mediate the relationship between personality traits and innovative behaviour. Results from previous studies have indicated a persisting lack of clear delineation of the relationships between personality traits and individual behaviours and outcomes such as innovative behaviour. Thus, to illuminate these correlations, researchers proposed using meditation or moderation (George and Zhou, 2001; Sung and Choi, 2009; Williams, 2004). The rationale for this assumption is that only certain personality traits, such as resilience, curiosity, and focus on opportunity, have value in helping individuals to adapt more easily to new or changing environments because they reframe the implications of change from threat to challenge (Bimrose and Hearne, 2012; Zacher, 2014; Zacher and Frese, 2009, 2011). Adaptive ability is likely to predict the ease with which individuals engage in creative and innovative behaviour. Previous research proposing that certain personality traits underlie human adaptation to the environment and influence psychological fitness (Hettema, 1979; Nettle, 2006), which serves as a proxy for problem-solving and innovative work behaviour, supports this view.

H5: *Career adaptability mediates the relationship between employee resilience and innovative behaviour.*
H6: *Career adaptability mediates the relationship between work-related curiosity and innovative behaviour.*
H7: *Career adaptability mediates the relationship between a focus on opportunity and innovative behaviour.*

Theoretical framework

The research model adopted in this study integrates the theories and reasoning outlined above and is presented in Fig. 1. The model proposes that employee

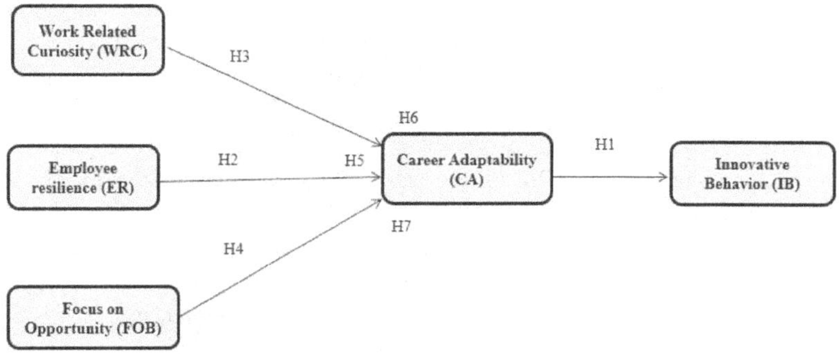

Fig. 1. A theoretical model of the study.

resilience, work-related curiosity, and focus on opportunity influence innovative work behaviour indirectly through career-related adaptability.

Methodology

Sample selection and data collection

Data were collected using a survey, consisting of two sequential questionnaires (Arabic and English versions), of a convenience sample of full-time front-desk employees of various five-star chain-branded hotels in Dubai. Five-star hotels were chosen because of the likely demand for high quality, innovative service offerings in this category (Bryman and Bell, 2015). Dubai has the highest concentration of five-star hotels in the UAE.

In the UAE government's Dubai Vision 2020 it is envisaged that Dubai will host 20 million tourists per year by 2020, tripling the current economic contribution of tourism to the Emirates' economy (Edgcumbe, 2013). The study specifically selected frontline hotel employees, i.e., those staff who have constant interaction with hotel customers. These employees deal daily with a diverse range of customers/guests who have distinctive needs and preferences. Frontline employees are expected to be responsive, knowledgeable, and able to offer solutions to customers whose needs fall outside the routine (Stock, 2016).

At the time of the study, there were 129 five-star hotels in Dubai. A list of these was prepared, along with the details of their human resources (HR) managers, to obtain formal permission to conduct the study. Access to these hotels was facilitated mainly by personal and professional contacts of the study's authors. Of this list, only 53 hotels agreed to participate in the study. A research assistant handed the questionnaire and a cover letter to obtain approval first from the hotel management. At the two-week follow-up, only 32 hotels confirmed their participation in the study. Some of the hotels refused to participate in this study because of the restriction policy from the general management and the fear of lack of confidentiality, despite verbal and written assurances from the researchers. Supervisors were then requested to inform frontline employees of the purpose of the study; the research assistant coordinated with each employee who agreed to take part in the study to explain its procedure.

The procedure for collecting data was as follows. Questionnaires were to be completed in two different time phases to limit the occurrence of common method bias and ensure that the temporal sequence of the independent and dependent variables was maintained (Podsakoff *et al.*, 2003). A reference number was assigned to each questionnaire to ensure that the same employee answered the questionnaire in each of the two phases. Recruits were informed that participation was voluntary and that all responses would be anonymous and subject to confidentiality. Supervisors at each hotel were asked to select one of the participants to coordinate the two-phase collection of completed questionnaires, which were returned directly to the research assistant in sealed envelopes. The first of the two-phase questionnaire survey was conducted on May 7, 2018 (time-1) with the research assistant personally distributing the questionnaires among 480 frontline employees of the participating hotels. The participants provided self-ratings on employee resilience, work-related curiosity, focus on opportunity, and career adaptability. A total of 397 completed questionnaires were received within one month, which represented a response rate of 82% at time-1. Two weeks later (June 20, 2018, time-2), the second set of questionnaires was distributed among these 397 participants who had completed the first questionnaire following the same procedure as with the time-1 survey. In the second survey, the participants provided ratings about innovative behaviour. On July 13, 313 completed questionnaires were collected, yielding a response rate of 78% at time-2. The overall response rate of 65% was acceptable average for such research type.

Measures

In the first of the two main sections, demographic data such as age, educational level, gender, and working experience were collected to create participant profiles. The second section referred to the main variables of the study, which were measured by closed questions whose responses were anchored on a Likert-type scale of a five-point range from strongly agree (5) to strongly disagree (1). Innovative behaviour was operationalised by six items adapted from Hu *et al.* (2009), and seven items from Luthans *et al.* (2007) were utilised by the employee resilience construct. Career adaptability was measured using five items adapted from Rottinghaus *et al.* (2005). Four items from Lang and Carstensen (2002) were used to assess participants' focus on opportunity. Finally, work-related curiosity was operationalised using ten items from Mussel (2013).

Analysis and results

Participant profile

Table 1 sets out the demographic profile of the participants in this study. Most of the participants were male, aged 21–30 years old, had a bachelor's degree, and years of work experience in the range between one and five.

Structural model testing

Construct relationships were analysed via structural equation modeling (SEM) in the Partial Least Squares (PLS) approach using SmartPLS.3 Software (Hansmann

Table 1. Participant profile.

Characteristic	Frequency	Percentage
Gender		
Male	196	62.6
Female	117	37.4
Age		
21–30	166	53
31–40	102	32.6
41–50	45	14.4
Educational level		
Diploma	43	13.8
Bachelor	219	70
Master	51	16.2
Work experience		
1–5	105	33.6
5–10	98	31.3
10–15	61	19.5
15–20	41	13.1
More than 20 years	8	2.5

and Ringle, 2004). PLS is appropriate for causal modeling in cases where sample sizes are small and models complex (Fornell and Bookstein, 1982; Hulland, 1999). The PLS approach requires a minimum sample size $n = 30$, and one that is ten times greater than (a) the number of items comprising the most formative constructs, or (b) the number of independent constructs directly influencing a dependent construct (Wixom and Watson, 2001). This study's sample size of 313 met these requirements. A PLS model is usually analysed and interpreted in two stages (Hulland, 1999). The measurement model is tested in the first stage by performing validity and reliability analyses of each of the measurements returned by the model. In the second stage, the structural model is tested by estimating the paths between its constructs to determine their significance, as well as the model's predictive ability. This sequence is followed to ensure that the measurements of the constructs are valid and reliable before conclusions about the significance of inter-construct relationships are drawn (Hulland, 1999).

Reliability and validity

As part of measurement evaluation, this study considers composite reliability, average variance extracted (AVE = convergent validity), outer loadings, Cronbach's alpha, cross loading and discriminant validity. To test the reliability of measurement model, Dijkstra–Henseler's rho (ρA) (an estimate of the reliability of construct scores), composite reliability and Cronbach's Alpha values are examined to ensure the reliability of the measurement model. All values of factor loadings, ρA, and Cronbach's Alpha are shown in Table 1, which are acceptable (more than 0.7) (Henseler *et al.*, 2016), justifying the reliability of constructs. Further, the AVE values for all exogenous constructs and the endogenous construct denote the convergent validity as the values are well above the minimum required level of 0.50 (see Table 2).

Furthermore, to assess the discriminant validity between constructs, Fornell and Larcker (1981) and cross-loading criterion were used. Referring to Table 3, the diagonals or numbers in bold are the AVE, while the other values represent the squared correlations, and thus off-diagonal values in the table are the correlations between the latent variables. In addition, as shown in Appendix A, comparing the loadings across the columns, an indicator's loadings on its own variable are in all cases higher than all of its cross loadings with other variables.

In addition, Henseler *et al.* (2016) indicated that Heterotrait–Monotrait (HTMT) ratio of correlations is required for examining discriminant validity in SmartPLS approach. They argued that both Fornell–Larcker criterion and cross loadings are not enough for evaluating discriminant validity and researchers need to report HTMT ratio of correlation. The threshold value for HTMT is below 0.9 (Teo *et al.*, 2008). Table 4 shows that all HTMT values are below the required value of 0.9. Through the results of bootstrapping for HTMT, the confidence intervals showed that the upper confidence intervals are below 1. The HTMT inference means that all HTMT values are significantly different from 1. Therefore, the discriminant validity of all constructs is met.

We also evaluated the quality of the structural model by using the R^2 of the dependent and mediating variables (Chin, 1998) and the Stone–Geisser Q-square test for predictive relevance (Hair *et al.*, 2014, p. 167). The R^2 value for the endogenous constructs in this case (innovative behaviour and career adaptability) was adequate (0.26 and 0.59, respectively) while most of the path coefficients were substantial and significant. Finally, like Chin *et al.* (2008) argued, researchers should be able to deploy the magnitude of R^2 and Stone–Geisser's Q^2 value as a criterion of the predictive value of assessing a model using PLS. Thus, a blindfolding technique in SmartPLS was employed to test the stability of the findings. The result of Q^2 calculation was greater than 0, i.e., $Q^2 = 0.15$ for innovative behaviour and $Q^2 = 0.39$ for career adaptability, signifying satisfactory predictive relevance (Hair *et al.*, 2014). Therefore, confidence in the model's stability and the predictive relevance requirement were satisfied. The goodness of fit (GoF) was not selected as a criterion for PLS-SEM because it cannot separate valid/invalid

Table 2. Construct reliability and validity.

Variable(s)	λi	Cronbach's alpha	Composite[b] reliability	AVE[a]	Dijkstra–Henseler's rho (ρA)
Innovative Behaviour		0.881	0.91	0.627	0.889
At work, I come up with innovative and creative notions	0.814				
At work, I try to propose my own creative ideas and convince others	0.834				
At work, I seek new service techniques or methods	0.749				
At work, I provide plans for developing new ideas	0.823				
I try to secure the resources needed to implement innovations	0.719				
Overall, I consider myself a creative member of my team	0.805				
Career Adaptability		0.897	0.924	0.71	0.902
I am good at adapting to new work settings	0.836				
I can overcome potential barriers that may exist in my career	0.861				
I enjoy trying new work-related tasks	0.861				
I can adapt to change in the world of work	0.892				
Others would say that I am adaptable to change in my career plans	0.757				
Resilience		0.888	0.913	0.603	0.893
When I have a setback (i.e., frustration) at work, I easily to recover from it and move on	0.62				
I usually manage difficulties one way or another at work	0.843				
I can get through difficult times at work because I've experienced difficulties before	0.747				
I learn from mistakes at work and improve the way I do my job	0.835				
I re-evaluate my performance and continually improve the way I do my work	0.819				
I respond effectively to feedback at work, even criticism	0.811				
I use change at work as an opportunity for growth	0.737				

Table 2. (*Continued*)

Variable(s)	λi	Cronbach's alpha	Composite[b] reliability	AVE[a]	Dijkstra–Henseler's rho (ρA)
Work-related curiosity		0.893	0.90	0.51	0.904
I am interested in how my contribution impacts this hotel	0.717				
I try to improve work processes by making innovative suggestions	0.753				
I enjoy developing a new theory	0.681				
Regarding practical problems, I'm also interested in the underlying causes	0.639				
When confronted with complex problems, I like to look for new solutions	0.726				
I enjoy pondering and thinking	0.63				
I am eager to learn	0.629				
I keep thinking about a problem until I've solved it	0.668				
I challenge already existing theories critically	0.723				
I carry on seeking information until I am able to understand complex issues	0.776				
Focus on opportunity		0.852	0.9	0.692	0.867
Many opportunities await me in my occupational future	0.854				
I expect that I will set many new goals in my occupational future	0.849				
My occupational future is filled with possibilities	0.85				
I could do anything I want in my occupational future	0.772				

Notes: [a]Average variance extracted (AVE) = (summation of the square of the factor loadings)/[(summation of the square of the factor loadings) + (summation of the error variances)]. [b]Composite reliability (CR) = (square of the summation of the factor loadings)/[(square of the summation of the factor loadings) + (square of the summation of the error variances)].

models and is not applicable to formative measurement models (Hair *et al.*, 2014, p. 185; Henseler and Sarstedt, 2013).

Hypothesis testing

After the validity and reliability testing, the hypothesised model was tested by SEM using SMART-PLS.3. Coefficient values and significance levels were used

Table 3. Mean, std. deviation and discriminant validity — Fornell–Larcker criterion.

Variable(s)	Mean	Std. Deviation	IB	CA	ER	WRC	FOP
IB	3.68	0.70	0.792[a]				
CA	3.83	0.67	0.516	0.842			
ER	3.83	0.76	0.49	0.719	0.775		
WRC	3.70	0.64	0.538	0.431	0.34	0.705	
FOP	3.54	0.75	0.574	0.593	0.546	0.449	0.832

Notes: [a]The off-diagonal values in the above matrix are the correlations between the latent constructs and diagonal are square values of AVEs.
IB = innovative behaviour, CA = career adaptability, ER = employee resilience, WRC = work-related curiosity, FO = focus on opportunity.

Table 4. Discriminant validity — Heterotrait–Monotrait ratio.

Variable(s)	IB	CA	ER	WRC	FOP
IB					
CA	0.566				
ER	0.537	0.805			
WRC	0.315	0.417	0.315		
FOP	0.646	0.672	0.612	0.474	

Notes: The criterion for HTMT is below or 0.90 (Gold and Arvind Malhotra, 2001; Teo *et al.*, 2008).
IB = innovative behaviour, CA = career adaptability, ER = employee resilience, WRC = work-related curiosity, FO = focus on opportunity.

to confirm/disconfirm the proposed correlatives. Analysis of the whole sample ($n = 313$) revealed a significant positive relationship between individual career adaptability and innovative behaviour ($\beta = 0.52$, $t = 9.36$, $p < 0.01$), supporting Hypothesis 1. Similarly, results for the three personality traits — employee resilience, work-related curiosity and focus on opportunity — showed positive and significant effects on employee career adaptability ($\beta = 0.54$, $t = 9.33$, $p < 0.01$), ($\beta = 0.15$, $t = 3.3$, $p < 0.01$) and ($\beta = 0.24$, $t = 4.39$, $p < 0.01$), respectively, supporting Hypotheses 2, 3, and 4. Further, the mediating role of career adaptability in the relationship of each of the traits and innovative behaviour was shown in the finding that career adaptability was a significant mediator of the relationships ($\beta = 0.28$, $t = 7.961$, $p < 0.01$), ($\beta = 0.10$, $t = 2.76$, $p < 0.01$) and ($\beta = 0.12$, $t = 3.47$, $p < 0.01$), respectively. Table 5 and Fig. 2 set out the detailed results of the data analysis.

Table 5. Summary of the PLS regression results.

Relationships	Variable	Coefficient	t-value	p-value	Result
Direct relationships	CA → IB	0.52	9.36	0.00	H1: Supported
	ER → CA	0.54	9.33	0.00	H2: Supported
	WRC → CA	0.15	3.30	0.00	H3: Supported
	FOP → CA	0.24	4.39	0.00	H4: Supported
Mediating effect 1	ER → CA → IB	0.28	7.96	0.00	H5: Supported
Mediating effect 2	WRC → CA → IB	0.10	2.76	0.00	H6: Supported
Mediating effect 3	FO → CA → IB	0.12	3.47	0.00	H7: Supported

Notes: $^{*}p < 0.05$, $^{**}p < 0.01$.
IB = innovative behaviour, CA = career adaptability, ER = employee resilience, WRC = work-related curiosity, FO = focus on opportunity.

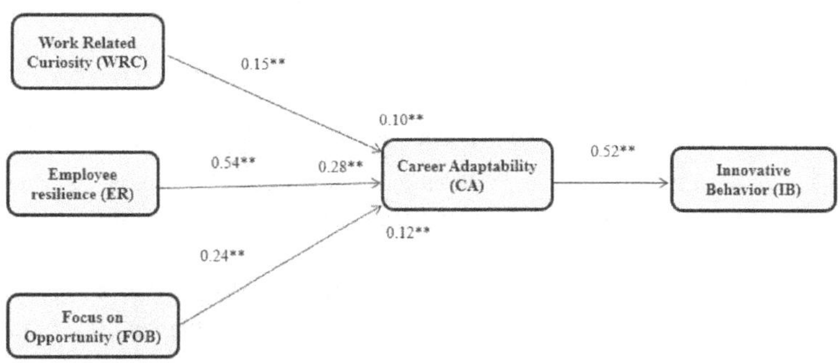

Note: $^{**}p < 0.01$.

Fig. 2. Illustration of the main findings.

Discussion and Conclusion

The main objective of the present study was to discover the potential drivers of innovative work behaviour. Two key points from this research stand out. The first is the considerable influence of career adaptability on innovative work behaviour. Career adaptability, or the capacity to cope with and capitalise on change in a future orientation, can be demonstrated by an employee's level of comfort with additional responsibilities, and the capacity for recovery when unexpected events impact career plans (Rottinghaus *et al.*, 2005). The highly adaptable employee indicates experience of several transitions during the life of a career and of various learning stages (Brown, 2015). In the hotel industry, changing jobs is not uncommon and reflects employees' aspirations to obtain different experience and new skills (CareerBuilder, 2014; Richardson, 2010). The greater scope of experiences, skills, and knowledge gained from job changes equips individuals with a broader perspective on work-related problem solving and innovative use of resources (Johnston, 2016; Savickas and Porfeli, 2012).

In the hotel industry innovative behaviour is expected of front-desk staff to fit a hotel's quality and innovative service image which underlies its organisational success (Naranjo-Valencia *et al.*, 2016; Rhee *et al.*, 2010). In a national survey in the United States of approximately 1000 travelers, Victorino *et al.* (2005) found that innovative service was a significant factor in selecting a hotel. A Nigerian study of four-star hotels by Igwe and Kalu (2017) similarly reported a strong and positive association between customer satisfaction and innovative service, and that the latter also influenced the booking decision. The importance of offering distinctive and problem-free service is paramount in hospitality enterprises, and so high-performing employees tend to be rewarded (Chandler *et al.*, 2000), which reinforces their motivation to make innovation part of their practice. Career adaptability is shown to be critical in determining career performance and workplace success (Autin *et al.*, 2017; Chan *et al.*, 2016; Nilforooshan and Salimi, 2016). Career construction theory states that individuals are capable of enacting change to improve their current circumstances (Crant, 2000, p. 41), which is supported by the demonstrable link between adaptive ability and innovative behaviour whereby employees initiate their own efforts to achieve their career goals.

Notwithstanding the plausibility of this explanation for the significant adaptability-innovation link, future studies should seek to validate the assertion by collecting data on the career transitions of hotel employees over time and determining whether and how career adaptability has translated to innovative performance. Equally important is the question of whether the desire to engage in innovative job performance drives hotel employees to change jobs and contribute further to the rates of staff turnover endemic in the hospitality industry.

Accepting the results for the link between career adaptability and enhanced innovative behaviour at work implies that certain personality constructs tend to influence career adaptability. Employees who are more resilient, curious, and opportunity-focused are also more career-adaptable. The conceptual premise of this study is that focus on opportunity incentivises individuals to visualise and prepare for future career possibilities by acquiring knowledge and skills and being more attuned and adapting to environmental change, assisted by curiosity about career opportunities (Savickas, 1997, 2005, 2013). Resilient employees also may draw on learning from an adverse experience to inform innovative performance in subsequent tasks. This adaptive potential makes resilient workers valuable to their organisation in times of changed or uncertain circumstances (Hind *et al.*, 1996).

These findings were anticipated because the personality constructs used in this study reflect career-related capabilities (Savickas, 2005) such as awareness and interpretation of the environment that allow individuals to adjust their mindset when current information does not fit (Gaglio and Katz, 2001). On this point, our result supports the differential perspective of career construction theory which describes how people develop a vocational personality and career-related abilities as adaptive strategies in the workplace (Savickas, 2005).

This result also offers a direction for future research. Past studies have tended to investigate the role of the "big five" personality traits in work-related outcomes such as burnout (Kim *et al.*, 2007; O'Neill and Xiao, 2010) but, to date, none has examined traits specific to career conduct. Speculation that the career-oriented personality may have an important role in employee turnover prevalence could proceed to theorise the link between three constructs — career-related personality, career adaptability, and turnover — in a single model.

Theoretical implications

The study has several implications for theory. The first speaks to the influence of three personality constructs on adaptive career performance. Our finding supports the contention of Borman (2004, p. 267) that narrower personality constructs could better explain a relatively specific criterion. Adhering to the Big Five personality model may not be useful for further theoretical development of the specific innovative behaviour–career performance link because the model pertains more closely to individuals' general pre-work, the residual components of personality. Our finding, by contrast, implies that the course of individuals' careers may be reflected in three personality constructs relating more directly to job performance, adaptability and response to change (Savickas, 2005). These personality constructs are meaningful and practical because they suggest that a career-oriented personality can be developed through self-effort, such that individuals become adaptive, curious, and resilient.

Another theoretical implication of this study is its highlighting of the value of testing an integrative model of career adaptability as it allows us to examine the indirect influence of career-related personality constructs on innovative behaviour. The integrative model helps clarify our understanding of how employee resilience, work-related curiosity, and focus on opportunity could drive employees to enact innovative work behaviour. Career adaptability was the elective explanatory mechanism in this study, although other mediating factors could be considered. However, this study primarily aimed to elucidate the role of vocational personality constructs in employees' propensity for career adaptability and, subsequently, their demonstrating innovative behaviour. The integrative model hence could constitute a critical first step in advancing our understanding of the development of a comprehensive explanatory framework for innovative behaviour viewed through the career lens.

Practical applications

Hospitality venues are characteristically dynamic workplaces whose employees are frequently challenged by unexpected events and/or excessive workloads. The public exposure of hotel employees makes explicit the requirement for creative problem solving and capacity for delivering innovative solutions and immediate response in a fast-paced environment (Chan *et al.*, 2015; Sigala and Kyriakidou, 2015). This study indicated that certain personality constructs contribute to frontline hotel employees' ability to cope and adapt to change and, in turn, prompting innovative behaviour. Our results pointed to significant benefits that human resource managers and practitioners in the hotel industry may gain in the recruitment of frontline personnel as well as in promoting and facilitating innovative behaviour.

Our results showed how trait curiosity is beneficial to innovative performance. Management should seek to cultivate work-related curiosity among their staff by welcoming questions, discussion and knowledge-sharing, and encouraging their employees to seek solutions to problems as they arise independently. Further, recruitment processes could include an assessment of curiosity in candidates for frontline hospitality employment that could figure more prominently in the selection process. Introducing training interventions which aim to foster work-related curiosity and emphasise other forms of divergent thinking may be useful.

Organisations can also establish strategies and means for selecting for and increasing employees' awareness of work-related opportunities. An organisational culture of learning and growth (Buckingham and Coffman, 1999; Sorakraikitikul and Siengthai, 2014) would be a basis for opportunity-seeking whereby employees of all educational backgrounds have access to professional development opportunities. Mentoring activities such as coaching and appraisal interviews should focus on employees' future options and include goal setting.

Resilience, as a set of personal abilities, temperament, and strategies, is plastic and can be developed (Krush *et al.*, 2013); developing a more resilient way of being is so useful that it should be an essential part of strategic human resource management. Resilience training and building programs in the workplace have been proven effective, reporting positive impacts on health, well-being, and performance (Sarkar and Fletcher, 2017; Robertson *et al.*, 2015). This is particularly relevant to stressful and time-constrained working environments such as those in the hotel industry.

As adaptive performance becomes an increasingly important attribute for employees in the labor market, the identification of individuals who can more positively adapt to change and uncertainty in workplace situations can provide businesses with a competitive edge. While there is general agreement that certain individuals are more likely to adapt well to dynamic work environments, firms are also able to influence their employees' adaptability. This study proposed that employee adaptability is a critical component leading to innovative behaviour in the hotel industry and that organisational interventions could promote frontline employees' adaptive capacities. That is, for practitioners concerned about the efficiency of measurements when designing staff recruitment guides, the non-developmental character of openness may preclude its being added to selection indicators. Leaders can develop organisational adaptability by fostering a supportive command climate where judicious accepting and taking of risks is acknowledged, new ideas receive valid consideration, there is access to knowledge and opportunities for collaboration and exchange of ideas, and where individual adaptability is rewarded so that it becomes fundamental to the organisation's culture. Similarly, job descriptions and enrichment programs should promote the conditions for developing high-activated positive mood work environments where, ideally, employees have autonomy, responsibility, and social interactions leading to innovative behaviour (Axtell *et al.*, 2000).

These results have especial relevance and utility for tourism and hospitality managers and policymakers in the UAE given the ongoing pressure for this sector to perform as a key economic contributor (Ahmed, 2015; Callen *et al.*, 2014; WTTC, 2016) in the shift from oil and gas dependency and diversification of industry. Therefore, this research provides the UAE hotel sector with an empirical framework for an integrated approach to developing innovative employee behaviour.

Limitations

Findings from this study should be interpreted with the following limitations taken into account. First, even though the order of constructs in our integrative model was informed by relevant theories such as the career construction theory, the causal link among constructs was not ascertained. It is possible that individuals develop career-related abilities or skills as an outcome of their innovative behaviour in accomplishing career performance. That is, in the delivery of innovative service, individuals discover those skills and abilities necessary for coping well in a pressured work environment. Nonetheless, further studies are required for determining the causal ordering of the constructs. Second, because the study was limited to frontline five-star hotel employees, the generalisability of its findings to larger populations and/or less prestigious hotels may be constrained — lower ranked hotels may be less well-resourced and, thus, less innovative than top-line hotels. It is generally accepted that an organisational culture of innovation stimulates more innovative employee performance (Chandler *et al.*, 2000).

References

Abbas, M and U Raja (2015). Impact of psychological capital on innovative performance and job stress. *Canadian Journal of Administrative Sciences/Revue Canadienne des Sciences de l'Administration*, 32(2), 128–138.

Abukhait, R, S Bani-Melhem and R Zeffane (2018). Empowerment, knowledge sharing, and innovative behaviors: Exploring gender differences. *International Journal of Innovation Management*. Available at https://doi.org/10.1142/S1363919619500063.

Ahmed, AZE (2015). The role of diversification strategies in the economic development for oil-depended countries: The case of UAE. *International Journal of Business and Economic Development*, 3(1), 47–57.

Akoum, IF (2008). Conducting business in the UAE: A brief for international managers. *Global Business and Organizational Excellence*, 27(4), 51–66.

Anwar, SA and MS Sohail (2004). Festival tourism in the United Arab Emirates: First-time versus repeat visitor perceptions. *Journal of Vacation Marketing*, 10(2), 161–170.

Arnone, MP, RV Small, SA Chauncey and HP McKenna (2011). Curiosity, interest and engagement in technology-pervasive learning environments: A new research agenda. *Educational Technology Research and Development*, 59(2), 181–198.

Asamsama, OH, BR Nelson, D Wiest and D Nelson (2011). Adaptability. In *Encyclopedia of Child Behavior and Development*, Goldstein S and JA Naglieri (eds.). Springer, Boston, MA.

Aspinwall, LG (2005). The psychology of future-oriented thinking: From achievement to proactive coping, adaptation, and aging. *Motivation and Emotion*, 29(4), 203–235.

Autin, KL, RP Douglass, RD Duffy, JW England and BA Allan (2017). Subjective social status, work volition, and career adaptability: A longitudinal study. *Journal of Vocational Behavior*, 99, 1–10.

Avey, JB, F Luthans and CM Youssef (2010). The additive value of positive psychological capital in predicting work attitudes and behaviors. *Journal of Management*, 36(2), 430–452.

Avey, JB, F Luthans and S Wernsing (2008). Can positive employees help positive organizational change? Impact of psychological capital and emotions on relevant attitudes and behaviors. *The Journal of Applied Behavioral Science*, 44(1), 48–70.

Axtell, CM, DJ Holman, KL Unsworth, TD Wall, PE Waterson and E Harrington (2000). Shopfloor innovation: Facilitating the suggestion and implementation of ideas. *Journal of Occupational and Organizational Psychology*, 73(3), 265–285.

Bagaeen, S (2015). Brand Dubai: The instant city; or the instantly recognizable city. *International Planning Studies*, 12(2), 173–197.

Berlyne, DE (1960). *McGraw-Hill Series in Psychology: Conflict, Arousal, and Curiosity*. New York, NY: McGraw-Hill Book Company.

Biemann T, H Zacher and DC Feldman (2012). Career patterns: A twenty-year panel study. *Journal of Vocational Behavior*, 81(2), 159–170.

Bimrose, J and L Hearne (2012). Resilience and career adaptability: Qualitative studies of adult career counseling. *Journal of Vocational Behavior*, 81(3), 338–344.

Borman, WC (2004). Introduction to the special issue: Personality and the prediction of job performance: More than the big five. *Human Performance*, 17(3), 267–269.

Brown, A (2015). Developing career adaptability and innovative capabilities through learning and working in Norway and the United Kingdom. *Journal of the Knowledge Economy*, 6(2), 402–419.

Bryman, A and E Bell (2015). *Business Research Methods*Oxford: Oxford University Press.

Buckingham, M and C Coffman (1999). *First, Break All the Rules*New York: Simon & Schuster.

Burns, E and AJ Martin (2014). ADHD and adaptability: The roles of cognitive, behavioral, and emotional regulation. *Journal of Psychologists and Counsellors in Schools*, 24(2), 227–242.

Buyukgoze-Kavas, A (2016). Predicting career adaptability from positive psychological traits. *The Career Development Quarterly*, 64(2), 114–125.

Callen, MT, R Cherif, F Hasanov, MA Hegazy and P Khandelwal (2014). *Economic Diversification in the GCC: Past, Present, and Future*. International Monetary Fund.

CareerBuilder (2014). Number of employers passing on applicants due to social media posts continues to rise — According to New CareerBuilder Survey. CareerBuilder, 1.

Chan, SH, X Mai, OM Kuok and SH Kong (2016). The influence of satisfaction and promotability on the relation between career adaptability and turnover intentions. *Journal of Vocational Behavior*, 92, 167–175.

Chan, SH, YKP Wan and OM Kuok (2015). Relationships among burnout, job satisfaction, and turnover of casino employees in Macau. *Journal of Hospitality Marketing and Management*, 24(4), 345–374.

Chandler, GN, C Keller and DW Lyon (2000). Unraveling the determinants and consequences of an innovation-supportive organizational culture. *Entrepreneurship Theory and Practice*, 25(1), 59–76.

Chen, SC, MC Wu and CH Chen (2010). Employee's personality traits, work motivation and innovative behavior in marine tourism industry. *Journal of Service Science and Management*, 3(2), 198–205.

Chin, WW (1998). The partial least squares approach to structural equation modelling. *Modern Methods for Business Research*, 295(2), 295–336.

Chin, WW, RA Peterson and SP Brown (2008). Structural equation modeling in marketing: Some practical reminders. *Journal of Marketing Theory and Practice*, 16(4), 287–298.

Collie, RJ and AJ Martin (2016). Adaptability: An important capacity for effective teachers. *Educational Practice and Theory*, 38(1), 27–39.

Crant, J (2000). Proactive behavior in organizations. *Journal of Management*, 26, 435–462.

Cullen, KL, BD Edwards, WC Casper and KR Gue (2014). Employees' adaptability and perceptions of change-related uncertainty: Implications for perceived organizational support, job satisfaction, and performance. *Journal of Business and Psychology*, 29(2), 269–280.

Edgcumbe, D (2013, May 5). DTCM unveils Dubai's tourism Vision for 2020. Available at http://www.hoteliermiddleeast.com/17095.

Egeland, B, E Carlson and LA Sroufe (1993). Resilience as process. *Development and Psychopathology*, 5(4), 517–528.

Feist, GJ (1998). A meta-analysis of personality in scientific and artistic creativity. *Personality and Social Psychology Review*, 2(4), 290–309.

Fleig-Palmer, MM, KW Luthans and BJ Mandernach (2009). Successful reemployment through resiliency development. *Journal of Career Development*, 35(3), 228–247.

Foo, MD, MA Uy and RA Baron (2009). How do feelings influence effort? An empirical study of entrepreneurs' affect and venture effort. *Journal of Applied Psychology*, 94(4), 1086–1094.

Fornell, C and DF Larcker (1981). Evaluating structural equation models with unobservable variables and measurement error. *Journal of Marketing Research*, 18(1), 39–50.

Fornell, C and FL Bookstein (1982). Two structural equations models: LISREL and PLS applied to consumer exit-voice theory. *Journal of Marketing Research*, 19(4), 440–452.

Gaglio, CM and JA Katz (2001). The psychological basis of opportunity identification: Entrepreneurial alertness. *Small Business Economics*, 16(2), 95–111.

George, JM and J Zhou (2001). When openness to experience and conscientiousness are related to creative behavior: An interactional approach. *Journal of Applied Psychology*, 86(3), 513–524.

Giambra, LM, CJ Camp and A Grodsky (1992). Curiosity and stimulation seeking across the adult life span: Cross-sectional and 6- to 8-year longitudinal findings. *Psychology and Aging*, 7(1), 150–157.

Giebels, E, RS de Reuver, S Rispens and EG Ufkes (2016). The critical roles of task conflict and job autonomy in the relationship between proactive personalities and innovative employee behavior. *The Journal of Applied Behavioral Science*, 52(3), 320–341.

Gielnik, MM, H Zacher and A Schmitt (2017). How small business managers' age and focus on opportunities affect business growth: A mediated moderation growth model. *Journal of Small Business Management*, 55(3), 460–483.

Gupta, V and S Singh (2014). Psychological capital as a mediator of the relationship between leadership and creative performance behaviors: Empirical evidence from the Indian R&D sector. *The International Journal of Human Resource Management*, 25(10), 1373–1394.

Hair, JF Jr, M Sarstedt, L Hopkins and G Kuppelwieser V (2014). Partial least squares structural equation modeling (PLS-SEM) An emerging tool in business research. *European Business Review*, 26(2), 106–121.

Hansmann, K-W and CM Ringle (2004). *SmartPLS Manual*. Hamburg: University of Hamburg.

Henseler, J and M Sarstedt (2013). Goodness-of-fit indices for partial least squares path modeling. *Computational Statistics*, 28(2), 565–580.

Henseler, J, G Hubona and PA Ray (2016). Using PLS path modeling in new technology research: Updated guidelines. *Industrial Management & Data Systems*, 116(1), 2–20.

Hettema, PJ (1979). *Personality and Adaptation*, Vol. 2. Amsterdam: Elsevier.

Hind, P, M Frost and S Rowley (1996). The resilience audit and the psychological contract. *Journal of Managerial Psychology*, 11(7), 18–29.

Hough, LM, FL Oswald and J Ock (2015). Beyond the Big Five: New directions for personality research and practice in organizations. *Annual Review of Organizational Psychology and Organizational Behavior*, 2(1), 183–209.

Hu, MLM, JS Horng and YHC Sun (2009). Hospitality teams: Knowledge sharing and service innovation performance. *Tourism Management*, 30(1), 41–50.

Huang, JL, AM Ryan, KL Zabel and A Palmer (2014). Personality and adaptive performance at work: A meta-analytic investigation. *Journal of Applied Psychology*, 99(1), 162–179.

Huang, JX, J Miao and B He (2013). High performance query expansion using adaptive co-training. *Information Processing and Management*, 49(2), 441–453.

Hulland, J (1999). Use of partial least squares (PLS) in strategic management research: A review of four recent studies. *Strategic Management Journal*, 20(2), 195–204.

Igwe, P and SE Kalu (2017). Service innovativeness and customer satisfaction of four-star hotels in Rivers State. *International Journal of Research in Business Studies and Management*, 4(3), 55–65.

Johnston, CS (2016). A systematic review of the career adaptability literature and future outlook. *Journal of Career Assessment*, 1, 1–28.

Jundt, DK, MK Shoss and JL Huang (2015). Individual adaptive performance in organizations: A review. *Journal of Organizational Behavior*, 36(S1), S53–S71.

Kantur, D and A İşeri-Say (2012). Organizational resilience: A conceptual integrative framework. *Journal of Management and Organization*, 18(6), 762–773.

Karatepe, OM and L Zargar Tizabi (2011). Work-related depression in the hotel industry: A study in the United Arab Emirates. *International Journal of Contemporary Hospitality Management*, 23(5), 608–623.

Karniol, R and M Ross (1996). The motivational impact of temporal focus: Thinking about the future and the past. *Annual Review of Psychology*, 47(1), 593–620.

Kashdan, TB, P Rose and FD Fincham (2004). Curiosity and exploration: Facilitating positive subjective experiences and personal growth opportunities. *Journal of Personality Assessment*, 82(3), 291–305.

Kim, HJ, KH Shin and WT Umbreit (2007). Hotel job burnout: The role of personality characteristics. *International Journal of Hospitality Management*, 26(2), 421–434.

Kim, MS and DW Koo (2017). Linking LMX, engagement, innovative behavior, and job performance in hotel employees. *International Journal of Contemporary Hospitality Management*, 29(12), 3044–3062.

Krush, MT, RAJ Agnihotri, KJ Trainor and S Krishnakumar, S (2013). The salesperson's ability to bounce back: Examining the moderating role of resiliency on forms of intra-role job conflict and job attitudes, behaviors and performance. *Marketing Management Journal*, 23(1), 42–56.

Kuntz, JR, K Näswall and S Malinen (2016). Resilient employees in resilient organizations: Flourishing beyond adversity. *Industrial and Organizational Psychology*, 9(2), 456–462.

Lang, FR and LL Carstensen (2002). Time counts: Future time perspective, goals, and social relationships. *Psychology and Aging*, 17, 125–139.

Li, ML and RD Green (2011). A mediating influence on customer loyalty: The role of perceived value. *Journal of Management and Marketing Research*, 7, 1–12.

Li, Y, Y Guan, F Wang, X Zhou, K Guo, P Jiang and Z Fang (2015). Big-five personality and BIS/BAS traits as predictors of career exploration: The mediation role of career adaptability. *Journal of Vocational Behavior*, 89, 39–45.

Linnenluecke, MK (2017). Resilience in business and management research: A review of influential publications and a research agenda. *International Journal of Management Reviews*, 19(1), 4–30.

Loewenstein, G (1994). The psychology of curiosity: A review and reinterpretation. *Psychological Bulletin*, 116(1), 75–98.

Luthans, F (2002). The need for and meaning of positive organizational behavior. *Journal of Organizational Behavior*, 23(6), 695–706.

Luthans, F, BJ Avolio, JB Avey and SM Norman (2007). Positive psychological capital: Measurement and relationship with performance and satisfaction. *Personnel Psychology*, 60(3), 541–572.

Madrid, HP, MG Patterson, KS Birdi, PI Leiva and EE Kausel (2014). The role of weekly high-activated positive mood, context, and personality in innovative work behavior: A multilevel and interactional model. *Journal of Organizational Behavior*, 35(2), 234–256.

Malachowski, CC, RM Chory and CJ Claus (2012). Mixing pleasure with work: Employee perceptions of and responses to workplace romance. *Western Journal of Communication*, 76(4), 358–379.

Martin, AJ, HG Nejad, S Colmar and GAD Liem (2013). Adaptability: How students' responses to uncertainty and novelty predict their academic and non-academic outcomes. *Journal of Educational Psychology*, 105(3), 728–746.

Mussel, P (2013). Intellect: A theoretical framework for personality traits related to intellectual achievements. *Journal of Personality and Social Psychology*, 104(5), 885–906.

Naranjo-Valencia, JC, D Jiménez-Jiménez and R Sanz-Valle (2016). Studying the links between organizational culture, innovation, and performance in Spanish companies. *Revista Latinoamericana de Psicología*, 48(1), 30–41.

Neal, A, G Yeo, A Koy and T Xiao (2012). Predicting the form and direction of work role performance from the Big 5 model of personality traits. *Journal of Organizational Behavior*, 33(2), 175–192.

Nettle, D (2006). The evolution of personality variation in humans and other animals. *American Psychologist*, 61(6), 622–631.

Ngo, HY and R Loi (2008). Human resource flexibility, organizational culture and firm performance: An investigation of multinational firms in Hong Kong. *The International Journal of Human Resource Management*, 19(9), 1654–1666.

Nilforooshan, P and S Salimi (2016). Career adaptability as a mediator between personality and career engagement. *Journal of Vocational Behavior*, 94, 1–10.

Niu, HJ (2014). Is innovation behavior congenital? Enhancing job satisfaction as a moderator. *Personnel Review*, 43(2), 288–302.

O'Neill, JW and Q Xiao (2010). Effects of organizational/occupational characteristics and personality traits on hotel manager emotional exhaustion. *International Journal of Hospitality Management*, 29(4), 652–658.

Oettingen, G and D Mayer (2002). The motivating function of thinking about the future: Expectations versus fantasies. *Journal of Personality and Social Psychology*, 83(5), 1198.

Ohme, M and H Zacher (2015). Job performance ratings: The relative importance of mental ability, conscientiousness, and career adaptability. *Journal of Vocational Behavior*, 87, 161–170.

Pendergast, WR (2003). Entrepreneurial contexts and traits of entrepreneurs. In Teaching Entrepreneurship to Engineering Students. Available at https://dc.engconfintl.org/teaching/8.

Peterson, C and ME Seligman (2004). *Character Strengths and Virtues: A Handbook and classification* (Vol. 1). Oxford: Oxford University Press.

Pham, TK, CH Pham and L Pham (2016). Top management support, organizational learning, innovative behavior, employee commitment and organizational performance of manufacturing companies in Hai Phong. *International Journal of Financial Research*, 7(3), 54–64.

Podsakoff, PM, SB MacKenzie, JY Lee and NP Podsakoff (2003). Common method biases in behavioral research: A critical review of the literature and recommended remedies. *Journal of Applied Psychology*, 88(5), 879–903.

Powell, C, T Nettelbeck and NR Burns (2016). Deconstructing intellectual curiosity. *Personality and Individual Differences*, 95, 147–151.

Pulakos, ED, RA Mueller-Hanson, RS O'Leary and MM Meyrowitz (2012). Building a high-performance culture: A fresh look at performance management. *Effective Practices Guidelines Series*. Alexandria, VA: SHRM Foundation.

Pulakos, ED, S Arad, MA Donovan and KE Plamondon (2000). Adaptability in the workplace: Development of a taxonomy of adaptive performance. *Journal of Applied Psychology*, 85(4), 612–624.

Raja, U and G Johns (2010). The joint effects of personality and job scope on in-role performance, citizenship behaviors, and creativity. *Human Relations*, 63(7), 981–1005.

Rhee, J, T Park and DH Lee (2010). Drivers of innovativeness and performance for innovative SMEs in South Korea: Mediation of learning orientation. *Technovation*, 30(1), 65–75.

Richardson, S (2010). Generation Y's perceptions and attitudes towards a career in tourism and hospitality. *Journal of Human Resources in Hospitality and Tourism*, 9(2), 179–199.

Roberts, BW (2018). A revised sociogenomic model of personality traits. *Journal of Personality*, 86(1), 23–35.

Robertson, IT, CL Cooper, M Sarkar and T Curran (2015). Resilience training in the workplace from 2003 to 2014: A systematic review. *Journal of Occupational and Organizational Psychology*, 88(3), 533–562.

Roehling, MV, MA Cavanaugh, LM Moynihan and WR Boswell (2000). The nature of the new employment relationship: A content analysis of the practitioner and academic literatures. *Human Resource Management*, 39(4), 305–320.

Rottinghaus, PJ, SX Day and FH Borgen (2005). The career futures inventory: A measure of career-related adaptability and optimism. *Journal of Career Assessment*, 13(1), 3–24.

Rudolph, CW, KN Lavigne and H Zacher (2017). Career adaptability: A meta-analysis of relationships with measures of adaptivity, adapting responses, and adaptation results. *Journal of Vocational Behavior*, 98, 17–34.

Safavi, HP and OM Karatepe (2018). High-performance work practices and hotel employee outcomes: The mediating role of career adaptability. *International Journal of Contemporary Hospitality Management*, 30(2), 1112–1133.

Sarkar, M and D Fletcher (2017). How resilience training can enhance wellbeing and performance. In MF Crane (ed.), *Managing for Resilience*, pp. 227–237. Routledge.

Savickas, ML (1997). Career adaptability: An integrative construct for life-span, life-space theory. *The Career Development Quarterly*, 45(3), 247–259.

Savickas, ML (2005). The theory and practice of career construction. In *Career Development and Counselling: Putting Theory and Research to Work*, SD Brown and RW Lent (eds.), 1st edn., pp. 42–70. Hoboken, NJ: John Wiley and Sons.

Savickas, ML (2013). Career construction theory and practice. In *Career Development and Counselling: Putting Theory and Research to Work*, SD Brown and RW Lent (eds.), 2nd edn., pp. 147–183. Hoboken, NJ: John Wiley and Sons.

Savickas, ML and EJ Porfeli (2012). Career adapt-abilities scale: Construction, reliability, and measurement equivalence across 13 countries. *Journal of Vocational Behavior*, 80(3), 661–673.

Schmitt, A, H Zacher and AH de Lange (2013). Focus on opportunities as a boundary condition of the relationship between job control and work engagement: A multi-sample, multi-method study. *European Journal of Work and Organizational Psychology*, 22(5), 505–519.

Seibert, SE, ML Kraimer and PA Heslin (2016). Developing career resilience and adaptability. *Organizational Dynamics*, 45(3), 245–257.

Seligman, ME (2002). Positive psychology, positive prevention, and positive therapy. *Handbook of Positive Psychology*, 2(2002), 3–12.

Shanker, R, R Bhanugopan, BI Van der Heijden and M Farrell (2017). Organizational climate for innovation and organizational performance: The mediating effect of innovative work behavior. *Journal of Vocational Behavior*, 100, 67–77.

Sigala, M and O Kyriakidou (2015). Creativity and innovation in the service sector. *The Service Industries Journal*, 35(6), 297–302.

Singh, H and S Prashar (2013). Factors defining shopping experience: An analytical study of Dubai. *Asian Journal of Business Research*, 3(1), 36–51.

Sorakraikitikul, M and S Siengthai (2014). Organizational learning culture and workplace spirituality: Is knowledge-sharing behaviour a missing link? *The Learning Organization*, 21(3), 175–192.

Southwick, SM, GA Bonanno, AS Masten, C Panter-Brick and R Yehuda (2014). Resilience definitions, theory, and challenges: Interdisciplinary perspectives. *European Journal of Psychotraumatology*, 5(1), 25338, doi: 10.3402/ejpt.v5.25338.

Stock, RM (2016). Understanding the relationship between frontline employee boreout and customer orientation. *Journal of Business Research*, 69(10), 4259–4268.

Stock, RM, AD Jong and NA Zacharias (2017). Frontline employees' innovative service behavior as key to customer loyalty: Insights into FLEs' resource gain spiral. *Journal of Product Innovation Management*, 34(2), 223–245.

Sung, SY and JN Choi (2009). Do big five personality factors affect individual creativity? The moderating role of extrinsic motivation. *Social Behavior and Personality: An International Journal*, 37(7), 941–956.

Sweetman, D, F Luthans, JB Avey and BC Luthans (2011). Relationship between positive psychological capital and creative performance. *Canadian Journal of Administrative Sciences/Revue Canadienne des Sciences de l'Administration*, 28(1), 4–13.

Tarofder, AK, SF Azam and AN Jalal (2017). Operational or strategic benefits: Empirical investigation of internet adoption in supply chain management. *Management Research Review*, 40(1), 28–52.

Teo, TSH, SC Srivastava and L Jiang (2008). Trust and electronic government success: An empirical study. *Journal of Management Information Systems*, 25(3), 99–132.

Tugade, MM and BL Fredrickson (2004). Resilient individuals use positive emotions to bounce back from negative emotional experiences. *Journal of Personality and Social Psychology*, 86, 320–33.

Victorino, L, R Verma, G Plaschka and C Dev (2005). Service innovation and customer choices in the hospitality industry. *Managing Service Quality: An International Journal*, 15(6), 555–576.

Voss, HG and H Keller (1983). *Curiosity and Exploration: Theories and Results*. New York, NY: Academic Press.

Wagner, A (2014). *Arrival of the Fittest: Solving Evolution's Greatest Puzzle*. London, UK: Penguin.

Wanberg, CR and JT Banas (2000). Predictors and outcomes of openness to changes in a reorganizing workplace. *Journal of Applied Psychology*, 85(1), 132–142.

Wang, C-H, K-Y Chen and S-C Chen (2012). Total quality management, market orientation and hotel performance: The moderating effects of external environmental factors. *International Journal of Hospitality Management*, 31(1), 119–129.

Waugh, CE, RJ Thompson and IH Gotlib (2011). Flexible emotional responsiveness in trait resilience. *Emotion*, 11(5), 1059–1067.

Williams, SD (2004). Personality, attitude, and leader influences on divergent thinking and creativity in organizations. *European Journal of Innovation Management*, 7(3), 187–204.

Wixom, BH and HJ Watson (2001). An empirical investigation of the factors affecting data warehousing success. *MIS Quarterly*, 25(1), 17–41.

Woods, SA, MJ Mustafa, N Anderson and B Sayer (2018). Innovative work behavior and personality traits: Examining the moderating effects of organizational tenure. *Journal of Managerial Psychology*, 33(1), 29–42.

WTTC (2016). Travel and Tourism Economic Impact 2016, World Travel and Tourism Council, London. Available at www.wttc.org/-/media/?les/reports/economic-impact-research/countries-2016/unitedarabemirates2016.pdf.

Youssef, CM and F Luthans (2007). Positive organizational behavior in the workplace: The impact of hope, optimism, and resilience. *Journal of Management*, 33(5), 774–800.

Zacher, H and M Frese (2009). Remaining time and opportunities at work: relationships between age, work characteristics, and occupational future time perspective. *Psychology and Aging*, 24(2), 487–493.

Zacher, H and M Frese (2011). Maintaining a focus on opportunities at work: The interplay between age, job complexity, and the use of selection, optimization, and compensation strategies. *Journal of Organizational Behavior*, 32(2), 291–318.

Zacher, H, RA Ambiel and APP Noronha (2015). Career adaptability and career entrenchment. *Journal of Vocational Behavior*, 88, 164–173.

Zacher, H. (2014). Career adaptability predicts subjective career success above and beyond personality traits and core self-evaluations. *Journal of Vocational Behavior*, 84(1), 21–30.

Zaitseva, NA (2013). *Management in Service Industry: Tourism and Hospitality*. Moscow: Academia Publishing House.

Zhou Y, A Wei, J Li, L Yan and J Li (2016) Groundwater quality evaluation and health risk assessment in the Yinchuan region, northwest China. *Expo Health*, 8(3), 443–456.

Chapter 3

THE ROLE OF EMPLOYEE INCENTIVES AND MOTIVATION ON ORGANISATIONAL INNOVATIVENESS IN DIFFERENT ORGANISATIONAL CULTURES[†]

PAAVO RITALA*

Strategy and Innovation
School of Business and Management
LUT University, Finland
ritala@lut.fi

MIKA VANHALA

School of Business and Management
LUT University, Finland

KATJA JÄRVELÄINEN

Head of Customer Success, Gapps, Finland

Published 20 December 2019

Organisational innovativeness is known to be affected by employee incentives and motivation, but the evidence is inconclusive regarding the organisational contexts and contingencies where this phenomenon takes place. To examine this issue, we adopt the Competing Value Framework of four types of organisational cultures, and hypothesise differences in the incentives–motivation–innovativeness relationships. Using an empirical study of 425 Finnish firms in technology industries, we found in general that intangible and tangible incentives facilitate both intrinsic and extrinsic motivation, but only intrinsic motivation leads to improved organisational innovativeness. Testing our model for subsamples that included clan, adhocracy, market, and hierarchy cultures, we found that results vary considerably between those. First, incentives have different implications to motivation under different organizational cultures. Further, intrinsic motivation leads to innovativeness under adhocracy, clan, and market culture, but not under hierarchy culture, and extrinsic motivation does not lead to innovativeness under any culture.

Keywords: Organisational innovativeness; incentives; motivation; organisational culture; competing values framework.

*Corresponding author.

[†]This article originally appeared in *International Journal of Innovation Management*, **24** 2050075-1-32

Introduction

Innovations and organisational renewal often emerge from the creative ideas and inputs of individual employees. Therefore, managers must stimulate this process by fostering an organisational culture that empowers creative individuals (Ahmed, 1998; Amabile, 1993, 1997; Amabile *et al.*, 1996 Özsomer *et al.*, 1997). To achieve this, it is important to create institutional surroundings in which creativity and innovation are accepted as basic cultural norms, and to develop related managerial practices (e.g., Amabile *et al.*, 1996; Ahmed, 1998; Büschgens *et al.*, 2013; Martins and Terblanche, 2003). However, achieving such an organisational environment is not easy. For instance, managers face many challenges in identifying optimal ways of motivating their employees to complete tasks (Behrens and Patzelt, 2018; Faisal Ahammad *et al.*, 2015; Stajkovic and Luthans, 2003), share knowledge, contribute new ideas and take initiatives (Foss *et al.*, 2009, 2015; Minbaeva *et al.*, 2003). Employees also respond differently to managerial practices and incentives, and motivational processes vary across different organisational cultures and environments (Krausert, 2014; Shalley *et al.*, 2000; Ryan and Berbegal-Mirabent, 2016). To understand organisational innovativeness, we must thus explore both practices that incentivise and motivate individuals, as well as take into account the cultural surroundings in which they are embedded.

Existing research provides substantial evidence of the links between organisational culture and innovativeness (e.g., Büschgens *et al.*, 2013; Brettel *et al.*, 2015; Matzler *et al.*, 2013; Wang *et al.*, 2010), and between organisational culture and incentives (e.g., Bushardt *et al.*, 2011; Kerr and Slocum, 1987; Li and Roloff, 2007), as well as between different forms of incentives and motivation (e.g., Deci *et al.*, 1999; Gagné and Forest, 2008). Some studies have also investigated the overall "big picture"; the links between incentives, (intrinsic) motivation, and creativity (e.g., Amabile, 1997, 1998; Burroughs *et al.*, 2011; Im *et al.*, 2012; Lee *et al.*, 2018) and the influence of organisational culture and incentives on creative behaviour in organisations (Amabile *et al.*, 1996 Amabile and Pratt, 2016; Martins and Terblanche, 2003).

In this study, we go deeper into the role of culture in organisational innovativeness in viewing it as a contingency factor (moderator) rather than a direct explanatory factor. This is because we view culture as a context within which individuals are incentivised and motivated, and ultimately behave (or not) in innovative ways. We expect that looking at the mechanisms of incentives and motivation within cultures — rather than culture as a whole — provides a more accurate view on when particular cultures are helpful for innovativeness and when they provide obstacles. By doing so, we respond to several calls regarding further research on organisational-specific contexts that regulate employee behaviour based on incentives (cf. Sung *et al.*, 2017, p. 303). Furthermore, recent studies have shown that organisations differ in major ways regarding their incentive systems and resulting in employee motivations that drive innovativeness (Behrens and Patzelt, 2018), pinpointing the role of contextual factors. To contribute towards these gaps in our understanding, this study examines *how organisational innovativeness is impacted by types of incentive and motivation within different organisational cultures.*

In attempting to explain this incentive–motivation–innovativeness linkage, we integrate arguments from three fields. First, we focus on *incentives* and *incentive systems* (Milne, 2007), that relate to organisational activity that seeks to motivate individuals to act in ways that are consistent with organisational objectives, such as creative or productive behaviour. Second, following the widely used approach (e.g., Miao *et al.*, 2007; Lau *et al.*, 2018) we draw on self-determination theory (SDT) (Deci and Ryan, 1985), which distinguishes between *extrinsic* and *intrinsic motivation*. Finally, we view organisational culture as a context for relationships between incentives, work motivation, and innovativeness (cf. de Witte and van Muijen, 1999, p. 498). In particular, we examine four organisational culture types — clan, adhocracy, market, and hierarchy — based on Quinn and Rohrbaugh's (1983) competing values framework (CVF), which has widely been used in an extensive body of empirical research (e.g., Chatman and O'Reilly, 2016).

Informed by these three perspectives, we will develop and test a model where intangible and tangible incentives affect intrinsic and extrinsic employee motivation and organisational innovativeness. We study these effects both within a general model and using subsamples of different cultural types (clan, adhocracy, market, hierarchy). Our empirical study of 425 Finnish firms confirms that intangible and tangible incentives facilitate various types of motivation, but only intrinsic motivation leads to improved organisational innovativeness. Interestingly, we find that these results vary considerably across different organisational cultures. For instance, the results suggest that it might be challenging to inspire creativity in hierarchical cultures, while clan and adhocracy cultures are the most feasible contexts for facilitating organisational innovativeness. Our results contribute to innovation management literature by providing systematic as well as detailed implications that help to understand how to best facilitate creative thinking and continuous learning among employees in organisational cultures of various kinds.

Conceptual Background

Organisational innovativeness

Organisational innovativeness can be defined as an organizational tendency towards adoption of ideas, behaviour, or processes that are new to that organisation

(Damanpour, 1991, 1996; Park and Kruse, 2014). According to Damanpour (1996), innovation encompasses the generation, development, and implementation of new ideas or behaviour, including new products or services, process technologies, organisational structures, and administrative systems. Accordingly, we explore organisational innovativeness as a holistic concept, referring to how a firm develops technical innovations that include new products, services, and production process technologies, as well as administrative innovations such as new procedures, policies, and organisational forms (Daft, 1978; Damanpour, 1991; Park and Kruse, 2014; Van de Ven, 1986). While technical innovations are linked to an organisation's basic work activities, administrative innovations relate more directly to management activities and the organisation's social structure, including policies governing recruitment, allocation of resources, structuring of tasks, authority, and reward (Daft, 1978; Damanpour, 1991). While acknowledging this heterogeneity, we are interested here in overall organisational innovation and how this is influenced by the interplay between incentives and employee motivation within different organisational cultures.

Incentives and motivation in organisations

Incentives are an important mechanism for the organisation to facilitate employee motivation. In this regard, the generic terms *incentive* or *incentive system* are used to encompass such concepts as reward, compensation, and recognition (Milne, 2007). The incentive system — which determines who gets rewarded and why — is an unequivocal statement of a company's values and beliefs (Kerr and Slocum, 1987). Incentives are used to reinforce the organisation's values, to promote outstanding performance, and to foster continuous learning by acknowledging desired behaviour and achievement (Milne, 2007). *Tangible incentive* systems — also referred to as reward, pay, or benefit systems — are strategic programs and plans for distributing financial rewards or penalties (Bento and White, 2003; Li and Roloff, 2007; Park and Sturman, 2016). A compensation package commonly includes direct and indirect pay, often in the form of benefits. At their best, compensation strategies as management tools can enhance a firm's effectiveness in meeting strategic objectives by influencing individual behaviour and encouraging high levels of performance (Milne, 2007). *Intangible incentives* include recognitions, nonfinancial awards or tokens of appreciation given selectively to employees to acknowledge their behaviour and commitment, which can be as basic as positive feedback or just saying thank you (Milne, 2007).

Motivation involves certain mental processes that arouse interest and energise, direct, and sustain goal-oriented behaviour and performance. Simply put, a person is motivated when they want to do something. While the behaviour of a motivated person is characteristically voluntary and volitional, motivation-enabling processes constantly shape how the individual is affected by their interaction with the surrounding environment, including the workplace (Cinar *et al.*, 2011; Ryan and Deci, 2000). In the present context, the focus is on employee work motivation and employee engagement, which have a significant influence on organisational performance and productivity, as more motivated employees perform better (Ahmed, 1998; Ankli and Palliam, 2012; Sokro, 2012; Stajkovic and Luthans, 2001, 2003). Understanding motivation is especially important in the context of organisational innovativeness because of its significant impact on employees' knowledge sharing behaviour (Stenius *et al.*, 2016; Shujahat *et al.*, 2019). If managers understand what moves their employees towards a desired goal, motivation can be used as a tool (Cinar *et al.*, 2011).

In this study, Deci and Ryan's (1985) SDT is applied in examining the origins of individual motivation in terms of two distinct and widely adopted types: intrinsic and extrinsic (cf. Hofeditz *et al.*, 2017; Miao *et al.*, 2007). *Intrinsic motivation* refers to doing something because it is inherently interesting, where the individual derives spontaneous satisfaction from the activity itself. *Extrinsic motivation* refers to doing something because it leads to a distinct outcome that may include tangible or intangible rewards. According to Amabile (1993) perceptions of intrinsic and extrinsic motivation may vary; while individuals may be more oriented towards one or the other, most people can be influenced by both intangible and tangible incentives.

Organisational culture

Organisational incentives, motivation, and resulting innovativeness have been broadly seen to be taking place in an organisational *context*, which affects how individuals and teams behave and perform regarding these phenomena. This context has been described with concepts such as work environment (Amabile and Pratt, 2016), organisational climate (Ekvall, 1996), innovative climate (Van der Vegt *et al.*, 2005), or more broadly, organisational culture (Brettel *et al.*, 2015; Matzler *et al.*, 2013; Naranjo-Valencia *et al.*, 2017). In this study, we focus on *organisational culture* since it provides a broad umbrella to understand how individuals are embedded to organisational norms, rules, and systems (Schein, 1985). Organisational culture involves a complex set of values, beliefs, assumptions, and symbols that define how a firm conducts its business (Barney, 1986). Hofstede (1998) characterises organisational culture as the collective mental programming that distinguishes the members of one organisation from those of another. Organisational culture can also be examined sociologically as an attribute possessed by organisations that enables researchers and managers to identify and empirically measure the differences between cultures (Cameron and Quinn, 2006).

As values are central to organisational culture, in this study we adopt Quinn and Rohrbaugh's (1983) *competing values framework* (CVF) to classify and compare different values as the most widely adopted typology of organisational culture (Chatman and O'Reilly, 2016). Utilising CVF is particularly useful for the current purposes as it has been subject to a major cross-contextual validation, and it has been demonstrated to explain differences in innovative behaviour and outputs of organisations (for reviews and meta-analyses, see Büschgens *et al.*, 2013 and Hartnell *et al.*, 2011). CVF assigns organisations to four different cultural types: clan, adhocracy, hierarchy, and market, based on two critical dimensions identified by Quinn and Rohrbaugh (1983): flexibility vs. control and external vs. internal orientation. In a *clan culture* (flexibility and internal orientation), the firm is seen as an extended family, where employees typically work in teams, participating a lot and openly sharing their insights. An *adhocracy culture* (flexibility and external orientation) emphasises innovative and entrepreneurial behaviour and values new challenges and risk taking. A *market culture* (control and external orientation) is competitive and results-oriented; personnel management is characterised by competitiveness, high demands, results orientation and a focus on achievement. Finally, a *hierarchy culture* (control and internal orientation) strives for stability, predictability, and smooth-running efficiency by being systematic and coordinated. In such a culture, personnel management emphasises conformity, efficiency, and security of employment.

The meta-analysis by Büschgens *et al.* (2013) broadly supports the important role of organisational culture in promoting or limiting innovativeness (see also Hartnell *et al.*, 2011). Their results show that innovativeness is most strongly and positively related to a developmental (adhocracy) culture, followed in descending order by group (clan) culture and rational (market) culture.[1] Conversely, organisational innovativeness is negatively related to a hierarchical culture. Additionally, Büschgens *et al.* (2013) found that innovation-supporting cultures do not seem to differentiate much between incremental and radical innovations and are probably equally supportive of both.[2] Similar findings have recently been found regarding the role of organisational culture types and entrepreneurial orientation — other cultures promote EO, while hierarchy culture suppresses it (Brettel *et al.*, 2015).

[1]Though these (and some other) researchers use different names to describe organisational cultures (namely group culture, developmental culture, rational culture, and hierarchical culture), their core values and dimensions are similar to the culture types identified by the CVF. Thus, the results of such studies are interpreted similarly across the two types of labelling.

[2]This evidence supports our choice in examining organisational innovativeness as a generic construct, rather than separating between incremental and radical innovation, for instance.

Further, Matzler *et al.* (2013) found that hierarchy and market cultures increase exploitation in the organisation, clan culture negatively impacts exploration, and finally, adhocracy increases both exploitation and exploration.

In this study, we view organisational culture as an organisational environment and a context within which individuals are incentivised and motivated, and ultimately behave (or not) in innovative ways. We expect that looking at the mechanisms of incentives and motivation within particular organisational cultures provides an useful view on when particular cultures are helpful for innovativeness and when they provide obstacles.

Hypotheses Development

Incentives, motivation and innovativeness

It is broadly established that incentives and incentive systems are used in organisations to facilitate employee motivation. In this regard, SDT suggests that extrinsic motivation can be controlled by external factors and intrinsic motivation by inherently interesting and satisfying things (Gagné and Deci, 2005; Ryan and Deci, 2000; Miao *et al.*, 2007).

Existing evidence quite widely agrees with the arguments of SDT. First, there is a broad base of studies that have provided support for the effects of intangible incentives on intrinsic motivation. For example, in an extensive meta-analysis, Deci *et al.* (1999) demonstrated that intangible incentives had a positive effect on intrinsic motivation while tangible rewards had the opposite effect. Supporting these findings, it has been shown that when the incentive schemes are changed from monetary and performance-based towards intangible one providing, e.g., social recognition intrinsic motivation will increase, and extrinsic motivation will decrease (cf. Kuvaas *et al.*, 2017). Ledford *et al.* (2013) also found that both tangible and intangible rewards play a role in motivation, and that while tangible rewards do not undermine intrinsic motivation, intangible incentives have a positive effect. Similarly, Moellers *et al.* (2018) found that if employees are stimulated through intangible, nonmonetary reward system, their passion and intrinsic motivation can be increased. Second, it has been broadly established that tangible incentives (e.g., merit-based rewards and monetary bonuses) are helpful in boosting extrinsic motivation as well as related issues such as job satisfaction and recruiting, and even intrinsic motivation (see, e.g., Law, 2016).

Overall, while there are also evidences suggesting nuances to these relationships (see, e.g., Amabile and Pratt 2016), it can be concluded that intrinsic motivation is especially affected by intangible and extrinsic motivation by tangible incentives (Yoon *et al.*, 2015). Based on the accumulated evidence and arguments, we would expect intangible incentives to be more closely linked to intrinsic motivation and tangible incentives to extrinsic motivation. Accordingly, we propose the following hypotheses.

Hypothesis 1(a)–(b): *Implementation of (a) intangible incentives is positively related to the perceived intrinsic motivation of personnel, and (b) tangible incentives is positively related to the perceived extrinsic motivation of personnel.*

While it is useful to understand how incentives help to boost individual motivation in organisations, it should also be acknowledged that different types of motivation have different implications for organisational goals, and in the case of the current study, organisational innovativeness. Indeed, since motivation directs and sustains goal-oriented behaviour and performance, the individual employee's motivation exerts a significant influence on organisational outcomes such as performance, productivity, or innovativeness (Ahmed, 1998; Ankli and Palliam, 2012; Kuvaas *et al.*, 2017; Sokro, 2012; Stajkovic and Luthans, 2001, 2003). In this regard, the accumulated evidence suggests that intrinsic motivation may exert a greater influence than extrinsic motivation on employee attitudes and performance in general, and that intrinsic motivation may be a key driver of creativity and innovativeness (Amabile, 1993; 1996; Amabile *et al.*, 1996; Ankli and Palliam, 2012; Cho and Perry, 2011; Ryan and Deci, 2000). Overall, the linkage between intrinsic motivation and organisational creativity and innovativeness is broadly established in various types of studies (for review and discussion, see Amabile and Pratt, 2016).

On the other hand, the relationship between extrinsic motivation and performance remains unclear, with evidence both for and against. While the relationship has been found to be positive for simple and standardised tasks, it seems small or even negative for more interesting and complex tasks (e.g., Bareket-Bojmel *et al.*, 2014; Kuvaas *et al.*, 2017; Weibel *et al.*, 2010). In addition, Cerasoli *et al.* (2014) found that when intrinsic motivation influences performance, the role of extrinsic motivation is less important. On the other hand, while some extrinsic motivators may weaken intrinsic motivation and its effect on performance (e.g. innovativeness), other factors may compensate; for example, Currie *et al.* (2015) reported that tangible incentives (e.g., performance-based compensation) can be significant drivers of employee innovative behaviours. However, it might be that such tangible incentives might spur intrinsic motivation, which would explain the increase in innovative and creative behaviour. Thus, we conclude that in general (i.e., not accounting specific cultural context), organisational innovativeness is mostly facilitated by intrinsic motivation of employees, and therefore we put forward the following hypothesis:

Hypothesis 2: *Perceived intrinsic motivation is positively related to organisational innovativeness.*

The contingency role of organisational culture

So far, we have discussed a general, baseline model of the interplay between incentives and motivation in relation to organisational innovativeness. However, different organisational practices do not occur in a vacuum, as contextual issues — notably organisational culture — play a role in how various incentives affect motivation (see for example Foss *et al.*, 2015). Thus, we build on the assumption that organisational behaviour is institutionally embedded, and that organisational culture is a useful construct in understanding the institutional environment of organisational processes and phenomena (see, for example, Kondra and Hurst, 2009). While the positive impact of tangible or intangible incentives on employee work motivation and performance remains a matter of ongoing dispute, we argue here that the optimal design of incentives depends crucially on contextual factors, and that the first step is to determine the appropriate incentives for the specific company and its employees (Pouliakas and Theodossiou, 2012; Sammer, 2007; Ryan and Berbegal-Mirabent, 2016). Therefore, we expect that the relationships between incentives and motivation and between motivation and innovativeness are likely to differ across cultures.

Regarding the relationship between incentives and motivation, we argue that the culture types can be grouped in to two categories. First, the choice of tangible and intangible incentive systems depends on the typical types of tasks appreciated in different cultures; while intangible incentives and intrinsic motivation underpin effective performance in problem solving or heuristic tasks, tangible incentives and extrinsic motivation may suffice for algorithmic tasks that are more automated or repetitive (Gagné and Deci, 2005). Problem solving and heuristic tasks are more related to the cultures where new ideas, knowledge sharing, and team-work are appreciated — that is — the clan and adhocracy cultures. Thus, under such cultural contexts intangible incentives provide to be particularly useful in facilitating intrinsic motivation. On the other hand, more mechanistic and performance oriented cultures (hierarchy and market cultures) provide a suitable setting for tangible rewards leading to extrinsic motivation. Indeed, it has been found that rewarding works differently across organisational cultures for instance, Kerr and Slocum (1987) suggested that a reward system in which mentor-like superiors evaluate subordinates on subjective criteria and provide frequent feedback, reflects a clan culture. On the other hand, a performance-based pay system that links rewards to quantitative performance measurement, with low levels of superior-subordinate interaction, is considered appropriate to a market culture.

In summary, we argue that clan and adhocracy cultures provide a context where intangible incentives are particularly effective in facilitating employees' intrinsic motivation. On the other hand, hierarchy and market cultures provide a more suitable context for tangible incentives leading to extrinsic motivation. We are not suggesting any negative effects here, given that all types of incentives can be beneficial to motivation, and they are not necessarily substitutes (Amabile and Pratt, 2016; Cerasoli *et al.*, 2014). However, we expect that the four organisational culture types as outlined in the CVF model provide particular benefits, the arguments which are summarised in the following two hypotheses:

Hypothesis 3a: *Clan and adhocracy cultures positively moderate the relationship between intangible incentives and intrinsic motivation.*
Hypothesis 3b: *Hierarchy and market cultures positively moderate the relationship between tangible incentives and extrinsic motivation.*

We also expect to see differences between the four cultures in terms of the relationship between motivation and organisational innovativeness, Aligned with Hypothesis 2, we focus particularly on the relationship between intrinsic motivation and organisational innovativeness, as we do not expect extrinsic motivation play a significant role.

In an adhocracy culture, the prevailing values of growth, stimulation, variety, and autonomy encourage employees to take risks and to apply their creativity (Hartnell *et al.*, 2011). On that basis, adhocracy culture is likely to be positively associated with innovativeness, and particularly adept for individuals who have intrinsic motivation to develop ideas and solutions, given that adhocracy culture does not provide much direction and managerial framework for goal-setting. Similarly, clan cultures also appear as innovation-friendly, given their openness and trust among employees (Brettel *et al.*, 2015; Cameron and Quinn, 2006) — features that are known to drive knowledge sharing as well as creativity in organisations. However, the fact that clan cultures rely heavily on participation, employee involvement, and open communication, might undermine innovation by the effects of group interdependence (see for example Braunscheidel *et al.*, 2010), limiting opportunities to identify novel solutions or challenge traditional approaches (e.g., Hartnell *et al.*, 2011; Sethi *et al.*, 2001). On the other hand, clan cultures still provide flexibility, high levels of knowledge sharing, and a trustful atmosphere for expressing ideas (e.g., Brettel *et al.*, 2015). Therefore, the role of intrinsic motivation is even further highlighted in clan cultures, where intrinsically motivated individuals could take the benefit of the open communication channels and knowledge sharing, while avoiding the limitations of group think.

In summary, we hypothesise that adhocracy and clan cultures are particularly feasible contexts for intrinsically motivated employees to contribute to organisational innovativeness, given their features that promote open and safe knowledge sharing, as well as collaboration among employees and teams.

Hypothesis 4a: *Adhocracy and clan cultures positively moderate the relationship between intrinsic motivation and organisational innovativeness.*

While adhocracy and clan cultures are contexts where intrinsic motivation plays a major role, we argue that market and hierarchy cultures are more aligned with extrinsically-motivated activities that focus on concrete performance targets. Performance and efficiency-oriented contexts do not align well with creative and innovative behaviour. Indeed, several authors have suggested that market culture's emphasis on group goal-setting and group performance in the interests of productivity and efficiency might be expected to undermine innovativeness (Braunscheidel *et al.*, 2010; Hartnell *et al.*, 2011; LePine, 2005).

There are many good reasons to argue why particular cultural contexts undermine the potential of intrinsic motivation for organisational innovativeness. For example, individuals with high performance orientation who undertake challenging tasks may not exhibit the adaptability needed for innovativeness and creativity. The high levels of competitiveness and even aggression that characterise market culture may work against innovativeness, and suppress individuals' intrinsic motivation for creativity. Furthermore, the formalisation of activities in a hierarchy culture (e.g., an emphasis on rules and regulations), in combination with the excessive role of authority and poor employee participation, may limit innovativeness (e.g., Naranjo-Valencia *et al.*, 2010, 2011; Lau *et al.*, 2018). In hierarchy cultures, the horizontal knowledge flows are often limited given the centralised communication schemes and top–down decision making (Song and Thieme, 2006). In market cultures, the horizontal knowledge flows might be limited for other reasons such as fast-paced work, competitive environment, and orientation towards individual performance. Therefore, these types of cultures often leave employees without power to push innovative ideas forward, and might discourage for those that would otherwise be motivated (e.g., Brettel *et al.*, 2015; Büschgens *et al.*, 2013). The following hypothesis summarises the negative contingency role of hierarchy and market cultures.

Hypothesis 4b: *Hierarchy and market cultures negatively moderate the relationship between intrinsic motivation and organisational innovativeness.*

Methods

Data collection

The following empirical analysis is based on quantitative survey data collected in 2014 from Finnish companies operating in technology-driven industries. Based on the NACE classification of economic activities in the European community, these include the electrical and electronics industry, mechanical engineering, metals, engineering and related technical consultancy, and the ICT industry. The electronics and metals sectors were selected because, as well as being technology-intensive, they received the greatest number of international patents in 2012 (Statistics Finland, 2013), which can be interpreted as one indicator of innovativeness. The ICT industry is included because of its rapid rate of technological progress and innovativeness, making it one of the fastest growing sectors in the EU (OECD, 2011).

By making the questionnaire available in both Finnish and English, it was possible to include company managers whose first language is not Finnish. The original measurement scales were translated into Finnish, ensuring that nothing was lost in translation. The questionnaire was pretested by two entrepreneurs holding managerial positions in their own companies and one HR professional working in an international company. Based on their comments and suggestions made by representatives of The Federation of Finnish Technology Industries, the questionnaire items were modified to ensure readability, clarity, and precision. For the English questionnaire, the scales were then back-translated (see Appendix A).

The dataset (obtained from the Amadeus database) included 3,704 companies that met the inclusion criteria. After eliminating unreachable and ineligible respondents, the final sample included 2,873 companies. In the four-week period during which the questionnaire was available, 425 valid responses were collected. Based on one key informant per company, the effective response rate was 15%. By industry, most of the respondents came from manufacturing (48%), information and communication (33%), and professional, scientific and technical activities (17%). The majority of respondents (76%) were current chief executive officers or vice presidents. The second largest group of respondents was HR managers and directors (9%), followed by chief operating officers and development managers (6%), chief finance officers and finance managers (3%), and chairmen and board members (2%). The remaining respondents (4%) included marketing directors, office managers, and sales directors. A majority (25%) had worked at their current company for 6–10 years while many had worked at the company (18%) or had held their current position (10%) for more than 20 years.

Measures

All variables other than organisational culture were measured using a 4-point Likert-type scale. Appendix A includes all the final items and measures as refined for reliability and validity. The rationale for these measures is elaborated in the following.

Our measurement design is focused on *organisational* level of analysis, as our aim in this study was to capture the existence of the phenomena and variance of those between, not within, companies. More specifically, we aimed to capture general level/types of incentives, motivation, and innovativeness within each company, and not of those for each individual they employ. Therefore, the level of the analysis in this study is the organisation and consequently we relied on individual respondents that represented highly knowledgeable persons from each company. In this regard, earlier studies have suggested that the cognitive maps of the highly ranked members of the organisation (e.g., Chief Executive Officer, HR director) can be seen to represent the essential aspects of all the members of the organisation and this approach have been utilised in previous studies (Lyles and Schwenk, 1992) also when motivation (DeVoe and Iyengar, 2004; Usugami and Park, 2006) has been under scrutiny. For instance, it is shown that there is a sufficient level of interdependence between managers' perceptions and employees' self-ratings of the motivation (DeVoe and Iyengar, 2004 see also Huber and Power, 1985). Thus, we believe the chosen measurement approach helps to examine the hypotheses in the context of the current study, regardless of its inherent limitations (the potential biases are further elaborated in "Assessment of bias" section).

Both *intangible* and *tangible incentives* were measured by three items that asked respondents how often different incentive policies were implemented in their company. These items were inspired by Kauhanen (2012) and Wood (1996). Items related to intangible incentives covered recognition, education, and flexible work arrangements while those related to tangible incentives concerned base salary, pay-for-performance commission, and rewarding new ideas. Scales ranged from *never* (1) to *often* (4).

Measures of perceived *intrinsic motivation* (five items) and *extrinsic motivation* (two items) were largely based on a scale developed by Tremblay (2009). We added two items to the intrinsic motivation scale: social bonds within the organisation (Baumeister and Leary, 1995) and meaningfulness of work (Guay *et al.*, 2000). Other items related to intrinsic motivation covered learning, challenges, and enjoying difficult work tasks. We added one further item on employee benefits (Kauhanen, 2012) to the extrinsic motivation scale, and the final version of this scale covered items on income and benefits. The scales ranged from *does not correspond at all* (1) to *corresponds a lot* (4).

Organisational innovativeness was measured by five items. The first of these was adapted from Wang *et al.* (2010) to measure the extent of new product and service innovations introduced to the market. The remaining four items were inspired by Damanpour (1991) and Park and Kruse (2014). These addressed the extent to which the company had adopted new technical and administrative innovations. The scale ranged from *not at all* (1) to *a lot* (4).

Organisational culture was measured using the instrument developed by Cameron and Quinn (2006) to present four types of organisational culture (clan, adhocracy, hierarchy, and market). Based on these descriptions, informants were asked to rate the extent to which each matched their own organisation; the question was framed as a forced choice, resulting in a rank-ordering.

We used four variables (age of company, number of employees, industry type, and R&D intensity) as control variables to account for any effect they might have on organisational innovativeness (Andersson *et al.*, 2004; Tu and Hall, 2004). Firm age was measured as the number of years since establishment, and number of employees was utilised as a proxy for firm size. Industry type was adapted from the NACE classification, and R&D intensity was measured as R&D expenditure as a percentage of total revenue.

Assessment of bias

The reliance on self-reported measures meant that common method variance might have biased the findings. Common method bias (CMB) is of particular concern when respondents are asked to address items that relate to both independent and dependent variables. Following relevant precedents from the literature (e.g., Minbaeva *et al.*, 2012; Vaccaro *et al.*, 2012), we took several steps to reduce the risk of such bias.

First, the survey design and administration explicitly assured respondent confidentiality (cf. Tsai and Ghoshal, 1998; Minbaeva *et al.*, 2012), so reducing any risk that respondents might alter their answers to align with the expectations of others. In addition, we consulted with practitioners in the field to improve the scale items and used clear and proper grammar to keep the survey compact (MacKenzie and Podsakoff, 2012). The fact that the survey asked experienced respondents to assess concrete constructs further reduced the possibility of CMB (see for example Rindfleisch *et al.*, 2008; MacKenzie and Podsakoff, 2012). Moreover, anchoring of the scales varied in our survey (different for incentives, motivation, and innovativeness), helping further to decrease the possibility of CMB (e.g., Podsakoff *et al.*, 2003; Rindfleisch *et al.*, 2008; MacKenzie and Podsakoff, 2012).

To further assess the risk of CMB, we performed statistical analyses that included Harman's one-factor test (Podsakoff *et al.*, 2003) and a principal component analysis that incorporated items from all of the constructs. We found that five factors accounted for the total variance, the largest of which accounted for 28% of the variance. In line with Podsakoff *et al.* (2003) and following the procedure suggested by Liang *et al.* (2008), a measurement model that included one method factor was also tested, allowing items to load both on their theoretical constructs and on a common method factor. Loadings on the method factor were substantially lower than those on construct factors. Finally, our analyses with the partial least squares (see the Results section below) revealed high discriminant validity which further decreases the concern of CMB (Ahammad *et al.*, 2017). Taken together, these tests suggest that common method bias was unlikely to be a major concern.

Results

We used partial least squares (PLS) for the analyses (version 3.2.7 of SmartPLS; see Ringle *et al.*, 2015) and followed the process suggested in the literature (see e.g., Hair *et al.*, 2014). To simultaneously address multiple and complex relationships (e.g., Ahammad *et al.*, 2017) among incentives, motivation, and organisational innovativeness, using PLS for structural equation modelling (SEM) is appropriate for the following reasons. First, PLS is exploratory in nature and is based on minimising the residual variance of the dependent variables. It therefore makes more modest demands on measures compared with other SEM techniques (Echambadi *et al.*, 2006; Hair *et al.*, 2014). In addition PLS-based structural modelling can be utilised with smaller sample sizes (Hair *et al.*, 2014). These features make PLS suitable for exploratory research questions also with small sample sizes (see e.g., Ahammad *et al.*, 2017), as in our culture sub-groups, where the smallest groups comprised 49 and 75 respondents (for the market and hierarchy cultures, respectively). As a first step in our analysis, we assessed the internal consistency and discriminant validity of the scales.

Internal consistency

To test for convergent validity, we examined construct reliability (CR), factor loadings, and Average Variance Extracted (AVE). In the CR test, all constructs returned a value above the 0.7 threshold (see Bagozzi and Yi, 1991). Secondly, the loadings were high and statistically significant for all items, indicating that all were related to their specific constructs, so verifying the posited relationships among indicators and constructs. Finally, AVE measures for all constructs exceeded the 0.5 cut-off (see Fornell and Larcker, 1981). Measures of CR and convergent validity are included in Appendix A.

Discriminant validity

Discriminant validity refers to the extent to which any one construct differs from the others. The square root of AVE should be greater than the variance between that construct and other constructs in the model (i.e., the correlation between two

Table 1. Discriminant validity

Construct	1	2	3	4	5
1. Intangible incentives	**0.71**				
2. Tangible incentives	0.34	**0.73**			
3. Intrinsic motivation	0.40	0.30	**0.81**		
4. Extrinsic motivation	0.25	0.30	0.29	**0.80**	
5. Organisational innovativeness	0.34	0.35	0.34	0.09	**0.74**

Notes: The square root of AVE associated with the construct is presented diagonally. Correlations between the constructs are presented in the lower left triangle.

constructs) (Fornell and Larcker, 1981). The constructs fulfilled this condition; in our model (see Table 1), the diagonal elements (square root of AVE) were greater than the off-diagonal elements in the corresponding rows and columns. In sum, the model assessments provided good evidence of the validity and reliability of concept operationalisation.

Correlation analysis

Table 2 presents means, standard deviations and a correlation matrix. As the matrix shows, there are significant correlations between the independent variables (incentives and motivation) and the dependent variables (motivation and innovativeness). This supports the expectation of interconnectedness between incentives and motivation and between motivation and innovativeness.

Testing the model

To test our research model, we estimated a path model reflecting the posited relationships between incentives, motivation, and organisational innovativeness, following the recommended procedures (see for example Hair *et al.*, 2014). As shown in Table 3, our research model explained about 18% of the variance in organisational innovativeness for the full sample. Moreover, in the full sample model, the R^2 value was 19% for intrinsic motivation and 11% for extrinsic motivation.

Path estimates for intangible incentives to intrinsic motivation ($B = 0.340$, $p = 0.000$) as well as tangible incentives to extrinsic motivation ($B = 0.172$, $p = 0.000$) confirmed our Hypothesis 1(a) and 1(b). We also found support for Hypothesis 2, suggesting a positive relationship between intrinsic motivation and organisational innovativeness. The path from intrinsic motivation to organisational innovativeness was positive and statistically significant ($B = 0.311$, $p = 0.000$).

Table 2. Correlation matrix.

Variable	Mean	SD	1	2	3	4	5	6	7	8
1. R&D intensity	0.28	2.05								
2. Employees	258.92	3037.85	−0.14							
3. Age	25.07	20.33	−0.042	0.404**						
4. Industry	7.11	4.12	0.27	−0.071	−0.376 **					
5. Intangible incentives	3.30	0.47	−0.032	0.039	−0.093	0.247 **				
6. Tangible incentives	2.51	0.67	−0.032	0.128 **	0.089	0.004	0.352**			
7. Intrinsic motivation	3.17	0.58	0.039	0.043	−0.147 **	0.291**	0.392**	0.221**		
8. Extrinsic motivation	2.34	0.64	0.042	0.049	−0.087	0.109*	0.243**	0.260**	0.265**	
9. Org. innovativeness	2.58	0.59	0.001	0.061	−0.041	−0.008	0.346**	0.346**	0.325**	0.082

Notes: $N = 425$. **Correlation is significant at the 0.01 level. *Correlation is significant at the 0.05 level.

In addition, even if not hypothesised, we also tested the effect for extrinsic motivation, and the results show that there was not a statistically significant path from extrinsic motivation to organisational innovativeness ($B = -0.012$, $p = 0.398$).

In addition, we wanted to explore the relationships between incentives, motivation, and organisational innovativeness within different organisational cultures. To that end, we tested four additional models to determine any effect of organisational culture in the previously tested paths, as in Hypotheses 3(a) and 3(b) and Hypotheses 4(a) and 4(b). We therefore conducted a sub-group analysis, splitting the sample into the four cultures: clan ($n = 174$), adhocracy ($n = 125$), hierarchy ($n = 75$), and market ($n = 49$) and running a separate PLS analysis for each of the four groups. Table 3 shows the results for the full sample and the four sub-samples.

For *clan culture*, the path from intangible incentives to intrinsic motivation ($B = 0.306$, $p = 0.000$) was significant and had a positive impact. The effect of tangible incentives on both intrinsic ($B = 0.136$, $p = 0.037$) and extrinsic (0.193, $p = 0.011$) motivation was also positive and significant. In addition, the effect of intrinsic motivation on organisational innovativeness ($B = 0.208$, $p = 0.013$) was significant and positive. For clan culture, then, the models show significant full paths from incentives (intangible and tangible) to organisational innovativeness, mediated by intrinsic motivation.

The model for *adhocracy culture* showed even more substantial path estimates, with otherwise similar findings. First, the path from intangible incentives to intrinsic motivation showed a positive impact ($B = 0.421$, $p = 0.000$). Second, the paths from tangible incentives to both intrinsic ($B = 0.145$, $p = 0.023$) and extrinsic ($B = 0.215$, $p = 0.027$) motivation were also significant. Finally, the path from intrinsic motivation to organisational innovativeness ($B = 0.337$, $p = 0.000$) was significant. The results for this model were similar to those for clan culture, with two significant paths all the way from incentives (intangible and tangible) through motivation (intrinsic) to organisational innovativeness.

In the case of *hierarchy culture*, there were significant paths from intangible incentives to both intrinsic ($B = 0.416$, $p = 0.000$) and extrinsic motivation ($B = 0.225$, $p = 0.027$). In addition, the path between tangible incentives and extrinsic motivation was positive and significant ($B = 0.321$, $p = 0.001$). Interestingly, hierarchy was the only culture in which neither intrinsic or extrinsic motivation had any effect on organisational innovativeness, indicating the absence here of any mediating effect.

In the model for *market culture*, there is also a significant path from incentives through motivation to organisational innovativeness, with a distinct empirical logic. This path runs from tangible incentives to intrinsic motivation ($B = 0.481$,

Table 3. Research model testing.

Path	Full sample ($N = 425$)	Clan ($N = 174$)	Adhocracy ($N = 125$)	Hierarchy ($N = 75$)	Market ($N = 49$)
Control variables					
R&D intensity→Organisational innovativeness	−0.039 (0.179)	−0.093 (0.210)	0.034 (0.319)	0.053 (0.340)	0.119 (0.146)
Employees→Organisational innovativeness	0.048 (0.253)	0.154 (0.037)	0.289 (0.004)	0.203 (0.089)	−0.158 (0.290)
Age→Organisational innovativeness	−0.014 (0.412)	−0.005 (0.477)	−0.292 (0.004)	−0.071 (0.339)	0.311 (0.091)
Industry (Manufacturing)→Organisational innovativeness	−0.012 (0.471)	−0.118 (0.500)	−0.189 (0.500)	0.011 (0.555)	0.167 (0.102)
Industry (Information and communication)→ Organisational innovativeness	0.078 (0.315)	−0.057 (0.500)	−0.232 (0.500)	0.212 (0.102)	0.332 (0.322)
Industry (Professional, scientific and technical activities)→Organisational innovativeness	−0.222 (0.044)	−0.330 (0.500)	−0.377 (0.500)	−0.281 (0.094)	0.006 (0.432)
Dependent variable					
Intangible incentives→Intrinsic motivation	0.340 (0.000)	0.306 (0.000)	0.421 (0.000)	0.416 (0.000)	−0.005 (0.490)
Intangible incentives→Extrinsic motivation	0.172 (0.000)	0.133 (0.081)	0.179 (0.136)	0.225 (0.027)	−0.004 (0.494)
Tangible incentives→Intrinsic motivation	0.185 (0.000)	0.136 (0.037)	0.145 (0.023)	0.102 (0.157)	0.481 (0.002)
Tangible incentives→Extrinsic motivation	0.238 (0.000)	0.193 (0.011)	0.215 (0.027)	0.321 (0.001)	0.515 (0.022)
Intrinsic motivation→ Organisational innovativeness	0.311 (0.000)	0.208 (0.013)	0.337 (0.000)	0.215 (0.146)	0.465 (0.001)
Extrinsic motivation→ Organisational innovativeness	−0.012 (0.398)	0.069 (0.247)	−0.048 (0.293)	0.119 (0.278)	0.090 (0.332)
R^2 for Intrinsic motivation	0.192	0.139	0.233	0.204	0.229
R^2 for Extrinsic motivation	0.114	0.072	0.100	0.189	0.263
R^2 for Organisational innovativeness	0.181	0.151	0.283	0.281	0.335

Note: P value for statistical significance is reported in parentheses.

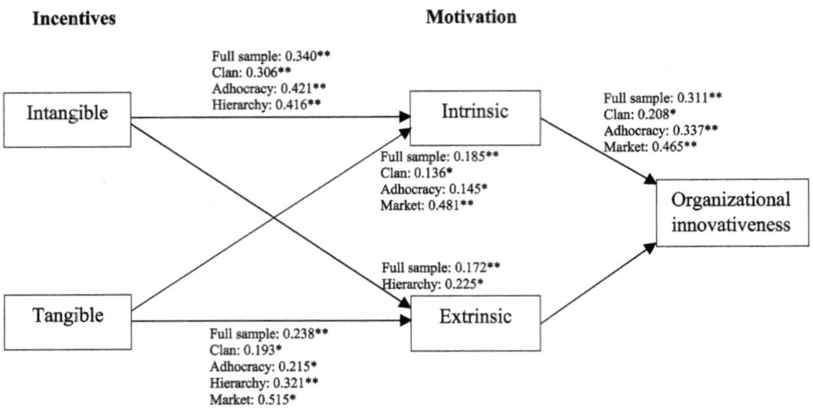

Fig. 1. Research model and significant paths (control variables omitted for clarity reasons).

$p = 0.002$) and from there to organisational innovativeness ($B = 0.465$, $p = 0.001$). In addition, there is a significant path with positive effect from tangible incentives to extrinsic motivation ($B = 0.515$, $p = 0.022$). It is notable that this was the only culture type in which intangible incentives played no role, as their effect on motivation had close-to-zero coefficients.

Based on these results, part of our hypotheses regarding the contextual and moderating role of organisational culture found support. Some paths were insignificant in certain cultures while significant in others, and the effect sizes varied a lot in different cultures. As Hypothesis 3(a) and 3(b) suggested, organisational culture affects the relationship between both types of incentives and both types of motivation (as discussed above). Hypothesis 4(a) and 4(b) concerning the role of organisational culture in how intrinsic motivation relate to organisational innovativeness were partially supported, as in adhocracy and clan cultures culture had a positive contingency role. Furthermore, hierarchy culture was the only culture under which the relationship between intrinsic motivation and innovativeness was not significant. However, regarding the role of market culture the results show that contrary to our Hypothesis 4(b) the effect of intrinsic motivation to organisational innovativeness is actually stronger within market culture. Figure 1 summarises the significant path coefficients of the structural model for the full sample, as well as for the four sub-groups.

Discussion and Conclusions

This study examined the interrelations among intangible and tangible incentives, employee motivation, and organisational innovativeness across various organisational cultures. The empirical survey of 425 respondents from Finnish technology industries provides interesting and novel evidence about how organisational innovativeness is facilitated in different organisational cultures, so making an important contribution to the relevant literature. In particular, the study contributes to the research stream examining managerial practices and employee motivation across various organisational contexts (e.g., Currie *et al.*, 2015; Foss *et al.*, 2009, 2015; Krausert, 2014). The implications are discussed in detail below.

The results for the full sample show that organisational innovativeness is facilitated mainly through intrinsic motivation, which is in turn augmented by both intangible and tangible incentives. Importantly, the results show that while extrinsic motivation is also increased by both types of incentives, it does not lead to organisational innovativeness. This clearly suggests that while incentive-motivation linkages are multiplex, intrinsic motivation ultimately mediates the effect of incentives on organizational innovativeness. Overall, these results support earlier claims that intrinsic motivation is a key driver of creativity (Amabile, 1993, 1996; Amabile *et al.*, 1996; Amabile and Pratt 1996; Ankli and Palliam, 2012; Behrens and Patzelt, 2018; Cho and Perry, 2011; Ryan and Deci, 2000).

Taking organisational culture into account, the path model reveals more detailed and interesting findings (for a summary, see Table 4). First, *clan* and *adhocracy* cultures support the fully mediated linkage between intangible and tangible incentives, intrinsic motivation, and organisational innovativeness. While clan culture is communicative and features strong relational ties, adhocracy is an innovative and entrepreneurial environment (cf. Cameron and Quinn, 2006). Based on our results, both of these cultures provide a good foundation for the use of both types of incentive to generate intrinsic motivation, leading ultimately to organisational innovativeness. However, this is likely to be achieved by different means; while clan culture may nurture employees who are easily intrinsically motivated by virtue of their embeddedness in the "extended family," adhocracy relies on entrepreneurial risk taking and innovative opportunity search. In both of these contexts, a variety of different types of incentives — both tangible and intangible — are useful in generating intrinsic motivation, ultimately leading to organisational innovation.

On the other hand, *market culture* seems to increase organisational innovativeness mainly by linking tangible incentives and intrinsic motivation. Organisations with market culture are distinctly oriented to the external environment and function primarily through economic market mechanisms such as monetary goals in pursuing competitiveness (Cameron and Quinn, 2006). In such cultures, our results suggest that tangible incentives can be used to facilitate both intrinsic and extrinsic motivation, leading to increased organisational innovativeness (contrary to our initial hypothesis). It was also interesting that only market culture lacked any linkage between intangible incentives and intrinsic motivation. This ineffectiveness of intangible incentives can be seen as partial support for the alleged detrimental effects of market culture to innovativeness (Braunscheidel *et al.*, 2010; Hartnell *et al.*, 2011; LePine, 2005). However, as our results suggest, tangible incentives can play an important complementary role in fostering motivation and innovative behaviour in such cultures.

Finally, the *hierarchy* is the only culture that fails to link any form of incentive or motivation to organisational innovativeness. This is perhaps unsurprising in light of the emphasis on control and efficiency (Büschgens *et al.*, 2013; Cameron and Quinn, 2006), but the results suggest that incentives can still increase motivation in such cultures. We found relationships between intangible incentives and intrinsic motivation, and between tangible incentives and extrinsic motivation. Indeed, regardless of these results, it is important to keep in mind that there are no intrinsically good or bad cultures; while hierarchy seems to diminish organisational innovativeness, it may impact positively on other organisational goals.

In sum, it seems that both intangible and tangible incentives play an important role in motivating people at work, especially in terms of the intrinsic motivation that is crucial for creativity and innovativeness (see Table 4 for summary of the results). Our findings broadly support the intrinsic motivational approach to organisational innovativeness and management (cf. Amabile and Pratt 2016), entailing a holistic view that embraces a broad range of incentives and policies. Our findings also highlight interesting differences among sub-groups, confirming that culture indeed matters. The results regarding innovativeness under different organisational cultures follow quite closely to those supported by the meta-analysis of Büschgens *et al.* (2013). However, our results provide further understanding of the interplay of employee incentives and motivation that facilitate —

Table 4. Results by type of organisational culture.

Path	Clan	Adhocracy	Hierarchy	Market
Incentives and motivation				
Intangible incentives→ Intrinsic motivation	x	x	x	—
Intangible incentives→ Extrinsic motivation	—	—	x	—
Tangible incentives→ Intrinsic motivation	x	x	—	x
Tangible incentives→ Extrinsic motivation	x	x	x	x
Motivation and organisational innovativeness				
Intrinsic motivation→ Organisational innovativeness	x	x	—	x
Extrinsic motivation→ Organisational innovativeness	—	—	—	—

in different ways — achieving organisational innovativeness. Altogether, the results of the current study enhance the understanding of how cultural and contextual factors contribute to the effects of employee incentives on behaviour (Sung *et al.*, 2017) and the role of cultural and institutional environments in organisational innovativeness (Ahmed, 1998; Martins and Terblanche, 2003; Matzler *et al.*, 2013; Vanhala and Ritala, 2016).

The study has some limitations in relation to research design and sampling. Our perception-based approach to measuring incentives, motivation, and innovativeness is likely to have influenced our results, and future research should collect these data from different sources. For instance, employees could be surveyed in organisational rather than cross-organisational settings (as here) to determine what incentivises and motivates them, using supervisor evaluation to assess innovative performance. Future research should also further investigate how incentives lead to motivation and ultimately to innovative behaviour; for example, more controlled research designs could be used to address these issues under experimental conditions. Equally, qualitative research could compare firms with differing cultures to further assess the present findings. A further limitation of the present study is our use of CVF to categorise organisational cultures. While this is the most widely used typological approach (Chatman and O'Reilly, 2016), it has attracted some criticism in the literature. For example, it could be asked whether competing values are actually competing, or whether they may be complementary, existing simultaneously for instance in organisations that emphasise time efficiency while also investing in innovativeness (Hartnell *et al.*, 2011; Chatman and O'Reilly, 2016 see also Brettel *et al.*, 2015). Future studies might take account of this issue by clustering or grouping firms with similar configurations in terms of different cultures types. It might also be useful to consider other typologies of organisational culture. In general, however, we believe that the present findings provide a useful foundation for future research on this topic.

Appendix A

Table A.1. Measurement items.

Concept	Item	Factor loading	CR	AVE
Incentives	*Using the scale below, indicate how often each of the following reward policies is implemented in your company. Answer each item according to the following scale*: 1: *never*, 2: *seldom*, 3: *sometimes*, 4: often. *In our company*. . .			

P. Ritala, M. Vanhala & K. Järveläinen

Table A.1. (*Continued*)

Concept	Item	Factor loading	CR	AVE
Intangible incentives	... personnel are given personal praises and acknowledgements from their superiors	0.741***	0.75	0.50
	... personnel are provided different training programs and educational courses to develop their competences	0.713***		
	... the management is understanding and flexible regarding work arrangements (e.g., working hours, leave of absence, telecommuting)	0.659***		
Tangible incentives	...employees base salary is increased if (s)he carries out her/his job duties well	0.743***	0.77	0.53
	... personnel are offered traditional, predefined pay-for-performance rewards (e.g., sales commission, production commission)	0.655***		
	... personnel are rewarded for ingenuity and new ideas (e.g., improvement ideas, innovations)	0.780***		
Motivation	*Using the scale below, indicate to what extent each of the following items corresponds to your perceptions as a manager to primary reasons why your personnel are currently engaged with their work duties.* *Answer each item according to the following scale*: 1: *does not correspond at all*, 2: *corresponds a little*, 3: *corresponds moderately*, 4: *corresponds a lot. The personnel of our firm engage in their work duties primarily because...*			
Intrinsic motivation	... they experience a strong social bond with work community and colleagues	0.665***	0.91	0.66
	... they derive pleasure from learning new things	0.882***		
	... they enjoy confronting new challenges and solving them	0.875***		
	... they enjoy being successful at difficult work tasks	0.835***		
	... they perceive their work to be meaningful and fun	0.781***		
Extrinsic motivation	... they can earn a lot of money doing this job	0.721***	0.78	0.65
	... they get good employee benefits	0.880***		

Table A.1. (*Continued*)

Concept	Item	Factor loading	CR	AVE
Organisational innovativeness	*Answer the questions according to the following scale*: 1: *not at all*, 2: *a little*, 3: *moderately*, 4: *a lot* *During the last 3 years, to what extent your firm has...*			
	... introduced new product and service innovations to the market?	0.767***	0.86	0.54
	... started using new products or services that are new to the firm?	0.788***		
	... brought to use technologies or technical processes that are new to the firm? (e.g., input materials, equipment, work flow mechanisms)	0.758***		
	... brought to use administrative procedures that are new to the firm?	0.712***		
	... brought to use organisational forms/structures that are new to the firm?	0.654***		

		Please, rate each of the following alternatives (A–D) in descending order on a scale from 1 – 4 *depending on the extent to which each description is similar to your own organisation.* (1 *being the most suitable description and* 4 *the least suitable description of your company. Use each of the values between* 1 *and* 4 *once.*)
Organisational culture	Clan	**A Firm as an extended family** The emphasis in this firm is on commitment, loyalty, participation, openness and mutual trust. Personnel development is emphasised and personnel are managed through mentoring and nurturing. Work is often done in teams and people tend to give a lot of themselves to the firm.
	Adhocracy	**B Innovative and entrepreneurial** The emphasis in this firm is on innovativeness, staying on the cutting edge, creating new challenges, and being entrepreneurial. Since the firm strives to be a product leader and innovator, trying new things and prospecting for opportunities are valued. Among personnel, freedom, uniqueness and risk taking is pronounced.
	Market	**C Competitive and results-oriented** The emphasis in this firm is on outpacing the competition, hitting stretch targets, and winning in the marketplace. Personnel management is characterised by hard-driving competitiveness, high demands, results-orientation and focus on achievement.

P. Ritala, M. Vanhala & K. Järveläinen

Appendix A.1. (*Continued*)

Hierarchy	**D Controlled and efficient** The firm is characterised by strong control, and formal rules and policies. By being systematic, the organisation strives towards stability, predictability and smooth-running efficiency. Dependable delivery, stable scheduling, and low-cost production are valued. Personnel management emphasises conformity, efficiency and security of employment.

Notes: ***Statistically significant at 0.005 significance level.

References

Ahammad, MF, SY Tarba, JG Frynas and A Scola (2017). Integration of non-market and market activities in cross-border mergers and acquisitions. *British Journal of Management*, 28, 629–648.

Ahmed, PK (1998). Culture and climate for innovation. *European Journal of Innovation Management*, 1, 30–43.

Amabile, TM (1993). Motivational synergy: Toward new conceptualizations of intrinsic and extrinsic motivation in the workplace. *Human Resource Management Review*, 3, 185–201.

Amabile, TM, R Conti, H Coon, J Lazenby and M Herron (1996). Assessing the work environment for creativity. *Academy of Management Journal*, 39, 1154–1184.

Amabile, TM (1997). Entrepreneurial creativity through motivational synergy. *The Journal of Creative Behavior*, 31, 18–26.

Amabile, TM (1998). How to kill creativity. *Harvard Business Review*, 76, 77–87.

Amabile, TM (2016). The dynamic componential model of creativity and innovation in organisations: Making progress, making meaning. *Research in Organisational Behavior*, 36, 157–183.

Andersson, S, J Gabrielsson and I Wictor (2004). International activities in small firms: Examining factors influencing the internationalization and export growth of small firms. *Canadian Journal of Administrative Sciences*, 21, 22–34.

Ankli, RE and R Palliam (2012). Enabling a motivated workforce: Exploring the sources of motivation. *Development and Learning in Organizations*, 26, 7–10.

Bagozzi, RP and Y Yi (1991). Multitrait-multimethod matrices in consumer research. *Journal of Consumer Research*, 17, 426–439.

Bareket-Bojmel, L, G Hochman and D Ariely (2014). It's (not) all about the Jacksons: Testing different types of short-term bonuses in the field. *Journal of Management*, 43, 534–554.

Barney, JB (1986). Organisational culture: Can it be a source of sustained competitive advantage? *Academy of Management Review*, 11, 656–665.

Baumeister, RF and MR Leary (1995). The need to belong: Desire for interpersonal attachments as a fundamental human motivation. *Psychological Bulletin*, 117, 497–529.

Behrens, J and H Patzelt (2018). Incentives, resources and combinations of innovation radicalness and innovation speed. *British Journal of Management*, 29, 691–711.

Bento, RF and LF White (1998). Participants' values and incentive plans. *Human Resource Management*, 37, 47–59.

Braunscheidel, MJ, NC Suresh and AD Boisnier (2010). Investigating the impact of organisational culture on supply chain integration. *Human Resource Management*, 49, 883–911.

Brettel, M, C Chomik and TC Flatten (2015). How organisational culture influences innovativeness, proactiveness, and risk-taking: Fostering entrepreneurial orientation in SMEs. *Journal of Small Business Management*, 53, 868–885.

Burroughs, JE, DW Dahl, CP Moreau, A Chattopadhyay and G Gorn (2011). Facilitating and rewarding creativity during new product development. *Journal of Marketing*, 75, 53–67.

Bushardt, SC, DW Glascoff and DH Doty (2011). Organisational culture, formal reward structure, and effective strategy implementation. *Journal of Organisational Culture Communications and Conflict*, 15, 57–70.

Büschgens, T, A Bausch and D Balkin (2013). Organisational culture and innovation: A meta-analysis review. *Journal of Product Innovation Management*, 30, 763–781.

Cameron, KS and RE Quinn (2006). *Diagnosing and Changing Organisational Culture — Based on the Competing Values Framework*, revised edition. San Francisco, CA: Jossey-Bass.

Cerasoli, CP, JM Nicklin and MT Ford (2014). Intrinsic motivation and extrinsic incentives jointly predict performance: A 40-year meta-analysis. *Psychological Bulletin*, 140, 980–1008.

Chatman, JA and CA O'Reilly (2016). Paradigm lost: Reinvigorating the study of organisational culture. *Research in Organisational Behavior*, 36, 199–224.

Cho, YJ and JL Perry (2011). Intrinsic motivation and employee attitudes: Role of managerial trustworthiness, goal directedness, and extrinsic reward expectancy. *Review of Public Personnel Administration*, 32, 382–406.

Cinar, O, C Bektas and I Aslan (2011). A motivation study on the effectiveness of intrinsic and extrinsic factors. *Economics and Management*, 16, 690–695.

Currie, G, N Burgess and JC Hayton (2015). HR practices and knowledge brokering by hybrid middle managers in hospital settings: The influence of professional hierarchy. *Human Resource Management*, 54, 793–812.

Daft, RL (1978). A dual-core model of organisational innovation. *Academy of Management Journal*, 21, 193–210.

Damanpour, F (1991). Organisational innovation: A meta-analysis of effects of determinants and moderators. *Academy of Management Journal*, 34, 555–590.

Damanpour, F (1996). Organisational complexity and innovation: Developing and testing multiple contingency models. *Management Science*, 42, 693–716.

P. Ritala, M. Vanhala & K. Järveläinen

Deci, EL (1971). Effects of externally mediated rewards on intrinsic motivation. *Journal of Personality and Social Psychology*, 18, 105–115.

Deci, EL and RM Ryan (1985). *Intrinsic Motivation and Self-Determination in Human Behavior*. New York: Plenum.

Deci, EL, RM Ryan and R Koestner (1999). A meta-analytic review of experiments examining the effects of extrinsic rewards on intrinsic motivation. *Psychological Bulletin*, 125, 627–668.

DeVoe, SE and SS Iyengar (2004). Managers' theories of subordinates: A cross-cultural examination of manager perceptions of motivation and appraisal of performance. *Organisational Behavior and Human Decision Processes*, 93, 47–61.

de Witte, K and JJ van Muijen (1999). Organisational culture. *European Journal of Work and Organisational Psychology*, 8, 497–502.

Echambadi, R, B Campbell and R Agarwal (2006). Encouraging best practice in quantitative management research: An incomplete list of opportunities. *Journal of Management Studies*, 43, 1801–1820.

Ekvall, G (1996). Organisational climate for creativity and innovation. *European Journal of Work and Organisational Psychology*, 5, 105–123.

Faisal A, M, SM Lee, M Malul and A Shoham (2015). Behavioral ambidexterity: The impact of incentive schemes on productivity, motivation, and performance of employees in commercial banks. *Human Resource Management*, 54, 45–62.

Fornell, C and DF Larcker (1981). Evaluating structural equation models with unobservable variables and measurement error. *Journal of Marketing Research*, 18, 39–50.

Foss, NJ, DB Minbaeva, T Pedersen and M Reinholt (2009). Encouraging knowledge sharing among employees: How job design matters. *Human Resource Management*, 48, 871–893.

Foss, NJ, T Pedersen, MR Fosgaard and D Stea (2015). Why complementary HRM practices impact performance: The case of rewards, job design, and work climate in a knowledge-sharing context. *Human Resource Management*, 54, 955–976.

Gagné, M and EL Deci (2005). Self-determination theory and work motivation. *Journal of Organisational Behavior*, 26, 331–362.

Gagné, M and J Forest (2008). The study of compensation systems through the lens of self-determination theory: Reconciling 35 years of debate. *Canadian Psychology*, 49, 225–232.

Guay, F, RJ Vallerand and C Blanchard (2000). On the assessment of situational intrinsic and extrinsic motivation: The Situational Motivation Scale (SIMS). *Motivation and Emotion*, 24, 175–213.

Hair, JF, M Sarstedt, L Hopkins and VG Kuppelwieser (2014). Partial least squares structural equation modeling (PLS-SEM) — An emerging tool in business research. *European Business Review*, 26, 106–121.

Hartnell, CA, AY Ou and A Kinicki (2011). Organisational culture and organisational effectiveness: A meta-analytic investigation of the competing values framework's theoretical suppositions. *Journal of Applied Psychology*, 96, 677–694.

Hofeditz, M, AM Nienaber, A Dysvik and G Schewe (2017). "Want to" versus "Have to": Intrinsic and extrinsic motivators as predictors of compliance behavior intention. *Human Resource Management*, 56, 25–49.

Hofstede, G (1998). Attitudes, values and organisational culture: Disentangling the concepts. *Organization Studies*, 19, 477–492.

Huber, GP and DJ Power (1985). Retrospective reports of strategic-level managers: Guidelines for increasing their accuracy. *Strategic Management Journal*, 6, 171–180.

Im, S, MM Montoya and JP Workman Jr (2012). Antecedents and consequences of creativity in product innovation teams. *Journal of Product Innovation Management*, 30, 170–185.

Kauhanen, J (2012). *Henkilöstövoimavarojen Johtaminen [Human Resource Management]*. Helsinki: Sanoma Pro.

Kerr, J and JW Slocum Jr (1987). Managing corporate culture through reward systems. *Academy of Management Executive*, 1, 99–108.

Krausert, A (2014). HRM systems for knowledge workers: Differences among top managers, middle managers, and professional employees. *Human Resource Management*, 53, 67–87.

Kondra, AZ and DC Hurst (2009). Institutional processes of organisational culture. *Culture and Organization*, 15, 39–58.

Kuvaas, B, R Buch, A Weibe, A Dysvik and CGL Nerstad (2017). Do intrinsic and extrinsic motivation relate differently to employee outcomes?. *Journal of Economic Psychology*, 61, 244–258.

Lau, CM, G Scully and A Lee (2018). The effects of organisational politics on employee motivations to participate in target setting and employee budgetary participation. *Journal of Business Research*, 90, 247–259.

Law, CC (2016). Using bonus and awards for motivating project employees. *Human Resource Management International Digest*, 24, 4–7.

Ledford, GE, B Gerhart and M Fang (2013). Negative effects of extrinsic rewards on intrinsic motivation: More smoke than fire. *World at Work Journal, Second Quarter*, 16, 17–29.

LePine, JA (2005). Adaptation of teams in response to unforeseen change: Effects of goal difficulty and team composition in terms of cognitive ability and goal orientation. *Journal of Applied Psychology*, 90, 1153–1167.

Li, L and ME Roloff (2007). Organisational culture and compensation systems: An examination of job applicants' attraction to organisations. *International Journal of Organisational Analysis*, 15, 210–230.

Liang, H, N Saraf, Q Hu and Y Zue (2008). Assimilation of enterprise systems: The effect of institutional pressures and the mediating role of top management. *MIS Quarterly*, 31, 59–87.

Lyles, MA and CR Schwenk (1992). Top management, strategy, and organisational knowledge structures. *Journal of Management Studies*, 29, 155–174.

MacKenzie, SB and PM Podsakoff (2012). Common method bias in marketing: Causes, mechanisms, and procedural remedies. *Journal of Retailing*, 88, 542–555.

Martins, EC and F Terblanche (2003). Building organisational culture that stimulates creativity and innovation. *European Journal of Innovation Management*, 6, 64–74.

Matzler, K, DE Abfalter, TA Mooradian and F Bailom (2013). Corporate culture as an antecedent of successful exploration and exploitation. *International Journal of Innovation Management*, 17(5), 1350025.

Miao, CF, KR Evans and S Zou (2007). The role of salesperson motivation in sales control systems — Intrinsic and extrinsic motivation revisited. *Journal of Business Research*, 60, 417–425.

Milne, P (2007). Motivation, incentives and organisational culture. *Journal of Knowledge Management*, 11, 28–38.

Minbaeva, D, T Pedersen, I Bjorkman, CF Fey and HJ Park (2003). MNC knowledge transfer, subsidiary absorptive capacity, and HRM. *Journal of International Business Studies*, 34, 586–599.

Minbaeva, D, K Mäkelä and L Rabbiosi (2012). Linking HRM and knowledge transfer via individual-level mechanisms. *Human Resource Management*, 51, 387–405.

Moellers, T, C Visini and M Haldimann (2018). Complementing open innovation in multi-business firms: Practices for promoting knowledge flows across internal units. *R&D Management*, 1–20. Doi:10.1111/radm.12343.

Naranjo-Valencia, JC, D Jiménez-Jiménez and R Sanz-Valle (2011). Innovation or imitation? The role of organisational culture. *Management Decision*, 49, 55–72.

Naranjo-Valencia, JC, R Sanz Valle and D Jiménez Jiménez (2010). Organisational culture as determinant of product innovation. *European Journal of Innovation Management*, 13, 466–480.

Naranjo-Valencia, JC, D Jimenez-Jimenez and R Sanz-Valle (2017). Organisational culture and radical innovation: Does innovative behavior mediate this relationship? *Creativity and Innovation Management*, 26, 407–417.

OECD (2011). OECD guide to measuring the information society 2011. Retrieved from http://browse.oecdbookshop.org/oecd/pdfs/free/9311021e.pdf.

Park, R and D Kruse (2014). Group incentives and financial performance: The moderating role of innovation. *Human Resource Management Journal*, 24, 77–94.

Park, S and MC Sturman (2016). Evaluating form and functionality of pay-for-performance plans: The relative incentive and sorting effects of merit pay, bonuses, and long-term incentives. *Human Resource Management*, 55, 697–719.

Podsakoff, PM, SB MacKenzie, J-Y Lee and NP Podsakoff (2003). Common method biases in behavioral research: A critical review of the literature and recommended remedies. *Journal of Applied Psychology*, 88, 879–903.

Quinn, RE and J Rohrbaugh (1983). A spatial model of effectiveness criteria: Towards a competing values approach to organisational analysis. *Management Science*, 29, 363–377.

Rindfleisch, A, A Malter, S Ganesan and C Moorman (2008). Cross-sectional versus longitudinal survey research: Concepts, findings, and guidelines. *Journal of Marketing Research*, 45, 261–279.

Ringle, CM, S Wende and J Becker (2015). *SmartPLS 3*. Boenningstedt: SmartPLS GmbH.

Ryan, JC and J Berbegal-Mirabent (2016). Motivational recipes and research performance: A fuzzy set analysis of the motivational profile of high performing research scientists. *Journal of Business Research*, 69, 5299–5304.

Ryan, RM and EL Deci (2000). Intrinsic and extrinsic motivations: Classic definitions and new directions. *Contemporary Educational Psychology*, 25, 54–67.

Sammer, J (2007). Weighing pay incentives: Incentive plans should motivate employees to perform at a higher level, not encourage them to engage in questionable behavior. *HR Magazine*, 52, 64–69.

Schein, EH (1985). *Organisational Culture and Leadership*. San Fransisco: Jossey-Bass.

Sethi, R, DC Smith and CW Park (2001). Cross-functional product development teams, creativity, and the innovativeness of new consumer products. *Journal of Marketing Research*, 38, 73–85.

Shalley, CE, LL Gilson and TC Blum (2000). Matching creativity requirements and the work environment: Effects on satisfaction and intentions to leave. *Academy of Management Journal*, 43, 215–223.

Shujahat, M, MS Sosa, S Hussain, F Nawaz, M Wang and M Umer (2019). Translating the impact of knowledge management processes into knowledge-based innovation: The neglected and mediating role of knowledge-worker productivity. *Journal of Business Research*, 94, 442–450.

SokroE (2012). Analysis of the relationship that exists between organisational culture, motivation and performance. *Problems of Management in the 21st Century*, 3, 106–119.

Stajkovic, AD and F Luthans (2001). Differential effects of incentive motivators on work performance. *Academy of Management Journal*, 4, 580–590.

Stajkovic, AD and F Luthans (2003). Behavioral management and task performance in organisations: Conceptual background, meta-analysis, and test of alternative models. *Personnel Psychology*, 56, 155–194.

Statistics Finland (2013). Patenting 2012. Retrieved from https://www.stat.fi/til/pat/2012/pat_2012_2013-10-31_en.pdf.

Sung, SY, JN Choi and SC Kang (2015). Incentive pay and firm performance: Moderating roles of procedural justice climate and environmental turbulence. *Human Resource Management*, 56, 287–305.

Tremblay, MA, CM Blanchard, S Taylor, LG Pelletier and M Villeneuve (2009). Work extrinsic and intrinsic motivation scale: Its value for organisational psychology research. *Canadian Journal of Behavioral Science*, 41, 213–226.

Tsai, W and S Ghoshal (1998). Social capital and value creation: The role of intrafirm networks. *Academy of Management Journal*, 41, 462–476.

Tu, C and GC Hall (2004). Internationalization and size, age and profitability in the United Kingdom. In *Handbook of Research on International Entrepreneurship*, L.-P. Dana (Ed.), pp. 596–613. Cheltenham: Edward Elgar.

Usugami, J and K-Y Park (2006). Similarities and differences in employee motivation viewed by Korean and Japanese executives: Empirical study on employee motivation management of Japanese-affiliated companies in Korea. *International Journal of Human Resource Management*, 17, 280–294.

Vaccaro, IG, JJP Jansen, FAJ Van Den Bosch and HW Volberda (2012). Management innovation and leadership: The moderating role of organisational size. *Journal of Management Studies*, 49, 29–51.

Van de Ven, AH (1986). Central problems in the management of innovation. *Management Science*, 32, 590–607.

Van der Vegt, GS, E Van de Vliert and X Huang (2005). Location-level links between diversity and innovative climate depend on national power distance. *Academy of Management Journal*, 48, 1171–1182.

Vanhala, M and P Ritala (2016). HRM practices, impersonal trust and organisational innovativeness. *Journal of Managerial Psychology*, 31, 95–109.

Wang, S, RM Guidice, JW Tansky and Z Wang (2010). When R&D spending is not enough: The critical role of culture when you really want to innovate. *Human Resource Management*, 49, 767–792.

Weibel, A, K Rost and M Osterloh (2010). Pay for performance in the public sector: Benefits and (hidden) costs. *Journal of Public Administration Research and Theory*, 20, 387–412.

Wood, S (1996). High commitment management and payment systems. *Journal of Management Studies*, 33, 53–77.

Yoon, HJ, SY Sung, JN Choi, KL Lee and S Kim (2015). Tangible and intangible rewards and employee creativity: The mediating role of situational extrinsic motivation. *Creativity Research Journal*, 27, 383–393.

Chapter 4

THE IMPACT OF ORGANISATIONAL SLACK ON INNOVATIVE WORK BEHAVIOUR: HOW DO TOP MANAGERS AND EMPLOYEES DIFFER?[§]

SUSANNE HÜGEL* and MARKUS KREUTZER†

EBS Universität, EBS Business School
Gustav-Stresemann-Ring 3, 65189 Wiesbaden, Germany
**susanne.huegel@myebs.de*
†markus.kreutzer@ebs.edu

Published 18 April 2019

In this paper, we advance our understanding of the relationship between slack and innovation in two ways. We distinguish between different slack types on the organisational level, and hypothesise and empirically test how they influence innovative work behaviour (IWB) of both employees and top managers on the individual level. Applying a multigroup analysis in PLS-SEM, we test our model with a sample of 403 individuals, 155 top managers and 248 employees, from the German real estate industry. We find support for our central argument that the influence of organisational slack on individuals' IWB differs according to the type of slack and the organisational role of the individual.

Keywords: Innovative work behaviour; innovation; organisational slack; resource availability; multigroup analysis.

Introduction

From a behavioural theory perspective, innovation represents an important form of organisational search that plays a key role for organisational renewal (Cyert and March, 1963; Salge, 2011; Teece, 2007). Additional time, resources, and freedom at work allow organisational members to reflect upon and experiment with innovative ideas (Kanter, 1988; Simsek, 2007; Yuan and Woodman, 2010). This "slack search" is pro-active, opportunity-driven, and triggered by resource availability,

*Corresponding author.

§This article originally appeared in *International Journal of Innovation Management*, **24** 2050022-1-44

in contrast to the reactive and problem-driven "problemistic search" (Cyert and March, 1963; Salge, 2011). Since the presence of organisational slack is considered critical for an organisation's ability to innovate (Bourgeois, 1981; Cyert and March, 1963), the concept of organisational slack and its impact on innovation constitutes an important area of research within the strategic management literature (Marlin and Geiger, 2015). While empirical studies provided diverse and inconsistent findings about the relationship between slack and innovation, the inverse U-shaped relationship is most widely suggested (e.g., Nohria and Gualti, 1996). However, more recent research questions the accuracy of the interpretation of results in previous studies (e.g., Lee, 2015), and indicates that different types of organisational slack can lead to different innovation outcomes (e.g., Jalilvand and Kim, 2013; Marlin and Geiger, 2015).

Besides the need for differentiation among slack dimensions, previous literature strongly focussed on slack as antecedent of innovation on the organisational level (Bourgeois, 1981), but rarely on the individual level. To the best of our knowledge, only Scott and Bruce (1994) empirically studied the impact of "resource supply" on individual "innovative behaviour" at work. However, their surprising findings in form of inconclusive and insignificant results might be attributed to the study's limitations. Most, if not all, studies solely focus on employees or subordinates, and thereby ignore the top management's behaviour, when investigating the individual's innovative work behaviour (IWB). In addition, the top management's central role in allocating and accumulating resources within the organisation remains disregarded, although the manner how top managers actually orchestrate slack resources is critical to innovation (Carnes *et al.*, 2017; Leitner and Meyer, 2013), and impacts the work surrounding in which employees are embedded. Each individual behaves in a certain way in a given surrounding based on his or her perception (Madrid *et al.*, 2014), which might also vary according to the different importance of an individual's job positions. Hence, hierarchy levels act as proxy for the access to resources (Kimberly and Evanisko, 1981; Yuan and Woodman, 2010). So far, the impact of different types of organisational slack on individuals' innovative behaviour at work, as well as the difference between top managers and employees remained unanswered and attracts our interest.

The purpose of this paper is to refine and further extend the findings of previous research on the relationship between organisational slack and innovative behaviour. We aim to explain the different roles of perceived slack in facilitating innovative behaviour of individuals belonging to different organisational levels. We therefore follow a threefold approach that (1) distinguishes between *different types* of organisational slack, (2) examines their impact on IWB at the *individual level*, and (3) contrasts top managers *with* employees. The insights of this deeper and more differentiated approach are highly relevant for the organisational

The Impact of Organisational Slack on Innovative Work Behaviour

management, and contributes to a more comprehensive understanding of the chain of effects within an organisation. We expect that different slack types will influence IWB differently, and that the effects of the different slack types will differ among top managers and employees, since they perceive these types differently given their role within the organisation.

First, the paper provides a review of prior research on IWB, organisational slack, and innovation, which addresses the detached research streams, the recent developments and their common linkages. After explaining the organisational context of the two organisational groups, the hypotheses are developed, and the research design and methodological approach are presented. Next, we empirically examine the research model using structural equation modelling including a multigroup analysis (MGA). Finally, the paper concludes with a discussion of results, and a section on theoretical and practical implications, limitations, and suggestions for future research.

Theoretical Background

Innovative work behaviour

Innovation plays a central role for the effectiveness, economic growth and long-term survival of organisations (Schumpeter, 1934; Yuan and Woodman, 2010), while the innovation *source* is strongly rooted in the organisational members' ability and willingness to demonstrate IWB (Axtell *et al.*, 2000; Damanpour and Wischnevsky, 2006; Ngan, 2015). Over recent years, there has been great interest among researchers to study IWB, which is well documented by the remarkable growth in the number of published papers (Anderson *et al.*, 2012). Scholars have introduced a wide range of concepts that count to the notion of "IWB", for instance, innovative behaviour (Scott and Bruce, 1994), individual innovativeness (Ishak, 2005), innovative job performance (Hammond *et al.*, 2011; Janssen, 2001), on-the-job innovation (Dorenbosch *et al.*, 2005), innovation-related behaviours (Ng *et al.*, 2010), and innovative behaviour in the workplace or at work (Carmeli and Spreitzer, 2009; Yuan and Woodman, 2010). A variety of factors have been studied as potential antecedentes of IWB from *organisational* characteristics and practices (e.g., organisational culture and climate (Scott and Bruce, 1994), supervisory behaviour and leadership style (Pieterse *et al.*, 2009; Scott and Bruce, 1994)), from *job* characteristics (e.g., job autonomy (Ramamoorthy *et al.*, 2005), coworker conflict (Janssen, 2003), job-related stress (Janssen, 2004)), or from *individual* persepctives (e.g., self-efficacy (Bandura, 1997), intrinsic interest (Yuan and Woodman, 2010)).

IWB is a discretionary and voluntary behaviour, since the amount and degree of this "extra-role behaviour" cannot be mandated by the organisation and is up to each individual (Janssen, 2000; Katz and Kahn, 1978). Hence, IWB is a form of work performance (Madrid *et al.*, 2014) that constitutes a particular key asset for the organisation from which it may benefit (Janssen, 2000; Ramamoorthy *et al.*, 2005). IWB is also closely related to "creativity at work", but they are not the same (Madrid *et al.*, 2014). In general, the innovation process involves two activities that are "the development *and* implementation of new ideas" (Van De Ven, 1986, p. 591). Creativity focusses exclusively on the development of novel and useful ideas (Amabile, 1988, 1996), which makes creativity an integrative component of the innovation process. Furthermore, creativity is associated with primarily *intra*-individual cognitive processes, and it can appear spontaneously and without purpose; innovation is mainly subject to *inter*-individual social-political dynamics at the workplace (Anderson *et al.*, 2012; Van De Ven, 1986). The individual's IWB is therefore a set of behaviours that embraces both creativity-oriented aspects, such as recognising opportunities and generating ideas for the identified opportunities, as well as implementation-oriented aspects, such as spreading ideas for the purpose of coalition building and implementing these new ideas (Janssen, 2000; de Jong and den Hartog, 2010; Reuvers *et al.*, 2008; Scott and Bruce, 1994).

Since innovation is often characterised by discontinuous, overlapping activities rather than separate, sequential stages (Kanter, 1988; Schroeder *et al.*, 1989), "individuals can be expected to be involved in any combination of these behaviours at any one time" (Scott and Bruce, 1994, p. 582). In analogy to the innovation process, IWB is considered a complex multistage process that consists of different activities at each stage. Although the different behavioural tasks that are required at each stage are interrelated, you may also engage in any of these behavioural tasks separately (Reuvers *et al.*, 2008; Scott and Bruce, 1994). Even though researches widely acknowledge the multidimensional nature of IWB in theory, they have usually operationalised IWB as a one-dimensional construct (e.g., Scott and Bruce, 1994; Reuvers *et al.*, 2008). Janssen (2000) was first to treat IWB as a multidimensional measure,[1] thereby encompassing three different behavioural tasks, namley idea generation, idea promotion, and idea realisation. de Jong and den Hartog (2010) considered for the first time "problem recognition", which has been regarded integral to "idea generation" in previous concepts, as a distinct behavioural task. They conceived IWB most comprehensively as a set of four different behaviours that relate to distinct stages of the innovation process. Moreover, the two scholars provided empirical evidence that employees higher on

[1]However, Janssen (2000) found high intercorrelations and inferred that additively combining all three dimensions into an overall scale of IWB might be the best.

IWBs show more innovative output. More recent advancements built on de Jong and den Hartog's (2010) four-dimensional conceptualization, which comprises the intentional identification, generation, promotion, and realisation of new ideas, and propose minor modifications, for instance, the specification as hierarchical construct and switching from supervisor- to self-ratings (Abstein *et al.*, 2014).

Organisational slack

The concept of "organisational slack" refers to the abundance of resources.[2] Cyert and March (1963) introduced this concept to the management literature in their seminal work on the behavioural theory of the firm. More specifically, they identify "slack search" and "problemistic search", which have opposing characteristics, as facilitators of organisational adaptation. Cyert and March (1963, p. 36) define slack as "the disparity between the resources available to the organisation and the payments required to maintain the coalition". Bourgeois (1981, p. 30) came up with a less focussed definition that conceives organisational slack as "cushion of actual or potential resources which allows an organisation to adapt successfully". Thereby, Bourgeois refers to the benefits of excess resources by suggesting that slack functions as buffer against unforeseen circumstances, as tool for strategic change processes, and as a means for innovation. Hence, slack reduces organisations' downside risk, which might potentially occur in change activities, and justifies resource-intensive processes of organisational search, which consume resources that would be lacking elsewhere in the organisations otherwise (Cyert and March, 1963; Lee, 2015; Leitner and Meyer, 2013; Singh, 1986).

In general, the existing research frames organisational slack as multidimensional concept, and differentiates between various categories that are further subdivided into different slack types. Most common categories differing among *available*, *recoverable*, and *potential* slack (e.g., Bourgeois and Singh, 1983), *absorbed* and *unabsorbed* slack (e.g., Singh, 1986), *specific* and *flexible* slack (e.g., Jalilvand and Kim, 2013) overlap with each other in large parts. The term *available slack*, corresponding with *unabsorbed* or *flexible slack*, refers to internal, readily deployable resources that are not yet committed for specific allocations. This category involves financial resources or time, which can be flexibly used, for example, as excess liquidity to support expenditures in existing assets or exploration-oriented opportunities. *Recoverable slack*, matching with *absorbed* or *specific* slack, applies to internal, highly specific and absorbed resources that

[2]From a dichotomous perspective, the terms "resource scarcity" and "resource constraints" are considered opposite of "resource availability", and thus, may also be found in the literature when the degree of organisational slack is determined (cf. Dolmans *et al.*, 2014).

would require certain time and effort to change, since these resources have already been internalised into the structure, processes, and routines of the organisation. This slack category includes human resources (e.g., specialised skilled labour), excess raw materials, or operational slack (e.g., underutilised capacities) among others that support exploitation-oriented opportunities. *Potential slack* is not attributed to current resources, but future expectations. The term refers to resources that are potentially available from the external environment, such as debt, loan and equity capital, as well as an organisation's potential of raising additional capital based on increasing credit worthiness or stock price in the future (Bourgeois and Singh, 1983; Geiger and Cashen, 2002; Herold *et al.*, 2006; Jalilvand and Kim, 2013; Lee, 2015; Singh, 1986). Owing to its speculative nature, uncertain occurrence, and limited knowledge throughout the organisation, potential slack is considered negligible for our study design and only briefly described for the sake of completeness.

While some scholars associate organisational slack positively, i.e., as an asset that may buffer against unforeseen circumstances and provides resources for innovative activities and change (Bourgeois, 1981; Cyert and March, 1963), other scholars consider slack negatively. In line with the neoclassical economics view, these scholars interpret slack as an inefficiency that results from an organisation's failure to use resources optimally (Nohria and Gualti, 1996; Nohria and Gulati, 1997; Simon, 1957). Although the two notions of slack appear to be paradoxical at first, more recent scholars are less black and white thinking and point to the need to balance the conflicting objectives of operating efficiently and nurturing opportunities (e.g., Herold *et al.*, 2006; Marlin and Geiger, 2015). While efficient organisations are considered to be the most profitable in the short-run, they are at risk to fall behind more resource-rich competitors who ensure their long-term market effectiveness by facilitating innovations with excess resources (Cheng and Kesner, 1997; Nohria and Gulati, 1997; Sharfman *et al.*, 1988). Thus, minimising slack for the sake of internal efficiency might be too short-sighted. According to the reasoning of Sharfman *et al.* (1988, p. 603), "there is an optimal level of slack for any given firm", or in other words, the same resource allocation pattern may not necessarily be appropriate for different organisation under different conditions. In either way, actively managing the organisation's slack resources is important and the top management has to be selective in the accumulation of resources (Cheng and Kesner, 1997).

Innovation, innovative work behaviour, and organisational slack

Most previous research on the relationship between organisational slack and innovation supports the assumption that highly available resources, among other

The Impact of Organisational Slack on Innovative Work Behaviour

organisational conditions, are likely to facilitate innovations, because these resources provide the buffer that is needed for developing and experimenting with ideas (Cyert and March, 1963; Kanter, 1988; Leitner and Meyer, 2013; Miller and Friesen, 1982; Patterson *et al.*, 2009; Subramanian and Nilakanta, 1996). Although there is empirical evidence that confirms the assumed positive relationship between slack and innovation (e.g., Aiken and Hage, 1971; Miller and Friesen, 1982; Greve, 2003), likewise contrary findings have been demonstrated. Slack has been found to have linear positive, linear negative, curvilinear, or insignificant effects on innovation among empirical studies (Herold *et al.*, 2006; Leitner and Meyer, 2013; Nohria and Gualti, 1996). Since many works on slack and innovation provided empirical evidence for an inverse U-shaped relationship (Lee, 2015), first presented by Nohria and Gualti (1996), research has widely accepted and advocated this relationship ever after. *Zero* slack, by nature, is considered a disadvantage for experimentation and innovation; *too much* slack is also considered a disadvantage, because high levels of slack lead to a relaxation of control mechanism and a decrease of discipline, which might outweigh the positive effects (cf. Nohria and Gualti, 1996). Lee (2015) critically analysed several studies, which report to have found an inverse U-shaped relationship between slack and innovation. The focus lied on the robustness and credibility of the studies' empirical results and interpretations. Only one study, however, passes the test that points to a clear inverse U-shaped relationship; all others have been found to provide merely inconsistent evidence.

Echoing the ambiguous research results, the relationship between slack and innovation points to two main conclusions: First, some researchers argue that the study results may vary based on the category or type(s) of slack that are used in the studies (Geiger and Cashen, 2002; Jalilvand and Kim, 2013; Marlin and Geiger, 2015). For example, Scott and Bruce (1994) operationalised slack as a global unidimensional variable comprising multiple (theoretically introduced) dimensions, namely personnel, funding, and time resources. Other studies were selective and focussed on a specific type or category of slack (e.g., Lee, 2015; Salge, 2011; George, 2005). More recent research by Geiger and Marlin (2015) took a configurational approach and found multiple ways of bundling different slack resources leading to similar positive innovation outcomes. Although the two researchers distinguish between slack categories that are commonly used (i.e., available, recoverable and potential slack), all of them are operationalised by financial statement data, and thereby ignorant to other types within each category. Second, the scholars examine the influence of slack on innovation at the organisational level like most researchers in this domain. The individual level has been largely neglected, although the actual orchestration of the resource portfolio *by* the individual (Carnes *et al.*, 2017), and the effect of resources *on* the individual are crucial for innovation. Amabile (1988) provides the explanation why the effect of slack resources on individual innovation might have received less attention in research, which is because the necessity of resources seems so obvious.

Hypotheses Development

Given the observations of Birkinshaw *et al.* (2011), successful innovations require close attention to both top-down and bottom-up efforts, whereby in particular the interplay is regarded as a decisive factor. The terms "top" and "bottom" refer to the two key groups within an organisation, namely the top management and employees (Kesting and Ulhøi, 2010; Klein and Sorra, 1996; Mayer and Gavin, 2005; Niehoff *et al.*, 1990). In particular, extending previous research, which has solely focussed on employees, to the top management is a common procedure (cf. Sirén *et al.*, 2018).[3] The top management is the uppermost authority, which plays a key role in explaining organisational outcomes (Hambrick, 2007; Hambrick and Mason, 1984). Top managers have the right and duty to make strategic decisions on a routine level, including decisions about innovation and resource allocation. Thereby, top managers are continually challenged to balance the trade-offs between running the business efficiently and having excess resources to buffer against unforeseen threats, to fuel strategic change or the pursuit of new opportunities (Jalilvand and Kim, 2013; Kesting and Ulhøi, 2010; Niehoff *et al.*, 1990). The employees' core task is usually on the operative and supportive level, i.e., they are responsible to implement management decisions and undertake assisting functions. Employees are mainly bounded by their given routines, while they typically possess lots of exclusive, in-depth and highly context-dependent operational knowledge, which they have acquired over time (Henderson and McAdam, 1997; Kesting and Ulhøi, 2010).

According to behavioural theory, boundedly rational actors envision an incomplete set of alternative actions (Cyert and March, 1963; Gavetti and Levinthal, 2000). Since cognition translates into actual behaviour, we assume that individuals will show different behaviour not only based on their unique personality, but also their personal perception, for example, on the availability of different resources. Since the individuals of each key group are embedded in similar frameworks

[3]We acknowledge that organisations are more diverse than a two-level categorisation into top managers and employees, which simplifies the organisational setting. However, it captures the two most important levels and differing viewpoints. In our robustness section, we test a three-fold division and further differentiate the employee level into middle managers and lower level employees (cf. Hornsby *et al.*, 2002).

The Impact of Organisational Slack on Innovative Work Behaviour

across organisations, it is not unlikely that their perception is similarly "filtered" and their scope of action similarly determined within each group. The individuals' IWB might therefore have similarities within each group, when certain contextual factors, such as the lack of a specific slack type, are similar. In this study, we focus on available and recoverable slack, and follow the predominant conceptualization of resource availability that distinguishes between managerial talent, skilled labour, material supplies, and reserves of capital (Miller and Friesen, 1982). We add "time" as a fifth slack type which is often included in studies on resource availability (e.g., Kesting and Ulhøi, 2010; Kuratko *et al.*, 1990; Kanter, 1985).

Managerial talent refers to the process of influencing others in order to increase the likelihood of a desired outcome, such as innovation (de Jong and den Hartog, 2007; Mumford *et al.*, 2002). According to Michaels *et al.* (2001, p. xiii), managerial talent is "some combination of a sharp strategic mind, leadership ability, emotional maturity, communications skills, the ability to attract and inspire other talented people, entrepreneurial instincts, functional skills, and the ability to deliver results". When top managers are asked about the managerial talent within their organisation, they are asked about their own skill set as well as their effectiveness as key decision makers to employ personnel that is also equipped with managerial talent. Top managers who are confident about their own capabilities and effectiveness would give a positive (self-) evaluation, which concurrently implies a positive statement about their self-efficacy (Bandura, 1997). Since there is a multitude of research, which confirms a positive relationship between self-efficacy and innovation (cf. Axtell *et al.*, 2000), as well as self-efficacy and IWB (cf. Janssen, 2005) on the employee level, it is highly likely to apply also to the top management level. Moreover, numerous studies have empirically shown that great leadership behaviours positively affect employees' IWB, for example, the support from supervisors (cf. Janssen, 2005) or a transformational leadership style (cf. Reuvers *et al.*, 2008). Since employees perform on the operative level, they are highly dependent on the top management's support, approval and decisions on resource allocation and orchestration (Carnes *et al.*, 2017; Kesting and Ulhøi, 2010). Hence, strong leadership skills within an organisation should highly stimulate employees' overall work ethic, as well as extra-role behaviour, such as IWB.

Hypothesis 1. *The perception of abundant managerial talent will encourage* (*a*) *top managers' IWB, as well as* (*b*) *employees' IWB.*

Skilled labour is considered a key factor of innovation both (cf. Leiponen, 2005) being a barrier to innovation, which refers to the lack of skills, expertise, and willingness in the employee pool (Hewitt-Dundas, 2006), as well as being a facilitator of innovation, because innovation is no longer just a task of scientists, specialists, or R&D staff (Dorenbosch *et al.*, 2005; Gupta and Singhal, 1993). An organisation backed with employees that possess a wide range of tacit knowledge, skills, and abilities is likely to be better positioned and more effective even if times become more turbulent (Patterson *et al.*, 2009). Hence, top managers might have few concerns about organisational failure and relax controls in such a setting, which has positive effects for their long-term orientation and own innovative efforts (Bromiley, 1991; Cyert and March, 1963; Nohria and Gualti, 1996). Therefore, we conclude that a workforce of qualified employees constitutes a (re)-source and enabler for top manager's innovative behaviour. Compared with less-skilled labour, skilled labour is characterised by various educational backgrounds and versatile career paths that lead to higher employability and (international) mobility, and thereby, to greater diversity in their target organisation. Employees benefit from diversity in terms of personal characteristics, expertise, and experiences when working in teams, because this diversity usually accelerates the individual's potential towards creativity and innovation (Gupta and Singhal, 1993; Kim and Choi, 2018; Østergaard *et al.*, 2011; Van De Ven, 1986). Stimulating human interaction is inevitably involved in IWB, which incorporates a social process where people build coalitions (Kanter, 1988; Van De Ven, 1986; West and Farr, 1990). In particular, lower level employees tend to share ideas first with their immediate network face-to-face and initiate innovations rather informally via interpersonal channels (Johnson *et al.*, 2001). Being surrounded by colleagues, well equipped with hard and soft skills can have a positive effect on the process to promote the idea more broadly as they are most likely capable of providing the needed support and security to do so. Both the support of work groups and colleagues that enhance the likelihood of the proposed ideas being adopted as well as the diversity of information, knowledge, and alternative points of view that enhance the occurrence of novel ideas (Hammond *et al.*, 2011; Kanter, 1988; Scott and Bruce, 1994; Van der Vegt and Janssen, 2003) should thrive in environments of skilled labour. However, even if more qualified people may appear beneficial for an employee's IWB at first, there is also a downside to the social interaction. Referring to research on resistance to change, innovative activities question the status quo, and therefore entail the risk of conflict with colleagues due to divergent personal interests and preferences leading to increased levels of stress (Bunce and West, 1994; Janssen, 2003; Patterson *et al.*, 2009). In addition, the perception of abundant qualified employees could facilitate a "lean-back-and-relax" mentality where employees assume (or expect) that others are sufficiently active, and thus, satisfice rather than optimise. This, in turn, may lead to an overall enhanced social inertia that often impedes recognising the opportunity or need for action, and the action itself (Tushman, 1997). Both feeling comfortable or avoiding conflict might negatively affect employees' IWB.

Hypothesis 2. *The perception of abundant skilled labour will encourage (a) top managers' IWB, but impede (b) employees' IWB.*

Material supply and its adequate availability contribute to innovation on the organisational level according to previous research (Amabile *et al.*, 1996; Cyert and March, 1963; Damanpour, 1991). Especially at the experimental stage of the innovation process, when tangible assets are consumed, excess material supply is beneficial. On the individual level, the pure existence of sufficient material might reduce top managers' concerns about failures, and enhance their cognitive efforts towards innovative activities (Bromiley, 1991; Cyert and March, 1963). Similarly, access to material resources is considered important for employees' creativity (Katz and Allen, 1988), because the material's instant availability encourages to "materialise" new ideas. However, it has been repeatedly observed that individuals tend to stick to the first feasible and affordable idea by default until they are pushed off (e.g., Ward, 1994, 2004). Individuals restrain to seek other superior novel solutions, because they initially follow a "path of least resistance". Getting off this path would require more cognitive effort, which individuals attempt to minimise according to the "cognitive least-effort principle" (Gray, 2000; Reichle *et al.*, 2000). Individuals need to be compelled to overcome their avoidance of cognitive effort, for instance, by not having everything that is needed readily at hand. The lack of material resources would therefore encourage individuals, especially those dealing with operational tasks, to think of different ways of doing their work, hence facilitate creativity and innovation. In the words of Csikszentmihalyi (1997), excessive resources can have a "deadening effect on creativity" (p. 321) by making it too comfortable for individuals. Nevertheless, we propose that material slack would positively affect IWB, because we expect a basic willingness to innovate that appreciates the opportunity to experiment and materialise.

Hypothesis 3. *The perception of abundant material supply will encourage (a) top managers' IWB, as well as (b) employees' IWB.*

Capital is considered a prominent determinant of innovation and creativity (Amabile, 1996; Damanpour, 1991). Excess capital resources provide the financial liquidity and increased certainty that the organisation can afford investment-intensive, long-term, open-ended and uncertain innovation search processes (Geiger and Cashen, 2002). Thus, slack capital encourages firms to pursue new ideas and allays concerns that the capital employed would be lacking elsewhere in the organisation (Cyert and March, 1963; Kim *et al.*, 2008). On the contrary, scarce capital resources will likely turn the organisation's focus to near-term survival and exploiting the existing (Levinthal and March, 1993). Hence, an unburdened consciousness that excess capital is available should inspire creativity and enables innovative activities in both groups.[4] The top management has a sensitive attitude towards financial matters, because it bears the responsibility for the budget (Williamson, 1963). Holding capital resources — the most generic form of slack and easiest to redeploy — is a strategic benefit and buffer for turbulent times and unexpected shortfalls (Greve, 2003; Shahzad *et al.*, 2016; Voss *et al.*, 2008). Due to the discretionary nature of capital resources, top managers may be more willing to deploy abundant capital resources in risky explorations than other more absorbed forms of slack (Voss *et al.*, 2008) and stimulated to pursue long-term aspirations. However, there is also a potential downside to the discretion of capital allocation: An increased or permanent financial surplus can leave so much discretionary power to the top management that they are at risk to fall into managerial opportunism (Williamson, 1963). The top managers' maximising behaviour is generally ambivalent and spans between the stakeholders' and their private interests. Opportunistic top managers might indulge in self-serving wasteful behaviours and misuse financial slack for their own empire building (Jensen and Meckling, 1976; Marlin and Geiger, 2015; Shahzad *et al.*, 2016). Conversely, financial scarcity is likely to shift the top managers' focus so that they operate the organisation more efficiently (Baker and Nelson, 2005), reduce the funds needed for experimentation in order to rebuild a financial cushion (Hoegl *et al.*, 2008), and also show a more efficient individual behaviour to the detriment of extra-role behaviour, such as IWB. Similarly, employees tend to adjust their activities and behaviours to what is deemed necessary. Research has shown that employees often excuse their limited performance by blaming the organisation for the budget constraints (Hoegl *et al.*, 2008). On the other hand, capital surplus should encourage the innovative behaviour of employees because they are rarely involved in decisions on capital allocation, hence less tempted to develop opportunistic behaviours thereof.

[4]Prior empirical research reported conflicting findings on the relationship between financial slack and firm innovation: In addition to the opposing views that present either a positive (e.g., Bourgeois, 1981; Hall, 2002; O'Brien, 2003) or negative (e.g., Williamson, 1964; Jensen and Meckling, 1976; Kraatz and Zajac, 2001) effect, scholars also suggested an inverse U-shaped relationship (e.g., Nohria and Gualti, 1996; Herold *et al.*, 2006; Kim *et al.*, 2008), which is again questioned by more recent scholars and remains an unsettled issue (e.g., Herold *et al.*, 2006; Lee, 2015). Despite the inconclusive findings, previous studies all refer to innovation as an outcome on the organisational level. Innovative work behaviour, however, refers to a set of innovation-related behaviours on the individual level. Therefore, we develop our hypothesis from an individual's activity-oriented rather than an organisation's result-oriented perspective.

The Impact of Organisational Slack on Innovative Work Behaviour

Hypothesis 4. *The perception of abundant financial slack will encourage* (*a*) *top managers' IWB, as well as the* (*b*) *employees' IWB.*

Time is a critical factor for innovation, because innovation requires time to think, process, adapt, and create (Lawson, 2001). Moreover, sufficient "time to think creatively about the problem, to explore different perspectives rather than having to impose an already determined approach" (Amabile, 1988, p. 147) enhances creativity. Having too little time can induce two different types of pressure: workload pressure and challenge (Amabile *et al.*, 1996). Since excessive "workload pressure" is negatively associated with creativity, IWB may suffer too. This might be the case, for instance, when the top management is occupied by turn-around management, high-frequently "fire-fighting" and/or working to capacity in their day-to-day business (Amabile, 1988). Then, initiating future goals may fall short, because there is too little time for creative and innovative endeavours due to the excess workload. By contrast, time pressure in form of "challenge" is positively associated with creativity and individual innovation behaviours (Amabile *et al.*, 1996; Wu *et al.*, 2014). Challenge based on time scarcity leads to higher activation, which stimulates individuals and may motivate them to attempt deviating from routines (Ohly and Fritz, 2010). Since time pressure represents a suboptimal condition that challenges the effort needed to achieve the expected goal, employees are encouraged to initiate new ideas and engage in novel approaches different from the status quo in order to accomplish their work on time (Fay and Sonnentag, 2002). On the contrary, employees with too much time available could also be a drawback that leads to redundant activities based on the limited strategic decision-making scope and management dependency (i.e., not knowing for sure how to reallocate a local time surplus so that it is useful for the organisation), or a shift towards "off-job" activities in favour of the work-life balance (O'Driscoll *et al.*, 1992). However, time scarcity is more likely to reflect reality.

Hypothesis 5. *The perception of having abundant time will encourage* (*a*) *top managers' IWB, but will impede the* (*b*) *employees' IWB.*

Method

Organisational context

We chose individuals from the German real estate industry as object of study. The real estate industry captures various fields of service-oriented activities, which become visible in the organisations' highly differentiated business profiles. Moreover, the real estate industry is highly interlinked with the real economy and the financial markets due to the real estates' characteristics as consumption and capital goods, as well as capital investments. However, it also constitutes a self-contained system within the economy due to the specific features of real estate objects, such as their immobility, location-specificity, long value chain and life-span, high-capital investments and life-cycle costs, as well as their special risk structure, which require profound know-how (Schulte *et al.*, 2005). Overall, the German real estate industry is an interesting sample that is comprised of personality and context variations corresponding to all the different job requirements within the industry (Hügel *et al.*, 2019).

Data collection procedure

In this study, we examine the effect of different types of (perceived) organisational slack on both employees' and top managers' IWB by using MGA. We surveyed members from all subsectors of the German real estate industry with a pretested questionnaire to gather individual-level data, and therefore performed a stepwise data collection. After identifying potential participants of the top management level via desk research, we sent a personalised contact request via "Xing"[5] that included a brief introduction and announcement of the forthcoming survey. In a second personalised message, we included the link to an online questionnaire and to a paper-based download version and asked the prospective participants to forward the link within their company to make use of the compiled network across the real estate industry. We also sent emails to industry members of various real estate networks, communities, and industry events who had made their contact details publicly available to collect the greatest possible amount of data on employee level. For a maximum industry coverage, we distributed survey invitations and the link to the questionnaire via indirect channels, for instance, posts in online real estate magazines, newsletter articles, and circular mails of various industry associations, institutions, and interest groups. Of course, respondents' participation in this study was strictly voluntary and the data subject to confidential treatment and anonymous use. Overall, we distributed 1,904 surveys (572 messages via Xing and 1,332 emails) directly over a period of almost 40 weeks.

Participants

The pool of study participants consists of both top management and employee level from all subsectors of the German real estate industry. A total of 813

[5]"Xing" is a career-oriented social media network for professionals, similar to but more popular than "LinkedIn" in Germany. According to data from Statista, "Xing" counted 12.7 million German speaking users in the DACH region (i.e., Germany, Austria, and Switzerland) as of the first quarter of 2017, LinkedIn counted 10 million German speaking users as of June 2017.

The Impact of Organisational Slack on Innovative Work Behaviour

responses were recorded and **403 valid responses** across all hierarchies from 197 different companies remained after eliminating partially completed answers, representing a response rate of 21.2%. Of these 403 participants, 48 work in companies who are younger than five years, respectively, 90 work in companies younger than 10 years. The final sample counted 155 top managers and 248 employees. Most top managers were male (94.2%), approximately between 46 and 55 years old (52.9%), and hold a postgraduate degree, i.e., Diploma, Master or MBA (69.7%), or Doctorate (11%). Their tenure mostly ranged between 1 and 5 years (42.6%), with a mean of 6.3 years. Their managerial positions were distinguished between member of the board or member of the management (56.8%), company owner or managing partner (35.5%), and partner[6] (7.7%). Employees were also male-dominated (74.6%), between 36 and 45 years old (41.9%), and had a university degree, i.e., Diploma, Master or MBA (68.5%), or Bachelor (14.1%). The employee tenure mostly ranged between 1 and 5 years (45.6%), with a mean of 5.6 years. Their job positions ranged between head of division (28.6%), head of department (27.4%), others with real estate-specific field of activity (39.1%), and others with administrative field of activity (4.9%).

Measures

For this study, we used self-reported measures derived from existing literature. In case, the measures were not available bilingually from the researchers directly, we applied the "committee approach" (Brislin, 1970). Two bilingual experts, German native-speaking academics, translated the items from their original language English into German followed by an independent review from a third bilingual person who controlled the translation's consistency and comprehensibility. The items of the core concepts were evaluated based on 7-point Likert scales ranging from (1) "I strongly disagree" via (4) "neither nor" to (7) "I strongly agree", control variables were categorical. All items of the questionnaire can be found in Appendix B.

Independent Variables. Organisational Slack. We used the four-item measure "resource availability" from Miller and Friesen (1982), which addresses the abundance of managerial talent, skilled labour, capital, and material supply within the firm. In addition, we employed "time" as a fifth relevant aspect, as in line with literature (e.g., Kesting and Ulhøi, 2010; Kuratko *et al.*, 1990; Kanter, 1985) real estate professionals mentioned "time" as critical factor for innovation in our plentiful a priori informal conversations. Originally, Miller and Friesen (1982) averaged all scale items to obtain one overall variable score for "resource

[6]A "partner" traditionally has co-ownership shares of a partnership, a "member of the board/member of the management" does not have ownership rights in contrast to a "company owner/managing partner".

availability". By contrast, we decided to treat each aspect separately by building five single-item measures to elaborate on their differences in effect. Since a single item solely and exclusively reflects the entire construct, thereby implies the complete absence of measurement error, the use of single-item measures in structural equation models is under debate in literature[7] (Fuchs and Diamantopoulos, 2009; Petrescu, 2013). This circumstance is considered problematic as "an observable measure never fully exhausts everything that is meant by a construct, i.e., constructs have surplus meaning" (Peter, 1981, p. 134). In our case, however, the perfect representation can be justified based on two criteria (cf. Fuchs and Diamantopoulos, 2009): First, the focal concept is highly "concrete" and easy-to-understand; and second, a "global" single-item question is reasonable due to our interest on the individual's overall perception of each aspect of resource availability, or, respectively, resource scarcity.

Dependent Variable: Innovative Work Behaviour (IWB): We measured IWB with a 10-item employee-rated scale taken from Abstein *et al.* (2014) who used a slightly modified version of de Jong and den Hartog's (2010) original supervisor-rated scale. IWB is comprised of four related dimensions, namely problem recognition, idea generation, idea championing, and idea realisation. Furthermore, the multidimensional measure is specified as a reflective first-order and formative second-order construct (type II) (Abstein *et al.*, 2014), which thereby advances Janssen's (2000) considerations on combining the dimensions additively. When intending to use self-reported measures in behavioural research (additional) supervisor or co-worker ratings are recommended to prevent confounding effects on the results, yielding potential misinterpretations due to, for example, consistency effects, implicit theories, or social desirability bias (Podsakoff *et al.*, 2003). Supervisor ratings, however, may have pitfalls too (de Jong and den Hartog, 2010). Supervisors might be less sensitive to all of their employees' genuine ideas and innovative activities due to their broad holistic view, whereas employees might be more subtle in their self-evaluation due to much more background information about their own innovative activities (Janssen, 2000; Madrid *et al.*, 2014). Moreover, previous research has shown that supervisor and self-ratings of employees' IWB correlate (Janssen, 2000; Scott and Bruce, 1994). We therefore conclude that self-reported measures are feasible to assess IWB, when potential common method bias is controlled for.

Controls: Consistent with previous research on IWB, we controlled for the individuals' demographics (*age*, *education*, and *gender*), as well as for job-related

[7]A detailed discussion and a decision guideline are provided by Fuchs and Diamantopoulos (2009), an empirical analysis on the use of single-item measures in published articles can be found in Sarstedt *et al.*'s (2016) article.

factors (*tenure*, *job position*, *firm age*, and *firm size*). For example, organisational members with higher *tenure*, especially in resource-rich settings, might have established comfort zones and routines that foster inertia leading to lower IWB. Also from a prospect theory perspective, peoples' tendency to place a higher value on avoiding loss than on realizing gains (Kahneman and Tversky, 1979) supports the assumption that longer tenures lead to more risk-averse (and less innovative) behaviour in order to conserve prior achievements (and this conservation might be visible in the abundance of available resources). On the other side, members with higher tenure could feel more confident to undertake more risky actions, for example, innovative search with uncertain outcome, due to their greater organisational experience (Simsek, 2007). Especially in resource-poor settings, organisational members should be more likely stimulated to draw on their experience in order to compensate the lacking resources. Furthermore, there is empirical evidence that firm size and firm age matter in the relationship between resource availability and innovation (Lee, 2015). *Firm size* depends on economies of scale and the organisation of the firm, and can act as proxy for the managerial discretion level (Mayers and Smith, 1994). Although larger firms have more and diverse resources, facilities, and knowledge to stimulate innovative activities (Damanpour and Wischnevsky, 2006), they suffer from increasing bureaucratic inflexibility. With increasing firm size, managerial discretion as well as employees' flexibility decrease due to greater bureaucratic control. Similarly, older firms have established organisational routines and bureaucratic mechanism over years, which jeopardise innovative activities of its members (Damanpour and Wischnevsky, 2006). The organisational inertia, an effect of firm maturity that limits the firm's ability to make change, is very likely to be an innovation inhibitor (Lee, 2015), although an old firm's solid and large knowledge base might support and encourage the seizing of ideas and new opportunities (Cohen and Levinthal, 1990). We operationalised "firm size" by the number of organisational members in the study's target country (i.e., Germany), and "firm age" by the number of years in business (i.e., the difference between the year of data collection and the founding year).

Results

For the evaluation of our research model, we followed a sequential procedure that started with an exploratory factor analysis (EFA)[8] to determine the factor structure of the multidimensional construct IWB. The preliminary analysis in SPSS

[8]We conducted the EFA three times, i.e., for the overall sample, employee only, and top management only. All three analyses indicated the same conclusion based on the high cross-loadings.

revealed high cross-loadings among its 10 items, which all loaded on one factor, and thereby indicated that IWB may be 1D. Although referring to Abstein *et al.* (2014) measure, which is specified as first-order reflective and second-order formative construct (type II), we were incapable to justify a multidimensional model, and thus, decided to proceed with a 1D IWB construct[9] in this study.

We used partial least square path modelling (PLS-SEM) to analyse the causal linear relationships between the latent and observed variables in our study. The variance-based PLS-SEM emphazis on the explained variance and predictiveness of a model rather than model fit indices as in covariance-based structural equation modelling (CB-SEM) (Roldán and Sánchez-Franco, 2012). PLS-SEM is also recommended, when the research goal is to identify the most important antecedents of a target construct (Hair *et al.*, 2011; Sarstedt *et al.*, 2014b), as in our case. PLS-SEM's ability to estimate higher-order formative constructs (e.g., IWB as it was initially expected in our study) is another advantage over the more commonly used CB-SEM (Chin, 2010), even though PLS-SEM may have drawbacks too. We employed SmartPLS (v.3.2.6) with default settings for the PLS algorithm, as suggested by the software developers Ringle, Wende, and Becker (i.e., path weighting scheme, maximum number of 300 iterations, and a stop criterion value of 10^{-7}). The bootstrapping settings were adjusted to 5,000 subsamples and the default retained for parallel processing, no sign changes, complete bootstrapping, bias-corrected and accelerated (BCa) bootstrap as the confidence interval method, two-tailed test type, and a significance level of 0.05.

We evaluated our model in three steps, which included the two-step diagnostic procedure that is recommended for a PLS-SEM evaluation (e.g., Chin, 2010; Hair *et al.*, 2014; Roldán and Sánchez-Franco, 2012; Sarstedt *et al.*, 2014b. First, the measurement model was assessed until satisfactory quality was established, then the structural model was evaluated, and finally the MAG was conducted. The two groups for comparison were defined according to the respondents' hierarchical level within the firm: The first group represents the *top management* level with 155 cases and comprises (1) company owners/managing partners, (2) members of the

[9]To be on the safe side, we also tested an alternative research model in SmartPLS in which IWB was specified as reflective first-order and formative second-order construct (type II). Since IWB is an *endogenous* variable with *unequal* number of indicators for each first-order construct in the alternative research model, we had to use the two-stage approach (Becker *et al.*, 2012; Hair *et al.*, 2014; Ringle *et al.*, 2012). Although the first-order met all reflective measures' quality criteria, the second order did not stand the test regarding the formative relation: First, the negative path coefficient does not really make sense, when items are supposed to cause a construct (cf. Cenfetelli and Bassellier, 2009, p. 692), and second, none of the four dimensions proved to significantly contribute to the higher-order construct (Table A.1). Thus, the multidimensional specification as reflective first-order and formative second-order construct appeared to be problematic.

board/members of the management, or (3) partners. The second group represents the *employee* level with 248 cases and comprises (4) division heads, (5) department heads, (6) others with real estate-specific field of activity, or (7) others with administrative field of activity.

Measurement model assessment

We evaluated all relevant reliability and validity criteria for the outer model(s)'s reflective measures across the overall and the two subgroups samples. In all three sample configurations, almost all loadings were above, or very close, to the recommended value of 0.7. Although IWB's item 5 "I often pay attention to issues that are not part of my daily work" showed the lowest loading with 0.597, researchers noted that 0.7 is rather a rule of thumb and loadings of at least 0.5 may still be acceptable if there are additional high-loading items in the same construct for comparison (Chin, 2010; Hair *et al.*, 2011). Thus, *indicator reliability* was considered satisfactory. Further calculations demonstrated good *construct reliability*, because both internal consistency, measured by Cronbach's alpha, and composite reliability (CR) yielded above the critical value of 0.7 (Hair *et al.*, 2014; Nunnally, 1978). The average variance extracted (AVE) values, which all were above the minimum threshold of 0.5, confirmed evidence of adequate *convergent validity* (Fornell and Larcker, 1981). Values below the 0.85 threshold for the heterotrait-monotrait ratio of correlations (HTMT)[10] indicated appropriate *discriminant validity* (Henseler *et al.*, 2015), as shown in Table A.2. Results of IWB's measurement model are illustrated in Table 1. Results for the single-item measures' measurement models (i.e., the resource availability measures) are not

Table 1. Results of IWB's measurement model.

	Item loadings												
Dataset	IWB1	IWB2	IWB3	IWB4	IWB5	IWB6	IWB7	IWB8	IWB9	IWB10	Scale CA	Scale CR	Scale AVE
Complete	0.748	0.727	0.782	0.720	0.614	0.721	0.767	0.783	0.782	0.732	0.908	0.923	0.546
Employees	0.717	0.710	0.798	0.667	0.652	0.708	0.757	0.782	0.776	0.730	0.904	0.920	0.535
Top management	0.775	0.769	0.712	0.769	0.597	0.772	0.739	0.745	0.743	0.692	0.904	0.920	0.537

Notes: CA = Cronbach's α; CR = composite reliability; AVE = average variance extracted.

[10]The HTMT approach is considered superior for variance-based SEM in comparison to the more frequently used Fornell–Larcker criterion (Fornell and Larcker, 1981) or the evaluation of cross-loadings (Chin, 1998b).

reported, because their loadings automatically have a value of 1 and the error term a value of 0 due to the inherent absence of measurement error that makes the construct become the measure (Fuchs and Diamantopoulos, 2009).

Structural model assessment

After validating the measurement model's quality, we assessed the main effects and fit indices of the structural model across all samples, and thereby, tested our hypotheses. We applied PLS-SEM-specific evaluation criteria, i.e., the relevance and significance of *path coefficients* (i.e., β and p), the exogenous constructs' *collinearity* (VIF), the endogenous latent variable's *predictive power* (R^2) and *predictive relevance* (Q^2) (Sarstedt *et al.*, 2014b), and the *standardised root mean square residual* (SRMR), which is currently the only approximate indicator of the overall model fit implemented for PLS path modelling (Henseler *et al.*, 2016).

Standardised path coefficients should be larger than 0.2 to be considered meaningful (Chin, 1998a); however, some researchers also acknowledge smaller path coefficients ($0.1 < \beta_i < 0.2$) if they are significant, and confirm the affected hypotheses (cf. Rudd *et al.*, 2008). Table 2 shows both subgroups' results. We tested potential collinearity among the exogenous constructs, illustrated in Table 3, but collinearity is no concern since all the variance inflation factor (VIF)

Table 2. Structural model paths and hypotheses.

		Complete			Employees			Top management	
Hypothesis	Structural path	β_i	t-value	HD	β_i	t-value	HD	β_i	t-value
H_4	RA1 > IWB	0.004	0.077	(+)	−0.089	1.311	(+)	**0.196**	1.929*
H_2	RA2 > IWB	−0.006	0.101	(−)	−0.186	2.314**	(+)	**0.262**	2.848***
H_3	RA3 > IWB	0.068	1.288	(+)	**0.173**	2.389**	(+)	−0.094	0.963
H_1	RA4 > IWB	**0.157**	2.148**	(+)	**0.292**	3.200***	(+)	0.024	0.207
H_5	RA5 > IWB	**0.123**	2.130**	(−)	0.007	0.091	(+)	**0.221**	2.268**
	FirmAge > IWB	0.049	1.081		0.093	1.619		−0.087	1.134
	FirmSize > IWB	0.061	0.961		0.052	0.700		0.018	0.166
	Age > IWB	−0.031	0.573		−0.002	0.030		−0.106	1.274
	Edu > IWB	−0.061	1.307		−0.039	0.605		−0.111	1.620
	Gender > IWB	−0.029	0.549		−0.013	0.198		−0.046	0.536
	Tenure > IWB	−0.067	1.205		0.000	0.005		−0.132	1.613
	Position > IWB	**−0.282**	4.713***		**−0.179**	2.719***		**−0.177**	2.110**

Notes: HD = Hypothesised direction; IWB = innovative work behaviour; RA1 = capital; RA2 = skilled labour; RA3 = material supply; RA4 = managerial talent; RA5 = time; Edu = education; path coefficient β and t-value based on a bootstrapping with $n = 5,000$; $^{***}p < 0.01$; $^{**}p < 0.05$; $^{*}p < 0.1$.

Table 3. VIF values of the exogenous constructs.

Dataset	RA1	RA2	RA3	RA4	RA5	FA	FS	Age	Edu	Gen	Ten	Pos
Complete	1.418	1.370	1.369	1.805	1.394	1.148	1.457	1.359	1.083	1.140	1.253	1.762
Employees	1.280	1.470	1.360	1.874	1.577	1.121	1.234	1.234	1.109	1.100	1.377	1.170
Top management	1.785	1.366	1.560	1.551	1.287	1.297	1.457	1.171	1.134	1.031	1.222	1.405

Notes: VIF = variance inflation factor; RA1 = capital; RA2 = skilled labour; RA3 = material supply; RA4 = managerial talent; RA5 = time; FA = firm age; FS = firm size; Edu = education; Gen = gender; Ten = tenure; Pos = position.

values are clearly below the conservative threshold of 3.3 (Petter *et al.*, 2007). Both *predictive power* (i.e., R^2) and *predictive relevance* (i.e., Q^2) point to a model's quality in terms of its ability to predict the endogenous constructs (Sarstedt *et al.*, 2014b). R^2 is also known as coefficient of determination and represents a measure of in-sample prediction, which is more of informative nature and its interpretation context-dependent (Sarstedt *et al.*, 2014a; Sarstedt *et al.*, 2014b). Small R^2 values are not inherently a problem and common, for example, in behavioural sciences[11] (Cohen, 1988), because it is hard to predict human behaviour that is largely affected by personal idiosyncrasies. Hence, R^2 values are particularly helpful to compare different models, or the explanatory power of a model across different datasets or data groups (Henseler *et al.*, 2016). The slack types altogether explain 15.0% of employees' IWB and 23.1% of top management's IWB, thereby proving moderate to large effects. The Stone–Geisser criterion Q^2 (Geisser, 1974; Stone, 1974) is a measure of out-of-sample prediction. We run the iterative blindfolding procedure, which is only applied to reflective latent variables, to obtain Q^2 values in terms of cross-validated redundancy with omission distance of 7 (Hair *et al.*, 2014). The values among all samples yielded larger than zero, and, therefore, demonstrated sufficient predictive relevance of the exogenous constructs (Hair *et al.*, 2011).

For a long period, PLS path modeling has been criticised for lacking a global goodness-of-fit measure (Dijkstra and Henseler, 2015). Henseler *et al.* (2016) introduce a new bootstrap-based approach in their updated guidelines and suggest assessing the overall model fit by the SRMR. While SRMR values of 0 represent a perfect fit (Byrne, 2008), values below the threshold of 0.08 indicate an adequate fit for PLS path models (Hu and Bentler, 1998, 1999), which our structural model

[11]As an example, Cohen (1988) defined values of $R^2 = 0.02$ as "small" effect size meaning that it accounts for 2% of the variance, $R^2 = 0.13$ as "medium" effect size, and $R^2 = 0.26$ as "large" effect size in his book on statistical power analysis for the behavioural sciences.

Table 4. Fit measures of the structural model.

Complete			Employees			Top management		
SRMR	R^2 (IWB)	Q^2 (IWB)	SRMR	R^2 (IWB)	Q^2 (IWB)	SRMR	R^2 (IWB)	Q^2 (IWB)
0.041	0.157	0.073	0.048	0.150	0.065	0.058	0.231	0.102

Notes: SRMR = standardised root mean square residual.

fulfils for all three samples. Table 4 summarises all fit measures (i.e., R^2, Q^2, and SRMR) of the structural model.

Multigroup analysis

We conducted a MGA in PLS path modelling (PLS-MGA), which has methodological advances over other existing approaches,[12] in order to take observed heterogeneity into account (Sarstedt *et al.*, 2011). PLS-MGA is a non-parametric method that allows to compare predefined data groups by testing the significance of group-related differences based on bootstrapping results (Henseler, 2012; Henseler *et al.*, 2009). We run PLS-MGA, which is implemented by default in SmartPLS, to test for group-specific differences in path coefficients and their significance at an α-level of 0.05. We conducted the final calculations with an MSExcel spreadsheet obtained from Henseler *et al.* (2009) to determine the conditional probability, i.e., the extent to which a population parameter differs across two subsamples. Table 5 illustrates the results of the PLS-MGA and the conditional probabilities, which show significant group differences on a 5% error level (i.e., p-values smaller than 0.05 or larger than 0.95 for a certain difference of parameter (Barajas-Portas *et al.*, 2017) for each type of perceived organisational slack on IWB. The conditional probabilities range between 79.59% and 90.15%, and verify that differences in path coefficients across groups are highly probable.

Although all *differences* among the paths are statistically significant, not all hypothesised *path relationships* are statistically significant and meaningful within each group, as indicated in Table 2. For the employee group, we can confirm Hypotheses 1–3, because these three paths have been found to have significant and

[12]Henseler (2007) initially introduced PLS-MGA to statistically assess differences between group-specific parameters in PLS path modelling. PLS-MGA's strengths, i.e., its ease and robustness, outperform the other two procedures available: The parametric test introduced by Keil *et al.* (2000) is limited due to its inherent assumption of normal distribution, whereas the permutation-based approach (Chin, 2003; Chin and Dibbern, 2010) requires symmetric group sample sizes to ensure similar statistical power. More detailed comparisons can be found in the articles of Henseler *et al.* (2009) and Sarstedt *et al.* (2011), an exemplary use of PLS-MGA in Henseler (2012).

Table 5. PLS-MGA parameter estimates and conditional probability.

Structural path	Difference β_i (|Employees - Top management|)	p-value (Employees vs. top management)	Conditional probability (%)
RA1 > IWB	0.285	**0.990**	84.00
RA2 > IWB	0.448	**0.999**	84.03
RA3 > IWB	0.267	**0.013**	84.03
RA4 > IWB	0.268	**0.034**	79.59
RA5 > IWB	0.213	**0.953**	83.29
FirmAge > IWB	0.180	**0.031**	89.94
FirmSize > IWB	0.033	0.407	81.60
Age > IWB	0.104	0.168	87.09
Edu > IWB	0.071	0.228	90.15
Gender > IWB	0.033	0.379	86.96
Tenure > IWB	0.132	0.123	85.98
Position > IWB	0.002	0.510	87.41

Notes: IWB = innovative work behaviour; RA1 = capital; RA2 = skilled labour; RA3 = material supply; RA4 = managerial talent; RA5 = time; Edu = education; path coefficient β based on bootstrapping with $n = 5,000$; α-level of 0.05 for $p < 0.05$ and > 0.95.

meaningful path coefficients: abundant managerial talent ($\beta_1 = 0.292$, $p < 0.01$) and material supply ($\beta_3 = 0.173$, $p < 0.05$) have positive effects on employees' IWB, whereas abundant skilled labour ($\beta_2 = -0.186$, $p < 0.05$) has a negative impact. For the top management group, the data supports Hypotheses 2, 4, and 5: abundant skilled labour ($\beta_2 = 0.262$, $p < 0.01$), excess capital ($\beta_4 = 0.196$, $p < 0.05$), and time surplus ($\beta_5 = 0.221$, $p < 0.05$) have significant positive effects on top managers' IWB. Although the control variable firm age showed a significant group difference ($\beta = 0.180$, $p < 0.05$), no meaningful and significant effects of firm age on IWB could be verified in any of the two subgroups.

Robustness checks

As we used self-reported data from a single source per case, common method variance might be problem (Podsakoff and Organ, 1986). Therefore, we applied widely accepted preventive practices regarding questionnaire design and diagnostic ex-post controls, as suggested by Podsakoff *et al.* (2003). First, the questionnaire was carefully constructed with a focus on a logical order, comprehensible wording, and unambiguous items. Second, participants were unaware of the nature of the relationships under investigation, because the questionnaire also collected data for another unrelated study, which thereby minimised potential over-justification effects. Third, we performed Harman's single factor test (Harman, 1976), one of the most commonly used ex-post tests (Podsakoff *et al.*, 2003), for the overall sample and each subgroup. The unrotated principal component factor analysis was carried out in SPSS. Results revealed multiple factors with no factor accounting for more than 26.6% of the total variance in the variables, also when fixed to one factor. In addition, we evaluated the correlation matrix of all constructs, because some researchers started raising concerns about Harman's single factor test. Correlations among the constructs are clearly below the critical threshold of 0.9 (Pavlou *et al.*, 2006; Podsakoff *et al.*, 2003), as illustrated in Table A.3 (Appendix A). Therefore, common method variance is unlikely to be a serious problem.

To assess potential nonresponse bias, we used the duration for completing the survey as a proxy, and compared fast and slow respondents within each group[13] by a *t*-test (Sax *et al.*, 2003). For the employee group, we found no statistically significant differences among fast and slow respondents, except for the variable "managerial talent". For the top management group, we found no statistically significant differences, except for IWB. When comparing its mean values, the slow respondents tend to assess their IWB higher than the fast respondents (Table A.4), and thereby indicating potential nonresponse bias.

We found the control variable *position* to be significant indicating that the variance differences in IWB might be on a finer level than the two subgroups of top managers and employees we used. For a better understanding of this influence, we further subdivided the employee group into *middle managers* composed of division heads (4) and department heads (5), and *lower level employees* composed of others with real estate-specific field of activity (6) and others with administrative field of activity (7). This split resulted in the following distribution: *top management* with 155 individuals, *middle management* with 139 individuals, and *lower level employees* with 109 individuals. As the MGA only works for pairwise comparisons, a two-step procedure is proposed for the comparison of three or more groups: When the initial global assessment, the omnibus test of group (OTG) differences, indicates *that* at least one path coefficient differs significantly across groups, *post-hoc* pairwise group comparisons determine between *which* groups the path coefficient differs by using standard approaches (e.g., the permutation test). Since a primary concern of multiple testings is the alpha inflation (i.e., Type I error), it is recommended to adjust the significance level by applying the Bonferroni correction or Šidák procedure (Hair *et al.*, 2018; Sarstedt *et al.*, 2011). Since the PLS-MGA has already verified that there are significant group

[13]In our case, the generally recommended distinction between early and late respondents (Armstrong and Overton, 1977) appeared inappropriate due to our stepwise multichannel data collection procedure, which implies that the last incoming responses are not necessarily from late respondents.

differences at least between two groups (i.e., employees overall vs top managers), we directly conducted pairwise comparisons across all possible constellations of the three groups (i.e., lower level employees, middle managers, and top managers). We used the recommended permutation test and applied the Šidák procedure (i.e., $1-(1-\alpha)^{1/m}$ with $m=$ number of comparisons) to adjust the significance level ($\alpha = 0.05$) yielding in a threshold of 0.01695 to evaluate the p-values in order to counteract the increase in the familywise error rate (Hair *et al.*, 2018).

Based on the pairwise comparisons, we did not detect significant differences between the samples of the lower level employees and the middle management. The differences that we found mainly delimited the top management group from the others: For the comparison between the top management and lower level employees, we found a substantial difference in the relationship between abundant skilled labour and IWB ($|\text{diff}\beta| = 0.482$; $p = 0.002$); for the top management and middle management samples, we found significant differences for all five hypothesized relationships (RA1 $\gg$ IWB: $|\text{diff}\beta| = 0.315$ and $p = 0.008$; RA2 $\gg$ IWB: $|\text{diff}\beta| = 0.386$ and $p = 0.007$; RA3 $\gg$ IWB: $|\text{diff}\beta| = 0.317$ and $p = 0.006$; RA4 $\gg$ IWB: $|\text{diff}\beta| = 0.436$ and $p = 0.013$; RA5 $\gg$ IWB: $|\text{diff}\beta| = 0.337$ and $p = 0.014$). Moreover, we assessed each of the groups' structural model to reflect upon the differences' origin in more detail. The employees' statistically significant and meaningful path relationships are distributed as followed: lower level employees experience a negative effect from abundant skilled labour on their IWB ($\beta_2 = -0.219$, $p < 0.1$) whereas the middle managers' IWB is positively influenced by abundant managerial talent ($\beta_1 = 0.460$, $p < 0.01$) and material supply ($\beta_3 = 0.223$, $p < 0.01$). Nevertheless, a distinct treatment of lower level employees and the middle managers was not justifiable since no substantial group differences were found in the permutation test results.

Discussion and Conclusion

Most previous research on the relationship of slack and innovation focussed only on the organisational level and disregarded the multidimensional nature of slack. Our study contributes to a more comprehensive understanding of how organisational slack influences individual's IWBs by examining differences among various slack types and roles within the organisation, i.e., between employees and top managers.

Our findings revealed significant differences between the impact of different types of organisational slack on employees (Fig. 1) and top managers (Fig. 2). Slack in the form of *managerial talent* shows a positive and significant link to employees' IWB. This underlines the important facilitating role of great

S. Hügel & M. Kreutzer

Fig. 1. Employees' path diagram with results and PLS-SEM estimates.

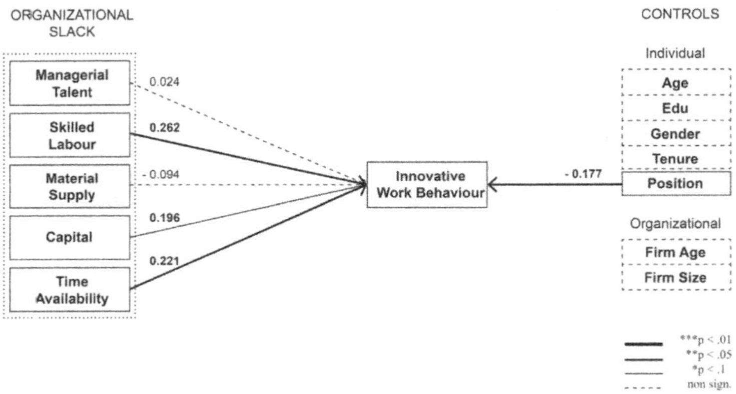

Fig. 2. Top managers' path diagram with results and PLS-SEM estimates.

management and the required leadership skills for stimulating IWB among employees. Our robustness tests showed that this positive influence on IWB only applies to middle managers. This might reflect that middle managers orient themselves more upwards compared to lower level employees. As subordinates middle managers might have a greater chance to stand out and be recognised for going the extra mile and being innovative (Ishak, 2005; Niehoff *et al.*, 1990) by the uppermost superiors compared to lower level managers. When managerial talent is high, recognition and appreciation for outstanding performance and extra-role behaviours are likely to increase, resulting in a stronger stimulation of middle managers by their leadership.

Slack in the form of *skilled labour*, however, was found to negatively influence employees' IWB. Employees with many other skilled colleagues around them may perceive a limited self-efficacy due to increased idea competition, and even feel threatened. They might also try to avoid any conflict by not questioning the status quo (cf. Janssen, 2003), seize the opportunity to establish a comfort zone, and switch to a satisficing instead of maximizing mentality (cf. Simon, 1955) since there are numerous skilled co-workers around them. In our robustness check, we could show that this influence only applies to lower level employees, not for middle managers. Slack resources in the form of *material supply* were found to encourage employees — and among them middle managers — to materialise and test new ideas. When the organisational environment is perceived to be materially equipped, concerns about (costly) failures are lower and cognitive efforts towards innovative activities induced (Bromiley, 1991; Cyert and March, 1963). Csikszentmihalyi's (1997) argument that excessive resources have a "deadening effect on creativity" (p. 321) is thus not supported on the middle manager level.

In contrast to the negative link between *skilled labour* and IWB on the employee level, we found this link to be positive on the top management level. Top managers' perception of being able to rely on a sufficiently sized and skilled employee body obviously increases their confidence in being well equipped for the future and makes them behave more innovatively. The specific knowledge and skills of employees are difficult to substitute quickly, and also required to implement the top management's novel ideas on the operative level (Kesting and Ulhøi, 2010). This divergent effect of slack in the form of skilled labour on top managers' vs. employees' behaviour implies a trade-off: Scarce skilled human resources impede top manager's IWB, but encourage employees' IWB and *vice versa*.[14] This might have implications for how top managers organize innovation within their firms as more bottom-up (when human resources are scarce and thereby innovative impulses from the employees are high) vs. top-down (when human resources are abundant and innovative impulses from top managers are high).

Furthermore, we could show that excess *time* positively influences top management's IWB. Top managers with time to reflect, explore, and think outside the box act more creatively and innovatively (Amabile, 1988; Lawson, 2001). This finding suggests that it pays off to protect top managers to a certain extent from day-to-day business. Along with time and skilled human resources, slack in the form of *capital* positively influences top managers' IWB as well. A financial cushion provides not only the liquidity needed, but also a comforting basis to

[14]This relies on the assumption that both groups' perception refers to the same labour group (e.g., a specific unit within the organisation).

engage in investment-intensive and open-ended innovative activities. Since *firm age* was neither influencing employees' nor top managers' IWB, we have no indication that the individuals' IWB depends on the company's life cycle (from start-up to incumbent phase).

From a methodological perspective, we identified a one-factor solution for IWB's specification based on high crossloadings among its items, although at first we have initially specified IWB as reflective first-order and formative second-order construct with four dimensions. Our insights are in-line with previous research that also found high intercorrelations among indicators attributed to the overlapping activities of the non-sequential multistage innovation process. However, previous research came up with different treatments: Janssen (2000) built an overall scale by combining IWB's dimensions additively; de Jong and den Hartog (2010) who found at least weak evidence for the four dimensions provided theoretical considerations, such as "real world innovation processes are reciprocal with overlapping stages" (p. 34); Abstein *et al.* (2014) specified the measurement model of IWB as a reflective first-order and formative second-order construct (type II). Our results indicated that IWB's items do not belong to sufficiently distinct dimensions, but they rather contribute to an overall construct directly. Having validated a 1D model, even though theory suggests that IWB should be multidimensional, does not necessarily constitute a conflict, because similar strong behaviours on all stages are not unlikely at a specific point in time.

Based on the gained insights on the influence of different slack types on individuals at different hierarchical levels, managers should be able to more consciously accumulate and better allocate slack resources in their organisations to thereby promote desired IWBs. For example, managers might not want to allocate all skilled labour in one place (or unit) to prevent a decrease of their IWB. By distributing skilled human resources throughout the organisation, these individuals have the freedom and stimulation to demonstrate superior, extra (innovation) efforts. The experience of being valued in respect thereof might also enhance their perception of managerial talent which would even increase these individuals' IWB. Particularly for service-oriented organisations, as in our study, a deliberate resource orchestration is important because their innovations are often developed jointly as a product of the client–provider interface during the process of service provision (Gallouj and Weinstein, 1997; Hügel *et al.*, 2019; Sundbo, 1997). Therefore, the IWBs of service providers' employees are crucial to their day-to-day business.

As any study also ours suffers from certain limitations. For example, we gathered data with the same method and from a single respondent and thus could suffer from common method bias. As a different study design, which *a priori* excluded common method issues, was not feasible, we tackled the potential bias

The Impact of Organisational Slack on Innovative Work Behaviour

with ex ante and ex post remedies. Furthermore, we had to employ somewhat coarse slack measures, i.e., single-item measures, due to the restricted length of the questionnaire. Single items clearly lag behind multiitem measures, because a single-item measure accounts for less differences and has lower predictive power, which can easily cause type II errors. Nevertheless, one can refer to single-item measures in case of study setting necessitates (Sarstedt *et al.*, 2016). As SmartPLS models linear relationships, potential non-linear relationships have not been considered. To do so, we would have had to use another analytical method and different software, for instance, quadratic regression model or piecewise regression model (cf. Lee, 2015), which could be the starting point for future research. Another limitation is the use of German data only, because the cultural context is likely to influence the perception and valuation of a specific resource. Besides cultural and economic effects, the sector type might also lead to relevant differences in the resource type importance. Our study participants are from service-oriented organisations of an "old economy" sector. As a result, resource types, effects might differ from those in manufacturing contexts or the "new economy". Hence, culture, economy, and sector dependencies are interesting fields for future research. Since the control variable job position was highly significant, future research could differentiate organisational levels or groups on an even more granular level. A follow-up study could investigate on the various positions that reflect power, prestige, and personnel responsibility within a company. Especially with respect to the top-level management, researchers could consider the influence of ownership structure, respectively, ownership rights which are implied in the distinct positions. Knowing that providing resources "over and above the "threshold of sufficiency" does not boost creativity" (Amabile, 1998, p. 83), another interesting field of research could be the examination of threshold and catalyst effects: What is the optimum amount of a specific resource type? What amount of one resource type is necessary to outweigh or boost another? And are there any beneficial patterns among certain resource types for one organisational group or the other?

In conclusion, this study emphasises that organisational slack predicts individuals' IWB to a considerable extent. Moreover, we understand that the influence of organisational slack on individual's IWB depends on the slack type and the individual's affiliation to an organisational level. Our findings suggest that continued work on the measurement of IWB and empirical verification (in different contexts) of the distinctiveness of its dimensions are necessary. We also demonstrated that organisational slack is not just "a facilitator" of organisational adaptation and innovation, but a multidimensional phenomenon with quite distinct effects that are worth to be aware of.

S. Hügel & M. Kreutzer

Appendix A

Table A.1. Results of IWB's alternative measurement model (second-order formative).

Second-order construct	First-order construct	VIF	β_i	t-value
Innovative work behaviour	Problem recognition	2.069	−0.225	0.628
	Idea generation	2.525	0.299	0.638
	Idea championing	2.334	0.405	1.505
	Idea realisation	3.313	0.211	0.746

Notes: VIF = variance inflation factor; path coefficient β and t-value based on a bootstrapping with $n = 5{,}000$; $^{***}p < 0.01$; $^{**}p < 0.05$; $^{*}p < 0.1$.

Table A.2. Results of HTMT.85 (per group).

		Age	Edu	FA	FS	Gen	IWB	Pos	RA1	RA2	RA3	RA4	RA5	Ten
Complete	Age													
(403)	Edu	0.018												
	FA	0.076	0.002											
	FS	0.009	0.06	0.275										
	Gen	0.131	0.092	0.023	0.007									
	IWB	0.089	0.076	0.095	0.091	0.048								
	Pos	0.395	0.040	0.102	0.385	0.297	0.266							
	RA1	0.031	0.016	0.115	0.294	0.099	0.047	0.182						
	RA2	0.116	0.118	0.035	0.013	0.007	0.122	0.006	0.161					
	RA3	0.012	0.043	0.044	0.094	0.120	0.119	0.089	0.467	0.170				
	RA4	0.125	0.105	0.169	0.104	0.006	0.307	0.249	0.112	0.468	0.239			
	RA5	0.104	0.129	0.026	0.018	0.056	0.225	0.002	0.088	0.311	0.213	0.480		
	Ten	0.323	0.174	0.152	0.195	0.025	0.064	0.110	0.087	0.148	0.051	0.057	0.021	
Employee	Age													
(248)	Edu	0.068												
	FA	0.118	0.022											
	FS	0.153	0.080	0.205										
	Gen	0.052	0.129	0.091	0.116									
	IWB	0.049	0.079	0.131	0.038	0.078								
	Pos	0.226	0.043	0.039	0.081	0.196	0.146							
	RA1	0.024	0.038	0.053	0.201	0.059	0.085	0.043						
	RA2	0.110	0.083	0.002	0.005	0.012	0.088	0.140	0.195					
	RA3	0.005	0.095	0.017	0.024	0.124	0.195	0.033	0.389	0.225				
	RA4	0.021	0.156	0.131	0.005	0.074	0.270	0.056	0.175	0.521	0.318			

Table A.2. (*Continued*)

		Age	Edu	FA	FS	Gen	IWB	Pos	RA1	RA2	RA3	RA4	RA5	Ten
	RA5	0.121	0.188	0.033	0.025	0.062	0.155	0.015	0.068	0.324	0.329	0.539		
	Ten	0.375	0.137	0.197	0.277	0.029	0.048	0.184	0.149	0.202	0.067	0.094	0.092	
TopMgmt	Age													
(155)	Edu	0.210												
	FA	0.112	0.037											
	FS	0.161	0.078	0.353										
	Gen	0.026	0.013	0.087	0.021									
	IWB	0.108	0.106	0.114	0.083	0.088								
	Pos	0.003	0.061	0.288	0.409	0.069	0.083							
	RA1	0.053	0.103	0.179	0.325	0.069	0.163	0.302						
	RA2	0.188	0.165	0.105	0.017	0.035	0.324	0.087	0.106					
	RA3	0.061	0.040	0.138	0.151	0.059	0.069	0.106	0.580	0.074				
	RA4	0.090	0.056	0.214	0.074	0.068	0.252	0.055	0.148	0.446	0.150			
	RA5	0.086	0.054	0.016	0.004	0.067	0.344	0.018	0.124	0.292	0.030	0.421		
	Ten	0.261	0.223	0.098	0.155	0.021	0.142	0.136	0.027	0.076	0.036	0.047	0.076	

Notes: TopMgmt = top management; Edu = education; FA = firm age; FS = firm size; Gen = gender; IWB = innovative work behaviour; Pos = position; RA 1 = capital; RA 2 = skilled labour; RA 3 = material supply; RA 4 = managerial talent; RA 5 = time; Ten = tenure.

Table A.3 Correlation matrix of the structural model's latent variables (per group).

		Age	Edu	FA	FS	Gen	IWB	Pos	RA1	RA2	RA3	RA4	RA5	Ten
Complete	Age	1.000												
(403)	Edu	−0.018	1.000											
	FA	−0.076	0.002	1.000										
	FS	0.009	0.060	−0.275	1.000									
	Gen	0.131	0.092	−0.023	−0.007	1.000								
	IWB	0.084	−0.071	0.094	−0.089	0.025	1.000							
	Pos	−0.395	−0.040	−0.102	0.385	−0.297	−0.266	1.000						
	RA1	−0.031	0.016	−0.115	0.294	−0.099	0.021	0.182	1.000					
	RA2	0.116	−0.118	0.035	0.013	−0.007	0.116	−0.006	0.161	1.000				
	RA3	−0.012	−0.043	−0.044	0.094	−0.120	0.114	0.089	0.467	0.170	1.000			
	RA4	0.125	−0.105	0.169	−0.104	−0.006	0.300	−0.249	0.112	0.468	0.239	1.000		
	RA5	0.104	−0.129	−0.026	−0.018	−0.056	0.214	−0.002	0.088	0.311	0.213	0.480	1.000	
	Ten	0.323	−0.174	−0.152	0.195	0.025	−0.017	−0.110	0.087	0.148	0.051	0.057	0.021	1.000
Employee	Age	1.000												
(248)	Edu	0.068	1.000											
	FA	−0.118	0.022	1.000										
	FS	0.153	0.080	−0.205	1.000									
	Gen	0.052	0.129	−0.091	0.116	1.000								
	IWB	0.015	−0.072	0.122	0.002	−0.026	1.000							
	Pos	−0.226	−0.043	0.039	0.081	−0.196	−0.147	1.000						

S. Hügel & M. Kreutzer

Table A.3 (*Continued*)

		Age	Edu	FA	FS	Gen	IWB	Pos	RA1	RA2	RA3	RA4	RA5	Ten
	RA1	0.024	−0.038	−0.053	0.201	−0.059	0.009	−0.043	1.000					
	RA2	0.110	−0.083	−0.002	−0.005	0.012	0.017	−0.140	0.195	1.000				
	RA3	−0.005	−0.095	0.017	0.024	−0.124	0.194	0.033	0.389	0.225	1.000			
	RA4	0.021	−0.156	0.131	0.005	−0.074	0.268	−0.056	0.175	0.521	0.318	1.000		
	RA5	0.121	−0.188	−0.033	−0.025	−0.062	0.156	0.015	0.068	0.324	0.329	0.539	1.000	
	Ten	0.375	−0.137	−0.197	0.277	0.029	0.022	−0.184	0.149	0.202	0.067	0.094	0.093	1.000
Top Mgmt	Age	1.000												
(155)	Edu	−0.210	1.000											
	FA	−0.112	−0.037	1.000										
	FS	0.161	0.078	−0.353	1.000									
	Gen	0.026	−0.013	0.087	0.021	1.000								
	IWB	−0.032	−0.104	−0.011	−0.019	−0.073	1.000							
	Pos	0.003	0.061	−0.288	0.409	−0.069	−0.055	1.000						
	RA1	0.053	0.103	−0.179	0.325	−0.069	0.151	0.302	1.000					
	RA2	0.188	−0.165	0.105	0.017	−0.035	0.317	0.087	0.106	1.000				
	RA3	0.061	0.040	−0.138	0.151	−0.059	0.032	0.106	0.581	0.074	1.000			
	RA4	0.090	−0.056	0.214	−0.074	−0.068	0.244	−0.055	0.148	0.446	0.150	1.000		
	RA5	0.087	−0.054	−0.016	−0.004	−0.067	0.337	0.018	0.124	0.292	0.030	0.421	1.000	
	Ten	0.261	−0.223	−0.098	0.155	−0.021	−0.095	−0.136	0.027	0.076	0.036	−0.047	−0.076	1.000

Notes: TopMgmt = top management; Edu = education; FA = firm age; FS = firm size; Gen = gender; IWB = innovative work behaviour; Pos = position; RA 1 = capital; RA 2 = skilled labour; RA 3 = material supply; RA 4 = managerial talent; RA 5 = time; Ten = tenure.

Table A.4. Result of the *T*-test for non-response bias.

	Mean value					
	Fast respondents		Slow respondents		Significance of *t*	
	Employees	TopMgmt	Employees	TopMgmt	Employees	TopMgmt
IWB°	5.38	5.68	5.57	6.05	0.17	0.03*
RA1	5.21	5.07	5.69	5.19	0.07	0.70
RA2	5.75	5.72	6.02	6.00	0.10	0.17
RA3	4.54	4.63	5.05	4.64	0.06	0.97
RA4	4.89	5.67	5.47	5.89	0.01*	0.25
RA5	4.49	4.42	4.91	4.53	0.09	0.73

Notes: °aggregated measure for non-response testing; TopMgmt = top management; IWB = innovative work behaviour; RA 1 = capital; RA 2 = skilled labour; RA 3 = material supply; RA 4 = managerial talent; RA 5 = time; * significance at the 0.05 level.

The Impact of Organisational Slack on Innovative Work Behaviour

Appendix B

Measurement Items and Controls

Innovative work behaviour

(7-point Likert scale: 1 = strongly disagree; 4 = neither nor; 7 = strongly agree)

For each of the following statements, please, indicate to what extent they apply to you:

Problem Recognition	
IWB1	I often look for opportunities to improve things.
IWB5	I often pay attention to issues that are not part of my daily work.
Idea Generation	
IWB4	I often search for new working methods, techniques or instruments.
IWB6	I often generate original solutions for problems.
IWB10	I often find new approaches to execute tasks.
Idea Championing	
IWB3	I often make important organisational members enthusiastic about my ideas.
IWB8	I often convince colleagues and supervisors about my ideas.
Idea Realisation	
IWB2	I often systematically introduce innovative ideas into work practices.
IWB7	I often contribute to the implementation of new ideas.
IWB9	I often put effort in the development of new things.

Organisational slack

(7-point Likert scale: 1 = strongly disagree; 4 = neither nor; 7 = strongly agree)

Please rate the abundance of the following resources for your firm. In our organisation, we have quite plentiful...

Resource availability	
RA1	Capital
RA2	Skilled labour
RA3	Material supply
RA4	Managerial talent
RA5	Time to reflect the current business development and to actively think about wider organisational problems.

Firm age

(year of founding)

S. Hügel & M. Kreutzer

Firm size

Number of employees in the target country	
1	Less than 5
2	5–10
3	11–50
4	51–100
5	101–250
6	251–500
7	501–1,000
8	More than 1,000
9	No answer

Position

	Top management level
1	Company owner/Managing partner
2	Member of the board/Member of the management
3	Partner
	Employee level
4	Head of division
5	Head of department
6	Others with real estate-specific field of activity
7	Others with administrative field of activity

Tenure

Number of years in the target country	
1	Less than 1
2	1–5
3	6–10
4	11–15
5	16–20
6	More than 20
7	No answer

Gender

(1 = Female/2 = Male)

The Impact of Organisational Slack on Innovative Work Behaviour

Age

	Number of years
1	Less than 26
2	26–35
3	36–45
4	46–55
5	More than 55
6	No answer

Education

	Highest successfully completed level of education
1	No educational qualification
2	Hauptschulabschluss (German)/Vocational School Leaving Certificate
3	Realschulabschluss (German)/Junior High School Degree
4	Abitur (German)/Senior High School Degree
5	Bachelor Degree
6	Master/MBA/Diploma Degree
7	Doctorate (PhD/Dr.)
8	No answer

References

Abstein, A, S Heidenreich and P Spieth (2014). Innovative work behaviour: The impact of comprehensive HR system perceptions and the role of work–life conflict. *Industry and Innovation*, 21(2), 91–116.

Aiken, M and J Hage (1971). The organic organization and innovation. *Sociology*, 5(1), 63–82.

Amabile, TM (1988). A model of creativity and innovation. *Research in Organizational Behavior*, 10(1), 123–167.

Amabile, TM (1996). *Creativity in Context*, 1st ed., Boulder, CO: Westview Press.

Amabile, TM, R Conti, H Coon, J Lazenby and M Lazenby (1996). Assessing the work environment for creativity. *The Academy of Management Journal*, 39(5), 1154–1184.

Anderson, N, K Potočnik and J Zhou (2012). Innovation and creativity in organizations: A state-of-the-science review, prospective commentary, and guiding framework Neil. *Journal of Management*, 40(5), 1297–1333.

Armstrong, JS and TS Overton (1977). Estimating nonresponse bias in mail surveys. *American Marketing Association*, 14(3), 396–402.

Axtell, CM, DJ Holman, KL Unsworth, TD Wall, PE Waterson and E Harrington (2000). Shopfloor innovation: Facilitating the suggestion and implementation of ideas. *Journal of Occupational and Organizational Psychology*, 73(3), 265–285.

S. Hügel & M. Kreutzer

Baker, T, and RE Nelson (2005). Creating something from nothing: Resource construction through entrepreneurial bricolage. *Administrative Science Quarterly*, 50(3), 329–366.

Bandura, A (1997). *Self-Efficacy: The Exercise of Control*, New York: W. H. Freeman.

Barajas-Portas, K, EM Artigas, LV Fernández and CN Alarcón (2017). Understanding corporate reputation through satisfaction in emerging markets. *International Journal of Sales, Retailing and Marketing*, 6(2), 17–31.

Becker, J-M, K Klein and M Wetzels (2012). Hierarchical latent variable models in PLS-SEM: Guidelines for using reflective-formative type models. *Long Range Planning*, 45(5–6), 359–394. Elsevier Ltd.

Birkinshaw, J, C Bouquet and J-L Barsoux (2011). The 5 myths of innovation. *MIT Sloan Mangagement Review*, 52(2), 40–53.

Bourgeois, LJ (1981). On the measurement of organizational slack. *Academy of Management Review*, 6(1), 29–39.

Bourgeois, LJ and JV Singh (1983). Organizational slack and political behavior among top management teams. *Academy of Management Proceedings*, 43, 43–47.

Brislin, RW (1970). Back-translation for cross-cultural research. *Journal of Cross-Cultural Psychology*, 1(3), 185–216.

Bromiley, P (1991). Testing a causal model of corporate risk taking and performance. *The Academy of Management Journal*, 34(1), 37–59.

Bunce, D and M West (1994). Changing work environments: Innovative coping responses to occupational stress. *Work & Stress: An International Journal of Work, Health & Organisations*, 8(4), 37–41.

Byrne, BM (2008). *Structural Equation Modeling with EQS: Basic Concepts, Applications, and Programming*. New York: Psychology Press.

Carmeli, A and GM Spreitzer (2009). Trust, connectivity, and thriving: Implications for innovative behaviors at work. *The Journal of Creative Behavior*, 43(3), 169–191.

Carnes, CM, F Chirico, MA Hitt, DW Huh and V Pisano (2017). Resource orchestration for innovation: Structuring and bundling resources in growth- and maturity-stage firms. *Long Range Planning*, 50(4), 472–486.

Cenfetelli, BRT and G Bassellier (2009). Interpretation of formative measurement in information systems research. *MIS Quarterly*, 33(4), 689–707.

Cheng, JLC and IF Kesner (1997). Organizational slack and response to environmental shifts: The impact of resource allocation patterns. *Journal of Management*, 23(1), 1–18.

Chin, WW, (1998a). Commentary: Issues and opinion on structural equation modeling. *MIS Quarterly*, 22(1), VII–XVI.

Chin, WW (1998b). The partial least squares approach to structural equation modeling. *Modern Methods for Business Research*, 295(2), 295–336.

Chin, WW (2003). A permutation procedure for multi-group comparison of PLS models. In *PLS and Related Methods: Proceedings of the International Symposium PLS' 03*, M Vilares, M Tenenhaus, P Coelho, VE Vinzi and A Morineau (eds.). pp. 33–43. Lisbon: Decisia.

Chin, WW (2010). How to write up and report PLS analyses. In *Handbook of Partial Least Squares — Concepts, Methods and Applications*, EV Vinzi, WW Chin, J Henseler and H Wang (eds.). pp. 655–690. Berlin: Springer-Verlag.

Chin, WW and J Dibbern (2010). An introduction to a permutation based procedure for multigroup PLS analysis: Results of tests of differences on simulated data and a cross cultural analysis of the sourcing of information system services between Germany and the USA. In *Handbook of Partial Least Squares — Concepts, Methods and Applications*, VE Vinzi, WW Chin, J Henseler and H Wang (eds.), pp. 171–193. Berlin: Springer-Verlag.

Cohen, J (1988). *Statistical Power Analysis for the Behavioral Sciences*, 2nd ed. Hillsdale, New Jersey: Lawrence Erlbaum Associates.

Cohen, WM and DA Levinthal (1990). Absorptive capacity: A new perspective on learning and innovation. *Administrative Science Quarterly*, 35(1), 128–152.

Csikszentmihalyi, M (1997). *Creativity: Flow and the Psychology of Discovery and Invention*. New York: Harper Collins.

Cyert, RM and JG March (1963). *A Behavioral Theory of the Firm*. Englewood Cliffs, New Jersey: Prentice Hall.

Damanpour, F (1991). Organizational innovation: A meta-analysis of effects of determinants and moderators. *The Academy of Management Journal*, 34(3), 555–590.

de Jong, JPJ and D den Hartog (2010). Measuring innovative work behaviour. *Creativity and Innovation Management*, 19(1), 23–36.

de Jong, JPJ and DN den Hartog (2007). How leaders influence employees' innovative behaviour. *European Journal of Innovation Management*, 10(1), 41–64.

Damanpour, F and DJ Wischnevsky (2006). Research on innovation in organizations: Distinguishing innovation-generating from innovation-adopting organizations. *Journal of Engineering and Technology Management*, 23(4), 269–291.

Dijkstra, TK and J Henseler (2015). Consistent and asymptotically normal PLS estimators for linear structural eEtions. *Computational Statistics and Data Analysis*, 81, 10–23.

Dolmans, SAM, E Van Burg, IM Reymen, MJ and AGL Romme (2014). Dynamics of resource slack and constraints: Resource positions in action. *Organization Studies*, 35(4), 511–549.

Dorenbosch, L, ML van Engen and M Verhagen (2005). On-the-job innovation: The impact of job design and human resource management through production ownership. *Creativity and Innovation Management*, 14(2), 129–141.

Fay, D and S Sonnentag (2002). Rethinking the effects of stressors: A longitudinal study on personal initiative. *Journal of Occupational and Health Psychology*, 7(2002), 221–234.

Fornell, C and DF Larcker (1981). Evaluating structural equation models with unobservable variables and measurement error. *Journal of Marketing Research*, 18(1), 39–50.

Fuchs, C and A Diamantopoulos (2009). Using single-item measures for construct measurement in management research: Conceptual issues and application guidelines. *Die Betriebswirtschaft*, 69(2), 195–211.

Gallouj, F and O Weinstein (1997). Innovation in services. *Research Policy*, 26(4–5), 537–556.

Gavetti, G and D Levinthal (2000). Looking forward and looking backward: Cognitive and experiential. *Administrative Science Quarterly*, 45(1), 113–137.

Geiger, SW and LH Cashen (2002). A multidimensional examination of slack and its impact on innovation. *Journal of Managerial Issues*, 14(1), 68–84.

Geisser, S (1974). A predictive approach to the random effects model. *Biometrika*, 61(1), 101–107.

George, G (2005). Slack resources and the performance of privately held firms. *The Academy of Management Journal*, 48(4), 661–676.

Gray, WD (2000). The nature and processing of errors in interactive behavior. *Cognitive Science*, 24(2), 205–248.

Greve, HR (2003). A behavioral theory of R&D expenditures and innovations: Evidence from shipbuilding. *The Academy of Management Journal*, 6, 685–702.

Gupta, AK and A Singhal (1993). Managing human resources for innovation and creativity. *Research Technology Management*, 36(3), 41–48.

Hair, JF, GTM Ringle, CM Ringle and M Sarstedt (2014). *A Primer on Partial Least Square Structural Equation Modeling (PLS-SEM)*. Thousand Oaks, CA: SAGE Publications.

Hair, JF, CM Ringle and M Sarstedt (2011). PLS-SEM: Indeed a silver bullet. *The Journal of Marketing Theory and Practice*, 19(2), 139–152.

Hair, JF, M Sarstedt, CM Ringle and SP Gudergan (2018). Modeling observed heterogeneity. *Advanced Issues in Partial Least Squares Structural Equation Modeling (PLS-SEM)*, pp. 135–174. Thousand Oaks, CA: Sage.

Hall, BH (2002). The financing of research and development. *Oxford Review of Economic Policy*, 18(1), 35–51.

Hambrick, DC (2007). Editor's forum — Upper echelons theory: An update. *Academi of Management Review*, 32(2), 334–343.

Hambrick, DC and PA Mason (1984). Upper echelons: The organization as a reflection of its top managers. *The Academy of Management Review*, 9(2), 193–206.

Hammond, MM, NL Neff, JL Farr, AR Schwall and X Zhao (2011). Predictors of individual-level innovation at work: A meta-analysis. *Psychology of Aesthetics, Creativity, and the Arts*, 5(1), 90–105.

Harman, HH (1976). *Modern Factor Analysis*. Chicago: University of Chicago Press.

Henderson, J and R McAdam (1997). Decision making in the fragmented organisation: A utility perspective. *Management Decision*, 39(6), 461–469.

Henseler, J (2007). A new and simple approach to multi-group analysis in partial least squares pathmodeling. In *PLS' 07 International Symposium on PLS and Related Methods — Causalities Explored by Indirect Observation*, H Martens, T Næs and M Martens (eds.), pp. 104–107. Ås: Matforsk.

Henseler, J (2012). PLS-MGA: A non-parametric approach to partial least squares-based multi-group analysis. In *Challenges at the Interface of Data Analysis, Computer Science, and Optimization: Studies in Classification, Data Analysis, and Knowledge Organization*, W Gaul, A Geyer-Schulz, L Schmidt-Thieme and J Kunze (eds.), pp. 495–501. Berlin: Springer Verlag.

Henseler, J, G Hubona and PA Ray (2016). Using PLS path modeling in new technology research: Updated guidelines. *Industrial Management & Data Systems*, 116(1), 2–20.

The Impact of Organisational Slack on Innovative Work Behaviour

Henseler, J, CM Ringle and M Sarstedt (2015). A new criterion for assessing discriminant validity in variance-based structural equation modeling. *Journal of the Academy of Marketing Science*, 43(1), 115–135.

Henseler, J, CM Ringle and RR Sinkovics (2009). The use of partial least squares path modeling in international marketing. In *New Challenges to International Marketing (Advances in International Marketing)*, RR Sinkovics and PN Ghauri (eds.), Vol. 20, pp. 277–319. Emerald Group Publishing Limited.

Herold, DM, N Jayaraman and CR Narayanaswamy (2006). What is the relationship between organizational slack and innovation? *Journal of Managerial Issues*, 18(3), 372–392.

Hewitt-Dundas, N (2006). Resource and capability constraints to innovation in small and large plants. *Small Business Economics*, 26(3), 257–277.

Hoegl, M, M Gibbert and D Mazursky (2008). Financial constraints in innovation projects: When is less more? *Research Policy*, 37, 1382–1391.

Hornsby, JS, DF Kuratko and SA Zahra (2002). Middle managers' perception of the internal environment for corporate entrepreneurship: Assessing a measurement scale. *Journal of Business Venturing*, 17, 253–273.

Hu, L and PM Bentler (1998). Fit indices in covariance structure modeling: Sensitivity to underparameterized model misspecification. *Psychological Methods*, 3(4), 424–453.

Hu, L and PM Bentler (1999). Cutoff criteria for fit indexes in coriance structure analysis: Conventional criteria versus new aAnatives. *Structural Equation Modeling: A Multidisciplinary Journal*, 6(1), 1–55.

Hügel, S, M Kreutzer and NB Rottke (2019). Firm innovativeness in service industries: A construct validation in the external environment and industry structure contexts. *International Journal of Innovation Management*, forthcoming.

Ishak, NA (2005). Promoting employees' innovativeness and organisational citizenship behaviour through superior-subordinate relationship in the workplace. *Research and Practice in Human Resource Management*, 13(2), 16–30.

Jalilvand, A and SM Kim (2013). Matching slack resources and investment strategies to achieve long-term performance: New perspectives on corporate adaptability. *Journal of Economic Asymmetries*, 10(1), 38–52.

Janssen, O (2000). Job demands, perceptions of effort-reward fairness and innovative work behaviour. *Journal of Occupational and Organizational Psychology*, 73(3), 287–302.

Janssen, O (2001). Fairness perceptions as a moderator in the curvilinear relationships between job demands, and job performance and job satisfaction. *Academy of Management Journal*, 44(5), 1039–1050.

Janssen, O (2003). Innovative behaviour and job involvement at the price of conflict and less satisfactory relations with co-workers. *Journal of Occupational and Organizational Psychology*, 76(3), 347–364.

Janssen, O (2004). How fairness perceptions make innovative bahvior more or less stressful. *Journal of Organizational Behavior*, 25(2), 201–215.

Janssen, O (2005). The joint impact of perceived influence and supervisor supportiveness on employee innovative behaviour. *Journal of Occupational and Organizational Psychology*, 78(4), 573–579.

Jensen, MC and WH Meckling (1976). Theory of the firm: Managerial behavior, agency cost, and ownership structure. *Journal of Financial Economics*, 3(4), 305–360.

Johnson, JD, WA Donohue, CK Atkin and S Johnson (2001). Communication, involvement, and perceived innovativeness. *Group & Organization Management*, 26(1), 24–52.

Kahneman, D and A Tversky (1979). Prospect theory: An analysis of decision under risk daniel. *Econometrica*, 47(2), 263–292.

Kanter, RM (1985). Supporting innovation and venture development in established companies. *Journal of Business Venturing*, 1, 47–60.

Kanter, RM (1988). When a thousand flowers bloom: Structural, collective, and social conditions for innovation in organizations. *Research in Organizational Behavior*, 10, 169–211.

Katz, D and RL Kahn (1978). *The Social Psychology of Organizations*. New York: John Wiley.

Katz, R and TJ Allen (1988). Project performance and locus of influence in the R&D matrix. In *Managing Professionals in Innovative Organizations: A Collection of Readings*, R Katz (ed.), pp. 469–484. Cambridge, MA: Ballinger.

Keil, M, BCY Tan, K-K Wei, T Saarinen, V Tuunainen and A Wassenaar (2000). A cross-cultural study on escalation of commitment behavior in software projects. *MIS Quarterly*, 24(2), 299.

Kesting, P and JP Ulhøi (2010). Employee-driven innovation: Extending the license to foster innovation. *Management Decision*, 48(1), 65–84.

Kim, H, H Kim and PM Lee (2008). Ownership structure and the relationship between financial slack and R&D investments: Evidence from korean firms. *Organization Science*, 19(3), 404–418.

Kim, MJ and JN Choi (2018). Group identity and positive deviance in work groups. *Journal of Social Psychology*, 158(6), 730–743.

Kimberly, JR and MJ Evanisko (1981). Organizational innovation: The influence of individual, and contextual adoption factors on hospital of technological and andministrative. *The Academy of Management Journal*, 24(4), 689–713.

Klein, KJ and J Sorra (1996). The challenge of innovation implementation. *The Academy of Management Review*, 21(4), 1055–1080.

Kraatz, MS and EJ Zajac (2001). How organizational resources affect strategic change and performance in turbulent environments: Theory and evidence. *Organization Science*, 12(5), 632–657.

Kuratko, DF, RV Montagno and JS Hornsby (1990). Developing an intrapreneurial assessment instrument for an effective corporate entrepreneurial environment. *Strategic Management Journal*, 11, 49–58.

Lawson, MB (2001). In praise of slack: Time is of the essence. *The Academy of Management Executive*, 15(3), 125–135.

The Impact of Organisational Slack on Innovative Work Behaviour

Lee, S (2015). Slack and innovation: Investigating the relationship in Korea. *Journal of Business Research*, 68(9), 1895–1905.

Leiponen, A (2005). Skills and innovation. *International Journal of Industrial Organization*, 23(5–6), 303–323.

Leitner, J and M Meyer (2013). Organizational slack and innovation. In *Encyclopedia of Creativity, Invention, Innovation and Entrepreneurship*, EG Carayannis (ed.), pp. 1412–1419. Springer.

Levinthal, DA and JG March (1993). The myopia of learning. *Strategic Management Journal*, 14, 95–112.

Madrid, HP, MG Patterson, KS Birdi, PI Leiva and EE Kausel (2014). The role of weekly high-activated positive mood, context, and personality in innovative work behavior: A multilevel and interactional model. *Journal of Organizational Behavior*, 35, 234–256.

Marlin, D and SW Geiger (2015). A reexamination of the organizational slack and innovation relationship. *Journal of Business Research*, 68(12), 2683–2690.

Mayer, RC and MB Gavin (2005). Trust in management and performance: Who minds the shop while the employees watch the boss? *Academy of Management Journal*, 48(5), 874–888.

Mayers, D and CW Smith Jr. (1994). Managerial discretion, regulation, and stock insurer ownership structure. *The Journal of Risk and Insurance*, 61(4), 638–655.

Michaels, E, H Handfield-Jones and B Axelrod (2001). *The War for Talent*. MA: Harvard Business School Press.

Miller, D and PH Friesen (1982). Innovation in conservative and entrepreneurial firms: Two models of strategic momentum. *Strategic Management Journal*, 3(1), 1–25.

Mumford, MD, GM Scott, B Gaddis and JM Strange (2002). Leading creative people: Orchestrating expertise and relationships. *The Leadership Quarterly*, 13, 705–750.

Ng, TWH, DC Feldman and SSK Lam (2010). Psychological contract breaches, organizational commitment, and innovation-related behaviors: A latent growth modeling approach. *Journal of Applied Psychology*, 95(4), 744–751.

Ngan, PT (2015). Organisational innovativeness: Motivation in an employee's innovative work behavior. *Scientific Bulletin – Economic Sciences*, 14, 86–97.

Niehoff, BP, CA Enz and RA Grover (1990). Impact of top-management actions on employee attitudes and perceptions. *Group & Organization Studies*, 15(3), 337–352.

Nohria, N and R Gualti (1996). Is slack good or bad for innovation? *The Academy of Management Journal*, 39(5), 1245–1264.

Nohria, N and R Gulati (1997). What is the optimum amount of organizational slack? A study of the relationship between slack and innovation in multinational firms. *European Management Journal*, 15(6), 603–611.

Nunnally, JC (1978). *Psychometric Theory*. New York: McGraw-Hill.

O'Brien, JP (2003). The capital structure implications of pursuing a strategy of innovation. *Strategic Management Journal*, 24(5), 415–431.

O'Driscoll, MP, DR Ilgen and K Hildreth (1992). Time devoted to job and off-job activities, interrole conflict, and affective experiences. *Journal of Applied Psychology*, 77(3), 272–279.

Ohly, S and C Fritz (2010). Work characteristics, challenge appraisal, creativity, and proactive behavior: A multi-level study. *Journal of Organizational Behavior*, 31(4), 543–565.

Østergaard, CR, B Timmermans and K Kristinsson (2011). Does a different view create something new? The effect of employee diversity on innovation. *Research Policy*, 40(3), 500–509.

Patterson, F, M Kerrin and G Gatto-Roissard (2009). Characteristics and behaviours of innovative people in organisations. *Literature Review Prepared for the NESTA Policy & Research Unit*, pp. 1–63.

Pavlou, PA, H Liang and Y Xue (2006). Understanding and mitigating uncertainty in online environments: A principal-agent perspective. *MIS Quarterly*, 31(1), 105–136.

Peter, JP (1981). Construct validity: A review of basic issues and marketing practices. *Journal of Marketing Research*, 18(2), 133–145.

Petrescu, M (2013). Marketing research using single-item indicators in structural equation models. *Journal of Marketing Analytics*, 1(2), 99–117.

Petter, S, DW Straub and A Rai (2007). Specifying formative constructs in IS research. *MIS Quarterly*, 31(4), 623–656.

Pieterse, AN, D Van Knippenberg, M Schippers and D Stam (2009). Transformational and transactional leadership and innovative behavior: The moderating role of psychological empowerment. *Journal of Organizational Behavior*, 31(4), 609–623.

Podsakoff, PM, SB MacKenzie, J-Y Lee and NP Podsakoff (2003). Common method biases in behavioral research: A critical review of the literature and recommended remedies. *The Journal of Applied Psychology*, 88(5), 879–903.

Podsakoff, PM and DW Organ (1986). Self-reports in organizational research: Problems and prospects. *Journal of Management*, 12(4), 531–544.

Ramamoorthy, N, PC Flood, T Slattery and R Sardessai (2005). Determinants of innovative work behaviour: Development and test of an integrated model. *Creativity and Innovation Management*, 14(2), 142–150.

Reichle, ED, PA Carpenter and MA Just (2000). The neural bases of strategy and skill in sentence — Picture verification. *Cognitive Psychology*, 40, 261–295.

Reuvers, M, ML van Engen, CJ Vinkenburg and E Wilson-Evered (2008). Transformational leadership and innovative work behaviour: Exploring the relevance of gender differences. *Creativity and Innovation Management*, 17(3), 227–244.

Ringle, CM, M Sarstedt and DW Straub (2012). Editor's comments: A critical look at the use of PLS-SEM. *MIS Quarterly*, 36(1), III–XVI.

Roldán, JL and MJ Sánchez-Franco (2012). Variance-based structural equation modeling: Guidelines for using partial least squares in information systems research. In *Research Methodologies, Innovations and Philosophies in Software Systems Engineering and Information Systems*, M Mora, O Gelman, A Steenkamp and MS Raisinghani (eds.), pp. 193–221.

The Impact of Organisational Slack on Innovative Work Behaviour

Rudd, JM, GE Greenley, AT Beatson and IN Lings (2008). Strategic planning and performance: Extending the debate. *Journal of Business Research*, 61(2), 99–108.
Salge, TO (2011). A behavioral model of innovative search: Evidence from public hospital services. *Journal of Public Administration Research and Theory*, 21(1), 181–210.
Sarstedt, M, A Diamantopoulos and T Salzberger (2016). Should we use single items? Better not. *Journal of Business Research*, 69(8), 3199–3203.
Sarstedt, M, J Henseler and CM Ringle (2011). Multigroup analysis in partial least squares (PLS) path modeling: Alternative methods and empirical results. In *Measurement and Research Methods in International Marketing (Advances in International Marketing)*, M Sarstedt, M Schwaiger and CR Taylor (eds.), Vol. 22, pp. 195–218. Emerald Group Publishing Limited.
Sarstedt, M, CM Ringle, J Henseler and JF Hair (2014a). On the emancipation of PLS-SEM: A commentary on rigdon (2012). *Long Range Planning*, 47(3), 154–160.
Sarstedt, M, CM Ringle, D Smith, R Reams and JF Hair (2014b). Partial least squares structural equation modeling (PLS-SEM): A useful tool for family business researchers. *Journal of Family Business Strategy*, 5(1), 105–115.
Sax, LJ, SK Gilmartin and AN Bryant (2003). Assessing response rate and nonreponse bias in web and paper surveys. *Research in Higher Education*, 44(4), 409–432.
Schroeder, R, AH Van de Ven, G Scudder and D Polley (1989). The development of innovation ides. In *Research on the Management of Innovation: The Minnesota Studies*, AH Van de Ven, H Angle and MS Poole (eds.), pp. 107–134. New York: Harper & Row.
Schulte, K, N Rottke and C Pitschke (2005). Transparency in the German real estate market. *Journal of Property Investment & Finance*, 23(1), 90–108.
Schumpeter, JA (1934). *Theory of Economic Development: An Inquiry into Profits, Capital, Credit, Interest, and the Business Cycle*. Cambridge: Harvard University Press.
Scott, SG and RA Bruce (1994). Determinants of innovative behaviour: A part model of individual innovation in the work place. *The Academy of Management Journal*, 37(3), 580–607.
Shahzad, AM, FT Mousa and MP Sharfman (2016). The implications of slack heterogeneity for the slack-resources and corporate social performance relationship. *Journal of Business Research*, 69(19), 5964–5971.
Sharfman, MP, G Wolf, RB Chase and DA Tansik (1988). Antecedents of organizational slack. *The Academy of Management Review*, 13(4), 601–614.
Simon, HA (1955). A behavioral model of rational choice. *The Quarterly Journal of Economics*, 69(1), 99–118.
Simon, HA (1957). *Administrative Behavior: A Study of Decision-Making Processes in Adminstrative Organization*, 2nd ed. New York: MacMillan.
Simsek, Z (2007). CEO tenure and organizational performance: An intervening model. *Strategic Management Journal*, 28(6), 653–662.
Singh, JV (1986). Performance, slack, and risk taking in organizational decision making. *The Academy of Management Journal*, 29(3), 562–585.

Sirén, C, PC Patel, D Örtqvist and J Wincent (2018). CEO burnout, managerial discretion, and firm performance: The role of CEO locus of control, structural power, and organizational factors. *Long Range Planning*, 51(6), 953–971.

Stone, M (1974). Cross-validatory choice and assessment of statistical predictions. *Journal of the Royal Statistical Society*, 36(2), 111–147.

Subramanian, A and S Nilakanta (1996). Organizational innovativeness: Exploring the relationship between organizational determinants of innovation, types of innovations, and measures of organizational performance. *Omega*, 24(6), 631–647.

Sundbo, J (1997). Management of innovation in services. *The Service Industries Journal*, 17(3), 432–455.

Teece, DJ (2007). Explication dynamic capabilities: The nature and microfoundations of (sustainable) enterprise performance. *Strategic Management Journal*, 28(13), 1319–1350.

Tushman, ML (1997). Winning through innovation. *Strategy & Leadership*, 25(4), 14–19.

Van der Vegt, GS and O Janssen (2003). Joint impact of interdependence and group diversity on innovation. *Journal of Management*, 29(5), 729–751.

Van De Ven, AH (1986). Central problems in the management of innovation. *Management Science*, 32(5), 590–607.

Voss, GB, D Sirdeshmukh and ZG Voss (2008). The effects of slack resources and environmental threat on product exploration and exploitation. *Academy of Management Journal*, 51(1), 147–164.

Ward, TB (1994). Structured imagination: The role of category structure in exemplar generation. *Cognitive Psychology*, 27(1), 1–40.

Ward, TB (2004). Cognition, creativity, and entrepreneurship. *Journal of Business Venturing*, 19(2), 173–188.

West, MA and JL Farr (1990). *Innovation and Creativity at Work: Psychological and Organizational Strategies*. Chichester: Wiley.

Williamson, OE (1963). Managerial discretion and business behavior. *The American Economic Review*, 53(5), 1032–1057.

Williamson, OE (1964). *The Economics of Discretionary Behavior: Managerial Objectives in a Theory of the Firm*. Englewood Cliffs, New Jersey: Prentice Hall.

Wu, C-H, SK Parker and JPJ de Jong (2014). Need for cognition as an antecedent of individual innovation behavior. *Journal of Management*, 40(6), 1511–1534.

Yuan, F and RW Woodman (2010). Innovative behavior in the workplace: The role of performance and image outcome expectations. *Academy of Management Journal*, 53(2), 323–342.

Chapter 5

INTERPERSONAL JUSTICE AND INNOVATIVE BEHAVIOURS: THE ROLE OF THE WORKGROUP†

ASMA DABOUSSI AYADI

Université de Tunis El Manar
Faculté des Sciences Économiques et de gestion de Tunis
Unité de Recherche Innovation, Stratégie et Organisation, Tunisia
asmadaboussi@ymail.com

CHI ZHANG

Kedge Business School, 680 Cours de la Libération
33405 Talence, France
chi.zhang@kedgebs.com

SAMIA KAROUI ZOUAOUI

Université de Tunis El Manar
Faculté des Sciences Économiques et de gestion de Tunis
Unité de Recherche Innovation, Stratégie et Organisation, Tunisia
samiazouaoui.fsegt@gmail.com

MARC OHANA*

Kedge Business School, 680 Cours de la Libération
33405 Talence, France
marc.ohana@kedgebs.com

Published 18 December 2019

In this research, we examine the effect of workgroup interpersonal justice (WIJ) (defined as the extent to which employees are treated with dignity and respect by their co-workers) on innovative work behaviours (IWB). Specifically, we first test the mediating role of group identification (GI) in this relationship. Next, we examine the moderating role of reflexivity of the group on this mediation effect. Based on 204 employees, our results showed that the indirect effect of the WIJ on IWB, through GI, is moderated by the reflexivity of the group. Theoretical and practical implications are discussed.

Keywords: Workgroup interpersonal justice; group identification; innovative work behaviours, reflexivity of the group.

*Corresponding author.

†This article originally appeared in *International Journal of Innovation Management*, **24** 2050073-1-18 © 2020 World Scientific Publishing Europe Ltd.

Introduction

The current organisational context, which is characterised by a turbulent, unpredictable and highly competitive environment, requires organisations to respond to unexpected events, to be inventive and to surpass themselves in order to face increasing hostile competitions (Anderson *et al.*, 2014; Fay *et al.*, 2015). Thus, innovation issues are becoming increasingly important in organisations. Organisations need to continually improve their products and services to ensure their survival, profitability and growth (Messmann and Mulder, 2012). Employees play a crucial role in this innovation process as they are the source of all ideas (Waenink, 2012). Therefore, employee's innovative work behaviours (IWB), which are defined as an intentional attempt to introduce and implement new ideas, products, processes or procedures as part of their work, group or organisation (West and Farr, 1990), are crucial in contemporary organisations (Anderson *et al.*, 2014).

Researchers have demonstrated that distributive justice (i.e., the fairness of decisions outcomes), procedural justice (i.e., the fairness of rules and procedures used to make these decisions), interpersonal justice (i.e., the degree of respect and propriety authority figures use when implementing procedures) and informational justice (i.e., the degree of respect and propriety authority figures use when implementing procedures) (Colquitt and Rodell, 2011) each can exert influence over a wide range of employee's attitudes and behaviours (Colquitt *et al.*, 2013). Among the four dimensions of organisational justice, interpersonal justice is particularly important in shaping employee behaviours (Judge *et al.*, 2006). However, there are various sources of justice (clients, supervisor, team and organisation) from which employees can make significant justice judgments, as they can hold them responsible for violating or complying with the norms of justice (Rupp and Cropanzano, 2002). Employees are able to differentiate the (un)just treatment they receive from their entire organisation or their supervisors (Rupp and Cropanzano, 2002) and also workgroup (Branscombe *et al.*, 2002). Most research on workplace justice focused on the (un)just treatment provided by the organisation and the supervisor (Colquitt *et al.*, 2013; Rupp *et al.*, 2014). To our knowledge, to date most previous researches have neglected the role of the workgroup in the relationship between justice and IWB. In addition, they examined mostly the mediating role of social exchange in this relationship (Xerri, 2014; Young, 2012). Very little attention has been paid to the role of social identity as a mediator in this relationship. Yet, social identity theory could explain the effects of perceptions of workgroup justice on IWB. This suggests that group members perceive interpersonal interactions as signals of appreciation, respect and status, which in turn will improve their identification within their group and creates positive behaviours such as IWB.

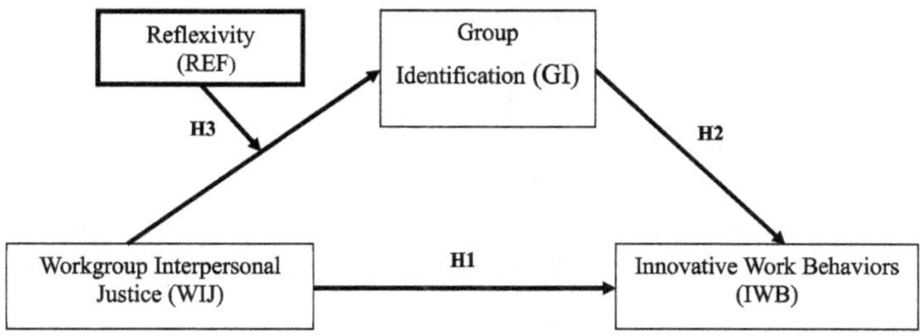

Fig. 1. Theoretical research model.

Based on the theory of social identity (Tajfel, 1970), our research proposes to test the influence of workgroup justice on IWB and to better understand the mechanism at stake in this relationship. By examining the mediating role of group identification (GI), our model provides an explanation of the psychological process underlying this relationship. Additionally, we identify a boundary conditions of mediation as they are relatively unexamined (Ambrose and Schminke, 2003). Researchers have therefore been called for more research integrating moderators into the literature on organisational justice (Shao *et al.*, 2013), as they can have a huge impact on the justice-outcomes relationship (Francis and Barling, 2005). Despite the difficulties inherent in detecting the effects of these moderators, we are interested in our research in the moderating effect of group reflexivity, i.e., the extent to which group members overtly reflect upon the group's objectives, strategies and processes and adapt them to current of anticipated endogenous or environmental circumstances (West, 1996). Reflexivity helps groups go beyond existing working practices to develop new understanding and methods that respond to emerging conditions and challenges. Groups with higher levels of reflexivity tend to be more innovative (Hoegl and Parboteeah, 2006; Tjosvold *et al.*, 2004). We thus expect that it influences the interpersonal justice IWB relationship. Figure 1 illustrates the proposed model.

Theoretical Framework and Hypothesis Development

Workgroup interpersonal justice and IWB

Given the growing importance of groups along with the flattening of organisational hierarchies, researchers have become more and more interested in the effects of group processes on employees' attitudes and behaviours (Lavelle *et al.*, 2007). Some empirical studies show that people identify co-workers as a source of justice, and differentiate them from other sources such as the supervisor or the organisation (Cropanzano *et al.*, 2011; Li *et al.*, 2013). Even if the relationship between justice and outcomes is expected to be the same whatever the focus of interest (Lavelle *et al.*, 2007), some researchers argue that the mechanism responsible for the effects of co-workers justice may well be different from that coming from another source (Li *et al.*, 2013; Ohana, 2016). Workgroups are therefore a source of justice that deserves to be studied.

Workgroup interpersonal justice (WIJ) refers to the perceived fairness of the interpersonal treatment that has been afforded to employees by their co-workers (Li *et al.*, 2013). Two rules govern this type of treatment: respect (being sincere and showing dignity) and propriety (using appropriate and non-detrimental language) (Bies and Moag, 1986). Daily interpersonal encounters are so common in groups that interpersonal justice often becomes more relevant and psychologically meaningful to employees. When employees feel that they are treated with respect and dignity by most of their colleagues, they will be more likely to develop a positive attitude towards them (Cropanzano *et al.*, 2011). In particular, IWB deserve to be studied. The link between organisational justice and IWB is not often examined (Simmers and McMurray, 2018). A study of Janssen (2004) examined the relationship between distributive justice and procedural justice of the supervisor and the IWB of nurses. According to this study, these two types of justice do not predict IWB. However, another study by Xerri (2014) indicates that procedural justice has a positive and direct effect on IWB, while interactional justice has a positive and indirect effect on IWB. These contradictory findings highlight the need for further empirical examinations of the relationship between organisational justice and IWB.

Indeed, when employees are treated in a respectful manner by their colleagues (i.e., do not use inappropriate language and gestures in their interactions), they may be more likely to be innovative. They will share new ideas, discuss these ideas with their colleagues, and try to implement them. Although no study shows this relationship, we can assume that IWB will be determined by interpersonal justice coming from the workgroup. We therefore formulate the following hypothesis:

H1: *WIJ is positively related to IWB.*

GI as a mediator between WIJ and IWB

The concept of GI derives from the social identity approach in social psychology. It is a person sense of identity based on the group(s) of which they are a member (Tajfel and Turner, 1986; Haslam, 2004). GI refers to a sense of belonging to a particular group coupled with a sense of commonality with members of that group (Ashforth and Mael, 1989; Sani *et al.*, 2015). It corresponds to the process by which employees perceive themselves in terms of values, goals, attitudes and behaviours that they share with their colleagues (Janssen and Huang, 2008). In other words, this process represents a personal, cognitive, emotional and behavioural link between the employee and his/her group (Henry *et al.*, 1999). It is mainly motivated by the need to define oneself and to create meaning in the life (Somech *et al.*, 2009).

The group engagement model (Tyler and Blader, 2003) offers a better insight of the potential link between WIJ, GI, and IWB. This model argues that GI is an essential element for understanding the psychological basis of employee engagement with their groups (Blader and Tyler, 2009). According to this model, interpersonal justice is a major dimension that individuals feel it to evaluate the interpersonal treatment faced within their workgroups (Tyler, 2000). A high level of WIJ improves the sense of individual respect and pride of being part of this group. This feeling improves also their identification with this group (Tyler and Blader, 2000). Members with strong identification to the group are intrinsically motivated to achieve its viability and success. For them, the success of the group is their own success. Furthermore, they intrinsically take care about the well-being of the group as well as its interests (Blader and Tyler, 2009). They will be more likely to behave positively on behalf of their group and go beyond their formal prescribed role. A study of Blader and Tyler (2009) shows the mediating role of organisational identification between procedural justice originating from the organisation and extra-role behaviours. Another study of De Cremer *et al.* (2005) indicates a link between interactional justice and citizenship behaviours through GI. Even if no study proves the mediating role of identification in the relationship between interpersonal justice and IWB for the workgroup, we thus hypothesise that:

H2: *GI is a mediator of the positive relationship between the WIJ and the IWB.*

Reflexivity of the group as a moderator between WIJ and IWB

Group members face obstacles as they try to coordinate effort, reinforce interpersonal relationships and integrate ideas. They need an important management to identify frustrations, develop and implement solutions (Tjosvold *et al.*, 2004) which refers to group reflexivity. Group reflexivity is defined as the extent to which group members overtly reflect upon the group's objectives, strategies and processes and adapt them to current of anticipated endogenous or environmental circumstances (West, 1996). It involves actions "*such as questioning, planning, exploratory learning, analysis, diverse explorations…learning at a meta level, reviewing past events with self-awareness, digestion, and coming to term over time with a new awareness*" (West, 1996, p. 560). Reflexivity help groups to understand their actual daily work and develop new knowledge and approaches that respond to emerging conditions and challenges (Tjosvold, 1991; Carter and West, 1998).

Uncertainty Management Theory (Lind and Van den Bos, 2002; Van den Bos and Lind, 2002) provides a better perspective to explain the moderation by group reflexivity of the indirect effect of WIJ on IWB through GI. According to this theory, one of the greatest challenges of one's life is facing various uncertainties that characterise his or her social relationships (Lind and Van den Bos, 2002; Van den Bos and Lind, 2002). Individuals need predictability in their immediate environment, as well as reduced uncertainty. Uncertainty is an aversive and alarming experience, which causes individuals to feel anxious about the control that they have about their lives and the quality of the results they may receive (Tangirala and Alge, 2006). It affects the individuals' knowledge, perceptions, feelings and behaviours (Van den Bos and Lind, 2002). Uncertainty threatens the self-esteem of individuals (Hogg, 2001), people try so to find a way to tolerate it and make it more cognitively manageable (Van den Bos and Lind, 2002).

In the context of the workgroup, employees pay more attention to equity-related information in order to cope with uncertainty (Tangirala and Alge, 2006). In fact, fair treatment received by their colleagues brings a decisional heuristic to restore the feeling of control and guide behaviour (Van den Bos, 2007). The more employees have uncertainty about their status, value and future prospects in their workgroup, the more they will tend to consider information about their treatment within the group. When group members are reflective, they will be able to identify frustrations, to develop and to implement appropriate solutions. Their sense of uncertainty will decrease (Tjosvold *et al.*, 2004). With the decreasing of uncertainty, the effect of fair treatment will be lower. Based on these arguments, we believe that the more reflective the workgroup is, the less uncertainty there is and the less the employees pay attention to the fair treatment within their workgroup. Therefore, we assume that the indirect effect of WIJ on IWB, through GI, will be moderated by the reflexivity of the group.

H3: *Group reflexivity moderates the positive indirect relationship between WIJ and IWB, so that this effect will be stronger when the reflexivity is lower compared to higher.*

Research Methodology

Sample

The hypotheses were tested with a sample of 204 employees working in a hospital and three clinics in Jendouba, a city in North-West Tunisia. The data were collected by questionnaires returned directly to the researchers. Employees were contacted by the researcher who explained the purpose of the study to them and assured them of the anonymity and confidentiality of their answers. Among 300 distributed questionnaires, 204 usable questionnaires were returned (response rate of 68%). Among these 204 individual employees, 67% are women. The average age of employees is between 26 and 35 years old. In terms of degree level, 42% hold a university degree. On average, 36% of employees had worked in their organisation for more than 10 years and 31% had worked in their workgroup for 3–10 years.

Measures

All the questionnaires were translated into French and back-translated into English to check the translation's accuracy. The items are measured by a 7-point Likert scale ranging from 1 = "strongly disagree" to 7 = "strongly agree".

***Workgroup Interpersonal Justice*:** The scale used was introduced by Rupp and Cropanzano (2002). Rupp and Cropanzano distinguished between supervisory interactional justice and organisational interactional justice. For supervisory interactional justice, four items were used to measure interpersonal justice and three items to measure informational justice. For organisational interactional justice, the same four items were used to measure interpersonal justice — except that supervisor was replaced by organisation — and four items to measure informational justice. In our study, we use the same four interpersonal items that in those scale and applied them to the workgroup by simply replacing supervisor/organisation by group members. An example of an item is "*My group members treats me with dignity and respect.*" Cronbach alpha of this scale equals 0.87.

***Innovative work behaviors*:** The scale used to measure IWB is composed of 17 items developed by Janssen (2000) and Scott and Bruce (1994). A sample item is "*I pay attention to issues that are no part of my daily work.*" Cronbach alpha equals 0.91.

***Group Identification*:** The six-item scale developed by Mael and Ashforth (1992) was used to measure GI. A sample item is "*When someone criticizes my workgroup, I take it as a personal insult.*" Cronbach alpha is 0.87.

***Reflexivity of the group*:** The scale used to measure reflexivity is composed by six items developed by Schippers *et al.* (2007) and Anderson and West (1998). An example of an item is "*We regularly discuss whether the workgroup is working effectively.*" Cronbach alpha of this scale equals to 0.90.

***Control variables*:** Gender, age, education level are the recurrent demographic variables controlled for analyses of organisational justice (Colquitt *et al.*, 2001). Tenure with the organisation and the group were also measured as control variables in our model.

Results

The correlations between variables, mean, standard deviation and internal reliability are presented in Table 1. The correlations are consistent with all the assumptions of the model: the WIJ is positively correlated both with GI ($r = 0.352$, $p < 0.01$) and with IWB ($r = 0.405$, $p < 0.01$), IWB is also positively correlated with group identification ($r = 0.362$, $p < 0.01$).

To ensure the convergent and discriminant validity of the variables of the model, we performed a confirmatory factor analysis by using Lisrel 8.8. The results of the CFA demonstrate that our measurement model presents a good fit to the data collected ($\chi^2 = 1118.11$, $df = 489$, RMSEA $= 0.08$, SRMR $= 0.07$, CFI $= 0.94$). Each relationship between the item and its latent variable is significant. Those results suggest that this model corresponds to an adequate representation of the data.

Our hypotheses predicts that the impact of WIJ on IWB is mediated by GI and moderated by reflexivity of the group (see Fig. 1). It thus corresponds to a moderated mediation. The data were thus analysed with the PROCESS macro and SPSS as suggested by Preacher and Hayes (2007).

Table 2 presents the results of regressions for simple mediation. The WIJ is significantly linked with IWB ($B = 0.22, p < 0.01$). However, after controlling for the mediator (GI), the coefficient is 0.09 ($p < 0.01$). This result shows a partial mediation such that WIJ exerts its influence directly and through GI ($B = 0.09$, Sobel Z-test $= 2.58$, $p < 0.01$). Mediation was confirmed by using bootstrap confidence intervals. These confidence intervals were calculated for 5,000 bootstrap samples. The confidence interval does not contain zero (Table 2), which supports a significant indirect relationship between the WIJ and the IWB through the GI. Given these results, both hypotheses 1 and 2 are confirmed.

Table 3 presents the results of the moderated mediation analysis for testing hypothesis 3. Hypothesis 3 predicts that group reflexivity acts as a moderator of the positive indirect relationship between WIJ and IWB through GI, meaning that this relationship would be weaker when reflexivity is high. This hypothesis was tested through the bootstrap procedure (Preacher *et al.*, 2007). The results presented in Table 3 show that reflexivity of the group has a significant moderating effect on the link between WIJ and GI ($B = -0.15$, $p < 0.01$). Furthermore, the results indicate that the conditional indirect effect of the WIJ on IWB (through GI) was lower when reflexivity was high. More precisely, this conditional indirect effect decreases when reflexivity increases and becomes insignificant at the 5% level for high levels of reflexivity. In order to interpret this moderating effect, Fig. 2 graphically represents the moderating effect of group reflexivity on the relationship between WIJ and GI. The diagram shows that in the case of high

Table 1. Mean, standard deviation and inter correlations.

Variables	M	SD	1	2	3	4	5	6	7	8
1. Gender	1.67	0.47	—							
2. Education	4.03	1.62	−0.03**	—						
3. Organisational tenure	2.91	1.02	−0.19**	−0.24**	—					
4. Group tenure	2.69	1.00	−0.15**	−0.25**	0.88**	—				
5. Reflexivity of the group	5.21	1.03	−0.01**	0.01	0.03	−0.01**	—			
6. Group identification	5.25	1.09	−0.06**	−0.01**	0.20*	0.17*	0.42**	—		
7. IWB	5.40	0.96	−0.10**	−0.01**	0.18*	0.14*	0.56**	0.36**	0.68**	—
8. Workgroup interpersonal justice	5.36	1.07	−0.08**	0.06	0.12*	0.10*	0.38**	0.35**	0.41**	0.35**

Notes: $n = 204$, $^{*}p < 0.05$, $^{**}p < 0.01$.

Table 2. Regression results for simple mediation.

Variables	Coefficients	T	P
WIJ * IWB	0.22	3.00	0.00
WIJ * GI	0.36	4.18	0.00
IWB * GI	0.24	3.39	0.00
IWB * WIJ mediated by GI	0.09	2.91	0.00

Sobel's indirect effect test and Bootstrap confidence interval based on 5,000 Bootstrap samples

			95% limits of the confidence interval			
	Value	SE	Z	P	LLCI	ULCI
Indirect effect	0.09	0.03	2.59	0.01	0.04	0.16

Notes: $n = 204$; WIJ = Workgroup Interpersonal Justice; IWB = Innovative work behaviours; GI = Group Identification.

reflexivity, the relationship between justice and identification is less strong. Hypothesis 3 is thus supported.

Discussion

Theoretical implications

The aim of this paper was to examine the relationship between WIJ, GI and IWB as well as the moderating role of reflexivity. The results of our research confirm our expectations that good interpersonal treatment of employees within their workgroup improves their identification with the group. As a result, they will be more likely to behave positively by displaying IWB. However, there are limiting conditions to this relationship because of the moderating role of reflexivity. When group members are reflexive, their sense of uncertainty about their status and value within their group will decrease. They will therefore be less sensitive to information about their treatment within the group.

Our results provide some contributions to existing research on organisational justice and IWB. First, this research offers a new perspective on the role of the workgroup in the relationship between organisational justice and IWB. Most previous research deals primarily with the relationship between organisational justice and extra-role behaviours of employees at the individual level (Barsky *et al.*, 2011). Recently, other researchers have begun to address this relationship at the workgroup level (Cropanzano *et al.*, 2011; Li *et al.*, 2013; Ohana, 2016). Our

Table 3. The results of the moderate mediation analysis.

Variable	B	SE	T	P
GI (Mediation variable)				
Constant	−2.28	1.58	−1.44	0.15
Age	0.08	0.08	1.06	0.29
Org Ten	0.13	0.14	0.98	0.33
Group Ten	−0.02	0.14	−0.11	0.91
WIJ	0.97	0.30	3.23	0.00
REF	1.18	0.31	3.73	0.00
WIJ * REF	−0.15	0.06	−2.65	0.01
IWB (Dependent variable)				
Constant	2.75	0.38	7.17	0.00
Age	0.08	0.07	1.12	0.26
Hospital	0.12	0.13	0.93	0.35
Group	−0.11	0.13	−0.82	0.41
WIJ	0.21	0.06	3.52	0.00
GI	0.23	0.06	3.82	0.00

Indirect Conditional Effect (s) of WIJ on IWB at Different Moderator Values (REF)

	REF	Effect	ES	L	U
GI	4.18	0.08	0.03	0.03	0.15
GI	5.22	0.04	0.02	0.01	0.09
GI	6.26	0.00	0.03	−0.07	0.05

Notes: $n = 204$; Org Ten = Organisational tenure; Group Ten = Group tenure; WIJ = Workgroup Interpersonal Justice; IWB = Innovative work behaviours; GI = Group Identification; REF = Reflexivity.

article shows that colleagues are a viable source of justice perceptions. Their fairness affects significantly employee attitudes and behaviours (Lavelle *et al.*, 2007; Liao and Rupp, 2005). Indeed, we contribute to the literature by demonstrating that WIJ influences IWB. When employees feel that they are treated with respect and dignity by most colleagues, they will be more likely to generate better ideas, to share ideas with co-workers and to implement these ideas successfully.

Second, our research explains the link between WIJ and IWB through GI. It offers additional empirical validation for the group's engagement model (Tyler and Blader, 2003), which confirms the idea that the relationship between WIJ and IWB is partially mediated by GI. Thus, our present research demonstrates the relevance of identification in the relationship between organisational justice and IWB. Although social identity has been suggested as an important mechanism in the

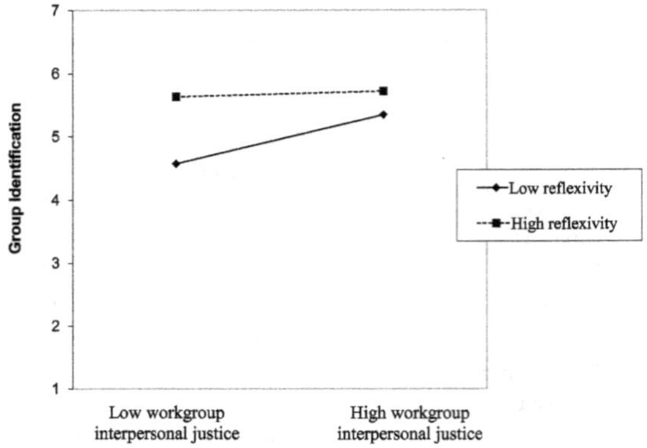

Fig. 2. Graph of interactions between WIJ, REF and GI.

relationship between organisational justice and extra-role behaviours (Blader and Tyler, 2009), this relationship has been mainly studied in terms of social exchange when it concerns IWB (Xerri, 2014; Young, 2012).Our results showed that the WIJ increases GI, which in turn leads to increased IWB. When colleagues treat others in a respectful and fair manner, employees feel obliged to adopt IWB. Therefore, future research could consider GI as an alternative mechanism explaining a strong relationship between WIJ and IWB in the absence of strong practice of exchange between employees. Future research could simultaneously explore the role of the two processes of identity and social exchange in the relationship between organisational justice and IWB in order to disentangle each effect.

Finally, our research shows the boundary conditions of the relationship between WIJ and IWB through the moderating role of reflexivity. Specifically, it points out that the indirect effect of WIJ on IWB through GI will be moderated by the group's reflexivity. In the context of workgroup, employees pay more attention to equity-related information in order to cope with uncertainty about their status, value and future prospects in their group. The fair treatment received by their colleagues provides a decision-making heuristic to reduce this feeling of uncertainty (Van den Bos, 2007). However, when workgroups are reflective, they will be able to develop and implement solutions that are suitable to their uncertain situation. As a result, employees are less concerned with the quality of treatment within their group. In other words, the more reflective the workgroups, the less uncertainty there is, the less the employees pay attention to the fair treatment within their workgroup. By demonstrating that group reflexivity moderates the relationship between organisational justice and IWB, this research contributes to the existing literature by bringing a better understanding of the boundary conditions of the impact of WIJ on innovative behaviours. It shows the need to explore these limiting conditions at a higher level of study, not just from an individual point of view. Consequently, we recommend that future research could explore other moderators of the impact of justice on innovative behaviour at the organisational or group level such as coordination, communication and cohesion.

Managerial implications

Our results reinforce the effect of perceptions of justice on employees' attitudes and behaviours at work. First, in order to enhance the spirit of solidarity within the organisation, fair treatment for all is required. This treatment includes employees' position, status and value within the organisation. In this way, they will be more likely to behave positively towards their organisation. This positive behaviour plays a crucial role in organisational reliability and success (Yuan and Woodman, 2010). However, employees with high levels of reflexivity will have less uncertainty about their status, value and future prospects in their organisation, and they pay less attention to fair treatment within their organisation. Hence, managers must encourage employees to take their time to reflect on their work habits, objectives (relevance, clarity, specificity and commitment), process and results, plan for change and implementation. This sense of security will help employees to be more reflective. In order to foster a sense of justice within the organisation, managers need to have special training in terms of organisational justice and practices that could effectively promote the perception of fairness (Skarlicki and Latham, 2005). The manager needs to explain his/her decisions to employees in a dignified and respectful manner. Yet, these training programs must go beyond the individual context with taking into account the effects of the influence of colleagues. They must introduce the notion of workgroup justice. Additionally, managers must ensure effective communication with their employees. The effective communicate between employees and their colleagues can influence the perception of employees in the way that their colleagues treat them fairly and encourages them to promote IWB.

Research limitations and future directions

Despite the important implications described above, our research has some limitations. First, our empirical research is limited to the Tunisian health sector. It would be interesting to replicate the study in other sectors and in other countries. In addition, the participants of our research were selected in different departments of the health sector. Although the results of our empirical research are fairly representative, they do not consider all employees working in this sector. Second, our empirical study is based on data obtained through self-administered questionnaires. This type of administration may cause problem of common method variance (Podsakoff *et al.*, 2003). However, the variables in our questionnaire are separated from each other by other variables not used in this study and the use of valid and reliable measurement scales can be considered as precautionary measures that help to reduce this problem. In consequence, we do not believe that the results presented in our research are biased through self-administration. Future research can complement data obtained through questionnaires administered from other sources such as supervisor and colleagues. Third, the cross-sectional nature of our data does not allow for having causal relationships between the WIJ, GI, and IWB. However, the causal relationships presented in our research are based on the argumentations and theoretical frameworks that are proved in previous research. To overcome this limitation, future research should use designed longitudinal data to test cause-and-effect relationships with greater precision. Additionally, literature reviews may reveal other moderating variables. Future research may consider other variables that affect the IWB of employees, such as conflict within the group, group cohesion and leadership. The inclusion of these variables would provide researchers with more in-depth results. Finally, in this research, we study the interactive effect of reflexivity and justice on innovative behaviour. Despite group reflexivity deals mainly about improving the way work is done (referring to procedural justice and not interpersonal justice such as in our paper), we can expect that the members of groups with higher reflexivity should actually be more perceived as fair. Therefore, it may be the case that high reflexivity should actually increase levels of justice. This direct relationship may be explored in future studies.

References

Ambrose, ML and M Schminke (2003). Organization structure as a moderator of the relationship between procedural justice, interactional justice, perceived organizational support, and supervisory trust. *Journal of Applied Psychology*, 88, 295–305.

Anderson, N, K Potočnik and J Zhou (2014). Innovation and creativity in organizations: A state-of the-science review, prospective commentary, and guiding framework. *Journal of Management*, 40(5), 1297–1333.

Anderson, NR and MA West (1998). Measuring climate for work group innovation: Development and validation of the team climate inventory. *Journal of Organizational Behavior*, 19, 235–258.

Ashforth, BE and F Mael (1989). Social identity theory and the organization. *The Academy of Management Review*, 14(1), 20–39.

Barsky, A, SA Kaplan and DJ Beal (2011). Just feelings? The role of affect in the formation of organizational fairness judgments. *Journal of Management*, 37(1), 248–279.

Bies, RJ and JS Moag (1986). Interactional justice: Communication criteria of fairness. In *Research on Negotiation in Organizations*, BH Sheppard, RJ Lewicki and M Bazerman (eds.), pp. 43–55. Greenwich, CT: JAI Press.

Blader, SL and TR Tyler (2009). Testing and extending the group engagement model: Linkages between social identity, procedural justice, economic outcomes, and extrarole behavior. *Journal of Applied Psychology*, 94, 445–464.

Branscombe, NR, R Spears, N Ellemers and B Doosje (2002). Intragroup and intergroup evaluation effects on group behavior. *Personality and Social Psychology Bulletin*, 28(6), 744–753.

Carter, SM and M West (1998). Reflexivity, effectiveness and mental health in BBC-TV production teams. *Small Group Research*, 29(5), 583–601.

Colquitt, JA, DE Conlon, MJ Wesson, COLH Porter and KY Ng (2001). Justice at the millennium: A meta-analytic review of 25 years of organizational justice research. *Journal of Applied Psychology*, 86(3), 425–445.

Colquitt, JA and JB Rodell (2011). Justice, trust, and trustworthiness: A longitudinal analysis integrating three theoretical perspectives. *Academy of Management Journal*, 54(6), 1183–1206.

Colquitt, JA, BA Scott, JB Rodell, DM Long, CP Zapata, DE Conlon and MJ Wesson (2013). Justice at the millennium, a decade later: A meta-analytic test of social exchange and affect-based perspectives. *Journal of Applied Psychology*, 98, 199–236.

Cropanzano, R, A Li and L Benson (2011). Peer justice and teamwork process. *Group & Organization Management*, 36(5), 567–596.

De Cremer, D, F Stinglhamber and R Eisenberger (2005). Effects of own versus other's fair treatment on positive emotions: A field study. *Journal of Social Psychology*, 145, 741–744.

Fay, D, H Shippton, MA West and M Patterson (2015). Teamwork and organizational innovation: The moderating role of the HRM context. *Creativity and Innovation Management*, 24, 261–277.

Francis, L and J Barling (2005). Organizational injustice and psychological strain. *Canadian Journal of Behavioural Science/Revue canadienne des sciences du comportement*, 37(4), 250–261.

Haslam, SA (2004). *Psychology in Organizations: The Social Identity Approach*, 2nd ed. London: Sage.

Henry, KB, H Arrow and B Carini (1999). A tripartite model of group identification: Theory and measurement. *Small Group Research*, 30, 558–581.

Hoegl, M and P Parboteeah (2006). Team reflexivity in innovative projects. *R&D Management*, 36(2), 113–125.

Hogg (2001). A social identity theory of leadership. *Personality and Social Psychology Review*, 5, 184–200.

Janssen, O (2000). Job demands, perceptions of effort-reward fairness and innovative work behaviour. *Journal of Occupational and Organizational Psychology*, 73(3), 287–302.

Janssen, O (2004). How fairness perceptions make innovative behavior more or less stressful. *Journal of Organizational Behaviour*, 25, 201–216.

Janssen, O and X Huang (2008). Us and me: Team identification and individual differentiation as complementary drivers of team members' citizenship and creative behaviors. *Journal of Management*, 34(1), 69–88.

Judge, TA, BA Scott and R Ilies (2006). Hostility, job attitudes, and workplace deviance: Test of a multilevel model. *Journal of Applied Psychology*, 91(1), 126–138.

Lavelle, J, D Rupp and J Brockner (2007). Taking a multifoci approach to the study of justice, social exchange, and citizenship behavior: The target similarity model. *Journal of Management*, 33, 841–866.

Li, A, R Cropanzano and J Bagger (2013). Justice climate and peer justice climate: A closer look. *Small Group Research*, 44, 563–592.

Liao, H and DE Rupp (2005). The impact of justice climate and justice orientation on work outcomes: A cross-level multifoci framework. *Journal of Applied Psychology*, 90, 242–256.

Lind, EA and K Van den Bos (2002). When fairness works: Toward a general theory of uncertainty management, In *Research in Organizational Behavior*, BM Staw and RM Kramer (eds.), Vol. 24, pp. 181–223. Boston, MA: Elsevier.

Mael, F and BE Ashforth (1992). Alumni and their alma mater: A partial test of the reformulated model of organizational identification. *Journal of Organizational Behavior*, 13, 103–123.

Messmann, G and RH Mulder (2012). Development of a measurement instrument for innovative work behaviour as a dynamic and context-bound construct. *Human Resource Development International*, 15(1), 43–59.

Ohana, M (2016). Voice, affective commitment and citizenship behavior in teams: The moderating role of neuroticism and intrinsic motivation. *British Journal of Management*, 27(1), 97–115.

Podsakoff, PM, SB MacKenzie, J-Y Lee and NP Podsakoff (2003). Common method biases in behavioral research: A critical review of the literature and recommended remedies. *Journal of Applied Psychology*, 88, 879–903.

Preacher, KJ, DD Rucker and AF Hayes (2007). Addressing moderated mediation hypotheses: Theory, methods, and prescriptions. *Multivariate Behavioral Research*, 42(1), 185–227.

Preacher, KJ and AF Hayes (2007). Asymptotic and resampling strategies for assessing and comparing indirect effects in multiple mediator models. *Behavior Research Methods*, 40(3), 879–891.

Rupp, DE and R Cropanzano (2002). The mediating effects of social exchange relationships in predicting workplace outcomes from multifoci organizational justice. *Organizational Behavior and Human Decision Processes*, 89, 925–946.

Rupp, DE, R Shao, KS Jones and H Liao (2014). The utility of a multifoci approach to the study of organizational justice: A meta-analytic investigation into the consideration of normative rules, moral accountability, bandwidth-fidelity, and social exchange. *Organizational Behavior and Human Decision Processes*, 123(2), 159–185.

Sani, F, V Madhok, M Norbury, P Dugard and JR Wakefield (2015). Greater number of group identifications is associated with healthier behaviour: Evidence from a Scottish community sample. *British Journal of Health Psychology*, 20(3), 466–481.

Schippers, MC, DN den Hartog and PL Koopman (2007). Reflexivity in teams: A measure and correlates. *Applied Psychology*, 56(2), 189–211.

Scott, SG and RA Bruce (1994). Determinants of innovative behavior: A path model of individual innovation in the workplace. *Academy of Management Journal*, 37(3), 580–607.

Shao, R, DE Rupp, DP Skarlicki and KS Jones (2013). Employee justice across cultures: A meta-analytic review. *Journal of Management*, 39, 263–301.

Simmers, CA and AJ McMurray (2018). Organisational justice and managing workplace innovation: How important are formal procedures? *International Journal of Innovation Management*, 23(3), 1–21.

Skarlicki, DP and GP Latham (2005). How can training be used to foster organizational justice? In *Handbook of Organizational Justice*, J Greenberg and JA Colquitt (eds.), pp. 499–522. Mahwah, NJ: Lawrence Erlbaum Associates.

Somech, A, HS Desivilya and H Lidogoster (2009). Team conflict management and team effectiveness: The effects of task interdependence and team identification. *Journal of Organizational Behavior*, 30, 359–378.

Tajfel, H (1970). Experiments in intergroup discrimination, scientific american. In *Introducing Psychological Research*, P Banyard and A Grayson (eds.), Vol. 223, pp. 69–73, 96–102. London: MacMillan Press.

Tajfel, H and JC Turner (1986). The social identity theory of inter-group behavior. In *Psychology of Intergroup Relations*, S Worchel and W Austin (eds.), Chicago: Nelson Hall.

Tangirala, S and BJ Alge (2006). Reactions to unfair events in computer-mediated groups: A test of uncertainty management theory. *Organizational Behavior and Human Decision Processes*, 100, 1–20.

Tjosvold, D, MML Tang and M West (2004). Reflexivity for team innovation in China: The contribution of goal interdependence. *Group & Organizational Management*, 29(5), 540–559.

Tjosvold, D (1991). *Team Organization: An Enduring Competitive Advantage*. Chichester, England: Wiley.

Tyler (2000). Social justice: Outcome and procedure. *International Journal of Psychology*, 35(2), 117–125.

Tyler, TR and SL Blader (2000). *Cooperation in Groups: Procedural Justice, Social Identity, and Behavioral Engagement*. Philadelphia: Psychology Press.

Tyler, TR and SL Blader (2003). The group engagement model procedural justice, social identity, and cooperative behavior. *Personality and Social Psychology Review*, 7, 349–361.

Van den Bos, K (2007). Hot cognition and social justice judgments: The combined influence of cognitive and affective factors on the justice judgment process. In *Advances in the Psychology of Justice and Affect*, D De Cremer (ed.), pp. 59–82. Greenwich, CT: Information Age Publishing.

Van den Bos, K and EA Lind (2002). Uncertainty management by means of fairness judgments. In *Advances in Experimental Social Psychology*, MP Zanna (ed.), Vol. 34, pp. 1–60. Boston, MA: Elsevier.

Waenink, E (2012). The effect of competences on innovative work behavior and the moderating role of human resource practices, Thesis, University of Twente, Enschede.

West, MA and JL Farr (eds.) (1990). *Innovation and Creativity at Work: Psychological and Organizational Strategies*. Oxford, England: John Wiley & Sons.

West, MA (1996). Reflexivity and work group effectiveness: A conceptual integration, In *Handbook of Work Group Psychology*, MA West (ed.), pp. 555–579. Chichester, UK: Wiley.

Xerri, M (2014). Examining the relationship between organisational justice, job satisfaction and the innovative behaviour of nursing employees. *International Journal of Innovation Management*, 18(1), 1–22.

Young, LD (2012). How to promote innovative behavior at work? The role of justice and support within organizations. *Journal of Creative Behavior*, 46(3), 220–243.

Yuan, F and RW Woodman (2010). Innovative behavior in the workplace: The role of performance and image outcome expectations. *Academy of Management Journal*, 53(2), 323–342.

Chapter 6

MANAGING THE IMPLEMENTATION OF INNOVATION STRATEGIES IN PUBLIC SERVICE ORGANISATION — HOW MANAGERS MAY SUPPORT EMPLOYEES INNOVATIVE WORK BEHAVIOUR[§]

SIGNE PHIL-THINGVAD* and KURT KLAUDI KLAUSEN†

Department of Political Science and Public Management
University of Southern Denmark, Denmark
**ssp@sam.sdu.dk*
†kkk@sam.sdu.dk

Published 30 December 2019

This paper examines which management strategies public managers may use to enhance innovative behavior among their employees. We focus on the implementation of a politically ambitious innovation strategy in a large Danish municipality. Based on a survey distributed to 1292 employees and 113 managers, we conduct a multi-level analysis focusing on how different management strategies (reported by the managers) and perceived management behavior (reported by the employees) affect the public employees' perceived idea generation, idea promotion, and idea realization. The results show that knowledge of the innovation strategy, encouraging management, a risk-tolerant culture and autonomy are important management tools, whereas strategic management communication and economic rewards do not correlate with any of the phases in innovative work behavior. We contribute with new evidence on how innovation is supported by public managers in the different phases of the innovation process, and we conclude by discussing the practical implications of the findings.

Keywords: Innovative behavior; management strategies; leadership.

Introduction

Throughout the Western world, rising costs of welfare services force politicians and managers to generate and implement strategies to ensure the level of welfare for future generations. In response to these challenges, many public organisations focus on innovation as the primary approach to driving down costs and handling increased demands for services (Borins, 2002, p. 467). Research has shown that innovation is often initiated by middle management and frontline workers (Borins,

§This article originally appeared in *International Journal of Innovation Management*, **24** 2050074-1-29

2011, p. 205), and innovative solutions are only effective in the public sector if they are proficiently implemented by frontline workers. But corporate strategies or "saying" are often decoupled from actual practice, i.e., from "doing" (Meyer and Rowen, 1983; Weick, 1995). The employees' work behaviour is therefore a very important element in public innovation, but so far only few studies have focused on this aspect (Bysted and Jespersen, 2013, p. 220; Günzel-Jensen *et al.*, 2017; Miao *et al.*, 2017).

In this study, we focus on innovative work behaviour among public employees and on the management that may enhance the implementation of the strategic intent. Innovation is often linked with major changes in the public sector, cutbacks or even layoffs (Klein *et al.*, 2010), and innovation potentially produce new and more demanding working conditions for the employees. Encouraging employees to engage in innovation can therefore be a challenge, and management is forced to create strategies to promote innovative work behaviour (Bysted and Jespersen, 2013). Thus, innovation encompasses the behaviour of both managers and employees. Recent research on the implementation of municipal innovation strategies in Denmark concludes that we often find a decoupling between the strategic intent and the actual work behaviour (Torp, 2016). Organisations that separate saying from doing potentialle become schizoid and loose their legitimacy while the employees loose their motivation (Brunsson, 1989; Weick, 1995). Consequently how the managerial strategic initiatives are linked to the employees' actual behaviour becomes crusial.

We will analyse and discuss how municipal managers may stimulate public employees to engage in innovative work behaviour.

Theories on managing innovation in public service organisations suggest that managers have several options in terms of ensuring innovation (Bysted and Jespersen 2013; Dorenbosch *et al.*, 2005) and thus bridge the cleavages and decoupling between strategic intent and actual practice. There is, however, still a both empirical and theoretical need to explore management mechanisms in depth (Bysted and Jespersen, 2013, p. 237) and conduct context-sensitive analyses within public service organisations on how managers can contribute to and strengthen the employees' innovative work behaviour (Svara, 2013, p. 193). We will examine which management strategies public managers may use in that endeavor.

We focus on the implementation of a politically ambitious innovation strategy in a large Danish municipality: "New Reality — New Welfare" in Odense Municipality (in short New–New). A single department (Department of Children and Youth) was chosen as the empirical case to minimise the contextual variation.[1]

[1]We would like to thank Pernille Carlsson and Dan Bonde Nielsen, who helped gather the data used in this paper. We would also like to thank Jesper Asring Hansen who has contributed to the statistical analyses.

We approach the analyses of innovation from a procedural perspective, following the existing research on innovative work behaviour (Scott and Bruce, 1994; Janssen, 2000, 2003, 2004; Bysted and Hansen, 2013; Bysted and Jespersen, 2014). Innovation is understood as a process consisting of different activities ranging from the initiation to the implementation of innovative ideas, which requires different individual patterns of behaviour (Scott and Bruce, 1994). We focus on three behavioural patterns among public employees: idea generation, idea promotion, and idea realisation (Scott and Bruce, 1994; Janssen, 2000, 2003, 2004) and scrutinise how employees' innovative work behaviour may be supported by different management strategies deduced partly from the literature on strategy and innovative work behaviour (for example, Mintzberg, 1994; Fernandez and Pitts, 2011; Zhang and Bartol, 2010; Janssen, 2004) and partly from the empirical context of "New–New". The analysis builds on a survey distributed to 1292 employees and 113 managers at Department of Children and Youth in Odense Municipality. To avoid common source bias and to achieve a more nuanced understanding of which management tools are actually affecting employees' innovative work behaviour, we use data from both managers and employees to measure the different management practices. We conduct a multilevel analysis focusing on how different management strategies and perceived management behaviour affect the innovative work behaviour among the employees.

We thereby contribute to the existing research on public innovation in several ways: First, we focus on innovative work behaviour among public employees, which is a highly important antecedent for public innovation (De Vries *et al.*, 2015, p. 147) but has not yet been thoroughly studied in the public sector (Bysted and Hansen, 2015; Bysted and Jespersen, 2015; Miao *et al.*, 2017; Günzel-Jensen *et al.*, 2017). Second, a recent review of public innovation emphasises that not all stages of innovation processes in the public sector are equally well covered. For example, more than half of the studies identified in the review focus on the diffusion or adoption stage in public innovations (De Vries *et al.*, 2015, p. 159). We clearly need more studies that follow innovation at all stages. The review also points out that the differences between the phases in the innovation process, especially relevant drivers or barriers, have not yet been sufficiently discussed (De Vries *et al.*, 2015, p. 159). Existing studies on innovative work behaviour do not examine all three behavioural patterns (Bysted and Jespersen, 2014; Bysted and Hansen, 2015; Miao *et al.*, 2017; Günzel-Jensen *et al.*, 2017); most of them treat innovative work behaviour as a unidimensional concept (Bysted and Hansen, 2015; Miao *et al.*, 2017; Günzel-Jensen *et al.*, 2017) and the different phases in innovative work behaviour are not covered. We contribute with a discussion of the three behavioural patterns in innovative work behaviour and focus on different management strategies as either drivers or barriers in all phases of innovative work behaviour. We do this in an attempt to qualify the discussion of public innovative work behaviour from a procedural perspective. Third, we scrutinise different management practices as underlying conditions for the employees' innovative work behaviour in a study of a specific innovation process in a large Danish municipal, which allows us to isolate and control for context-specific organisational factors in the analysis. Control for such contextual factors is highly important as research has shown that many antecedents are linked to the specific organisational context (De Vries *et al.*, 2015, p. 157). By conducting a context-sensitive analysis of a specific case, we supplement the few existing studies on innovative work behaviour in the public sector, which all address these questions at a macro-level and across organisational contexts (Bysted and Jespersen, 2014; Günzel-Jensen *et al.*, 2017; Miao *et al.*, 2017).

In the next section, we will define innovative work behaviour and discuss how public managers may support such behaviour among their employees. We propose six hypotheses related to (1) the management of meaning, (2) developing the institutional setup and (3) facilitating motivation. These three levels are drawn from the literarture on strategic management and supplement each other in our attempt to scrutinise how managers may bridge the gap between strategic intent and actual practice of innovative behaviour among the employees. Strategic communication (the use of narratives in the management of meaning) address all employees as does the nourishing of a favourable institutional setup such as a culture for innovation, while facilitating motivation (using rewards and feedback) is aimed at the individual level. The following section presents the research design and discusses the methods used. Finally, we present our findings and discuss our results with focus on theoretical and practical implications.

Innovation

We follow a traditional understanding of innovation as "*production or adoption of useful ideas and idea implementation* (Kanter, 1988; Van de Ven, 1986)" (in Scott and Bruce, 1994, p. 581). We thereby view innovation as a process that concerns generation, promotion, and realisation of new ideas in organisations. New ideas may be related to new products and new processes and may come from various places. They do not necessarily have to be new in the sense that no one has tried them out before; they may also be adopted from other organisations (Scott and Bruce, 1994). However, new products or new processes should represent discontinuity with existing practice (Osborne and Brown, 2005).

Innovation in the public sector

Innovation has been discussed within the private sector for a long time. Until recently, relatively little was known about the contingencies, processes and impacts of innovation in the public sector (Osborne and Brown, 2013, p. 1). The public sector is often stigmatised by its critics as a rigid bureaucracy, characterised by stagnation and inertia and much less flexibility than the private sector (Sørensen and Torfing, 2011; Svara, 2013). This made other scholars argue that the dominant form of creative output in the public sector was process innovation (see Bysted and Jespersen, 2014, p. 219) and that other forms of innovation faced severe challenges in the public sector (Bartlett and Dibben, 2002). However, due to demographic changes, economic crises and rising costs in the public sector, innovation (including process innovation) has become extremely important (Torfing, 2012) and has taken a prominent position on the political agenda (Borins, 2002, p. 467).

A number of studies have shown that innovation in the public sector mainly comes from middle managers and front-staff, and not from politicians or senior managers (Borins, 2006; Borins, 2001a). It is an interesting conclusion that public managers do not have to be innovative. Instead their role is to secure the implementation of innovative strategies — to frame, encourage and support the innovative work behaviour among their employees by establishing the right conditions in the daily practice (Borins, 2002, p. 467). Hence, we are interested in how the institutional and managerial setup can avoid a decoupling between a top-down driven innovation strategy and practice.

Innovative work behaviour

The vast majority of studies follow Scott and Bruce's understanding of employees' innovative work behaviour. They describe innovation as a multi-stage process: generation of new or adopted ideas; sponsorship and support of the ideas; and implementation of prototypes in the organisation (Scott and Bruce, 1994, p. 582). Scott and Bruce thereby perceive innovation as a process consisting of different activities requiring different individual behaviours.

Janssen offers the following widely used definition of innovative work behaviour: *The intentional creation, introduction and application of new ideas within a work role, group or organisation, in order to benefit role performance, the group, or the organisation* (Janssen, 2000, p. 288). Janssen furthermore states that innovative work behaviour consists of *idea generation, idea promotion and idea realisation* (Janssen, 2000, p. 288). In this way, Janssen expands the last phase of the innovation process to idea realisation, which can be understood as the actual implementation of the innovative ideas in the organisations. With Janssen's definition, innovative work behaviour includes simple and complex innovations in an organisation made by an individual, a group or by the entire organisation, from idea generation to implementation.

While innovative work behaviour has become an important concept in the literature on innovation, most of the empirical studies have been conducted within the private sector (for example, Janssen, 2000, 2003, 2004; Aryee *et al.*, 2012; Scott and Bruce, 1994). Exceptions are Bysted and Jespersen (2014), Bysted and Hansen (2015), Günzel-Jensen and Colleagues (2017) and Miao and colleagues (2017). Since innovation has become so prominent on the public agenda, we are in strong need of more substantial and genuine knowledge about innovative behaviour in the public sector especially in local governments (Svara, 2013).

Moreover, drivers and barriers to innovation are not necessarily the same in the public and the private sector (Osborne and Brown, 2013; Borins, 2001a). Osborne and Brown argue that management of innovation is an entirely different task than management of developmental changes, which was previously the dominant management approach in the public sector (Osborne and Brown, 2013, p. 3). The increased focus on innovation in the public sector challenges the existing management approach and places new demands on management to ensure that innovative ideas are generated, promoted and realised. However, in general, we still lack knowledge about which management mechanisms may support innovative work behaviour among employees in the public sector (Bysted and Jespersen, 2014). In the following, we will discuss some management tools that may affect employees' innovative work behaviour and develop hypotheses for our analyses.

How management may ensure strong innovative work behaviour among employees

Our discussion of management tools that facilitate innovative work behaviour among employees are divided into three equally important levels: (1) *the management of meaning*, (2) *developing the institutional setup*, and (3) *facilitating motivation.*

These levels are drawn from the strategic management literature, which states that alignment and adjustment are indispensible for the implementation of strategies (Miles and Snow, 1978; Mintzberg, 1994). (1) If the original strategic intent for innovative behaviour is not found meaningful amongst those who are supposed to implement it, they are less likely to make it their own project. Hence, sensemaking (Weick, 1995) such as story-telling and goal specification as a part of the management of meaning becomes vital to implementation. (2) The institutional setup (Scott, 1995) of a particular organisation may inherently bear on norms such as culture that may enforce or inhibit behavioural changes, and this accordingingly (following, e.g., Schein, 2010) can and should be managed. (3) Finally individual motivation is important when implementing strategies in this case innovation (Miron *et al.*, 2004) and should also be taken into account. Below, we will further clarify, how these three levels relate to innovative behaviour.

First, management may affect employees' behaviour by framing organisational meaning, by invoking meaning to the strategy of innovation through strategic communication. Strategic narratives (Barry and Elms, 1997), and communicating the importance of and reasons for the strategic imperative of innovation are viewed as important in several studies (Fernandez and Rainey, 2006; Borins, 2011). It is emphasised that management communication should be a continuous process and that it should be both vertical and horizontal (Fernandez and Rainey, 2006). Especially top management should engage on a continuous basis and keep communicating about the organisational changes to convince employees of the importance of being innovative (Fernandez and Pitts, 2011). Also communication from the middle management has been shown to be of utmost importance in regard to public innovation. Borins (2011) concludes that most new ideas are generated at that level. Thus, management should ensure that the purpose of the innovation process is communicated clearly to the organisation's employees. Both the level and the nature of the communication is important, as is the actual knowledge of the innovation strategy among the employees. In this case, we, therefore, also look at the employees' actual knowledge of the specific innovation strategy. Our first two hypotheses are:

H1: *The more effort management puts into strategic communication of new goals, the more innovative work behaviour is expected among employees.*

H2: *The more knowledge employees have about the innovation strategy (New–New), the more innovative work behaviour is expected among them.*

We expect a positive relationship between both strategic communication and knowledge and all phases in innovative work behaviour. However, we expect strategic communication to have strongest impact on the idea realisation phase, since implementation has been shown to be greatly affected by communication from management (Fernandez and Rainey, 2006). We expect knowledge of New–New among the employees to be equally important in all phases of innovative work behaviour, since knowledge of the management's intentions is a basic premise for fostering behaviour (Jacobsen and Andersen, 2015) and thereby avoid a decoupling between strategy and practice.

Second, managers may pave the way for innovative behaviour by nourishing a favourable institutional setup characterised by trust, and by developing a culture where innovation is seen as a legitimate and "appropriate" work behaviour.

Thus, to avoid a decoupling between an innovation strategy and employees' practice it is necessary that public managers support a culture characterised by support and trust (Bysted and Jespersen, 2014, p. 224; Scott and Bruce, 1994). There are several management strategies that can help to create such a culture. First, management should recognise the innovative behaviour during the whole process, not just at the innovative outcome (Bysted and Jespersen, 2014, p. 224; Clegg, 2002; Dobni and Luffman, 2000). Encouraging management, i.e., recognition of and feedback to employees who engage in the creation of new ideas and are willing to take a risk, has a positive influence on innovative work behaviour (Chandler *et al.*, 2000; Clegg 2002). We, therefore, hypothesise that:

H3: *The more the manager encourages employees to innovate, the more employees will engage in innovative work behaviour.*

We expect this effect to be strongest for idea generation and promotion. Encouraging employees' attempts to generate ideas may help create a culture in which both failure and success are accepted (Bysted and Jespersen, 2014, p. 224). And securing a culture where risks are tolerated and the discussion of ideas is encouraged is important for an employee's ability to discuss innovative ideas with others in the organisation (idea promotion). Even though we also expect a positive relationship between encouraging management and idea realisation, the fear of risks might be smaller in the idea realisation phase, when the manager most likely has accepted the innovative idea and decided to implement it in the organisation.

However, in general there is a tendency for employees to avoid the uncertainty and stress that can be associated with changes (Janssen, 2003, p. 349). Several studies point out that employees are often afraid to innovate because of simple resistances to changes (see Fernandez and Rainey, 2006, p. 82) and that employees associate innovative behaviour with risktaking (Bysted and Jespersen, 2014, p. 224; Yuan and Woodman, 2010). Furthermore, since innovation has been used rhetorically in discussions of the need to reduce the public sector (Klein *et al.*, 2010), public employees often associate innovation with cutbacks (Bysted and Jespersen, 2014, p. 225) and layoffs. We therefore also hypothesise that:

H4: *If employees perceive that the organisational culture has a low degree of risk avoidance, they will be more engaged in innovative work behaviour.*

We expect this relationship to be equally strong for all phases of innovative work behaviour since uncertainty and stress among employees is inherently present in all phases (Janssen, 2004). Furthermore, culture is a general underlying premise for employees' reactions to organisational changes (Piderit, 2000; van der Panne *et al.*, 2003).

Third, managers have to facilitate innovation at the individual and motivational level in the organisation by including employees in the decision-making processes, by delegating responsibility and autonomy to employees and by using incentives (for example, pecuniary incentives such as bonuses). While the relation between performance and extrinsic rewards is thoroughly discussed and empirically tested, the relationship between extrinsic rewards and innovative work behaviour is much less theorised (Fernandez and Pitts, 2011). External economic rewards can be a powerful motivational tool in the public sector despite restrictions on using them. Bysted and Jespersen (2014) argue that financial rewards increase innovative work behaviour. However, they only find a weak positive correlation between salary bonuses and idea generation, and the correlation seems to be weaker among public than among private employees. Still there seem to be a positive correlation, so we propose that:

H5: *The more managers use economic rewards, the more employees will engage in idea generation.*

We only expect this relationship to be significant in the idea generation phase. Fernandez and Pitts show that employees who experienced that their creativity and innovation attempts were rewarded would continue to generate new ideas and search for better ways of doing things (2011, p. 212). It should be noted, however, that the study made it impossible to differentiate between the effects of external rewards (such as economic bonuses) and internal rewards (such as recognition and promotion). On the other hand, idea promotion is a subtle and invisible behaviour that takes places both in and outside the organisation and it might be both a formal and informal task, which makes it hard for a manager to pinpoint and reward. Idea realisation takes place in the implementing phase, which often involves a group, and this may also prevent the use of individual rewards.

Finally, research has shown that innovative work behaviour is encouraged by giving employees autonomy (Fernandez and Pitts, 2011, p. 206). Borins (2011) also point out the importance of including employees in managerial decision-making processes regarding innovation. Autonomy thus gives employees freedom to act more creatively and innovatively (Fernandez and Pitts, 2011, p. 206; Zhang and Bartol, 2010, p. 117). Our final hypothesis is:

H6: *The more autonomy employees perceive they have in their work, the more they will engage in innovative work behaviour.*

We expect autonomy to be equally important for all phases in innovative work behaviour. When employees have an impact on daily tasks, and when they get to decide how to solve tasks, they will come up with new ideas (idea generation)

(Bysted and Hansen, 2013, p. 8) and it may be easier for them to promote their ideas in different settings. Finally, autonomy has been shown to have a significant effect on positive reactions to organisational changes (Piderit, 2000; Shalley and Gilson, 2004), which makes it more likely for autonomous employees to engage positively in idea realisation.

Methods and Data

While the private sector is percieved as dynamic and innovative, the public sector is often depicted as a rigid bureaucracy (Osborne and Plastric, 1997). Our case New–New illustrates the efforts of a local authortity to change this image and become more innovative.

The methodological procedure and the case

Our study was originally designed as a mixed methods study. We gathered qualitative data on the development, the translation and the practical implementation of New–New in Odense Municipality, by collecting and analysing all relevant documents about the innovation process and by conducting interviews with key respondents at the administrative and political level. However, in this paper, we only draw on the qualitative data in the following description of the case (for further analyses, see Klausen *et al.*, 2016).

The case: New Reality–New Welfare

Odense Municipality is the third largest city in Denmark. The department of Children and Youth has about 6,000 employees, 33 schools and some 150 kindergartens. As in all other Danish municipalities, the global financial crisis and the following economic recession created a new strategic situation, imposing budget restrictions and cutbacks in the entire organisation.

New–New was decided upon as a politically sanctioned corporate innovation strategy in June 2011. The main idea in the new corporate strategy was to infuse the entire organisation with a sense of urgency and the insight that if reality is economic scarcity and increasing demand on municipal services, the appropriate response is to reinvent the current production of welfare services. In other words, New–New was supposed to legitimise innovative endeavors throughout the organisation and require each group and individual to generate novel solutions, but it was also an effort to produce more with less.

The board of directors decided on a platform for communicating New–New in 2011. The main idea was to make sure that managers knew about New–New and made it their own priority to disseminate the idea of innovation. Employees were addressed more indirectly (primarily through newsletters and the intranet). The framing of the strategy with the name "New Reality–New Welfare" represented a punchline for a strategic narrative that made it possible to translate the innovation idea into sub-strategies in various parts of the organisation without loss of the original intention. Translating any strategy into meaningful sub-strategies is of utmost importance since it is the translated narratives that may affect work behaviour (Weick, 1995; Madsen, 2013).

To support this agenda, the municipality presented a new HR strategy including two codes of conducts that dictated how New–New was to affect the work behaviour of managers and employees: The first code of conduct, "Leadership under development", was launched in 2011. Leaders were now expected to think in "wholes" in culture, process, innovation and relations in order to stimulate the implementation of New–New. This approach to innovation obliged managers to be open-minded towards and encourage the formation of new ideas and the sharing of knowledge among employees (autonomy and freedom of thinking anew), to encourage dialogue, a risk-taking culture and open-mindedness that could promote organisational learning and avoid defensive reasoning and skilled incompetence (Klausen *et al.*, 2016). The second code of conduct, "Employee fundamentals — developing together", was launched in 2013. It stipulated, among other things, that employees were expected to let loose their creativity and new ideas, to be open-minded about the potential of others, see diversity as a potential resource, and be willingly to work in new directions towards personal and collective development (Klausen *et al.*, 2016). The employees were basically expected to engage in all phases of innovative work behaviour.

Finally, in 2014 a new organisational design to support implementation of New–New in the entire department was launched. Figure 1 documents the new organisational design to show the translation of New–New into the Department of Children and Youth.

Overall, Odense Municipality developed and implemented a thorough top-down innovation strategy from 2011 to 2014.

After gathering qualitative data on the implementation of New–New from 2011 to 2014, we conducted a quantitative study in 2015 to examine managers' and employees' reactions and behaviour related to New–New. We distributed a survey on innovative work behaviour, management and psychosocial work environment to 113 managers and 1292 (nested) employees at the Department for Children and Youth in Odense Municipality. The response rate was 91% among the managers and 65% among the employees. The employees and managers were sampled by

S. Phil-Thingvad & K. K. Klausen

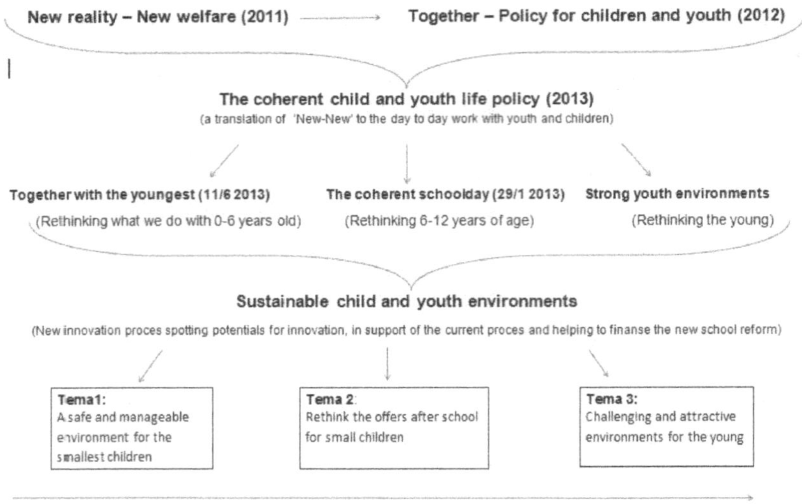

Fig. 1. Reorganising of the department April 1 st 2014 to support the implementation of New–New.

randomly selected institutions in the area of daycare and primary schools. 79% of the employee sample were female, and the respondents' ages ranged from 20 to 69 years ($M = 44.96$, SD = 9.72). Average seniority (organisational tenure) was 7 years (SD = 3.96).

Quantitative measures

To avoid common source bias, we distributed a survey to both the managers and the employees at the Department of Children and Youth in Odense Municipality. In our analyses, we use the employees' answers to measure the degree of innovative work behaviour. An important issue when determining how to measure management strategies is whether to use leaders' self-reported behaviours or employees' assessments of leadership behaviours. Both approaches may come at a cost. If we use leaders' self-reported behaviours as measures, social desirability bias may inflate the measures (Fleenor *et al.*, 2010). However, it is not given that the errors that inflate the leaders' self-ratings are correlated with employee ratings of their own behaviours (Jacobsen and Andersen, 2017). Therefore, we use both the immediate manager and employee ratings of management tools. We believe that this is a good measure of the association between strategic management tools and innovative work behaviour since it provides a measure of both the managers' intentions and employees' perception of the management approach. Below, we briefly describe our measures (see Appendix A for a more detailed overview).

Innovative work behaviour. To assess innovative work behaviour, we used Janssen's (2001) scale. The scale was translated into Danish and pilot tests were conducted with two practitioners and two academics.[2] This scale has been used in different variations in several studies on innovative work behaviour (see, for example, Janssen, 2000, 2001, 2003; 2004; Bysted and Hansen 2013; Bysted and Jespersen, 2014). An index was constructed for idea generation (Chronbachs alpha = 0.87), idea promotion (Chronbachs alpha = 0.83) and idea realisation (Chronbachs alpha = 0.88).

Strategic communication. It was tested through the managers' answers to three items, inspired by Zhang and Barthols' study on creative process engagement (2010). An index was constructed measuring the level and nature of the managers' communication. The index was tested and had a Chronbach's alpha of 0.69.

The employees' knowledge about New–New was tested by the following question sent to the employees: "I know the purpose of New–New".

Encouraging management was tested through the managers' answers to two items developed with inspiration from the encouraging management scale in QPS Nordic (General Nordic Questionnaire for psychological and social factors at work). To make sure the encouragement was related to innovation, the questions were slightly altered based on ideas from Fernandez and Rainey (2006, p. 171) and Borins (2000). The index was tested and had a Chronbach's alpha of 0.82.

Culture of risk avoidance. We used three questions to measure the employees' perception of whether their organisational culture is characterised by *risk avoidance*. The questions were inspired by Miron *et al.* (2004, p. 182–183). The exact phrasing of the questions was aligned with the official management guidelines (ledestjerne 2) in New–New. The index was tested and had a Chronbach's alpha of 0.74.

Economic rewards. Whether the managers used economic rewards related to innovative work behaviour was tested by a single question: "I reward my employees economically if they try out new and different approaches".

Autonomy. To measure the perception of autonomy among the employees, we used QPS Nordic's autonomy index, which is a classic and validated measure

[2]Because of too high similarities in question 4 and 5 after translation of the items, the two questions were combined into one.

of autonomy (Wännerström *et al.*, 2009). The index was tested and had a Chronbach's alpha of 0.84.

Controls. Age was measured as years from birthday, gender was measured as (male = 1, female = 0), number of working hours per week, seniority (number of years), and job position had six categories (teacher, head teacher, pedagogue, pedagogical assistant, pedagogical helper, and other).

Strategy for the analyses. Since we sampled subunits in the organisation (schools and kindergartens), we use multi-level modelling. We choose fixed effects models to control for differences between groups and thus only estimate variation at the individual level, which is relevant to our hypotheses. We have 62 schools and kindergartens in the sample with immediate managers who participate in the survey. We apply the fixed effects at the level of top managers above immediate managers where we have 21 schools and kindergartens. We use the answers from the immediate supervisors because the interactions between the immediate supervisors and their employees seem most relevant to this study. In order to compare the coefficients in the models, we report a model in which all independent variables are normalised between 0 and 1.

Results

Descriptive statistics and correlation matrices are reported in Appendix B. The directions between the dependent and independent variables are as expected. Some of the independent variables, for instance autonomy and risk-tolerant culture, are correlated. However, we do argue that granting employees autonomy is theoretically distinguishable from a risk-tolerant culture. Both measures are validated in previous research and there is still substantial unshared variation, so we perceive the similarity to be unproblematic for our research purposes. The descriptive statistics lend support to our theoretical framework, but they do not answer our hypotheses, and multilevel analyses with fixed effects were therefore conducted. Table 1 shows the results of the analyses.

In New–New, the top management has worked strategically with innovation, which was initiated as a top-down process. We argued in hypothesis 1 that it is important that managers communicate strategically about the goals in the organisation to ensure innovative work behaviour among employees. However, the data do not support this hypothesis in any part of the innovation process. There were no significant relationships between strategic communication and idea generation, promotion or realisation. On the other hand, hypothesis 2, that employees will engage more in innovative work behaviour the more they know about the innovation strategy (New–New), finds support in the analysis. As expected,

Table 1. Outcome: Innovative work behaviour among the employees.

	Idea generation		Idea promotion		Idea realisation	
	Coeff.	Std. err.	Coeff.	Std. err.	Coeff.	Std. err.
Age	−0.714***	0.26	−1.03***	0.283	−0.452	0.285
Male	−0.047	0.103	0.041	0.111	−0.064	0.113
Number of working hours	0.126	0.237	0.143	0.258	0.133	0.259
Tenure (number of years)	−0.047	0.198	−0.139	0.215	−0.202	0.217
Education (ref teacher)						
Pedagogical assistant	0.025	0.277	−0.115	0.3	−0.255	0.302
Pedagogical helper	−0.484**	0.197	−0.24	0.214	−0.357*	0.215
Pedagogue	0.017	0.142	−0.096	0.154	−0.188	0.155
Head teacher	0.087	0.151	0.191	0.164	0.163	0.165
Other	0.174	0.183	0.021	0.199	−0.053	0.2
Meaning at organisational level						
Communication	−0.41	0.362	−0.13	0.393	−0.032	0.396
Knowledge about New–New	0.486***	0.179	0.595***	0.194	0.744***	0.196
Daily practice at collective level						
Encouraging management	−0.277	0.297	0.599*	0.323	0.077	0.326
Risk tolerant culture	1.136***	0.313	1.819***	0.34	1.481***	0.343
Motivation at individual level						
Economic rewards for innovation	−0.277	0.311	0.224	0.339	0.151	0.341
Autonomy	0.847***	0.28	1.829***	0.304	1.353***	0.307
Constant						
Observations	533		533		533	
Number of organisations	21		21		21	
Fixed effects	YES		YES		YES	
R^2 (within)	0.141		0.259		0.183	
R^2 (between)	0.082		0.284		0.281	
R^2 (overall)	0.133		0.246		0.177	

Notes: $^*p < 0.1$, $^{**}p < 0.05$, $^{***}p < 0.01$.

knowledge of New–New among the employees is highly significantly ($p < 0.01$) correlated with innovative work behaviour throughout the innovation process (idea generation, promotion and realisation). A one-unit increase in knowledge of New–New is associated with a 0.122 increase in idea generation, a 0.149 increase in idea promotion and a 0.186 increase in idea realisation.

We also argued that the management should try to affect innovation via the institutional setup. Hypothesis 3 proposed that the more managers encourage employees to innovate the more employees will engage in innovative work behaviour. We expected the effect to be strongest in relation to idea generation and promotion. However, this hypothesis was not strongly supported by the data. For idea generation and idea realisation there were no significant relationships, but there was a weak significant correlation between encouraging management and idea promotion ($p < 0.1$). This is a surprising result, which we will inspect further in our discussion. Another important aspect of the institutional setup is organisational culture. Hypothesis 4 suggested that employees will engage more in all phases of innovative work behaviour if they experience an organisational culture with a low degree of risk avoidance. This hypothesis is strongly supported in the analyses. The results show that the more the culture is characterised by low risk avoidance the more engaged employees are in idea generation, promotion and realisation. A one-unit increase in low risk avoidance is associated with a 0.189 increase in idea generation, a 0.303 increase in idea promotion and a 0.247 increase in idea realisation ($p < 0.01$).

Finally, we argued that management also had to ensure innovation by affecting *the individual motivation* using economic incentives and by giving employees enough autonomy to motivate innovation. In hypothesis 5, we followed the argumentation of Bysted and Jespersen (2014) that the more managers use economic rewards the more employees will engage in idea generation. However, this hypothesis was not supported in our data. In hypothesis 6, we proposed that the more autonomy employees have the more they engage in all phases of innovative work behaviour. This hypothesis was strongly supported in our data. For all types of innovative work behaviour there were a positive and highly significant ($p < 0.01$) relationship between autonomy and innovative behaviour. A one-unit increase in autonomy is associated with a 0.212 increase in idea generation, a 0.457 increase in idea promotion and a 0.338 increase in idea realisation.

If we look at the normalised coefficient, we can compare the effect of the different management tools on innovative work behaviour among the employees in this data. A clear pattern stands out across idea generation, idea promotion and idea realisation, namely that the strongest impact on innovative work behaviour seems to come from a risk-tolerant organisational culture and autonomy.

Discussion and Conclusion

Innovative work behaviour among public employees is pointed out as important when western societies face challenges in welfare provision. However, we still need more knowledge about how managers may stimulate public employees to engage in innovative work behaviour. In this study, we focused on three strategically important levels, namely (1) the management of meaning, (2) the development of an institutional setup and (3) the facilitation of individual motivation.

With regard to *managing the overall organisational meaning*, we proposed that the more effort managers put into strategic communication the more innovative work behaviour can be expected among employees. However, the data did not support this hypothesis in its narrow sense in any part of the innovation process, which is surprising. The reason may be the focus in the questions included in the communication index. The questions take a classic strategic approach to communication and focus on overall goal clarification and how the goals are connected to the overall strategy in the organisation. This kind of communication may support routine behaviour in the organisation. It depends on the strategy. In our case, New–New was a part of the strategy, but broader goals were emphasised as well in the overall strategy. If the questions had focused more specifically on strategic communication related only to New–New, the result may have been different. On the other hand, hypothesis 2, that employees will engage more in innovative work behaviour the more they know about the innovation strategy, finds support in the analysis for all parts of the innovation process (idea generation, promotion and realisation). New–New was implemented as a top-down process, so it is not surprising that knowledge of the strategy is important for the employees' engagement in innovative work behaviour. These results support the argument that context-sensitive measures are highly important when we study innovation in the public sector (De Vries *et al.*, 2015). Studies might not be able to find important antecedents for innovative work behaviour if they only scrutinise their research questions at a macro-level or across organisational contexts since such antecedents may be dependent on their actual implementation in the organisation. Therefore, the overall conclusion must be that topmanagements' strategic communication may not directly affect the employees' innovative work behaviour. However, it may have an indirect effect since the employees' knowledge about the innovation strategy (which stems from their immediate manager, who is responsible for making them aware of the strategy and for translating the original strategic intent into a meaningful local narrative) seems to be strongly correlated with their innovative work behaviour.

Regarding *managing the institutaional setup*, we focused on encouraging management. We expected that the more the managers encourage employees to innovate the more the employees will engage in innovative work behaviour, especially idea generation and idea promotion. This hypothesis was only supported in relation to idea promotion in the analyses. To scrutinise this surprising result further, we ran all the analyses with the employees' reports of how encouraging they perceived their managers to be in relation to innovation. The results from these analyses showed that the more the employees perceived their managers to encourage them to innovate the more they engaged in innovative work behaviour (in all three phases). When we used the employees' perceptions of encouraging management it significantly correlated with innovative work behaviour: and it was a factor as important as a risk-tolerant organisational culture and more important than autonomy (the analyses are reported in Appendix C). The reason is probably that employees' perceived managerial practices have greater influence on employee behaviour than the managers intended practices (Jacobsen and Andersen, 2015). Therefore, we will only make a very cautious conclusion that encouragement from management seems to matter in relation to innovative work behaviour. However, there is a need for more thorough studies of which phases of the innovation process and in which ways encouragement affects employees' innovative work behaviour. Furthermore, the analyses showed, as expected, that a risk-tolerant organisational culture is highly significantly correlated with all phases of innovative work behaviour. Several studies have theorised risk tolerance as one of the most vital preconditions for innovation in public organisations (Brown and Osborne, 2013; Dumay *et al.*, 2013). However, Bysted and Hansen (2015) did not find a positive relation between risk tolerance and innovative behaviour after control for autonomy, expectancy clarity, and room for innovation. Still, our study shows that risk tolerance is the most important managerial strategy compared to frequently examined causes of innovation such as autonomy, encouraging management, communication, and rewards. This result might point to one important difference between innovation in the public and the private sector. Research has emphasised that public managers have to operate within a wider field of actors (including elected politicians and citizens/users) (Hartley, 2013, p. 57). Politicians are important catalysts in this regard, since they are held accountable for the public innovations in the medias and they risk losing votes to their political opponents (ready to attack them) if the innovations fail. They may therefore put a pressure on the public organisations to be less risk tolerant, and this pressure causes a less risk willing climate, where it is hard to develop the necessary level of trust to support innovative behaviour (Hartley, 2013, p. 54). However, further inquiry is needed to determine how risk tolerance interacts with other managerial and organisational factors in the public sector.

Looking at *managing the individual motivation* in the organisation we did not find that economic rewards were significantly related to idea generation as suggested by Bysted and Jespersen (2014). This result might also be caused by the public context, where the possibility to use economic incentives is much more restricted than in the private sector. Furthermore studies (especially in public service motivation) have argued that public employees are primarily intrinsically motivated, and that economic rewards might crowd out the intrinsic motivation among public employees (e.g., Houston, 2000; Frey and Jegen, 2002). We, therefore, propose that future studies should look into the more complex pathways between different kinds of rewards, extrinsic and intrinsic motivation and innovative work behaviour among public employees. Finally, the results revealed that the more autonomy the employees have the more they engage in all phases of innovative work behaviour. Thus, the data support existing findings in the private sector that autonomy gives employees freedom to act more creatively and innovatively (Fernandez and Pitts, 2011, p. 206; Zhang and Bartol, 2010, p. 117) and it seems to be at all levels of innovative work behaviour. The literature suggests that public managers have to handle a greater degree of formalisation and bureaucratisation (Rainey, 2009) which makes it harder to provide the necessary autonomy and reduces innovation in the public sector. However, there are considerable variation within as well as across sectors when it comes to formalisation and bureaucratisation (Rainey and Chun, 2005), and overall Hartley shows that existing evidence do not support clear differences between the sectors in this regard (Hartley, 2013, p. 52).

Like all studies, our analyses have some limitations that should be addressed. First, the cross-sectional nature of the data prohibits us from making causal claims. Endogeneity may account for some of the covariation between the variables. We chose the Department of Children and Youth in Odense Municipality to minimise contextual variation. However, this minimisation of variation comes at a price, since it limits the generalisability of the findings. Further research is needed to determine whether the findings concerning management strategies from this study are generalisable to other public or private settings. We use both leader and employee ratings of behaviours to mitigate problems with common source bias. However, when employees' and leaders' self-reported behaviours are used as measures, social desirability bias may inflate the measures (Fleenor *et al.*, 2010). This might be the reason why we did not find a significant correlation between innovative work behaviour and the managers' answers to how encouraging their management were. A floor effect may be present that prevents us from reliably estimating the effects of lower levels of management strategies and employees' innovative behaviour. However, it is not given that the errors that inflate the leaders' self-ratings are correlated with employee ratings of their own behaviours (Jacobsen and Andersen, 2017).

We conclude by focusing on some practical implications of the results. In this study, we contribute with novel evidence on how innovation is supported by public managers in the different phases of the innovation process in a large local government. Even though strategical communication of goals did not relate directly to any of the phases in innovative work behaviour, our results suggest that managers should still place an effort in communication to enhances the employees' knowledge of the strategy, which is important for their innovative behaviour. We saw remarkable differences in managing the institutional setup for the different phases of innovative work behaviour. Encouraging employees and signaling that risks are tolerated is more strongly related to idea promotion than to the other two phases of innovative behaviour. This may be due to the political nature of this phase in the innovation process (Janssen, 2004, p. 204). Managers have to ensure that employees' career prospects are not harmed by entering the political game of building organisational support for a new idea. Thus, it becomes particularly important for the promotion of new ideas that managers signal that risky attempts are not punished. To enhance innovative work behaviour managers should work with the culture to ensure that it is acceptable to take risks and try out new solutions even though they may fail during the process. This is especially important in the public sector (Flemig *et al.*, 2016). Finally, it seems that autonomy at the individual level is equally important for all three phases in the innovation process. Therefore, managers should be keen on giving employees autonomy to try new solutions to existing problems. In this regard, it becomes especially important that the managers find a way to balance bureaucratic rules with innovative work behaviour so it is possible to grant public employees enough autonomy to support their innovative behaviour.

The hypocracy of decoupling — separating saying and doing, may lead to schizoid organisations, but such cleavages can be bridged. This study shows that corporate innovation strategies such as New–New have at chance of being implemented to the extent that they are supported by managers who enable the processes by ways of infusing knowledge and meaning, by creating af favourable institutional setup and by supporting individual motivation and thereby encouraging innovative behaviour.

Appendix A. Measures

Idea generation

I generate new ideas to solve problems
I search for new work methods, techniques, or instruments
I contribute with original solutions to our problems

Answering categories: Never (1), Rarely (2), Occasionally (3), Sometimes (4), Often (5), Mostly (6), Always (7).

Cronbach's alpha: 0.867.

Idea promotion

I am good at getting support for innovative ideas
I make important people in my organisation enthusiastic about innovative ideas

Answering categories: Never (1), Rarely (2), Occasionally (3), Sometimes (4), Often (5), Mostly (6), Always (7).

Cronbach's alpha: 0.835.

Idea realisation

I translate innovative ideas into useful solutions
I introduce innovative ideas in a systematic way
I evaluate the usefulness of innovative ideas

Answering categories: Never (1), Rarely (2), Occasionally (3), Sometimes (4), Often (5), Mostly (6), Always (7).

Cronbach's alpha: 0.883.

Communication strategy (leader ratings)

I help my employees understand how the goals they are working to achieve fit with organisational visions and goals
I help my employees understand how their daily work fits in a bigger picture
I help my employees understand how important their work is for the organisation's effectiveness

Answering categories: Completely disagree (1), Disagree (2), Neither agree nor disagree (3), Agree (4), Completely agree (5).

Cronbach's alpha: 0.695.

Knowledge of New–New

I know what the purpose of the vision 'New reality – new welfare' is

Answering categories: Completely disagree (1), Disagree (2), Neither agree nor disagree (3), Agree (4), Completely agree (5).

Encouragement (leader ratings)

My employees have my full support to try out new and different solutions
I give praise to my employees when they try out new and different solutions

Answering categories: To a very low extent (1), To a low extent (2), To some extent (3), To a high extent (4), To a very high extent (5).

Cronbach's alpha: 0.821.

2050074-21

S. Phil-Thingvad & K. K. Klausen

Risk tolerant culture

We are not afraid to fail when we try out new things in my organisation
I am not afraid to take risks in an attempt to change habits and practices
New ideas are not suppressed–nor in the early stages, when their value is unclear

Answering categories: Completely disagree (1), Disagree (2), Disagree to some extent (3), Neither agree nor disagree (4), Agree to some extent (5), Agree (6), Completely agree (7).

Cronbach's alpha: 0.743.

Economic rewards (leader ratings)

I reward my employees with economic incentives when they try out new and different solutions

Answering categories: To a very low extent (1), To a low extent (2), To some extent (3), To a high extent (4), To a very high extent (5).

Autonomy

I have influence on decisions regarding my work
I have influence on who I work with
I have influence on the amount of work that I do
I have influence on my work tasks
My immediate supervisor encourages me to participate in important decisions

Answering categories: Never (1), Rarely (2), Sometimes (3), Often (4), Always (5).

Cronbach's alpha: 0.843.

Control variables

Gender: Female (0), Male (1).

Age (measured in years): 20–25 (0), 26–30 (1), 31–35 (2), 36–40 (3), 41–45 (4), 46–50 (5), 51–55 (6), 56–60 (7), 61–65 (8), 66–70 (9).

Tenure (measured in years): 0–2 (0), 3–4 (1), 5–6 (2), 7–8 (3), 9–10 (4), 11–12 (5), 13–14 (6), 15–16 (7), 17–18 (8), 19–20 (9), 21–22 (10), 23–24 (11), 25 years (12), more than 25 years (13).

Job position: Teacher, Head teacher, Pedagogue, Pedagogical helper, Pedagogical assistant, Other.

Appendix B. Descriptive Statistics

Table B.1. Descriptive Statistics.

Variable	*N*	Mean	St. dev.	Range
Idea generation	709	4.773	1.051	2–7
Idea promotion	708	4.218	1.193	1–7
Idea realisation	708	4.262	1.171	1–7
Encouraging management	74	4.589	0.474	3–5
Communication	74	4.041	0.454	3–5
Economic rewards	74	1.195	0.499	1–3
Knowledge about New–New	686	3.319	1.041	1–5
Risk tolerant culture	714	5.203	1.051	1–7
Autonomy	702	3.296	0.788	1–5
Age	753	4.39	1.937	0–9
Tenure	703	4.747	4.242	0–14
Gender	768	0.212	0.409	0–1

Table B.2. Correlation matrix.

Variable	[1]	[2]	[3]	[4]	[5]	[6]	[7]	[8]	[9]	[10]	[11]	[12]
[1] Id. gen.	1											
[2] Id. pro.	0.68	1										
[3] Id. rea.	0.7	0.77	1									
[4] En. management	−0.01	0.08	0.03	1								
[5] Communication	0.07	0.02	0.04	−0.34	1							
[6] Econ. Rewards	−0.01	0.06	0.03	−0.2	0.01	1						
[7] Knowledge N–N	0.21	0.26	0.27	−0.07	0.12	0.03	1					
[8] Risk tol. cult.	0.27	0.38	0.31	0.02	0.1	0.1	0.27	1				
[9] Autonomy	0.26	0.42	0.35	0.03	0.06	0.09	0.36	0.52	1			
[10] Age	−0.08	−0.09	−0.03	0.11	−0.09	0.04	0.09	0.01	0.09	1		
[11] Tenure	−0.06	−0.06	−0.03	0.03	−0.11	0.01	0.04	−0.03	0.04	0.59	1	
[12] Gender	−0.03	−0.01	−0.02	0.01	0.00	0.02	−0.15	−0.05	−0.08	−0.04	0.03	1

Appendix C. Employee Ratings Only

Table C.1. Innovative work behaviour among the employees.

	Idea generation		Idea promotion		Idea realisation	
	Coeff.	Std. err.	Coeff.	Std. err.	Coeff.	Std. err.
Age	−0.594**	0.235	−0.809***	0.247	−0.493*	0.258
Male	−0.009	0.097	0.022	0.105	−0.064	0.107
Number of working hours	0.217	0.199	0.314	0.208	0.298	0.219
Tenure (number of years)	−0.045	0.175	−0.023	0.186	−0.148	0.193
Education (ref teacher)						
Pedagogical assistant	0.0261	0.238	−0.063	0.239	−0.188	0.26
Pedagogical helper	−0.41**	0.17	−0.383**	0.177	−0.449**	0.187
Pedagogue	0.0283	0.128	−0.05	0.132	−0.127	0.14
Head teacher	0.07	0.144	0.214	0.152	0.212	0.159
Other	0.115	0.167	0.088	0.176	−0.038	0.184
Meaning at organisational level						
Communication	−0.341	0.281	0.045	0.292	0.352	0.309
Knowledge about New–New	0.616***	0.165	0.586***	0.176	0.75***	0.182
Daily practice at collective level						
Encouraging management	0.798***	0.291	1.206***	0.311	0.57*	0.321
Risk tolerant culture	0.795***	0.282	1.199***	0.299	1.071***	0.311
Motivation at individual level						
Economic rewards for innovation	−0.148	0.195	0.51**	0.205	0.169	0.215
Autonomy	0.759**	0.306	1.108***	0.326	0.889***	0.337
Constant						
Observations	606		606		606	
Number of organisations	21		21		21	
Fixed effects	YES		YES		YES	
R^2 (within)	0.156		0.285		0.202	
R^2 (between)	0.164		0.44		0.317	
R^2 (overall)	0.165		0.295		0.206	

Notes: *$p < 0.1$, **$p < 0.05$, ***$p < 0.01$.

References

Aryee, S, FO Walumbwa, Q Zhou and CA Hartnell (2012). Transformational Leadership, Innovative Behavior and Task Performance: Test of Mediation and Moderation Processes. *Human Performance*, 25(1), 1–25, doi: 10.1080/08959285.2011.631648.

Barry, D and M Elms (1997). Strategy retold: Towards a narrative view of strategic discourse. *Academy of Management Review*, 22(2), 429–452.

Bartlett, D and P Dibben (2002). Public sector innovation and entrepreneurship: Case studies from local government. *Local Government Studies*, 28(4), 107–121, doi: 10.1080/714004159.

Borins, S (2000). Loose cannons and rule breakers, or enterprising leaders? Some evidence about innovative public managers. *Public Administration Review*, 60(6), 498–507.

Borins, S (2006). *The Challenge of Innovating in Government.* Innovation Series (Second Edition) IBM Center for The Business of Government.

Borins, S (2001a). Innovation, success and failure in public management — Some methodological reflections. *Public Management Review*, 3(1), 3–17.

Borins, S (2001b). Public management innovation — Toward a global perspective. *American Review of Public Administration*, 31(1), 5–21.

Borins, S (2002). Leadership and Innovation in the Public Sector. *Leadership & Organization Development Journal*, 23(8), 467–476.

Borins, S (2011). Making narrative count: A narratological approach to public management innovation. *Journal of Public Administration and Theory*, 22(1), 143–164.

Brown, L and S Osborne (2013). Risk and innovation. *Public Management Review*, 15(2), 186–208.

Brunsson, N (1989). *The Organization of Hypocricy*, Chichester: John Willey & Sons.

Bysted, R and JR Hansen (2015). Comparing public and private sector employees innovative behaviour: Understanding the role of job and organizational characteristics, job types and subsectors'. *Public Management Review*, 17(5), pp. 698–717, doi: 10.1080/14719037.2013.841977.

Bysted, R and KR Jespersen (2014). Exploring managerial mechanism that Influence Innovative Work Behavior: Comparing private and public employees. *Public Management Review*, 16(2), 217–241.

Chandler, GN, C Keller and DW Lyon (2000). Unraveling the determinants and consequences of an innovation-supportive organizational culture. *Entrepreneurship Theory and Practice*, 59–76.

Clegg, C, K Unsworth, O Epitropaki and G Parker (2002). Implicating Trust in the Innovation Process. *Journal of Occupational and Organizational Psychology*, 75, 409–422.

De Vries, H, V Bekkers and L Tummers (2016). Innovation in the public sector: A systematic review and future research agenda. *Public Administration*, 94(1), pp. 146–166, doi: 10.1111/padm.12209.

Dobni, CB and G Luffman (2000). Market orientation and market strategy profiling: An empirical test of environment-behavior-action coalignment and its performance implications. *Management Decision*, 38(8), 503–519.

Dorenbosch, L, ML Engen and M Verhagen (2005). On-the-job innovation: The impact of job design and human resource management through production ownership. *Creativity and Innovation Management*, 14, 129–141.

Dumay, J, J Rooney and L Marini (2013). An intellectual capital-based differentiation theory of innovation practice. *Journal of Intellectual Capital*, 14(4), 608–633.

Fernandez, S and DW Pitts (2011). Understanding Employee Motivation to Innovate: Evidence from Front Line Employees in United States Federal Agencies. *Australian Journal of Public Administration*, 70(2), 202–222.

Fernandez, S and HG Rainey (2006). Managing successful organizational change in the public sector. *Public Administration Review*, 66(2), 168–176.

Fleenor, JW, JW Smither, LE Atwater, PW Braddy and RE Sturm (2010). Self-other rating agreement in leadership: A review. *The Leadership Quarterly*, 21(6), 1005–1034.

Flemig, S, S Osborne and T Kinder (2016). Risky business—Reconceptualizing risk and innovation in public services. *Public Money & Management*, 36(6), 425–432, doi: 10.1080/09540962.2016.1206751.

Frey, B and R Jegen (2002). Motivation crowding theory. *Journal of Economic Surveys*, 15(5), 589–611, doi.org/10.1111/1467-6419.00150.

Günzel-Jensen, F, JR Hansen, ML Jakobsen and J Wulff (2018). A two-pronged approach? Combined leadership styles and innovative behavior. *International Journal of Public Administration*, 41(12), 957–970, doi.org/10.1080/01900692.2017.1303711.

Hartley, J (2013). Public and private features of innovation. In *Handbook of Innovation in Public Services*, S Osborne and L Brown (Eds.), Edward Elwar, Cheltenham, UK. Northampton, MA, USA ISBN 978 1 84980 974 0.

Houston, DJ (2000). Public-service motivation: A multivariate test. *Journal of Public Administration Research and Theory*, 10(4), 713–728.

Jacobsen, CB and LB Andersen (2015). Is leadership in the eye of the beholder? A study of intended and perceived leadership practices and organizational performance. *Public Administration Review*, 75(6), 829–841.

Janssen, O (2000). Job demands, perceptions of effort — Reward fairness and innovative work behaviour. *Journal of Occupational and Organizational Psychology*, 73(3), 287–302.

Janssen, O (2003). Innovative behavior and job involvement at the price of conflict and less satisfactory relations with co-workers. *Journal of Occupational and Organizational Psychology*, 76(3), 347–364.

Janssen, O (2004). How fairness perceptions make innovative behavior more or less stressful. *Journal of Organizational Behavior*, 25(2), 201–215.

Klausen, KK, S Pihl-Thingvad, P Carlsson and J Jessen Hansen (2016). 1 udg. *Medarbejdere og ledere i innovationsprocessen "Ny Virkelighed - Ny velfærd, En surveyundersøgelse i Børn- og Ungeforvaltningen i Odense Kommune.* Forskningsrapport, Syddansk Universitet. Institut for Statskundskab.

Klein, PG, JT Mahoney, AM Mcgahan and CN Pitelis (2010). Toward a theory of public entrepreneurship. *European Management Review*, 7(1), 1–15.

Madsen, SO (2013). *Lederen som oversætter*, Ph.D theses Copenhagen: CBS.

Meyer, J and B Rowen (1983). Institutionalized organizations: Formal structure as myth and ceremony. *American Journal of Sociology*, 83(2), 340–363.

Miao, Q, A Newman, G Schwarz and B Cooper (2017). How leadership and public service motivation enhance innovative behavior. *Public Administration Review*, 78(1), 71–81.

Miles, RE and CC Snow (1978). *Organizational Strategy, Structure and Process*. Stanford: Stanford Business Classics.

Mintzberg, H (1994). *The Rise and Fall of Strategic Planning*, New York: Prentice Hall.

Miron, E, M Erez and E Naveh (2004). Do personal characteristics and cultural values that promote innovation, quality and efficiency compete or complement each other? *Journal of Organizational Behavior*, 25(2), 175–199.

Osborne, S and K Brown (2005). *Managing Change and Innovation in Public Service Organizations*, New York: Routledge.

Osborne, S and L Brown (2013). Introduction: Innovation in public services, in *Handbook of Innovation in Public Services*, S Osborne and L Brown (Eds.), Edward Elwar, Cheltenham, UK. Northampton, MA, USA, ISBN 978 1 84980 974 0.

Osborne, D and P Plastric (1997). *Banishing Bureaucracy*, New York: Penguin.

Piderit, SK (2000). Rethinking resistance and recognizing ambivalence: A multidimensional view of attitudes toward an organizational change. *The Academy of Management Review*, 25(4), 783–794.

Rainey, H and Y Chun (2005). Public and private management compared. In *Oxford Handbook of Public Management*, E Ferlie, L Lynn and C Pollitt (Eds.), Oxford: Oxford University Press, pp. 72–102.

Rainey, H (2009). *Understanding and Managing Public Organizations*. San Francisco, CA: Jossey Bass.

Schein, E (2010). *Organizational Culture and Leadership*, San Francisco Jossey-Bass.

Scott, SG and RA Bruce (1994). Determinants of innovative behavior — A path model of individual innovation in the workplace. *Academy of Management Journal*, 37(3), 580–607.

Scott, WR (1995). *Institutions and Organizations*, Thousand Oaks: Sage.

Shalley, CE and LL Gilson (2004). What leaders need to know: A review of social and contextual factors that can foster or hinder creativity. *The Leadership Quarterly*, 15(1), 33–53.

Svara, J (2013). Leading succesful innovation in local public services. In *Handbook of Innovation in Public Services*, S Osborne and L Brown (Eds.), Edward Elwar, Cheltenham, UK. Northampton, MA, USA, ISBN 978 1 84980 974 0.

Sørensen, E and J Torfing (2011). *Samarbejdsdrevet innovation i den offentlige sektor*. In *Samarbejdsdrevet innovation – i den offentlige sektor, København: Jurist- og Økonomforbundets Forlag*. E. Sørensen and J Torfing (Eds.), pp. 19–39.

Torfing, J (2012). Samarbejdsdrevet innovation I den offentlige sektor. *SJPR*, 16(1), pp. 27–46.

Torp, WM (2016). *Offentlig ledelse i udvikling*, Ph.D. theses, Roskilde: RUC.

van der Panne, G, C van Beers and A Kleinknecht (2003). Success and failure of innovation: A literature review. *International Journal of Innovation Management*, 7(3), 309–338.

Wännerström, I, U Petterson, M Åsberg, Å Nygren and P Gustavsson (2009). Psychometric properties of scales in the General Nordic Questionnaire for Psychological and Social Factors at Work (QPSNordic): Confirmatory factor analysis and prediction of certified long-term sickness absence, *Scandinavian Journal of Psychology*, 50, 231–244.

Weick, KE (1995). *Sensemaking in Organizations*. Sage: Thousand Oaks.

Yuan, FR and RW Woodman (2010). Innovative behavior in the workplace: The role of performance and image outcome expectation. *Academy of Management Journal*, 53(2), 323–334.

Zhang, X and KM Bartol (2010). The influence of creative process engagement on employee creative performance and overall job performance: A curvilinear assessment. *Journal of Applied Psychology*, 95(5), 862–873.

Chapter 7

FOSTERING EMPLOYEES' INNOVATIVE WORK BEHAVIOUR IN HEALTHCARE ORGANISATIONS[†]

DANIELA CARLUCCI

Department of European and Mediterranean Cultures
Environment and Cultural Heritage (DICEM)
University of Basilicata Via Lanera 20, 75100, Matera, Italy
daniela.carlucci@unibas.it

MATTEO MURA

Department of Management
University of Bologna, Bologna, Via Terracini, 28 Italy
matteo.mura@unibo.it

GIOVANNI SCHIUMA

Department of Mathematics, Computer Sciences and Economics (DIMIE)
University of Basilicata, Via dell'Ateneo Lucano
10, 85100, Potenza, Italy
giovanni.schiuma@unibas.it

Published 18 April 2019

Healthcare workers' innovative work behaviour plays a key role in generating innovation. To date determinants of innovative work behaviour are not completely detected and there is a call for additional empirical evidence on organizational-level factors influencing individual's innovation.

This study empirically explores the relationships between organizational climate, organisation's openness to innovation, and innovative work behaviour in the context of a public sector healthcare organization.

A survey has been conducted on employees of a large Italian public sector hospital. Data collected on 560 professionals have been analyzed through Structural Equation Modelling technique.

The results show that organisational climate affects employees' innovative work behavior both directly and indirectly through organisation's openness to innovation. Specifically our findings highlight that organization's openness to innovation partially mediates the relationship between organizational climate and employees' innovative work behavior.

[†]This article originally appeared in *International Journal of Innovation Management*, **24** 2050014-1-28

D. Carlucci, M. Mura & G. Schiuma

The results should lead managers to consider the importance of organizational climate and openness to innovation as effective levers to pull in order to improve employees' innovative work behavior.

Keywords: Organisational climate; innovative work behaviour; openness to innovation; healthcare organizations.

Introduction

Healthcare (HC) organisations have to continuously face a trade-off between high quality of delivered service and cost reduction. In order to cope with these apparently opposing demands, these organisations are increasingly relying on innovation as a fundamental driver of continuous quality improvement as well as cost reduction (Barlow, 2017; Moreira *et al.*, 2017; Omachonu and Einspruch, 2010; Thakur *et al.*, 2012). However, although crucial, the generation and the adoption of innovation in HC are not effortless.

HC organisations can be viewed as complex adaptive systems where the interrelated processes of generation, implementation, and widespread adoption of innovative ideas reflect the complexity of the system (Plsek, 2003). This complex system is characterised by the presence of multiple actors and interest groups which have different views of the meaning of getting and staying healthy (Kanter, 2011) and, in turn, of the innovation process and its results. Moreover, in HC organisations the generation of new knowledge can emerge from anyone, in any part of the system, at any time. Indeed, different stimuli from different HC stakeholders, internal and external to organisation, can trigger innovation and many new solutions in HC can be initiated by actors such as government, patients, or physicians (Omachonu and Einspruch, 2010). Moreover, regulation and political pressures can influence the pace and spread of innovation.

In such a view, the openness of HC organisations to the external environment and their capacity to mobilise stakeholders' experience and creativity in the search for novel and sustainable solutions are becoming more and more critical. On the other hand, it remains important for organisations to contextualise the experienced solutions, since, although the development and implementation of new ideas can be informed also by external viewpoints or what has worked elsewhere, external knowledge, ideas and solutions have to take account of the local structures and processes (e.g., relationships, mental models, etc.). In this regard HC employees' capability in capturing external knowledge and solutions and adapting them to organisational context is essential.

Usually the search for improved services or new solutions is triggered by feedbacks from patients, physicians and staff, almost on daily basis (Omachonu and Einspruch, 2010). Especially patients are a valuable source for new ideas on how to improve satisfaction and engagement practices. Innovation in healthcare is, in fact, frequently related to uncovering and addressing opportunities for efficiencies that may be hidden in the day-to-day work of care delivery and that are context sensitive. Therefore, if in a hospital innovation can take forms such as, for example, new surgical procedures, devices and tests, new forms of health professional training and management, new financing and service delivery models, etc., in a nursing home innovation can regard special rehabilitation, computerisation of medical records, the use of specialised care settings, such as beds for patients with particular diseases, e.g., Alzheimer's disease, AIDS, dialysis, etc. R&D units, where they exist, represent important catalysers of innovation, where researchers, healthcare personnel, public and private organisations, patients share and generate knowledge to find innovative treatments and look for ideas for new products or procedures to help further improve patient care.

In such a context, one of the most crucial features of innovation dynamics in HC organisations is healthcare workers' attitude of capturing, generating and applying new knowledge (e.g., Åmo, 2006; De Jong and Den Hartog, 2007; Thakur *et al.*, 2012 and performing an innovative work behaviour (Scott and Bruce, 1994). Employees distinguishing for an innovative behaviour at work have a visionary way of thinking on challenges and changes, make available or distribute their knowledge to others, and shape their ideas in a committed and self-acting way. They communicate openly over their ideas and manage to inspire other people for them.

Building the right conditions to enable employees to break free from the daily work and support their intrinsic interest to generate innovations is not effortless for organisations. Several factors, both individual and organisational, intervene in fostering and nourishing employees' innovative work behaviour.

Research has explored the factors affecting individual innovative work behaviour referring to three levels of analysis, i.e., individual, work group, and organisation (see Amabile, 1996; Amabile and Gryskiewicz, 1987; Anderson *et al.*, 2004; Anderson and West, 2001).

In their paper, Anderson *et al.* (2004) present an overview of the main factors which have been regularly found across numerous primary source studies to be facilitators of innovation at the different levels of analysis. The authors argue that research has accumulated on a wide range of factors found to be associated with innovation in the workplace. According to the scholars, at individual level factors include personality, characteristics of proactivity, self-confidence and originality, motivation, and cognitive ability. At the wok-level, job characteristics such as autonomy and job demands further determine whether the person will engage in innovative behaviour. While at work group level, factors include team structure, team composition (heterogeneity), team climate, mood states, team member characteristics, team processes and leadership style. Finally, at organisational level, the factors influencing innovation at workplace are numerous and range from individual characteristics (e.g., the open-mindedness of the CEO and supervisory behaviour) to organisational characteristics such as knowledge structure, size, strategy and resources, culture and climate.

Innovation at workplace depends, indeed, on several heterogeneous factors. Their effect on individual innovative behaviour have been analysed through different methodological approaches and in different fields.

Focussing on healthcare field, Kessel *et al.* (2012) pointed out that in this field the individual innovative behaviour has not traditionally been a compulsory aspect of daily practice but rather something beyond the scope of healthcare professionals' prescribed work behaviour. However nowadays due to the current relevance of innovation for HC organisation, research on the topic is becoming increasingly important (Kessel *et al.*, 2012).

In the last years, some scholars have examined some antecedents of healthcare workers' innovative behaviour, such as the influence from management and colleagues (Åmo, 2006), workplace relationships (Xerri, 2013), the guidelines and the flexibility in taking on extra roles in the workplace (Kessel *et al.*, 2012), transformational leadership (Sanders and Shipton, 2012), satisfaction with teamwork and satisfaction with training opportunities (Xerri and Stuart, 2017).

However, as underlined by Kessel *et al.* (2012) the understanding of individual, work group, and organisation factors affecting healthcare workers' innovative work behaviour, remains very limited. There is a need for additional theoretical advances and empirical evidence on individual, team and organisational antecedents of individual's innovation in healthcare (Kessel *et al.*, 2012; Patterson *et al.*, 2005).

This study focusses on two organisational factors, namely organisational climate and organisation's openness to innovation, and seeks to analyse their relationships with healthcare workers' innovative behaviour. It is reasonable to assume that individual innovative behaviour is more likely to occur in a work context characterised by, for instance, a positive organisational climate and conducive openness to change and willingness to experiment new ideas. However, more research is needed to corroborate this statement, especially in the under-explored healthcare sector.

In particular, to date, relatively few studies have examined the effects of organisational climate on employees' innovative behaviour (e.g., Imran *et al.*, 2010; Scott and Bruce, 1994). Regarding HC context some studies have analysed the impact of some specific factors of organisational climate, such as workplace relationships, empowerment and leadership upon innovative behaviour of a particular category of HC workers, i.e., nursing employees (Bagheri and Akbari,

2018; Chang *et al.*, 2008; Xerri, 2013). However, to date, to our knowledge, there are not studies that have examined comprehensively the role of organisational climate in fostering the innovative behaviour of HC employees. Analogously even if the openness to change and willingness to experiment new ideas, i.e., organisation's openness to innovation, are likely to influence employees' innovative work behaviour (e.g., Scott and Bruce, 1994), this relationship still remains unexplored.

As a result, how organisational climate, organisation's openness to innovation and HC workers' innovative behaviour interact is still an open question. In this context, this study aims to address the following leading research question: How organisational climate and organisation's openness to innovation relate to healthcare workers' innovative behaviour? For this purpose, a structural equation model, in which organisational climate was hypothesised to affect employees' innovative work behaviour directly and indirectly through employees' perception of organisation's openness to innovation, is developed and tested.

The remainder of this paper is organised as follows. Next section presents the theoretical background and the research hypotheses. Method section illustrates the research methodology, followed by the presentation of the results. The final section details the discussion and the practical implications.

Conceptual Framework

Nowadays, in a rapid changing environment, innovation in healthcare has to respond to a variety of social, technological, economic and medical issues (Akenroye, 2012; Omachonu and Einspruch, 2010; Varkey *et al.*, 2008). According to Akenroye (2012), currently there is a multidimensional plethora of forces driving the need for innovation in the health sector. These forces include unstable operational landscape, technological change, budgetary cuts, persistent and long terms health problems, changing patients' needs, supply chain necessities, social concerns, sustainability obligations.

In such environment HC organisations are called upon to nourish and exploit their innovative competences (Varkey *et al.*, 2008) in order to cope with various challenges ranging from clinical, technological and medical issues, to organisational, managerial, social and environmental matters. This, in turn, requires an involvement of the entire organisation in looking for improved or new delivered services. Nowadays, innovation cannot be confined to specialists, scientists and other R&D professionals, rather organisations have to encourage and develop the innovative potential of all their employees — or in other words, their innovative work behaviour (Scott and Bruce, 1994) — if they want to sustain their competitive advantage (Getz and Robinson, 2003). Encouraging commitment and risk-taking and promoting creativity and innovation within and among employees represent key factors in long-term organisational survival. In HC organisations an active role of employees in innovation processes is particularly desirable. In their daily works care providers interact with a multitude of patients and face as many care situations. This allows them to better understand how the services may fit into the patient's life and health to continuously face expected and unexpected problems, and to look for new and/or improved solutions. Certainly a high level of treatments and processes are up to less innovation and alteration on a daily basis.

However, the existing several issues, e.g., technological, clinical, managerial, organisational, social, etc., are stimulating more and more healthcare organisations to look for solutions in various domains and to continuously improve their services over time.

In such context, the active role of HC workers in understanding issues and formulating innovative solutions, is becoming crucial.

Scholars (e.g., De Jong and Den Hartog, 2007; Farr and Ford, 1990; Scott and Bruce, 1994) have described the intentional generation, promotion and realisation of new ideas within a work role, group or organisation, in order to benefit role performance, the group or the organisation as innovative work behaviour.

Innovative work behaviour typically includes exploration of opportunities and the generation of new ideas, but can also include behaviours directed towards implementing changes, applying new knowledge or improving processes to enhance personal and/or business objectives (De Jong and Den Hartog, 2008). In HC settings, employees' innovative work behaviour can be regarded as "everything from altering routines or making use of new remedies, to simplifying work, to improving the service provided to the end-user, or to being able to give the end user new offers" (Åmo, 2006; p. 231). Examples of innovative work behaviour in HC organisations include physicians developing new criteria for the diagnosis of patients or promoting new therapeutic methods; nurses engaging in teamwork to develop new guidelines for patient–nurse and family–nurse communication; physiotherapists adopting scientific evidence and international guidelines to modify rehabilitation approaches and techniques (e.g., Kessel *et al.*, 2012; Radaelli *et al.*, 2014).

The construct of innovative work behaviour is closely related to individual creativity. However, some differences between the two constructs have to be highlighted (De Jong and Den Hartog, 2010; Scott and Bruce, 1994). Eemployee's creativity refers to the production of new and useful ideas concerning products, services, processes and procedures (Amabile, 1996), while innovative work behaviour. also includes the promotion and implementation of ideas (Radaelli *et al.*, 2014). Unlike creativity, innovative work behaviour has a clearer applied component and is expected to result in innovative outputs. Therefore, creativity

Fostering Employees' Innovative Work Behaviour in Healthcare Organisations

can be seen as a crucial component of innovative work behaviour, most evident in the beginning of the innovation process when problems are recognized and ideas are generated in response to a perceived need for innovation (West, 2002).

Management research has devoted significant attention to innovative work behaviour in order to understand how to bring out the wealth of creativity and innovation inherent in employees via effective management practices (see e.g., Amabile, 1996). Nevertheless, to date, the conditions that promote the innovative performance of employees in organisations as well as the factors that affect process innovation at the individual level still remain to be explored more in depth (Oldham and Cummings, 1996). Specifically referring to HC settings, few studies have adequately examined the innovative behaviour of HC workers (Radaelli *et al.*, 2014; Xerri, 2013). In particular, the understanding of factors affecting healthcare workers' innovative work behaviour, is still limited (Kessel *et al.*, 2012). There is a need for additional theoretical advances and empirical evidence on individual, work group, and organisational antecedents of individual's innovation in healthcare (Patterson *et al.*, 2005).

Management literature suggests that OC is an organisational factor associated with employees' capacity to be innovative (e.g., Axtell *et al.*, 2000; Imran *et al.*, 2010; Shanker *et al.*, 2017). Supportive climates encourage individual innovation whereas environments characterised by distrust, personal hostilities, limited autonomy and unclear work goals inhibit the implementation of ideas. An organisational context where individuals can focus on their work, are able to participate in decision making, can think freely and communicate their opinions and ideas openly, supports interaction and knowledge sharing among employees thus stimulating employees' innovative work behaviour.

A further organisational factor influencing employee's innovative work behaviour is the organisation's openness to innovation, that is organisation's openness to change and willingness to experiment with ideas. Research has found that the organisation's ability to promote open, ongoing contacts among employees or information seeking from multiple sources, influences individual's creativity (Shalley *et al.*, 2004). Organisation's openness to innovation, indeed, facilitates the building of absorptive capacity (Cohen and Levinthal, 1990). In fact, it involves a greater interaction with external sources and enables an organisation to learn from partners, access external information, and transform and integrate that information into its existing knowledge base (Wang and Ahmed, 2007). This in turn stimulates employees to absorb and exploit new knowledge in internal process of innovation (Fosfuri and Tribó, 2008).

To date theoretical and empirical research on how organisational cliamte and openness to innovation, are related to employees' innovative behaviour are still limited (Imran *et al.*, 2010; Scott and Bruce, 1994). This is particularly valid in HC services, where more studies exploring the factors affecting innovative behaviour of employees are invoked (Xerri, 2013).

This paper seeks to enrich knowledge around the influence of organisational climate and openness to innovation on innovative behaviour of HC employees. Coherently, we investigate the role of organisational climate as a driver for employees' innovative work behaviour and openness to innovation. Additionally, we propose organisation's openness to innovation to positively mediate the effect of organisational climate on employees' innovative behaviour. The following section details the relationships among the model constructs by formulating specific research hypotheses.

Hypotheses development

Organisational climate and innovative work behaviour

Past research suggests that organisational climate can affect employees' capacity to be innovative (Axtell *et al.*, 2000; De Jong and Den Hartog, 2007; Imran *et al.*, 2010; Scott and Bruce, 1994; Shanker *et al.*, 2017). Organisational climate is a relatively enduring characteristic of an organisation which distinguishes it from other organisations and which reflects the prevalent norms, values and attitudes of the organisation's culture. It is connected to employees' shared perceptions of their organisation with respect to factors such as autonomy, trust, cohesiveness, support, recognition, and fairness, as well as to employees' interactions and structural features of the organisation.

Moreover, climate represents signals individuals receive about organisational expectations for behaviour and potential outcomes of behaviour (Scott and Bruce, 1994). Individuals use these signals to formulate expectations and to regulate their own behaviour to meet the organisations' expectation. Referring to innovative behaviour, if employees perceive a climate that values problem solving behaviour, is open to experimentation, is tolerant of failure and supports risk taking, they are more likely to be persistent, creative and helpful when faced with unexpected problems (Wolf *et al.*, 2012). Moreover, where there is a cooperative climate, individuals are more inclined to work together, to share and develop tacit knowledge, to generate new knowledge and to promote each other's performance and learning, by creating a fertile soil for innovative behaviour development (Bock *et al.*, 2005).

Regarding HC context, hitherto few studies have examined the effects of organisational climate on employees' innovative behaviour. This is not surprising if we consider that the phenomenon of innovative behaviour has been widely addressed in the area of business management, technology, engineering, and education, but it was not much discussed in the area of health care (Asurakkody and Shin, 2018; Kessel *et al.*, 2012). A small number of empirical studies have focussed on innovative behaviour in healthcare (e.g., Knol and Van Linge, 2009; Kessel *et al.*, 2012). Most of them analysed the impact of some specific dimensions of organisational cliamte on workers' innovative behaviour and frequently their setting of investigation was the nurses' category. For example, Bagheri and Akbari (2018) examined the influence of leadership, that many scholars have described as a dimension of organisational climate (e.g., James and McIntyre, 1996; Neal *et al.*, 2000; Wienand *et al.*, 2007), on nurses' innovation work behaviour. They concluded that leadership is effective in enhancing nurses' innovation work behaviour and more attention needs to be focused on developing entrepreneurial leadership competencies and on nurturing nurse leaders. Xerry (2013) analysed the effects of a further dimension of organisational cliamte, i.e., workplace relationships (James and McIntyre, 1996; Patterson *et al.*, 2005; Neal *et al.*, 2000), upon the individual innovativeness of nurses. The results from this study support previous literature suggesting that workplace relationships are positively related to the effort on an employee to be innovative. Knol and Van Linge (2009) investigated the relationships between empowerment and nurses' innovative behaviour and found that empowerment is statistically significant predictor of innovative behaviour. Despite the variety of the research perspectives and findings, what is undeniable is the empirical support for organisational climate's effect on healthcare workers' innovative behaviour. Thus we propose the following:

Hypothesis 1. *Organisational climate positively affects employees' innovative work behaviour.*

Organisation's openness to innovation and innovative work behaviour

The concept of openness to innovation used in this study refers to an organisation's attitude to be open to external environment and, more generally, to change and flexibility. It is an organisational trait that has become increasingly important for innovation dynamics, both at individual and organisational level. The focus on organisation's openness in studies of innovation reflects a wider trend in the research of firm behaviour that suggests that the network of relationships between an organisation and its external environment can play an important role in fostering innovation performance. In this trend, the seminal work of Cohen and Levinthal (1990) on absorptive capacity represented a milestone for studies on the links between organisation's ability to absorb external knowledge and innovation performance. Interacting with external sources, an organisation can learn from partners, acquire information and transform them in new knowledge to exploit in innovation processes.

The recent theory of employee-driven innovation (Høyrup, 2010), based on the assumption that all employees have the potential for creative thinking, and are able to contribute to innovation and change, highlights that orientation towards improvement, change and openness to new ideas, represent important organisational characteristics that increase employees' responsibility for change and innovation.

With reference to HC context and its increasing need for innovation, organisation's openness to external environment is becoming more and more relevant. In particular, the need to spread knowledge much more widely, bringing into the innovation process a wider range of stakeholders, such as providers, other hospitals, research centres, universities, communities, governments/payers, and mobilising their experience and creativity in the search for novel and sustainable solutions, is growing. This is also because healthcare organisations, are more and more becoming an open and complex system (Spaulding *et al.*, 2015), where networking and knowledge sharing are crucial factors for initiating and developing changes (e.g., new policies, procedures, practices or technologies).

At an individual level, the contact with heterogeneous stakeholders facilitates cognitive processes related to creativity and innovation, such as divergent, autonomous, and flexible thinking, and fosters innovation.

Together with the openness to external knowledge, also the continuous tendency of an organisation to improve work processes or forms of work organisation as well as employees' skills, contributes to encourage the individual propensity to engage in change and innovative activities. In particular, as outlined by Weiner (2009), when organisation's change commitment is high, organisational members are more likely to initiate change, exert greater effort in support of change, exhibit greater persistence in the face of obstacles during implementation, and develop actions supporting the change that exceed job requirements or role expectations.

In sum, the exposure to appropriate knowledge, an orientation towards change and adaptation to external environment, the organisational responsiveness to stakeholders' needs and a collective aspiration to continuous improvement within the organisational environment, can promote innovative potential of HC employees. Thus, we propose the following:

Hypothesis 2. *Organisation's openness to innovation positively affects employees' innovative work behaviour.*

Organisational climate and organisation's openness to innovation

In the last decades some studies have stressed that a positive organisational climate can promote organisational interest and efforts in keeping up with change and

Fostering Employees' Innovative Work Behaviour in Healthcare Organisations

innovation. In particular, these studies (e.g., Ahmed, 1998; Eby *et al.*, 2000; Isaksen *et al.*, 2003) outlined that an organisation where organisational climate encourages communication and a timely and accurate information sharing among employees, cultivates employees' capability in managing and solving problems, nurtures trust and guarantees equal opportunities for training and participation for employees, is more open to change and continuous development.

Additionally, some authors (e.g., Garcia Morales *et al.*, 2006), analysing the determinants of innovative conduct in organisations, have revealed that some components of organisational climate, such as leadership style and the organisational attention to people, encourage the generation and maintenance of organisational orientation toward creativity, change and innovation. Others scholars (Eby *et al.*, 2000; Weiner, 2009) have stressed the importance of flexible organisational policies and procedures and a positive organisational climate in promoting organisational readiness for change.

Based on the above the following hypothesis is proposed:

Hypothesis 3. *Organisational climate positively affects an organisation's openness to innovation.*

Taken together we propose the following:

Hypothesis 4. *An organisation's openness to innovation positively mediates the relationship between organisational climate and innovative work behaviour.*

Figure 1 details the proposed research hypotheses.

Method

In order to validate the proposed hypotheses, we conducted a survey in a large public Italian hospital, having the employee as the unit of analysis. The hospital

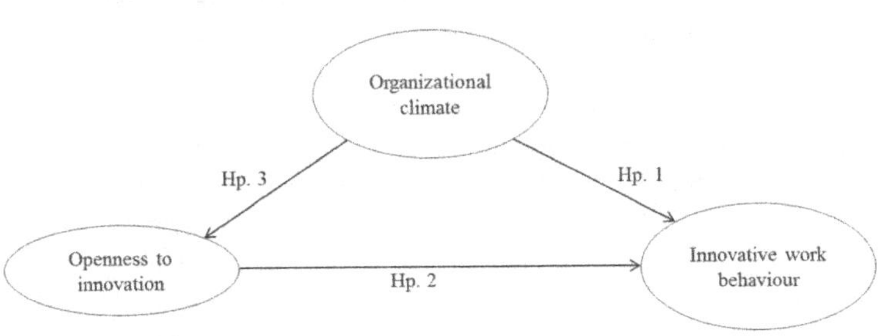

Fig. 1. Research framework.

counts 1,130 hospital beds, 1,500 employees, 36,000 hospitalisations per year, 47 complex operative units and 11 departments. Four focus groups were organised prior to survey administration. The aim of the focus groups was to gather information on the organisation and present the study's purpose.

The participants in the focus groups were department heads, heads of nursing, directors of wards, quality manager, responsible for quality at department level, physicians, nurses and technicians. The focus groups involved the hospital departments as follows: focus group I: oncology, nephrology–urology, neuroscience; focus group II: surgery, internal medicine, high specialties of heart and great vessels; focus group III: rehabilitation and long-term care; focus group IV: diagnostic and therapeutic services, accident and emergency, department of women's and children's health. A total of 80 health employees participated in the focus groups (i.e., 40% head nurses; 25% physicians, the rest others). The focus groups were facilitated by a moderator (researcher) and the HC quality manager. A researcher took field notes. Each focus group lasted an average of 45 min and a focus group guide was developed to facilitate the discussion and team working.

The focus groups revealed that HC workers perceive organisational climate as a factor which significantly influences the quality of the delivered service, their capacity to satisfy patient and productivity as well as the capacity to innovate. Additionally, the employees highlighted some dimensions of organisational climate that are particularly important for improving individual performance. In particular, they believe that to invest energy and extra efforts in their daily activities, they need to be motivated. The motivation, in turn, is perceived as closely related to performance assessment and management of the reward system as well as to an equal guarantee of career for all.

Moreover, discussions showed that the workers' interest in the change and innovation, is linked to a clear understanding of hospital's strategy as well as to the existence of an organisation open to experimentation and problem solving, tolerant of failure and with fair relationships among colleagues. The focus groups findings have corroborated the idea funding the study that healthcare workers' attitude to innovate is linked both to their perception of organisational climate and organisation's openness to change and new ideas.

The survey has involved most of departments which attended the focus groups. In particular, it has involved six departments: (1) High specialties of heart and great vessels; (2) Surgery; (3) Oncology; (4) Internal medicine; (5) Department of Women's and Children's Health; (6) Diagnostic and therapeutic services. The selection of these departments was carried out with the top management of the hospital.

Before implementing the survey, a small pre-test of the survey questionnaire was undertaken to solicit feedback from a panel of employees. Moreover, the

Fostering Employees' Innovative Work Behaviour in Healthcare Organisations

questionnaire has been submitted also to the hospital's quality department in order to obtain feedbacks and comments as well. No data were collected as part of this pilot as the purpose was simply to evaluate the acceptability and understandability of the questionnaire to respondents and enhance face validity of the measurement scales. Based on these feedbacks, some redundant or ambiguous items were modified or deleted. No new items were added. The final questionnaire comprised 41 items. In order to allay any suspicions and hence reduce response bias, prior to the survey administration all respondents were informed that responses would be kept completely confidential and results would have been shown in an aggregate form.

Sample

A total of 560 usable questionnaires were returned (response rate 51%). The sample encompassed various hospital's professionals such as physicians (18%), nurses (63%), technicians (12%), healthcare assistants (4%), and other (3%). We conducted a chi-square test in order to test whether the sample was representative of the hospital's population in terms of job category and no significant difference emerged.

Measures

All measures were five-point Likert-type scales derived from existing literature in the fields of organisational behaviour, innovation management, and HC management (see Appendix A for details of the measures).

Organisational climate. Different methods for evaluating organisational climate and operationalising its components have been proposed, however, few measures with demonstrated reliability and validity have been produced (Patterson *et al.*, 2005). Specifically referring to the HC sector, studies focusing on organisational c, imate and its evaluation have been very limited (Wienand *et al.*, 2007). In this study organisational climate measure is drawn from Wienand *et al.* (2007). It is a measure which has been validated in several Italian public hospitals and represents the most widely adopted instrument to measure climate in an HC setting. This proposed measure operationalises organisational climate as a second-order construct reflected by six first-order factors, such as: (1) Job satisfaction, (2) Organisational communication, (3) Perceived quality of care, (4) Team working and spirit, (5) Leadership style, (6) Performance assessment and rewarding system.

Organisation's openness to innovation. Perception of organisation's openness to innovation was adapted from Avallone and Paplomatas (2005). This measure describes, among others, the organisation's openness to the external environment and, more generally, to change and flexibility in the use of new technologies, the attitude to recognise and address the problems and mistakes of the past and to experiment new forms of organisations, the openness to customers' needs and requests, the development of innovative skills in employees, the establishment of collaborative relationships with other organisations.

Innovative work behaviour. Innovative work behaviour has been measured in a variety of ways in private sector organisations. However not all of the proposed approaches transfer appropriately from the private to the HC public sector. The most promising approach to measuring innovative work behaviour in this sector is that of self-reports or supervisor-reports of whether or not an employee contributed certain innovative behaviours from a list. The list of behaviours is often based on the literature on the stages of innovation (idea generation, idea promotion, and idea realisation). In line with the work of Scott and Bruce (1994), Janssen's (2000, 2001) proposed a scale with three items for each stage. He formulated items specifically tapping idea generation, idea promotion and idea implementation, but found strong correlations, and concluded that his items could best be combined and used as a single additive scale. In this study, we used the approach of Janssen (2000, 2001) by using his employees' self-rating of innovative work behaviour.

Control *variables.* We included several *control variables* that may influence the hypothesised relationships. Previous work has shown that organisational climate and innovative work behaviour can be significantly related to a number of demographic and position variables. We thus included: (i) *organisational tenure* (natural logarithm of years). People, who work for a longer period in their current job, are likely to develop skills that are relevant and specific to the domain, thereby, tackling problems in a more focussed and relevant way (Amabile, 1996); (ii) *job category* (dummy variables for physician, nurse, technician, HC assistant); task routineness and a low amount of discretion granted employees in performing their job have previously been reported to influence the relationship between climate and performance (Middlemist and Hitt, 1981); (iii) *gender* (dummy variable).

Analytical procedure

The proposed model was tested using the Partial Least Squares (PLS) approach for structural equations modelling. PLS has been shown to provide higher statistical power than covariance-based Structural Equation Model (SEM) (e.g., Lisrel) when dealing with samples of small or moderate size. Moreover, PLS does not make assumptions about data distributions to estimate model parameters, observation independence, or variable metrics. PLS generates estimates of standardised regression coefficients (beta values) for the model's paths, which are then used to measure relationships among latent variables. PLS also generates factor loadings for measurement items, which are interpretable similarly to loadings generated by principal component factor analysis. This study employed the SmartPLS software version 2.0. The model was analysed in two steps: firstly, the measurement model was assessed and the reliability, convergent and discriminant validity of the model constructs were evaluated; secondly, the structural model was evaluated by examining the size and significance of the path coefficients and the R^2 values of the dependent variables.

Common method variance. Since all data were collected from individual respondents in a cross-sectional study, the potential for common method variance (CMV) is a concern (Siemsen *et al.*, 2010). Following Podsakoff *et al.* (2003), we took procedural measures to minimise the impact of CMV by randomising the sequence of items in the survey, guaranteeing anonymity and confidentiality to respondents, emphasising that there were no correct or incorrect answers, asking respondents to provide independent and honest answers.

Additionally, in order to evaluate the extent to which CMV might influence our empirical findings, we carried out an analysis using a single-method-factor approach as suggested by Podsakoff *et al.* (2003) and Liang *et al.* (2007). Results of this test showed that CMV was not problematic (results of this test are available from the authors upon request).

Findings

Measurement model

Cronbach's alpha, composite reliability and average variance extracted (AVE) were calculated to assess the reliability of the constructs. All these coefficients were higher than the recommended thresholds thus supporting the reliability of all the measures adopted (Table 1). Also, convergent validity of the scales was supported, with loadings higher than 0.60 and highly statistically significant ($p > 0.001$). In order to assess the discriminant validity of the constructs using the PLS approach it is necessary that the square root of each factor's AVE is larger than its correlations with other factors. Table 2 shows that the square root of all the AVEs was larger than all other cross correlations, therefore supporting discriminant validity. Note that, coherently with Wienand *et al.* (2007), we modeled organisational climate as a second-order construct reflected by Job satisfaction, Organisational communication, Perceived quality, Team spirit, Performance assessment, Leadership style. Discriminant validity is supported for both the first-

Table 1. Descriptive statistics and reliability.

Construct	Mean	SD	AVE	Composite reliability	Cronbachs alpha
1. Job satisfaction	3.110	0.724	0.539	0.822	0.719
2. Organisational communication	2.157	0.757	0.666	0.888	0.833
3. Perceived quality	2.741	0.647	0.557	0.861	0.797
4. Team spirit	2.826	0.775	0.709	0.880	0.795
5. Performance assessment	2.023	0.620	0.587	0.945	0.936
6. Leadership style	2.485	0.859	0.633	0.957	0.950
7. Organisational climate	2.557	0.577	0.412	0.950	0.945
8. Innovative work behaviour	3.041	0.795	0.747	0.922	0.888
9. Openness to innovation	2.833	0.870	0.644	0.942	0.929

Table 2. Discriminant validity.

	1	2	3	4	5	6	7	8	9
1. Job satisfaction	0.734								
2. Organisational communication	0.470	0.816							
3. Perceived quality	0.513	0.496	0.746						
4. Team spirit	0.506	0.351	0.508	0.842					
5. Performance assessment	0.549	0.604	0.730	0.519	0.766				
6. Leadership style	0.642	0.517	0.624	0.668	0.696	0.796			
7. Organisational climate	0.701	0.714	0.832	0.659	0.947	0.781	0.642		
8. Innovative work behaviour	0.398	0.316	0.361	0.346	0.304	0.472	0.400	0.864	
9. Openness to innovation	0.511	0.358	0.526	0.499	0.565	0.718	0.548	0.502	0.802

Note: $N = 560$. On the diagonal the square root of the AVE.

order constructs of organisational climate and the second-order construct as well (see lower right quadrant in Table 2).

Structural model

Figure 2 shows the standardised PLS path coefficients and *t*-values.

The results of both the measurement and the structural models show that organisational climate is a second-order construct reflected by Job satisfaction, Organisational communication, Perception of quality of care, Team working and spirit, Leadership style, Performance assessment and rewarding system. Referring to the research hypotheses, Hypotheses 1 and 2 posit organisational climate and organisation's openness to innovation to positively affect employees' innovative work behaviour. The results show that organisational climate positively and significantly affects innovative work behaviour ($\beta = 0.142$, $p > 0.01$), thus

Fostering Employees' Innovative Work Behaviour in Healthcare Organisations

Fig. 2. Results of the structural model.

providing support for Hypothesis 1. The results also show that organisation's openness to innovation positively and significantly affects innovative work behaviour ($\beta = 0.400$, $p > 0.001$), thus providing support for Hypothesis 2. Hypothesis 3 suggests that organisational climate positively affects organisation's openness to innovation and our results provide support for this hypothesis ($\beta = 0.621$, $p > 0.001$). Finally, in order to test whether organisation's openness to innovation mediates the relationship between organisational climate and innovative work beahviour, the procedure proposed by Baron and Kenny (1986) was followed and adapted to SEM context by using the approach proposed by Bass *et al.* (2003). We firstly analysed a path model exclusively linking organisational climate to organisation's openness to innovation (Step 1). This model showed that organisational climate positively and significantly affects organisation's openness to innovation ($\beta = 0.628$, $p > 0.001$). Then we developed a model linking organisational climate to innovative work behaviour, without considering the effect of organisation's openness to innovation (Step 2). This model showed organisational climate to positively and significantly affect innovative work behaviour ($\beta = 0.392$, $p > 0.001$). Finally, (Step 3), we included organisation's openness to innovation in the model proposed in Step 2. Evidence of full mediation is present if organisational climate (the independent variable) is significant in Steps 1 and 2, but not significant in Step 3. Partial mediation is present if organisational climate (the independent variable) is significant in Steps 1, 2 and 3, but the strength of the relationship is reduced in Step 3 when compared to Step 2. As our results show the effect of organisational climate on innovative work behaviour is reduced from Step 2 to Step 3 (β value from 0.392 to 0.142), however the significant level of the beta coefficient — although reduced — still remains significant at $p > 0.01$. Taken together these results suggest that an organisation's openness to innovation partially mediates the effect of organisational climate on employees' innovative work behaviour. The proposed model explains 39% of the variance of organisation's openness to innovation and 27% of the variance of innovative work behaviour. Control variables did not show any significant relationship.

Conclusions and Implications

In this study, we developed and tested a model in which organisational climate was hypothesised to affect employees' innovative work behaviour directly and indirectly through employees' perception of organisation's openness to innovation. The rationale behind the study refers, on the one hand, to the increasing importance of innovation within HC organisations and, on the other hand, to the lack of studies exploring the link between organisational climate, openness to innovation and innovative work behaviour in HC organisations. Overall the results of this study lend support to the role of organisational climate and openness to innovation in fostering innovative behaviour of HC employees. Our findings show that organisational climate affects innovative work behaviour both directly and indirectly through organisation's openness to innovation. Specifically, the results highlight that an organisation's openness to innovation partially mediates the relationship between organisational climate and employees' innovative work behaviour. These findings support previous studies in this area (e.g., Amabile, 1996; Imran *et al.*, 2010) and extend existing lines of research concerning the importance of organisational climate for the dynamics surrounding innovation — and in particular individual innovation — in HC organisations. These results prove to be particularly valuable since innovative behaviour has received scant attention in the public sector, and in particular in HC, and studies have mainly focussed on individuals' innovative behaviour as intuitive problem-solving styles relatively difficult to change (Kessel *et al.*, 2012; Scott and Bruce, 1994). HC organisations have significantly increased their interest towards innovation conceived as a critical lever of improved and sustainable service. The results of this study suggest that in order to encourage employees' innovative behaviour, managers of HC organisations should strive to improve both organisational cliamte and organisation's openness to innovation. Managers need to be sensitive to the climate perceived by workers in daily activities and to the ways the organisation relates to the external environment in the search for novel and sustainable solutions. Our findings suggest that organisational climate can be modelled as a second-order construct reflected by job satisfaction, organisational communication, perception of quality of care, team working and spirit, leadership style, performance assessment and rewarding system. In such a view, managers should consider the multifaceted nature of organisational climate and be comprehensive in targeting the different climate factors. Therefore, HC managers should attempt to create conditions for an effective information and knowledge sharing within the organisation. Providing greater access to information gives employees a greater sense of personal meaning and influence within the organisation (Knight-Turvey, 2006) and can stimulate their innovative behaviour. Moreover in large, bureaucratic organisations the wide access to information and an effective communication are essential to support innovation dynamics (Patterson *et al.*, 2009). Managers should also build great awareness of continuous quality improvement among employees since this can create a significant commitment to improve the delivered service. Furthermore, managers should cultivate a diverse workforce and encourage the development of networking to promote knowledge sharing and innovative ways of working. This is because the cohesiveness of a work group determines the degree to which individuals believe that they can introduce ideas without personal censure and collaborative effort among peers is crucial to idea generation. In fact, even if a worker can be creative and generate ideas, implementation typically depends upon the approval, support and resources of others. Ensuring that the organisation's infrastructure is aligned with an innovative culture — i.e., the compensation and performance management systems recognize and reward those who engage in innovative behaviour — represents a further challenge for HC managers. Practice shows that organisations that actively promote and reward innovation are most effective at bringing individual innovation (Patterson *et al.*, 2009). However, looking at research literature the relation between reward and innovative work behaviour appears ambiguous. Some scholars (see Sanders *et al.*, 2010) argue that rewards seem to undermine employees' motivation to engage in innovative work behaviour at least when their motivation is intrinsic in nature. On the other hand, other scholars (e.g., Zhang and Begley, 2011) state that when organisations use compensation systems to signal their employees that extra role behaviours such as innovative work behaviour are recognised and valued, employees will then perceive the engagement in innovative behaviour as worthwhile. In a wider perspective it is arguable that the impact of reward on innovative behaviour mainly depends on the attitude that employees have towards innovative behaviour and how they perceive the use of compensation systems. Moreover, rewards are not necessarily financial. Practical support and valuing problem solving behaviour, tolerance of failure and valuing risk taking can be extremely effective in this policy area. Incorporating specific training and development interventions into current management development programmes to promote the behaviours that enhance innovative working, is a further issue that should capture managers' attention. These interventions should be directed also to shape a more motivating and collaborative leadership style, that encourages risk-taking among employees. Several studies show that leadership is a critical catalyst for innovative working (e.g., Patterson *et al.*, 2009). In order to promote innovative work behaviour, leaders should be more inspiring, motivating and collaborative, and able to generate a shared commitment amongst employees. Moreover, they should devote specific time for developing new ideas, offering informational feedback and engaging in creative goal setting. The research also suggests that an organisation's openness to innovation is conducive to employees' innovative behaviour. Therefore, building a work environment open to change, responsive to stakeholders' wants and needs, oriented to the development and acquisition of new skills, open to experimentation of new technologies and forms of organisation, oriented to the building and exploitation of internal and external networks as vital sources of innovation, represents a further managerial challenge to deal with.

Although the proposed model may be a useful tool for any HC organisation that considers organisational climate a core element to manage for improving its innovation capacity, we acknowledge some limitations on this study. First, while the hypothesised model represents a step forward previous studies in the field, we believe that the relationships among the investigated constructs are fairly complex. As such, future studies could expand the proposed model by introducing new factors at the individual level (e.g., employees' knowledge sharing behaviour) rather than at the organisational level (e.g., organisation's social capital; top management team behavioural integration) as well as exploring further moderation and mediation effects. Second, since the data collected in this study refer to a single institutional setting, the robustness and generalisability of findings should be tested in other HC contexts (e.g., palliative care organisations) or industries (e.g., manufacturing). Additionally, while the self-reported measure of innovative work behaviour might be more subtle than leader-scores (Janssen, 2000), the latter measure provides an assessment of innovative work behaviour that is procedurally independent of the participants' self-reports of job demands and perceived effort–reward fairness. Therefore, future research should consider the adoption of a supervisor assessment of employees' innovative behaviour. Finally, the cross-sectional design of this study precluded making inferences about causality, therefore future studies could employ longitudinal data in order to clarify the causal relations among the investigated variables.

Appendix A

Table A.1. Details of measures.

Organisational climate *Please assess to what extent the following statements characterise what your organisation practices* (1 = *Not at all*, 2 = *A little*, 3 = *Some what*, 4 = *A lot, and* 5 = *Very much*)

Factor	*Items*	*Factor*	*Items*
Job satisfaction	Recognition of one's on-the-job daily achievements Personal involvement in decision processes which could affect one's job Feeling of self-direction in daily work situations Job satisfaction	*Leadership style*	Consideration of the employees' opinions by the director of the unit when decisions are made Clarity of the incentive system in the unit Adequate management of internal conflicts Continuous education programs offered and promoted
Knowledge and communication of organisational objectives and assets	Knowledge of the organisational structure of the General Management Knowledge of the department's structure Knowledge of the organisation's action plan Knowledge of the organisation's mission and vision		Comprehensibility of projects and aims of the unit Propensity to advise others to work in the unit Clear aims stated by the unit's chief Participation in decisions undertaken within the unit
Performance assessment and rewarding systems	Clarity of the organisation's incentive system Concern of the General Management about the employees' needs Efficacy of the General Management's system of internal communication among the various sectors of the organisation		Support for improvement of competence Encouragement by the unit's chief to improve professional knowledge Simplicity of roles and assignment of tasks within the unit

Table A.1. (*Continued*)

Organisational climate *Please assess to what extent the following statements characterise what your organisation practices* (1 = *Not at all*, 2 = *A little*, 3 = *Some what*, 4 = *A lot, and* 5 = *Very much*)

Factor	*Items*	*Factor*	*Items*
	Clarity in the assignment of job specifications by General Management		Adequacy of technical equipment
	Recognition of good results by the organisation		Efficacious flow of information within the unit
	Aims clearly defined by the General Management	*Team working and spirit*	Propensity to teamwork within the unit
	Consistency between the incentive system and the organisation's goal		Propensity to teamwork within the organisation
	Ability of the system to reward individual performance		Concern for the patients' requests shown by the colleagues in the unit
	Clarity in the way the General Management evaluates performance	*Quality of care*	Concern of colleagues in the organisation about patients' needs
	Efficacious flow of information within the organisation		Concern of the General Management about customers' complaints
	Propensity to advise others to work in the organisation		Quality of services provided by the organisation
	Respect for enterprisingness within the organisation		Being proud to work in the organisation
			Possibility of decision making for the chiefs of the units

Table A.1. (*Continued*)

Innovative work behaviour *Please assess in your job how often you (1 = never 2 = occasionally 3 = fairly often 4 = often 5 = always)*		***Openness to innovation*** *Please assess to what extent the following statements characterise what your organisation practices (1 = Not at all, 2 = A little, 3 = Some what, 4 = A lot, and 5 = Very much)*	
Factor	*Items*	*Factor*	*Items*
Innovative work behaviour	Generate original solutions for problems Mobilize support for innovative ideas Search out new working methods, techniques, or instruments Transform innovative ideas into useful applications	*Openness to innovation*	Improving work processes Benchmarking with other organisations Acknowledging and facing problems and past mistakes Meeting customers 'requests Adding new professionals Developing employees' innovative competencies Establishing collaborative relationships with other organisations Experimenting with new form of work organisation

References

Abbey, A and J Dickson (1983). R&D work climate and innovation in semiconductors. *Academy of Management Journal*, 26, 362–368.

Ahmed, PK (1998). Culture and climate for innovation. *European Journal of Innovation Management*, 1(1), 30–43.

Akenroye, TO (2012). Factors influencing innovation in healthcare: A conceptual synthesis. *The Innovation Journal*, 17(2), 1.

Amabile, T and SS Gryskiewicz (1987). Creativity in the R&D laboratory. Center for Creative Leadership.

Amabile, TM (1996). *Creativity in Context*. Boulder: Westview Press.

Åmo, B (2006). Employee innovation behaviour in health care: The influence from management and colleagues. *International Nursing Review*, 53(3), 231–237.

Anderson, NR and MA West (1998). Measuring climate for work group innovation: Development and validation of the team climate inventory. *Journal of Organizational Behavior: The International Journal of Industrial, Occupational and Organizational Psychology and Behavior*, 19(3), 235–258.

Anderson, N, CK De Dreu and BA Nijstad (2004). The routinization of innovation research: A constructively critical review of the state-of-the-science. *Journal of Organizational Behavior*, 25(2), 147–173.

Asurakkody, TA and SY Shin (2018). Innovative behavior in nursing context: A concept analysis. *Asian Nursing Research*, 12(4), 237–244.

Avallone, F and A Paplomatas (2005). *Salute Organizzativa: Psicologia del Benessere nei Contesti Lavorativi*. Milano: Raffaello Cortina Editore.

Axtell, CM, DJ Holman, KL Unsworth, TD Wall, PE Waterson and E Harrington (2000). Shop-floor innovation: Facilitating the suggestion and implementation of ideas. *Journal of Occupational and Organizational Psychology*, 73, 265–285.

Bagheri, A and M Akbari (2018). The impact of entrepreneurial leadership on nurses' innovation behavior. *Journal of Nursing Scholarship*, 50(1), 28–35.

Barlow, J (2017). *Managing Innovation in Healthcare*. Singapore: World Scientific.

Baron, RM and DA Kenny (1986). The Moderator-mediator variable distinction in social psychological research: Conceptual, strategic, and statistical considerations. *Journal of Personality and Social Psychology*, 516, 1173–1182.

Bass, BM, BJ Avolio, DI Jung and Y Berson (2003). Predicting unit performance by assessing transformational and transactional leadership. *Journal of Applied Psychology*, 88(2), 207–218.

Bock, GW, RW Zmud, YG Kim and JN Lee (2005). Behavioral intention formation in knowledge sharing: Examining the roles of extrinsic motivators, social-psychological forces, and organizational climate. *MIS Quarterly*, 29(1), 87–111.

Chang, LC, CH Liu and EHW Yen (2008). Effects of an empowerment-based education program for public health nurses in Taiwan. *Journal of Clinical Nursing*, 17(20), 2782–2790.

Fostering Employees' Innovative Work Behaviour in Healthcare Organisations

Cohen, WM and DA Levinthal (1990). Absorptive capacity: A new perspective on learning and innovation. *Administrative Science Quarterly*, 35(1), 128–152.

Dawson, JF, V González-Romá, A Davis and MA West (2008). Organizational climate and climate strength in UK hospitals. *European Journal of Work and Organizational Psychology*, 17(1), 89–111.

De Jong, JPJ and DN Den Hartog (2007). How leaders influence employees' innovative behavior. *European Journal of Innovation Management*, 10(1), 41–64.

De Jong, JPJ and DN Den Hartog (2008). *Innovative Work Behavior: Measurement and Validation*. Zoetermeer: IEM.

Eby, LT, DM Adams, JEA Russel and SH Gaby (2000). Perceptions of organizational readiness: Factor related to employees' reactions to the implementation of team based selling. *Human Relation*, 53, 419–442.

Farr, JL and CM Ford (1990). Individual innovation. In *Innovation and Creativity at Work: Psychological and Organizational Strategies*, MA West and JL Farr (Eds.), pp. 63–80. Oxford, England: John Wiley & Sons.

Fosfuri, A and JA Tribó (2008). Exploring the antecedents of potential absorptive capacity and its impact on innovation performance. *Omega*, 36(2), 173–187.

Getz, I and AG Robinson (2003). Innovate or die: Is that a fact?, *Creativity and Innovation Management*, 12(3), 130–136.

Høyrup, S (2010). Employee-driven innovation and workplace learning: Basic concepts, approaches and themes. *Transfer: European Review of Labour and Research*, 16, 143–154.

Imran, R, T Saeed and A Fatima (2010). Organizational climate as a predictor of innovative work behavior. *African Journal of Business Management*, 4(15), 3337–3343.

Isaksen, SG, KJ Lauer and GV Wilson (2003). An examination of the relationship between personality type and cognitive style. *Creativity Research Journal*, 15(4), 343–354.

James, LR and MD McIntyre (1996). *Perceptions of Organizational Climate. Individual Differences and Behavior in Organizations*, pp. 416–450, San Francisco: Jossey–Bass.

Janssen, O (2000). Job demands, perceptions of effort-reward fairness, and innovative work behavior. *Journal of Occupational and Organizational Psychology*, 73, 287–302.

Janssen, O (2001). Fairness perceptions as a moderator in the curvilinear relationships between job demands, and job performance and job satisfaction. *Academy of Management Journal*, 44, 1039–1050.

Kanter, M (2011). Why Innovation Is So Hard in Health Care - and How to Do It Anyway. Retrieved 31, January 2015, Available at: http://blogs.hbr.org/innovations-in-health-care/2011/02/why-innovation-is-so-hard-in-h.html.

Kessel, M, H Hannemann-Weber and J Kratzer (2012). Innovative work behavior in healthcare: The benefit of operational guidelines in the treatment of rare diseases. *Health Policy*, 105, 146–153.

Knight-Turvey, N (2006). Influencing employee innovation through structural empowerment initiatives: The need to feel empowered. *Entrepreneurship Theory and Practice*, 43, 313–324.

Knol, J and R Van Linge (2009). Innovative behaviour: The effect of structural and psychological empowerment on nurses. *Journal of Advanced Nursing*, 65(2), 359–370.

Länsisalmi, H, M Kivimäki and R Ruoranen (2006). Innovation in healthcare: A systematic review of recent research. *Nursing Science Quarterly*, 19(1), 66–72.

Liang, H, N Saraf, Q Hu and Y Xue (2007). Assimilation of enterprise systems: The effect of institutional pressures and the mediating role of top management. *MIS Quarterly*, 31(1), 59–87.

Middlemist, R and M Hitt (1981). Technology as a moderator of the relationship between perceived work environment and subunit effectiveness. *Human Relations*, 34, 517–532.

Morales, VJ, FJ Llorens-Montes and AJ Verdu-Jover (2006). Antecedents and consequences of organizational innovation and organizational learning in entrepreneurship. *Industrial Management & Data Systems*, 106(1), 21–42.

Moreira, MR, M Gherman and PS Sousa (2017). Does innovation influence the performance of healthcare organizations? *Innovation*, 19(3), 335–352.

Neal, A, MA Griffin and PM Hart (2000). The impact of organizational climate on safety climate and individual behavior. *Safety Science*, 34(1–3), 99–109.

Oldham, G and A Cummings (1996). Employee creativity: Personal and contextual factors at work. *The Academy of Management Journal*, 39(3), 607–634.

Omachonu, V and N Einspruch (2010). Innovation in healthcare delivery systems: A conceptual framework. *The Innovation Journal: The Public Sector Innovation Journal*, 15(1), 1–20.

Patterson, F, M Kerrin, G Gatto-Roissard and P Coan (2009). Everyday innovation how to enhance innovative working in employees and organizations, Nesta Report, December.

Patterson, MG, MA West, VJ Shackleton, JF Dawson, R Lawthom, S Maitlis, DL Robinson and AM Wallace (2005). Validating the organizational climate measure: Links to managerial practices, productivity and innovation. *Journal of Organizational Behaviour*, 26(4), 379–408.

Plsek, P (2003). Complexity and the adoption of innovation in health care. *Accelerating Quality Improvement in Health Care: Strategies to Accelerate the Diffusion of Evidence-Based Innovations*. Washington, DC: National Institute for Healthcare Management Foundation and National Committee for Quality in Health Care.

Podsakoff, PM, SB MacKenzie, JY Lee and NP Podsakoff (2003). Common method biases in behavioral research: A critical review of the literature and recommended remedies. *Journal of Applied Psychology*, 88(5), 879–903.

Radaelli, G, E Lettieri, M Mura and N Spiller (2014). Knowledge sharing and innovative work behaviour in healthcare: A micro-level investigation of direct and indirect effects. *Creativity and Innovation Management*, 23(4), 400–414.

Sanders, K and H Shipton (2012). The relationship between transformational leadership and innovative behaviour in a healthcare context: A team learning versus a cohesion perspective. *European Journal of International Management*, 6(1), 83–100.

Sanders, K, M Moorkamp, N Tprka, S Groeneveld and C Goeneveld (2010). How to support innovative behaviour? The role of LMX and satisfaction with HR practices. *Technology and Investment*, 1, 59–68.

Schneider, B, D Bowen, ME Erhart and KM Holcombe (2000). The climate for service: Evolution of a construct. In *Handbook of Organizational Culture and Climate*, NM Ashkanasy, C Wilderom and MF Peterson (Eds.), Thousand Oaks: Sage.

Scott, SG and RA Bruce (1994). Determinants of innovative behavior: A path model of individual innovation in the workplace. *Academy of Management Journal*, 37(3), 580–607.

Shalley, CE, J Zhou and GR Oldham (2004). The effects of personal and contextual characteristics on creativity: Where should we go from here? *Journal of Management*, 30(6), 933–958.

Shanker, R, R Bhanugopan, BI Van der Heijden and M Farrell (2017). Organizational climate for innovation and organizational performance: The mediating effect of innovative work behavior. *Journal of Vocational Behavior*, 100, 67–77.

Siegel, S and W Kaemmerer (1978). Measuring the perceived support for innovation in organizations. *Journal of Applied Psychology*, 63, 553–562.

Siemsen, E, A Roth and P Oliveira (2010). Common method bias in regression models with linear, quadratic, and interaction effects. *Organizational research methods*, 13(3), 456–476.

Spaulding, A, BA Kash, CE Johnson and L Gamm (2017). Organizational capacity for change in health care: Development and validation of a scale. *Health Care Management Review*, 42(2), 151–161.

Thakur, R, SH Hsu and G Fontenot (2012). Innovation in healthcare: Issues and future trends. *Journal of Business Research*, 65(4), 562–569.

Varkey, P, A Horne and KE Bennet (2008). Innovation in health care: A primer. *American Journal of Medical Quality*, 23(5), 382–388.

Wang, CL and Ahmed, PK (2007). Dynamic capabilities: A review and research agenda. *International Journal of Management Reviews*, 9(1), 31–51.

Weiner, BJ (2009). A theory of organizational readiness for change. *Implementation Science*, 4(1), 67.

West, MA (2002). Sparkling fountains or stagnant ponds: An integrative model of creativity and innovation implementation in work groups. *Applied Psychology*, 51(3), 355–387.

Wienand, U, R Cinotti, A Nicoli and M Bisagni (2007). Evaluating the organisational climate in Italian public healthcare institutions by means of a questionnaire. *BMC Health Service Research*, 7, 73, Available at: http://www.biomedcentral.com/1472-6963/7/73.

Wolf, DAP, CN Dulmus and E Maguin (2012). Empirically supported treatment's impact on organizational culture and climate. *Research on Social Work Practice*, 22(6), 665–671.

Xerri, MJ and SR Reid (2018). Human resources and innovative behaviour: Improving nursing performance. *International Journal of Innovation Management*, 22(2), 1850019.

Xerri, M (2013). Workplace relationships and the innovative behaviour of nursing employees: A social exchange perspective. *Asia Pacific Journal of Human Resources*, 51(1), 103–123.

Xerri, M (2013). Workplace relationships and the innovative behaviour of nursing employees: A social exchange perspective. *Asia Pacific Journal of Human Resources*, 51(1), 103–123.

Zhang, Y and T Begley (2011). Perceived organizational climate, knowledge transfer and innovation in China-based research and development companies. *The International Journal of Human Resource Management*, 22(1), 34–56.

Chapter 8

INDIVIDUAL INNOVATIVE WORK BEHAVIOUR: EFFECTS OF PERSONALITY, TEAM LEADERSHIP AND CLIMATE IN THE US CONTEXT[§]

ABDELRAHMAN ZURAIK

Middle East University (MEU)
Queen Alia Airport Street, Amman, Jordan
dr.a.zuraik@gmail.com

LOUISE KELLY[*] and LOREN R. DYCK[†]

University of La Verne, 1950 3rd St.
La Verne, CA 91750, United States
[*]lkelly@laverne.edu
[†]ldyck@laverne.edu

Published 15 January 2020

This paper is the first to empirically investigate the connections between the Big Five personality factors, ambidextrous team leadership, organisational climate of US workers that supports innovation, and individual innovative work behaviour. A self-report survey was used to obtain data from 215 team members in US-based corporations. We provide an empirically tested model of the positive influence of Openness to Experiences, Extraversion and Conscientiousness personality traits on individual innovative work behaviour. Results also confirm that supervisors' leadership behaviours and a supportive organisational climate of innovation have a moderating influence on this set of relationships. Individuals can develop their individual innovative work behaviour. Supervisors can adopt higher levels of opening behaviours and executives can create a climate supportive of innovation to boost individual innovative work behaviour. This study further demonstrates that Big Five personality traits interact with supervisor behaviours and a supportive climate to foster individual innovative work behaviour.

Keywords: Individual innovative work behaviour; ambidextrous leadership; creativity; personality traits; team leader behaviours; innovation; Big Five; innovation climate.

[§]This article originally appeared in *International Journal of Innovation Management*, **24** 2050078-1-30 © 2020 World Scientific Publishing Europe Ltd.

Introduction

Some literature highlights employee individual personality characteristics as significant drivers of innovation outcomes (Ali, 2019; Sackett *et al.*, 2017). However, other research suggests that models combining personality or individual factors with organisational factors are the best way to explain innovation outcomes (Jeong and Shin, 2019; Liu *et al.*, 2017; Martinaityte *et al.*, 2019). Specifically, this present research examines the interaction of individual factors with contextual variables, such as a climate supportive of innovation. Combining the individual and contextual factors can give a fuller explanation of innovation outcomes (Anderson *et al.*, 2014; Mansfield and Wagner, 1975). This argument is consistent with the multi-dimensional measure of individual innovation behaviour delineated by Kleysen and Street (2001), whose' finding suggests that integrated models, i.e., ones that combine individual factors with organisational factors, have greater explanatory power for innovation outcomes.

The purpose of this present research is to examine innovation at the level of individual employee contribution. Specifically, in this research, we examine the role of individual team members and what drives individual innovative work behaviour. This study considers individual personality factors as well as organisational contextual factors that contribute to individual innovative work behaviour.

The current research looks at individual innovative work behaviour in the context of the United States (US). The US context puts a high value on an individualistic culture which provides a contrast to many countries in the world that have more of a collectivist orientation. The US score according to Hofstede's model is the highest at 91 in the individualism dimension (Clearly Cultural, 2019). In addition, the US economy is designed to be more of a free market economy and lacks many of the social programmes found in social democracies such as Canada, Australia or much of Western Europe. This means there is an even greater emphasis on the role of the individual and the individual's impact on economic and business outcomes (Christie *et al.*, 2003). Therefore, in the US free market economy, there is an emphasis on the empowerment of individuals (Rinne *et al.*, 2012). The US consistently ranks in the top 10 of the most innovative countries in the world (Global Innovation Index, 2019). Finally, US culture is further defined by having a lower power distance using Hofstede's model, with a low power distance index score of 40, which puts the US in the middle as compared with other countries. As such, the US is an ideal setting for studying the factors that drive individual work behaviour (Buda and Elsayed-Elkhouly, 1998).

Innovation as a People-Driven Process

Innovation is defined as "any idea, practice or material artefact perceived to be new by the relevant unit of adoption" (Zaltman *et al.*, 1973, p. 158). It is an innovation even if it existed before the adopter's awareness of it (Rogers, 1995). Therefore, innovation is a "people-intensive business process" (Kuczmarski, 1996, p. 91).

Van de Ven and Poole (2000) refer to the innovation process as a "temporal sequence of events that occur as people interact with others to develop and implement their innovation ideas within an institutional context" (p. 32). As a multistep discontinuous process, innovation begins with ideation or idea generation in response to a problem. The idea then gets developed or "elaborated," moves through the pursuit of sponsors or champions to promote the idea, and ends with the implementation of the innovation (Perry-Smith and Mannucci, 2017). However, it is not a lock-step process, yet not entirely random either (Caniëls *et al.*, 2014). Van de Ven *et al.* (1999) call it an "innovation journey" that involves nonlinear dynamic systems with recurring patterns that occur, over time, of divergent behaviours, such as creating ideas paired with convergent actions such as implementing ideas.

As part of this nonlinear cycle, Schroeder *et al.* (2000) found the innovation process begins with a "shock" caused by some significant change to the organisation such as new leadership or an operational crisis to initiate innovation action and gain people's attention. Managing people's attention is a central problem in the management of innovation as people tend to protect existing processes instead of paying attention to new ones, especially in successful organisations (Van de Ven, 1986). To facilitate this attention-getting shock, Katz (1964) states that organisations must encourage "innovative and spontaneous behaviour" (p. 132) from its employees to ensure the organisation's ability to manage the unexpected. Organisations that motivate innovative practices are more likely to see them occur (Amabile, 1988).

However, individual innovative work behaviour is also a function of personal characteristics, ability and the environment (Choi, 2004; Angle, 2000). Innovative behaviour is often associated with creativity. However, as we have defined in our study, the innovation process includes both the creation of new ideas and the implementation of them (West, 2002). Effectively then, creativity adds to the front-end of the innovation process with divergent thinking and the creation of new ideas. However, the open question that remains is to determine how personality impacts individual innovative work behaviour.

Personality and Individual Innovative Work Behaviour

The role of different personality traits in individual innovation has a long history (Sackett *et al.*, 2017). Major literature reviews conducted 50 years ago

(Stein, 1968) document the association between personality and individual innovative work behaviour. Developing an organising framework for the plethora of personality traits was an important step in linking personality and individual innovative work behaviour. The model that subsequently emerged as an accepted taxonomy of personality traits is called the "Big Five" which currently remains as the most influential model (Ali, 2019; Goldberg, 1981; Rossberger, 2014).

The Big Five is inclusive of five dimensions and is often referred to as the Five Factor Model (Goldberg, 1993). The five factors are as follows:

(I) Extraversion or surgency (talkative, assertive and energetic);
(II) Agreeableness (good-natured, cooperative and trustful);
(III) Conscientiousness (orderly, responsible and dependable);
(IV) Emotional stability vs. neuroticism (calm, not neurotic and not easily upset);
(V) Intellect or Openness (intellectual, imaginative and independent-minded) (John and Srivastava, 1999, p. 105).

Findings from personality and individual innovation studies

Meta-analyses confirm personality as an individual difference in the workplace and link personality to components of the innovation process such as creativity thereby raising interest in identifying the personality traits associated with individual innovative work behaviour (Sackett *et al.*, 2017). Extraversion is a personality trait of individuals who are talkative and assertive with a high activity level (Goldberg, 1993). These are warm, enthusiastic and outgoing individuals who seek to experience positive versus negative emotions (Rossberger, 2014) which can lead to behaviour change (Dyck, 2017, 2018). Specifically, prior research strongly supports a positive association between Extraversion and individual innovative work behaviour (Ali, 2019; Guo *et al.*, 2017; King *et al.*, 1996; Patterson and Zibarras, 2017).

Therefore, we predict that Extraversion will positively impact individual innovative work behaviour.

Hypothesis 1a: *Extraversion personality has a positive relationship with individual innovative work behaviour.*

However, the literature is less clear and consistent concerning Agreeableness, Conscientiousness and Emotional Stability and their respective associations with individual innovative work behaviour. For instance, King *et al.* (1996) found that Agreeableness not only was negatively associated with creative accomplishments and explained that individuals high in agreeableness may be "nice" people, but also conflict avoidant and conformity seeking versus demonstrating independent behaviour. However, the results from Guo *et al.* (2017) study lead the researchers to reject the hypothesis that Agreeableness is negatively related to individual innovation despite yet further prior work by Furnham *et al.* (2009) who did find a negative relationship between Agreeableness and divergent thinking.

Further complicating the understanding of Agreeableness, is Hsieh *et al.*'s (2011) study which found a significant positive effect on individual innovative work behaviour for technology innovations. Ali (2018) likewise found a significant positive association between Agreeableness and individual innovative work behaviour. Steel *et al.* (2012) explain the findings of a positive relationship between Agreeableness and individual innovation as individuals with high levels of Agreeableness demonstrate an ability to manage social networks and successfully interact with key stakeholders to build trust and cooperation necessary for innovation implementation.

Therefore, we propose a non-directional relationship between Agreeableness and individual innovative work behaviour.

Hypothesis 1b: *Agreeableness personality trait has a relationship with individual innovative work behaviour.*

Mixed findings continue in the literature also for Conscientiousness. These inconsistent study results for Conscientiousness can be explained, at least in part, by the broad array of characteristics or facets which the domain represents (Costa and McCrae, 1995). Conscientious individuals prefer intentionality versus spontaneity (Patterson and Zibarras, 2017) and are dutiful or dependable as well as achievement oriented (Moon, 2001). Furthermore, Conscientious individuals are often seen as intelligent, persistent and self-disciplined with a long-term view (Ali, 2019; Rossberger, 2014).

At face value, all these facets of Conscientiousness seem likely to be positively associated with individual innovative work behaviour. Some studies have supported this assertion such as Ali (2018) who found a positive and significant association between Conscientiousness and individual innovative work behaviour. Earlier researches (Hsieh *et al.*, 2011; Taggar, 2002) have also demonstrated that Conscientiousness can predict individual innovative behaviour especially certain facets of Conscientiousness such as drive, ambition and perseverance.

However, yet other research has found a negative association between Conscientiousness and individual innovative work behaviour (Feist, 1998) especially at moderate and high levels of creativity (King *et al.*, 1996). In explaining their finding of a negative relationship between Conscientiousness and individual innovation, Guo *et al.* (2017) state that Conscientious individuals may prefer to avoid change and keep their routines. Researchers with similar findings

(Feist, 1998; Sung and Choi, 2009), likewise identify impulse control and rule following by conscientious individuals as reasons for avoiding change and not exploring new ideas.

Therefore, we propose a non-directional relationship between Conscientiousness and individual innovative work behaviour.

Hypothesis 1c: *Conscientiousness personality trait has a relationship with individual innovative work behaviour.*

The final personality trait with inconclusive results regarding its association with individual innovative work behaviour is Emotional Stability or its inverse, Neuroticism. Feist (1998) found that artistic individuals were more neurotic and displayed characteristics such as anxiety, insecurity and excitability in comparison to non-artistic individuals who were less neurotic and displayed Emotional Stability characteristics such as calmness, ego strength and personal adjustment. Gelade (1997) also found that advertising and design creatives were significantly more neurotic than professionals and managers in non-creative occupations. However, subsequently, Gelade (2002) determined that creative style or the degree to which an individual's problem-solving approach is unconventional and results in unorthodox ideas is unrelated to Neuroticism. Likewise, King *et al.* (1996) found that Neuroticism was unrelated to either creative ability or creative achievements.

In contrast to the positive results and study findings of no relationship, there is lots of evidence that there is a negative relationship between neuroticism and individual innovative work behaviour. For instance, Ali (2018), Guo *et al.* (2017), Hsieh *et al.* (2011), indicate that more neurotic individuals demonstrate less individual innovative work behaviour than less neurotic individuals. Guo *et al.* (2017) explains that an individual's ability to demonstrate Emotional Stability by remaining calm despite time and budget pressures may facilitate individual innovative behaviour. The foregoing findings regarding Emotional Stability tend to indicate that individual innovative work behaviour is not dependent upon neurotic or emotionally stable behaviour.

Therefore, we propose a non-directional relationship between Emotional Stability and individual innovative work behaviour.

Hypothesis 1d: *Emotional Stability personality trait has a relationship with individual innovative work behaviour.*

Taken together the inconsistent associations between individual innovative work behaviour and Agreeableness, Conscientiousness and Emotional Stability, respectively, highlight the need to provide more clarity for these dimensions of personality and their possible effects on individual innovative work behaviour.

Early work by McCrae (1987) established that the personality domain of Openness to Experiences is related to the creativity component or initial idea-generating phase of the individual innovation process along the path to new idea implementation. In major literature reviews decades later (Hammond *et al.*, 2011; Sackett *et al.*, 2017), Openness to Experiences was confirmed as the best predictor of innovative behaviours. For administrative innovations such as in the provision of hotel services, Yesil and Sozbilir (2013) found Openness to Experiences positively associated with individual innovation behaviour. In recent research by Ali (2018), Openness to Experiences was also positively related to individual innovation behaviour. Guo *et al.* (2017) provide further support in a study that showed Openness to Experiences was positively related to individual creativity. Study participants who like to explore, and who are divergent thinkers, curious, open-minded and unconventional tend to score high on Openness to Experiences (Guo *et al.*, 2017; McCrae, 1987). Overall, the research suggests that Openness to Experiences is perhaps the most important personality trait for individual innovation behaviour in the workplace.

Therefore, we propose that Openness to Experiences will positively impact individual innovative work behaviour.

Hypothesis 1e: *Openness to Experiences personality trait has a positive relationship with individual innovative work behaviour.*

Individual Innovation and Team Leadership

An individual's innovation contribution does not occur in a vacuum because most innovation occurs in teams. Individual innovation is influenced by team processes and team leadership (Taggar, 2002). In particular, team leadership can be expected to have an influence on an individual's innovation outcomes (Katzenbach and Smith, 2015; Eisenbeiss *et al.*, 2008). The relationship among team members and with their team leader and leadership clarity on expectations at different stages of the innovation process, have been linked to individual innovation outcomes (Yuan and Woodman, 2010; West *et al.*, 2003). Team leader influence includes the clarity of leadership as perceived by the team members (West, 2002). This concept of clarity works well with the findings of Zacher and Rosing (2015), where team member innovation is highest when the complementary leadership behaviours of opening and closing are high and well-defined.

When a leader communicates clearly to the team members that this is the time in the innovation process to generate unfettered new ideas, employees will be less risk-averse and more emboldened to share their perspectives (Zuraik and Kelly, 2019).

Likewise, employees will be more willing to engage in innovation implementation behaviour when a leader creates clarity that, due to the time constraints of the project, for instance, now is the time to close in on an implementation plan and assign roles, responsibilities and deadlines. According to Zacher and Rosing (2015), it is the clarity and interaction of the two complementary leadership behaviours that produce team innovation. We use this finding and extrapolate it to the individual innovation outcome, predicting that there will be a moderating impact of the team leadership style on the relationship between personality and individual innovation. Ambidextrous leadership provides some insight as to how the leader's choice impact individual innovation outcomes.

Rosing *et al.*'s (2011) model of team leader behaviour and innovation introduces a team ambidextrous leadership dimension as a determinant of team innovation. Specifically, the model introduces the concept of opening and closing behaviour of the team lead as a driver of team innovation performance. Opening behaviour (OB) encourages that blue-sky, opened ended and exploratory thinking whereas closing behaviour (CB) refers to the assigning of roles, tasks, milestones and deliverables that form an essential part of project planning in team performance. The CB of the team leader corresponds to Hirst *et al.*'s (2011) identification of the bureaucratic practices of centralisation and formalisation. OB, on the other hand in the Rosing *et al.* model, speaks to the divergent, exploratory behaviour that is unfettered by bureaucratic processes, or at least is not unduly constrained by risk management or risk aversion. Many of the dimensions of OB are like the creativity dimension found in much of the individual innovation behaviour literature. According to Rosing *et al.*'s work, the pursuit of innovation is best aided by ambidextrous team leadership which is a concept that integrates OB and CB at the team leadership level (Rosing *et al.*, 2011). However, Rosing *et al.* (2011) argue that both OB and CBs are necessary for effective innovation.

Reflecting on all the personality dimensions, one can infer that OB with its exploratory stance strengthens the innovation outcomes of all five personality dimensions. The expansive energy of the OB helps to unleash and extend the positive innovation outcomes from personality factors such as Openness to new Experiences and Extraversion.

In contrast, the CBs can be seen as detrimental to the positive and expansive effect of the personality dimensions. For example, if a team lead introduces rules, roles, deadlines and other control functions, although this may be positive for efficiency and innovation implementation behaviours, it could have a dampening down effect on the innovation process of those fuelled by a desire and Openness to new experience. Ultimately, many who have personality dimensions closely linked to innovation may chafe and feel resentful with the typical, bureaucratic constraints of the project of the project planning process such as assigning roles and deadlines to team members. Although these common sense CBs are to be expected in the innovation process, they can dampen down the positive effect of pro-innovation personality characteristics of Openness to new Experience and Extraversion, among others.

In the research to date, there has been no exploration of the interaction of team leader ambidextrous behaviours and team members personality traits, and how this might influence individuals' innovative work behaviours. In other words, how can team leader opening and CBs moderate the relationship between the individual team members' personality traits and individual team members' innovative work behaviour? Therefore, we propose:

Hypothesis 2a: *Team leader OB moderates the relationship between the individual team members' personality traits and individual team members' innovative work behaviour.*

Hypothesis 2b: *Team leader closing behaviour moderates the relationship between the individual team members' personality traits and individual team members' innovative work behaviour.*

Regarding Hypotheses 2a and 2b, it is noteworthy that we are recognising team leader OB and team leader CB as two separate constructs and measure them with two separate unipolar scales as we explain in the Methods section. Therefore, a team leader who does not practice OBs, may or may not practice CBs. Likewise, a team leader who does not practice CBs, may or may not practice OBs.

Climate

From a system theory perspective, teams do not operate in a vacuum but rather in an environmental and organisational context (Kast and Rosenzweig, 1972; Rice, 2013). The effect of the contextual factor of climate on individual employee performance is well documented (Calantone *et al.*, 2002; Gibson and Birkinshaw, 2004). There is significant research that examines the impact of climate on employee outcomes such as morale, engagement and performance (Marinova *et al.*, 2018; Salanova *et al.*, 2005). Pirola-Merlo and Mann (2004) found that an organisation's climate for creativity and innovation is a significant factor that directly influences an individual team member's innovation.

In organisational climate where innovative job performance is rewarded and valued, there is a higher level of individual innovative work behaviour (Anderson *et al.*, 2014). The perceived organisational support, whether financial or emotional, for innovation, is a crucial driver of the climate for innovation (Anderson and West, 1998).

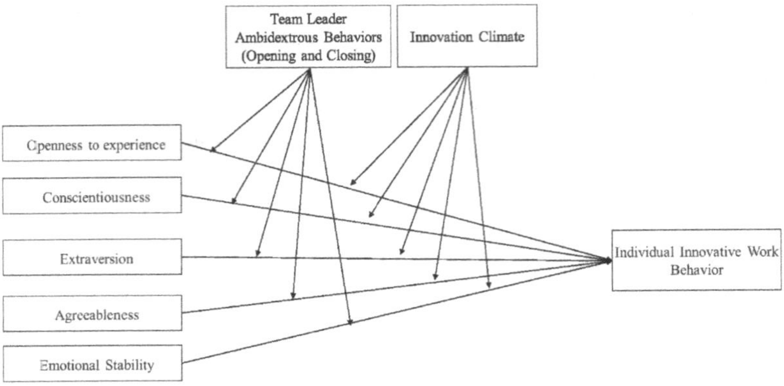

Fig. 1. The research model.

There are individual factors (Scott and Bruce, 1994) and contextual factors (Lin, 2007) which influence individual innovative work behaviour. Workplace climate supportive of innovation is a key determinant of individual innovative behaviour (Scott and Bruce, 1994; Ahmed, 1998). Climate for innovation has a significant impact on the relationship between individual personality factors and individual innovative work behaviour. Therefore, we expect:

Hypothesis 3: *Innovation climate moderates the relationship between an individual team member's personality dimensions and their individual innovative work behaviour.*

The research model for our study is shown in Fig. 1.

Method

A quantitative approach was used for analysing the data collected for hypothesis testing. The main goal of this paper was to test whether the ambidextrous behaviours of the team leader combined within a supportive innovation climate can moderate the relationship between a team members' personality traits and their individual innovative work behaviour. Self-reported scores from a Big Five dimensions instrument, self-report scores from an organisational innovation climate instrument, self-report scores from a team leader's opening and CBs instrument and self-reported scores from an individual innovative work behaviour instrument have been used in data analysis. The data were subjected to correlation, regression and confirmatory factor analysis to determine the strength, direction, validity and significance of the relationships among those variables.

Qualtrics LLC, a private research company, based in Utah, USA was hired to distribute the survey questionnaires, and collect data from a diverse demographic of the target sample on behalf of the researchers. Participants from US companies in diverse industries were approached through email and asked to participate in this study.

The selection of participants was based on specific criteria. First, participants had to be full-time employees who were reporting to a supervisor, manager or team leader. Second, they had to be working in companies that have been in operation for more than three years with more than 100 employees. This size of the businesses is classified as the starting size for the business to be considered a medium size business in US (Small Business Administration, 2016), in which, this type of companies has an explicit organisational climate identity. Finally, the participant had to be a member of an active team in his/her company.

Three hundred twenty-seven surveys from nine industries were collected using a Qualtrics research panel over a 30-day period. All the surveys that were received met the selection criteria. However, some surveys showed questionable validity (i.e., straight lining and random answers). These surveys were removed from the statistical analysis leaving the overall sample size as 215.

As shown in the descriptive table (Table 1). Participants ranged from 18 to 64 years old. The majority of the respondents (45.2%) were millennials

Table 1. Descriptive table.

	Age of the participants	
Age	*n*	%
18–24	10	4.7
25–34	87	40.5
35–44	61	28.4
45–54	33	15.3
55–64	24	11.2
	Age of the companies	
Years in business	*n*	%
3–5	7	3.3
5–10	15	7.0
> 10	193	89.8
	Size of the companies	
Number of employees	*n*	%
100–500	49	22.8

Table 1. (*Continued*)

	Size of the companies	
Number of employees	*n*	%
501–5000	75	34.9
> 5000	91	42.3
	Gender of participants	
	n	%
Male	49	22.8
Female	166	77.2
	Gender of supervisors	
	n	%
Male	122	56.7
Female	93	43.3
	Industries of the participants	
	n	%
Education	6	2.8
Fast-moving consumer goods (FMCG)	24	11.2
Finance/insurance	25	11.6
Health care	32	14.9
Technology/communication	25	11.6
Transportation	4	1.9
Professional services	15	7.0
Manufacturing	21	9.8
Utilities	7	3.3
Other	56	26.0
	Departments of the participants	
	n	%
Sales/marketing	24	11.2
Finance/accounting	19	8.8
Human resources	8	3.7
Management/administration	37	17.2
Manufacturing	7	3.3
Operations	55	25.6
Research and development (R&D)	7	3.3
Other	58	27.0

(18–34 years old); the second largest group (38.7%) was generation X (35–54 years old) and the least represented group (11.2%) was baby boomers (55–65 years old). The size of the companies represented in this study ranged from medium- to large-sized companies. The majority of respondents were working in large organisations. Specifically, 42% of the sample was working in businesses that had more than 5,000 employees, whereas only 23% were working in medium-sized companies. The gender representation at the different organisational levels of the sample varied. Most of the respondents were female ($n = 166$). Female employees tend to participate in surveys more and express their feelings about their workplace more in comparison to male employees (Simon and Nath, 2004) which can justify the dominance of female participation in this collected sample.

Measures

Personality traits were measured using the 10-Item Personality Inventory TIPI (Gosling *et al.*, 2003). This scale was created as a brief measure of the Big Five dimensions of personality (John and Srivastava, 1999). TIPI has shown good convergent validity with other widely used five-factor model scales and has demonstrated good test-retest reliability (Gosling *et al.*, 2003; Muck *et al.*, 2007). The measure covers personality dimensions of Openness to Experiences, Conscientiousness, Extraversion, Agreeableness and Emotional Stability. Each item consists of two descriptors that represent a pole of the Big Five personality dimensions and is rated on seven-point Likert scales ranging from 1 (strongly disagree) to 7 (strongly agree). A sample of the items is: Regarding my personality traits "I see myself as extraverted, enthusiastic," "I see myself as reserved, quiet," "I see myself as dependable, self-disciplined" and "I see myself as disorganised, careless".

The team leader ambidextrous behaviours scale was developed by Rosing *et al.* (2011). These two scales measure team leader opening and CBs. Participants were asked to rate their team leader's leadership/Supervisor/Manager behaviours using two sets of items on a 5-point scale ranging from 1 (not at all) to 5 (frequently, if not always). A sample of the items for opening leadership behaviours is: "My Supervisor allows different ways of accomplishing a task," "My supervisor encourages risk-taking," "My Supervisor gives possibilities for independent thinking and acting" and "My Supervisor encourages learning from errors." The Cronbach's alpha for this scale was 0.91. A sample of the items for closing leadership behaviours is: "My Supervisor monitors and controls goal attainment," "My Supervisor establishes routines," "My Supervisor takes corrective actions," "uniform accomplishment of task" and "My Supervisor sticks to plans." The Cronbach's alpha for this scale was 0.83.

The climate scale measures the shared expectations and perceptions of the employees of policies, practices and procedures as well as the observed behaviours related to being supported and rewarded by the organisations (Ostroff *et al.*, 2003). The Supportive Climate for Innovation scale was developed by Scott and Bruce (1994). It includes 16 items that measure the degree to which individuals view the organisation they work for as being open to change, and the level of support an organisation provides its employees who are taking initiative and exploring innovative approaches. It represents the explicit and implicit signals employees receive concerning organisational expectations about innovation. The climate measure includes two main sets of items. The first set includes items that support creativity. Some examples are: "Our ability to function creatively is respected by the leadership," "This organisation publicly recognises those who are innovative." The second set consists of tolerance of differences. Some examples are: "The reward system here benefits mainly those who don't rock the boat," "The best way to get along in this organisation is to think the way the rest of the group does." Each item is rated on a scale from 1 (strongly disagree) to 5 (strongly agree). The Cronbach's alpha coefficient for the Supportive Innovation Climate is 0.92.

Participants were asked to rate their individual innovative work behaviour by rating their outcomes using a validated and reliable scale also developed by Scott and Bruce (1994). The six items for innovation performance was used by participants to rate their innovative work behaviours. A sample of the items is: "I promote and champion ideas to others," "I investigate and secure funds needed to implement new ideas" and "I develop adequate plans and schedule for the implementation of new ideas." The questions were answered on a five-point Likert scale ranging from 1 (strongly disagree) to 5 (strongly agree). The Cronbach's alpha for the scale is 0.94.

Researchers emphasise using control variables to help avoid coming up with misleading findings (Bernerth and Aguinis, 2016). The analyses should be conducted with and without the controls to make sure there is no change in the resulting explanation. Otherwise, a possible alternative explanation could potentially be revealed when including a control variable in the study. Individual innovative work behaviour can be influenced by different demographic factors such as participant and team leader gender (Reuvers *et al.*, 2008). The industry that the organisation belongs to can affect the innovation levels they are trying to achieve. The function that participants are performing in the company may also have different innovation level requirements based upon more fixed versus flexible operations. The size and the age of the firm may also affect the climate that supports innovation. A smaller and younger firm may have more focus on innovative objectives because of its agility and the newness of its ideas than a larger and older firm.

Results

Study instruments were subjected to a Confirmatory Factor Analysis (CFA) to determine their validity and to verify the factor structure of the observed variables. Variables Means, Standard Deviations and the Reliability of Instruments are presented in Table 2.

The Cronbach's alpha value for the OB was 0.89 which is higher than the minimum reliability threshold. In contrast, an integrated CFA on the items of all scales, where each item constrained to load only on the factor for which it is the proposed indicator, yields an acceptable fit to the data ($\chi^2 = 9.66$, $\chi^2/\text{df} = 1.074$, $p = 0.378$, comparative fit index [CFI] = 0.99, root-mean-square error of approximation [RMSEA] = 0.019). Moreover, the Cronbach's alpha value for the CB innovation was 0.85 and the integrated CFA yields an acceptable data fit ($\chi^2 = 13.44$, $\chi^2/\text{df} = 1.034$, $p = 0.414$, comparative fit index [CFI] = 0.99, root-mean-square error of approximation [RMSEA] = 0.013). The Cronbach's alpha value for innovation climate instrument was 0.94, and the CFA results were ($\chi^2 = 181$, $\chi^2/\text{df} = 2.06$, $p < 0.001$, [CFI] = 0.96, [RMSEA] = 0.07). On the other hand, the Cronbach's alpha value for the individual innovative work behaviour was 0.82. The CFA results were ($\chi^2 = 9.71$, $\chi^2/\text{df} = 1.21$, $p = 0.286$, [CFI] = 0.99, [RMSEA] = 0.032). Therefore, the CFA Model Fit Statistics for study instruments meet the accepted thresholds and the factors which are unlike the TIPI measurement which was not designed with these confirmatory testing (Gosling *et al.*, 2003). TIPI was designed to measure broad domains with two items per dimension only. Therefore, alpha testing could be misleading when calculated on scales with such small numbers of items (Kline, 2000).

To control for possible alternative explanations, the relevant control variables have been included in the analysis. Industry, department and the size of the organisation were tested using an ANOVA statistical technique which compared groups and checked to see if there were significant mean differences in the outcome variables. Findings confirmed that there were no significant mean differences in individual innovative work behaviour ($p > 0.05$). The gender of the team leaders/supervisors showed a significant mean difference in individual innovative work behaviour ($p < 0.05$). Therefore, it was included in the regression analysis as well as the gender of the participants.

Table 2. Variable means, standard deviations, and the reliability of instruments.

IV — Big 5-Participants traits		
Items	*M*	SD
I see myself as		
1. Extroverted, enthusiastic	4.73	1.72
2. Critical, quarrelsome	2.67	1.44
3. Dependable, self-disciplined	6.26	0.91
4. Anxious, easily upset	2.94	1.58
5. Open to new Experiences, complex	5.79	1.09
6. Reserved, quiet	3.80	1.69
7. Sympathetic, warm	2.25	1.01
8. Disorganised, careless	6.07	1.17
9. Calm, emotionally stable	2.45	1.19
10. Conventional, uncreative	5.28	1.37

MV1 — Climate that support innovation	The Cronbach's alpha = 0.94	
Items	*M*	SD
How do you rate the innovation performance of your organisation?		
1. Creativity is encouraged here	3.93	1.16
2. Our ability to function creatively is respected by the leadership	3.87	1.13
3. Around here, people are allowed to try to solve the same problems in different ways	3.87	1.15
4. The main function of members in this organisation is to follow orders which come down through channels	2.40	1.15
5. Around here, a person can get in a lot of trouble by being different	3.72	1.26
6. This organisation can be described as flexible and continually adapting to change	3.96	1.04
7. A person cannot do things that are too different around here without provoking anger	3.63	1.30
8. The best way to get along in this organisation is to think the way the rest of the group does	3.30	1.28
9. People around here are expected to deal with problems in the same way	3.41	1.25
10. This organisation is open and responsive to change	3.94	1.13
11. The people in charge around here usually get credit for others' ideas	3.18	1.38
12. In this organisation, we tend to stick to tried and true ways	2.71	1.14
13. This place seems to be more concerned with the status quo than with change	3.55	1.16
14. The reward system here encourages innovation	3.48	1.26
15. This organisation publicly recognises those who are innovative	3.58	1.23

Innovative Work Behaviour: Personality, Leadership and Climate in the US

Table 2. (*Continued*)

MV1 — Climate that support innovation	The Cronbach's alpha = 0.94	
Items	*M*	SD
16. The reward system here benefits mainly those who do not rock the boat	3.28	1.28
MV2 — Supervisor ambidextrous behaviours	The Cronbach's alpha = 0.89	
(a) Opening behaviours	*M*	SD
According to your interaction with your supervisor/team leader/manager, how do you rate his/her leadership behaviours?		
1. My supervisor allows different ways of accomplishing a task	3.84	1.06
2. My supervisor encourages experimentation with different ideas	3.57	1.15
3. My supervisor encourages risk taking	2.70	1.22
4. My supervisor gives possibilities for independent thinking and acting	3.76	1.19
5. My supervisor gives room for my own ideas	3.75	1.20
6. My supervisor allows for errors	3.11	1.11
7. My supervisor encourages learning from errors	3.84	1.14
(b) Closing behaviours	The Cronbach's alpha = 0.85	
1. My supervisor monitors and controls goal attainment	3.71	1.16
2. My supervisor establishes routines	3.59	1.18
3. My supervisor takes corrective actions	3.65	1.18
4. My supervisor insists that rules be followed	3.94	1.05
5. My supervisor pays attention to the uniform accomplishment of task	3.57	1.15
6. My supervisor gives sanctions for errors	2.83	1.16
7. My supervisor sticks to plans	3.63	1.03
DV — individual innovative work behaviour	The Cronbach's alpha = 0.82	
Items	*M*	SD
How do you rate your innovation performance?		
1. I search out new technologies, processes, techniques and/or product ideas	3.95	0.88
2. I generate creative ideas	4.17	0.77
3. I promote and champion ideas to others	4.00	0.89
4. I investigate and secure funds needed to implement new ideas	2.81	1.28
5. I develop adequate plans and schedule for the implementation of new ideas	3.62	1.14
6. I am innovative at work	4.10	0.79

Hypothesis testing

A hierarchical regression analysis was used to test whether the ambidextrous behaviours of the team leader combined within a supportive innovation climate can moderate the relationship between a team member's personality traits and their individual innovative work behaviour. Table 3 presents the correlations between the study variables. Table 4 shows the results of the hierarchical regression analyses for individual innovative work behaviour. The predictors entered in the hierarchical regression analysis are gender, Big Five personality dimensions, team leader OB and CBs and Innovation climate. Baseline Models 1, 2, 3 and 4 contain the control variable (gender of the individual and team leader). Models 2, 3 and 4 present the effects of Big Five personality dimensions. Models 3 and 4 introduce the effects of the moderator, team leader OB and CBs and Innovation climate. Finally, Model 4 introduces the potential interactions of team leader behaviours and Innovation climate with the Big Five personality dimensions. However, before the creation of the interaction terms, the independent variables were mean centred to mitigate the inter-correlation effect of the predictors (Aiken *et al.*, 1991).

According to the standardised regression coefficients in Table 4, findings in the Model 4 show that while the gender of the participants had no significant influence on individual innovative work behaviour ($\beta = 0.008, p > 0.05$), the gender of the team leader had a significant negative impact on individual innovative work behaviour ($\beta = -0.17, p < 0.01$). The proposed relationship between each of the personality dimensions Openness to Experiences, Extraversion and Conscientiousness of employees and individual innovative work behaviour is statistically supported ($\beta_1 = 0.32, p < 0.001$, $\beta_2 = 0.16, p < 0.01$ and $\beta_3 = 0.17, p < 0.05$), respectively. However, the positive influence of the Openness to Experiences dimension is higher than Extraversion or Conscientiousness personality dimensions. In contrast, the proposed relationship between personality dimensions Agreeableness and Emotional Stability of the employee and individual innovative work behaviour failed statistically to be supported. Findings confirmed these traits have non-significant relationships with individual innovative work behaviour ($\beta_1 = -0.08, p > 0.05$ and $\beta_2 = 0.07, p > 0.05$), respectively. On the other hand, the moderator variables, OBs, CBs and Innovation climate also have no significant direct effect on individual innovative work behaviour ($\beta_1 = 0.3, p > 0.05$; $\beta_2 = -0.3$, $p > 0.05$; $\beta_3 = 0.12$, $p > 0.05$), respectively.

Regarding interactions, findings confirmed that there are only two significant interactions between Openness to Experiences personality dimension and both moderators team leader CBs and Innovation climate ($\beta_1 = -0.17$, $p < 0.01$; $\beta_2 = 0.27$, $p < 0.001$), respectively. The interaction effects of our research are shown in Fig. 2.

Table 3. Correlations, means and standard deviations.[a]

	M	SD	(1)	(2)	(3)	(4)	(5)	(6)	(7)	(8)	(9)	(10)	(11)
(1) Individual Innovative Work Behaviour	3.78	0.71	—										
(2) Individual Gender[b]	1.77	0.42	−0.04	—									
(3) Team leader Gender[b]	1.43	0.50	−0.18**	0.30**	—								
(4) Extraversion	4.26	1.47	0.34**	0.07	−0.03	—							
(5) Agreeableness	5.54	0.98	0.05	0.08	0.14*	0.04	—						
(6) Conscientiousness	6.16	0.87	0.30**	0.05	0.04	0.16*	0.34**	—					
(7) Emotional Stability	5.30	1.23	0.28**	−0.10	−0.01	0.11	0.40**	0.51**	—				
(8) Openness to Experiences	5.53	0.99	0.49**	0.07	−0.02	0.35**	0.17*	0.33**	0.31**	—			
(9) Innovation Climate	3.49	0.87	0.30**	0.02	−0.17*	0.19**	0.22**	0.28**	0.31**	0.26**	—		
(10) Opening Behaviours	3.51	0.90	0.30**	−0.11	−0.14*	0.18**	0.12	0.18**	0.26**	0.24**	0.62**	—	
(11) Closing Behviours	3.56	0.82	0.12	−0.11	−0.08	0.13	0.15*	0.07	0.14*	0.16*	0.22**	0.22**	—

Notes: [a]$n = 215$, [b]1 = male, 2 = female, $*p < 0.05$, $**p > 0.01$.

Table 4. Results of hierarchical regression analyses: effects of personality traits moderated by team leader ambidextrous behaviours and Innovation climate on individual innovative work behaviour.[a]

	Individual innovative work behaviour			
	Model 1	Model 2	Model 3	Model 4
Control variables				
Individual gender[b]	0.02	−0.02	−0.01	0.00
Team leader gender[b]	−0.19**	−0.16**	−0.13*	−0.17**
Personality traits effect				
Conscientiousness		0.13	0.12	0.17*
Extraversion		0.17***	0.16**	0.16**
Openness to Experiences		0.37***	0.35***	0.32***
Agreeableness		−0.08	−0.09	−0.08
Emotional stability		0.11	0.08	0.07
Moderator effect				
Opening behaviours			0.10	0.03
Closing behaviours			−0.01	−0.03
Innovation climate			0.06	0.12
Interaction effect				
Conscientiousness OBs				0.11
Extraversion × OBs				0.01
Openness to Experiences × OBs				−0.14
Agreeableness × OBs				−0.08
Emotional Stability × OBs				−0.17
Conscientiousness × CBs				−0.07
Extraversion × CBs				0.00
Openness to Experiences × CBs				−0.17**
Agreeableness × CBs				0.03
Emotional stability × CBs				−0.01
Conscientiousness × Innovation climate				0.13
Extraversion × Innovation climate				−0.12
Openness to Experiences × Innovation climate				0.27***
Agreeableness × Innovation climate				0.13
Emotional stability × Innovation climate				−0.06
R^2	0.03*	0.33**	0.35**	0.43**
ΔR^2	0.03*	0.30**	0.02	0.08*

Notes: $n = 215$, [a]standardised regression coefficients are reported. [b]1 = male, 2 = female, *$p < 0.05$, **$p < 0.01$, ***$p < 0.001$.

We used the scatterplot to see the impact of organisational climate in predicting individual innovative work behaviour among two levels of team leader CBs and Innovation climate. One standard deviation below the mean considered (low level) and one standard deviation above the mean considered (high level) as included in Fig. 2. The interaction effect between the Openness to Experiences trait and

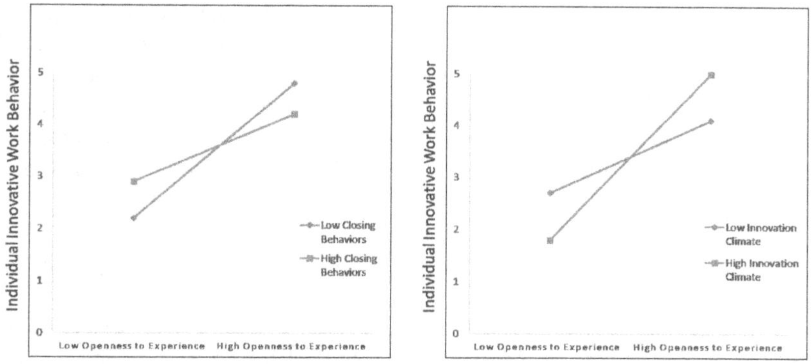

Fig. 2. The effect of interactions between team leader CBs and Innovation climate with Openness to Experience personality dimension on individual innovative work behaviour.

Innovation climate is positively related to individual innovative work behaviour. A higher level of supportive climate of innovation enhanced and synergised the relationship between Openness to Experiences and individual innovative work behaviour. Nevertheless, the interaction effect between Openness to Experiences and team leader CBs is negatively related to individual innovative work behaviour. CBs act as a buffer variable for the relationship between Openness to Experiences and individual innovative work behaviour. A higher level of team leader CBs reduces the positive influence of the Openness to Experiences on individual innovative work behaviour.

The total effect size of model 3 is large and significant ($R^2 = 0.35$, $p < 0.01$). But in model 4 the interaction terms between personality dimensions and both team leader CBs and Innovation climate significantly increased the effect size by 8% ($R^2 = 0.43$, $p < 0.001$). This interaction means 43% of the variance in individual innovative work behaviour is explained by the main predictors, Openness to Experiences, Conscientiousness, and Extraversion of the team member and the interaction of Openness to Experiences with both Innovation climate and team leader CBs.

Finally, the beta (β) weights of the predictors confirmed that the Openness to Experiences personality trait has a major positive influence in driving individual innovative work behaviour compared to other traits. Nevertheless, while this influence can be boosted by high levels of a climate that supports innovation, it can also be hindered by team leader CBs.

Briefly stated, the above findings of Table 4 showed that these personality traits (Openness to Experiences, Extraversion and Conscientiousness) of team members have a significant influence on their individual innovative work behaviour.

However, the findings also showed that there are two significant moderation relationships between Openness to Experiences personality trait of the team member and both innovation climate and CBs of the team leader. In other words, CB of the team leader may hinder Openness to Experiences influence on individual innovative work behaviour. In contrast, Innovation climate may boost the influence of Openness to Experiences on individual innovative work behaviour.

Discussion

This research demonstrates the crucial role that Big Five personality traits play in individual innovative work behaviour. The study also delineates the moderation influence of a supportive climate for innovation and ambidextrous team leader behaviours providing some additional insights through a contextual research design. The results showed a direct positive influence of three of the Big Five personality traits on individual innovative work behaviour. These traits include Openness to Experiences, Extraversion and Conscientiousness. However, the influence of the Openness to Experiences dimension is higher than the Extraversion or the Conscientiousness dimension. Results also confirmed that there was no relationship between Agreeableness and Emotional Stability personality traits with individual innovative work behaviour.

Our findings are consistent with McCrae (1987) who demonstrated that the personality domain of Openness to Experiences is related to the creativity component of the individual innovation process. Guo *et al.* (2017) also showed Openness to Experiences and Extraversion were positively related to individual creativity. Through a major literature review, Sackett *et al.* (2017) confirmed Openness to Experiences as the best predictor of creative behaviours followed by Extraversion and Conscientiousness. Individuals with high levels of Openness to Experiences are curious, imaginative, independent and divergent thinkers who are willing to embrace and are attracted to new ideas (Hammond *et al.*, 2011; McCrae, 1987). Extroverted individuals are energetic, experience positive emotions, and actively engage with their respective social networks (Rossberger, 2014) which increases their innovative performance (Hsieh *et al.*, 2011). Therefore, our findings regarding the relationship of Big Five personality traits with individual innovative work behaviour are consistent with the preponderance of research.

As Caniëls *et al.* (2014) suggest, the explanation of our results may rest in part with the framework that we used to measure individual innovative work behaviour. Earlier, we explained that the innovation process is viewed by many researchers as a sequence of events (Van de Ven and Poole, 2000), a multi-step discontinuous process (Perry-Smith and Mannucci, 2017), and even a journey involving nonlinear dynamic systems with recurring patterns of divergent and convergent behaviours (Van de Ven *et al.*, 1999). Therefore, we used Scott and Bruce's (1994) measure of individual innovative work behaviour because it recognises innovation as a process requiring employees to generate and implement ideas. Given this view of individual innovation as a process of many phases, Caniëls *et al.* (2014) suggest that each phase may have different antecedents. It is conceivable that individuals who are more Open to Experiences will be more likely to demonstrate behaviours consistent with the early phases of the innovation process that involve creative and divergent thinking than individuals who are less Open to Experiences. As a corollary found in our study and supported by prior research, conscientiousness has a positive effect on the later stages of individual innovative work behaviour when implementing the innovation where the individual's persistence and self-discipline are needed (Ali, 2019; Hsieh *et al.*, 2011).

Although our results showed no relationship between Agreeableness and Emotional Stability personality traits with individual innovative work behaviour, this is consistent with prior research. Furnham *et al.* (2009), for instance, did not find a significant relationship between Agreeableness and divergent thinking in their study of over 3,000 adult managers. This finding makes sense since by the very nature of the personality trait, as Agreeableness refers to one's expression of warmth (Goldberg, 1981) and acting in a "conciliatory, cooperative and agreeable" (Goldberg, 1990, p. 1218) manner. In contrast, the idea generating phase of innovation can include navigating the conflict of sharply opposing perspectives and priorities in response to a "shock" to the organisation that requires divergent thinking (Schroeder *et al.*, 2000). This conflict stage puts someone who only wants to "get along well with others" in an uncomfortable position.

Emotional stability too can be at odds with individual innovative work behaviour as we found in our study. For instance, Van de Ven (1986) theorizes that one of the central problems of innovation management is managing the attention of employees. Getting employees to pay attention to new ideas particularly in successful companies whose attention is focused on protecting the status quo of current practices and procedures is very difficult. Emotional stability characterised by calmness and exhibiting poise, in contrast to Neuroticism characterised by anxiousness and nervousness, can run counter to standing out in a crowd of other ideas waiting to be developed and implemented (Goldberg, 1981). In fact, prior research positively associates Neuroticism with creativity given the alternative and the highly creative perspectives of neurotic individuals (Wang *et al.*, 2014).

We further explored this relationship between Big Five personality traits and individual innovative work behaviour by introducing moderating variables: Innovation climate and ambidextrous team leaders. We found only Openness to Experiences to interact with team leader ambidextrous behaviours and a supportive

Innovation climate. The Innovation climate can boost the impact of Openness to Experiences on individual innovative work behaviour. However, team leader ambidextrous behaviours, specifically CBs, buffered and hindered the impact of the Openness to Experiences personality dimension on individual innovative work behaviour.

Our research has some interesting findings regarding the moderating effect of team leadership. We found that individual innovative work behaviour of team members with high Openness to Experiences decreases when team leadership exhibits strong CB. This finding confirms Hirst *et al.*'s (2011) model suggesting bureaucratic practices have a negative impact on innovation. We found the personality characteristic most correlated with innovation performance, i.e., Openness to Experiences, is extremely vulnerable to the anti-innovation impact of CBs. Our findings reinforce the conclusions of Hirst *et al.* (2011) that CB by the team leader constrains the creative and innovation expression of the individual team member who has high Openness to Experiences. The managerial implication of this finding is that those team members with high Openness to Experiences should not be subject to too much CB by a team leader.

The research design used gender as a control variable. The analysis showed female team supervisors had a negative impact on team member innovation work behaviours while male supervisors had a positive impact on this relationship. There was no clear explanation for this. This is a surprising finding that merits further research on the influence of gender on innovation leadership but is beyond the scope of the current research.

Our research confirmed Pirola-Merlo and Mann's (2004) findings that Innovation climate has a strong effect on individual innovative work behaviour. This was a significant moderating effect in the case of team members with high Openness to Experiences. Therefore, team members with high Openness to Experiences are likely to have higher individual innovative work behaviour and this relationship is even stronger with high levels of Innovation climate support.

Limitations

As with any other research, this study was subject to potential limitations. First, the gender representation of participants in this study was imbalanced. Three quarters of the participants were female which could limit the generalizability of findings. Second, the statistical analyses were based on self-report surveys. Self-report data is a common limitation of survey-based studies and may lead to inflated correlations due to shared variance. Finally, this study is based solely on a United States' sample which also can reduce the generalizability of the results.

Recommendations for future research

Future studies should consider how our research model contributes to individual innovative work behaviour in companies in different cultural or industry contexts. Also, it is important to look at other individual factors, such as gender, and how they modify the impact of leadership style on individual innovative work behaviour and organisational climate.

Implications of study findings

Results of this study contribute to innovation theory by confirming that personality traits, team leader behaviours, and a supportive climate for innovation work together to create a new strategic model to foster individual innovative work behaviour. There is a clear reaffirmation of the primacy of Openness to Experiences as a driver of individual innovation work behaviour. However, the results suggest that executives need to spend considerable time and resources ensuring that the climate is supportive of innovation. The findings of this study can also be used in leadership development and training programs to demonstrate how leadership behaviours of the supervisor in conjunction with a supportive Innovation climate promote and foster innovation performance.

Conclusion

This study provides strong support for the impact of Big Five personality traits on individuals' innovative work behaviour. Openness to Experiences, Extraversion and Conscientiousness can enrich individual innovative work behaviour. Our research highlights the importance of a climate that supports innovation to enhance the positive relationship with certain personality traits. Finally, team leaders' high CBs can diminish innovation. Therefore, to foster individual innovative work behaviour, organisations should ensure that team leaders are trained in and practice ambidextrous leadership behaviours and the organisational climate is supportive of innovation.

References

Ahmed, PK (1998). Culture and climate for innovation. *European Journal of Innovation Management*, 1(1), 30–43.

Aiken, LS, SG West and RR Reno (1991). *Multiple Regression: Testing and Interpreting Interactions*. Sage.

Ali, I (2019). Personality traits, individual innovativeness and satisfaction with life. *Journal of Innovation & Knowledge*, 4(1), 38–46, doi: https://doi.org/10.1016/j.jik.2017.11.002.

Amabile, TM (1988). A model of creativity and innovation in organizations. *Research in Organizational Behavior*, 10(1), 123–167.

Anderson, NR and MA West (1998). Measuring climate for work group innovation: Development and validation of the team climate inventory. *Journal of Organizational Behavior*, 9(3), 235–258.

Anderson, N, K Potočnik and J Zhou (2014). Innovation and creativity in organizations: A state-of-the-science review, prospective commentary, and guiding framework. *Journal of Management*, 40(5), 1297–1333.

Angle, HL (2000). Psychology and organizational innovation. In *Research on the Management of Innovation: The Minnesota Studies*, AH Van de Ven, HL Angle and MS Poole (Eds.), pp. 135–170. New York: Oxford University Press.

Bernerth, JB and H Aguinis (2016). A critical review and best-practice recommendations for control variable usage. *Personnel Psychology*, 69(1), 229–283.

Buda, R and SM Elsayed-Elkhouly (1998). Cultural differences between Arabs and Americans: Individualism-collectivism revisited. *Journal of Cross-Cultural Psychology*, 29(3), 487–492.

Calantone, RJ, ST Cavusgil and Y Zhao (2002). Learning orientation, firm innovationcapability, and firm performance. *Industrial Marketing Management*, 31(6), 515–524.

Caniëls, MC, K De Stobbeleir and I De Clippeleer (2014). The antecedents of creativity revisited: A process perspective. *Creativity and Innovation Management*, 23(2), 96–110.

Choi, JN (2006). Organisational active learning: Implications for innovation adoption and implementation. *International Journal of Innovation and Learning*, 3(2), 198.

Christie, PMJ, IWG Kwon, PA Stoeberl and R Baumhart (2003). A cross-cultural comparison of ethical attitudes of business managers: India, Korea and the United States. *Journal of Business Ethics*, 46(3), 263–287.

Clearly Cultural: Making Sense of Cross Cultural Communication (2019). Retrieved on Oct 14, 2019, http://clearlycultural.com/geert-hofstede-cultural-dimensions/i.

Costa, Jr PT and RR McCrae (1995). Domains and facets: Hierarchical personality assessment using the revised NEO personality inventory. *Journal of Personality Assessment*, 64(1), 21–50.

Dyck, LR (2017). Resonance and dissonance asymmetry in effective physician–patient relationships. *The Journal of the Royal College of Physicians of Edinburgh*, 47(4), 314–323. doi: 10.4997/JRCPE.2017.403.

Dyck, LR (2018). The impact of resonance and dissonance on effective physician–patient communication. In *Individual, Relational, and Contextual Dynamics of Emotions: Research on Emotion in Organizations*, L Petitta and NM Ashkanasy (Eds.), Vol. 14, pp. 139–162. Bingley, UK: Emerald Publishing Ltd.

Eisenbeiss, SA, D van Knippenberg and S Boerner (2008). Transformational leadership and team innovation: Integrating team climate principles. *Journal of Applied Psychology*, 93(6), 1438.

Feist, GJ (1998). A meta-analysis of personality in scientific and artistic creativity. *Personality and Social Psychology Review: An Official Journal of the Society for Personality and Social Psychology, Inc.*, 2(4), 290–309.

Furnham, A, J Crump, M Batey and T Chamorro-Premuzic (2009). Personality and ability predictors of the "Consequences" Test of divergent thinking in a large non-student sample. *Personality and Individual Differences*, 46(4), 536–540, doi: 10.1016/j.paid.2008.12.007.

Gelade, GA (1997). Creativity in conflict: The personality of the commercial creative. *The Journal of Genetic Psychology*, 158(1), 67–78.

Gelade, GA (2002). Creative style, personality, and artistic endeavor. *Genetic, Social, and General Psychology Monographs*, 128(3), 213–234.

Gibson, CB and J Birkinshaw (2004). The antecedents, consequences, and mediating role of organizational ambidexterity. *Academy of Management Journal*, 47(2), 209–226.

Global Innovation Index (2019). retrieved on Oct 14, 2019, https://www.globalinnovationindex.org/Home.

Goldberg, LR (1981). Language and individual differences: The search for universals in personality lexicons. *Review of Personality and Social Psychology*, 2(1), 141–165.

Goldberg, LR (1990). An alternative "description of personality": The big-five factor structure. *Journal of Personality and Social Psychology*, 59(6), 1216.

Goldberg, LR (1993). The structure of phenotypic personality traits. *American Psychologist*, 48(1), 26–34, doi: 10.1037/0003-066X.48.1.26.

Gosling, SD, PJ Rentfrow and WB Swann (2003). A very brief measure of the Big-Five personality domains. *Journal of Research in Personality*, 37(6), 504–528.

Guo, J, Q Su and Q Zhang (2017). Individual creativity during the ideation phase of product innovation: An interactional perspective. *Creativity and Innovation Management*, 26(1), 31–48.

Hammond, MM, NL Neff, JL Farr, AR Schwall and X Zhao (2011). Predictors of individual-level innovation at work: A meta-analysis. *Psychology of Aesthetics, Creativity, and the Arts*, 5(1), 90–105, doi: 10.1037/a0018556.

Hirst, G, D Van Knippenberg, CH Chen and CA Sacramento (2011). How does bureaucracy impact individual creativity? A cross-level investigation of team contextual influences on goal orientation–creativity relationships. *Academy of Management Journal*, 54(3), 624–641.

Hsieh, H-L, J-R Hsieh and I-L Wang (2011). Linking personality and innovation: The role of knowledge management. *World Transactions on Engineering and Technology Education*, 9(1), 38–44.

Jeong, I and SJ Shin (2019). High-performance work practices and organizational creativity during organizational change: A collective learning perspective. *Journal of Management*, 45(3), 909–925.

John, OP and S Srivastava (1999). The Big Five trait taxonomy: History, measurement, and theoretical perspectives. *Handbook of Personality: Theory and Research*, 2(1999), 102–138.

Kast, FE and JE Rosenzweig (1972). General systems theory: Applications for organization and management. *Academy of Management Journal*, 15(4), 447–465.

Katzenbach, JR and DK Smith (2015). *The Wisdom of Teams: Creating the High-Performance Organization*. Harvard Business Review Press.

Katz, D (1964). The motivational basis of organizational behavior. *Systems Research and Behavioral Science*, 9(2), 131–146.

King, LA, LM Walker and SJ Broyles (1996). Creativity and the five-factor model. *Journal of Research in Personality*, 30(2), 189–203.

Kleysen, RF and CT Street (2001). Toward a multi-dimensional measure of individual innovative behavior. *Journal of Intellectual Capital*, 2(3), 284–296.

Kline, P (2000). *A Psychometrics Primer*. Free Assn Books.

Kuczmarski, TD (1996). *Innovation: Leadership Strategies for the Competitive Edge*. NTC Publishing Group.

Lin, HF (2007). Knowledge sharing and firm innovation capability: An empirical study. *International Journal of Manpower*, 28(3/4), 315–332.

Liu, D, Y Gong, J Zhou and JC Huang (2017). Human resource systems, employee creativity, and firm innovation: The moderating role of firm ownership. *Academy of Management Journal*, 60(3), 1164–1188.

Mansfield, E and S Wagner (1975). Organizational and strategic factors associated with probabilities of success in industrial R&D. *The Journal of Business*, 48, 179–198.

Marinova, SV, X Cao and H Park (2018). Constructive organizational values climate and organizational citizenship behaviors: A configurational view. *Journal of Management*, 5(5), 2045–2071.

Martinaityte, I, C Sacramento and S Aryee (2019). Delighting the customer: Creativity-oriented high-performance work systems, frontline employee creative performance, and customer satisfaction. *Journal of Management*, 45(2), 728–751.

McCrae, RR (1987). Creativity, divergent thinking, and Openness to Experiences. *Journal of Personality and Social Psychology*, 52(6), 1258.

Moon, H (2001). The two faces of conscientiousness: Duty and achievement striving in escalation of commitment dilemmas. *Journal of Applied Psychology*, 86(3), 533–540, doi: 10.1037/0021-9010.86.3.535.

Muck, PM, B Hell and SD Gosling (2007). Construct validation of a short five-factor model instrument. *European Journal of Psychological Assessment*, 23(3), 166–175.

Ostroff, C, AJ Kinicki and MM Tamkins (2003). *Organizational Culture and Climate*. Wiley Online Library.

Patterson, F and LD Zibarras (2017). Selecting for creativity and innovation potential: Implications for practice in healthcare education. *Advances in Health Sciences Education*, 22(2), 417–428.

Perry-Smith, JE and PV Mannucci (2017). From creativity to innovation: The social network drivers of the four phases of the idea journey. *Academy of Management Review*, 42(1), 53–79.

Pinchot, III G (1985). Intrapreneuring: Why you don't have to leave the corporation to become an entrepreneur. *University of Illinois at Urbana-Champaign's Academy for Entrepreneurial Leadership Historical Research Reference in Entrepreneurship.*

Pirola-Merlo, A and L Mann (2004). The relationship between individual creativity and team creativity: Aggregating across people and time. *Journal of Organizational Behavior*, 25(2), 235–257.

Reuvers, M, ML van Engen, CJ Vinkenburg and E Wilson-Evered (2008). Transformational leadership and innovative work behaviour: Exploring the relevance of gender differences. *Creativity & Innovation Management*, 17(3), 227–244, doi: 10.1111/j.1467-8691.2008.00487.x.

Rice, AL (2013). *The Enterprise and its Environment: A System Theory of Management Organization*. Milton Park, Abingdon, Oxon: Routledge.

Rinne, T, GD Steel and J Fairweather (2012). Hofstede and Shane revisited: The role of power distance and individualism in national-level innovation success. *Cross-Cultural Research*, 46(2), 91–108.

Rogers, EM (1995). *Diffusion of Innovations*, 4th edition. New York: The Free Press.

Rosing, K, M Frese and A Bausch (2011). Explaining the heterogeneity of the leadership-innovation relationship: Ambidextrous leadership. *The Leadership Quarterly*, 22(5), 956–974.

Rossberger, RJ (2014). National personality profiles and innovation: The role of cultural practices. *Creativity & Innovation Management*, 23(3), 331–348, doi: 10.1111/caim.12075.

Sackett, PR, F Lievens, CH Van Iddekinge and NR Kuncel (2017). Individual differences and their measurement: A review of 100 years of research. *Journal of Applied Psychology*, 102(3), 254–273, doi: 10.1037/apl0000151.

Salanova, M, S Agut and JM Peiró (2005). Linking organizational resources and work engagement to employee performance and customer loyalty: The mediation of service climate. *Journal of Applied Psychology*, 90(6), 1217.

Schroeder, RG, AH Van de Ven, GD Scudder and D Polley (2000). The development of innovation ideas. In *Research on the Management of Innovation: The Minnesota Studies*, AH Van de Ven, HL Angle and MS Poole (Eds.), pp. 107–134. New York: Oxford University Press.

Scott, SG and RA Bruce (1994). Determinants of innovative behavior: A path model of individual innovation in the workplace. *The Academy of Management Journal*, 37(3), 580–607, doi: 10.2307/256701.

Simon, RW and LE Nath (2004). Gender and emotion in the United States: Do men and women differ in self-reports of feelings and expressive behavior? *American Journal of Sociology*, 109(5), 1137–1176.

Small Business Administration (2016). Table of Small Business Size Standards Matched to North American Industry Classification System Codes. Retrieved from https://www.sba.gov/sites/default/files/files/Size_Standards_Table.pdf.

Stein, MI (1968). Creativity. In *Handbook of Personality Theory and Research*, EF Borgatta and WW Lambert (Eds.), pp. 900–942. Chicago: Rand McNally.

Steel, GD, T Rinne and J Fairweather (2012). Personality, nations, and innovation: Relationships between personality traits and national innovation scores. *Cross-Cultural Research*, 46(1), 3–30.

Sung, SY and JN Choi (2009). Do big five personality factors affect individual creativity? The moderating role of extrinsic motivation. *Social Behavior & Personality: An International Journal*, 37(7), 941–956.

Taggar, S (2002). Individual creativity and group ability to utilize individual creative resources: A multilevel model. *Academy of Management Journal*, 45(2), 315–330.

Van de Ven, AH (1986). Central problems in the management of innovation. *Management Science*, 32(5), 590–607.

Van de Ven, AH, DE Polley, R Garud and S Venkataraman (1999). *The Innovation Journey*. New York: Oxford University Press, Inc.

Van de Ven, AH and MS Poole (2000). Methods for studying innovation processes. In *Research on the Management of Innovation: The Minnesota Studies*, AH Van de Ven, HL Angle and MS Poole (Eds.), pp. 31–54. New York: Oxford University Press.

Wang, S, RA Noe and Z-M Wang (2014). Motivating knowledge sharing in knowledge management systems. *Journal of Management*, 40(4), 978–1009, doi: 10.1177/0149206311412192.

West, MA (2002). Sparkling fountains or stagnant ponds: An integrative model of creativity and innovation implementation in work groups. *Applied Psychology: An International Review*, 51(3), 355–387.

West, MA, CS Borrill, JF Dawson, F Brodbeck, DA Shapiro and B Haward (2003). Leadership clarity and team innovation in health care. *The Leadership Quarterly*, 14(4), 393–410.

Yesil, S and F Sozbilir (2013). An empirical investigation into the impact of personality on individual innovation behaviour in the workplace. *Procedia-Social and Behavioral Sciences*, 81, 540–551.

Yuan, F and RW Woodman (2010). Innovative behavior in the workplace: The role of performance and image outcome expectations. *Academy of Management Journal*, 53(2), 323–342.

Zacher, H and K Rosing (2015). Ambidextrous leadership and team innovation. *Leadership & Organization Development Journal*, 36(1), 54–68.

Zaltman, G, R Duncan and J Holbek (1973). *Innovations and Organizations*. New York: Wiley.

Zuraik, A and LKelly (2019). The role of CEO transformational leadership and innovation climate in exploration and exploitation. *European Journal of Innovation Management*, 22(1), 84–104.

Section 2

Absorptive Capacity

Chapter 9

HOW FIRMS ABSORB EXTERNAL KNOWLEDGE — MODELLING AND MANAGING THE ABSORPTIVE CAPACITY PROCESS†

DJERDJ HORVAT*

Fraunhofer Institute for Systems and Innovation Research ISI
Breslauer Straße 48, 76139 Karlsruhe, Germany
djerdj.horvat@isi.fraunhofer.de

CARSTEN DREHER

Freie Universität Berlin, Thiel allee 73
14195 Berlin, Germany
carsten.dreher@fu-berlin.de

OLIVER SOM

Management Center Innsbruck MCI
Universitätsstraße 15,6020 Innsbruck, Austria
oliver.som@mci.edu

Published 10 September 2018

This paper contributes to the literature and management practice by opening the "black box" of firms' absorptive capacity (AC) processes. Following a process research approach and based on in-depth comparative case studies of four German manufacturing companies, we develop and empirically validate a procss model of the firm-internal AC process. Our model integrates the different single elements (e.g., individuals, teams, departments) as well as the different linear and nonlinear causal interactions that constitute the firm's ability to identify, adopt, implement and exploit external information and knowledge. Furthermore, the paper elaborates on various organizational leverages to increase the effectiveness of the identified process flows. The findings provide explanatory insight into the organisational prerequisites of AC. Thus, the paper simultaneously contributes to enhance the academic and management's understanding of firms' AC by identifying its constitutional key elements, their different kinds of processual interrelation as well as organisational prerequisites and points of leverage to modify, measure, and improve the AC of a company.

Keywords: Absorptive capacity; organisation; innovation; management; case study; qualitative research; process approach.

*Corresponding author.

†This article originally appeared in *International Journal of Innovation Management*, **24** 1950041-1-35 © 2019 World Scientific Publishing Europe Ltd.

Introduction

To become and remain competitive, firms need to effectively address rapid technological changes by continuously developing and implementing innovative solutions. This is complicated by the fact that the innovation environment of many firms today is becoming increasingly volatile, uncertain, complex and ambiguous (Bennett and Lemoine, 2014; Caiazza and Volpe, 2017; Yang *et al.*, 2017). For instance, ongoing technological dynamics like additive manufacturing, new materials or the rapid shift towards digitalised value creation and the internet of things are accompanied by disruptive potentials that challenge and, in the worst case, could even devaluate the existing knowledge base of established firms (Christensen, 2013). The increasing pace (e.g., in the field of digital economy) or complexity (e.g., additive manufacturing) of such dynamics make it almost impossible for firms to develop and update all the necessary knowledge and knowhow in-house. In consequence, firms are increasingly forced to explore and exploit external sources of relevant innovation knowledge (Amniattalab and Ansari, 2016; Galati, 2015; Galati and Bigliardi, 2016; Henttonen and Lehtimäki, 2017; Hoyer *et al.*, 2010; Martín-de Castro, 2015; Nooteboom, 2009; O'Hern and Rindfleisch, 2010; Petti and Zhang, 2016; Zubielqui *et al.*, 2016) — or, as Chesbrough pointed out — to reshape their innovation strategy towards Open Innovation (Chesbrough, 2003; Chesbrough *et al.*, 2006).

In this respect, a firm's capacity to acquire new knowledge from a variety of external sources, integrate it with internal knowledge and exploit it to create and deploy innovative outcome, its so-called absorptive capacity (AC), plays a crucial strategic role (Cohen and Levinthal, 1990). Moreover, as a bundle of underlying routines and processes, AC represents a kind of "dynamic capability" that drives the creation of the knowledge for innovating; knowledge that is essential to adapt existing or develop entirely new organisational capabilities (Eisenhardt and Martin, 2000; Teece *et al.*, 1997; Zahra and George, 2002).

Since Cohen and Levinthal's (1990) very first publications on AC, this construct has been widely researched in theoretical and empirical studies over the last, almost, 30 years. One of the most frequently cited AC approaches is a recent framework that aims to define the underlining process and its dimensions (Easterby-Smith *et al.*, 2008; Filippini *et al.*, 2012; Marabelli and Newell, 2014; Patterson and Ambrosini, 2015). The roots of this framework go back to the studies by Zahra and George (2002) as well as Todorova and Durisin (2007) that explain knowledge absorption as a process in which knowledge moves from one component to another, thereby defining the firm's innovative capability.

Zahra and George (2002) introduced a perspective of AC based on dynamic capabilities (Eisenhardt and Martin, 2000; Teece *et al.*, 1997; Zollo and Winter, 2002) and defined AC as a set of organisational routines and strategic processes by which firms acquire, assimilate, transform and exploit essential knowledge in order to modify existing or develop new organisational capabilities (Zahra and George, 2002, p. 186). Moreover, they divided these processes into two separate but complementary dimensions: potential (PACAP) and realized (RACAP) and emphasise the importance of managing the equilibrium between them to achieve and maintain competitiveness. Todorova and Durisin (2007) explained AC as an iterative process rather than the linear one presented by Zahra and George and detailed the sequences of its components as well as emphasizing its dynamic nature. Following these two seminal works, Patterson and Ambrosini (2015) were the first to provide more clarity on the constitutional elements and their interrelations of the AC process based on empirical evidence from a qualitative process study. In their paper, they suggest a reconceptualised AC model, emphasizing the iterative and dynamic nature of the AC process.

Despite previous studies emphasizing the managerial relevance of AC, there are still no satisfactory answers to the question about what the process of AC actually looks like inside a company, and how its effectiveness can be managed (Cohen and Levinthal, 1990; Marabelli and Newell, 2014; Patterson and Ambrosini, 2015; Todorova and Durisin, 2007; van Wijk *et al.*, 2008; Volberda *et al.*, 2010; Zahra and George, 2002). To answer this question, the single constitutive elements of the AC process and the interactive flows between them (Patterson and Ambrosini, 2015; Todorova and Durisin, 2007) have to be examined empirically as do the complex inter-relationships resulting from the influence of various upstream organisational or social mechanisms (Jansen *et al.*, 2005; van den Bosch *et al.*, 2006; Volberda *et al.*, 2010). In other words, the process flow patterns as well as their supporting organisational frame conditions have to be taken into account beyond the basic AC components identified in previous studies (Todorova and Durisin, 2007; Zahra and George, 2002). Moreover, the existing literature still tells us very little about how external knowledge is actually transformed and combined with existing internal stocks of knowledge in order to modify or develop new organisational capabilities and thereby influence companies' innovation performance. Knowing more about these organisational prerequisites would help innovation managers to improve their firms' AC effectiveness by facilitating the adaptation and development of innovation routines and capabilities.

Our paper addresses this research gap by further exploring the underlying components and iterative sequences of events, and thus trying to explain in detail how the development and change resulting within the process occurs (van de Ven and Poole, 2005). To do so, the paper builds on the one hand on recent process-based approaches of AC research (Easterby-Smith *et al.*, 2008; Filippini *et al.*, 2012; Marabelli and Newell, 2014; Patterson and Ambrosini, 2015; Todorova and Durisin, 2007; Zahra and George, 2002). On the other hand, it follows a process research method (Garud *et al.*, 2013; Poole *et al.*, 2000; van de Ven and Poole, 1995, 2005) using an in-depth case study of four German medium-sized manufacturing companies. The following research questions are addressed: *Which firm-internal elements and interactions between them are constitutive for a firms' ability to identify, absorb, implement and exploit external information and knowledge? What are the organisational prerequisites to manage the AC performance?* The paper will present a process model of firms' AC to answer these questions.

The findings of the paper contribute to a better understanding of firms' AC processes, both from an academic and managerial perspective. To the best of our knowledge this paper is the first contribution that tries to explore how firm-internal AC unfolds at the micro-level of its single elements and their causal interrelations building the AC process. By integrating them into a descriptive model of AC process flows the findings provide a fruitful starting point for further research on firms' AC. Secondly, as the presented model highlights the single elements and their interlinkages, it can be used by innovation managers to improve and assess their firm's AC.

The paper is organised as follows: First, the theoretical background and the paper's underlying conceptual framework of an improved process-based AC approach are introduced. The theoretical background is based on previous process-based AC research as well as seminal studies on social prerequisites influencing the AC process within firms. Then, the research design of the qualitative, process study and the database used to access the AC process are described and discussed. An in-depth comparative case study of four companies was conducted to explore the constitutive elements of AC as well as their causal interactions on the micro-level. Given that the reality of the absorptive capacity process is expected to be highly complex and to analyse the process within its natural organisational environment, allowing for real-life interventions on social processes, practices and contexts, a qualitative research method has been chosen. Besides other qualitative methodology, an action research was conducted, which will be explained in the section accordingly of this paper. Furthermore, visual mapping strategy is used to depict the process components and the complex process flows resulting from the interaction of the process components with different organisational prerequisites. The closing section highlights conclusions that can be drawn from these findings as well as implications for further research and particularly the management of AC processes in practice.

Conceptualisation of the Absorptive Capacity Process

Constitutive elements of a firm's absorptive capacity

AC represents the organisational ability to recognize the value of new external information, assimilate it and apply it as a knowledge resource for commercial purposes (Cohen and Levinthal, 1990). From the resource-based view of strategic management, it can be defined as an organisational routine composed of processes "[...] by which firms acquire, assimilate, transform, and exploit knowledge to produce a dynamic organisational capability" (Zahra and George, 2002, p. 186). In this context, a dynamic capability represents "[. . .] the firm's ability to integrate, build, and reconfigure internal and external competences to address rapidly changing environments" (Teece *et al.*, 1997, p. 516). Understood as a dynamic capability, the AC drives the creation of knowledge that is essential to adapt existing or develop new organisational capabilities and plays a significant role in helping a firm adapt to environmental changes (Eisenhardt and Martin, 2000; Teece *et al.*, 1997; Zahra and George, 2002).

Zahra and George (2002) began to clarify the concept of AC with respect to its domain and operationalisation by distinguishing two dimensions. The first represents the "potential AC" (PACAP) and captures the firm's capabilities for the acquisition and assimilation of new knowledge from external sources. The second is what the authors call, "realized AC" (RACAP). This comprises the firm's capabilities for the transformation and further economic exploitation of the assimilated knowledge.

Viewed through the lens of dynamic capabilities, the PACAP aims at exploring new potentials to enhance the effectiveness of existing routines or the opportunity to form new ones by generating variations based on newly acquired knowledge and their further internal interpretation and legitimisation (Zahra and George, 2002; Zollo and Winter, 2002). On the other hand, in transformation, the newly acquired knowledge is combined and integrated with existing knowledge (Zahra and George, 2002; Camisón and Forés, 2010) and is used to replicate or test novel solutions (Zollo and Winter, 2002). As such, it describes the development and refinement of "[. . .] internal routines that facilitate the transference and combination of previous knowledge with the newly acquired or assimilated knowledge" (Camisón and Forés, 2010, p. 709). It represents a core capability for the maximum exploitation of existing knowledge on the one hand, by interpreting and combining this in different ways, and new knowledge on the other, by integrating this with existing knowledge. The transformed knowledge is then applied further in diverse contexts and integrated into the firm's operational processes, enabling the refinement, extension and leveraging of existing capabilities or the creation of new ones (Zahra and George, 2002; Zollo and Winter, 2002). Consequently, firms with well-developed RACAP are more likely to achieve a competitive advantage by exploiting existing knowledge. However, as argued by Zahra and George (2002) and others, competitive advantages based on exploitation may result in competence traps (Gupta *et al.*, 2006). Thus, PACAP is a precondition to renewing substantially the internal knowledge stock in a dynamic technological environment in terms of more novel innovations. "But in a context where technological, regulatory, and competitive conditions are subject to rapid change, persistence in the same operating routines quickly becomes hazardous. Systematic change efforts are needed to track the environmental change" (Zollo and Winter, 2002). In other words, firms also need to be capable of deriving appropriate problem-solving ideas as new opportunities based on new knowledge (Kim, 1998). This could help to avoid competence traps and continuously develop innovative solutions. Overall, firms should manage both PACAP and RACAP effectively to successfully convert (external and internal) knowledge into a superior incremental and more radical innovation performance.

Some authors have examined the different practical implications that PACAP and RACAP may have for innovative outcomes. For example, Jansen (2005) proved empirically that firms with well-developed transformative capabilities (as part of RACAP) are more likely to generate exploitative innovations. Consequently, by implementing the relevant strategic instruments to increase RACAP, firms can enhance their level of incremental innovations. Moreover, he emphasizes that RACAP plays only a moderate role in the case of explorative innovation (Jansen, 2005). Consequently, a firm is more likely to increase its innovation output by combining both PACAP and RACAP. In other words, while it may be sufficient to focus solely on RACAP if firms intend to base their innovation strategy mainly on incremental innovation, this does not hold for innovation strategies aiming at higher degrees of novelty. In this case, firms need to develop capabilities in both AC dimensions. These findings highlight the essential role of transformative learning as a connector between exploration and exploitation.

Todorova and Durisin (2007) review Zahra and George's (2002) explanation of knowledge transformation as an alternative process to assimilation. Based on cognitive theories of individual learning, they argue that if the newly acquired knowledge is a good match to the firm's cognitive schemes, the exploitation of the acquired knowledge will directly follow the assimilation phase without any need for transformation. In contrast, if the new knowledge is not a good fit with existing internal knowledge, the existing cognitive structures should be modified or transformed accordingly. Furthermore, they argue, "[...] pieces of knowledge that an organisation tries to absorb may move backward and forward between assimilation and transformation processes before they are successfully incorporated into the organisational knowledge structures and ready for exploitation" (Todorova and Durisin, 2007, p. 779).

In rapidly changing and volatile environments, the constant need to absorb new technological knowledge from various external sources becomes crucial for sustainable innovation performance and competitive advantages. This knowledge is partly tacit in nature and represents an important source of continuous innovation. However, before a firm can integrate new knowledge from different backgrounds into its already existing knowledge base, it should be able to interpret, analyse and codify it, regardless of whether it relates to the firm's existing knowledge base and structure (Camisón and Forés, 2010). Thus, as Camisón and Forés (2010, p. 709) argue, "This phase comes before the acquired knowledge can be diffused and integrated into the firm's existing internal routines, processes and knowledge". Firms need to be able to codify the newly acquired knowledge before they can integrate it into their existing knowledge stocks and apply it to meet the conditions necessary to achieve the desired value (Camisón and Forés, 2010; Horvat, 2015; Zahra and George, 2002; Zollo and Winter, 2002). During this process, proposals to change existing routines are generated, and strengths and weaknesses in the proposed variations to the current set of routines are identified (Zollo and Winter, 2002). Accordingly, given the aim of this paper to develop a conceptual model of firm-internal AC processes controlling different intra- as well as inter-organisational knowledge networks (Van Wijk, 2008) the two capacities assimilation and transformation should be examined as separate, but complementary capabilities (Ambrosini *et al.*, 2009; Camisón and Forés, 2010; Horvat, 2015).

Table 1. Overview of the main AC components.

Authors Components	Cohen and Levinthal (1990)	Zahra and George (2002)	Todorova and Durisin (2007)	Camisón and Forés (2010)
Identification and seeking	Recognize the value of new, external knowledge	Knowledge acquisition	Recognize the value of new, external knowledge	Acquisition capacity
Processing	Assimilate new external information	Assimilation	Assimilation or transformation	Assimilation capacity
Integration		Transformation		Transformation capacity
Exploitation	Apply it to commercial ends	Exploitation	Value creation	Application or exploitation capacity

Table 1 summarizes the previously discussed strands of literature on the different components of firms' AC. As these build the conceptual cornerstones for firms' AC, they will be included in the model as well as in the empirical analysis.

Causal interactions within firm-internal AC processes

Firstly, the basic structure of an integrated AC process model (Fig. 1) builds upon the contribution of Zahra and George (2002). Therefore, we define the AC process as a sequence of events grouped into four components and two dimensions: acquisition and assimilation (PACAP), transformation and exploitation (RACAP). It is thus assumed that the AC process elements focussing on the identification and assessment of external knowledge differ, both in their nature and management, from those AC process elements that are referring to the transformation and implementation of new knowledge inside the company.

Secondly, the development of an AC process model connects to the work of Todorova and Durisin (2007). In contrast to Zahra and George, they depict knowledge absorption rather as an iterative process characterised by a feedback loop between the process components or stages. Hence, we do not consider firms' AC as one linear sequence of process stages in which one task needs to occur and have to be completed before the next starts, but instead in the form of a non-linear

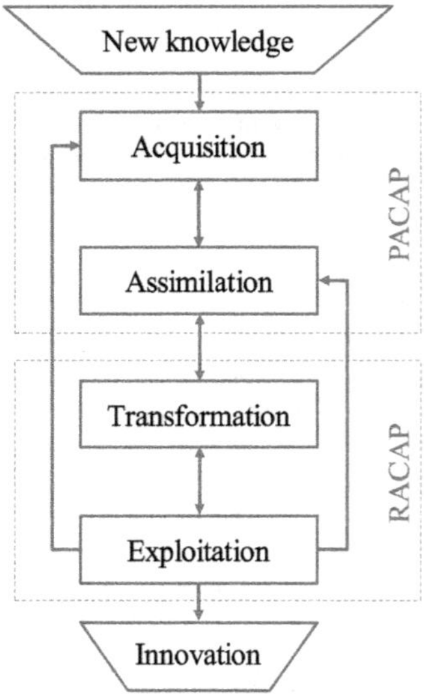

Fig. 1. Integrated model of firms' AC processes (own illustration).

process with different flow patterns and feedback loops. By including this element of feedback loops, the proposed process model of AC highlights the dynamic nature of firms' AC processes as well as the option of organisational learning.

Thirdly, the paper of Patterson and Ambrosini (2015) emphasize that AC is an iterative process in accordance with Todorova and Durisin (2007) and reject the more linear process model of Zahra and George. They investigate the AC process empirically by further detailing its key activities, events and moderators and examining the duration and sequence of each phase. For the operationalisation of AC in their analysis, they used the absorption of intellectual property rights (IPRs) in European biopharmaceutical firms as a knowledge resource for drug discovery and development. In contrast to Zahra and George (2002), however, Patterson and Ambrosini indicate that knowledge assimilation occurs not only in one component or step in the AC process but should be recognized as taking place continuously throughout the acquisition, transformation and exploitation phases. For this reason, they split the component of assimilation into two sub-components: "assimilate before" and "assimilate after acquisition". Likewise, applying the model of Todorova and Durisin (2007), they additionally separate the "search for" and "recognition of value" components into two sub-components which occur before the acquisition (i.e., activities related strongly to explicit knowledge) like contract negotiation and signing.

Unfortunately, Patterson and Ambrosini neglect the effect of the technology-related, tacit knowledge. Moreover, the impact of different organisational prerequisites of AC on the structure and characteristics of firm-internal process flows remains unclear, which makes it difficult to apply their contribution directly to the context of AC management. Without paying sufficient attention to the drivers or enablers of the different AC components, it is hardly possible to make recommendations to management on how to facilitate the flows and thus the effectiveness of firms' AC processes. Moreover, Patterson and Ambrosini indicate time durations in their AC operationalisation for each component of the process based on the industry average. However, as innovation is usually accompanied by complex problem-solving, time should be considered a relative component in AC process flows rather than the key factor that determines the sequence of activities within process phases (Hobday *et al.*, 2000; Muir *et al.*, 2013).

Finally, following the very idea of Zahra and George (2002) that companies need to effectively manage the balance between their PACAP and RACAP processes to achieve a superior level of their overall AC, we propose that this can be achieved by adjusting the process flows, e.g., by designing or reducing intentionally feedback flows within and between the AC components to increase the effectiveness of the overall AC process. By effectiveness, we understand the performance level, which the firm's AC process achieves from the perspective of the company. Hence, effectiveness in this paper is conceptualised in a subjective, qualitative manner and not in terms of a standardised, quantitative performance ratio which, by the way, is, to best of our knowledge, not available in existing literature to date. Consequently, the effectiveness of AC process management cannot be compared between the single cases. Based on the contribution of Patterson and Ambrosini (2015), we propose instead that it should refer to the firm-internal, subjectively perceived AC performance "before" and "after" several measures were taken to improve the AC performance.

Organisational prerequisites of the AC process

Process flow patterns and their supporting frame conditions beyond the basic AC components identified above have to be taken into account to explain why firms are characterised by different levels of AC. "Examining differing effects of organisational prerequisites of AC process dimensions would not only clarify how AC can be developed, but also reveal why firms have difficulties in managing dimensions of AC successfully" (Volberda *et al.*, 2010, p. 942).

In the literature, capabilities are often conceptualised in the context of problem-solving (Schreyögg and Kliesch-Eberl, 2007; Zahra and George, 2002). In this understanding, problem-solving represents different critical situations for organisations (Kim, 1998), because various internal and external factors have to be managed (Zahra and George, 2002). The action and the appropriate resources for solving a specific problem mainly depend on its complexity (Hobday *et al.*, 2003). Solving complex problems requires a combination of cognitive and habitual acts and thereby involves more than just explicit knowledge. In this context, AC is largely a function of prior related knowledge that entails more than just the stock of general or explicit knowledge. According to Cohen and Levinthal (1990), this represents much wider related knowledge domains, basic skills, problem-solving methods, prior learning experiences, shared language, etc.

As firms are distributed knowledge systems (Tsoukas, 1996), Cohen and Levinthal (1990) describe AC as an organisational construct that "[...] is not resident in any single individual but depends on the links across a mosaic of individual capabilities" (Cohen and Levinthal, 1990, p. 133) which, as a whole, facilitate the solving of complex problems. With this view, Cohen and Levinthal (1990) emphasize the foundations of absorptive capacity in knowing and interacting individuals. In this context, Nonaka (1994) argues that organisational knowledge creation "[...] should be understood in terms of a process that "organisationally" amplifies the knowledge created by individuals, and crystallizes it as a part of the knowledge network of organisation" (Nonaka, 1994, p. 17). Thus, when examining a firm's AC, besides prior related knowledge, different organisational prerequisites have to be taken into account. These prerequisites compass the promotion of personal interaction and knowledge management systems, and thus abetting the knowledge exchange across disciplinary and hierarchical boundaries within the firm (van den Bosch *et al.*, 2006). Moreover, these organisational prerequisites can be found in terms of combinative capabilities, enabling the firm to synthesize already existing and newly acquired knowledge (Kogut and Zander, 1992; Eisenhardt and Martin, 2000) into new or modified stocks of organisational knowledge that can be practically applied. Other studies about organisational prerequisites of AC include cross-functional teams and gatekeepers, job rotation, participation in decision-making, power relationships, formalisation of rules, procedures, communication and connectedness and socialisation (van den Bosch *et al.*, 1999; Zahra and George, 2002; Jansen *et al.*, 2005; van den Bosch *et al.*, 2006; Todorova and Durisin, 2007). Empirical research has highlighted the different influences of some of these prerequisites on PACAP and RACAP. Three main types of organisational prerequisites are usually analysed: coordination capabilities, system capabilities and socialisation capabilities (Jansen *et al.*, 2005). For example, according to Jansen *et al.* (2005), coordination capabilities in the form of cross-functional interfaces, participation in decision-making and job rotation influence mainly the firms' PACAP, while the socialisation capabilities associated with connectedness, trust and cooperation primarily strengthen RACAP.

As such, prerequisites are likely to influence all AC-related processes of knowledge absorption (Todorova and Durisin, 2007) and they should not be expected to act as moderating factors between generating problem-solving ideas in assimilation and integrating them with the current knowledge stock in transformation as originally proposed by Zahra and George (2002). Because of their universal character, we do not understand these prerequisites as being a part of the firm's ACAP generally. Accordingly, organisational prerequisites are considered separately in all phases of the knowledge absorption process analysis, because it can be expected that they contribute significantly to better understanding how firms can manage the balance between PACAP and RACAP to improve their AC. Hence, we extend the proposed conceptual framework of the firm-internal AC process flow by considering organisational prerequisites and their effects (Fig. 2).

Finally, a firm's overall AC defined as an organisational (dynamic) capability is thus assumed to be composed by the process elements of PACAP, RACAP, and the interlinkages between them in terms of feedback interactions, as well as the more general organisational prerequisites building the foundation of the overall AC.

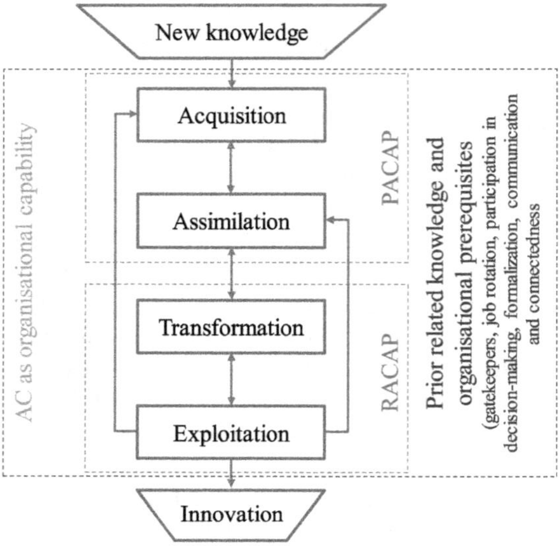

Fig. 2. Conceptual framework of the process-based AC approach.

Research Design, Method and Sampling

Building on the previously outlined conceptual framework (see Fig. 2), we use the innovation process research approach (Garud *et al.*, 2013; Poole *et al.*, 2000; van de Ven and Poole, 1995, 2005) to explain different patterns of movements through the components of AC process linked to the design of several organisational prerequisites. To explore the causal links between AC components, we chose an inductive case study method (Eisenhardt, 1989; Yin, 2009) embedded in a setting of an action research with real-life interventions on social processes, practices and contexts. The analysis takes an exploratory research design using case studies. Its aims are to obtain new insights into the elements and causal interactions that build firm-internal AC processes as well as to derive managerial options for actions to improve the obtained AC level.

To empirically explore and validate the conceptual model of the firm-internal AC process, we conducted case studies in four companies of the German manufacturing industry. The cases were identified by theoretical sampling targeted towards analytical instead of statistical generalisation (Yin, 2009). We looked for a sample of manufacturing companies representing different contextual and structural characteristics which are likely to affect the nature of the AC process in terms of the number of employees, sector affiliation, value chain position and product complexity (see Table 2). Firstly, we selected manufacturing companies

Table 2. Composition of firm sample for case study analysis.

Company characteristics	A	B	C	D
Number of employees	1000	500	200	55
Sector	Electronic	Furniture	Metal and automotive	Electronic
Value chain position	Parts/components supplier	Finished products	Parts/components supplier	Parts/components supplier
Product complexity	High	Medium	Low to medium	Rather low

characterised by the common feature of developing and producing technological solutions that are completely and entirely tailored to the needs of their customers. This means they pursue an innovation strategy that builds upon product or technical process innovations. Such companies need to be able to constantly adapt their internal processes and routines to new external requirements. Thus, the capability to absorb new technological knowledge plays a crucial role for their innovativeness and success on the market (Som, 2012). Secondly, based on a cross-case analysis, the further aim was to identify and examine any differences and/or recurrent patterns between the cases to develop and validate the proposed process model of AC.

The first company (A) develops electric motors as well as various additional hardware and software components for electronic drive systems. The company's main strength is the development and production of completely customised drive solutions that are characterised by high product flexibility. The second company (B) is a furniture manufacturing company that designs, develops and produces swivel, executive, visitor and kids chairs as well as alternative seating solutions for a range of customer groups – business, mid-range, low-end products, etc. The in-house design department continuously develops new, highly innovative and ergonomically designed products for customers all over the world. The third one (C) is a highly innovative company in the aluminium processing industry that produces technical extruded parts and assemblies. It specializes in cold forming by impact extrusion combined with innovative processing techniques with the emphasis on aluminium use. Each solution is completely and entirely customised to the client's requirements. The fourth company (D) is a manufacturer of electric heating components that also develops and produces customer-tailored parts and components.

We collected data from multiple information sources, targeting data triangulation and high reliability (Yin, 2009). The process of data collection was divided into two stages (see Fig. 3). In the first stage, an in-depth case study of a manufacturing company from the electronic sector (company A) was conducted. We conducted 15 semi-structured interviews with engineering professionals as

D. Horvat, C. Dreher & O. Som

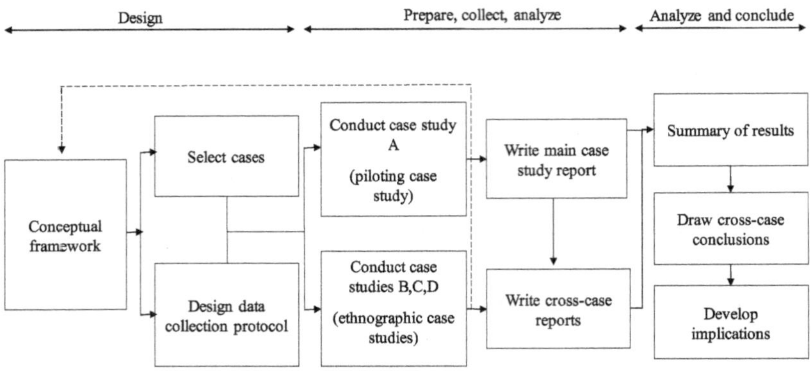

Fig. 3. Case Study design and approach.

well as another eight narrative interviews with company managers. In addition to the interviews, we attended numerous internal meetings and analysed a variety of company documents. This contextual material included paper and electronic documents related to project conversations and presentations. The aim of this piloting case study was to identify the basic process flow patterns and use the very detailed and different kinds of information and data to develop the initial AC process model.

In the second stage, additional case studies with three additional manufacturing companies (B, C and D) were conducted as part of a three-year research project funded by the German Ministry of Education and Research. Two semi-structured interviews were held at each company with leading engineers in the development/innovation departments. Another two narrative interviews were conducted with the companies' managers. In addition to the interview data, information was gathered from non-recorded conversations as well as document analysis. Moreover, the research team engaged in direct, non-participant observation of organisational actions, employees' routines and social interactions to gather potentially insightful data in terms of interpersonal conversations and knowledge exchanges. On the one hand, these three additional case studies were intended to gain further information about the firms' internal AC process flows and the organisational prerequisites that function as prerequisites to AC-related process activities and thus to better understand the explanatory factors for different flow patterns in AC processes. On the other hand, they were intended to empirically validate and evaluate the draft AC process model and identify possible needs for modification.

We applied the qualitative content analysis approach according to Mayring (2010). Category formation was both deductive and inductive. Targeting high

1st order codes		2nd order codes	Aggregate dimensions	
Activities	**Prerequisite**		**Elements**	**Dimensions**
Solving technical problem situations in production process and product development			Triggers	
Knowledge seeking, internet, suppliers, research institutions, cooperation etc.	Prior related knowledge, cross-functional interfaces, density of linkages, participation, team leader	linear/ feedback flows	Acquisition	PACAP
Knowledge exchange in team, knowledge processing and selecting, definition of problem solving solutions			Assimilation	
Design, prototyping, tests and experiments	Prior related knowledge, cross-functional interfaces, participation, density of linkages, team leader, formalization		Transformation	RACAP
Knowledge searching within the data base, implementation for large scales, large series production etc.	Density of linkages, formalization		Exploitation	

Fig. 4. Category system of the qualitative content analysis.

construct validity, the analysis started by defining the aggregate dimensions as the main categories based on the conceptual model (see Fig. 2) (Yin, 2009). With respect to these categories, process activities and their organisational prerequisites were inductively identified in the data and subsequently grouped into 1st-order codes using Atlas.ti software. Axial coding was then performed, searching for relationships between and among these categories (activities and prerequisites), and grouping them into 2nd-order codes that represent the process flows (Corley and Gioia, 2004). Finally, the inductively constructed 1st-and 2nd-order codes were matched with the deductively formed aggregate dimensions. The main purpose of this approach was to develop a unified category system (see Fig. 4) following the "Gioia Methodology" (Gioia *et al.*, 2013) to enable further repetitions of procedure and target the same results (Yin, 2009). We used visual mapping as a strategy for sense making (Langley, 1999) to overcome the complexity by summarising a large quantity of information in simple terms. This method can simultaneously display multiple dimensions, their constituent components and complex non-linear relationships, and as such is suitable for depicting process flows.

Results

Triggers activating the AC process

In terms of the operationalisation of the AC process, we focused our empirical research on problem situations in development and design projects, where

Table 3. Activation triggers of the AC process.

Activation trigger	Representative quotations
Technical problem situation in production process	"Our engineers in the development department are also working to support our production [. . .] It happens very often that they have to solve some technical problems in the production processes and they need information from, for example, tool producers." (case A, interview 8)
	"Someone from production comes with a certain technical problem. Then I have to interview my colleagues working in production and sometimes I observe the processes too. My first task is to understand what is going on and what the problem really is. Then I can start trying to solve the problem in my development team." (case C, interview 2)
Technical problem situation in product development	"The effectiveness of the product development process depends among others on how quickly we can recognize problem situations [. . .] Such situations are completely normal, and our objective is to react as quickly as possible and to further advance the development." (case A, interview 14)
	"As we are developing products that consist of parts produced by our suppliers, we need to obtain information about these parts to be able to combine them with other parts." (case B, interview 2)
	"We are developing our products further based on the feedback of our customers [. . .] If we receive a complaint, for example, we work on further improving the product with the main objective to avoid similar complaints in the future" (case D, interview 1)

engineers need additional technical knowledge to solve the problems. Since solving a technical problem is understood as goal formulation, we considered the AC process as purposeful sequences of actions or process flows following thereby the *teleological theory of change* in organisations (van de Ven and Poole, 1995). In the investigated manufacturing companies, these situations are either related to certain stages or technologies in the production process — process innovation — or to innovations in product development (see Table 3).

Prerequisites, elements and causal interactions of the PACAP dimension

The empirical data retrieved from case study research provide evidence for acquisition and assimilation activities as well as for organisational prerequisites that facilitate knowledge seeking and processing.

Regardless of the type of problem — whether related to product or technical process innovation — engineers are actively seeking new knowledge from external sources either by direct communication with external actors, e.g., suppliers, research partners or clients, or by researching external data sources, e.g., component catalogues of suppliers or open source programme codes. Once they have acquired the necessary information, they use it either to solve the problem individually or to channel it into knowledge processing — assimilation — which normally occurs in a cross-functional team within the firm.

Which of these approaches is used depends on problem complexity, on the one hand, and on the experiences and previous knowledge of the engineers involved, on the other hand (see Table 4). Usually, an interdisciplinary team is brought together to generate a set of problem-solving ideas if the problem is complex and the engineers cannot solve it directly due to lack of knowledge or experience. This team uses cross-functional interfaces such as regular team meetings, task forces or even internal portals and databases for knowledge exchange. As the team represents an organisational environment characterised by lateral forms of communication among and across functional boundaries, the density of linkages or the connectedness between team members has significant influence on the effectiveness of knowledge assimilation. The team leaders take on the role of an intra-organisational boundary spanner or gatekeeper with the function of facilitating knowledge exchange within the team, enabling a better exchange of ideas or proposals.

We identified two typical process flow patterns in PACAP (see Fig. 5), from examining the different situations resulting from various combinations of team members' problem-solving activities that are leveraged by various organisational prerequisites. The process of PACAP flows linearly if the acquisition of new knowledge and its assimilation within the team result directly in suitable ideas to solve the problem. In other words, the acquired knowledge is instantly translated into a set of problem-solving ideas. Such a situation usually occurs if the problem is less complex or the intra-organisational knowledge exchange functions well across cross-functional interfaces.

Failures or unexpected difficulties in knowledge exchange and in assimilation can emerge if cross-functional collaboration does not function well, resulting from, e.g., the demotivation of team members, insufficient integration of team members in decision-making and low density of linkages within the team. Such situations induce feedback loops within the PACAP that are repeated until a suitable problem-solving idea is generated. Eventually, this could cause time delays that threaten the effectiveness of the PACAP process and thus the success of the project. Therefore, the role of team leader is to facilitate and coordinate intra-team collaboration and communication with the aim to reduce or control the number of feedback loops within the PACAP. Figure 5 provides an overview of the common patterns observed about PACAP across all case companies.

Table 4. Prerequisites of the PACAP dimension.

Prerequisite	Representative quotations
Prior related knowledge	"We have to deal with new technical problem situations that we didn't have before on a daily basis. But this is very common because we are working with new technologies in the electronics industry - new components, new software etc [...] Our problem is the lack of experience and of course the lack of knowledge in such situations." (case A, interview 6)
	"I know in which areas my colleagues are really good. So, I always know whom to ask if I have a question. And if I ask the right person, in most cases, let's say in 90 percent, I got the answer really quickly." (case A, interview 7)
	"We are using new materials and components for our chairs, and we have to test them first to know-how they behave. [...] Our designers and engineers do not have experience with these components, and they have to learn first to work with them properly." (case B, interview 3)
	"To develop a new product for our customers, we often have to learn about some new materials or new production technologies [...] The know-how accumulated during years of working in the firm is very important to us [...] Without our experienced engineers, we would have to buy basic knowledge and that would have a very negative influence on our competitiveness." (case C, interview 4)
	"I think it depends on the knowledge we have. If we know a lot about the problem, the new information we gather can lead us to the right solution. Otherwise it is only a medium-term solution which has to be developed further." (case D, interview 1)
Cross-functional interfaces	"Every Monday we have team meetings where we discuss the current problems in product development [...] We also use our internal database for knowledge exchange." (case A, interview 6)
	"If I have a technical problem and I cannot solve it alone I have to inform my team leader. He analyses the problem and brings together a team of colleagues from different backgrounds, for example, mechanical and electrical." (case A, interview 3)
	"We always form expert teams with employees with different experiences and knowledge [...] sometimes even machine operators take part in project teams because they have more practical knowledge [...] We then meet regularly once or twice a week" (case D, interview 2)
Density of linkages	"I think we can only perform well if we work as a team. [...] For me it would be very difficult to work alone on complex problems." (case B, interview 1)
	"As we are a small company, we know everything about each other. I think this has a very positive influence on our collaboration and team work." (case D, interview 1)

Table 4. (*Continued*)

Prerequisite	Representative quotations
Participation	"For me it is very important to be involved in important decisions in [case B] As a designer, I'm also working on the company's image and it motivates me to work effectively." (case B, interview 2) "Our engineers are active elements of our company. This means they are involved in technology and development-related decisions and they appreciate this very much." (case C, interview 4)
Team leader	"Without our team leader it would be difficult to manage the communication with our colleagues from other units who are involved in the problem." (case A, interview 11) "One of my functions in the company is to coordinate team work [...] Sometimes I have to motivate my colleagues." (case B, interview 4) "When we come across a problem we have an idea, if not an exact one, we can at least estimate who could be responsible for the problem which is tied to a specific product or technology. Then we can refer to this person." (case A, interview 3)

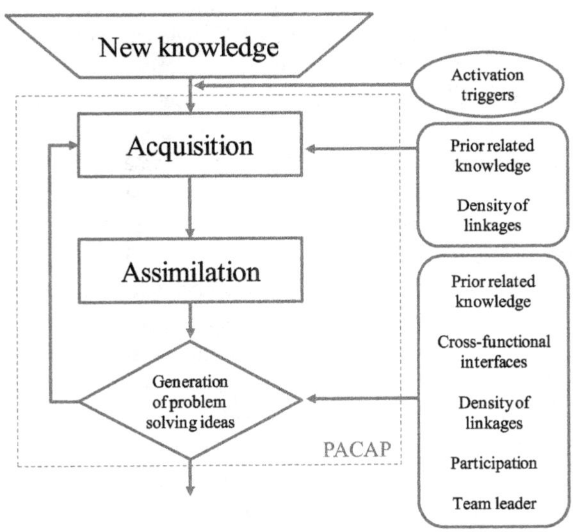

Fig. 5. Process flows in the PACAP.

Prerequisites, elements and causal interactions of the RACAP dimension

Having identified the firm-internal process flows in PACAP, the analysis then examines what happens to the generated problem-solving ideas in terms of

RACAP. Based on the findings from interviews, observations and secondary data analysis, two main process components of RACAP can be identified in line with Zahra and George (2002): (1) integration or transformation and (2) exploitation of external knowledge.

The generated set of problem-solving ideas as the outcome of assimilation is further used in the team to solve one-off problems occurring in innovation projects. This is done by integrating newly assimilated knowledge with already existing knowledge. Ideally, the problem is solved instantly by implementing the newly assimilated knowledge. However, because of the complexity of technical problems, the newly assimilated knowledge is normally combined with existing knowledge in a different way or, it is experimented with until the problem is solved. The effectiveness of the process is therefore characterised by the performance level, the problem is solved by implementing the defined problem-solving ideas.

The data shows that, besides prior knowledge and experiences with similar technical issues, the intra-organisational setting in terms of organisational prerequisites in which the knowledge exchange occurs, plays a crucial role for process effectiveness (see Table 5). In all the analysed companies, cross-functional interfaces represent a platform for combining the inter-disciplinary team members' relevant knowledge with newly assimilated knowledge. But such an interface alone is not sufficient for problem solving. Motivating team members to achieve the desired results and combinative capabilities are additional organisational prerequisites to knowledge integration. According to the interviews, the motivation of the engineers working on projects depends primarily on how deeply they are involved in project-relevant decision-making processes. If they have already participated actively in decision making, they are more focused on positive outcomes of innovation projects, because of their sense of belonging.

Combinative capabilities enable newly assimilated knowledge to be applied and synthesized with the team's already existing knowledge, thereby facilitating the modification of its existing problem-solving routines (Kogut and Zander, 1992; van den Bosch *et al.*, 1999). The empirical research provides evidence for three factors with relevance for the presence of combinative capabilities: (1) density of linkages between the organisational members, (2) the role of team leaders in facilitating knowledge exchange and (3) the formalisation of procedures.

The density of linkages facilitates knowledge transfer within the team, thereby enabling the combination of individual (tacit) knowledge components, which are usually difficult to exchange. Combining intra-organisational knowledge with newly assimilated knowledge makes knowledge integration more effective and helps to refine existing routines in the organisation. If there is low connectedness between team members, the role of team leader becomes crucial for success. As a moderator in the process, the team leader takes on the function of a boundary

Table 5. Prerequisites of transformation.

Prerequisites	Representative quotations
Prior related knowledge	"In some projects we can work faster. But in almost every single project we need some external information which is missing. So we learn constantly." (case A, interview 8) "How fast we can solve a problem situation clearly depends on our experiences with similar problems in previous projects. If we have had experiences with similar problems, we are less afraid to test new ideas" (case B, interview 1) "There is always at least one of us in the team who is not familiar with similar technical issues. I think this is very important because otherwise we would approach every problem situation in the same way" (case D, interview 3)
Cross-functional interfaces	"We have team meetings to discuss the results of our prototyping. Sometimes we have a lot of prototypes and we test them one by one" (case A, interview 3) "Even if we have developed ideas for how we could solve a problem, we continue to work together to test our ideas. First, we develop a work plan and assign responsibilities [. . .] we have team meetings regularly where we talk about the results and problems in testing the ideas [...] of course there are many of them, and this is the reason why we meet so often. We want to solve emerging issues before they become huge problems" (case D, interview 1)
Participation	"I like to be included in team work when my colleagues have technical problems to solve, because I know that my opinion and expertise are appreciated" (case A, interview 1) "I think our engineers are much more creative in generating solutions when they know that their ideas will be included in decisions within the project" (case B, interview 3)
Density of linkages	"Our experiments are very important to us because we are testing prototypes for example, with new materials we haven't used before [...] the knowledge of every single team member is important to succeed in developing the right solution" (case B, interview 2) "We have teams in which the members can work better with each other. [. . .] it is much easier when you know what your colleagues know and can do, it makes the work much easier and more effective" (case D, interview 1)
Team leader	"I think, how effective we are in testing the pilots also depends on our team leader [. . .] he is in direct contact with management and is involved in decision making" (case A, interview 4) "I am the person in the team who has to know as much as possible about the production process [...] I must keep everything under control" (case C, interview 2)
Formalisation	"I have a complete solution which is working properly and after that I produce the documentation for it. [...] the software either works properly or not. I only have to distribute the document about the working software but not about the process of how I developed the solution" (case A, interview 6) "For our experiments and pilot tests we have developed clear check lists which we use in all our projects. [...] Of course, we further improve these tools, but they are a good basis for our work and improve the quality of piloting" (case B, interview 2)

spanner who facilitates the exchange of knowledge and its integration with newly assimilated knowledge (Aldrich and Herker, 1977; Tushman and Scanlan, 1981). Moreover, the leader is in charge of motivating team members in their work and thereby enhancing the effectiveness of the problem-solving process.

Formalising the integration procedures in the form of written instructions and prescribed documentation methods contributes further to the routinisation of procedures and plays a crucial role in sustaining the effectiveness of the integration process. However, we were also able to identify negative effects of formalisation on the transformation process. Formalisation often reduces the creativity of team members and hinders innovations in organisational routines.

If organisational prerequisites do not support this process, there is the possibility that combining new knowledge with already existing knowledge does not lead to the desired results. Based on our empirical investigation, we identified two patterns of feedback process flows (see Fig. 6). First, the process of integration is repeated with the aim of finding the right solution to one-off problem solving — we call this the "experiment flow". Second, if the solution cannot be found after a certain number of repetitions, the search for additional knowledge is mounted.

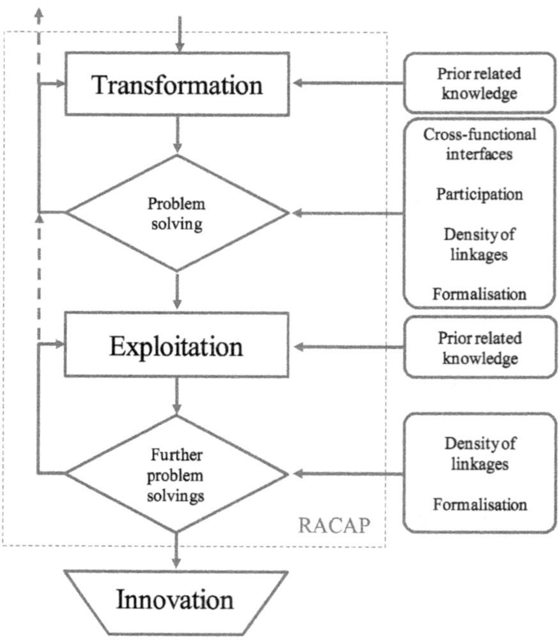

Fig. 6. Process flows in the RACAP.

Both feedback loops are harmless and represent ordinary operational procedures if they occur in a controlled manner. However, if they are not properly controlled, they can result in serious process delays causing lower levels of company AC.

Finally, the new knowledge elements found during transformation are combined in a different way in the phase of exploitation. Problem solving in the company is routinised through repetitive utilisation of integrated knowledge, or by testing the problem-solving results in different manners and contexts (Nonaka, 1994; Zollo and Winter, 2002). Hence, the establishment of a proper organisational environment fosters this process connotatively (Jansen *et al.*, 2005). The intra-organisational density of linkages or member connectedness is the most important characteristic of this environment because this facilitates access to the relevant technological knowledge for the different organisational units (see Table 6). In contrast to assimilation and integration, the results of our analysis do not indicate any relevance of cross-functional interfaces at all. One possible explanation for this is that problems are usually solved locally or individually based on the knowledge — problem-solving routines — previously generated in the company. Even without regular team meetings, a high density of linkages between employees (engineers) facilitates the use of this already generated knowledge to

Table 6. Prerequisites to exploitation.

Prerequisites	Representative quotations
Density of linkages	"There is a lot of knowledge from previous projects, but the question is how to get the relevant information to solve a particular problem. [...] I know products and projects very well because I have been working in the company for 21 years and my colleagues often ask me whether I have experienced similar problem situations." (case B, interview 2)
	"Each problem-solving process is unique and to find the right piece of information within our company, I have to know about the activities of my colleagues." (case C, interview 2)
	"We work very closely with each other and so we learn from each other. Sometimes we have situations which some of us in the team already know from previous projects and which could be useful for solving the task." (case A, interview 5)
Formalisation	"We test the developed solutions in our production and if we are satisfied with the results we use them further on. [...] normally we develop instructions for our machine operators who have to implement the new solutions in their everyday activities [...] of course their activities become routine over time." (case interview 3)
	"The problem is that we don't have a formalised method for documentation of our problem-solving processes. Therefore, it is really difficult to reproduce the process." (case C, interview 2)

solve problems. Moreover, the reliance on established rules and procedures — or formalisation — which make knowledge more accessible intra-organisationally and its exploitation more efficiently plays an equally significant role here (Kogut and Zander, 1992; Jansen *et al.*, 2005).

Routinisation fails if the integrated knowledge does not lead to solving similar problem situations after a few iterations. This is different to transformation, where the experimental repetition of integration in a controlled manner is normal (see Fig. 6). If exploitation fails, the integration process within the RACAP is repeated with the aim of further adjusting the problem-solving routines in the organisation. Unfortunately, such a situation frequently results in running a new PACAP process, thereby negatively influencing the companies' AC level.

Success story of improving the effectiveness of the AC process

To present how the effectiveness of the AC process can be improved by leveraging effects of implementing new or adjusting existing organisational prerequisites, we summarise a success story of company C from our case study. In the framework of a three-year research project funded by the German Ministry of Education and Research, we had the opportunity to conduct interviews at different times and thus to research on the improvements in AC processes in-depth which relates to defining and implementing product and process innovations in the company.

Company C is a manufacturer in aluminium processing industry. To maintain competitiveness on turbulent markets, the company needs to be able to continuously offer flexibility combined with a high quality/price ratio. One of the crucial prerequisites for achieving this goal is the adoption and effective usage of innovative manufacturing techniques in production. Technological knowledge, or knowledge related to innovation in production processes, is thus seen as a critical resource, not only for engineering and construction but also for the production department in the company. Since its internal knowledge creation and learning-by-doing often do not provide sufficient process innovation knowledge, the capacity to absorb new technological knowledge from external sources takes up a crucial strategic role for the company.

The company's innovation activities are mainly driven by market needs. Traditionally, the innovation processes from analyzing customers' requirements to developing innovation plans were managed solely by the technical department within the company. In terms of AC, the technical department was solely responsible for the PACAP of the company. Once the technical department had developed a technical solution, they sent it to production for implementation. If new knowledge was needed, it was acquired by the technical department from external knowledge sources (e.g., customers, suppliers, universities or research organisations). Sometimes, the innovation also included the adoption of a completely new equipment in production. In such cases, the technical department worked closely with suppliers in developing new solutions. Unfortunately, the production department was until then only in charge of implementing innovation (RACAP) without being involved in development processes (PACAP) itself, which influenced negatively the effectiveness of implementation of the innovation in production (see Fig. 7). On the one hand, it caused problems with acceptance of innovation plans in production that hamper the adaptation of new processes. On the other hand, the lack of knowledge in production department in terms of the innovations caused delays in implementation due to frequent feedback loops to the technical department. Finally, the lower effectiveness in implementing innovation caused also problems in projects' efficiency.

To solve these issues, the company established new positions of 'process developers' who have been positioned as boundary spanners between the technical development department and production (see Fig. 8). Experienced employees with good reputation and know-how from the production department are now involved

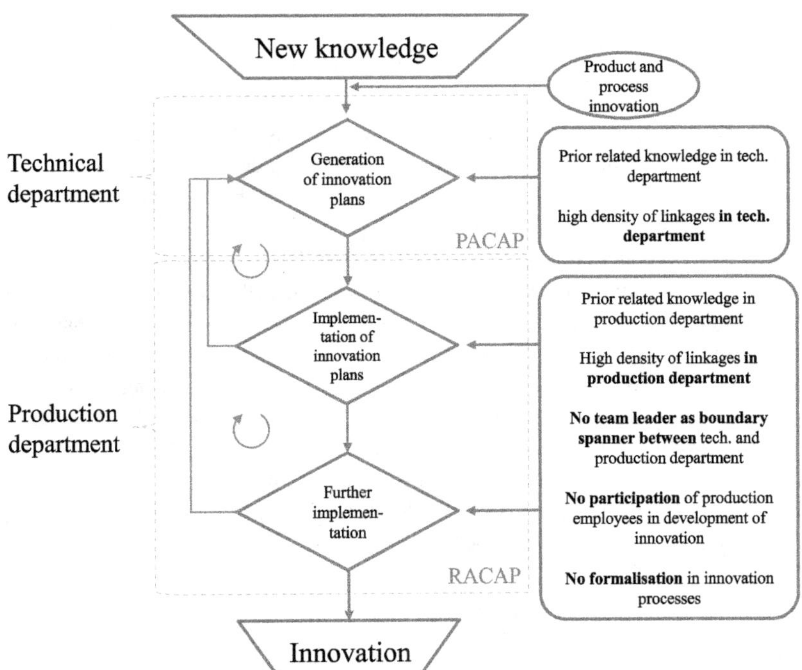

Fig. 7. Issues in AC process of the company C.

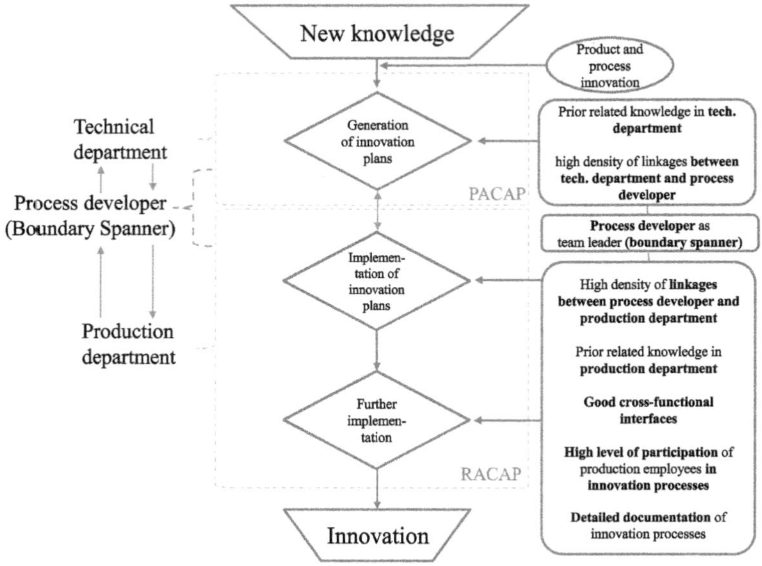

Fig. 8. Solving issues in AC process of company C.

in the development of product and process innovations in the technical department at an early stage. Once innovative solutions have been developed to a production-ready stage, these employees are responsible for managing the transfer and implementation of the new solutions in the production. Because of the high participation of production employees in innovation development, the acceptance of plans (ideas) is much higher than before. Interestingly, the positive effects on the knowledge flows are not limited to production and the technical department solely, but also spilled-over to other departments in the company, like marketing and sales. Due to the improved cross-functional collaboration in terms of intra-organisational knowledge flows, the company observed not only higher levels of effectiveness in their product and process innovation (PACAP), but also with regard to the implementation of innovative solutions in the production (RACAP). Finally, via significant reduction in feedback loops from RACAP to PACAP, the company has achieved a higher effectivity in their AC process.

Discussion and implications for AC research and management

Following the concept of Zahra and George (2002) and starting from the gaps in existing AC process concepts (Easterby-Smith *et al.*, 2008; Filippini *et al.*, 2012; Marabelli and Newell, 2014; Patterson and Ambrosini, 2015), this paper proposes a more complex and dynamic view of firms' AC in a new conceptual model of the firm-internal AC process. Pursuing the main objective of this paper, we adopted a process research approach (Garud *et al.*, 2013; Poole *et al.*, 2000; van de Ven and Poole, 1995, 2005) and conducted an explorative, in-depth examination of the process and knowledge flows, not only between the PACAP and the RACAP but also within these two dimensions. Moreover, the paper highlights the links between various organisational prerequisites and the effectiveness of process flows.

Following Zahra and George (2002), we consider AC to be a process made up of the two dimensions PACAP and RACAP. The first dimension consists of components for acquiring and assimilating external knowledge. The results show that the component of acquisition comprises a set of problem-solving activities aimed at seeking and acquiring knowledge from external sources (Henderson and Clark, 1990; Kim, 1998; Schreyögg and Kliesch-Eberl, 2007). According to the empirical analysis, and in line with Zahra and George's concept, both activities represent components of the acquisition capability and because of their mutual interdependence should not be considered separately, as suggested by Todorova and Durisin (2007) as well as by Patterson and Ambrosini (2015). Moreover, due to differences in the knowledge acquired from different intra- and inter-organisational sources, and therefore from different organisational cultures, systems and practices, we propose — in line with Zahra and George (2002) as well as Camisón and Forés (2010) — that the acquired knowledge should be first internally selected via assimilation as well as analysed and discussed in the group with other colleagues with the aim to, firstly, understand it properly, and secondly, define suitable problem-solving ideas. "These sets of ideas, initially in embryonic and partly tacit form, are then subject to internal selection pressures aimed at the evaluation of their potential for enhancing the effectiveness of existing routines or the opportunity to form new ones" (Zollo and Winter, 2002) and comply with the generative variation and internal selection stages of Zollo and Winter's "Knowledge Evolution Cycle". To sum up, our case study exploration shows that assimilation activities are most likely to be implemented after external knowledge has been acquired. However, it also turned out that if not enough problem-solving ideas can be generated during assimilation based directly on the acquired knowledge, these processes will be repeated — we called this the "feedback loop of PACAP".

Processes in PACAP are influenced by both prior related knowledge in explicit and tacit form (Cohen and Levinthal, 1990) and by organisational prerequisites that facilitate knowledge exchange and intra-organisational processing across disciplinary boundaries (Gupta and Govindarajan, 2000; Jansen, 2005; van den Bosch *et al.*, 1999). Overall, the findings indicate that the integration of cross-functional teams with skilled team leaders as well as the establishment of close links between inter-disciplinary members represent important leverages for managers to increase firms' capabilities of knowledge acquisition and assimilation. Moreover, in contrast to previous empirical work (Jansen *et al.*, 2005; van Wijk *et al.*, 2008), the results indicate that participation in decision-making as an organisational prerequisite plays an important role in motivating team members, not only to seek new knowledge, as proposed in the previous empirical literature (Jansen *et al.*, 2005), but also to assimilate this effectively. Without the feeling of belonging, the motivation is likely to be lower for teams to work on solving a technical problem situation in a project led by someone else.

Managers can increase the level of their firms' PACAP (Jansen *et al.*, 2005) by adjusting the organisational prerequisites identified in the analysis. If they want to improve the process of generating problem-solving ideas, they need to reduce the number of feedback loops within the PACAP process. To do so, they should first establish an inter-disciplinary team with the relevant tacit knowledge (routines and capabilities) and ensure its members are closely connected. This team should be headed by a team leader with the relevant knowledge and experience and awareness of the team members' individual capabilities. The leader is responsible for the team's effectiveness and must manage the process flows and results. In case of, e.g., uncontrolled repetitions within the PACAP — perennial acquisition and assimilation — resulting in ineffective outcomes, the team leader is in charge of defining measures to improve this AC process.

According to the results presented in this paper, the problem-solving ideas generated during the assimilation stage represent only hypothetical solutions or ideas for the actual problem solving that then occurs by testing these defined solutions on the concrete problem situation. This takes place by experimenting practically with the problem-solving ideas, or as Zahra and George (2002) express it, integrating the newly assimilated knowledge with existing knowledge in different ways (Zahra and George, 2002). As such, this activity complies with Zollo and Winter's concept of searching for unique solutions or replication (Zollo and Winter, 2002). Because this involves the first practical usage of the assimilated knowledge, this activity belongs to the phase of RACAP and plays an important role in adjusting existing or even developing new organisational routines (Zahra and George, 2002; Zollo and Winter, 2002). Hence, the assimilation and transformation components of AC should be considered as distinct, but complementary capabilities rather than as alternative components of AC, as proposed by Todorova and Durisin (2007).

Likewise, the existence of cross-functional interfaces like team meetings is an important organisational prerequisite (Gupta and Govindarajan, 2000; Jansen *et al.*, 2005) for integrating new external knowledge with existing stocks of knowledge (that are often tacit in nature). Moreover, combinative capabilities characterised by a high density of linkages between the team members as well as the motivation that results from the sense of belonging, facilitate knowledge integration and the adjustment of organisational routines to problem situations (Jansen *et al.*, 2005). Besides team-related prerequisites, the results also indicate the relevance of process formalisation and standardisation, e.g., written rules, procedures and instructions for increasing the AC level of knowledge integration and transformation (Jansen *et al.*, 2005; van Wijk *et al.*, 2008).

Finally, the exploitation of newly transformed (tacit) knowledge occurs in diverse contexts, built on unique/limited scope application in transformation. In this retention phase, the term used by Zollo and Winter, organisational routines emerge and are stabilized through repetition. These stable routines represent the carriers of new knowledge in the company. They are then applied to other tasks by diffusing to the spatially dispersed parts of the company allowing the company "[...] to refine, extend, and leverage existing competencies or to create new ones by incorporating acquired and transformed knowledge into its operations" (Zahra and George, 2002, p. 190).

Besides prior knowledge about the form of learning skills (Cohen and Levinthal, 1990), the findings of this paper also reveal that the density of intra-organisational linkages as well as formalisation and standardisation have a positive impact on further application of the newly transformed knowledge throughout the whole company. These prerequisites facilitate intra-organisational access to the relevant knowledge (Jansen *et al.*, 2005; van Wijk *et al.*, 2008). For example, formal exchange mechanisms like working manuals and documentation to retain new knowledge, increase the likelihood of unit members finding the right solutions effectively and efficiently. Similarly, good intra-organisational connectedness (e.g., knowledge management as a part of innovation management) facilitates faster and easier access to the required components of knowledge along the different AC stages.

Compard to the PACAP, managers can also adjust their firms' RACAP by setting up the appropriate organisational prerequisites. One effective measure to improve a firm's RAPAC could be written rules for data preservation regarding the technical issues and problem situations encountered. Moreover, practising team building can enhance the density of linkages by developing trust and the willingness to cooperate among team members.

Summary and Outlook

Building upon previous research, this paper aims to provide exploratory insight on the constitutive elements and their causal interactions along firms' AC process. It disentangles the PACAP and RACAP (Zahra and George, 2002) dimensions by conceptualising each of their related capabilities as four interacting elements of firms' process of absorbing external knowledge. Describing how these process phases are linked based on Zollo and Winter's (2002) Knowledge Evolution Cycle, the paper offers a novel approach to opening the "black box" of the firm-internal absorptive capacity process by developing and empirically validating an integrated, conceptual process model of AC. Secondly, based on four in-depth case studies of the German manufacturing industry, the paper identifies the influence of organisational prerequisites on the effectiveness of processes within and between firms' PACAP and RACAP. These results can be used as starting points to advance the debate on the AC of firms and its performance potentials.

Firstly, the results show that the AC of firms should be understood as a complex and non-linear flow of activities and processual sequences that relate to various strands of innovation, organisation and management research (e.g., organisational learning, leadership, boundary spanning and knowledge management). These findings are in line with previous conceptual approaches to AC as a non-linear process (Patterson and Ambrosini, 2015) that features numerous feedback and feedforward loops (Marabelli and Newell, 2014). By developing and validating a conceptual model of the firm-internal AC process within and between PACAP and RACAP using the process research approach (Garud *et al.*, 2013; Poole *et al.*, 2000; van de Ven and Poole, 1995, 2005), the paper makes an important contribution to the academic debate on AC. Furthermore, the results also underline that the understanding of firms' AC is not necessarily fully in line with single theoretical models like those of Zahra and George (2002), Todorova and Durisin (2007) or Patterson and Ambrosini (2015). Instead, our findings show that various elements of all models can be found in the empirical reality of firms' AC. Thus, future research might also benefit from using such an integrated model instead of focusing solely on dedicated features or sticking to particular assumptions of different approaches.

Secondly, the insights gained from the analysis can serve as a starting point for the development of new operationalisations and measurement concepts for firms' AC. The existing theoretical and empirical research is only able to partially deal with this complexity. Hence, to overcome the predominantly R&D-focussed way of measuring AC at company level in the tradition of Cohen and Levinthal's seminal contribution, the process model of AC developed here can be used as a basis for developing a holistic AC measurement framework that helps to structure and connect the indicators to the various components and stages of the firm-internal AC process.

Finally, the conceptual process model of firms' AC presented in this paper and the identified organisational prerequisites and drivers of the firms' AC performance make a valuable contribution to management practice by shedding some first explorative light into the black box of firms' AC process flows. So far, the AC of firms was considered as either given or not, and was hardly accessible to practical strategic management as component of firms' dynamic capabilities (Eisenhardt, 1989; Eisenhardt and Martin, 2000; Teece *et al.*, 1997; Zollo and Winter, 2002).

By providing a process-based approach that can be used to assess and design firms' PACAC and RACAP, our findings can help to support the strategic decision-making of managers to increase their firms' AC and innovativeness. We suggest that managers should focus, especially on minimising feedback loops within the AC process when addressing AC performance. Hence, by analysing the activities within the four AC components — acquisition, assimilation, transformation and exploitation — and the influences of various organisational prerequisites which facilitate the intra-organisational knowledge exchange, the paper identifies leverage points to optimize process performance in PACAP and RACAP. Moreover, the results show that managers should strive for synchronisation and an optimal relation between the two different modes: exploitation of existing capabilities and exploration of new prospects (ambidexterity) (Camisón and Forés, 2010; Horvat, 2015; Jansen *et al.*, 2005; Zahra and George, 2002).

We recognize that our analysis suffers from some limitations which could serve as the starting points for future research on firms' AC. First, our AC process model does not explicitly differentiate between the acquisition of explicit (codified) and implicit (tacit) knowledge. Given the methodological approach used, it can be assumed that the model mainly covers the acquisition of explicit stocks of external knowledge which can be transferred more easily between social entities. Therefore, it would be interesting to further explore the extent to which the acquisition of implicit knowledge plays a role in PACAP, and whether the model must be modified or extended as a result. Second, the model at present does not account for different environmental settings in which the AC process takes place. For instance, the AC process flow might vary across different types of external partners, different knowledge sources or different institutional frameworks for knowledge acquisition and assimilation. Another open question is what the AC process model might look like in terms of long-term, inter-organisational knowledge exchange processes, and to what degree it is determined by factors that are rooted in the firm's external environment. Thirdly, given the inherent restrictions of the in-depth case study method, the developed process model of AC is valid only in the context of manufacturing companies. While the firms were carefully selected to account for a broad coverage of different size categories, industries, positions in the value chain, and levels of product complexity, it is unclear to what degree the process model presented in this paper can be applied to other industries and economic sectors. Fourthly, because of the qualitative conceptualisation based on subjective self-perception of the AC effectiveness, we can neither perform inter-firm comparisons within our sample, nor provide a standardised ration that can be compared to firms outside our sample. Hence, our findings are limited in terms of the uncertainly that the sample firms are outperforming other companies in terms of their AC effectiveness. The AC process model presented in this paper can serve as a basis to develop these kinds of new indicators and measurement concepts to better assess the AC performance of firms in a standardised manner. Finally, the identified organisational prerequisites of the firm-internal AC process are rather generic ones to ensure effective organisational processes in general instead of being particularly targeted towards external knowledge absorption. This appears reasonable if AC is understood as an organizational capability being embedded in the existing organisational setting and routine configuration inside the firm. However, further insight is needed here to find out whether and to what extent AC build upon specific and/or general organisational prerequisites. Maybe this also requires other types of empirical analysis, as interviewees might find it difficult to disentangle the specific aspects accounting for external knowledge absorption, if they aware of them at all.

References

Aldrich, H and D Herker (1977). Boundary spanning roles and organization structure. *Academy of Management Review*, 2(2), 217–230.

Ambrosini, V, C Bowman and N Collier (2009). Dynamic capabilities: An exploration of how firms renew their resource base. *British Journal of Management*, 20(1), 9–S24.

Amniattalab, A and R Ansari (2016). The effect of strategic foresight on competitive advantage with the mediating role of organisational ambidexterity. *International Journal of Innovation Management*, 20(3), 377–400.

Bennett, N and GJ Lemoine (2014). What a difference a word makes: Understanding threats to performance in a VUCA world. *Business Horizons*, 57(3), 311–317.

Caiazza, R and T Volpe (2017). Innovation and its diffusion: Process, actors and actions. *Technology Analysis & Strategic Management*, 29(2), 181–189.

Camisón, C and B Forés (2010). Knowledge absorptive capacity: New insights for its conceptualization and measurement. *Journal of Business Research*, 63(7), 707–715.

Chesbrough, H (2003). The logic of open innovation: Managing intellectual property. *California Management Review*, 45(3), 33–58.

Chesbrough, H, W Vanhaverbeke and J West (2006). *Open Innovation: Researching a New Paradigm.* (Oxford University Press) on Demand.

Christensen, CM (2013). *The Innovator's Dilemma: When New Technologies Cause Great Firms to Fail.* (Harvard Business Review Press, Boston, Mass).

Cohen, WM and DA Levinthal (1990). Absorptive capacity: A new perspective on learning and innovation. *Administrative Science Quarterly*, 35(1), 128–152.

Corley, KG and DA Gioia (2004). Identity ambiguity and change in the wake of a corporate spin-off. *Administrative Science Quarterly*, 49(2), 173–208.

Easterby-Smith, M, M Graca, E Antonacopoulou and J Ferdinand (2008). Absorptive capacity: A process perspective. *Manage. Learn*, 39(5), 483–501.

Eisenhardt, KM (1989). Building theories from case study research. *Academy of Management Review*, 14(4), 532–550.

Eisenhardt, KM and JA Martin (2000). Dynamic capabilities: What are they? *Strategic Management Journal*, 21, 1105–1121.

Filippini, R, WH Güttel, P Neirotti and A Nosella (2012). The different modes for absorbing knowledge: An analytic lens on absorptive capacity from a process perspective. *International Journal of Knowledge Management Studies*, 5(1–2), 45–65.

Galati, F (2015). At what level is your organization managing knowledge? *Measuring Business Excellence*, 19(2), 57–70.

Galati, F and B Bigliardi (2016). The unintended effect of the Orphan Drug Act on the adoption of open innovation. *Science and Public Policy*, 43(6), 840–848.

Garud, R, P Tuertscher and AH van de Ven (2013). Perspectives on innovation processes. *Academy of Management Annals*, 7(1), 775–819.

Gioia, DA, KG Corley and AL Hamilton (2013). Seeking qualitative rigor in inductive research: Notes on the Gioia methodology. *Organizational Research Methods*, 16(1), 15–31.

Gupta, AK and V Govindarajan (2000). Knowledge flows within multinational corporations. *Strategic Management Journal*, 21, 473–496.

Gupta, AK, KG Smith and CE Shalley (2006). The interplay between exploration and exploitation. *Academy of Management Journal*, 49(4), 693–706.

Henderson, RM and KB Clark (1990). Architectural innovation: The reconfiguration of existing product technologies and the failure of established firms. *Administrative Science Quarterly*, 35(1), 9–30.

Henttonen, K and H Lehtimäki (2017). Open innovation in SMEs: Collaboration modes and strategies for commercialization in technology-intensive companies in forestry industry. *European Journal of Innovation Management*, 20(2), 329–347.

Hobday, M, G Dosi and L Marengo (2000). Problem-solving behaviours, organizational forms and the complexity of tasks. EM Working Paper Series no. 2000/06.

Horvat, D (2015). Absorptive capacity, auswärtigen Niederlassungen multinationaler Unternehmen: Eine vergleichende Analyse der Wissensabsorptionsprozesse zweier Unternehmen aus der Antriebstechnik. Hamburg: Kovač.

Hoyer, WD, R Chandy, M Dorotic, M Krafft and SS Singh, (2010). Consumer cocreation in new product development. *Journal of Service Research*, 13(3), 283–296.

Jansen, JJP (2005). *Ambidextrous Organizations: A Multiple-Level Study of Absorptive Capacity, Exploratory and Exploitative Innovation and Performance*, no. 55, Erasmus University Rotterdam.

Jansen, JJP, Van Den Bosch, Frans AJ and HW Volberda, (2005). Managing potential and realized absorptive capacity: How do organizational antecedents matter? *Academy of Management Journal*, 48(6), 999–1015.

Kim, L (1998). Crisis construction and organizational learning: Capability building in catching-up at Hyundai motor. *Organization Science*, 9(4), 506–521.

Kogut, B and U Zander (1992). Knowledge of the firm, combinative capabilities, and the replication of technology. *Organization Science*, 3(3), 383–397.

Langley, A (1999). Strategies for theorizing from process data. *Academy of Management Review*, 24(4), 691–710.

Marabelli, M and S Newell (2014). Knowing, power and materiality: A critical review and reconceptualization of absorptive capacity. *International Journal of Management Reviews*, 16(4), 479–499.

Martín-de Castro, G (2015). Knowledge management and innovation in knowledge-based and high-tech industrial markets: The role of openness and absorptive capacity. *Industrial Marketing Management*, 47, 143–146.

Mayring, P (2010). *Qualitative Inhaltsanalyse: Grundlagen und Techniken* eleventh., aktual. und überarb. Aufl. Weinheim: Beltz.

Muir, T, K Beswick and J Williamson (2013). Approaches to problem solving: Developing an understanding of naïve, routine and sophisticated problem-solving behaviours.

Nonaka, I (1994). A dynamic theory of organizational knowledge creation. *Organization Science*, 5(1), 14–37.

Nooteboom, B (2009). *A Cognitive Theory of the Firm: Learning, Governance and Dynamic Capabilities*. Edward Elgar Publishing.

O'Hern, MS and A Rindfleisch (2010). Customer co-creation. In *Review of Marketing Research*, Emerald Group Publishing Limited, 84–106.

Patterson, W and V Ambrosini (2015). Configuring absorptive capacity as a key process for research intensive firms. *Technovation*, 36, 77–89.

Petti, C and S Zhang (2016). The role of absorptive capacity in Chinese firms. *Measuring Business Excellence*, 20(2), 1–12.

Poole, MS, AH van de Ven, K Dooley and ME Holmes (2000). *Organizational Change and Innovation Processes: Theory and Methods for Research*, Oxford University Press.

Schreyögg, G and M Kliesch-Eberl (2007). How dynamic can organizational capabilities be?: Towards a dual-process model of capability dynamization. *Strategic Management Journal*, 28, 913–933.

Som, O (2012). *Innovation without R&D: Heterogeneous Innovation Patterns of Non-R&D-Performing Firms in the German Manufacturing Industry*. Wiesbaden: Springer Science & Business Media.

Teece, DJ, G Pisano and A Shuen, (1997). Dynamic capabilities and strategic management. *Strategic Management Journal*, 18, 509–533.

Todorova, G and B Durisin (2007). Absorptive capacity: Valuing a reconceptualization. *Academy of Management Review*, 32(3), 774–786.

Tsoukas, H (1996). The firm as a distributed knowledge system: A constructionist approach. *Strategic Management Journal*, 17(S2), 11–25.

Tushman, ML and TJ Scanlan (1981). Boundary spanning individuals: Their role in information transfer and their antecedents. *Academy of Management Journal*, 24(2), 289–305.

van de Ven, AH and MS Poole (1995). Explaining development and change in organizations. *Academy of Management Review*, 20(3), 510–540.

van de Ven, AH and MS Poole (2005). Alternative approaches for studying organizational change. *Organization Science*, 29(8–9), 1187.

van den Bosch, F, R van Wijk and HW Volberda (2006). Absorptive capacity: Antecedents, models and outcomes. ERIM Report Series Reference no. ERS-2003-035-STR, Erasnus Research Institute of Management (ERIM), The Netherlauds.

van den Bosch, FransAJ, HW Volberda and M de Boer (1999). Coevolution of firm absorptive capacity and knowledge environment: Organizational forms and combinative capabilities. *Organization Science*, 10(5), 551–568.

van Wijk, R, JJP Jansen and MA Lyles, (2008). Inter- and intra-organizational knowledge transfer: A meta-analytic review and assessment of its antecedents and consequences. *Journal of Management Studies*, 45(4), 830–853.

Volberda, HW, NJ Foss and MA Lyles, (2010). Absorbing the concept of absorptive capacity: How to realize its potential in the organization field. *Organization Science*, 21(4), 931–951.

Yang, Y, J Hong, G Song and S Hong, (2017). Technology policy, technology strategy and innovation performance: Evidence from Chinese aircraft and spacecraft manufacturing. *Science and Public Policy*, 44(5), 620–630.

Yin, RK (2009). *Case study Research: Design and Methods*, Los Angeles, CA.: Sage.

Zahra, SA and G George (2002). Absorptive capacity: A review, reconceptualization, and extension. *Academy of Management Review*, 27(2), 185–203.

Zollo, M and SG Winter, (2002). Deliberate learning and the evolution of dynamic capabilities. *Organization Science*, 13(3), 339–351.

Zubielqui, GC de, J Jones and L Lester (2016). Knowledge inflows from market- and science-based actors, absorptive capacity, innovation and performance — a study of SMEs. *International Journal of Innovation Management*, 20(6).

Chapter 10

THE SYNERGISTIC ROLE OF INDIVIDUAL ABSORPTIVE CAPACITY AND INDIVIDUAL AMBIDEXTERITY IN OPEN INNOVATION: A MODERATED-MEDIATION MODEL†

SIDDHARTH GAURAV MAJHI*

Information Systems Area
Indian Institute of Management Ranchi, Jharkhand, India
siddharth.majhi16fpm@iimranchi.ac.in

SAURAV SNEHVRAT

Strategic Management Area
XLRI – Xavier School of Management
Jamshedpur, Jharkhand, India
saurav@xlri.ac.in

SANJAY CHAUDHARY

Strategic Management Area
O.P. Jindal Global University, Sonepat, Haryana, India
SanjayChaudhary@jgu.edu.in

ARINDAM MUKHERJEE

Information Systems Area
Indian Institute of Management Ranchi, Jharkhand, India
arindam.m@iimranchi.ac.in

Published 31 January 2020

Managers employed in the dual gatekeeper-shepherd roles in open innovation contexts need to combine external knowledge inflows with existing internal knowledge to drive innovative work behaviour. This study explores how such managers leverage knowledge sources at the firm boundary, to drive innovation activities, by using their individual-level capabilities of absorptive capacity and ambidexterity. To collect data for the study, 121 technology managers employed in four large automotive equipment manufacturing firms in India were surveyed using an online questionnaire. Structural equation modelling

*Corresponding author.

†This article originally appeared in *International Journal of Innovation Management*, **24** 2050083-1-30 © 2020 World Scientific Publishing Europe Ltd.

(PLS-SEM) was used to examine the direct, moderation and mediation relationships hypothesised in the study. The results demonstrate the synergistic roles played by individual absorptive capacity and individual ambidexterity in enhancing the innovative behaviour of managers operating in an open innovation context. This study contributes to the theory related to the understudied individual-level analyses of open innovation and offers recommendations for managers looking to increase their innovativeness at work.

Keywords: Open innovation; individual ambidexterity; individual absorptive capacity; innovative work behaviour; structural equation modelling.

Introduction

Innovative work behaviour (IWB) of managers plays a vital role in the success of firms operating in turbulent environmental conditions characterised by rapid technological change and increased competition (Gupta *et al.*, 2017). As firms in emerging markets lack access to advanced knowledge and capabilities (Bogers *et al.*, 2019; Fu *et al.*, 2014), these firms need to draw on external knowledge sources to augment and facilitate internal innovation processes in order to promote innovativeness by helping them explore new opportunities and translate these opportunities into new products and services (Foss *et al.*, 2013; Leiponen and Helfat, 2010; Guerrero and Urbano, 2017; Hertenstein and Williamson, 2018). This puts the spotlight on open innovation practices that help manage knowledge flows across the organisational boundary (Chesbrough, 2003a,b; Chesbrough and Bogers, 2014; Ollila and Ylström, 2017; Wikhamn and Styhre, 2019).

Open innovation is defined as "a distributed innovation process based on purposively managed knowledge flows across organizational boundaries, using pecuniary and non-pecuniary mechanisms in line with the organization's business model" (Chesbrough and Bogers, 2014, p. 17). Through the adoption of open innovation practices, firms are increasingly asking their employees to identify, assimilate and utilise external knowledge (Chesbrough and Bogers, 2014; Ter Wal *et al.*, 2017).

Recent research points towards the critical role of individual employees and managers, i.e., human capital factors such as firm managerial capabilities (Cirera and Maloney, 2017), in promoting open innovation in emerging economies (Badir *et al.*, 2019). A number of researchers have discussed the growing interest in examining open innovation at the individual level (for example, see Enkel *et al.*, 2017; Lowik *et al.*, 2017), because it is ultimately the individuals who ensure that open innovation is brought into practice (Bogers *et al.*, 2017; West and Bogers, 2017). In this paper, we adopt a capabilities-based perspective on open innovation (Lichtenthaler and Lichtenthaler, 2009) and focus on the role of managerial knowledge-related capabilities in promoting IWB. Individuals performing the roles of boundary spanners or knowledge workers are especially called upon to search for and identify external knowledge (Fleming and Waguespack, 2007) and act as the drivers of subsequent knowledge creation and innovation (Felin and Hesterly, 2007; Grant, 1996) through the mechanisms of knowledge sharing and integration (Lowik *et al.*, 2017). Since the knowledge base of individual employees plays a fundamental role in external search and absorption of external knowledge (Cohen and Levinthal, 1990), investigation of open innovation processes at the individual level of analysis has gained importance in academic studies.

While studies have begun to address the question of individuals' relevance for practices of open innovation, little is known about how individual managers manage the external knowledge absorption process and how it affects their ability to deliver innovative outcomes for their firms (Badir *et al.*, 2019; Bogers *et al.*, 2017; Podmetina *et al.*, 2013; Ter Wal *et al.*, 2017; Volberda *et al.*, 2010). Previous research has emphasised the need for managers to utilise knowledge-related capabilities (such as absorptive capacity and ambidexterity) in order to adequately capture the potential effects of open innovation activities (Cheng and Shiu, 2015). Prior research has emphasised the critical role of absorptive capacity in the open innovation paradigm as it helps in the identification and acquisition of external knowledge (Cohen and Levinthal, 1990; Lichtenthaler and Lichtenthaler, 2009; Ter Wal *et al.*, 2017; Zahra and George, 2002). Also, scholars have demonstrated that individual absorptive capacity positively influences IWB (Lowik *et al.*, 2017). However, recent studies suggest that absorptive capacity may hinder the development of radically new knowledge (Lichtenthaler, 2016).

Since internal and external knowledge plays complementary roles in innovation performance (Faems *et al.*, 2010; Foss *et al.*, 2011; West and Bogers, 2014), it is essential to balance these two types of knowledge (Cassiman and Veugelers, 2006). Individual ambidexterity refers to managers' behavioural orientation to combine knowledge exploration and exploitation activities and thus plays a critical role in the balancing of external and internal knowledge for achieving IWB. However, there is a gap in the understanding of how individuals leverage their absorptive capacity and ambidextrous capability to use both external and internal knowledge in an open innovation context in order to incorporate innovative behaviour in their work practices. Motivated by this, the research question driving this study is:

What is the role of managers' individual-level knowledge-related capabilities (absorptive capacity and ambidexterity) in driving their IWB in an open innovation context?

To test the hypothesised relationships, we collected survey data from a sample of 121 managers employed in a techno-commercial role in four large automotive equipment manufacturing firms in India. These managers are primarily responsible for open innovation-related activities and play a dual gatekeeper-shepherd role (Ter Wal *et al.*, 2017). These managers are expected to both recognise and acquire relevant knowledge from external sources and then utilise the gained external knowledge for driving IWB. Analysis of the collected data reveals that individual managers leverage their potential absorptive capacity and realised absorptive capacity to enhance their IWB and that individual ambidexterity plays a critical mediating role in this relationship.

This paper contributes to the extant academic literature in many ways. It offers greater clarity on the under-studied role of managers in open innovation by examining how the individual level capabilities of absorptive capacity and ambidexterity help in the IWB of managers. An additional contribution lies in the serial operationalisation of individual absorptive capacity as individual potential absorptive capacity and individual realised absorptive capacity throwing light on the underlying components of individual absorptive capacity in a richer manner. By demonstrating the critical mediating role of individual ambidexterity in the relationship between individual absorptive capacity and IWB, this paper brings out the synergistic role of two distinct individual-level knowledge-related capabilities in enhancing managerial innovation outcomes.

The paper has been organised as follows. We begin by reviewing the relevant literature on managerial IWB, individual ambidexterity and individual absorptive capacity to develop the hypotheses for our study. Then, we describe the research methodology and the obtained results. Finally, we analyse the results and discuss the implications for theory and practice before concluding the paper by stating the limitations and avenues for future research.

Theoretical Background and Hypotheses

Recent studies have pointed out that the individual level of analysis has largely remained unexplored in the research on open innovation (Lowik *et al.*, 2017). The discussion at the individual level is essential because, while the adoption of open innovation practices is a firm-level strategic decision, it is ultimately the people employed in the firm who play a critical role in implementing and utilising the open innovation mentality (Giannopoulou *et al.*, 2011; Herzog, 2011) and enable, support and facilitate open innovation (Ollila and Yström, 2017). The role of managers in combining internal and external sources of knowledge to effect innovation is crucial (Pedrosa *et al.*, 2013; Slowinski *et al.*, 2009).

Individual absorptive capacity

Absorptive capacity was first defined by Cohen and Levinthal (1990, p. 128) as "the ability of a firm to recognize the value of new, external information, assimilate it, and apply it to commercial ends." Being an important organisational capability, absorptive capacity has been widely researched in the areas of strategy and organisation theory (Distel, 2019). Since researchers have strongly argued that organisational absorptive capacity is rooted in individual absorptive capacity (Cohen and Levinthal, 1990; Volberda *et al.*, 2010), there has been an increasing interest in the investigation of individual absorptive capacity (Enkel *et al.*, 2017; Martinkenaite and Breunig, 2016; Sjödin *et al.*, 2019).

Some researchers have empirically found support for the primacy of individual factors as against organisational factors, for the cause of knowledge creation (Matusik and Heeley, 2005). Individual absorptive capacity can be defined as the ability of an individual to recognise, assimilate and utilise new knowledge flowing from external sources (Enkel *et al.*, 2017; Lewin *et al.*, 2011; Todorova and Durisin, 2007). We follow prior research (Enkel *et al.*, 2017; Lowik *et al.*, 2017; Todorova and Durisin, 2007; Zahra and George, 2002) in conceptualising individual absorptive capacity as consisting of four different individual activities.

The *identification* or *recognition* activity requires individuals to interact with the external environment and then recognise and acquire relevant knowledge. Secondly, individuals seek to *assimilate* knowledge by articulating it, storing in their memory and retrieving it when need arises (Zollo and Winter, 2002). Thirdly, individuals leverage their cognitive and creative skills to *transform* the assimilated knowledge. Finally, individuals *exploit* the transformed knowledge and apply it in the creation of new products, services and processes. Following the accepted convention (Zahra and George, 2002), we refer to the identification/recognition and assimilation activities collectively as individual potential absorptive capacity and the transformation and exploitation activities as individual realised absorptive capacity.

Sequential operationalisation of individual absorptive capacity

Moving forward, at the firm level of analysis, researchers have argued that one reason for the contradictory findings regarding the consequences of absorptive capacity on organisational outcomes is the inaccurate operationalisation of absorptive capacity as a one-dimensional construct (Fosfuri and Tribo, 2008; Jansen *et al.*, 2005). Hence, a sequential operationalisation of absorptive capacity at the firm level, first proposed by Zahra and George (2002), has been empirically supported by later research (Fosfuri and Tribo, 2008; Jansen *et al.*, 2005).

At the individual level of analysis, Tian and Soo (2018) separate individual absorptive capacity into the complementary dimensions of individual potential absorptive capacity and individual realised absorptive capacity. Ojo and Raman (2016, p. 729) note that "individual members of the firm are responsible for the acquisition of external knowledge and in order to clarify the individual level of ACAP, the associated dimensions need to be isolated," and proceed to isolate individual-level absorptive capacity into potential and realised dimensions. The distinction between potential and realised absorptive capacity is important, because the new knowledge obtained from sources external to the firm need to be first identified and assimilated (i.e., potential absorptive capacity) before it can be transformed and utilised (i.e., realised absorptive capacity).

Thus, while potential absorptive capacity (PACAP) may make an individual receptive to acquisition and assimilation of external knowledge without guaranteeing the utilisation of this knowledge (Todorova and Durisin, 2007; Zahra and George, 2002), it is the realised absorptive capacity (RACAP) that allows an individual to leverage the absorbed knowledge, and thus PACAP and RACAP play complementary roles (Todorova and Durisin, 2007; Zahra and George, 2002). Such a sequential operationalisation brings a more productive understanding of the construct of individual absorptive capacity. Hence, we hypothesise:

Hypothesis 1. *The individual potential absorptive capacity of a manager enhances his or her individual realised absorptive capacity.*

Moreover, the relationship between potential and realised absorptive capacity is further contingent on enabling mechanisms (Zahra and George, 2002). At the firm level, social integration mechanisms have been argued to be the facilitators of the sharing and, ultimately, the integration of knowledge by reducing the gap between PACAP and RACAP (Sheremata, 2000; Zahra and George, 2002).

The exploitation of assimilated external knowledge is dependent on the individual's ability to secure support from the organisation (Enkel *et al.*, 2017). Knowledge absorption processes are also dependent on the influence of power and organisational politics (Easterby-Smith *et al.*, 2008; Jones, 2006). Hence, individuals who have identified and assimilated external knowledge (i.e., potential absorptive capacity) are more likely to be able to transform and utilise this knowledge in their work activities (i.e., realised absorptive capacity), if they possess the authority to make decisions independently (i.e., have decision-making authority (DMA)). Here, it refers to "the extent to which a manager has DMA over how and which tasks the manager performs and his or her ability to solve problems and to set goals" (Mom *et al.*, 2009, p. 814). Increased DMA allows managers to focus on both short-term and long-term needs and be in a better position to secure support from other organisational members and circumvent organisational politics and power play. Hence, we hypothesise:

Hypothesis 2. *The DMA of a manager moderates the relationship between his or her potential absorptive capacity and realised absorptive capacity.*

Individual absorptive capacity and IWB

In technology-intensive industries characterised by fast-changing and competitive environments (Shih and Susanto, 2011) and non-standardised and non-routine work activities (Zhang and Bartol, 2010), innovation becomes imperative for all employees (Axtell *et al.*, 2000; Dorenbosch *et al.*, 2005). In such contexts, employees need to look beyond mature routines and focus on the development and implementation of new ideas, approaches or procedures (Shih and Susanto, 2011).

IWB is defined as "the intentional creation, introduction, and application of new ideas within a work role, group or organization, in order to benefit role performance, the group, or the organization" (Janssen, 2000, p. 288). IWB helps an individual generate, promote and realise ideas in order to modify herself as well as the work environment (Janssen, 2000). Extant literature considers IWB to be a complex behaviour comprising of three distinct behavioural tasks — idea generation, idea promotion and idea realisation (Janssen, 2000, 2001; Janssen and Van Yperen, 2004). These innovation processes require managers to engage in discontinuous activities and extra-role behaviours (Janssen, 2000), and they "can be expected to be involved in any combination of these behaviours at any time" (Scott and Bruce, 1994, p. 582).

Prior research notes the positive relationship between individual-level capabilities and innovative behaviour (Kang and Lee, 2017; Lowik *et al.*, 2017; Radaelli *et al.*, 2014; Sun *et al.*, 2019; Wang *et al.*, 2017). Individual absorptive capacity enhances the IWB of managers (Lowik *et al.*, 2017). Individual absorptive capacity enables managers to access and utilise external knowledge more effectively through proactive identification of events, trends and changes (Sun *et al.*, 2019). Access to a broader pool of knowledge enhances idea generation and implementation (Dahlander *et al.*, 2016), which further enhances IWB. Similarly, higher individual absorptive capacity facilitates the acquisition of tacit knowledge and sensitive information (Badir and O'Connor, 2015), thus enhancing the IWB. To summarise, individual potential absorptive capacity (recognition and assimilation activities) and individual realised absorptive capacity (transformation and exploitation activities) help individuals in idea generation (Kanter, 1988; Scott and Bruce, 1994; West and Farr, 1990) and idea implementation (Zahra and George, 2002), respectively. Hence, we hypothesise the following.

Hypothesis 3a. *The individual potential absorptive capacity of a manager enhances his or her IWB.*
Hypothesis 3b. *The individual realised absorptive capacity of a manager enhances his or her IWB.*

Individual ambidexterity

Following Mom *et al.* (2007), we focus on the exploration and exploitation activities of managers in this study, thus differing from organisation-level activities of exploration and exploitation (March, 1991). Exploration requires managers to try new things, deviate from routinised behaviour and not rely on existing knowledge. On the contrary, exploitation involves incremental improvement of existing activities and reliance on previous experience. Managers' exploration activities include experimentation with new technologies, business processes and markets (McGrath, 2001), new rules, routines and systems (Zollo and Winter, 2002), adoption of a long-term orientation (Tushman and O'Reilly, 1996) and the reconsideration of extant beliefs and decisions (Rivkin and Siggelkow, 2003). In contrast, managers' exploitation activities include the use and refinement of existing knowledge (Levinthal and March, 1993), improvement and extension of existing technologies, products and processes (March, 1991), the adoption of a short-term orientation (Tushman and O'Reilly, 1996) and the extension of existing beliefs and decisions (Rivkin and Siggelkow, 2003).

Individual absorptive capacity and individual ambidexterity

Recent studies suggest that absorptive capacity may hinder the development of radically new knowledge bases/resources due to the probability of reduced variety and limited search (Lichtenthaler, 2016). Such findings underscore the need for managers and firms to balance their acquisition of knowledge between radical and incremental knowledge bases. Research also notes the complementarity of internal and external knowledge for innovation performance (Faems *et al.*, 2010; Foss *et al.*, 2011; West and Bogers, 2014) and the importance of balancing the two (Cassiman and Veugelers, 2006). If the managers of a firm are to take advantage of knowledge from external sources through the processes of exploration and exploitation, they will require high levels of absorptive capacity which resides in factors like cognition, motivation, action and interaction (Volberda *et al.*, 2010). Hence, we argue that individual ambidexterity plays a critical role in helping managers balance the use of radical and incremental knowledge in their work.

Managers in the gatekeeper role need to simultaneously explore and exploit different sources of knowledge in order to elicit advantages from an optimal knowledge mix (Crescenzi and Gagliardi, 2018). The innovative performance of managers is closely related to their ability to combine the knowledge inflows from both external and internal sources (Teece *et al.*, 1997). Since it is the absorptive capacity of managers which helps them identify, acquire and assimilate external knowledge and integrate it with internal knowledge in order to utilise the same (Arora and Gambardella, 1994), it follows that individual absorptive capacity of managers is critical to leverage ambidexterity advantages of simultaneous exploration and exploitation of external and internal knowledge. Summarily, sufficient level of absorptive capacity aids in ambidexterity or the simultaneous pursuit of exploration and exploitation (Kranz *et al.*, 2016; Limaj and Bernroider, 2019; Rothaermel and Alexandre, 2009; Solís-Molina *et al.*, 2018). Hence, we hypothesise:

Hypothesis 4a. *The individual potential absorptive capacity of managers has a positive effect on their individual ambidexterity.*
Hypothesis 4b. *The individual realised absorptive capacity of managers has a positive effect on their individual ambidexterity.*
Hypothesis 4c. *Individual realised absorptive capacity mediates the relationship between individual potential absorptive capacity and individual ambidexterity of managers.*

Individual ambidexterity and IWB

Engaging in innovative behaviour at the workplace is considered to be an extra-role behaviour (Janssen, 2000; Katz and Kahn, 1978), and this requires individuals to go beyond their prescribed role expectations (standard job performance) (Janssen, 2001) and simultaneously engage in discretionary innovation-related activities (Katz and Kahn, 1978). Thus, individual ambidexterity will help enhance IWB because it requires a balancing of the in-role and extra-role work behaviours (i.e., standard job performance and IWB, respectively).

Innovation has an aspect of duality associated with it — *generation* of new and useful ideas and the *implementation* of these ideas (Anderson *et al.*, 2014; West and Farr, 1990). Extant research has noted the role of individual ambidexterity in helping innovative workers deal with this duality (Rosing and Zacher, 2017).

Innovation is often characterised by tensions, contradictions and paradoxes (Bledow *et al.*, 2009; MironSpektor *et al.*, 2011), and individual ambidexterity helps in the integration of such contradictory requirements and paradoxical tensions in order to facilitate innovative behaviour (Rosing and Zacher, 2017). Innovative workers are likely to experience more conflict with resisting co-workers who may obstruct their innovative ideas (Janssen, 2003). Also, such innovative workers would have to balance exploitative activities (regular job performance) with exploratory activities (IWB). Thus, ambidextrous managers who are adept at effectively balancing the opposing activities of exploration and exploitation are more likely to successfully engage in IWB (Bledow *et al.*, 2009; Rosing *et al.*, 2011; Rosing and Zacher, 2017). Thus, we hypothesise

Hypothesis 5. *Individual ambidexterity of managers enhances their IWB.*

Individual absorptive capacity and IWB: The mediating role of individual ambidexterity

Researchers adopting a capabilities perspective on the open innovation paradigm note that while absorptive capacity is an influential concept in this context, it focuses on the utilisation of external knowledge within the firm while neglecting other essential knowledge processes such as internal knowledge generation (Lane *et al.*, 2006; Lichtenthaler and Lichtenthaler, 2009; Zahra and George, 2002). Thus, it is essential to consider various knowledge-related capabilities such as exploration, retention and exploitation both inside and outside the boundaries of the organisation (Lichtenthaler and Lichtenthaler, 2009). Many scholars emphasise the need to combine internal and external knowledge in innovation processes (Andersen and Drejer, 2008; Hargadon and Sutton, 1997). Mom *et al.* (2009, p. 812) define individual ambidexterity or manager-level ambidexterity as "a manager's behavioural orientation toward combining exploration and exploitation related activities within a certain period of time." Thus, individual ambidexterity as a managerial capability will play a critical role in the leveraging of individual absorptive capacity for IWB.

Based on Hypotheses 4a, 4b, 4c and 5 presented earlier, we see that individual absorptive capacity has a positive effect on individual ambidexterity and, in turn, individual ambidexterity enhances the IWB of managers. Hence, we hypothesise,

Hypothesis 6a. *Individual ambidexterity mediates the relationship between individual realised absorptive capacity and IWB of managers.*

Hypothesis 6b. *Individual realised absorptive capacity and individual ambidexterity mediate the relationship between individual potential absorptive capacity and IWB of managers.*

The following model (Fig. 1) depicts the relationships hypothesised by us in this study.

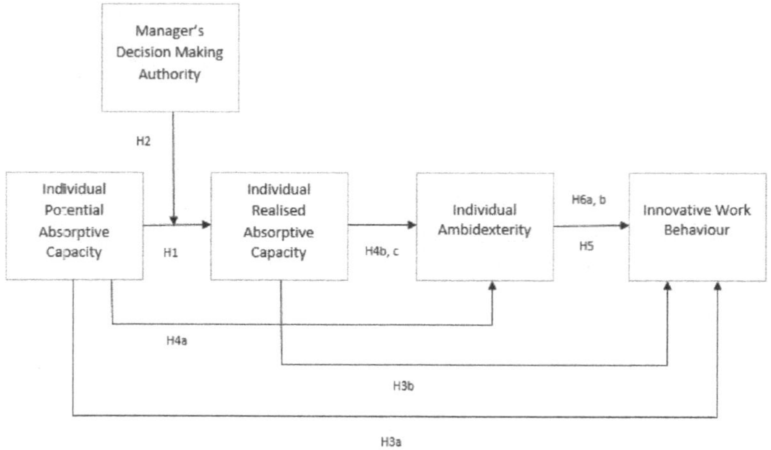

Fig. 1. Model of the relationships hypothesised in this study.

Research Methodology

Sampling and data collection

This study uses a quantitative method and a deductive approach to examine the relationship between individual absorptive capacity, individual ambidexterity and IWB. To eliminate industry-specific differences, we collected data from four leading firms belonging to the automotive equipment manufacturing industry in India (average size = 7237.5 employees, average R&D intensity = 0.02185). The sample firms are mobility solution providers offering automotive aftermarket solutions in India. These organisations offer automotive components, replacement parts as well as service solutions for service SMEs. The automotive equipment manufacturing industry experiences a rapid pace of change, making it an appropriate context for studying the use of individual-level capabilities in absorbing external knowledge for innovation (Enkel *et al.*, 2017).

Our sample consists of technology managers who act as gatekeepers of technological innovation and also as carriers of new knowledge into and across the firm (Ebers and Maurer, 2014). These technology managers perform techno-commercial jobs in the technical sales department of the sample firms. They enable the bidirectional exchange of information with external partners (e.g., service SMEs, suppliers) and facilitate internal development of low-cost automotive solutions by Indian service SMEs. These managers interact with the external environment to recognise new technology resources, combine acquired new knowledge regarding automotive servicing with existing internal knowledge and are also responsible for dissemination of acquired internal as well as external knowledge to create new solutions at service SMEs. Such managers are the primary change agents in organisations (Jones, 2006) and are expected to need and have higher individual absorptive capacity due to their position at the interface of different organisational units (internal firm environment) and the external firm environment (Cohen and Levinthal, 1990; Lowik *et al.*, 2016). These managers play a critical role in the creation and exchange of new knowledge and are most likely to contribute to the innovation output of firms (Rothaermel and Hess, 2007).

To collect the survey data for our study, we randomly sampled 50 technology managers each in the four chosen firms. All the 200 managers were sent a personalised email containing the link to an online questionnaire in September 2018. We sent them three rounds of reminders, once every month. By the end of December 2018, 130 responses were returned, resulting in a 65% response rate. We eliminated nine responses from further analysis because of missing data. Hence, the final sample used for analysis consisted of 121 observations.

Measures

All the constructs were measured using multiple items, either directly derived or adapted with minor modifications from existing literature. A 7-point Likert scale ranging from 1 (strongly disagree) to 7 (strongly agree) was used to measure the items (Podsakoff *et al.*, 2003). Before conducting the final data collection effort, the survey instrument was pilot-tested with a sample of 25 respondents randomly drawn from our sampling frame. Based on the responses to the pilot survey and the comments of the respondents, we made some minor refinements to the questionnaire in order to change some unclear wording.

Individual ambidexterity

We assessed individual ambidexterity using the procedures and scales developed and validated by Mom *et al.* (2007, 2009). Since there are two separate scales for individual exploration and individual exploitation, we followed past research to measure individual ambidexterity in two steps (Kauppila and Tempelaar, 2016; Menguc and Auh, 2008). Exploration and exploitation were first assessed using separate seven-item orthogonal scales, which were borrowed from Mom *et al.* (2007). We found acceptable reliability of the scales used for individual exploration (alpha = 0.79, CR = 0.85) and individual exploitation (alpha = 0.82, CR = 0.87). Secondly, we derived an indicator for individual ambidexterity by computing a multiplicative interaction between exploration and exploitation. Such a multiplicative interaction has been argued to be the most appropriate measure of ambidexterity by previous researchers (Kauppila and Tempelaar, 2016; Mom *et al.*, 2009), and this approach is also consistent with the theoretical conceptualisation of ambidexterity (Tushman and O'Reilly, 1996).

Individual potential absorptive capacity

To assess individual potential absorptive capacity, we used seven items corresponding to the recognition and assimilation dimensions of the individual absorptive capacity scale developed by Lowik *et al.* (2016, 2017). The scale was found to be reliable (alpha = 0.85, CR = 0.89).

Individual realised absorptive capacity

To assess individual realised absorptive capacity, we used seven items from the individual absorptive capacity scale developed by Lowik *et al.* (2016, 2017) corresponding to the transformation and exploitation dimensions. The scale was found to be reliable (alpha = 0.83, CR = 0.88).

Manager's DMA

We used an existing four-item scale to assess a manager's DMA in performing his or her tasks and in the ability to set goals. Originally developed by Dewar *et al.* (1980), this scale has been used in previous studies related to individual absorptive capacity and individual ambidexterity (Mom *et al.*, 2009). The scale was found to be reliable (alpha = 0.74, CR = 0.85).

IWB

We assessed the IWB of managers by using a nine-item scale developed by Janssen and Van Yperen (2004). This scale is meant for supervisors to report the performance of employees and was hence adapted to make it a self-reported scale. Prior research has noted that employees are best suited to self-report IWBs and such employee self-reports have been found to be correlated with supervisor ratings (Gupta *et al.*, 2017). The scale was found to be reliable (alpha = 0.88, CR = 0.91).

Control variables

To account for the possibility of spurious relationships arising due to socio-demographic and inter-firm differences in the dependent variables, we used the following control variables in this study. We controlled for (1) age (in years), (2) gender, (3) experience (in years), (4) highest level of education obtained (graduate, post-graduate or doctorate), (5) size of the firm (natural logarithm of the number of employees) and (6) R&D intensity of the firm (computed as the ratio between R&D investments and sales revenue). Further, to control for inter-firm differences, we created dummy variables for each firm and included these dummy variables in the analysis. For both the dependent variables (IA and IWB), we also controlled for the effect of the manager's DMA.

Analytical techniques

Partial least squares analysis

We chose to use partial least squares-based structural equation modelling (PLS-SEM) using Smart PLS 3.2.8 for testing the hypothesised relationships in this study because of three reasons, which are in line with the accepted recommendations (Benitez *et al.*, 2019; Cepeda-Carrion *et al.*, 2019; Chin, 2010; Hair *et al.*, 2016). First, our research was exploratory. Secondly, variance-based PLS-SEM is more suitable for small samples, compared with covariance-based SEM. Thirdly,

PLS enforces less strict restrictions regarding distributional assumptions related to normality of the observations.

We used the Smart PLS 3.2.8 package for the analysis. To review the significance levels of the hypothesised relationships, we used the bootstrapping procedure in order to examine the *t*-statistics of all the indicators. We ran the bootstrap procedure with the recommended number of 5000 samples and did not accept sign changes during the bootstrapping (Hair *et al.*, 2016).

Moderation and mediation analysis

We tested the moderation and mediation effects hypothesised in the model in two ways — using Smart PLS 3.2.8 and the PROCESS tool of SPSS 23. Smart PLS offers features to test the moderation and mediation effects (Hair *et al.*, 2016), and we followed the accepted recommendations to conduct the analysis. We used the Sobel's *Z*-test for testing the significance of the mediation effects (Hypotheses 4c, 6a and 6b). To confirm the moderation and mediation effects, we also used the latent variable scores obtained from Smart PLS to analyse the effects using the bootstrapping procedure (with 5000 resamples) in the PROCESS tool (Hayes, 2013) in SPSS.

Results and Analysis

Checking for common method bias

If the variance is attributable to the measurement method rather than the construct, it leads to method bias (Podsakoff *et al.*, 2003). A specific case of the method bias is the common method bias (CMB), and it occurs when data are collected using only a single instrument (Burton-Jones, 2009). During the survey design, we used methodological recommendations (Podsakoff *et al.*, 2003) and tried to minimise risk from CMB by (a) taking care to reduce item ambiguity through pre-testing, (b) maintaining anonymity of respondents through the use of an online platform for survey administration and (c) separation of the scales for independent and dependent variables.

After data collection, we used Harman's single factor test (Harman, 1967), in which the proportion of variance explained by the unrotated single factor can indicate level of risk from CMB. We found that the single factor accounted for only 27.57% of the variance and this indicates that CMB is not a serious problem in this study.

Assessment of the measurement model

We assessed the reflective measurement model by evaluating the internal consistency (Cronbach's alpha, composite reliability), convergent validity (indicator reliability, average variance extracted (AVE)) and discriminant validity.

We assessed the internal consistency reliability using both the traditional measure of Cronbach's alpha as well as the composite reliability. It is recommended to consider and report both these criteria because Cronbach's alpha tends to underestimate the reliability, whereas composite reliability (CR) tends to overestimate the same (Hair *et al.*, 2016). For all the constructs used in our study except IWB (CR = 0.91), the alpha and CR scores were found to lie in the recommended range of 0.7–0.9 (Hair *et al.*, 2016; Nunnally, 1978) (Table 2).

We assessed the convergent validity using the outer loadings of each item (indicator reliability) and AVE. While the rule of thumb is to have outer loadings greater than 0.7, slightly lower values are acceptable in social science research (Hair *et al.*, 2016). Therefore, following the recommended procedure, we decided to retain items that had outer loadings higher than 0.6 if removing them did not lead to increase in composite reliability or AVE (see Table 1 for factor loadings).

Table 1. Construct measurement summary and factor loadings.

Item description	Factor loading
Manager's Decision-Making Authority (DMA)	
DMA_1: I can undertake little action until my supervisor approves a decision	0.62
DMA_3: If I want to make my own decisions, I will be quickly discouraged	0.90
DMA_4: I have to ask my supervisor before I do almost anything	0.89
Individual Ambidexterity (IA) (Single item construct)	
Individual exploration × Individual exploitation	Single item
Individual exploration	
"In the last year, to what extent did you engage in..."	
EXPLOR_1: Searching for new possibilities with respect to products/services, processes or markets	0.79
EXPLOR_2: Evaluating diverse options with respect to products/services, processes or markets	0.74
EXPLOR_3: Focusing on strong renewal of products/services or markets	0.77
EXPLOR_4: Activities requiring quite some adaptability of you	0.72
EXPLOR_5: Activities requiring you to learn new skills or knowledge	0.65
Individual exploitation	
"In the last year, to what extent did you engage in ..."	
EXPLOIT_1: Activities of which a lot of experience has been accumulated by yourself	0.78
EXPLOIT_3: Activities of which it is clear to you how to conduct them	0.68
EXPLOIT_5: Activities which you can properly conduct by using your present knowledge	0.83
EXPLOIT_6: Activities which clearly fit into existing company policy	0.75
EXPLOIT_7: Activities which you carry out as if it were routine	0.77
Individual Potential Absorptive Capacity (IPACAP)	
IPACAP_1: I am always actively looking for new knowledge for my work	0.67

Table 1. (*Continued*)

Item description	Factor loading
IPACAP_2: I intentionally search for knowledge in many different domains to look "outside the box"	0.70
IPACAP_4: I easily identify what new knowledge is most valuable to us	0.70
IPACAP_5: I frequently share my new knowledge with colleagues to establish a common understanding	0.83
IPACAP_6: I translate new knowledge in such a way that my colleagues understand what I mean	0.85
IPACAP_7: I communicate newly acquired knowledge that might be of interest for our unit	0.78
Individual Realised Absorptive Capacity (IRACAP)	
IRACAP_1: I often sit together with colleagues to come up with new ideas	0.79
IRACAP_2: I attend meetings with people from different departments to come up with new ideas	0.82
IRACAP_3: I develop new insights from the knowledge that is available within our firm	0.73
IRACAP_4: I can turn existing knowledge into new ideas	0.77
IRACAP_6: I exploit new knowledge to create new products, services, or work methods	0.74
IWB	
IWB_1: I create new ideas for improvements	0.77
IWB_2: I mobilise support for innovative ideas	0.77
IWB_3: I search for new working methods or techniques	0.69
IWB_5: I transform innovative ideas into useful application	0.79
IWB_6: I generate original solutions to problems	0.71
IWB_7: I introduce innovative ideas in a systematic way	0.78
IWB_8: I make important organisational members enthusiastic for innovative ideas	0.67
IWB_9: I thoroughly evaluate the application of innovative ideas	0.71

Table 2. Descriptive statistics, construct reliability, convergent and divergent validity.

	Mean	SD	AVE	CA	CR	DMA	IA	IWB	IPACAP	IRACAP
DMA	4.21	1.22	0.66	0.74	0.85	**0.81**				
IA	26.42	5.26	Single item	Single item	Single item	0.10	**1.00**			
IWB	5.29	0.84	0.54	0.88	0.91	0.18	0.48	**0.74**		
IPACAP	5.65	0.88	0.58	0.85	0.89	0.31	0.56	0.47	**0.76**	
IRACAP	5.42	0.98	0.59	0.83	0.88	0.34	0.66	0.47	0.70	**0.77**

The AVE for all constructs was higher than the recommended value of 0.5, thus establishing their convergent validity (Table 2).

We confirmed the discriminant validity by examining the cross-loadings and applying the Fornell–Larcker criteria. None of the indicators loaded higher on any construct than its own. For each construct, the square root of AVE was higher than the inter-construct correlations, confirming the discriminant validity (Table 2). Based on recent methodological recommendations (Benitez *et al.*, 2019), we also examined and confirmed the discriminant validity using the HTMT (heterotrait-to-monotrait) ratio.

Assessment of the structural model

We estimated the structural model using the bias-corrected and accelerated (Bca) bootstrapping procedure with 5000 resamples. We checked all the predictors for multicollinearity using VIF values, which were much lower than the recommended value of 5 for each construct (Hair *et al.*, 2016). We assessed the overall model fit by using standardised root mean square residual (SRMR) as the index for model validation, following accepted recommendations of PLS-SEM research (Hair *et al.*, 2016; Henseler *et al.*, 2014). For SRMR, values below 0.08 are considered favourable for CB-SEM (Hu and Bentler, 1999), whereas some relaxation of this value (up to 0.10) is acceptable when using PLS-SEM (Hair *et al.*, 2016). The estimation of our model using the PLS algorithm indicated an SRMR value of 0.089, which is acceptable and shows the goodness of fit of our model. The model quality indices for individual realised absorptive capacity ($R^2 = 52.2\%$, and adjusted $R^2 = 51\%$), individual ambidexterity ($R^2 = 45\%$, and adjusted $R^2 = 44.1\%$) and IWB ($R^2 = 30.2\%$ and adjusted $R^2 = 28.4\%$) were found to be satisfactory.

None of the control variables was found to have a statistically significant effect on the dependent variables. All the hypothesised relationships, except H3a and H3b, were found to be statistically significant for our sample (Table 3 and Fig. 2).

Moderation analysis

Using PLS-SEM, the moderating effect of a manager's DMA on the relationship between the individual potential absorptive capacity and the individual realised

Table 3. Results of the testing of hypotheses (direct effects).

Hypothesis	Path	Coefficient	T-value	p-value	Result
H1	IPACAP −> IRACAP	0.613***	8.334	0.000	Accepted
H3a	IPACAP −> IWB	0.251	1.638	0.101	Not accepted
H3b	IRACAP −> IWB	0.135	0.840	0.401	Not accepted
H4a	IPACAP −> IA	0.207*	2.421	0.016	Accepted
H4b	IRACAP −> IA	0.512***	6.083	0.000	Accepted
H5	IA −> IWB	0.247*	2.415	0.016	Accepted

Notes: ***$p < 0.001$, **$p < 0.01$, *$p < 0.05$. IPACAP, individual potential absorptive capacity; IRACAP, individual realised absorptive capacity; DMA, manager's decision making authority; IA, individual ambidexterity; IWB, innovative work behaviour.

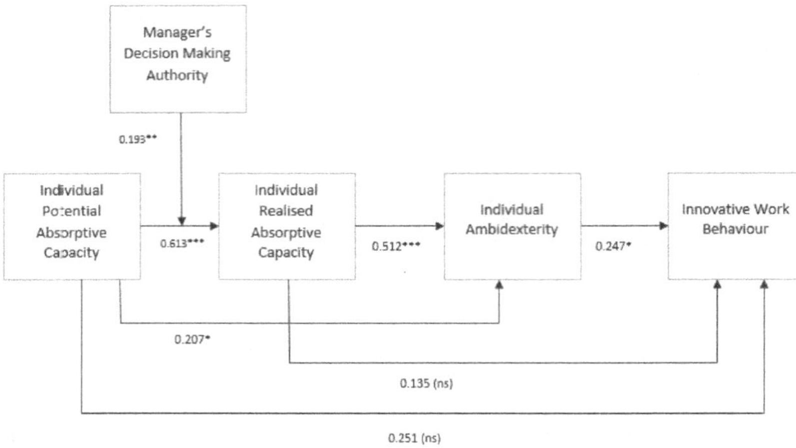

Fig. 2. Results of hypotheses testing.

absorptive capacity was found to be statistically significant ($p = 0.009$), thus supporting Hypothesis 2. The moderation effect was also tested using the PROCESS tool (Hayes, 2013) in SPSS, using the latent variable scores obtained from Smart PLS. The analysis using the Model 1 specification also showed the moderation effect to be significant ($p = 0.0061$, 95% CI = [0.0549, 0.3233]) and that this effect increases the R-square by 3.12%.

Figures 3(a) and 3(b) depict the moderation effect of the manager's DMA on the relationship between individual potential absorptive capacity and individual realised absorptive capacity, as tested in Smart PLS and SPSS PROCESS tool, respectively. Thus, higher the DMA of managers, higher is their ability to transform and utilise the external knowledge that has been identified and assimilated.

Mediation analysis

Table 4 shows the results of the mediation analysis conducted using Sobel's Z-test method. The results show that Hypotheses 4c, 6a and 6b are valid for our sample. Further, we see that IRACAP partially mediates the relationship between IPACAP and IWB. In contrast, IA fully mediates the relationship between IRACAP and IWB. Similarly, IRACAP and IA fully mediate the relationship between IPACAP and IWB.

We also confirmed the mediation effects using the bootstrapping procedure in the PROCESS tool of SPSS. We found support for Hypotheses 4c, 6a and 6b since the 95% confidence intervals were [0.2345, 0.5142], [0.0777, 0.3364] and [0.0268, 0.4937], respectively.

Individual Absorptive Capacity and Individual Ambidexterity in Open Innovation

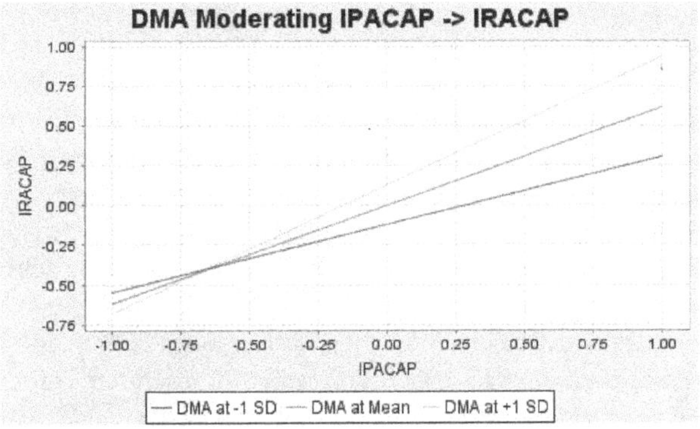

(a)

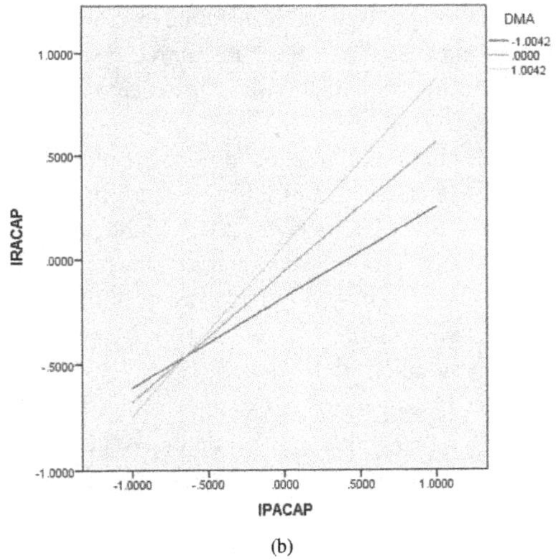

(b)

Fig. 3. (a) Moderation effect of DMA on IPACAP -> IRACAP (PLS-SEM) and (b) Moderation effect of DMA on IPACAP -> IRACAP (SPSS Process).

Table 4. Mediation analysis using Sobel's *Z*-test.

Hypothesis	IV −> M −> DV	Direct effect	Indirect effect	Total effect	*Z*-score	Result
H4c	IPACAP −> IRACAP −> IA	0.207*	0.314***	0.521***	4.91***	Accepted
H6a	IRACAP −> IA −> IWB	0.135	0.126*	0.261*	2.25*	Accepted
H6b	IPACAP −> IRACAP −> IA −> IWB	0.251	0.077*	0.328*	2.17*	Accepted

Discussion

Theoretical implications

Many managers, acting as gatekeepers, are additionally expected to contribute towards the implementation of new knowledge in their respective firms. This paper focuses on managers involved in such dual roles and the factors affecting their innovative behaviour in open innovation settings. In doing so, the study explores the relevance and importance of two capabilities, absorptive capacity and ambidexterity, at the individual level.

Utilising multiple hypotheses, the paper tests various direct and indirect relationships between a sequential conceptualisation of absorptive capacity (divided into potential and realised absorptive capacity), individual ambidexterity and IWB at the managerial level on a sample spanning four automobile equipment-manufacturing firms in India. The role-related details of the sampled managers are discussed in the methodology section. It is found that individual ambidexterity moderates the relationship between realised absorptive capacity and IWB, whereas manager's DMA moderates the relationship between individual potential and realised absorptive capacity.

Various extant studies have explored the importance of absorptive capacity and ambidexterity for various measures of firm performance (Cao *et al.*, 2009; He and Wong, 2004; Kim *et al.*, 2016; Kranz *et al.*, 2016; Lichtenthaler, 2016). Although some work has been done on both individual ambidexterity and absorptive capacity (Enkel *et al.*, 2017; Seo *et al.*, 2015), there is a lack of clarity on the difference between the two constructs at the individual level. This is because both constructs deal with exploration and exploitation of knowledge and may seem similar from a distance. However, using existing theory, this paper differentiates between the effects of the two constructs. While individual absorptive capacity is visualised as the sequential exploration and exploitation of new knowledge by the manager, individual ambidexterity is visualised as the balance between two different kinds of new knowledge: incremental and radical.

Dual-role managers need to be able to sequentially explore and exploit new knowledge streams. However, this is not enough to consistently display IWB. Also, such managers need to balance their choice between incremental and radically new knowledge. Individual ambidexterity, visualised as the balance dimension (Cao *et al.*, 2009) between radical and incremental knowledge, captures the manager's ability to distribute her efforts across entirely new as well as relatively explored knowledge frontiers. Focusing on the hitherto unexplored dynamics between ambidexterity and absorptive capacity at the individual level, this paper adds to the understanding of IWB in an open innovation setting.

To account for the possibility of spurious relationships arising due to socio-demographic and inter-firm differences in the dependent variables, we control for variables like age of the manager, gender, experience, education, size of the firms and R&D intensity. These control variables add to the robustness of the hypothesised model.

Further, this paper finds that the DMA accorded to a manager enables her to convert potential absorptive capacity to its realised form. This finding adds to the overall understanding of absorptive capacity at the individual level. We checked for the possibility that DMA may directly affect IWB, but found the effect to be statistically insignificant.

This study also contributes to the open innovation literature by explicating the role of individual managers in identifying and implementing new knowledge originating outside the firm boundaries. In such open innovation settings, this paper adds to the understanding and underpinnings of innovative managerial work behaviour.

Finally, this study also contributes to the micro-foundations stream of research (Felin *et al.*, 2012; Teece, 2007, 2012), which seeks to understand how capabilities are created through the actions and interactions of individual managers in the workplace. By adopting a serial operationalisation of individual absorptive capacity, this study delves into the intricacies of individual absorptive capacity and the crucial moderating role of managerial DMA. It is important to note that the manifestation of realised absorptive capacity is a necessary condition for individual ambidexterity. DMA captures the impact of organisational settings on the manager's ability to translate knowledge exposure to assimilated and useful knowledge for the firm. The model confirms the critical role of firms in promoting freedom in decision-making leading to the assimilation and use of external knowledge. Finally, this study adds hitherto scant empirical evidence on the relationships between individual absorptive capacity, individual ambidexterity and the individual ambidexterity–work behaviour link.

Managerial implications

This study shows how managers in the dual role of gatekeepers and shepherds (Ter Wal *et al.*, 2017) can drive innovation with the help of both external and internal sources of knowledge, by leveraging their capabilities of absorptive capacity and ambidexterity. Since we offer greater clarity on individual absorptive capacity by separating the complementary dimensions of potential ACAP and realised ACAP, this can offer guidance to technology managers about the need to develop distinct competencies to tap into these two distinct dimensions of ACAP (Hafkesbrink and Schroll, 2016). This will help managers develop appropriate skills to be able to engage in different types of knowledge absorption activities in a better manner, which is a crucial imperative for managers in gatekeeping roles (Ter Wal *et al.*, 2017) who are often limited by the availability of time and attention (Ocasio, 1997). We also demonstrate the distinct yet synergistic roles played by both absorptive capacity and ambidextrous capability in leveraging maximum benefit from open innovation activities. This shows the need for managers to focus on developing these capabilities in tandem for driving innovation activities more effectively.

Limitations and further research

Although this study provides valuable insights into the relationships between the important constructs of absorptive capacity, ambidexterity and IWB in an open innovation setting, it does have some noteworthy limitations apart from the usual ones associated with quantitative empirical studies using survey data. The study considers only managers in dual roles (involved in both identification and implementation of new knowledge). More research is required on whether the hypothesised model would hold in the case of managers having differing roles.

The study considers the impact of managerial DMA on individual managerial abilities and behaviour. Manager's DMA may be influenced by the group and firm-level variables. Future studies could consider the impact of other firm-level variables on individual absorptive capacity and ambidexterity. Besides, this study utilises a sample of technology managers from four automobile equipment-manufacturing firms in India. Further studies could test whether the found relationships hold in other country and industry settings. Specifically, similar tests in different service industries would add valuable knowledge to the extant literature. Finally, this study focuses on IWB of individual managers as the outcome variable. Studies could also test the impact of individual absorptive capacity and ambidexterity on other work-related outcome variables like task performance and overall managerial performance.

References

Andersen, PH and I Drejer (2008). Systemic innovation in a distributed network: The case of Danish wind turbines, 1972–2007. *Strategic Organization*, 6(1), 13–46. doi: 10.1177/1476127007087152.

Anderson, N, K Potočnik and J Zhou (2014). Innovation and creativity in organizations. *Journal of Management*, 40(5), 1297–1333. doi: 10.1177/0149206314527128.

Arora, A and A Gambardella (1994). Evaluating technological information and utilizing it. *Journal of Economic Behavior and Organization*, 24(1), 91–114. doi: 10.1016/0167-2681(94)90055-8.

Axtell, CM, DJ Holman, KL Unsworth *et al.* (2000). Shopfloor innovation: Facilitating the suggestion and implementation of ideas. *Journal of Occupational and Organizational Psychology*, 73(3), 265–285. doi: 10.1348/096317900167029.

Badir, YF and GC O'Connor (2015). The formation of tie strength in a strategic alliance's first new product development project: The influence of project and partners' characteristics. *Journal of Product Innovation Management*, 32(1), 154–169. doi: 10.1111/jpim.12222.

Badir, YF, B Frank and M Bogers (2019). Employee-level open innovation in emerging markets: Linking internal, external, and managerial resources. *Journal of the Academy of Marketing Science*. doi: 10.1007/s11747-019-00674-6.

Benitez, J, J Henseler, A Castillo *et al.* (2019). How to perform and report an impactful analysis using partial least squares: Guidelines for confirmatory and explanatory IS research. *Information and Management*, doi: 10.1016/j.im.2019.05.003.

Bledow, R, M Frese, N Anderson *et al.* (2009). A dialectic perspective on innovation: Conflicting demands, multiple pathways, and ambidexterity. *Industrial and Organizational Psychology*, 2(3), 305–337. doi: 10.1111/j.1754-9434.2009.01154.x.

Bogers, M, A-K Zobel, A Afuah *et al.* (2017). The open innovation research landscape: Established perspectives and emerging themes across different levels of analysis. *Industry and Innovation*, 24(1), 8–40. doi: 10.1080/13662716.2016.1240068.

Bogers, M, A Burcharth and H Chesbrough (2019). Open innovation in Brazil: Exploring opportunities and challenges. *International Journal of Innovation*, 7(2), 178–191.

Burton-Jones, A (2009). Minimizing method bias through programmatic research. *MIS Quarterly*, 33(3), 445–471.

Cao, Q, E Gedajlovic and H Zhang (2009). Unpacking organizational ambidexterity: Dimensions, contingencies, and synergistic effects. *Organization Science*, 20(4), 781–796. doi: 10.1287/orsc.1090.0426.

Cassiman, B and R Veugelers (2006). In search of complementarity in innovation strategy: Internal R&D and external knowledge acquisition. *Management Science*, 52(1), 68–82. doi: 10.1287/mnsc.1050.0470.

Cepeda-Carrion, G, J-G Cegarra-Navarro and V Cillo (2019). Tips to use partial least squares structural equation modelling (PLS-SEM) in knowledge management. *Journal of Knowledge Management*, 23(1), 67–89. doi: 10.1108/JKM-05-2018-0322.

Cheng, CCJ and EC Shiu (2015). The inconvenient truth of the relationship between open innovation activities and innovation performance. *Management Decision*, 53(3), 625–647. doi: 10.1108/MD-03-2014-0163.

Chesbrough, H and M Bogers (2014). Explicating open innovation: Clarifying an emerging paradigm for understanding innovation. In *New Frontiers in Open Innovation*, H Chesbrough, W Vanhaverbeke and J West (eds.), pp. 3–28. Oxford: Oxford University Press.

Chesbrough, HW (2003a). *Open Innovation: The New Imperative for Creating and Profiting from Technology*. Boston, MA: Harvard Business School Press.

Chesbrough, HW (2003b). The logic of open innovation: Managing intellectual property. *California Management Review*, 45(3), 33–58.

Chin, W (2010). How to write up and report PLS analyses. In *Handbook of Partial Least Squares: Concepts, Methods and Applications*, V Esposito Vinzi, W Chin, J Henseler *et al.* (eds.), pp. 655–690. Heidelberg: Springer.

Cirera, X and WF Maloney (2017). *The Innovation Paradox: Developing-Country Capabilities and the Unrealized Promise of Technological Catch-up*. Washington, DC.

Cohen, WM and DA Levinthal (1990). Absorptive capacity: A new perspective on learning and innovation. *Administrative Science Quarterly*, 35(1), 128. doi: 10.2307/2393553.

Crescenzi, R and L Gagliardi (2018). The innovative performance of firms in heterogeneous environments: The interplay between external knowledge and internal absorptive capacities. *Research Policy*, 47(4), 782–795. doi: 10.1016/j.respol.2018.02.006.

Dahlander, L, S O'Mahony and DM Gann (2016). One foot in, one foot out: How does individuals' external search breadth affect innovation outcomes? *Strategic Management Journal*, 37(2), 280–302. doi: 10.1002/smj.2342.

Dewar, RD, DA Whetten and D Boje (1980). An examination of the reliability and validity of the Aiken and Hage scales on centralization, formalization, and task routines. *Administrative Science Quarterly*, 25, 120–128.

Distel, AP (2019). Unveiling the microfoundations of absorptive capacity: A study of Coleman's Bathtub Model. *Journal of Management*, 45(5), 2014–2044. doi: 10.1177/0149206317741963.

Dorenbosch, L, ML van Engen and M Verhagen (2005). On-the-job innovation: The impact of job design and human resource management through production ownership. *Creativity and Innovation Management*, 14(2), 129–141. doi: 10.1111/j.1476-8691.2005.00333.x.

Easterby-Smith, M, M Graça, E Antonacopoulou *et al.* (2008). Absorptive capacity: A process perspective. *Management Learning*, 39(5), 483–501. doi: 10.1177/1350507608096037.

Ebers, M and I Maurer (2014). Connections count: How relational embeddedness and relational empowerment foster absorptive capacity. *Research Policy*, 43(2), 318–332. doi: 10.1016/j.respol.2013.10.017.

Enkel, E, S Heil, M Hengstler *et al.* (2017). Exploratory and exploitative innovation: To what extent do the dimensions of individual level absorptive capacity contribute? *Technovation*, 60–61, 29–38. doi: 10.1016/j.technovation.2016.08.002.

Faems, D, M De Visser, P Andries *et al.* (2010). Technology alliance portfolios and financial performance: Value-enhancing and cost-increasing effects of open innovation. *Journal of Product Innovation Management*, 27(6), 785–796. doi: 10.1111/j.1540-5885.2010.00752.x.

Felin, T and WS Hesterly (2007). The knowledge-based view, nested heterogeneity, and new value creation: Philosophical considerations on the locus of knowledge. *The Academy of Management Review*, 32(1), 195–218. doi: 10.2307/20159288.

Felin, T, NJ Foss, KH Heimeriks *et al.* (2012). Microfoundations of routines and capabilities: Individuals, processes, and structure. *Journal of Management Studies*, 49(8), 1351–1374. doi: 10.1111/j.1467-6486.2012.01052.x.

Fleming, L and DM Waguespack (2007). Brokerage, boundary spanning, and leadership in open innovation communities. *Organization Science*, 18(2), 165–180. doi: 10.1287/orsc.1060.0242.

Fosfuri, A and J Tribo (2008). Exploring the antecedents of potential absorptive capacity and its impact on innovation performance. *Omega*, 36(2), 173–187. doi: 10.1016/j.omega.2006.06.012.

Foss, NJ, K Laursen and T Pedersen (2011). Linking customer interaction and innovation: The mediating role of new organizational practices. *Organization Science*, 22(4), 980–999. doi: 10.1287/orsc.1100.0584.

Foss, NJ, J Lyngsie and SA Zahra (2013). The role of external knowledge sources and organizational design in the process of opportunity exploitation. *Strategic Management Journal*, 34(12), 1453–1471. doi: 10.1002/smj.2135.

Fu, X, J Li, H Xiong *et al.* (2014). Open innovation as a response to constraints and risks: Evidence from China. *Asian Economic Papers*, 13(3), 30–58.

Giannopoulou, E, A Yström and S Ollila (2011). Turning open innovation into practice: Open innovation research through the lens of managers. *International Journal of Innovation Management*, 15(3), 505–524. doi: 10.1142/S1363919611003465.

Grant, RM (1996). Toward a knowledge-based theory of the firm. *Strategic Management Journal*, 17(S2), 109–122. doi: 10.1002/smj.4250171110.

Guerrero, M and D Urbano (2017). The impact of Triple Helix agents on entrepreneurial innovations' performance: An inside look at enterprises located in an emerging economy. *Technological Forecasting and Social Change*, 119, 294–309.

Gupta, V, S Singh and A Bhattacharya (2017). The Relationships between leadership, work engagement and employee innovative performance: Empirical evidence from the Indian R&D context. *International Journal of Innovation Management*, 21(7), 1750055. doi: 10.1142/S1363919617500554.

Hafkesbrink, J and M Schroll (2016). Ambidextrous organisational and individual competencies in OI: The dawn of a new research agenda. In *Open Innovation: A Multifaceted Perspective*, A-L Mention and M Torkkeli (eds.), pp. 517–570. doi: 10.1142/9789814719186_0020.

Hair, JF, GTM Hult, C Ringle *et al.* (2016). *A Primer on Partial Least Squares Structural Equation Modeling (PLS-SEM)*, 2nd edn. Thousand Oaks, CA: Sage Publications.

Hargadon, A and RI Sutton (1997). Technology brokering and innovation in a product development firm. *Administrative Science Quarterly*, 42(4), 716. doi: 10.2307/2393655.

Harman, HH (1967). *Modern Factor Analysis*, 2nd edn. Chicago: University of Chicago Press.

Hayes, AF (2013). *Introduction to Mediation, Moderation, and Conditional Process Analysis: A Regression-Based Approach*. New York, NY: Guilford Press.

He, Z-L and P-K Wong (2004). Exploration vs. exploitation: An empirical test of the ambidexterity hypothesis. *Organization Science*, 15(4), 481–494. doi: 10.1287/orsc.1040.0078.

Henseler, J, TK Dijkstra, M Sarstedt *et al.* (2014). Common beliefs and reality about PLS. *Organizational Research Methods*, 17(2), 182–209. doi: 10.1177/1094428114526928.

Hertenstein, P and PJ Williamson (2018). The role of suppliers in enabling differing innovation strategies of competing multinationals from emerging and advanced economies: German and Chinese automotive firms compared. *Technovation*, 70–71, 46–58.

Herzog, P (2011). *Open and Closed Innovation*, 2nd edn. Wiesbaden: Gabler. doi: 10.1007/978-3-8349-6165-5.

Hu, L and PM Bentler (1999). Cutoff criteria for fit indexes in covariance structure analysis: Conventional criteria versus new alternatives. *Structural Equation Modeling: A Multidisciplinary Journal*, 6(1), 1–55. doi: 10.1080/10705519909540118.

Jansen, JJP, FAJ Van Den Bosch and HW Volberda (2005). Managing potential and realized absorptive capacity: How do organizational antecedents matter? *Academy of Management Journal*, 48(6), 999–1015. doi: 10.5465/amj.2005.19573106.

Janssen, O (2000). Job demands, perceptions of effort-reward fairness and innovative work behaviour. *Journal of Occupational and Organizational Psychology*, 73(3), 287–302. doi: 10.1348/096317900167038.

Janssen, O (2001). Fairness perceptions as a moderator in the curvilinear relationships between job demands, and job performance and job satisfaction. *Academy of Management Journal*, 44(5), 1039–1050. doi: 10.5465/3069447.

Janssen, O (2003). Innovative behaviour and job involvement at the price of conflict and less satisfactory relations with co-workers. *Journal of Occupational and Organizational Psychology*, 76(3), 347–364. doi: 10.1348/096317903769647210.

Janssen, O and NW Van Yperen (2004). Employees' goal orientations, the quality of leader-member exchange, and the outcomes of job performance and job satisfaction. *Academy of Management Journal*, 47(3), 368–384. doi: 10.2307/20159587.

Jones, O (2006). Developing absorptive capacity in mature organizations. *Management Learning*, 37(3), 355–376. doi: 10.1177/1350507606067172.

Kang, M and M-J Lee (2017). Absorptive capacity, knowledge sharing, and innovative behaviour of R&D employees. *Technology Analysis and Strategic Management*, 29(2), 219–232. doi: 10.1080/09537325.2016.1211265.

Kanter, R (1988). When a thousand flowers bloom: Structural, collective, and social conditions for innovation in organizations. In *Research in Organizational Behavior*, BM Staw and LL Cummings (eds.), pp. 169–221. Greenwich, CT: JAI Press.

Katz, D and R Kahn (1978). *The Social Psychology of Organizations*, 2nd ed. New York: Wiley.

Kauppila, OP and MP Tempelaar (2016). The social-cognitive underpinnings of employees' ambidextrous behaviour and the supportive role of group managers' leadership. *Journal of Management Studies*, 53(6), 1019–1044. doi: 10.1111/joms.12192.

Kim, B, E Kim and NJ Foss (2016). Balancing absorptive capacity and inbound open innovation for sustained innovative performance: An attention-based view. *European Management Journal*, 34(1), 80–90. doi: 10.1016/j.emj.2015.10.002.

Kranz, JJ, A Hanelt and LM Kolbe (2016). Understanding the influence of absorptive capacity and ambidexterity on the process of business model change — The case of on-premise and cloud-computing software. *Information Systems Journal*, 25(6), 477–517.

Kranz Johann, J, A Hanelt and LM Kolbe (2016). Understanding the influence of absorptive capacity and ambidexterity on the process of business model change — The case of on-premise and cloud-computing software. *Information Systems Journal*, 26(5), 477–517. doi: 10.1111/isj.12102.

Lane, PJ, BR Koka and S Pathak (2006). The reification of absorptive capacity: A critical review and rejuvenation of the construct. *Academy of Management Review*, 31(4), 833–863. doi: 10.5465/amr.2006.22527456.

Leiponen, A and CE Helfat (2010). Innovation objectives, knowledge sources, and the benefits of breadth. *Strategic Management Journal*, 31(2), 224–236. doi: 10.1002/smj.807.

Levinthal, DA and JG March (1993). The myopia of learning. *Strategic Management Journal*, 14(S2), 95–112. doi: 10.1002/smj.4250141009.

Lewin, AY, S Massini and C Peeters (2011). Microfoundations of internal and external absorptive capacity routines. *Organization Science*, 22(1), 81–98. doi: 10.1287/orsc.1100.0525.

Lichtenthaler, U (2016). Absorptive capacity and firm performance: An integrative framework of benefits and downsides. *Technology Analysis and Strategic Management*, 28(6), 664–676. doi: 10.1080/09537325.2015.1131258.

Lichtenthaler, U and E Lichtenthaler (2009). A capability-based framework for open innovation: Complementing absorptive capacity. *Journal of Management Studies*, 46(8), 1315–1338. doi: 10.1111/j.1467-6486.2009.00854.x.

Limaj, E and EWN Bernroider (2019). The roles of absorptive capacity and cultural balance for exploratory and exploitative innovation in SMEs. *Journal of Business Research*, 94, 137–153. doi: 10.1016/j.jbusres.2017.10.052.

Lowik, S, J Kraaijenbrink and A Groen (2016). The team absorptive capacity triad: A configurational study of individual, enabling, and motivating factors. *Journal of Knowledge Management*, 20(5), 1083–1103. doi: 10.1108/JKM-11-2015-0433.

Lowik, S, J Kraaijenbrink and AJ Groen (2017). Antecedents and effects of individual absorptive capacity: A micro-foundational perspective on open innovation. *Journal of Knowledge Management*, 21(6), 1319–1341. doi: 10.1108/JKM-09-2016-0410.

March, JG (1991). Exploration and exploitation in organizational learning. *Organization Science*, 2(1), 71–87. doi: 10.1287/orsc.2.1.71.

Martinkenaite, I and KJ Breunig (2016). The emergence of absorptive capacity through micro–macro level interactions. *Journal of Business Research*, 69(2), 700–708. doi: 10.1016/j.jbusres.2015.08.020.

Matusik, SF and MB Heeley (2005). Absorptive capacity in the software industry: Identifying dimensions that affect knowledge and knowledge creation activities. *Journal of Management*, 31(4), 549–572. doi: 10.1177/0149206304272293.

McGrath, RG (2001). Exploratory learning, innovative capacity, and managerial oversight. *Academy of Management Journal*, 44(1), 118–131. doi: 10.5465/3069340.

Menguc, B and S Auh (2008). The asymmetric moderating role of market orientation on the ambidexterity–firm performance relationship for prospectors and defenders. *Industrial Marketing Management*, 37(4), 455–470. doi: 10.1016/j.indmarman.2007.05.002.

Miron-Spektor, E, F Gino and L Argote (2011). Paradoxical frames and creative sparks: Enhancing individual creativity through conflict and integration. *Organizational Behavior and Human Decision Processes*, 116(2), 229–240. doi: 10.1016/j.obhdp.2011.03.006.

Mom, TJM, FAJ van den Bosch and HW Volberda (2007). Investigating managers' exploration and exploitation activities: The influence of top-down, bottom-up, and horizontal knowledge inflows. *Journal of Management Studies*, 44(6), 910–931. doi: 10.1111/j.1467-6486.2007.00697.x.

Mom, TJM, FAJ van den Bosch and HW Volberda (2009). Understanding variation in managers' ambidexterity: Investigating direct and interaction effects of formal structural and personal coordination mechanisms. *Organization Science*, 20(4), 812–828. doi: 10.1287/orsc.1090.0427.

Nunnally, JC (1978). *Psychometric Theory*, 2nd edn. New York: McGraw-Hill.

Ocasio, W (1997). Towards an attention-based view of the firm. *Strategic Management Journal*, 18(S1), 187–206.

Ojo, AO and M Raman (2016). The role of prior experience and goal orientation in individual absorptive capacity. *Industrial Management and Data Systems*, 116(4), 723–739. doi: 10.1108/IMDS-05-2015-0187.

Ollila, S and A Yström (2017). An investigation into the roles of open innovation collaboration managers. *R and D Management*, 47(2), 236–252. doi: 10.1111/radm.12197.

Pedrosa, ADM, M Välling and B Boyd (2013). Knowledge related activities in open innovation: Managers' characteristics and practices. *International Journal of Technology Management*, 61(3/4), 254. doi: 10.1504/IJTM.2013.052670.

Podmetina, D, D Volchek, J Dbrowska *et al.* (2013). Human resource practices and open innovation. *International Journal of Innovation Management*, 17(6), 1340019. doi: 10.1142/S1363919613400197.

Podsakoff, PM, SB MacKenzie, J-Y Lee *et al.* (2003). Common method biases in behavioral research: A critical review of the literature and recommended remedies. *Journal of Applied Psychology*, 88(5), 879–903. doi: 10.1037/0021-9010.88.5.879.

Radaelli, G, E Lettieri, M Mura *et al.* (2014). Knowledge sharing and innovative work behaviour in healthcare: A micro-level investigation of direct and indirect effects. *Creativity and Innovation Management*, 23(4), 400–414. doi: 10.1111/caim.12084.

Rivkin, JW and N Siggelkow (2003). Balancing search and stability: Interdependencies among elements of organizational design. *Management Science*, 49(3), 290–311. doi: 10.1287/mnsc.49.3.290.12740.

Rosing, K, M Frese and A Bausch (2011). Explaining the heterogeneity of the leadership-innovation relationship: Ambidextrous leadership. *The Leadership Quarterly*, 22(5), 956–974. doi: 10.1016/j.leaqua.2011.07.014.

Rosing, K and H Zacher (2017). Individual ambidexterity: The duality of exploration and exploitation and its relationship with innovative performance. *European Journal of Work and Organizational Psychology*, 26(5), 694–709. doi: 10.1080/1359432X.2016.1238358.

Rothaermel, FT and AM Hess (2007). Building dynamic capabilities: Innovation driven by individual-, firm-, and network-level effects. *Organization Science*, 18(6), 898–921. doi: 10.1287/orsc.1070.0291.

Rothaermel, FT and MT Alexandre (2009). Ambidexterity in technology sourcing: The moderating role of absorptive capacity. *Organization Science*, 20(4), 759–780. doi: 10.1287/orsc.1080.0404.

Scott, SG and RA Bruce (1994). Determinants of innovative behavior: A path model of individual innovation in the workplace. *Academy of Management Journal*, 37(3), 580–607. doi: 10.2307/256701.

Seo, YW, SW Chae and KC Lee (2015). The impact of absorptive capacity, exploration, and exploitation on individual creativity: Moderating effect of subjective well-being. *Computers in Human Behavior*, 42, 68–82. doi: 10.1016/j.chb.2014.03.031.

Sheremata, WA (2000). Centrifugal and centripetal forces in radical new product development under time pressure. *Academy of Management Review*, 25(2), 389–408. doi: 10.5465/amr.2000.3312925.

Shih, H and E Susanto (2011). Is innovative behavior really good for the firm? *International Journal of Conflict Management*, 22(2), 111–130. doi: 10.1108/10444061111126666.

Sjödin, D, J Frishammar and S Thorgren (2019). How individuals engage in the absorption of new external knowledge: A process model of absorptive capacity. *Journal of Product Innovation Management*, 36(3), 356–380. doi: 10.1111/jpim.12482.

Slowinski, G, E Hummel, A Gupta *et al.* (2009). Effective practices for sourcing innovation. *Research-Technology Management*, 52(1), 27–34. doi: 10.1080/08956308.2009.11657546.

Solís-Molina, M, M Hernández-Espallardo and A Rodríguez-Orejuela (2018). Performance implications of organizational ambidexterity versus specialization in exploitation or exploration: The role of absorptive capacity, *Journal of Business Research*, 91(September 2017), 181–194. doi: 10.1016/j.jbusres.2018.06.001.

Sun, Y, X Wang, Z Zhang *et al.* (2019). How do IT users' attributes influence innovative use of IT: The mediating role of individual absorptive capacity. *IEEE Access*, 7, 50718–50733. doi: 10.1109/ACCESS.2019.2911197.

Teece, DJ (2007). Explicating dynamic capabilities: The nature and microfoundations of (sustainable) enterprise performance. *Strategic Management Journal*, 28(13), 1319–1350. doi: 10.1002/smj.640.

Teece, DJ (2012). Dynamic capabilities: Routines versus entrepreneurial action. *Journal of Management Studies*, 49(8), 1395–1401. doi: 10.1111/j.1467-6486.2012.01080.x.

Teece, DJ, G Pisano and A Shuen (1997). Dynamic capabilities and strategic management. *Strategic Management Journal*, 18(7), 509–533.

Ter Wal, ALJ, P Criscuolo and A Salter (2017). Making a marriage of materials: The role of gatekeepers and shepherds in the absorption of external knowledge and innovation performance. *Research Policy*, 46(5), 1039–1054. doi: 10.1016/j.respol.2017.03.003.

Tian, AW and C Soo (2018). Enriching individual absorptive capacity. *Personnel Review*, 47(5), 1116–1132. doi: 10.1108/PR-04-2017-0110.

Todorova, G and B Durisin (2007). Absorptive capacity: Valuing a reconceptualization. *Academy of Management Review*, 32(3), 774–786. doi: 10.5465/amr.2007.25275513.

Tushman, ML and CA O'Reilly (1996). Ambidextrous organizations: Managing evolutionary and revolutionary change. *California Management Review*, 38(4), 8–29. doi: 10.1080/09652540903536982.

Volberda, HW, NJ Foss and MA Lyles (2010). Perspective — Absorbing the concept of absorptive capacity: How to realize its potential in the organization field. *Organization Science*, 21(4), 931–951. doi: 10.1287/orsc.1090.0503.

Wang, J, J Yang and Y Xue (2017). Subjective well-being, knowledge sharing and individual innovation behavior. *Leadership and Organization Development Journal*, 38(8), 1110–1127. doi: 10.1108/LODJ-10-2015-0235.

West, J and M Bogers (2014). Leveraging external sources of innovation: A review of research on open innovation. *Journal of Product Innovation Management*, 31(4), 814–831. doi: 10.1111/jpim.12125.

West, J and M Bogers (2017). Open innovation: Current status and research opportunities. *Innovation*, 19(1), 43–50. doi: 10.1080/14479338.2016.1258995.

West, MA and JL Farr (1990). Innovation at work. In *Innovation and Creativity at Work: Psychological and Organizational Strategies*, pp. 3–13. Chichester: John Wiley & Sons.

Wikhamn, BR and A Styhre (2019). Open innovation groundwork. *International Journal of Innovation Management*, 2050013. doi: 10.1142/S1363919620500139.

Zahra, SA and G George (2002). Absorptive capacity: A review, reconceptualization, and extension. *Academy of Management Review*, 27(2), 185–203. doi: 10.5465/AMR.2002.6587995.

Zhang, X and KM Bartol (2010). Linking empowering leadership and employee creativity: The influence of psychological empowerment, intrinsic motivation, and creative process engagement. *Academy of Management Journal*, 53(1), 107–128. doi: 10.5465/amj.2010.48037118.

Zollo, M and SG Winter (2002). Deliberate learning and the evolution of dynamic capabilities. *Organization Science*, 13(3), 2002.

Chapter 11

THE EFFECTS OF COGNITIVE DIVERSITY AND COHESIVENESS ON ABSORPTIVE CAPACITY†

RADOSLAW NOWAK
School of Management
New York Institute of Technology
1855 Broadway, New York, NY 10023-7692, USA
rnowak@nyit.edu

Published 23 April 2019

While investigating organisational factors related to a firm's ability to innovate, this study identifies two new antecedents of absorptive capacity. Drawing from literatures on innovation management and organisational studies, the paper puts forward a model linking absorptive capacity to a unit's cognitive diversity and cohesiveness, empirically testing their effects on potential absorptive capacity (PACAP) and realised absorptive capacity (RACAP). Statistical tests are conducted using original survey data collected in the healthcare industry. Future research and implications for practitioners are discussed.

Keywords: Absorptive capacity; potential absorptive capacity; realised absorptive capacity; cognitive diversity; group cohesiveness.

Introduction

Absorptive capacity is defined as the firm's ability to recognise value, incorporate, and exploit new information emerging in the market (Cohen and Levinthal, 1990). Subsequent empirical studies have investigated the role of absorptive capacity in various empirical settings, mostly concentrating on its outcomes such as innovation and performance. Nevertheless, the research question of how organisations could reinforce their absorptive capacity has been also perceived as a key priority in this field of research (e.g., Schleimer and Pedersen, 2013; Fosfuri and Tribó, 2008; Volberda *et al.*, 2010; Jansen *et al.*, 2005). Consequently, to respond to calls for further empirical examination of its antecedents, this study investigates the role of two new mechanisms related to absorptive capacity.

Prior research emphasises the difference between two distinctive components of absorptive capacity, therefore identifying: (1) potential absorptive capacity

†This article originally appeared in *International Journal of Innovation Management*, **24** 2050019-1-23 © 2020 World Scientific Publishing Europe Ltd.

(hereafter referred to as PACAP) — its externally-oriented function regulating influx of new and valuable, exogenous ideas generated in the market; (2) realised absorptive capacity (hereafter referred to as RACAP) — the internally focused function facilitating transformation and exploitation of newly updated stocks of knowledge (Zahra and George, 2002). Although PACAP and RACAP operate together as integral parts of one organisational system, jointly delineating a firm's ability to innovate, the two functions clearly fulfill distinctive organisational roles. Consequently, the strength of PACAP and RACAP could be impacted by different organisational factors (Zahra and George, 2002). Based on this assumption, this paper aims to contribute to research by exploring the role of cognitive diversity and cohesiveness in the context of PACAP and RACAP.

The first objective of this study is to examine the role of cognitive diversity. Cognitive diversity is a group level construct capturing the breadth of knowledge, thinking styles, beliefs, and perspectives residing within a given group (Kilduff *et al.*, 2000; Harrison *et al.*, 1998). Although cognitive diversity was studied in numerous empirical settings, research has produced largely inconclusive results concerning its effects on group-level outcomes (e.g., Milliken and Martins, 1996). Nevertheless, it clearly established that cognitive diversity is related to organisational learning processes — it influences collective information processing, in turn affecting how units address emergent organizational problems (e.g., Mitchell *et al.*, 2017). Based on such findings, this paper examines the relationship between a unit's cognitive diversity and PACAP. In their model, Zahra and George (2002) identify the process of information comprehension — or the ability to recognize the meaning and value of new information — as the critical function fulfilled by PACAP. Furthermore, the authors explain that such comprehension of new incoming information can occur only in units who already possess so-called "related knowledge" — knowledge related to new information generated in the market. This key role of knowledge "relatedness" has been also strongly emphasized in other studies (e.g., Kogut and Zander, 1992). To expand on this concept, the present paper proposes that cognitive diversity should be positively related to PACAP, because it reinforces a unit's ability to comprehend the meaning and value of new incoming information. By expanding the scope of heterogeneous knowledge, ideas, and perspectives residing within a unit, higher levels of cognitive diversity should also enlarge the stocks of related knowledge, in turn enabling the comprehension of a broader scope of new exogenous information incoming from the market — this should reinforce the strength of PACAP.

The second objective of this paper is to explore the effect of a unit's cohesiveness. Cohesiveness is group-level construct defined by research as the degree of members' affiliation, belonginess, and commitment to a unit as a whole and collectively pursued objectives (e.g., Wech *et al.*, 1998; Mullen and

Copper, 1994). Ample empirical studies have examined the role of cohesiveness in numerous organisational settings, demonstrating its positive effects on group-level outcomes (e.g., Wech *et al.*, 1998). Therefore, showing that cohesiveness can lead to the development of collective identity as it increases trust, which in turn, translates into higher levels of cooperation among employees (Beal *et al.*, 2003; Wech *et al.*, 1998).

According to Zahra and George (2002), the process of knowledge creation and exploitation is the key function fulfilled by RACAP. However, prior literature has identified the critical problem of knowledge "stickiness," referring to structural barriers that can impede knowledge transfers within and across organisational units (Szulanski, 1996; Nonaka, 1994). Thereby, research established that the process of knowledge exploitation is significantly hindered, when the internal mechanisms of social integration are weak. To contribute to literature, this paper proposes that a unit's cohesiveness should be positively related to RACAP. According to prior findings, higher cohesiveness increases levels of trust and collaboration among employees (e.g., Beal *et al.*, 2003; Wech *et al.*, 1998), consequently, it should reduce structural barriers that could otherwise hinder internal transfers of newly created knowledge. Based on this assumption, this paper proposes that higher levels of cohesiveness should strengthen a unit's ability to exploit newly created knowledge — this should reinforce the strength of RACAP.

To summarize, this study aims to contribute to research by exploring the role of two new factors that could explain variance in the strength of absorptive capacity. Hence, this paper answers the following research questions: (1) can a unit's cognitive diversity be positively related to PACAP? (2) Can a unit's cohesiveness be positively related to RACAP? (see Fig. 1). To empirically test the proposed relationships, this study uses a survey dataset collected from healthcare organisations. The unit of analysis in the study are emergency departments from 104 hospitals located across the Unites States. In the subsequent sections, this paper presents: (1) a review of relevant literatures regarding absorptive capacity, cognitive diversity, and cohesiveness; (2) the analysis of the relationships among the constructs, which leads to the hypotheses development; (3) methodology, results, and findings; (4) finally, the paper presents recommendations for future research and practice and discusses the study's limitations.

Literature Review and Hypotheses

Absorptive capacity

Absorptive capacity is described in the literature as a firm's ability to identify, transform, and utilize exogenous information to generate innovation (Zahra and

George, 2002; Cohen and Levinthal, 1990). Ample research has studied the role of absorptive capacity in various settings such as organisational learning (e.g., Lane and Lubatkin, 1998), a firm's problem-solving capacity (e.g., Kim, 1997), as well as the group decision-making processes (e.g., Malhotra *et al.*, 2005). Because absorptive capacity is widely recognised as a group-level ability to access, process, and utilise incoming exogenous information to create and exploit new knowledge, this study proposes that a unit's cognitive diversity and cohesiveness could be positively related to the strength of absorptive capacity.

In their seminal paper, Cohen and Levinthal (1990) identify absorptive capacity as a critical component of a firm's innovative capabilities describing the construct as "*the ability of a firm to recognise the value of new, external information, assimilate it, and apply it to commercial ends*." (1990, p. 128). Furthermore, the authors explain that current stocks of organisational knowledge — a key collective resource residing within a unit — should enable such units to recognize the value of new emergent information incoming from the market, and subsequently utilize it with the objective of implementing new innovative solutions. While expanding on this notion, Zahra and George (2002) reconceptualise absorptive capacity in the way that highlights its two distinctive components. Therefore, the authors introduce the capacity's two critical functions — externally-focused PACAP and internally focused RACAP. While PACAP connects a unit to its external environment in turn transferring valuable exogenous ideas into a unit, RACAP aims to carefully incorporate such new information and select optimal internal applications that should lead to process improvements.

In their model, Zahra and George (2002) note the complementarity of PACAP and RACAP, also emphasising that the two functions are highly dependent and work together as a firm's innovative ability. Furthermore, the authors also note that the strength of PACAP and RACAP could vary across organisations. In practical terms, depending on a firm's business strategy, some firms may allocate more resources to develop stronger PACAP. Concurrently, other firms, pursuing different strategic objectives, may rely mostly on RACAP as its core competency. This division reinforces the notion that PACAP and RACAP are responsible for performing distinctive organisational tasks.

PACAP and RACAP

In their model of absorptive capacity, Zahra and George (2002) describe the construct as a firm's continuously evolving dynamic capabilities enabling firms to access new valuable external information, and in turn exploit it internally to generate new innovative solutions. The authors introduce two core functions of absorptive capacity: (1) the externally-focused PACAP connects a firm to its external stakeholders channeling valuable exogenous ideas into a firm; (2) the internally-focussed RACAP facilitates transformation of exogenous information, enabling subsequent exploitation of newly created knowledge, in turn generating performance gains. Although the essence of this model assumes the key distinction between the two core functions, Zahra and George (2002) strongly emphasise their interdependence. Subsequent research also demonstrates the positive association between PACAP and RACAP based on one fundamental assumption — higher levels of PACAP should allow firms to develop stronger RACAP by increasing levels of firm-specific knowledge that drives up levels of knowledge exploitation. At the same time, stronger RACAP, by enlarging the stocks of existing organisational knowledge, should allow a firm to become more responsive to a broader scope of new exogenous information, thus resulting in stronger PACAP (e.g., Volberda *et al.*, 2010). This positive association of PACAP and RACAP has been confirmed by numerous empirical studies conducted in various organisational contexts (e.g., Nowak, 2017; Leal-Rodríguez *et al.*, 2014; Chang *et al.*, 2013). Consequently, based on such prior findings this paper confirms:

Hypothesis 1: *A unit's PACAP is positively related to such a unit's RACAP.*

Cognitive diversity

Diversity in the workplace is defined as the distribution of differences among employees with respect to common attributes (Harrison and Klein, 2007). Research points out that such differences may generate both positive and negative organisational outcomes (Milliken and Martins, 1996). Although diversity expands a scope of knowledge and expertise that units can use during the decision-making process, nevertheless, it also leads to higher levels of disagreements, in turn generating conflict (e.g., van Knippenberg and Schippers, 2007). Prior research has made significant progress in explaining when diversity could benefit organisations, nonetheless, numerous calls for additional empirical studies exploring the effect of diversity on group-level outcomes still emerge (e.g., Guillaume *et al.*, 2017). To answer such calls, this paper examines the role of cognitive diversity in the context of absorptive capacity.

Cognitive diversity is defined in terms of the breadth of knowledge, ideas, perspectives and beliefs existing within a given unit (Kilduff *et al.*, 2000). Early research in management studies recognised some crucial benefits associated with diversity in organisational knowledge, proposing that heterogeneity of knowledge can influence how a unit will interpret reality and what solutions it will select to address emergent organisational problems (Weick, 1979; Cyert and March, 1963; Simon, 1957). Subsequent research also confirms that cognitive diversity should be regarded as a key factor impacting the group decision making processes, affecting how a firm's resources are allocated, and in turn, what core competencies will be developed (e.g., Kilduff *et al.*, 2000; Harrison *et al.*, 1998; Miller *et al.*, 1998). Furthermore, recent studies on innovation management find a positive effect of cognitive diversity in the context of a unit's ability to generate new innovate solutions (Mitchell *et al.*, 2017). In this study, the authors establish a positive effect of cognitive diversity on innovation by showing that the breadth of expertise residing within cross-functional groups enables such groups to identify and implement more innovative solutions resulting in process improvements (Mitchell *et al.*, 2017). Building on such findings, this paper proposes that a unit's cognitive diversity should be positively related to the strength of PACAP.

PACAP and cognitive diversity

As an organisational function, PACAP is responsible for obtaining and comprehending new valuable information emerging in the environment (Zahra and George, 2002). Because stronger PACAP delineates a unit's ability to comprehend and assimilate a wider scope of exogenous information generated in the market, this paper proposes that cognitive diversity, signifying a scope of heterogeneous knowledge, thinking styles, and perspectives residing within a unit (e.g., Kilduff *et al.*, 2000), should increase this unit's ability to process and comprehend a broader scope of new incoming information, thus it should be positively related to PACAP.

In the model created by Zahra and George (2002), PACAP is composed of two core components. First, acquisition is a unit's ability to acquire externally generated information. As such, this function determines speed, intensity, and direction of external searches that a unit may undertake due to activation triggers such as internal performance problems. The second component, assimilation is responsible for interpretation and comprehension of the newly acquired information. Consequently, assimilation comprises internal processes that are necessary to realise the meaning and value of incoming information. In other words, assimilation determines what new external information will be recognized by a unit as valuable, and subsequently used to generate innovation.

As pointed out by Teece (1981), the process of knowledge comprehension, which enables the recognition of the meaning and value of new information, can be very challenging, because it requires the existence of some prior knowledge related to new incoming information. This key condition was described by Cohen and Levinthal (1990) who write that "*the ability to evaluate and utilise outside knowledge is largely a function of the level of prior related knowledge*" (1990, p. 128). In practical terms, to comprehend the meaning and value of new exogenous information, a unit must already possess some overlapping or related knowledge that will enable the process of comprehension. Building on this assumption, this paper proposes that such a process of comprehension should be reinforced in units possessing high levels of cognitive diversity.

Zahra and George (2002) point out the linear relationship between the acquisition and assimilation functions of PACAP. Thus, a unit's ability to assimilate new information should be dependent on its ability to acquire new information. As demonstrated by prior research, cognitive diversity encompasses a scope of ideas, perspectives, and beliefs within a unit, thus it expands collective stocks of heterogeneous knowledge residing in such a unit (e.g., Kilduff *et al.*, 2000). Prior research also finds that units with higher levels of cognitive diversity are able to utilise a broader range of new information, when making key strategic decisions regarding the development of their core competencies (Miller *et al.*, 1998). Moreover, cognitively diverse units consider a wider range of alternatives, because the breadth of relevant task-related knowledge expands their overall problem-solving capacity (Hambrick *et al.*, 1996), influencing how key organisational issues are being framed (Cheng *et al.*, 2003). Based on such findings, this paper empirically tests the notion that higher levels of cognitive diversity should expand a unit's stocks of heterogeneous knowledge related to new information incoming from the market. Thus, it should reinforce a unit's ability to comprehend the meaning and value of a broader scope of new exogenous information:

Hypothesis 2: *By enabling comprehension of a broader scope of new information, a unit's cognitive diversity should positively moderate the relationship between such a unit's acquisition and assimilation functions.*

Cohesiveness

Prior literature recognises that a unit's cohesiveness is a key factor influencing social processes occurring within a group, pointing out that cohesiveness could explain variance in group-level outcomes (e.g., Lvina *et al.*, 2018; Beal *et al.*, 2003; Gully *et al.*, 1995). Given this role of cohesiveness, the present paper investigates the relationship between a unit's cohesiveness and its absorptive capacity.

Early literature defined group cohesiveness as "*the forces which are acting on the members to stay in a group*" (Festinger, 1950, p. 274), whereas later studies strongly emphasise that a unit's cohesiveness entails both the extent to which its members want to belong to such a unit, and the degree of shared commitment to complete collectively pursued tasks. In that way, the literature identified two key dimensions of cohesiveness — its social and task-oriented dimensions. Based on prior research, in this study a unit's cohesiveness is defined as the degree of members' affiliation, belonginess, and commitment to both a unit as a whole and to specific objectives that the unit pursues (e.g., Wech *et al.*, 1998; Mullen and Copper, 1994). Numerous studies empirically examined the role of cohesiveness in various organisational settings, establishing that cohesiveness increases social integration within a unit (Hackman, 1992). While explaining organisational effects of cohesiveness, scholars point out that stronger cohesiveness boosts "*social attraction*" toward a unit (Lott and Lott, 1965), resulting in the development of collective identity (e.g., Wech *et al.*, 1998). When such collective identity emerges, members become "*closely knitted*," and in turn, they become more committed to the unit and its objectives. This process produces higher levels of trust, higher motivation, and stronger collective commitment. When collective attributes shared by members of a given unit become stronger, they intensify the process of social integration (e.g., Roccas and Brewer, 2002; Ashforth and Mael, 1989).

Because prior research strongly emphasizes that the process of knowledge creation and exploitation should depend on social integration and a quality of social exchanges among employees (e.g., Szulanski, 1996; Spender, 1996; Nonaka, 1994), this paper empirically tests the notion that a unit's cohesiveness should be positively related to its RACAP.

RACAP and cohesiveness

According to Zahra and George (2002), RACAP enables a unit to exploit newly created knowledge. In their model, the authors highlight that the strength of RACAP relies on its two critical components — transformation and exploitation. First, Zahra and George (2002) explain that transformation "*denotes a firm's capability to develop and refine the routines that facilitate combining existing knowledge and the newly acquired and assimilated knowledge*" (2002, p. 190). In practical terms, it signifies that a unit's transformation processes are responsible for updating existing organisational knowledge with some new valuable components that were identified as valuable by PACAP. The second component of RACAP, exploitation is the function that allows to expand existing competencies or to create new core competencies by incorporating knowledge newly created during the stage of transformation (Zahra and George, 2002). According to prior research, the process of knowledge exploitation requires strong mechanisms of social integration (Spender, 1996; Szulanski, 1996), consequently, this paper proposes that a unit's cohesiveness should be related to the strength of RACAP.

Zahra and George (2002) theorize that social integration mechanisms are instrumental in the context on absorptive capacity, because they moderate the relationship between PACAP and RACAP. Nevertheless, other researchers strongly emphasize the critical role of social integration in the process of knowledge exploitation (e.g., Spender, 1996). Consequently, while expanding on the model introduced by Zahra and George (2002), this paper empirically tests the notion that a unit's cohesiveness should be related to the strength of RACAP by moderating the linear relationship between this unit's transformation and exploitation functions.

While examining the process of knowledge exploitation, Cohen and Levinthal (1990) emphasize the critical role of individuals by noting that to facilitate the stage of knowledge exploitation "*employees must be able to apply new external knowledge to commercial ends*" (1990, p. 128). Thus, implying that social exchanges among individual employees may be required for the newly transformed knowledge to find its optimal process application. As identified by prior research, higher cohesiveness generates stronger commitment to a unit and its collective tasks as it reinforces social attraction and collective pride, in turn increasing cooperation among individuals comprising a given unit (Rosh *et al.*, 2012; Beal *et al.*, 2003). By increasing quality of social exchanges and by enabling collaboration, higher cohesiveness should reinforce the channels of formal and informal dissemination of new knowledge that was created during the stage of transformation. Consequently, as it reduces social barriers that could otherwise hinder the process of new knowledge exploitation, a unit's cohesiveness should reinforce the strength of RACAP, thus:

Hypothesis 3: *By reducing structural barriers hindering internal dissemination of newly created knowledge, a unit's cohesiveness will positively moderate the relationship between such a unit's transformation and exploitation functions.*

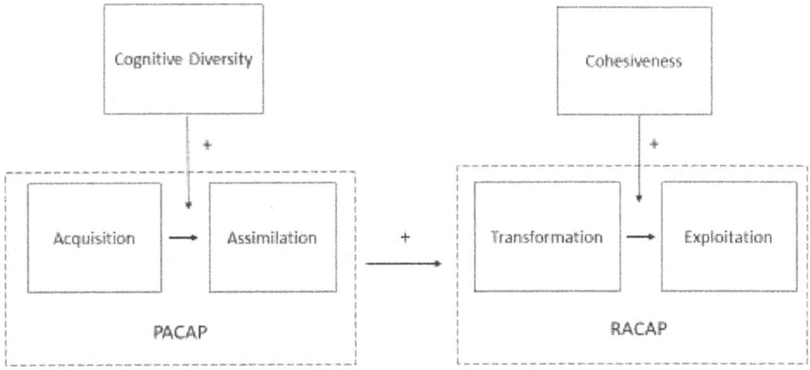

Fig. 1. The effects of cognitive diversity and cohesiveness on absorptive capacity.

Methods

Empirical setting

During the last couple of decades, the healthcare industry in the United States has gained a lot of attention due to vast political and economic changes that had generated a high degree of market turbulence. For organisations operating in such a highly dynamic environment, strong internal competencies that facilitate necessary adjustments to shifting exogenous conditions become critical (Teece *et al.*, 1997). Research on healthcare management suggests that due to a high degree of external changes, healthcare organisations must innovate in form of new medical services or more effective methods of service delivery (e.g., Avgar *et al.*, 2011). Because prior research established that cognitive diversity can critically influence the development of firm's core competencies (Harrison *et al.*, 1998), it seems plausible to empirically test the proposed model in this empirical setting.

Sample and data collection

An invitation to participate in this research were extended to all hospitals collaborating with a consulting firm that provides staffing service to numerous healthcare organisations across the United States. The invited hospitals are located in economically diverse regions including the South, Northeast, and Central states of the United States. In total, over 200 hospitals were invited to participate in the study. An emergency department was a unit of analysis in this study. For each participating emergency department, the surveys were sent to all employees employed by such departments. Consequently, almost 2,000 individuals were asked to fill out the surveys that were distributed electronically. The survey included all instruments measuring the latent constructs included in the proposed model, specifically, each department's cognitive diversity, cohesiveness, and absorptive capacity. When multiple employees from one emergency department responded, the mean values for all items were calculated. Overall almost 490 responses were received. This produced an individual level response rate of around 25%. The final sample used to perform statistical analyses included 104 emergency departments.

Measurements

All three constructs included in the theorised model are latent. Therefore, surveys should be viewed as an appropriate way to operationalise such constructs (e.g., Hinkin, 1998). To reduce common method bias, this study followed the procedure recommended by prior research (e.g., Podsakoff *et al.*, 2003). Consequently, only validated instruments were used to measure the constructs included in the tested model.

Cognitive Diversity: This measure of cognitive diversity was adopted from previous research. This instrument was introduced by Van der Vegt and Janssen (2003) and captures how members of a group differ in their knowledge, skills, opinions, beliefs, etc. ($m = 3.7$; s.d. $= 0.9$). Subsequently, this instrument was extensively used in prior empirical studies (e.g., Shin *et al.*, 2012). The employees of emergency departments were asked to indicate to what extent they agree with the statements such as: "*the members of our group differ in their ways of thinking*," "*the members of our group differ in their knowledge and skills*;" "*the members of our group differ in how they see the world*," "*the members of our group differ their beliefs about what is right or wrong*." As recommended by prior research, any latent constructs should be analysed by using the CFA procedure (Jöreskog and Sörbom, 1993). Consequently, the range of loadings for cognitive diversity was calculated at 0.78–0.89 and should be viewed as acceptable.

Cohesiveness: The instrument as also extensively used and validated in prior studies (e.g., Wech *et al.*, 1998). This scale captures members' commitment to collective tasks and to a group as a whole ($m = 4.2$; s.d. $= 0.8$). The participants were asked to indicate the extent to which they agree/disagree with the statements such as: "*there is a high spirit of teamwork among employees in my department*;" "*employees in my department take a personal interest in one another*;" "*employees in my department are usually aware of important events and situations*." The CFA procedure revealed the acceptable range of loadings for this construct at 0.79–0.88.

Absorptive Capacity: This instrument was developed by Jansen *et al.* (2005) and measures PACAP: acquisition ($m = 4.0$; s.d. $= 0.8$) and assimilation ($m = 3.7$; s.d. $= 0.8$) and RACAP: transformation ($m = 4.1$; s.d. $= 0.8$) and exploitation ($m = 3.7$; s.d. $= 0.6$). I decided to use this instrument, because the survey introduced by Jansen *et al.* (2005) captures a firm's competencies embedded in organisational structure, processes, and knowledge sharing routines. Moreover, it clearly distinguishes among the key functions of PACAP (acquisition and assimilation), and RACAP (transformation and exploitation) — this distinction was a crucial assumption in the proposed model. This scale was also widely validated by many previous empirical studies (e.g., Jansen *et al.*, 2005). The sample questions included in this instrument are: "*we collect industry information through informal means*," "*other departments of our hospital are hardly visited (reversed)*," "*our department quickly analyzes the usefulness of new external information to existing knowledge*," "*new opportunities to serve our patients are quickly understood*," "*we record and store newly acquired knowledge for future reference*," "*it is clearly known how activities within our department are organized and should be performed.*" The recommended CFA analysis revealed that the loadings for PACAP ranging from 0.73 to 0.94 and the loadings for RACAP ranging between 0.77–0.95. Therefore, these results should be also viewed as acceptable.

Control Variables: Group-level controls (hospital size and age, per capita income in a county, competition) were obtained from the secondary data sources (e.g., American Hospital Association). *Income* ($m = 26$, s.d. $= 4.8$) was measured as median household income in a county where each hospital is located. Strategy research recognizes that *firm size* is one of the key factors that can impact the development of firm's internal capabilities and performance (e.g., Kimberly and Evanisko, 1981). It was measured as the number of beds in each hospital (serving capacity) ($m = 233$, s.d. $= 51$). *Age* of each hospital ($m = 58$, s.d. $= 16$). *Competition* ($m = 0.9$, s.d. $= 0.6$) is a key factor affecting a firm's operation. It was measured as the number of other hospitals operating in the same county.

Data analysis procedure

Prior research has identified alternative research approaches that could be used to empirically test proposed models. The present study uses the multiple regression method recommended in cases when the proposed model includes a moderating effect (Baron and Kenny, 1986). The analysis follows the hierarchical regression procedure, which according to prior literature, can reveal the changes in predictability of independent variables entered at different stages of the analysis. Thus, it shows how predictors explain variance above what was already predicted by variables entered earlier in the analysis (Preacher *et al.*, 2007; Cohen, 2001; Baron and Kenny, 1986). To test the interactive effects, the centering of independent variables was done as recommended by Aiken and West (1991). All statistical tests were conducted by using Stata 14.

First, to determine whether the common method variance could influence the study's findings, the Harman's single-factor test was performed (Podsakoff *et al.*, 2003). Based on this test, all latent variables were forced to load onto one factor. Such a model showed poor fit of data, thus confirming that multiple factors existed within the analyzed data (Podsakoff *et al.*, 2003). Second, the confirmatory factor analysis (CFA) was performed to examine the convergent validity of all latent constructs included in the model. Finally, testing the hypothesized relationship proposed in the model was performed. Consequently, the null model captures only effects of control variables (Model 1). Subsequently, the relationship between PACAP and RACAP was tested in Model 2. The moderating effect of acquisition and cognitive diversity (ACQ*COG) regressed on assimilation is shown in Model 3, while Model 4 shows the interactive effect of transformation and cohesiveness (TRA*COH) regressed on exploitation. As the last step, to confirm the moderating effects, the interactive effects were plotted in accordance with the procedure recommended by prior research (Aiken and West, 2001).

Results

Table A.1 presents descriptive statistics including the means, standard deviations, and inter-scale correlations for the variables included in the proposed model.

Following research recommendations, this study used hierarchical multiple regressions to test the proposed relationships (e.g., Preacher *et al.*, 2007). Hypothesis 1 suggested the main effect of PACAP and RACAP. Hypothesis 2 proposed the positive moderating effect of acquisition and cognitive diversity on the process of assimilation. Hypothesis 3 suggested the positive moderating effect of a unit's transformation and cohesiveness on exploitation. These results are included in Table A.2.

Model 1 in Table A.2 shows the effects of control variables only. Model 2 in Table A.2 shows the main effect of PACAP on RACAP. As expected, this coefficient is robust and statistically significant ($b = 0.36$; $p < 0.01$), thereby Hypothesis 1 can be supported. Model 3 shows the interactive effect of acquisition and cognitive diversity (ACQ*COG) regressed on assimilation, revealing a significant positive coefficient ($b = 0.15, p < 0.05$). Model 4 reveals the positive interactive coefficient representing the joint effect of transformation and cohesiveness (TRA*COH) regressed on exploitation ($b = 0.12, p < 0.05$). As the last step, the interactive effects were plotted following the procedure described by Aiken and West (2001). These plots examine whether the magnitude of the interactive effects was different at high versus low levels (1 standard deviation above and below the means) of interacting variables. The plots confirm the interactive effects.

In summary, based on the analysed data, empirical tests reveal the following findings: (1) PACAP is significantly related to RACAP; (2) the interactive effect of acquisition and cognitive diversity (ACQ*COG) on assimilation is statistically significant; (3) the interactive effect of transformation and cohesiveness (TRA*-COH) on exploitation is also significant.

Discussion

By revealing two new mechanisms related to the strength of absorptive capacity, this study's contributes to research on innovation management, workplace diversity, and group dynamics in the following ways: (1) it explains how cognitive diversity and cohesiveness could be instrumental in the context of PACAP and RACAP; (2) clarifies that cognitive diversity could lead to positive organisational outcomes when it increases a unit's ability to assimilate a broader scope of new knowledge emerging in the market; (3) finally, it reveals that a unit's cohesiveness can reinforce the process of knowledge exploitation. In the following section, this paper provides a detailed analysis of its theoretical and practical contribution.

Contribution to research

Scholars have called for new empirical studies that would further investigate what mechanisms could explain heterogeneity of internal resources (e.g., Felin *et al.*, 2012), as well as new antecedents of absorptive capacity (e.g., Volberda *et al.*, 2010). Prior research has also emphasised that various organisational factors could impact either the strength of PACAP or RACAP (Zahra and George, 2002). While building on this assumption, the present study contributes to research by demonstrating the critical role of a unit's cognitive diversity and cohesiveness in the context of absorptive capacity.

First, this paper finds a positive interactive effect of acquisition and cognitive diversity on assimilation — the key function of PACAP. Not only, this finding corroborates with prior research, suggesting that cognitive diversity affects the process of strategic decision-making, thus impacting the development of core competencies (e.g., Miller *et al.*, 1998). Moreover, it expands on prior findings by revealing when cognitive diversity may become beneficial — when it increases a unit's openness and sensitivity to a broader scope of new exogenous information generated by the market. By enlarging the pool of heterogeneous knowledge and perspectives existing within a given unit, higher levels of cognitive diversity expand the stocks of knowledge that could help identify the meaning and value of new exogenous information. In turn, enhancing the ability to assimilate a broader scope of new valuable information that could be used to generate innovation. Additionally, this study's finding also emphasizes a key role played by cognitive diversity in the context of expanding a firm's dynamic capabilities (Teece *et al.*, 1997). By increasing levels of openness and sensitivity to a broader scope of exogenous changes, cognitive diversity increases a level of knowledge "relatedness" (Kogut and Zander, 1992) between a given unit and its task environment. This could enable such a unit to recognise and respond to a broader scope of key exogenous developments mandating the need for internal process improvements.

Second, to the extent of my knowledge, the association between a unit's cohesiveness and the ability of innovate has never been examined in any empirical studies. In this way, this study contributes to research on cohesiveness and group-level outcomes (Wech *et al.*, 1998), social mechanisms reinforcing the strength of absorptive capacity (e.g., Armstrong and Lengnick-Hall, 2013), and to the literature on social antecedents of knowledge commercialization (e.g., Hansen, 2002). The study's findings clarify the role of cohesiveness during the process of innovation. The interactive effect of cohesiveness and transformation on the stage of exploitation shows that stronger cohesiveness can increase innovative output by reducing structural barriers hindering the process of dissemination of newly created knowledge. By demonstrating that internal cohesiveness may be instrumental in building more innovative organisational systems, it reveals a necessity to establish organizational practices that promote high quality of social interactions, collective commitment to organisational objectives, and collaboration in the workplace.

Another key contribution of this study lies in demonstrating that organisations could strategically invest into their internal resources to reinforce either their PACAP or RACAP. Therefore, this finding supports the notion, that depending on specific strategic goals, firms may want to increase levels of cognitive diversity or cohesiveness to boost either their externally or internally-oriented capabilities. To illustrate, for firms operating in a highly dynamic industries, higher levels of cognitive diversity may become essential in strengthening their openness and alertness to new emergent opportunities such as new technological developments. For firms operating in more turbulent environments, greater investments in the development of cognitive diversity may result in creating a more "open" system, thus allowing such organisations to scrutinise external markets and better comprehend the magnitude of critical external changes. Conversely, by investing a firm's resources into the development of internal cohesiveness, organisations may create a more integrated system that will reduce the key problem of knowledge "stickiness," thereby reinforcing the ability to implement necessary internal process improvements.

Although not related to the field of innovation management, it should be noted that this study also contributes to the literature on workplace diversity and group dynamics. Diversity research has not fully clarified when and how diversity in attributes could become detrimental or advantageous (e.g., Bell *et al.*, 2011). This study's findings contribute to this field of research by showing that cognitive diversity may help create a more open organisational system by reinforcing a unit's core competencies required to better comprehend the meaning and magnitude of external changes. Thus, it reinforces key connections between such a unit and its external stakeholders. Moreover, in the context of group dynamics, the study reveals a new positive role of internal cohesiveness in the context of innovation.

Practical implications

This study contributes to practice by providing a set of implementable actions for managers who aim to increase the effectiveness of their organisations. First, the findings suggest that cognitive diversity in the workforce could reinforce a firm's connections with its key external stakeholders, and thus could increase a firm's ability to innovate. Consequently, some specific actions related to innovation management should be proposed. First, to promote a firm's innovative capabilities, managers may want to utilise a firm's existing human capital to enhance the breadth of cognitive resources in the externally-oriented organisational functions — such utilisation of cognitive diversity should support the development of diverse connections with diverse external stakeholders. Furthermore, for companies with low levels of cognitive diversity, updating general recruitment strategies in the way that will bring in more diverse human capital should also become critical — it may generate more cognitive heterogeneity within a firm's human resources. To illustrate, if a company has traditionally used only one university to hire all data analysts, this could lead to highly homogeneous cognitive resources in that specific organisational function. By including new target schools (e.g., schools offering novel experiential training to students), such a company could expand a level of its cognitive resources, thus increasing its overall innovative capabilities.

Another important managerial implication is related to the role of cohesiveness and its impact on the processes of knowledge exploitation. In this case, managers may want to consider incorporating formal and information employee socialisation mechanisms resulting in higher levels of institutional trust (e.g., Zucker, 1986). For example, well-designed formal training programs could provide opportunities to reinforce social ties, and thus enhance a firm's social capital. Also, establishing very clear and transparent policies at the firm-level (e.g., regulating the process of promotion) should be highly recommended, as transparency in the decision making may increase employee perception of organizational fairness (e.g., Greenberg, 1990), boosting overall quality of social interactions, and thus promoting social integration. Overall, this paper contributes to practice by increasing managerial awareness of the mechanisms that could be utilised as strategic resources to positively impact group performance.

Future research and limitations

Although this paper identifies two new factors related to absorptive capacity, our understanding of how the ability to innovate could be strengthened is still lacking. Consequently, other empirical studies focusing on identifying new mechanisms related to absorptive capacity should be encouraged — they may help reveal new sources of variance in resource heterogeneity across firms. Moreover, identifying new contextual variables impacting information flows across organisations could help better explain the relationship between PACAP and RACAP (e.g., formal and informal communication channels within a firm). Additionally, research on organisational psychology identifies numerous individual-level predictors of group-level outcomes (e.g., a manager's leadership style, an executive's personality traits). Further empirical studies in strategic management could also aim to incorporate other micro-level factors. Examining such individual-level antecedents could expand our understanding of the role played by key individuals in the context of absorptive capacity (e.g., Nowak, 2018). Finally, further studies examining the effect of cognitive diversity on the development of other core competences could also help us better understand when and how cognitive diversity could benefit firms and when it could actually hinder their performance.

Every study has some important limitations that should be discussed. First, in the case of this research, empirical tests were done using the data collected only in one industry. Thus, incorporating a cross-industry research design in the future could reveal new valuable insights as it could help further address an issue of how environmental factors (e.g., more stable environments) could impact the proposed model. Because the data were collected in the industry experiencing high levels of external changes — this industry specific condition could affect the generalisability of the findings. Second, the data used in the study were cross-sectional, thus no claims of casual relationship between constructs can be made, because cross-sectional data could produce biased inferences (Bowen and Wiersema, 1999). A longitudinal design could help more accurately estimate causal influences within the proposed model. Third, another key limitation is related to common method bias. However, as explained in the methodology section, to reduce the impact of this bias on the findings, this study followed the procedure recommended by prior research (Podsakoff *et al.*, 2003). Finally, a relatively small sample size can also affect the study's results. Nonetheless, it should be noted that this study meets basic requirements of an absolute, minimum sample (size of N = 50) recommended in prior research (Comfrey and Lee, 1992; Barrett and Kline, 1981).

Conclusion

This study answers numerous calls for more empirical research identifying organisational antecedents of absorptive capacity. While building on the model introduced by Zahra and George (2002), the study contributes to prior literature by putting forward and empirically testing the model relating the strength of absorptive capacity to two organizational mechanisms: (1) a unit's cognitive diversity enabling the comprehension of a broader scope of newly acquired information: (2) a unit's cohesiveness reducing social barriers hindering internal transfers of newly created knowledge. The paper suggests that high cognitive diversity could become advantageous, because it expands a unit's "relatedness" or openness to a broader scope of new exogenous developments emerging in the market. In turn, reinforcing the ability to better understand and assimilate a broader scope of valuable information that can be used to generate innovation. Furthermore, the findings reveal that a unit's cohesiveness could act as an important social integrator. By reducing structural barriers hindering the process of exploitation of new knowledge created during the stage of transformation, high cohesiveness reduces the key problem of knowledge "stickiness," thereby enhancing the unit's exploitation capabilities. Moreover, for practitioners, this study suggests a set of specific recommendations that managers may consider to reinforce their firm's ability to innovate.

Acknowledgement

I would like to thank the editor and anonymous reviewers for their very insightful suggestions, which helped me improve and develop this research.

Appendix A

Table A.1. Descriptive statistics.

Variables	M	SD	1	2	3	4	5	6	7	8	9	10
1. Acquisition	4.0	0.8	1.0									
2. Assimilation	3.8	0.7	0.49	1.0								
3. Transformation	4.1	0.8	0.26	0.29	1.0							
4. Exploitation	3.7	0.6	0.22	0.20	0.48	1.0						
5. Cognitive Diversity	3.7	0.9	0.26	0.23	0.08	0.05	1.0					
6. Cohesiveness	4.2	0.8	0.05	0.11	0.20	0.22	−0.06	1.0				
7. Age	58	16	−0.02	0.05	0.07	0.08	0.3	0.11	1.0			
8. Income	26	4.8	0.16	0.12	0.13	0.13	0.10	0.12	0.09	1.0		
9. Competition	0.9	0.6	0.18	0.12	0.14	0.11	0.13	0.10	0.13	0.12	1.0	
10. Size	238	53	−0.06	0.04	−0.04	0.01	0.09	0.04	0.10	0.07	0.08	1.0

Notes: $n = 104$; correlations 0.15 and above are significant.

Table A.2. Results of hierarchical regression analyses (standardised coefficients reported).

	RACAP		Assimilation	Exploitation
Variables	Model 1	Model 2	Model 3	Model 4
Age	0.1 (0.01)	0.0 (0.01)	0.03 (0.02)	0.04 (0.03)
Income	0.15* (0.07)	0.14* (0.06)	0.10 (0.07)	0.07 (0.06)
Competition	0.15* (0.06)	0.13* (0.06)	0.10 (0.06)	0.08 (0.06)
Size	−0.03 (0.03)	−0.01 (0.02)	0.02 (0.02)	0.00 (0.01)
Cognitive Diversity		−0.02 (0.02)	0.11 (0.06)	−0.01 (0.02)
Cohesiveness		0.13* (0.06)	0. 04 (0.05)	0.10 (0.06)
PACAP		0.36** (0.10)		0.14* (0.08)
Acquisition			0.26* (0.10)	
Transformation				0.21* (0.09)
ACQ*COG			0.15* (0.06)	
TRA*COH				0.12* (0.05)
Adj. R-squared	0.19	0.37	0.35	0.42

Notes: $n = 104$; $*p < 0.05$; $**p < 0.01$; $***p < 0.001$.

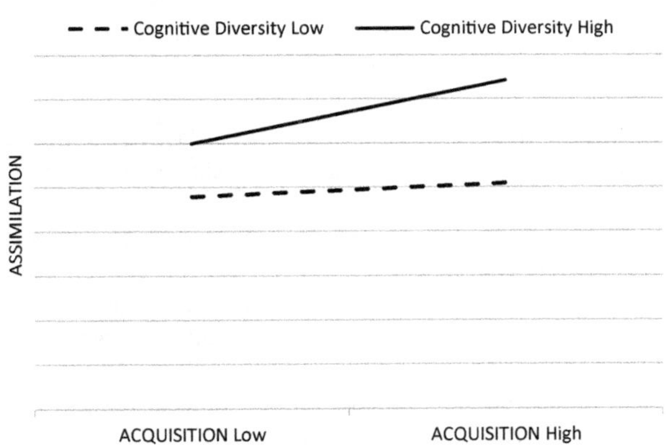

Fig. A.1. The interactive effect of acquisition and cognitive diversity.

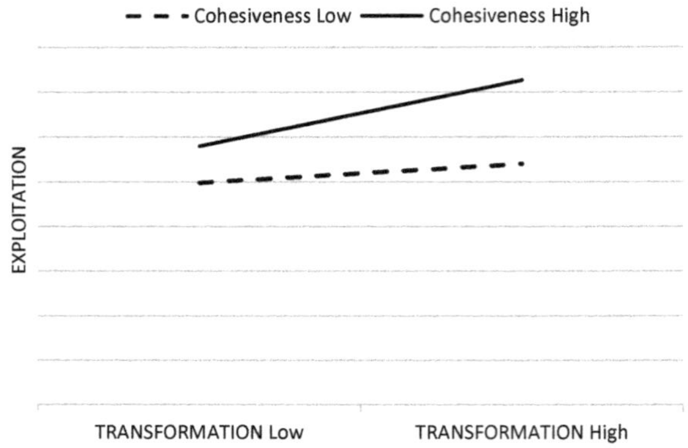

Fig. A.2. The interactive effect of transformation and cohesiveness.

References

Aiken, LS and SG West (1991). *Multiple Regression: Testing and Interpreting Interactions*. New York: Sage.

Ancona, DG and DF Caldwell (1992). Bridging the boundary: External activity and performance in organizational teams. *Administrative Science Quarterly*, 37(4), 634–665.

Armstrong, CE and CA Lengnick-Hall (2013). The Pandora's box of social integration mechanisms: Can they make it more difficult to realize absorptive capacity? *Journal of Strategy and Management*, 6(1), 4–26.

Ashforth, BE and F Mael (1989). Social identity theory and the organization. *Academy of Management Review*, 14(1), 20–39.

Avgar, AC, RK Givan and M Liu (2011). Patient-centered but employee delivered: Patient care innovation, turnover intentions, and organizational outcomes in hospitals. *ILR Review*, 64(3), 423–440.

Barrett, PT and P Kline (1981). The observation to variable ratio in factor analysis. *Personality Study and Group Behavior*, 1(1), 23–33.

Baron, RM and DA Kenny (1986). The moderator–mediator variable distinction in social psychological research: Conceptual, strategic, and statistical considerations. *Journal of Personality and Social Psychology*, 51(6), 1173.

Beal, DJ, RR Cohen, MJ Burke and CL McLendon (2003). Cohesion and performance in groups: A meta-analytic clarification of construct relations. *Journal of Applied Psychology*, 88(6), 989.

Bowen, HP and MF Wiersema (1999). Matching method to paradigm in strategy research: Limitations of cross-sectional analysis and some methodological alternatives. *Strategic Management Journal*, 20(7), 625–636.

Chang, S, Y Gong, SA Way and L Jia (2013). Flexibility-oriented HRM systems, absorptive capacity, and market responsiveness and firm innovativeness. *Journal of Management*, 39(7), 1924–1951.

Cheng, MM, PF Luckett and AK Schulz (2003). The effects of cognitive style diversity on decision-making dyads: An empirical analysis in the context of a complex task. *Behavioral Research in Accounting*, 15(1), 39–62.

Cohen, BH (2001). *Explaining psychological statistics*, 2nd edn. New York: Wiley.

Cohen, WM and DA Levinthal (1990). Absorptive capacity: A new perspective on learning and innovation. *Administrative Science Quarterly*, 35(1), 128–152.

Comfrey, AL and HB Lee (1992). *A First Course in Factor Analysis*. Hillsdale, NJ: Erlbaum.

Cyert, RM and JG March (1963). *A Behavioral Theory of the Firm*. Englewood Cliffs, NJ, Vol. 2, No. 4, pp. 169–187.

Felin, T, NJ Foss, KH Heimeriks and TL Madsen (2012). Microfoundations of routines and capabilities: Individuals, processes, and structure. *Journal of Management Studies*, 49(8), 1351–1374.

Festinger, L (1950). Informal social communication. *Psychological Review*, 57, 271–282.

Fosfuri, A and JA Tribó (2008). Exploring the antecedents of potential absorptive capacity and its impact on innovation performance. *Omega*, 36(2), 173–187.

Guillaume, YR, JF Dawson, L Otaye-Ebede, SA Woods and MA West (2017). Harnessing demographic differences in organizations: What moderates the effects of workplace diversity? *Journal of Organizational Behavior*, 38(2), 276–303.

Gully, SM, DJ Devine and DJ Whitney (1995). A meta-analysis of cohesion and performance: Effects of level of analysis and task interdependence. *Small Group Research*, 26(4), 497–520.

Hackman, JR (1992). Group influences on individuals in organizations. In *Handbook of Industrial and Organizational Psychology*, MD Dunnette and LH Hough (Eds.), Vol. 3, 2nd edn., pp. 199–267. Palo Alto, CA: Consulting Psychologists Press.

Hambrick, DC, TS Cho and MJ Chen (1996). The influence of top management team heterogeneity on firms' competitive moves. *Administrative Science Quarterly*, 659–684.

Hansen, MT (2002). Knowledge networks: Explaining effective knowledge sharing in multiunit companies. *Organization Science*, 13(3), 232–248.

Harrison, DA and KJ Klein (2007). What's the difference? Diversity constructs as separation, variety, or disparity in organizations. *Academy of Management Review*, 32(4), 1199–1228.

Hinkin, TR (1998). A brief tutorial on the development of measures for use in survey questionnaires. *Organizational Research Methods*, 1(1), 104–121.

Jansen, JJ, FA Van Den Bosch and HW Volberda (2005). Managing potential and realized absorptive capacity: How do organizational antecedents matter? *Academy of Management Journal*, 48(6), 999–1015.

Jöreskog, KG and D Sörbom (1993). LISREL 8: Structural Equation Modeling with the SIMPLIS Command Language. Mooresville, IL: Scientific Software International.

Kogut, B and U Zander (1992). Knowledge of the firm, combinative capabilities, and the replication of technology. *Organization Science*, 3(3), 383–397.

Kilduff, M, R Angelmar and A Mehra (2000). Top management-team diversity and firm performance: Examining the role of cognitions. *Organization Science*, 11(1), 21–34.

Kim, L (1997). The Dynamics of Samsung's Technological Learning in Semiconductors. *California Management Review*, 39(3), 86–100.

Lane, PJ and M Lubatkin (1998). Relative absorptive capacity and interorganizational learning. *Strategic Management Journal*, 19(5), 461–477.

Leal-Rodríguez, AL, JL Roldán, JA Ariza-Montes and A Leal-Millán (2014). From potential absorptive capacity to innovation outcomes in project teams: The conditional mediating role of the realized absorptive capacity in a relational learning context. *International Journal of Project Management*, 32(6), 894–907.

Lott, AJ and BE Lott (1965). Group cohesiveness as interpersonal attraction: A review of relationships with antecedent and consequent variables. *Psychological Bulletin*, 64(4), 259.

Lvina, E, G Johns and C Vandenberghe (2018). Team political skill composition as a determinant of team cohesiveness and performance. *Journal of Management*, 44(3), 1001–1028.

Miller, CC, LM Burke and WH Glick (1998). Cognitive diversity among upper-echelon executives: Implications for strategic decision processes. *Strategic Management Journal*, 19(1), 39–58.

Milliken, FJ and LL Martins (1996). Searching for common threads: Understanding the multiple effects of diversity in organizational groups. *Academy of Management Review*, 21(2), 402–433.

Mitchell, R, B Boyle, R O'brien, A Malik, K Tian, V Parker, and V Chiang (2017). Balancing cognitive diversity and mutual understanding in multidisciplinary teams. *Health Care Management Review*, 42(1), 42–52.

Mullen, B and C Copper (1994). The relation between group cohesiveness and performance: An integration. *Psychological Bulletin*, 115(2), 210.

Nonaka, I (1994). A dynamic theory of organizational knowledge creation. *Organization Science*, 5(1), 14–37.

Nowak, R (2017). Demystifying Absorptive Capacity: Focus on Firm Size and Employee Empowerment. *International Journal of Innovation Management*, 21(6), 1–19.

Nowak, R (2018). Executive's Personality and Group Performance: The Mediating Effect of Absorptive Capacity. *International Journal of Innovation Management*, 22(6), 1–29.

Olson, BJ, S Parayitam and Y Bao (2007). Strategic decision making: The effects of cognitive diversity, conflict, and trust on decision outcomes. *Journal Of Management*, 33(2), 196–222.

Podsakoff, PM, SB MacKenzie, JY Lee and NP Podsakoff (2003). Common method biases in behavioral research: A critical review of the literature and recommended remedies. *Journal of Applied Psychology*, 88(5), 879.

Preacher, KJ, DD Rucker and AF Hayes (2007). Addressing moderated mediation hypotheses: Theory, methods, and prescriptions. *Multivariate Behavioral Research*, 42(1), 185–227.

Roccas, S and MB Brewer (2002). Social identity complexity. *Personality and Social Psychology Review*, 6(2), 88–106.

Rosh, L, LR Offermann and R Van Diest (2012). Too close for comfort? Distinguishing between team intimacy and team cohesion. *Human Resource Management Review*, 22(2), 116–127.

Schleimer, SC and T. Pedersen (2013). The driving forces of subsidiary absorptive capacity. *Journal of Management Studies*, 50(4), 646–672.

Shin, SJ, TY Kim, JY Lee and L Bian (2012). Cognitive team diversity and individual team member creativity: A cross-level interaction. *Academy of Management Journal*, 55(1), 197–212.

Simon, HA (1957). *Models of Man; Social and Rational.* Oxford, England: Wiley.

Spender, JC (1996). Making knowledge the basis of a dynamic theory of the firm. *Strategic Management Journal*, 17(S2), 45–62.

Szulanski, G (1996). Exploring internal stickiness: Impediments to the transfer of best practice within the firm. *Strategic Management Journal*, 17(S2), 27–43.

Teece, DJ (1981). The market for know-how and the efficient international transfer of technology. *The Annals of the American Academy of Political and Social Science*, 458(1), 81–96.

Teece, DJ, G Pisano and A Shuen (1997). Dynamic capabilities and strategic management. *Strategic Management Journal*, 18(7), 509–533.

Van Knippenberg, D and MC Schippers (2007). Work group diversity. *Annual Review of Psychology*, 58, 515–541.

Volberda, HW, NJ Foss and MA Lyles (2010). Perspective—absorbing the concept of absorptive capacity: How to realize its potential in the organization field. *Organization Science*, 21(4), 931–951.

Wech, BA, KW Mossholder, RP Steel and N Bennett (1998). Does work group cohesiveness affect individuals' performance and organizational commitment? A cross-level examination. *Small Group Research*, 29(4), 472–494.

Weick, KE (1979). Cognitive processes in organizations. *Research in Organizational Behavior*, 1(1), 41–74.

Zahra, SA and G George (2002). Absorptive capacity: A review, reconceptualization, and extension. *Academy of Management Review*, 27(2), 185–203.

Zucker, LG (1986). Production of Trust: Institutional sources of economic structure, 1840–1920. *Research in Organizational Behavior*, 8, 53–111.

Chapter 12

EXPLORING THE INDIVIDUAL: AN EMPIRICAL INVESTIGATION OF INTERRELATIONSHIPS BETWEEN DIMENSIONS OF ABSORPTIVE CAPACITY[§]

KATJA-MARIA PREXL[*,‡], MARCO HUBERT[†,§],
MIRJA HUBERT[†,¶] and ANTJE GONERA[*,||]

[*]*Innovation Research, Division Food Science*
NOFIMA AS, PO Box 210, Ås 1431, Norway
[†]*Department of Management, Aarhus University*
Fuglesangs Allé 4, Aarhus, Denmark
[‡]*katja-maria.prexl@nofima.no; kmp@katjamariaprexl.com*
[§]*mah@mgmt.au.dk*
[¶]*mirja.hubert@mgmt.au.dk*
[||]*Antje.Gonera@nofima.no*

Published 21 January 2020

Absorptive capacity (AC) describes new knowledge absorption and its use for innovation on an organisational level. In this paper, we explore the role of individual AC (IAC) for corporate innovation. We focus on the individual and relationships among the capability dimensions of existing AC models. A quantitative online survey allows us to empirically explore and underline the role of the individual in AC. Our findings contribute to and extend existing theories of AC, by confirming the multidimensionality of IAC, shed light on the view of transformation and exploitation as alternative paths and their effect on different innovation processes. Our research highlights the individual's central role in innovation and introduces, explores and evaluates individual capacities to absorb new knowledge. This in consequence will influence processes and structures within a company with regard to innovation and human resource management.

Keywords: Absorptive capacity; external knowledge; innovation performance; knowledge management; individual.

Introduction

As innovation strength and agility have become essential to corporate survival and competitiveness, one of the primary challenges for corporations is how to keep up

*Corresponding author.

§This article originally appeared in *International Journal of Innovation Management*, **24** 2050077-1-29

with trends and increase corporate and individual innovation (Hubert *et al.*, 2017; Lengnick-Hall, 1992; Rohrbeck and Schwarz, 2013; Rubera and Kirca, 2012; Teece *et al.*, 1997; Tidd and Bessant, 2013). Therefore, economic success strongly depends on the ability to address rapidly changing contexts by identifying, implementing and facilitating new knowledge and new knowledge sources into an organisation (Alexander *et al.*, 2016; Bessant and Trifilova, 2017; Chauvet, 2010; Ter Wal *et al.*, 2015).

A corporation's ability to find and identify new knowledge and opportunities, generate ideas, and develop and implement those ideas for corporate innovation is mainly associated with the concept of absorptive capacity (Bessant and Trifilova, 2017; Enkel *et al.*, 2017; Weiblen and Chesbrough, 2015). The concept of absorptive capacity emphasises evaluating, adapting and exploiting new sources of knowledge to increase a company's competitiveness, flexibility and agility (Cohen and Levinthal, 1990; Lane and Lubatkin, 1998; Martinkenaite and Breunig, 2016; Volberda *et al.*, 2010). Indeed, different conceptualisations of absorptive capacity identified various dimensions (e.g., recognition/acquisition, assimilation, transformation and utilisation/exploitation) and have been applied to a wide range of studies. The importance of understanding of absorptive capacity thus continues to grow (Bessant and Trifilova, 2017; Camisón and Forés, 2010; Lewin *et al.*, 2011; Marabelli and Newell, 2014; Mariano and Walter, 2015; Noblet *et al.*, 2011; van den Bosch *et al.*, 2003).

However, despite a consensus about the relevance of absorptive capacities to the economic success of corporations (Dahlander and Gann, 2010; Huizingh, 2010; Kalogerakis *et al.*, 2010), there is an ongoing debate about a concrete conceptualisation of absorptive capacity and the interplay of its dimensions (Jansen *et al.*, 2005; Lane *et al.*, 2006; Mariano and Walter, 2015; Todorova and Durisin, 2007; van den Bosch *et al.*, 2003; Zahra and George, 2002).

Furthermore, although some evidence suggests that individuals play a key role in innovation management (Matusik and Heeley, 2005; McAdam *et al.*, 2010; Schoenmakers and Duysters, 2010; Ter Wal *et al.*, 2015; Tian and Soo, 2018), most of the literature has focused on the organisational level rather than the individual (Tidd and Bessant, 2013; Volberda *et al.*, 2010). Recent conceptual and empirical studies on absorptive capacity have started to investigate the individual level and its central role in corporations of integrating new knowledge (Salter *et al.*, 2015; Ter Wal *et al.*, 2015; Tian and Soo, 2018; Yildiz *et al.*, 2019). Nevertheless, there is still a need for further empirical research in the field of absorptive capacity and the role and impact of individuals (Volberda *et al.*, 2010).

Against this background, the aim of our research is to provide three main contributions. First, we contribute to an acknowledgement of absorptive capacity as a multidimensional process and clearly distinguish *between the dimensions* and clarify *the specific roles* of each dimension — namely, acquisition, assimilation, transformation and exploitation. In more detail, by empirically comparing different process models of absorptive capacity, we clarify whether (1) assimilation and transformation are alternative paths that affect exploitation, which in consequence solely affects the generation of innovation (Model 1); or (2) transformation and exploitation are alternative paths that affect the generation of innovation separately (Model 2). Second, we contribute to and extend knowledge about *the individual* and its *central role in generating innovation*. Thus, we focus on how individuals are associated with the different dimensions of absorptive capacity in order to better understand their role in the company's innovation management process. Third, we provide additional empirical evidence to the investigation and interrelationship of *(individual) absorptive capacity dimensions* by extending existing research (e.g., Enkel *et al.*, 2017; Yildiz *et al.*, 2019) to a *cross-industry setting*.

The paper is organised as follows: In 'Theoretical Background' section, we review the theoretical background and existing literature on the concepts of absorptive and individual absorptive capacity. We discuss the definitions, operationalisation, contextualisation and importance of empirically researching individuals' absorptive capacity. We then present our conceptual framework and the different competing models, which divide individual absorptive capacities into distinct dimensions. In 'Model Comparison of Alternative Dimension Pathways' section, we describe our research method and empirical analysis and then present our results. In 'Method and Results' section, we discuss the developed conceptual model and the results. Finally, in sections 'Discussion and Theoretical Implications', 'Managerial Implications' and 'Conclusion, Limitations, and Future Research', we conclude by discussing the theoretical and managerial implications and future research directions in light of our findings.

Theoretical Background

The concept of absorptive capacity

The concept of absorptive capacity derives from the economics of competition and innovation, the psychology of learning and managerial cognition, and the perspective of resources and dynamic capabilities (Volberda *et al.*, 2010). On an organisational level, absorptive capacity is defined as an organisation's capacity and ability to absorb and use different types of knowledge and to create new knowledge by addressing the required competencies for absorbing external information and ideas (Bessant *et al.*, 2005; Christensen *et al.*, 2005;

Cohen and Levinthal, 1990; Dahlander and Gann, 2010). Cohen and Levinthal (1990) first introduced the term *absorptive capacity* and defined it as a three-dimensional process of recognition, assimilation and the application of new external knowledge to commercial ends. These capacities depend to a high degree on prior related knowledge and can influence the innovation performance of the firm. Zahra and George (2002) re-conceptualised absorptive capacity and introduced the transformation dimension. They mainly distinguished between *potential absorptive capacity* (pAC), which comprises the dimensions of acquisition and assimilation of new knowledge, and *realised absorptive capacity* (rAC), which comprises the dimensions of transformation and exploitation of new knowledge within an organisation.

In contrast, Todorova and Durisin (2007) differentiated between knowledge that fits preexisting knowledge — it only has to be assimilated — and knowledge that does not fit the internal structures and thus must be transformed. Consequently, they also integrated the new dimension of transformation introduced by Zahra and George (2002), but not as the next step after new knowledge assimilation. Instead, they suggested two alternative paths: after new knowledge is recognised and acquired, (1) it can be assimilated if it fits preexisting knowledge and structures, or (2) it can yield transformation. This is the case when new ideas are incompatible and cannot be adjusted to existing structures and knowledge. Todorova and Durisin (2007) assumed that for the step of transformation, structures of the organisation must be altered in order to adjust to new knowledge. Both paths will finally result in exploitation of knowledge (Todorova and Durisin, 2007).

Individual absorptive capacity

Individuals are critical sources for sustainable corporate development and competitiveness, and they drive innovation performance and capability. They can act as facilitators of information exchange by sharing their experience, motivation and knowledge with others in the corporation (Felin and Foss, 2006; Jansen *et al.*, 2005; Minbaeva *et al.*, 2003; Szulanski, 1996). This view is supported by Zahra and George (2002) and Matusik and Heeley (2005), who valued the absorptive abilities of individuals within corporations and the active exchange of knowledge and experience. Matusik and Heeley (2005) demonstrated that the *individual's absorptive abilities are an essential component of absorptive capacity's multiple dimensions*. For corporations, using new internal and external knowledge from outside their existing knowledge base (i.e., not solely from internal ideas and preexisting knowledge) is a primary factor in helping them innovate and compete. Unlike corporations, individuals absorb new knowledge by first recognising it based on their individual experiences, characteristics and abilities and then converting and using that knowledge (e.g., Escribano *et al.*, 2009; Lane *et al.*, 2001; Ter Wal *et al.*, 2011). Several scholars espousing the knowledge-based view of the firm also deem the individual as the primary actor in knowledge creation (Felin and Foss, 2006; Grant, 1996; Tian and Soo, 2018; Yildiz *et al.*, 2019). Volberda *et al.* (2010) emphasised absorptive capacity as 'a multilevel construct [that] should be studied at the individual, unit, firm, and interfirm level of analysis' (p. 937) because it is influenced by individual competencies (Criscuolo *et al.*, 2014; Hafkesbrink and Schroll, 2016) and circumstances (Cohen and Levinthal, 1990).

The four dimensions of individuals' absorptive capacity

The multidimensional conceptualisation of absorptive capacity yielded many revisions and modifications in the literature (e.g., Camisón and Forés, 2010; Daspit and Souza, 2013; Escribano *et al.*, 2009; Leal-Rodríguez *et al.*, 2014; Patterson *et al.*, 2009; Volberda *et al.*, 2010). Table 1 gives an overview of selected studies and their proposed dimensionality of absorptive capacity.

In accordance with different conceptualisations of absorptive capacity shown in Table 1 and discussed in the literature (Cohen and Levinthal, 1990; Daspit and Souza, 2013; Flatten *et al.*, 2011; Todorova and Durisin, 2007; van den Bosch *et al.*, 1999; Zahra and George, 2002), we identified four main dimensions — acquisition, assimilation, transformation and exploitation — to *investigate individuals' absorptive capacity.*

The first (I)AC dimension is *acquisition*, which comprises experience, qualifications, commitment and existing knowledge to seek and recognise valuable new information or sources and to appraise new knowledge and integrate it into the corporate knowledge base (Camisón and Forés, 2010; Chauvet, 2010; Szulanski, 1996). Intensity, speed and the direction of acquiring new knowledge all influence the quality of the knowledge base and corporate planning paths (Zahra and George, 2002). There is ongoing scientific discussion about whether the first step should be *knowledge acquisition* or *recognising the value of knowledge*. The original model of (Cohen and Levinthal, 1990) assumed that recognising the value of knowledge is the starting point of the absorptive capacity process. Zahra and George (2002) later introduced the term *acquisition of knowledge* as the starting point and defined it as a 'firm's capability to identify and acquire externally generated knowledge that is critical to its operations' (p. 189). Todorova and Durisin (2007) then adopted the knowledge acquisition step, but reintroduced the step of recognising the value before the acquisition of knowledge. They argued that the capability to learn depends largely on the ability to evaluate and recognise new and relevant external knowledge.

Table 1. Overview of selected studies on AC dimensions.

Study	Dimension 1	Dimension 2	Dimension 3	Dimension 4
Cohen and Levinthal (1990)	Recognition	Assimilation	Application/commercialisation	
Heeley (1997)	Acquisition	Dissemination	Technical competence	
Lane and Lubatkin (1998); Lane *et al.* (2001)	Acquisition	Dissemination	Commercialisation	
Zahra and George (2002)	Potential AC (acquisition and assimilation)	Realised AC (transformation and exploitation)		
Jansen *et al.* (2005)	Recognition	Assimilation	Transformation	Exploitation
Lane *et al.* (2006)	Exploratory learning (recognition and understanding)	Transformative learning (assimilation of valuable new knowledge)	Exploitative learning (new knowledge and commercial outputs generated by assimilation and by combining new with existing knowledge)	
Todorova and Durisin (2007)	Recognition	Acquisition	Assimilation or transformation	Exploitation
Liao *et al.* (2007)	Acquisition	Dissemination	Transformation	
Lichtenthaler (2009)	Recognition/realisation and acquisition	Preservation/maintenance and reactivation	Transmutation and application	
Escribano *et al.* (2009)	Acquisition	Assimilation	Exploitation	
Enkel *et al.* (2017)	Identification	Assimilation	Utilisation	

Exploring the Individual

The second dimension is *assimilation*, the process of analysing, interpreting, understanding, learning and storing new knowledge (Szulanski, 1996). Knowledge is transferred to the company through knowledge sharing, socialisation and co-ordination (Jansen *et al.*, 2005). The process of *knowledge assimilation* is of great importance because, if external knowledge is only acquired or created but not assimilated, it cannot be used extensively (Holsapple, 2003). Regarding important antecedents of knowledge assimilation, Cohen and Levinthal (1990) stated that one of the most important factors for successful knowledge assimilation is prior knowledge. Thus, ideas not covered by a corporation's search zone might easily be overlooked (Rosenkopf and Nerkar, 2001). If external knowledge does not fit the existing heuristics in a company, assimilation and comprehension are more difficult and take longer, depending on embodied heuristics, context or the existence of specific assets in the firm (Zahra and George, 2002). In contrast, Todorova and Durisin (2007) assumed that external knowledge can be assimilated by an organisation only if that knowledge fits preexisting cognitive structures. If this is not the case, an alternative path of transformation is exhibited instead of assimilation.

The third dimension is *transformation*, which is the process of developing and refining routines to reorganise new internal and external knowledge when combining it with existing internal knowledge structures. According to Zahra and George (2002), transformation is about 'adding or deleting knowledge or simply [...] interpreting the same knowledge in a different manner' (p. 190). This dimension is considered important for creating synergies and for recodification, and it therefore depends on understanding knowledge (Chauvet, 2010) through such means as recodification and questioning (Flatten *et al.*, 2011; Liao *et al.*, 2007; Szulanski, 1996), and on knowledge internalisation, such as through integration (Flatten *et al.*, 2011; Jansen *et al.*, 2005; Szulanski, 1996). Scanned but untransformed assimilated knowledge can be stored in the knowledge base for future use (Zahra and George, 2002) and for improving the capacity to continuously use new knowledge (e.g., Wang and Chen, 2010). Whereas Zahra and George (2002) assumed that knowledge is first assimilated and then transformed, Todorova and Durisin (2007) saw knowledge transformation as an alternative to knowledge assimilation; knowledge can thus be either assimilated or t-ransformed.

The fourth dimension, *exploitation*, denotes the skills of effectively using external knowledge to create something new (Flatten *et al.*, 2011; Zahra and George, 2002; Yildiz *et al.*, 2019). Exploitation depends on knowledge use and implementation, such as by creating core competencies, harvesting resources and intensifying knowledge (Cohen and Levinthal, 1990; Lane *et al.*, 2006; Lane and Lubatkin, 1998).

Model Comparison of Alternative Dimension Pathways

Model 1: Assimilation and transformation as alternative pathways

Model 1 is based on Todorova and Durisin (2007). Assuming a positive relationship between recognising the value and acquisition of knowledge, they argued that assimilation and transformation act as independent processes. Todorova and Durisin (2007) agreed on the new dimension of transformation introduced by Zahra and George (2002), but didn't define it as the next step after knowledge assimilation; instead, they theorised that transformation represents an alternative process to assimilation (Marabelli and Newell, 2014; Patterson and Ambrosini, 2015; Todorova and Durisin, 2007).

Drawing on cognitive learning theories, Todorova and Durisin (2007) argued that knowledge can be assimilated only if it fits the individual's preexisting cognitive structures. In this case, the new information is only marginally adjusted and can then be implemented in the existing cognitive structures. However, if new knowledge is incompatible with cognitive premises, the process of knowledge assimilation is not possible. New cognitive structures have to be developed, and the absorption of knowledge yields a transformation process in the individual and the organisation. After knowledge yields assimilation or transformation, the next steps are exploitation and then innovation (Cohen and Levinthal, 1990; Lane *et al.*, 2006; Ter Wal *et al.*, 2011; Volberda *et al.*, 2010).

Therefore, Model 1 assumes an underlying process of the individual's absorptive capacity as follows:

> **Model 1 proposition:** *The dimension of individuals' acquisition capacity (ACQ) positively affects the dimension of individuals' assimilation capacity (AS) and individuals' transformation capacity (TR) as alternative paths. Both dimensions will positively affect individuals' exploitation capacity (EX), which in consequence will lead to different perceived outcomes of innovations (see Fig.1(a)).*

Model 2: Transformation and exploitation as alternative pathways

Model 2 is based on absorptive capacity as conceptualised by Zahra and George (2002), with its distinction between the individual's potential (acquisition, assimilation) and realised (transformation, exploitation) absorptive capacity.

Similar to the proposition of Model 1 (Todorova and Durisin, 2007), in Model 2 there is a clear dependency between the individual's acquisition and assimilation capacity, which Zahra and George (2002) define as the individual's pAC.

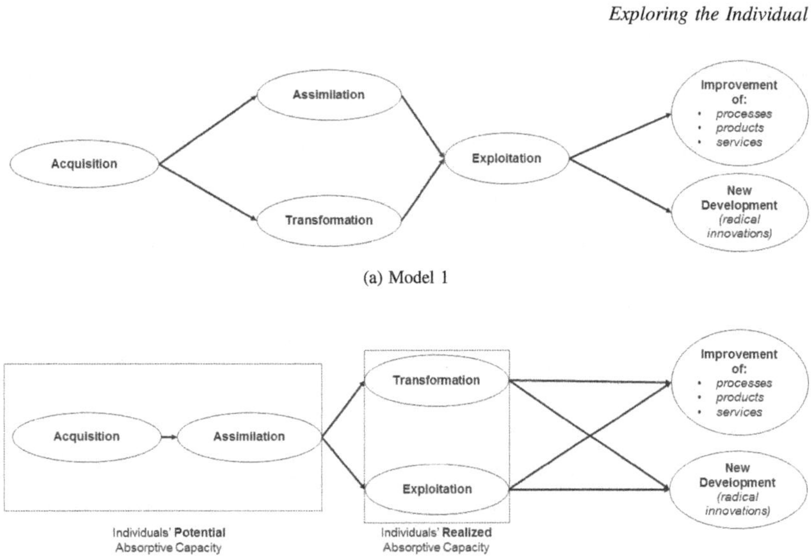

(a) Model 1

(b) Model 2

Fig. 1. Conceptual models.

Thus, individuals need to be capable of identifying knowledge sources and collecting new knowledge (acquisition), as well as of converting and internalising the explored knowledge into the organisation (assimilation) (Kogut and Zander, 1992).

However, in contrast to Model 1, Model 2 expects a difference with regard to the roles of individuals' TR and EX within the absorptive capacity process. Both are components of rAC (Zahra and George, 2002) and might create alternative paths of refining, reinterpreting and/or facilitating existing and newly assimilated knowledge into innovation outcomes.

Individuals' TR is considered important for creating synergies with existing knowledge through knowledge internalisation, recodification and refinement (Chauvet, 2010; Criscuolo *et al.*, 2014; Flatten *et al.*, 2011; Jansen *et al.*, 2005; Liao *et al.*, 2007; Szulanski, 1996; Zahra and George, 2002). Therefore, individuals' TR could mainly affect the innovation process and its outcomes by anchoring and reframing assimilated knowledge into already existing products, services or processes.

Individuals' EX is considered important for creating synergies with existing knowledge to create new goods, services, knowledge or organisational forms (Nooteboom *et al.*, 2007; Zahra and George, 2002).

Therefore, Model 2 assumes an underlying process of individuals' absorptive capacity:

> **Model 2 proposition:** *The dimension of individuals' acquisition capacity (ACQ) positively affects the dimension of individuals' assimilation capacity (AS) (potential absorptive capacity). Individuals' assimilation capacity (AS) will positively affect the dimensions of individuals' transformation capacity (TR) and individuals' exploitation capacity (EX) as alternative paths. Both will in consequence lead separate from each other to different outcomes of innovations (see Fig.1(b)).*

Method and Results

Participants and survey setup

In this paper, German organisations from different knowledge intensive industries with high innovation pace (e.g., engineering, manufacturing, university and financial services such as banking or insurance) were approached through personal and social networks and invited to participate. Seven out of 30 interested organisations agreed to participate. Employees within these companies were randomly selected and asked to participate in an online survey. On average, 12.71 employees per company (SD = 7.11, median = 10, range = 5–25) participated in the survey, resulting in a final sample of 89 employees (36 females; age: $M = 31.19$, SD = 8.72; age ranged from 19 to 58 years; no differences between genders were found with regard to age, $t(1, 87) = 0.55$, $p = 0.59$).

The largest group of participants had 1–2 years of experience within their respective positions (21 participants) and within their respective companies (17); followed by 3–6 months (14), 0–3 months (12) and 2–3 years (10) with regard to their position within the company; and then 3–4 years (10), 0–3 months (9) and 2–3 years (8) for time at the company itself. The longest time in a given position was 9–10 years (1 participant), and within a company, 30–35 years (1 participant).

We asked participants to answer questions related to the four derived dimensions: individuals' capacity for acquisition, assimilation, transformation and exploitation (Enkel *et al.*, 2017; Flatten *et al.*, 2011). The questions were translated into German to facilitate comprehension and were adapted slightly to the individual context. The translations were discussed in a back-and-forth translation process with an independent translator whose native language is English and with academics in the field of absorptive capacity research. Scales based on previous research were adapted when necessary for the individual level. The items were rated on a 7-point scale to describe agreement with different statements (from 1 = *strongly disagree* to 7 = *strongly agree*).

Furthermore, participants answered questions about the extent of their participation in (1) developing and improving existing processes, products and services (1 = 0%, 2 = 1–20%, 3 = 21–40%, 4 = 41–60%, 5 = 61–80% and 6 = 81–100%), and (2) about the extent of their participation in the development of new (radical) developments (1 = 0%, 2 = 1–20%, 3 = 21–40%, 4 = 41–60%, 5 = 61–80%, and 6 = 81–100%). See Table 2 for an overview of items and definitions of each construct.

Data analysis and results

For the assessment of the measurement model and the path estimations of the two competing models (Models 1 and 2) and a total (saturated) model (Model 3), we applied a partial least squares (PLS) algorithm by using SmartPLS 3 as the underlying toolbox (Ringle *et al.*, 2015). The PLS algorithm was applied with path as the weighting scheme and a maximum of 300 iterations (stop criterion $(10^\wedge - X) = 7$). To calculate significance, we applied a bootstrapping approach with 5.000 subsamples (parallel processing) and a bias-corrected and accelerated (BCa) bootstrap as a confidence interval method (Ringle *et al.*, 2015).

Assessment of the measurement model

Regarding the assessment of the measurement model, standard criteria for construct reliability and validity as well as discriminant validity were applied (Hair *et al.*, 2017). The outer loadings (standardised factor loading) showed almost overall appropriate loadings greater than 0.7. Cronbach's alpha (CA), composite reliability (CR) and average variance extracted (AVE) for all latent (reflective) constructs were acceptable and exceeded the minimum threshold values suggested in the literature (CA > 0.8, CR > 0.7, AVE > 0.5) (Fornell and Larcker, 1981; Hair *et al.*, 2017), except for individuals' ACQ. See Table 3 for an overview of factor loadings, construct reliability and validity. Bootstrapping showed significance for all of the criteria ($p < 0.001$).

Discriminant validity of the latent constructs was examined using the criterion proposed by Fornell and Larcker (1981). As all squared correlations among latent variables were smaller than their average variances extracted, discriminant validity was given for all constructs. In addition, applying the heterotrait–monotrait ratio (HTMT) recommended for PLS modelling (Hair *et al.*, 2017, 2019a, b), all

Table 2. Overview of measurements in the survey.

Construct/items	Definition
Acquisition (based on Enkel *et al.*, 2017)	
1. I systematically analyse the advantages and weaknesses of existing products and services on the market.[a] 2. First, I thoroughly abstract specific problems to later transfer them to another context.[a] 3. I regularly attend lectures, seminars, and exhibitions outside our industry to pursue the latest technological developments in other industries. 4. I purposefully define new search fields as a reaction to identified changes in the company environment or foreign industries. 5. When interacting with others, I always try to obtain information on the latest market needs or new technologies. 6. I regularly exchange information with colleagues from foreign business areas within the company to gain knowledge on alternative technologies.	The individual's ability to identify, realise, and acquire relevant new knowledge from external or internal sources. The individual continuously monitors, scans, explores, and stays alert for 'useful' ideas (Cohen and Levinthal, 1990; Flatten *et al.*, 2011, p. 100; Marabelli and Newell, 2014; Zahra and George, 2002, p. 189). Enkel *et al.* (2017) developed six identification and acquisition ability items inspired by other authors or slightly adapted already existing scales (Jansen *et al.*, 2005; Ter Wal *et al.*, 2011).
Assimilation (based on Enkel *et al.*, 2017)	
1. I process external knowledge quickly to get a feeling for how it can be used effectively in our company. 2. I participate rigorously in the assessment of the benefits of external ideas. 3. I strongly endeavor to critically assess the potential value of external knowledge with respect to our business requirements. 4. I frequently analyse how external expertise could be linked with the business requirements of my company. 5. I strongly endeavor to understand how external knowledge can be linked with my company's current research and development activities. 6. I regularly reconcile new technologies with ideas for new products, services, and processes. 7. I take time to translate external knowledge to guarantee that it is understood by my colleagues.	The individual's processes of interpreting, analysing, understanding or storing new external knowledge (Szulanski, 1996). Enkel *et al.* (2017) developed the 10 assimilation items through inspiration by other authors or slight adaptation of already existing scales (Jansen *et al.*, 2005; Ter Wal *et al.*, 2011).

Exploring the Individual

Table 2. (*Continued*)

Construct/items	Definition
8. I endeavor to prepare external knowledge so that it gains the necessary attention. 9. I have a central function in the preparation of external knowledge for other departments in the company. 10. I frequently meet with colleagues to explain and discuss new knowledge that I have gained externally.	
Transformation (based on Flatten *et al.*, 2011) 1. I have the ability to structure and use collected knowledge. 2. I am accustomed to absorbing new knowledge, as well as to preparing it for further purposes and making it available. 3. I successfully link existing knowledge with new insights. 4. I am able to apply new knowledge in my daily work.	Transformation means developing and refining routines that reorganise external knowledge when combining it with existing (internal) knowledge structures and assimilated knowledge for further use in the future (Zahra and George, 2002, p. 190). Four items were slightly adapted and validated to measure individual transformation capability based on Flatten *et al.* (2011), who developed items measuring organisational AC.
Exploitation (based on Enkel *et al.*, 2017) 1. When dealing with external ideas that I believe will be resisted in the company, I strongly engage in implementing the ideas. 2. I take risks to convince decision-makers of the adoption and utilisation of external knowledge. 3. I would do almost anything to get my external ideas adapted by the company. 4. When an external idea appeals to me, I energetically work on making sure that the idea is implemented, even if the idea was not originally mine. 5. I am willing to take action to guarantee that the potential of external ideas that I believe in is realised.	Exploitation denotes the skills of effectively using formerly external knowledge to create something new for company operations (Flatten *et al.*, 2011, p. 100; Zahra and George, 2002, p. 190). It is the individual efforts to utilise external knowledge. Enkel *et al.* (2017) describe seven items of the individual exploitation/utilisation capabilities through inspiration by Jansen *et al.* (2005) and Ter Wal *et al.* (2011) and by slightly adapting existing items. The study used only the five exploitation items.

Table 2. (*Continued*)

Construct/items	Definition
Incremental Innovation (scale based on and inspired by intensive literature review, including Chandy and Tellis, 1998; Jansen *et al.*, 2006; McGrath, 2001; Tidd and Bessant, 2013)	
To what extent did you participate in the following activities in the firm? (a) Improvements of products (b) Improvements of services (c) Improvements of processes	Very low or no novelty level (Garcia and Calantone, 2002). Exploitative nature of innovation: doing more or less the same thing, but with small changes, variants or imitation. It denotes highly structured and well-known processes to improve products, services, and/or processes. High degree of path-dependency: no or very low learning capacity.
Radical/New Innovation (scale based on and inspired by intensive literature review, including Chandy and Tellis, 1998; Jansen *et al.*, 2006; McGrath, 2001; Tidd and Bessant, 2013)	
To what extent did you participate in the following activities in the firm? • Entirely new, radical developments	Very high novelty level (Garcia and Calantone, 2002). Explorative nature of innovation: doing something new and unknown and substantially different (e.g., calling automobiles *horseless carriages* to introduce the innovation). Occasionally but not directly plannable with higher-risk new requirements and flexible approaches. Dealing with uncertainty. No path-dependency: knowledge-leveraging and high and increasing learning capacity.

[a]Both items were step-by-step excluded from the main analysis because of their low factor loadings of 0.26 and 0.501, respectively.

Table 3. Factor loadings, construct reliability and validity.

Construct	Item	Standardised loadings	Mean (SD)	CA	CR	AVE
ACQ	ACQ1	0.645	4.42 (1.18)	0.689	0.810	0.518
	ACQ2	0.711				
	ACQ3	0.708				
	ACQ4	0.805				
AS	AS1	0.778	4.85 (1.04)	0.898	0.916	0.523
	AS2	0.740				
	AS3	0.707				
	AS4	0.731				
	AS5	0.779				
	AS6	0.700				
	AS7	0.710				
	AS8	0.702				
	AS9	0.728				
	AS10	0.643				
TR	TR1	0.720	4.74 (1.27)	0.801	0.867	0.622
	TR2	0.770				
	TR3	0.802				
	TR4	0.856				
EX	EX1	0.839	5.72 (0.89)	0.875	0.909	0.668
	EX2	0.873				
	EX3	0.843				
	EX4	0.826				
	EX5	0.692				
Improvement of Processes	ImProc	—	3.38 (1.53)			
Improvement of Products	ImProd	—	2.55 (1.69)	—	—	—
Improvement of Services	ImSrv	—	3.04 (1.67)	—	—	—
New, Radical Development	NRD	—	2.74 (1.72)	—	—	—

constructs showed values of HTMT < 0.85 (Hair *et al.*, 2017). See Table 4 for the discriminant validity measures according to Fornell and Larcker (1981) and Hair *et al.* (2017). Bootstrapping showed significance for all of the criteria ($p < 0.001$).

As suggested by Podsakoff *et al.* (2003), potential common method bias was addressed, for instance, by varying scale end points and formats, reassuring respondents about the anonymity of their answers, and using established measurements. In addition, we applied a full collinearity test suggested for a PLS approach (Kock, 2015; Kock and Lynn, 2012). The full collinearity test showed that all variance inflation factors were smaller than the proposed threshold of 3.3.

Table 4. Discriminant validity.

Construct	*ACQ*	*AS*	*TR*	*EX*	*ImProc*	*ImProd*	*ImSrv*	*NRD*
ACQ	**0.720**							
AS	0.665 (0.808)	**0.723**						
TR	0.397 (0.523)	0.628 (0.717)	**0.788**					
EX	0.377 (0.484)	0.623 (0.696)	0.451 (0.513)	**0.817**				
ImProc	0.338 (0.400)	0.420 (0.439)	0.428 (0.469)	0.365 (0.387)	—			
ImProd	0.319 (0.385)	0.394 (0.409)	0.239 (0.246)	0.527 (0.547)	0.391 (0.391)	—		
IMSrv	0.370 (0.439)	0.341 (0.356)	0.252 (0.264)	0.352 (0.364)	0.600 (0.600)	0.519 (0.519)	—	
NRD	0.379 (0.467)	0.495 (0.511)	0.341 (0.368)	0.609 (0.629)	0.451 (0.451)	0.736 (0.736)	0.499 (0.499)	—

Main analysis and model testing

First, with regard to Model 1 (see Fig. 1(a)), ACQ significantly predicted individuals' AS ($\beta = 0.700$, $p < 0.001$) and individuals' TR ($\beta = 0.423$, $p < 0.001$). However, only individuals' AS showed a significant relation towards individuals' EX ($\beta = 0.556$, $p < 0.001$) but not individuals' TR ($\beta = 0.104$, $p = 0.442$). Individuals' EX showed significant effects on improving (1) the process ($\beta = 0.365$, $p < 0.001$), (2) the product ($\beta = 0.527$, $p < 0.001$) and (3) the service ($\beta = 0.352$, $p < 0.01$), as well as working on entirely new (radical) developments ($\beta = 0.610, p < 0.001$). Furthermore, significant indirect effects on improving the (1) process ($\beta = 0.142$, $p = 0.015$), (2) product ($\beta = 0.205$, $p = 0.001$) and (3) service ($\beta = 0.137, p = 0.013$), as well as working on entirely new, radical developments ($\beta = 0.237$, $p < 0.001$), were found through the connection of individuals' acquisition–assimilation–exploitation capacities.

Second, with regard to Model 2 (see Fig. 1(b)), ACQ significantly predicted individuals' AS ($\beta = 0.692$, $p < 0.001$). Individuals' AS significantly predicted TR ($\beta = 0.627, p < 0.001$) and exploitation capacity (EX, $\beta = 0.622, p < 0.001$). With regard to the innovation outcomes, individuals' TR showed significant effects only on improving the process ($\beta = 0.330$, $p = 0.001$), but not on improving the product ($\beta = 0.001$, $p = 0.995$), improving the service ($\beta = 0.116$, $p = 0.269$), or entirely new, radical developments ($\beta = 0.083$, $p < 0.374$). Individuals' EX showed significant effects on improving the product ($\beta = 0.528$,

Table 5. Overview of model comparison.

	Model 1		Model 2		Saturated model (Model 3)	
Relationship	Beta	R^2	Beta	R^2	Beta	R^2
Acquisition (ACQ) → Assimilation (AS)	0.700**	0.490	0.692**	0.479	0.665**	0.442
Acquisition (ACQ) → Transformation (TR)	0.423**	0.179		0.393	−0.038	0.396
Assimilation (AS) → Transformation (TR)			0.627**		0.654**	
Acquisition (ACQ) → Exploitation (EX)		0.392		0.386	−0.063	0.396
Assimilation (AS) → Exploitation (EX)	0.556**		0.622**		0.604**	
Transformation (TR) → Exploitation (EX)	0.104				0.097	
Acquisition (ACQ) → ImpProcess		0.133		0.221	0.124	0.242
Assimilation (AS) → ImpProcess					0.080	
Transformation (TR) → ImpProcess			0.330**		0.261*	
Exploitation (EX) → ImpProcess	0.365**		0.219*		0.151	
Acquisition (ACQ) → ImpProduct		0.278		0.279	0.131	0.297
Assimilation (AS) → ImpProduct					0.046	
Transformation (TR) → ImpProduct			0.001		−0.056	
Exploitation (EX) → ImpProduct	0.527**		0.528**		0.474**	
Acquisition (ACQ) → ImpService		0.124		0.135	0.275*	0.191
Assimilation (AS) → ImpService					−0.022	
Transformation (TR) → ImpService			0.116		0.049	
Exploitation (EX) → ImpService	0.352**		0.301**		0.240	
Acquisition (ACQ) → New Development		0.372		0.378	0.122	0.401
Assimilation (AS) → New Development					0.100	
Transformation (TR) → New Development			0.083		0.004	
Exploitation (EX) → New Development	0.610**		0.573**		0.499**	

$p < 0.001$), improving the service ($\beta = 0.301$, $p = 0.001$), and new (radical) developments ($\beta = 0.573$, $p < 0.001$), but not on improving the process ($\beta = 0.219$, $p = 0.054$). Furthermore, significant indirect effects on improving the process ($\beta = 0.143$, $p = 0.005$) were found through the connection of individuals' acquisition–assimilation–transformation capacities. Significant indirect effects on improving the product ($\beta = 0.227$, $p < 0.001$), improving the service ($\beta = 0.129$, $p = 0.018$) and new radical developments ($\beta = 0.247$, $p < 0.001$) were found through the connection of individuals' acquisition–assimilation–exploitation capacities.

A saturated model (Model 3) controlling for all direct and indirect multidimensionality effects confirms the outcome of Model 2 with regard to (1) major significant direct and indirect relations, (2) the distinction between transformation and exploitation as alternative paths and (3) the similar improved values in explained variances (R^2) for Models 2 and 3 compared to Model 1. See Table 5 for an overview of the results for the different models.

Discussion and Theoretical Implications

Despite strong interest in the conceptualisation of absorptive capacity, there is still an ongoing debate on how the main dimensions of absorptive capacity — acquisition, assimilation, transformation and exploitation — relate to each other and affect innovation potential and outcomes. Therefore, this study extends studies on individuals' absorptive capacities and their contributions to developing and improving different outcomes of innovation (Volberda *et al.*, 2010; Tian and Soo, 2018; Yildiz *et al.*, 2019).

Against this background, two competing models (Models 1 and 2) and one saturated model (Model 3) were analysed. The analysis showed that, based on the explained variances (R^2) and compared to the control model (Model 3), Model 1, which tests individuals' AS and TR as alternative paths, is inferior to Model 2, which tests individuals' TR and EX as alternative paths (see Table 5). Therefore, the results show a clear distinction between individuals' TR and EX and their differentiated impact on innovation outcomes. Furthermore, both components of individuals' *realised* absorptive capacities strongly depend upon individuals' *potential* absorptive capacities. See Fig. 2 for an overview of the significant paths (solid) and insignificant paths (dotted).

First, in line with both models (Models 1 and 2; see Fig. 1), an individual's capacity to acquire new knowledge and identify new knowledge sources is critical to the individual's absorptive capacity process, forming the foundation for subsequent AS (Todorova and Durisin, 2007; Zahra and George, 2002).

Exploring the Individual

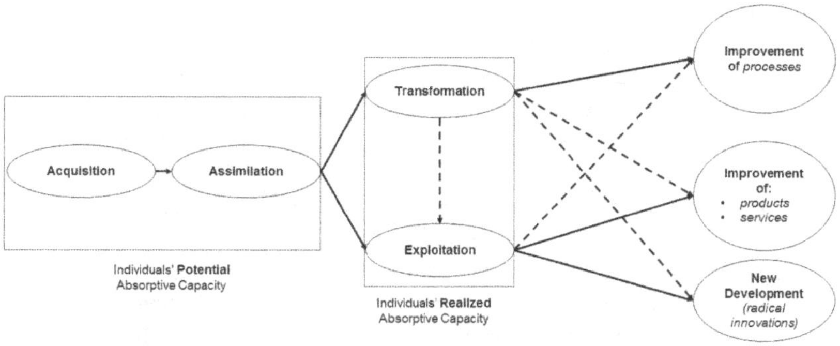

Fig. 2. Overview of results and final model.

Consequently, *individuals' absorptive capacity process* encourages individuals to value new information and to scan for its indicators by exploring, interpreting, understanding and using the new information. This has been confirmed by the positive relationship between these two capacities, which indicates that individuals' AS is associated with higher levels of ACQ (Todorova and Durisin, 2007). Therefore, individuals need to be alert and willing to identify important indicators of new knowledge (Gaglio and Katz, 2001), which is a prerequisite for individuals' AS of new knowledge.

Second, in contrast to Model 1, our analyses (Model 2) emphasise the importance of individuals' AS as a necessary requirement to influence both the TR and EX of individuals, which are components of an individuals' rAC. Indeed, an individual's AS does not seem to be an alternative path towards the individuals' TR (Model 1, Todorova and Durisin, 2007). Instead, assimilation is acting as a mediating antecedent between components of the individuals' pAC and rAC (Model 2; Zahra and George, 2002). Assimilation depends on individuals' capacity to interpret, formalise, and comprehend new information and fit it into their existing cognitive structures (e.g., Jansen *et al.*, 2005; Lichtenthaler, 2009; Zollo and Winter, 2002). Individual attempts to assimilate external knowledge enable exploration, but such efforts require the openness, commitment and motivation to recognise the value of the knowledge, transfer it to the corporate knowledge base, and either transform it into internal processes or exploit it in new products (Daspit and Souza, 2013; Hafkesbrink and Schroll, 2016; Minbaeva *et al.*, 2003; Salter *et al.*, 2015).

Third, our findings (Models 2 and 3) validate a distinction between dimensions of individuals' realised absorptive capacities — namely, individuals' TR and EX. While both dimensions are positively influenced by the individual's

AS (Zahra and George, 2002), they seem to be distinguishable paths of rAC and consequently differ in their impact on innovation performance (see Fig. 2). This confirms that individuals can have multifold but unequally distributed capacities that might lead to different flows of activities (Bradford and Saad, 2014; Marabelli and Newell, 2014; Patterson and Ambrosini, 2015; Todorova and Durisin, 2007). Therefore, recognising individuals' differences in either transforming or exploiting new knowledge or having both capacities is important for corporate strategy and innovation management (Jansen *et al.*, 2006; Rothaermel and Alexandre, 2009; Rothaermel and Hess, 2007; Sun and Anderson, 2010; Yildiz *et al.*, 2019).

Fourth, the results of Model 2 show that the internal organisation-related focus of the outcome on improving organisational processes is significantly mediated by a sequence of individuals' capacities to acquire, assimilate and transform knowledge. In contrast, a more external and market-related focus on improving products and services and working on radical developments (Cohen and Levinthal, 1990) is significantly mediated by a sequence of individuals' capacity to acquire, assimilate and exploit knowledge. These results support research assuming that transformation capacities are stronger when related to processes of internal recodification and refinement (Chauvet, 2010; Criscuolo *et al.*, 2014; Flatten *et al.*, 2011; Jansen *et al.*, 2005; Liao *et al.*, 2007; Szulanski, 1996; Zahra and George, 2002). In contrast, EX is often considered as valuable for creating new goods and/or services or organisational forms (Nooteboom *et al.*, 2007; Zahra and George, 2002).

In summary, our research contributes to the existing knowledge and conceptualisation of (the individual's) absorptive capacity by (1) acknowledging the multidimensionality of the construct, (2) connecting the individual's pAC with the individual's *realised* capacity (Zahra and George, 2002), (3) adding insights on the existence of the individual's TR and EX as two alternative paths and (4) illuminating the different innovation outcomes associated with the dimensions of the individual's realised absorptive capacities.

Managerial Implications

This research can improve the understanding of current developments of the absorptive capacity concept and the critical role of individuals on the micro- and macro-levels (Volberda *et al.*, 2010) as observations at the individual level have been argued to be the most appropriate type of data and object to focus on (Felin and Foss, 2006) and offers several managerial implications.

First, by continuously scanning for indicators and weak signals and exploring new knowledge, corporations stay alert to useful ideas so as to face the challenges of dynamic environments, quickly changing requirements, and the absolute necessity to innovate and in radically new ways (Arnold and Thuriaux, 1998). Therefore, we believe that corporations must gain competence on how employees acquire, assimilate, transform and exploit knowledge in specific contexts. This also means that companies need to develop mechanisms that deal with differences in their employees' capacities without demotivating those employees. Thus, it is important (1) to understand new internal knowledge by using individuals' neglected or ignored experiences and knowledge bases; (2) to gain know-how inside and outside the corporate environment, anticipate the ideas that emerge in reaction to possible scenarios, and launch promising innovations at the right time; (3) to avoid failing to react appropriately and (4) to facilitate performance on the different levels of disruption (Garcia and Calantone, 2002).

Second, implementing and encouraging innovation activities that promote engagement among individuals will increase new knowledge absorption and facilitate the individual's capabilities and their interconnections (Yildiz *et al.*, 2019). In addition, innovation depends on developing and modifying activities in order to renew and transfer knowledge and to differentiate between the corporate and individual levels. The role of an organisation is to develop decision-making structures and networks of intra-firm relationships through which individual absorptive capacities can be leveraged and deployed (Tortoriello, 2015). At the same time, the successful exchange and transfer of knowledge depends on the willingness of individuals and corporations to take part in innovation processes, and knowledge is more easily transferred between sources and recipients with experiences and knowledge bases that have similar characteristics, backgrounds and circumstances (Fox *et al.*, 1988; Phelps *et al.*, 2007; Reagans and McEvily, 2003). Therefore, it is not enough to build on single capacities and competences to absorb new knowledge. Requirements (e.g., of individual and organisational resources), barriers (e.g., lack of acceptance), and conditions have to be considered as much as competence, willingness and motivation to increase individual absorption capabilities and foster innovation (e.g., Abrell *et al.*, 2018; Horvat *et al.*, 2018; Schweisfurth and Raasch, 2018).

When referring to individuals' potential and realised absorptive capabilities, acquisition and assimilation can be largely managed by hiring certain profile people (T-shaped) and by setting the expectation to scout for new knowledge in non-familiar areas outside the existing heuristics in a company. To succeed with knowledge absorption, individuals must be motivated and capable of evaluating technological and organisational feasibility, desirability and viability. The capacities of transformation and exploitation could be cultural or systemically supported by enabling and empowering individuals to realise their capacity towards a specific innovation outcome. Absorptive capacity processes are challenging but absorption efforts especially on the individual level are worth (for the individual and the group and organisation level) (e.g., Nowak, 2018). Individual engagements are key to secure absorption of new external knowledge and might enable to explore in more depth the individuals' capabilities (e.g. Lichtenthaler and Lichtenthaler, 2010; Zuñiga-Collazos *et al.*, 2019) from an more open innovation perspective in collaborations and co-creative approaches to foster entirely new radical developments (e.g., Barchi and Greco, 2018; Horvat *et al.*, 2018).

Conclusion, Limitations, and Future Research

Our study has some limitations and offers opportunities for further insights. Our research sample focuses on seven German corporations in different knowledge intense, fast moving industries. Future studies should be expanded to include a larger sample of companies across more industry sectors in Germany and other European countries. Additionally, the number of individual participants in each corporation and department would also be increased. By broadening the database potential cultural, industrial, behavioural and contextual bias can be further reduced. A more detailed investigation in this research field supplemented by qualitative interviews might advance the understanding of and insights into individuals' absorptive capacity and open-up for more opportunities of the analysis, and theoretical and managerial implications to further develop and build on an individual absorptive capacity measurement scale. Only few studies actually measure and correlate absorptive capacity, especially on the individual level (e.g., Enkel *et al.*, 2017; Tian and Soo, 2018; Schweisfurth and Raasch, 2018).

In addition, our results have not been validated through cross-country empirical research. We know less about how corporations in less knowledge intense and less innovative companies foster employees' acquisition and assimilation of new knowledge. Doing so will encourage corporations to develop individual absorptive capacities and specific (innovation) management practices considering different internal and external context and capabilities.

In our study, we discovered that the dimensions of individuals' realised absorptive capacities — transformation and exploitation — establish alternative paths that influence innovation outcomes. This finding indicates that individual capacity dimensions are not a process flow of activities but are special individual capacities instead; the way they are connected increases new knowledge absorption and engagement in innovations and performances differently (see Fig. 2). In addition, this finding develops and improves the cognitive structure, individual learning, motivation and bootlegging, and it increases the effectiveness of using a new knowledge base in the future. We hope that the findings of our empirical research will open the way for further systematic research and analyses of (individual) absorptive capacity using possible new methods and approaches in this research field.

References

Abrell, Th, A Benker and M Pihlajamaa (2018). User knowledge utilization in innovation of complex products and systems: An absorptive capacity perspective. *Creativity and Innovation Management*, 27, 169–182.

Alexander, AT, A-K Neyer and KRE Huizingh (2016). Introduction to the special issue: Transferring knowledge for innovation. *R&D Management*, 46(2), 305–311. doi: 10.1111/radm.12195.

Amniattalab, A, and R Ansari (2016). The effect of strategic foresight on competitive advantage with the mediating role of organizational ambidexterity. *International Journal of Innovation Management*, 20(3), 377–400.

Arnold, E and B Thuriaux (1998). *Developing Firms' Technological Capabilities*. Brighton: Technopolis.

Barchi, M and M Greco (2018). Negotiation in open innovation: A literature review. *Group Decision and Negotiation*, 27, 343–374.

Bessant, J, B Phelps and R Adams (2005). *External Knowledge: A Review of the Literature Addressing the Role of External Knowledge and Expertise at Key Stages of Business Growth and Development*. London, UK: AIM Research.

Bessant, J and A Trifilova (2017). Developing absorptive capacity for recombinant innovation. *Business Process Management Journal*, 23(6), 1094–1107.

Bradford, J and M Saad (2014). Towards a method for measuring absorptive capacity in firms. *Technology Management and Sustainable Development*, 13(3), 237–249.

Camisón, C and B Forés (2010). Knowledge absorptive capacity: New insights for its conceptualization and measurement. *Journal of Business Research*, 63(7), 707–715. doi: 10.1016/j.jbusres.2009.04.022.

Carmines, EG and RA Zeller (1979). *Reliability and Validity Assessment*. Thousand Oaks, CA: Sage Publications.

Chandy, RK and GJ Tellis (1998). Organizing for radical product innovation: The overlooked role of willingness to cannibalize. *Journal of Marketing Research*, 35(4), 474–487.

Chauvet, V (2010). Absorptive capacity: Scale development and implications for future research. *International Management*, 19(1), 113–129.

Christensen, J, M Olesen and J Kjaer (2005). The industrial dynamics of open innovation: Evidence from the transformation of consumer electronics. *Research Policy*, 34(10), 1533–1549.

Cohen, WM and DA Levinthal (1990). Absorptive capacity: A new perspective on learning and innovation. *Administrative Science Quarterly*, 35(1), 128–152.

Cowan, R and N Jonard (2009). Knowledge portfolios and the organization of innovation networks. *Academy of Management Review*, 34(2), 320–342.

Criscuolo, P, A Salter and ALJ Ter Wal (2014). Going underground: Bootlegging and individual innovative performance. *Organization Science*, 25(5), 1287–1305. doi: 10.1287/orsc.2013.0856.

Crossan, MM, HW Lane and RE White (1999). Organizational learning framework: From intuition to institution. *Academy of Management Review*, 24(3), 522–537.

Dahlander, L and DM Gann (2010). How open is innovation? *Research Policy*, 39(6), 699–709. doi: 10.1016/j.respol.2010.01.013.

Daspit, JJ and DED Souza (2013). Understanding the multi-dimensional nature of absorptive capacity. *Journal of Managerial Issues*, 25(3), 299–316.

Enkel, E, S Heil, M Hengstler and H Wirth (2017). Exploratory and exploitative innovation: To what extent do the dimensions of individual level absorptive capacity contribute? *Technovation*, 60–61, 29–38. doi: 10.1016/j.technovation.2016.08.002.

Escribano, A, A Fosfuri and JA Tribó (2009). Managing external knowledge flows: The moderating role of absorptive capacity. *Research Policy*, 38(1), 96–105. doi: 10.1016/j.respol.2008.10.022.

Felin, T and NJ Foss (2006). Individuals and organizations: Thoughts on a micro-foundations project for strategic management and organizational analysis. In *Research Methodology in Strategy and Management*, DJ Ketchen and DD Bergh (eds.), Vol. 3, pp. 253–288. Bingley, UK: Emerald Group Publishing Limited.

Filippini, R, WH Guettel, P Neirotti and A Nosella (2012). The different modes for absorbing knowledge: An analytical lens on absorptive capacity from a process perspective. *International Journal of Knowledge Management Studies*, 5(1–2), 45–65.

Flatten, TC, A Engelen, SA Zahra and M Brettel (2011). A measure of absorptive capacity: Scale development and validation. *European Management Journal*, 29(2), 98–116. doi: 10.1016/j.emj.2010.11.002.

Fornell, C and DF Larcker (1981). Evaluating structural equation models with unobservable variables and measurement error. *Journal of Marketing Research*, 18, 39–50.

Fox, DG, RL Ellison and KL Keith (1988). Human-resource management: An index and its relationship to readiness for change. *Public Personnel Management*, 17(3), 297–302.

Gaglio, CM and JA Katz (2001). The psychological basis of opportunity identification: Entrepreneurial alertness. *Small Business Economics*, 16(2), 95–111.

Garcia, R and R Calantone (2002). A critical look at technological innovation typology and innovativeness terminology: A literature review. *Journal of Product Innovation Management*, 19(2), 110–132.

Grant, RM (1996). Toward a knowledge-based theory of the firm. *Strategic Management Journal*, 17, 109–122. doi: 10.1002/smj.4250171110.

Hafkesbrink, J and M Schroll (2016). Ambidextrous organizational and individual competencies in open innovation: The dawn of a new research agenda. In *Open Innovation: A Multifaceted Perspective*, AL Mention and M Torkkeli (eds.), pp. 517–570. Singapore: World Scientific Books.

Hair, JF, GTM Hult, CM Ringle and M Sarstedt (2017). *A Primer on Partial Least Squares Structural Equation Modeling (PLS-SEM)*, 2nd Ed. Thousand Oaks, CA: Sage.

Hair, JF, M Sarstedt and CM Ringle (2019a). Rethinking some of the rethinking of partial least squares. *European Journal of Marketing*, 53(4), 566–584.

Hair, JF, JJ Risher, M Sarstedt and CM Ringle (2019b). When to use and how to report the results of PLS-SEM. *European Business Review*, 31(1), 2–24.

Heeley, MB (1997). Appropriating rents from external knowledge: The impact of absorptive capacity on firm sales growth and research productivity. *Frontiers of Entrepreneurship Research*, 17, 390–404.

Holsapple, CW (2003). *Handbook on Knowledge Management*. Berlin: Springer-Verlag.

Horvat, D, C Dreher and O Som (2018). How firms absorb external knowledge — Modelling and managing the absorptive capacity process. *International Journal of Innovation Management*, 23(1), 1363–9196. doi: 10.1142/S1363919619500415.

Hubert, M, A Florack, R Gattringer, T Eberhardt, E Enkel and P Kenning (2017). Flag up!–Flagship products as important drivers of perceived brand innovativeness. *Journal of Business Research*, 71, 154–163.

Huizingh, EKRE (2010). Open innovation: State of the art and future perspectives. *Technovation*, 31, 2–9. doi: 10.1016/j.technovation.2010.10.002.

Jansen, JJP, FAJ van den Bosch and HW Volberda (2005). Managing potential and realised absorptive capacity: How do organisational antecedents matter? *Academy of Management Journal*, 48(6), 999–1015. doi: 10.5465/AMJ.2005.19573106.

Jansen, JJP, FAJ Van Den Bosch and HW Volberda (2006). Exploratory innovation, exploitative innovation, and performance: Effects of organizational antecedents and environmental moderators. *Management Science*, 52(11), 1661–1674, doi: 10.1287/mnsc.1060.0576.

Kaish, S and B Gilad (1991). Characteristics of opportunities search of entrepreneurs versus executives: Sources, interests, general alertness. *Journal of Business Venturing*, 6(1), 45–61.

Kalogerakis, K, C Lüthje and C Herstatt (2010). Developing innovations based on analogies: Experience from design and engineering consultants. *Journal of Product Innovation Management*, 27(3), 418–436. doi: 10.1111/j.1540-5885.2010.00725.x.

Kock, N (2015). Common method bias in PLS-SEM: A full collinearity assessment approach. *International Journal of e-Collaboration (IJeC)*, 11(4), 1–10.

Kock, N and GS Lynn (2012). Lateral collinearity and misleading results in variance-based SEM: An illustration and recommendations. *Journal of the Association for Information Systems*, 13(7), 546–580.

Kogut, B and U Zander (1992). Knowledge of the firm, combinative capabilities, and the replication of technology. *Organization Science*, 3, 383–397.

Lane, PJ, BR Koka and S Pathak (2006). The reification of absorptive capacity: A critical review and rejuvenation of the construct. *Academy of Management Review*, 31(4), 833–863. doi: 10.5465/AMR.2006.22527456.

Lane, PJ and M Lubatkin (1998). Relative absorptive capacity and interorganizational learning. *Strategic Management Journal*, 19(5), 461–477.

Lane, PJ, JE Salk and MA Lyles (2001). Absorptive capacity, learning, and performance in international joint ventures. *Strategic Management Journal*, 22(12), 1139–1161. doi: 10.1002/smj.206.

Leal-Rodríguez, AL, JL Roldán, JA Ariza-Montes and A Leal-Millán (2014). From potential absorptive capacity to innovation outcomes in project teams: The conditional mediating role of the realized absorptive capacity in a relational learning context. *International Journal of Project Management*, 32(6), 894–907.

Lengnick-Hall, CA (1992). Innovation and competitive advantage: What we know and what we need to learn. *Journal of Management*, 18(2), 399–429.

Lewin, AY, S Massini and C Peeters (2011). Microfoundations of internal and external absorptive capacity routines. *Organization Science*, 22(1), 81–98. doi:10.1287/orsc.1100.0525.

Liao, SH, WC Fei and CC Chen (2007). Knowledge sharing, absorptive capacity, and innovation capability: An empirical study of Taiwan's knowledge-intensive industries. *Journal of Information Science*, 33(3), 340–359.

Lichtenthaler, U (2009). Absorptive capacity, environmental turbulence, and the complementarity of organizational learning processes. *Academy of Management Journal*, 52(4), 822–846. doi: 10.5465/AMJ.2009.43670902.

Lichtenthaler, U and E Lichtenthaler (2010). Technology transfer across organizational boundaries: Absorptive capacity and desorptive capacity. *California Management Review*, 53(1), 154–170.

Marabelli, M and S Newell (2014). Knowing, power and materiality: A critical review and reconceptualization of absorptive capacity. *International Journal of Management Reviews*, 16(4), 479–499. doi: 10.1111/ijmr.12031.

March, JG (1991). Exploration and exploitation in organizational learning. *Organization Science*, 2(1), 71–87. doi: 10.1287/orsc.2.1.71.

Mariano, S and C Walter (2015). The construct of absorptive capacity in knowledge management and intellectual capital research: Content and text. *Journal of Knowledge Management*, 19(2), 372–400. doi: 10.1108/JKM-08-2014-0342.

Martinkenaite, I and KJ Breunig (2016). The emergence of absorptive capacity through micro-macro level interactions. *Journal of Business Research*, 69(2), 700–708. doi: 10.1016/j.jbusres.2015.08.020.

Matusik, SF and MB Heeley (2005). Absorptive capacity in the software industry: Identifying dimensions that affect knowledge and knowledge creation activities. *Journal of Management*, 31(4), 549–572. doi: 10.1177/0149206304272293.

McAdam, M, R McAdam, B Galbraith and K Miller (2010). An exploratory study of principal investigator roles in UK university proof-of-concept processes: An absorptive capacity perspective. *R&D Management*, 40(5), 455–473. Retrieved from http://10.0.4.87/j.1467-9310.2010.00619.x.

McGrath, RG (2001). Exploratory learning, innovative capacity, and managerial oversight. *Academy of Management Journal*, 44(1), 118–131.

Minbaeva, DB, T Pedersen, I Björkman, CF Fey and HJ Park (2003). Subsidiary absorptive. *Journal of International Business Studies*, 34(6), 586–599.

Noblet, J-P, E Simon and R Parent (2011). Absorptive capacity: A proposed operationalization. *Knowledge Management Research & Practice*, 9(4), 367–377. doi: 10.1057/kmrp.2011.26.

Nooteboom, B, W van Haverbeke, G Duysters, V Gilsing and A van den Oord (2007). Optimal cognitive distance and absorptive capacity. *Research Policy*, 36(7), 1016–1034. doi: 10.1016/j.respol.2007.04.003.

Nowak, R (2018). Executive's personality and group performance: The mediating role of absorptive capacity. *International Journal of Innovation Management*, 22(6), 1850047.

O'Reilly, C and ML Tushman (2011). Organizational ambidexterity in action: How managers explore and exploit. *California Management Review*, 53(4), 5–22.

Patterson, F, M Kerrin and G Gatto-Roissard (2009). Characteristics & behaviours of Innovative people in organisations. Literature review prepared for the NESTA Policy & Research Unit, pp. 1–63. Retrieved from http://www.nesta.org.uk/library/documents/characteristics-behaviours-interim-summary.pdf.

Patterson, W and V Ambrosini (2015). Configuring absorptive capacity as a key process for research intensive firms. *Technovation*, 36, 77–89. doi: 10.1016/j.technovation.2014.10.003.

Phelps, R, R Adams and J Bessant (2007). Models of organizational growth: A review with implications for knowledge and learning. *International Journal of Management Reviews*, 9(1), 53–80.

Podsakoff, PM, SB MacKenzie, JY Lee and NP Podsakoff (2003). Common method biases in behavioral research: A critical review of the literature and recommended remedies. *Journal of Applied Psychology*, 88(5), 879–903.

Reagans, R and B McEvily (2003). Network structure and knowledge transfer: The effects of cohesion and range. *Administrative Science Quarterly*, 48(2), 240–267.

Ringle, CM, S Wende and J-M Becker (2015). *SmartPLS 3*. Boenningstedt: SmartPLS GmbH, http://www.smartpls.com.

Rohrbeck, R and JO Schwarz (2013). The value contribution of strategic foresight: Insights from an empirical study of large European companies. *Technological Forecasting and Social Change*, 80(8), 1593–1606. doi: 10.1016/j.techfore.2013.01.004.

Rosenkopf, L and A Nerkar (2001). Beyond local search: Boundary-spanning, exploration, and impact in the optical disk industry. *Strategic Management Journal*, 22(4), 287–306.

Rothaermel, FT and MT Alexandre (2009). Ambidexterity in technology sourcing: The moderating role of absorptive capacity. *Organization Science*, 20(4), 759–780. doi: 10.1287/orsc.1080.0404.

Rothaermel, FT and AM Hess (2007). Building dynamic capabilities: Innovation driven by individual-, firm-, and network-level effects. *Organization Science*, 18(6), 898–921. doi: 10.1287/orsc.1070.0291.

Rubera, G and AH Kirca (2012). Firm innovativeness and its performance outcomes: A meta-analytic review and theoretical integration. *Journal of Marketing*, 7, 130–147.

Salter, A, ALJ Ter Wal, P Criscuolo and O Alexy (2015). Open for ideation: Individual-level openness and idea generation in R&D. *Journal of Product Innovation Management*, 32(4), 488–504. doi: 10.1111/jpim.12214.

Schoenmakers, W and G Duysters (2010). The technological origins of radical inventions. *Research Policy*, 39(8), 1051–1059. doi: 10.1016/j.respol.2010.05.013.

Sun, PYT and MH Anderson (2010). An examination of the relationship between absorptive capacity and organizational learning, and a proposed integration. *International Journal of Management Reviews*, 12(2), 130–150. doi: 10.1108/JKM-08-2014-0342.

Schweisfurth, TG and Ch Raasch (2018). Absorptive capacity for need knowledge: Antecedents and effects for employee innovativeness. *Research Policy*, 47, 687–699.

Szulanski, G (1996). Exploring internal stickiness: Impediments to the transfer of best practice within the firm. *Strategic Management Journal*, 17(Winter Special Issue), 27–43.

Teece, DJ, G Pisano and A Shuen (1997). Dynamic capabilities and strategic management. *Strategic Management Journal*, 18(7), 509–533. doi: 10.1002/(SICI)1097-0266(199708)18:7<509::AID-SMJ882>3.0.CO;2-Z.

Ter Wal, A, P Criscuolo and A Salter (2011). Absorptive capacity at the individual level: An ambidexterity approach to external engagement. In *Paper presented at the Druid Society Conference 2011*, Copenhagen.

Ter Wal, A, P Criscuolo and A Salter (2015). Making a marriage of materials: The role of gatekeepers and shepherds in the absorption of external knowledge and innovation performance. *Research Policy*, 46, 1039–1054. doi: 10.1016/j.respol.2017.03.003.

Tian, AW and C Soo (2018). Enriching individual absorptive capacity. *Personnel Review*, 47(5), 1116–1132.

Tidd, J and J Bessant (2013). *Management Innovation: Integrating Technological, Market and Organizational Change*, 5th Ed. West Sussex: John Wiley & Sons.

Todorova, G and B Durisin (2007). Absorptive capacity: Valuing a reconceptualization. *Academy of Management Review*, 32(3), 774–786. doi: 10.5465/AMR.2007.25275513.

van den Bosch, FAJ, R van Wijk and HW Volberda (2003). Absorptive capacity: Antecedents, models, and outcomes. In *Handbook of Organizational Learning and Knowledge Management*, M Easterby-Smith and M Lyves (eds.), pp. 278–301. Oxford: Blackwell Publishing.

van den Bosch, FAJ, HW Volberda and M de Boer (1999). Coevolution of firm absorptive capacity and knowledge environment: Organizational forms and combinative capabilities. *Organization Science*, 10(5), 551–569. doi: 10.1287/orsc.10.5.551.

Volberda, HW, NJ Foss and MA Lyles (2010). Perspective: Absorbing the concept of absorptive capacity: How to realize its potential in the organization field. *Organization Science*, 21(4), 931–951. doi: 10.1287/orsc.1090.0503.

von Hippel, E (1998). Economics of product development by users: The impact of "sticky" local information. *Management Science*, 44(5), 629–644.

Wang, H and W-R Chen (2010). Is firm-specific innovation associated with greater value appropriation? The roles of environmental dynamism and technological diversity. *Research Policy*, 39(1), 141–154. doi: 10.1016/j.respol.2009.09.015.

Weiblen, T and HW Chesbrough (2015). Engaging with startups to enhance corporate innovation. *California Management Review*, 57(2), 66–90. doi: 10.1525/cmr.2015.57.2.66.

Yams, NB (2017). Integrated model of innovation competence. *Journal of Creativity and Business Innovation*, 3, 140–169.

Yildiz, HE, A Murtic, U Zander and A Richtnér (2019). What Fosters individual-level absorptive capacity in MNCs? An extended motivation–ability–opportunity framework. *Management International Review*, 59(1), 93–129.

Zahra, SA and G George (2002). Absorptive capacity?: A review and extension. *Academy of Management Review*, 27(2), 185–203. doi: 10.5465/APBPP.2000.5438568.

Zollo, M and SG Winter (2002). Deliberate learning and the evolution of dynamic capabilities. *Organization Science*, 13(3), 339–351.

Zuñiga-Collazos, A, N Lozada and G Perdomo-Charry (2019). Effect of absorptive capacity acquired on organisational performance. *International Journal of Innovation Management*, https://doi.org/10.1142/S1363919620500486.

Section 3

Organizational Innovation

Chapter 13

EFFECT OF ABSORPTION CAPACITY ACQUIRED ON ORGANISATIONAL PERFORMANCE†

ALEXANDER ZUÑIGA-COLLAZOS

Faculty of Economic Sciences
Universidad de San Buenaventura, Cali, Colombia
azuniga01@usbcali.edu.co

NELSON LOZADA*

Department of Administrative Sciences
University of Antioquia, Medellin, Colombia
nelson.lozada@udea.edu.co

GEOVANNY PERDOMO-CHARRY

Business School, CEIPA University. Medellín, Colombia
geovanny.perdomo@ceipa.edu.co

Published 5 August 2019

Emerging markets have achieved important growth through innovation in services and industrial sectors. However, both research and empirical evidence about innovation development is very limited in Latin America. Innovation-based absorption capacity of different companies is one of the main keys to this growth. This empirical study analysed the relationships between absorption capacity and organisational performance (OP) in a sample of 227 firms in Medellin, Colombia. The findings show that enterprises developing the absorption capacity acquired (ACA) may have better probabilities to improve OP. This study argues that companies whose managers motivate their employees to use information within sources from their industry may have higher probabilities to improve organisational profit and growth.

Keywords: Absorption capacity acquired; organisational performance; SEM; emerging markets.

Introduction

The region of Latin America occupies intermediate positions in the Global Innovation Index and is lagging behind developed countries (Dutta *et al.*, 2018),

*Corresponding author.

†This article originally appeared in *International Journal of Innovation Management*, **24** 2050048-1-19

which occurs partly because the cultural ties of innovator behaviour have a domino effect that negatively affects not only politics but also the economy (Poveda, 2015) since it is reflected on the actions of business organisations and their members — what has been called the contagion effect (Gino *et al.*, 2009; Thoumi, 2012).

According to literature in the 2000s, the notion of dynamics of innovation based on absorption capacity (AC) has expanded over the levels of organisational analysis, both individual and organisational and inter-organisational and environment, and a significant number of studies are analysed multidimensionally; recognising further development and contribution to the AC as a construct that generates new knowledge for the present and the future of the organisation, which means that AC is seen as a realised and potential capability (Zahra and George, 2002; Fosfuri and Tribó, 2008; Grimpe and Sofka, 2009; Mihalache *et al.*, 2014).

During the decade of 2010, AC has been conceived as a construct of second order that has first-order variables such as (1) acquisition, (2) assimilation, (3) transformation and (4) exploitation of knowledge at multiple levels and dimensions of the organisation and its environment (Camisón and Forés, 2010; Engelen *et al.*, 2014; Flatten *et al.*, 2011; Kostopoulos *et al.*, 2011. However, studies to understand the dynamics of innovation (Zuñiga-Collazos *et al.* 2015) or knowledge management (Cuesta Santos and Valencia Rodríguez, 2014) in companies from developing countries such as Colombia is limited (Vasco Uribe and Perdomo-Charry, 2015). Especially, empirical evidence to study the relationship between each of these dimensions of AC is limited. Consequently, this suggests that there is a gap in how to better understand the way each AC dimension is related to other variables such as OP. This study analyses the impact of absorption capacity acquired (ACA) on organisational performance (OP) in a representative sample of companies located in the city of Medellin-Colombia.

Conceptual Framework

For Perdomo-Charry *et al.* (2017) "The ways firms face rapid technological changes, entrepreneurial aggressiveness, and the short lifecycles of technology can be found in their inside as well as in their environment (Camisón and Forés, 2010). Some firms may face changes more rapidly than others due to their capability to recognise, assess, assimilate and apply newly acquired external knowledge (Camisón and Forés, 2010; Cepeda-Carrion *et al.*, 2012; Enkel and Heil, 2014; Escribano *et al.*, 2009; Flatten *et al.*, 2011; Fosfuri and Tribó, 2008; Jansen *et al.*, 2005; Javalgi *et al.*, 2014; Jiménez-Barrionuevo *et al.*, 2011; Kostopoulos *et al.*, 2011; Leal-Rodríguez *et al.*, 2014; Malhotra *et al.*, 2005)" (2017, p. 10).

Academic works conducted by Cohen and Levinthal (1990) have generated a great amount or literature framed mainly under four research lines contributing to this study: organisational learning (Cohen and Levinthal, 1990; Kim, 1998), knowledge management (Szulanski, 1996), strategic alliances (Lane and Lubatkin, 1998), and innovation management (Mowery and Oxley, 1995; Veugelers, 1997; Liu *et al.*, 2013).

In fact, Cohen and Levinthal (1990) were pioneers in addressing the concept of AC as a complex process (Cohen and Levinthal, 1990; Lane and Lubatkin, 1998; Todorova and Durisin, 2007); they establish AC as a unidimensional variable when measuring it, and the most common way of measuring AC centres on research and development topics (Tsai, 2001). However, subsequent research expanded the AC concept to an organisational level in order to encompass the richness of the construct (Zahra and George, 2002; Jiménez-Barrionuevo *et al.*, 2011), where for first-order constructs composing AC are proposed as a second-order construct: acquision, assimilation, transformation and exploitation, the first one being the object of analysis in this research.

Absorption capacity acquired

Development, evolution and adoption of the AC construct, variables, approaches and dimensions by various authors, are presented in the following matrix of analysis (Table 1).

According to Table 1, the work of Zahra and George (2002) has allowed several authors (Volberda *et al.*, 2010; Jansen *et al.*, 2005), on one hand, to advance and deepen their studies on how organisational management affects the realised and potential AC; and on the other hand, to work separately on both capacities, potential absorptive capacity (Fosfuri and Tribó, 2008) and realised absorptive capacity (Flatten *et al.*, 2011a, 2011b), and the effect of potential absorptive capacity on the opening to new changes or organisational knowledge (Liao *et al.*, 2003) and on innovation performance (Fosfuri and Tribó, 2008; Flatten *et al.*, 2011b).

This study specifically addresses the acquisition capacity studied by Zahra and George (2002) in the potential sub-dimension of the absorption capacities, wherein acquisition refers to a firm's capability to initiate, identify, value, acquire and gather relevant knowledge that is critical to its operations from external sources. Besides, according to these authors there is limited empirical evidence. In the same way, they suggest that the ACA can be obtained by the organisation through: (1) The permanent search for relevant information in the company' industry; (2) Motivation fostered by managers through which employees use information sources based on the sector to which the company belongs; (3) Managers expect

Table 1. Absorption capacity dimensions.

Variables	Description	Perspectives	Authors	Dimensions
Assess, assimilate and Apply	**Assess:** The company has basic prior knowledge. Assimilate: Internalising knowledge from external sources. **Apply:** Ability to solve problems.		Cohen and Levinthal (1990), Lane and Lubatkin (1998)	Multidimensional
		Relative absorptive capacity of a Company to another	Lane and Lubatkin (1998)	Multidimensional
Acquire Apply	**Acquire:** Evaluation of the usefulness of knowledge and the ability to transfer to another company. **Apply:** Ability to solve problems.		Arbussá and Coenders (2007)	Two-dimensional
Acquire Assimilate Transform Exploit	***Acquire:*** *Evaluation of the usefulness of knowledge and the ability to transfer to another company.* **Assimilate:** To understand the external knowledge through the organisation routines.	Sub-dimension: Potential	Zahra and George (2002), Mihalache *et al.* (2014), Volberda *et al.* (2010).	Multidimensional
	Transform: Links the previous two dimensions to combine and achieve new entrepreneurial opportunities. **Exploit:** Creating new routines to generate knowledge, which results in new goods, processes, system, etc.	Sub-dimension: Realised		

that employees are familiar with information from other different industries to which the company belongs.

Organisational performance

Improving OP has been one of the main topics of interest in management (Neely, 1999). More particularly, there is considerable interest in OP measurement systems (OPMS) (Choong, 2014). Its origin can be traced back to the late 1960/early 1970 where many forms of measures, metrics, indicators and methods of measurement and performance measurement were proposed and introduced into the workplace (Kaplan and Norton, 1992, 1996; White, 2008). In its evolution, research in OPMS has become a highly prescriptive or historical approach, with very few authors venturing into the scientific, mathematical or logical perspectives wherein measurement researchers debate for or against a particular measurement system (Gunasekaran and Kobu, 2007; Petersen *et al.*, 2009; Sole and Schiuma, 2010). According to Choong (2014), research in OPMS has pointed the need for proper definitions or cohesive framework according to specific research interests.

OP has been traditionally analysed by managers emphasising financial indicators of organisations. However, previous literature defends the use of an ampler range of performance measurement, beyond financial indicators (Quinn and Rohrbaugh, 1983; Venkatraman and Ramanujam, 1986). These authors suggest that the concept of OP includes different dimensions, which correspond to four basic models of organisational effectiveness: the human relations model, the internal process model, the open system model and the rational goal model. This last model is of specific interest to this research because it is a very important dimension about OP related to organisational means and ends (Quinn and Rohrbaugh, 1983), from an emphasis on important processes (e.g., planning and goal setting) to an emphasis on final outcomes (e.g., productivity, return on investment, profit growth, sales growth and market share increase).

Recent studies by Achtenhagen *et al.* (2013) prove that there is a direct and positive relationship in the relationship between organisational knowledge stocks and flows and the performance of firms in the biotechnology industry; the authors also suggest that a company's geographic locations, it alliances with other organisations and institutions, and R + D investments are very representative in knowledge flows, whereas pending and granted patents are indicative of the existence of business knowledge.

Furthermore, the findings by Decarolis and Deeds (1999) and Zeng *et al.* (2010) confirm that vertical and horizontal cooperation with customers, suppliers and other companies play a more specific role in companies' innovation processes given that through horizontal cooperation with research institutions, universities or colleges and government agencies they acquire better absorptive capacities. In the same study, Zeng *et al.* (2010) find that there are significantly positive relationships between cooperation among companies, institutions and intermediary organisations, and that there is also better organisational performance when cooperation takes place between firms and research, development and innovation entities.

The previous dynamic favours the four key aspects related to organisational performance as proposed by Nybakk and Jenssen (2012), who examine the differences between open innovation practices in firms, the impact of public financing to improve external relations, the strengthening of firms' R + D outsourcing and the role of human resources in research, development and innovation processes.

ACA and organisational performance

The literature reveals that researchers in their empirical studies have applied two types of approaches to the AC: (1) the one-dimensional approach, where capacity is assessed using either a unique measure through proxies variables whose nature changes from one study to other, or two-dimensional measures that reflect various aspects of the construct (Chen *et al.*, 2009) and (2) the multidimensional approach, which considers the theoretical basis of the construct and can be considered as a more optimal alternative over traditional constructs/approaches (Chen *et al.*, 2009).

To the best of our knowledge, few studies report the use of the second type of approach to AC. This may be explained by implementation problems when differentiating phases (Murovec and Prodan, 2009). In fact, few empirical studies capture the robust theoretical arguments and multidimensionality of the AC construct. In spite of this, it has been found that several multidimensional scales have been proposed in recent years (Comisón and Fóres, 2010; Jiménez-Barrionuevo *et al.*, 2011; Liao *et al.*, 2003; Mihalache *et al.*, 2014) all these authors follow the conceptualisation of Zahra and George (2002), who have re-conceptualised the construct in order to contribute to the weakness of the one-dimensional measurement.

Linked to components of absorptive capacity, the potential AC and realised AC have been used by Mihalache *et al.* (2014) to investigate organisational background. The measure proposed by Mihalache *et al.* (2014) is derived from the subcomponents of the potential AC and that could be empirically applied. Based on these new contributions, Camisón and Forés (2010) have developed an AC scale of 16 items considering the background and components. Jiménez-Barrionuevo *et al.* (2011) have measured the concept through internal factors, resulting in an 18-item scale.

The literature shows that the relation between absorption capabilities of innovation in the organisations and performance is positive (Chen *et al.*, 2009;

Jiménez-Jiménez and Sanz-Valle, 2011; Tsai, 2001). In the same way Ali *et al.* (2016) argue that absorption capabilities are some of the most important determinants of a firm's ability to acquire, assimilate and effectively utilise new knowledge to increase innovation, which at the same time could directly affect OP. Consequently, firms make efforts to increase AC to acquire new and external knowledge, which contributes to achieving higher performance (Ali *et al.*, 2016).

Recent studies revealed that AC is seen as having a mediating and moderating role with respect to organisational performance; particularly it was found that the acquisition dimension does not have a direct effect on performance, but the dimension of use does have a direct effect on firm performance. The dimensions of acquisition and use have a positive effect on strategic agility and the latter positively affects organisational performance. It was also revealed, on one hand, that the dimensions of acquisition and use have an indirect effect on firm performance through strategic agility (Kale *et al.*, 2018; Solís-Molina *et al.*, 2018) and, on the other hand, evidence of the influence of AC, linear and nonlinear way, on the relationship between internationalisation and innovation (Filippetti *et al.*, 2017). These results indicate that the AC must be re-evaluated in accommodation businesses, and perhaps even in the service industry, with a different scale and model.

Solís-Molina *et al.* (2018) were able to determine in an emerging country how the rise in ambidexterity and the specialisation in exploitation or exploration affect the organisation's performance. The moderating role of the AC is tested with the introduction of bidirectional interactions of the AC with exploitation and exploration, and a three-way interaction with exploitation and exploration outcome. It is estimated how the effect on performance raises exploration, when exploitation remains at low levels. On the other hand, the effect of ambidexteriry is calculated as the impact of the exploitation (or exploration) increase on performance when exploration (or exploitation) remains at high levels.

Firms with acquired absorption capabilities are more likely to have a better understanding of new technologies, which can generate new ideas for developing new products, processes and management innovation (Tsai, 2001). These capabilities could certainly impact OP. Therefore, the following hypothesis is proposed.

Hypothesis: *Absorption capacities acquired have a positive effect on organizational performance.*

Methodology

The aim of this study is to analyse the effect of acquired absorption capacities on organisational performance obtaining empirical evidence. For this reason, a quantitative methodology is proposed seeking to test the previously posited

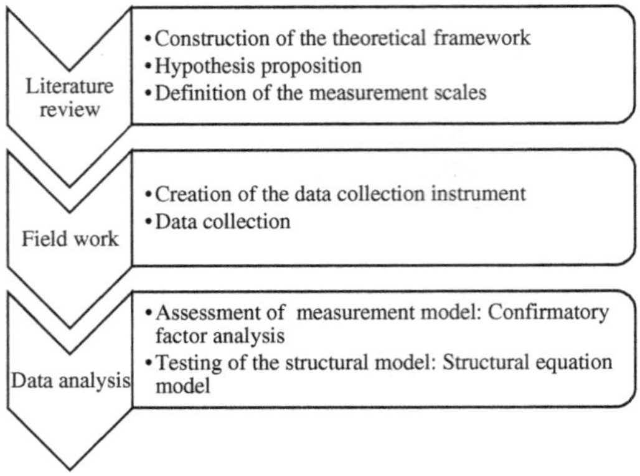

Fig. 1. General research model.

hypothesis, which has been supported by the theoretical framework and is founded on the measurement scales validated in the literature; it must be noted that for this case a multivariate analysis is required due to the different relationships between the latent variables. Figure 1 presents the general research model 1.

The study methodology followed three phases: literature review, field research and data analysis. The first one was applied for understanding the state-of-the art and the second one for hypothesis testing. The results of the first phase have been used to build the theoretical framework of this study, and then to design the questionnaire for primary data collection. The questionnaire was designed based on ACA and OP structures. A Likert 5-point scale was used to measure the ACA and OP, where 1 represented no importance and 5 highest importance. To validate the questionnaire, a factor analysis was used. To check factors reliability, a Cronbach's alpha coefficient was calculated, obtaining > 0.800 for both cases.

To verify the model, a confirmatory factor analysis was deployed to test the relationships between the latent variables and their items. The measurement model (confirmatory factor analysis) permitted to examine the relation between items or questions in the questionnaire and the constructs. The relations cannot be evaluated until it is proven that the items measure the related latent variables of the questionnaire. Hence, to prove that the concepts were well measured, a confirmatory factor analysis has been utilised. Factor loading determined the strength of the relationship between the factors (i.e., the latent variables) and the observed variables. Factor loading is a value between zero and one. A factor loading below 0.3 is considered as a poor relation and refutable (Kline, 1994; Brown, 2006). A factor loading between 0.03 and 0.6 is acceptable, and a loading over 0.6 is completely desirable (Kline, 1998). Finally, in order to validate the relationships, a

Effect of ACA on Organisational Performance

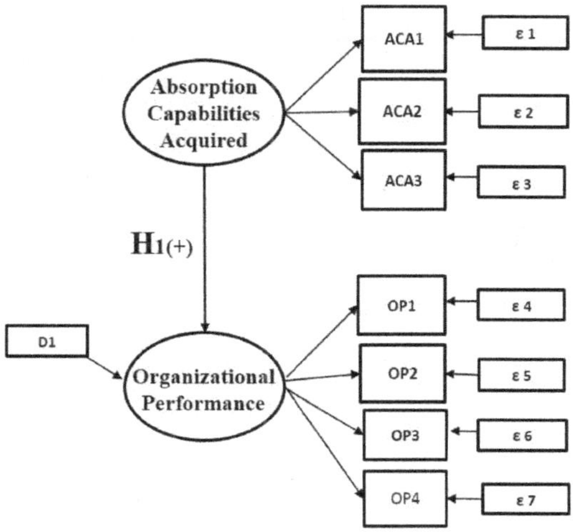

Fig. 2. Conceptual model.

structural equation model (SEM) with a maximum likelihood and robust estimation method was used to test the measurement model of the conceptual model. In addition, the SEM was used to test the hypothesis in the structural model of the conceptual model. The data was analysed using EQS 6.3.

In line with the literature and the specific focus of this research, the questionnaire used in this study asked the firms about the evolution of acquired AC according to Flatten *et al.* (2011a, 2011b), and OP during the previous three years using items proposed by Akgün *et al.* (2007) and Ellinger *et al.*, 2002. The conceptual model for this study and its relationships can be seen in Fig. 2.

Sample

Initially, in order to determine an appropriate sample size, the literature suggests that adopting an excessively large sample may cause loss of resources, whereas an extra small sample may yield unreliable results. Besides, an important issue in factor analysis and structural equation modelling (SEM) is the determination of a minimum sample size (Kline, 2010; McQuitty, 2004). Although there is no consensus on the sample size required for factor analysis and SEM (Schreiber *et al.*, 2006), many researchers recommend a sample size of at least 200 units (Garver and Mentzer, 1999; Hoe, 2008). Since this study is based on SEM, a sample size of 227 was randomly selected to be surveyed using questionnaires.

A. Zuñiga-Collazos, N. Lozada & G. Perdomo-Charry

Table 2. Characteristics of the firms in the sample.

Sector	Frequency	Percentage
Business management activities; management consulting activities	51	22.55
Information and communications	36	15.69
Education	27	11.76
Clothing manufacturing	18	7.84
Human health attention and social assistance activities	13	5.88
Accommodation and food services	13	5.88
Wholesaling and retailing; motor vehicle and motorcycle repair	11	4.90
Manufacturing of metal products, except machinery and equipment	9	3.92
Manufacturing of chemical substances and products	9	3.92
Other manufacturing activities	9	3.92
Transport and storage	7	2.94
Manufacturing of electric devices and equipment	4	1.96
Manufacturing of dental and medical instruments, devices and materials (including furniture)	4	1.96
Manufacturing of games, toys and puzzles	2	0.98
Financial and insurance activities	2	0.98
Real estate activities	2	0.98
Water distribution; waste water evacuation and treatment, waste management	2	0.98
Other service activities	7	2.94
Size by number of employees		
Medium	56	25
Small	171	75

A survey was designed and applied to a representative sample of 227 managers and directors responsible for the innovation area of firms in the city of Medellin, Colombia. The survey was conducted between February and May 2016 by means of an electronic mail sent to a population of 2100 firms participating in a regional program for strengthening innovation capabilities, obtaining a response rate of 10.8%. The data collected for the study contain a sample of different service and industrial sector firms. The companies surveyed are small and medium enterprises (SMEs); according to the Ministry of Commerce, Industry, and Tourism of Colombia, the sample included firm size of 1–200 workers (Table 2).

Results

This study followed a two-step approach to analyse and interpret the SEM results: (1) assessment measurement model and (2) testing of the structural model.

Correlations, means, standard deviations and reliabilities can be observed in Table 3. The means obtained can be considered relatively low for both variables,

Table 3. Correlations, means, standard deviations, reliability.

Variables	*M*	SD	1	2
· ACA	3.36	1.24	(0.873)	
· Organisational performance (OP)	3.35	1.06	0.498*	(0.926)

$N = 227$; alpha reliability is show on the diagonal. $*p < 0.05$.

which were between 3.35 and 3.36, and with similar standard deviations between 1.06 and 1.24. The correlation value for the latent variables are above the adequate level (0.498) with significance at $p < 0.05$.

The measurement model met all the general validity requirements (see Appendix A). First, all items loadings are above 0.778 or 0.931 and are significant at $p < 0.05$ level, indicating convergent validity at each item level. Second, Cronbach's alpha values are greater than 0.85 and composite reliability greater than 0.94, which suggests very good reliability. Third, the AVE values of all the constructs are greater than 0.50 at the construct level. These results confirm the existence of discriminant validity.

In order to evaluate the structural model, this study examined the predictor in the structural model for possible collinearity. The results show minimal collinearity along with the VIF outputs below the threshold of 5. Therefore, collinearity among the predictor construct in the structural model is not an issue. According to Falk and Miller (1992), the R2 value of latent variables is above the adequate level. Following the rules of thumb R2 values between variables is 0.498 with significance at $p < 0.05$.

As can be seen, this measurement model obtained optimal values in the following indices: BBNFI, BBNNFI, CFI and IFI. Considering Ullman (2001), values greater than 0.90 in BBNFI and BBNNFI indices indicate that the goodness of fit of the model is appropriate, thus meeting the respective condition values. Moreover, Hu and Bentler (1999) explain that values greater than 0.90 in the CFI index mean acceptable goodness of fit and values above 0.95 mean that the model is very good, which can be seen in the score of this index (0.970). In addition, the RMSEA value measurement model obtained can be considered appropriate. Browne and Cudeck (1993) explain that values between 0.05 and 0.08 in the RMSEA indicate the presence of an acceptable model.

The value obtained by this model was closed to zero (0.01). It is also important to see how the load factors of every item differ. For the factor of Absorption capabilities acquired the most important variable due to high weight load (0.931) is the motivation from management to the employees in order to use information sources within our industry, followed by the search for relevant information concerning their industries as everyday business task in their companies (0.800);

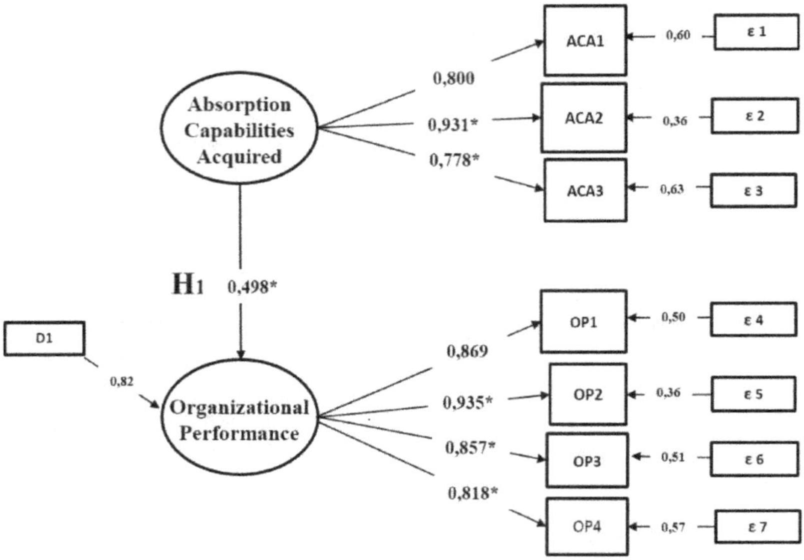

Notes: $N = 227$. X^2 (42.11) = 13 *df.* NFI = 0.957, NNFI = 0.951, CFI = 0.970, RMSA = 0.100; $^*p < 0.05$.

Fig. 3. Results of the structural model.

and thirdly, the management expects that the employees deal with information beyond their industries (0.778). In the case of the OP factor, the most important variable is Profit Growth (0.935) followed by the other three variables with relatively similar values, but high load as follows: return on investment (0.870), sales growth (0.857) and market share increase (0.818). Finally, all these results go in accordance with Hair *et al.* (2005) showing the existence of a direct and positive relationship between ACA and OP. Consequently, the results corroborate the hypothesis proposed in this study in which ACA has a positive effect on OP. The results appear in Fig. 3.

Discussion and Conclusions

While the results show a better understanding of the relationship between ACA and organisational performance (OP) in the real sector, they also provide important empirical evidence supporting the theoretical conceptualizations and empirical validations explained by Chen *et al.* (2009); Murovec and Prodan (2009), Comisón and Fóres (2010), Jiménez-Barrionuevo *et al.* (2011), Liao *et al.* (2003),

Mihalache *et al.* (2014), Zahra and George (2002), Jiménez-Jiménez and Sanz-Valle (2011), Tsai (2001) and Ali *et al.* (2016).

Moreover, these results support the empirical evidence for companies located in less developed countries, wherein the dynamics and context are a very different context. This could be justified by the difference(s) in the factor loadings of each item. However, it is interesting to observe that among the enterprises in the sample the most important variable, due to high weight load in ACA, is the motivation from management to the employees to use information sources within their industrial sector. In the case of the OP factor, the most important variable is profit growth. Therefore, this study suggests that companies where managers motivate their employees in order to use information within sources from their industry may have better probabilities to improve their profit growth.

Certainly, there exists a direct and significant relationship between ACA and OP. This relation has a positive and direct effect. In other words, firms that develop ACA may have better probabilities to improve their OP.

In fact, the research findings give credibility to the idea set forth by Achtenhagen *et al.* (2013), in what geographical location is important for firm performance in the context of accumulating the necessary knowledge to achieve a competitive advantage, obtain positive impacts in R + D activities and increase intensity in firm performance. Such claim is supported in the change and transformation process that the city of Medellin has recently undergone, being the first city (including institutions and organisations) to invest around 3.2% of the annual national GDP in science, technology and innovation (Ruta, 2018).

Implications, Limitations and future research

As the main theoretical contribution, the study obtains empirical evidence confirming the positive relationship existing between ACA and OP in a context of small and medium enterprises in an emerging economy; multiple aspects significant for the managerial practice are derived from the above: (1) the relevance of establishing innovation management areas for good firm performance is observed, something that appears to be obvious but which in the context of emerging economies is not a common practice in the case of small and medium enterprises; (2) the importance for the company to manage mechanisms and processes allowing the employees access to sector information is highlighted; (3) managers must see to it that company culture incorporates the continuous monitoring of the sector as a normal and accepted practice, which requires special attentions since in some contexts this practice is not well regarded. On one hand, some managers could consider this a waste of time as a distractor from company mission issues and, from another perspective, there will be people and team's jealousy and ego towards information and knowledge coming from outside.

Finally, this study presents some limitations. In order to expand the sample to a larger number of cities in the country, it is recommended that future studies consider an ampler sample size including other cities (of Colombia). On the other hand, future research may direct efforts to identify correlations of other ACA variables such as assimilation, transformation and exploitation absorption capabilities and OP from financial and nonfinancial perspectives.

Acknowledgements

This article is part of research results derived from the study: "Efecto de la co-creación de valor y la coinnovación sobre el desempeño innovador en las PYMES de Medellín-Antioquia", This work was supported by Universidad de Antioquia, under project number 21530004-FAPP01 (CODI), and the Fundación Universitaria Ceipa, Medellín. Approved by internal call in 2017.

Appendix A

Table A.1. Scale items. Results of confirmatory factor analysis.

		Factor loadings	Composite reliability	AVE
ACA	Absorption Capabilities Acquired (α = 0.873) (Adopted from Flatten*et al.*, 2011a, 2011b)		0.941	0.842
ACA1	The search for relevant information concerning our industry is every-day business in our company.	0.800		
ACA2	Our management motivates the employees to use information sources within our industry	0.931		
ACA3	Our management expects that the employees deal with information beyond our industry.	0.778		
OP	Organisational Performance OP ($\alpha = 0.926$) (Adopted from: Akgün *et al.*, 2007; Ellinger *et al.*, 2002)		0.940	0.872
OP1	Return on investment	0.870		
OP2	Profit growth	0.935		
OP3	Sales growth	0.857		
OP4	Market share increase	0.818		

References

Achtenhagen, E, A Melin and O Naldi (2013). Dynamics of business models — Strategizing, critical capabilities and activities for sustained value creation. *Long Range Planning*, 46(6), 427–442.

Akgün, AE, H Keskin, JC Byrne and S Aren (2007). Emotional and learning capability and their impact on product innovativeness and firm performance. *Technovation*, 27(9), 501–513.

Ali, M, KAS Kan and M Sarstedt (2016). Direct and configurational paths of absorptive capacity and organizational innovation to successful organizational performance. *Journal of Business Research*. Advance online publication.

Arbussà, A and G Coenders (2007). Innovation activities, use of appropriation instruments and absorptive capacity: Evidence from Spanish firms. *Research Policy*, 36(10), 1545–1558.

Brown, TA (2006). *Confirmatory Factor Analysis for Applied Research*. New York: Guilford Press.

Browne, MW and R Cudeck (1993). Alternative ways of assessing model fit. In *Testing Structural Equation Models*, KA Bollen and JS Long (eds.), pp. 136–162. Newbury Park, CA: Sage.

Camisón, C and B Forés (2010). Knowledge absorptive capacity: New insights for its conceptualization and measurement. *Journal of Business Research*, 63(7), 707–715.

Cepeda-Carrion, G, JG Cegarra-Navarro and D Jimenez-Jimenez (2012). The Effect of Absorptive Capacity on Innovativeness: Context and information systems capability as catalysts. *British Journal of Management*, 23(1), 110–129.

Chen, Y-S, M-JJ Lin and C-H Chang (2009). The positive effects of relationship learning and absorptive capacity on innovation performance and competitive advantage in industrial markets. *Industrial Marketing Management*, 38(2), 152–158.

Choong, KK (2014). Has this large number of performance measurement publications contributed to its better understanding? A systematic review for research and applications. *International Journal of Production Research*, 52(14), 4174–4197.

Cohen, WM and DA Levinthal (1990). Absorptive capacity: A new perspective on learning and innovation. *Administrative Science Quarterly*, 35, 128–152.

Cuesta Santos, A and M Valencia Rodríguez (2014). *Indicadores de gestión humana y de Conocimiento en la Empresa*. Ecoe Ediciones.

Decarolis, DM and D Deeds (1999). The impact of stocks and flows of organizational knowledge of firm performance: An empirical investigation of the biotechnology industry. *Strategic Management Journal*, 20(1), 953–968.

Dutta, S, B Lanvin and S Wunsch-Vincent (2018). *Global Innovation Index 2018: Energizing the World with Innovation. Cornell University, INSEAD, and WIPO.* Ithaca, Fontainebleau, and Geneva.

Ellinger, AD, AE Ellinger, B Yang and SW Howton (2002). The relationship between the learning organization concept and firm's financial performance: An empirical assessment. *Human Resource Development Quarterly*, 13(1), 5–21.

Engelen, A, H Kube, S Schmidt and TC Flatten (2014). Entrepreneurial orientation in turbulent environments: The moderating role of absorptive capacity. *Research Policy*, 43(8), 1353–1369.

Enkel, E and S Heil (2014). Preparing for distant collaboration: Antecedents to potential absorptive capacity in cross-industry innovation. *Technovation*, 34(4), 242–260.

Falk, RF and NB Miller (1992). *A Primer for Soft Modeling*. Akron, OH: Univ. Akron Press.

Flatten, TC, A Engelen, SA Zahra and M Brettel (2011a). A measure of absorptive capacity: Scale development and validation. *European Management Journal*, 29(2), 98–116.

Flatten, TC, GI Greve and M Brettel (2011b). Absorptive capacity and firm performance in SMEs: The mediating influence of strategic alliances. *European Management Review*, 8(3), 137–152.

Fosfuri, A and J Tribó (2008). Exploring the antecedents of potential absorptive capacity and its impact on innovation performance. *Omega*, 36(2), 173–187.

Garver, MS and JT Mentzer (1999). Logistics research methods: Employing structural equation modeling to test for construct validity. *Journal of Business Logistics*, 20(1), 33–57.

Gino, F, S Ayal and D Ariely (2009). Contagion and differentiation in unethical behavior: The effect of one bad apple on the barrel. *Psychological Science*, 20(3), 393–398. https://doi.org/10.1111/j.1467-9280.2009.02306.x.

Grimpe, C and W Sofka (2009). Search patterns and absorptive capacity: Low- and high-technology sectors in European countries. *Research Policy*, 38(3), 495–506.

Gunasekaran, A and B Kobu (2007). Performance measures and metrics in logistics and supply chain management: A review of recent literature (1995–2004) for research and applications. *International Journal of Production Research*, 45(12), 2819–2840.

Hair, J, R Anderson, R Tatham and W Black (2005). Análisis Multivariante. 5ta. Edición, Prentice Hall, España.

Hoe, SL (2008). Issues and procedures in adopting structural equation modeling technique. *Journal of Applied Quantitative Methods*, 3(1), 76–83.

Hu, L and P Bentler (1999). Cutoff criteria for fit indexes in covariance structure analysis: Conventional criteria versus new alternatives. *Structural Equation Modelling*, 6, 1–55.

Filippetti, A, M Frenz and G Ietto-Gillies (2017). The impact of internationalization on innovation at countries' level: The role of absorptive capacity. *Cambridge Journal of Economics*, 41, 413–439, doi: 10.1093/cje/bew032.

Jansen, JJP, FAJ Van Den Bosch and HW Volberda (2005). Managing potential and realized absorptive capacity: How do organizational antecedents matter? *Academy of Management Journal*, 48(6), 999–1015.

Javalgi, RG, KD Hall and ST Cavusgil (2014). Corporate entrepreneurship, customer-oriented selling, absorptive capacity, and international sales performance in the international B2B setting: Conceptual framework and research propositions. *International Business Review*, 23(6), 1193–1202.

Jiménez-Barrionuevo, MM, VJ García-Morales and LM Molina (2011). Validation of an instrument to measure absorptive capacity. *Technovation*, 31(5–6), 190–202.

Jiménez-Jiménez, D and R Sanz-Valle (2011). Innovation, organizational learning and performance. *Journal of Business Research*, 64(4), 408–417.

Kale, E, A Aknar and Ö Başar (2018). Absorptive capacity and firm performance. The mediating role of strategic agility. *International Journal of Hospitality Management*, 75, 1–8.

Kaplan, RS and PN Norton (1992). The balanced scorecard: Measures that drive performance. *Harvard Business Review*, 70(1), 71–79.

Kaplan, RS and PN Norton (1996). Using the balanced scorecard as a strategic management system. *Harvard Business Review*, 74(1), 75–85.

Kim, DH (1998). The link between individual and organizational learning. *The Strategic Management of Intellectual Capital*, Capitulo, 4, 41–62.

Kline, P (1994). *An Easy Guide to Factor Analysis*. New York, NY: Routledge.

Kline, RB (1998). *Principles and Practice of Structural Equation Modeling*. New York: Guilford Press.

Kline, Rex B (2010). *Principles and Practice of Structural Equation Modeling*, Series Editor's Note by Todd D. Little. New York: The Guilford Press.

Kostopoulos, K, A Papalexandris, M Papachroni and G Ioannou (2011). Absorptive capacity, innovation, and financial performance. *Journal of Business Research*, 64(12), 1335–1343.

Lane, PJ and M Lubatkin (1998). Relative absorptive capacity and interorganizational learning. *Strategic Management Journal*, 19(5), 461–477.

Leal-Rodríguez, AL, JA Ariza-Montes, JL Roldán and AG Leal-Millán, (2014). Absorptive capacity, innovation and cultural barriers: A conditional mediation model. *Journal of Business Research*, 67(5), 763–768.

Liao, J, H Welsch and M Stoica (2003). Organizational absorptive capacity and responsiveness: An empirical investigation of growth-oriented SMEs. *Entrepreneurship Theory and Practice*, 28(1), 63–85.

Liu, H, W Ke, KK Wei and Z Hua (2013). The impact of IT capabilities on firm performance: The mediating roles of absorptive capacity and supply chain agility. *Decision Support Systems*, 54(3), 1452–1462.

Malhotra, A, S Gosain and OA Sawy El (2005). Absorptive capacity configurations in supply chains: Gearing for partner-enabled market knowledge creation. *MIS Quarterly*, 29(1), 145–187.

McQuitty, S (2004). Statistical power and structural equation models in business research. *Journal of Business Research*, 57(2), 175–183.

Mihalache, OR, JJP Jansen, Bosch, FAJ Van den and HW Volberda (2014). Top management team shared leadership and organizational ambidexterity: A moderated mediation framework. *Strategic Entrepreneurship Journal*, 8(2), 128–148.

Mowery, DC and J Oxley (1995). Inward technology transfer and competitiveness: The role of national innovation systems. *Cambridge Journal of Economics*, 19(1), 67–93.

Murovec, N and I Prodan (2009). Absorptive capacity, its determinants, and influence on innovation output: Cross-cultural validation of the structural model. *Technovation*, 29(12), 859–872.

Neely, A (1999). The performance measurement revolution: Why now and what next? *International Journal of Operations & Production Management*, 19(2), 205–228.

Nybakk, E and JI Jenssen (2012). Innovation strategy, working climate, and financial performance in traditional manufacturing firms: An empirical analysis. *International Journal of Innovation Management*, 16(2), 26.

Perdomo-Charry, G, A Zuñiga-Collazos and NE Lozada (2017). Absorptive capacity (AC): Knowledge generation and its evolution from variable to construct. *Revista Espacios*, 38, 10–19.

Petersen, JA, L McAlister, DJ Reibstein, WS Russell, V Kumar, G Atkinson and G Atkinson (2009). Choosing the right metrics to maximize profitability and shareholder value. *Journal of Retailing*, 85(1), 95–111.

Poveda, AC (2015). Corruption, economic development, and insecurity in Colombia. In *Business Law and Ethics: Concepts, Methodologies, Tools, and Applications*, IGI Global (ed.), pp. 373–387. Hershey, PA. https://doi.org/10.4018/978-1-4666-4474-8.ch009.

Quinn, RE and J Rohrbaugh (1983). A spatial model of effectiveness criteria: Towards a competing values approach to organizational analysis. *Management Science*, 29(3), 363–377.

Ruta, N (2018). Informe de gestión de la corporación Ruta N sobre el plan de ciencia, tecnología de innovación del año.

Schreiber, JB, A Nora, FK Stage, EA Barlow and J King (2006). Reporting structural equation modeling and confirmatory factor analysis results: A review. *Journal of Educational Research*, 99, 323–337.

Sole, F and G Schiuma (2010). Using performance measures in public organizations: Challenges of Italian public administrations. *Measuring Business Excellence*, 14(3), 70–84.

Solis-Molina, M, M Hernández-Espallardo and A Rodríguez-Orejuela (2018). Performance implications of organizational ambidexterity versus T specialization in exploitation or exploration: The role of absorptive capacity. *Journal of Business Research*, 91, 181–194. https://doi.org/10.1016/j.jbusres.2018.06.001.

Szulanski, G (1996). Exploring internal stickiness: Impediments to the transfer of best practice within the firm. *Strategic Management Journal*, 17(2), 27–43.

Thoumi, FE (2012). Colombian organized crime: From drug trafficking to parastatal bands and widespread corruption. In *Traditional Organized Crime in the Modern World: Responses to Socioeconomic Change*, D Siegel and H van de Bunt (eds.), pp. 131–148. Boston, MA: Springer US. https://doi.org/10.1007/978-1-4614-3212-8_7.

Todorova, G and B Durisin (2007). Absorptive capacity: Valuing a reconceptualization. *Academy of Management Review*, 32(3), 774–786.

Tsai, W (2001). Knowledge transfer in intraorganizational networks: Effects of network position and absorptive capacity on business unit innovation and performance. *Academy of Management Journal*, 44(5), 996–1004.

Ullman, JB (2001). Structural equation modeling. In *Using Multivariate Statistics*, BG Tabachnick and LS Fidell (eds.), 4th Ed., Needham Heights, MA: Allyn & Bacon.

Vasco Uribe, CE and G Perdomo-Charry (2015). *"Balance de organizaciones para el desarrollo 20 años despus" Misión de Ciencia, Educación y Desarrollo. Balance 20 años despus*. En: Colombia ISBN: 978-958-734-162-1 Ed: Procuraduría General de la Nación. Instituto de Estudios del Ministerio Público, 1, 5 - 65.

Venkatraman, N and V Ramanujam (1986). Measurement of business performance in strategy research: A comparison of approaches. *Academy of Management Review*, 11(4), 801–814.

Veugelers, R (1997). Internal R&D expenditures and external technology sourcing. *Research Policy*, 26(3), 303–315.

Volberda, HW, NJ Foss and MA Lyles (2010). Perspective-absorbing the concept of absorptive capacity: How to realize its potential in the organization field. *Organization Science*, 21(4), 931–951.

White, L (2008). The use of performance measures and their outcomes. *Journal of American Academy of Business*, 13(1), 133–137.

Zahra, SA and G George (2002). Absorptive capacity: A review, reconceptualization, and extension. *Academy of Management Review*, 27(2), 185–203.

Zeng, SX *et al.* (2010). Relationship between cooperation, networks and innovation performance of SMEs. *Technovation*, 30, 181–194.

Zuñiga-Collazos, A, R Harrill, NR Escobar-Moreno and M Castillo-Palacio (2015). Evaluation of the determinant factors of innovation in Colombia's tourist product. *Tourism Analysis*, 20(1), 117–122.

Chapter 14

HR PRACTICES, KNOWLEDGE SHARING AND PROTECTION ACTIVITIES, AND PERFORMANCE — A MODERATION MODEL†

JORGE F. S. GOMES

ISEG — Lisbon School of Economics and Management
University of Lisbon, Rua Miguel
Lupi, 20, 1249-078, Lisbon, Portugal
jorgegomes@iseg.ulisboa.pt

PIA HURMELINNA*

Oulu Business School
University of Oulu
P. O. Box 4600, 90014 Oulu, Finland
pia.hurmelinna@oulu.fi

HEIDI OLANDER

School of Business and Management
Lappeenranta University of Technology
P. O. Box 20, 53851 Lappeenranta, Finland
heidi.olander@lut.fi

Published 31 May 2017

Innovation and HRM practices are connected, but the nature of these linkages may not be completely understood. Practical examples where knowledge securing practices limit efficiency of creative work, and where rewarding established ways of work prevent new approaches from being tried, suggest that there are challenges. In this study, we examine the relationships between different forms of HRM practices, knowledge sharing and protection (i.e., knowledge activities), and performance outcomes. Our findings from empirical analysis among 150 firms suggest that HRM practices are positively related to subjective overall performance and innovation performance, and that knowledge sharing likewise has such a relationship with performance outcomes. Furthermore, when knowledge sharing is accompanied with HR practices targeted to securing knowledge, innovation performance can be improved. Knowledge securing also comes in play when it is combined with HR practices of personnel compensation and appraisal; in this case

*Corresponding author.

†This article originally appeared in *International Journal of Innovation Management*, **24** 1740003-1-19 © 2017 World Scientific Publishing Europe Ltd.

J. F. S. Gomes, P. Hurmelinna & H. Olander

subjective performance is diminished. This leads us to suggest that companies might benefit from smart HRM systems.

Keywords: Human resource management; performance; innovation; knowledge sharing; knowledge protection.

Introduction

In relation to innovation, human resource management (HRM) practices can be argued to function directly, through e.g., influencing creativity (Sanders *et al.*, 2014), or indirectly, e.g., through shaping an innovative climate (Pereira and Gomes, 2012); HRM practices seek such aims by securing the availability and presence of employees with innovative capabilities, promoting knowledge exchange, facilitating motivation, and fostering innovative climate (Sanders *et al.*, 2014). On top of these goals, HR practices can be utilised to secure the uniqueness of knowledge assets and innovative knowledge that form the basis for capturing value and gaining adequate return from the investments put in innovative activities. How willing and able employees are to take care of confidential knowledge, and to look after the interests of their organisation, are important issues both in terms of theory and practice (Porter Liebeskind, 1997; Hurmelinna-Laukkanen and Puumalainen, 2007).

The challenge is that distinct HRM practices may encourage conflicting aims, or that they tend to promote one issue at a time — that is, they stimulate those features that they focus on — thus failing/forgetting the need to serve multiple, and not always consistent, organisational goals. For example, on one hand personnel compensation and appraisal are likely to facilitate productivity in the focus areas (that is, employees' search for rewards and recognition makes them act in a manner that fits the existing [production] systems), but on the other hand it cannot be taken for granted that they would ensure knowledge exchange or trial and error type of activities. Also, it has sometimes been questioned if such HR practices help employees to protect knowledge assets (Bulgurcu *et al.*, 2010). In the same vein, knowledge sharing may become limited: it may be that rivalry over appreciation and compensation makes individuals guard their knowledge. Similarly, training personnel on knowledge protection and introducing information security policies, is likely to promote protection-related aspects, but such practices may not be helpful in terms of promoting knowledge sharing that would facilitate creative behaviour and innovative climate. In fact, those practices that support knowledge protection may even collide with practices supporting knowledge sharing (see Hannah and Robertson, 2016, on challenges faced by employees with regard to following the rules set on handling confidential knowledge). Dealing with these aspects is, therefore, a multidimensional and a highly relevant managerial issue;

HR Practices, Knowledge Sharing and Protection Activities, and Performance

managing HRM for innovation and efficiency is managing complex paradoxes and calls for balancing both at individual and organisational levels.

These aspects seem to go quite unnoticed in existing literature. Although leadership, management, and HR issues are frequently connected to innovativeness and innovation activities, often the focus is on creativity, both in terms of finding the ways to enhance it, and in terms of removing obstacles to creativity and innovation (Ribeiro *et al.*, 2011). The paradoxical nature of HRM practices, where stability and change, and sharing and protection of knowledge may collide, is a research area that calls for further examination (Hannah and Robertson, 2016).

This study addresses the questions of *how different forms of HRM practices, and knowledge sharing and protection activities relate to different performance types, and how aligning HR-practices with knowledge sharing and protection activities is related to performance*? In the following, we first discuss HRM systems and practices, and explicate how they have varying linkages to knowledge sharing and protection, and how these might then be related to performance outcomes — innovation and more comprehensive types. Empirical examination among 150 firms provides practical insight into these issues. Discussion on the findings and conclusions completes the paper.

HRM systems and practices supporting innovation

The connection between HRM and innovation has attracted research since Miles and Snow (1978) first introduced their ideas about the connections between innovation strategies and the HRM function. In the following decades, advancements in the area were important, however, there is still much that has not been thoroughly studied or fully understood. The so-called 'black box' of HRM research (Ferris *et al.*, 1998; Gomes and Sanders, 2012) indicates that the mechanisms to explaining influences of an organisation's strategies on its performance through the HRM system, are still relatively undefined. In short, there are already a few studies that touch upon the issue of connecting HRM to innovation and other performance outputs (Guest, 2011), but research has yet to show a comprehensive and clear picture of such connections in modern organisations. These aspects would benefit from closer examination: which HR management practices are associated with various performance outcomes and how — e.g., in relation to which activities — are questions with high relevance.

HRM practices — connection to knowledge protection and sharing

Knowledge protection and sharing are activities where the opposing goals come visible and where HRM practices therefore become challenged. So far, these activities have been considered in a few instances with HR issues. Bulgurcu *et al.* (2010) and Hannah and Robertson (2016), for example, build their studies on the issues of confidentiality, and consider the reasons for employees not to follow the knowledge securing practices of a firm. In some cases, this failure to *protect knowledge* (i.e., emergence of unwanted leakages, is about unawareness, sometimes it is simple neglected, and in some cases the rules are deliberately bent or broken so as to allow efficient work (Bulgurcu *et al.*, 2010). Rarely the question is about employees abusing the organisation, even if such cases could be possible due to disappointment with the (former) employer (see Olander *et al.*, 2016 for redundancy-related knowledge mobility), or knowingly neglecting confidentiality rules in order to benefit oneself (Husted *et al.*, 2013). Most often mishaps in knowledge protection activity are about the inability to understand the damage that breaking knowledge protection rules causes (Husted and Michailova, 2010; Ritala *et al.*, 2015). Managers can address these issues through continuous monitoring, and by evaluating, for example, the trustworthiness of employees already during the recruitment interviews (Olander and Hurmelinna-Laukkanen, 2015). In general, the HR practices that are targeted towards limiting unwanted knowledge flows, i.e., *knowledge securing practices*, can cover means such as non-disclosure agreements, confidentiality clauses, enforcing non-competition agreements (applicable only with certain employees), educating employees on confidentiality issues, motivational aspects for following information security rules, sanctions for breaking the rules, and controlling and restricting access (Baughn *et al.*, 1997; Bulgurcu *et al.*, 2010; Hannah, 2005; Hannah and Robertson, 2016; Olander and Hurmelinna-Laukkanen, 2015; O'Neill and Adya, 2007; Porter Liebeskind, 1996, 1997).

Promotion of knowledge sharing has likewise been discussed in earlier studies (e.g., Cabrera and Cabrera, 2005; Donate and Guadamillas, 2015). It is frequently noted that employees are highly important for an organisation as they possess information and knowledge that is needed and valuable in process improvement and innovation creation (e.g., Alegre *et al.*, 2013; Camelo-Ordaz *et al.*, 2011). *Knowledge sharing activity* allows spread of the knowledge through various channels. In this sense, HRM can support — even ensure — knowledge sharing activity. HRM can facilitate presence of knowledgeable employees that have enough common ground to efficiently share and utilise knowledge, and also generate new intellectual assets. In particular, *recruitment* and dismissal practices are of importance in this regard (see e.g., Bae and Lawler, 2000). At the same time, increasing security about the job, ensuring person–job and person–organisation fit (see e.g., Boon *et al.*, 2011), and promoting *commitment and involvement* may boost the levels of knowledge sharing among the established personnel (Camelo-Ordaz *et al.*, 2011) . *Compensation and appraisal* practices may, likewise, play a central role in this kind of activity (Delery and Doty, 1996; Sanders *et al.*, 2014). Surely, there is a risk of internal competition becoming so fierce that individual employees start to guard their knowledge, or a possibility of suboptimal alignment of incentive systems, but in general, these practices could be considered to be relevant for knowledge sharing.

A more notable challenge is, as suggested above, that knowledge protection and sharing are by default at least partly opposing; knowledge that is heavily protected from being transferred is not likely shared efficiently, and knowledge that is disseminated openly and extensively cannot really be kept within a specific sphere for exclusive utilization (see e.g., Hannah and Robertson, 2016). This also has implications in the area of HRM. As Hurmelinna-Laukkanen *et al.* (2016, P. 166) note, even if the need for both knowledge sharing and protection has been acknowledged, "how to achieve these seemingly contradicting goals is another issue, which is yet to be resolved (Kale *et al.*, 2000; Yang *et al.*, 2014)." If this can be accomplished, the performance of an organisation may be positively affected. These issues are discussed in the following.

Impact on performance and research goal

Earlier studies have suggested that HRM systems are related to the financial and innovation performance of the firm (Boselie *et al.*, 2005; Hurmelinna-Laukkanen and Gomes, 2012). This thought comes from the expectation that when employees know what is expected from them and are motivated to act according to the goals of their organisations, they will be engaged, motivated, and committed, and hence better results can be achieved. At the same time, the difficulties of connecting HRM directly to performance have been acknowledged, and therefore empirical studies have been exploring the role of various factors in the HRM-performance connection (see e.g., Boselie *et al.*, 2005; Guest, 1997; Wright and Gardner, 2003).

The current research follows this line of enquiry, by examining the relationships between HRM practices and performance, on one hand, and knowledge sharing and protection activities, on the other hand. The reasoning is that, in some industries more than in others, balancing knowledge sharing with knowledge protection is a critical capacity that companies need to develop, and HRM practices can play a pivotal role in such capacity building. In fact, following the above sections, industries which are heavily dependent on information and knowledge, need to have in place a set of HRM practices that are capable of stimulating employees' urge to share ideas, creativity, and knowledge, but also the wisdom to protect knowledge from leaving the organisation. Whether or not this is achieved, is a matter of designing the right set of HRM practices and securing their positive impact on performance.

Given the relatively exploratory nature of this study, a set of hypotheses was put forward based on a research model in which performance depends, first, on HRM practices and, second, knowledge sharing and protection activities as antecedents. Moreover, these antecedents are considered to operate in interaction.

The first two hypotheses state a positive relationship between HRM practices and performance. Performance in the current research was measured in two ways: subjective (evaluation on the overall performance of the firm) and innovation performance (introduction of innovation in different areas):

H1: *There is a positive relationship between the different HR practices and subjective performance.*

H2: *There is a positive relationship between the different HR practices and innovation performance.*

Furthermore, following from the above discussion, performance is also likely to be affected by specific knowledge related activities and management practices, such as sharing and protection of knowledge. This leads to formulating the following hypotheses:

H3a: *There is a positive relationship between knowledge sharing activities and subjective performance.*

H3b: *There is a positive relationship between knowledge protection activities and subjective performance.*

H4a: *There is a positive relationship between knowledge sharing activities and innovation performance.*

H4b: *There is a positive relationship between knowledge protection activities and innovation performance.*

Finally, following especially from the above notion that HR practices likely yield best results when they are aligned with firm goals and activities, the interaction of HR practices and knowledge activities is taken under examination. HRM may influence the linkages between knowledge activities and performance, especially considering the match of HR practices to firm goals in this respect. Literature has established a clear influence of HRM on performance, but the linkages of knowledge protection and sharing activities with performance are more ambiguous, which increases the need to consider these issues. In sum, a moderator-type of research seemed to be appropriate to capture these complex relationships between the three subject matters. The following shows the rationale on a general level:

H5a: *The different HRM practices moderate the relationship between knowledge sharing activities and subjective performance.*

HR Practices, Knowledge Sharing and Protection Activities, and Performance

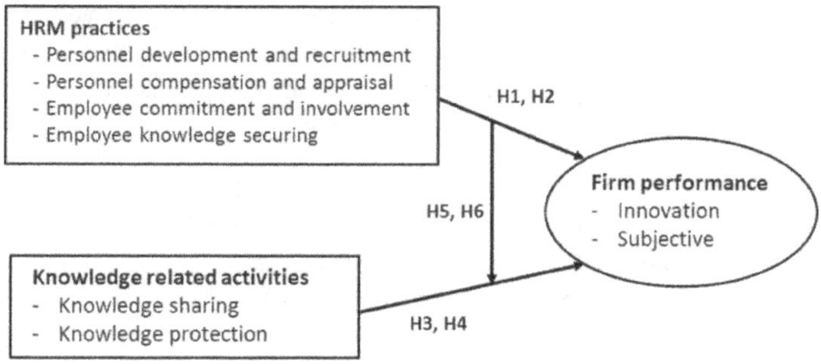

Fig. 1. The conceptual model.

H5b: *The different HRM practices moderate the relationship between knowledge protection and subjective performance.*

H6a: *The different HRM practices moderate the relationship between knowledge sharing and innovation performance.*

H6b: *The different HRM practices moderate the relationship between knowledge protection and innovation performance.*

Figure 1 illustrates our hypotheses and how they shape relationships between the concepts under examination.

Methods

Procedure and participants

The data were collected from 150 technology-oriented firms (a 12% return rate) using a survey conducted in Finland during 2012. The initial sample included all members of the Federation of Finnish Technology Industries, a national industry association, which comprised 1,273 firms from machinery and metal, electronics, information technology, and planning and consulting industries. The sample selection had a threshold of at least 10 employees per firm. Following key informant logic (Kumar *et al.*, 1993), the questionnaires were sent to professionals with a sufficient level of seniority to be able to respond to the questions, i.e., to the Chief Executive Officer of each firm.

Measures

The data were collected with the help of a structured questionnaire that consisted of scales from previous studies, and some original item sets. The scales used in this study were aimed to measure individual perceptions of HR practices, two performance dimensions, and knowledge protection and sharing activities. The following variables were captured in the questionnaire (Appendix A shows all the items, as well as the scales and original sources):

(A) HRM practices: literature discusses extensively what an HRM practice might be. Due to the limited consensus regarding what an HRM practice is, or what the most central HRM practices are, the current work followed several authors (see Appendix A), and comprised four HRM practices, of which the last one is expected to capture specific HR practices that target securing of knowledge:

   (i) Personnel Development and Recruitment: 15 items (Alpha = 0.93)
   (ii) Personnel Compensation and Appraisal: 9 items (Alpha = 0.82)
   (iii) Employee Commitment and Involvement: 12 items (Alpha = 0.92)
   (iv) Employee Knowledge Securing practices: 5 items (Alpha = 0.75)

(B) Efficiency of Knowledge-related activities: as exposed above, these were divided into sharing and protecting knowledge activities:

   (v) Knowledge Sharing activities: 6 items (Alpha = 0.87)
   (vi) Knowledge Protection activities[1]: 4 items (Alpha = 0.86)

(C) Performance: two forms of performance were used:

   (vii) Subjective Performance: 13 items (Alpha = 0.82)
   (viii) Innovative Performance: 4 items (Alpha = 0.74)

Analyses and Findings

Data analyses was carried out with correlation, regression, and hierarchical regression analyses. Following the example of earlier studies, four variables were utilised as controls: share of R&D from turnover, size and age of the organization, and turnover. Due to the non-normality character of some of the control and independent variables, scales transformation was performed before the main analyses. Table 1 shows the descriptive statistics and the correlations between the main variables.

From Table 1, one can observe an interesting pattern of correlations. Firstly, HRM practices seem to be statistically associated with both subjective and

[1]Small values indicate high efficiency in knowledge protection: any emerging negative relationship therefore suggest a positive relationship with the other variable.

HR Practices, Knowledge Sharing and Protection Activities, and Performance

Table 1. Correlation matrix and descriptive statistics.

	Mean (SD)	(1)	(2)	(3)	(4)	(5)	(6)	(7)
Knowledge protection activities	2.1 (1.16)	−0.144	0.026	0.039	0.019	−0.202*	−0.109	−0.020
1. Knowledge sharing activities	4.1 (1.39)		0.511**	0.359**	0.492**	0.160	0.257**	0.343**
2. Per. development and recruitment	4.4 (1.06)			0.633**	0.713**	0.157	0.437**	0.569**
3. Pers. compensation and appraisal	4.4 (0.90)				0.644**	0.116	0.302**	0.491**
4. Commitment and involvement	5.3 (1.02)					0.101	0.305**	0.529**
5. Knowledge securing practices	5.3 (1.15)						0.089	0.010
6. Subjective performance	4.2 (0.82)							468**
7. Innovative performance	4.36 (0.93)							

Notes: *Correlation is significant at the 0.05 level (two-tailed), ** Correlation is significant at the 0.01 level (two-tailed).

innovative performance measures, which sanction the value and effectiveness of HRM practices in the respondent companies.

Subsequent multiple regression analyses taking the four HR practices (development and recruitment, compensation and appraisal, commitment and involvement, and knowledge securing) together show that the predictive value of practices is higher for innovative performance ($R_a^2 = 0.377$), than for subjective performance ($R_a^2 = 0.267$). Regressions also indicate that the variable development and recruitment practices is the most important predictor for innovation performance ($B = 0.312$, t-value $= 3.432$, $p = 0.001$), followed by compensation and appraisal ($B = 260$, t-value $= 2.561$, $p = 0.012$). Employee knowledge securing practices point toward a negative relationship, although only moderately significant one ($B = -0.099$, t-value $= -1.636$, $p = 0.105$). Personnel development and recruitment also is positively related to subjective performance ($B = 0.352$, t-value $= 3.684$, $p = 0.000$). A small multicollinearity effect was detected between the first three practices. All in all, these results only partially support H1 and H2, but it still is likely that some HRM practices influence performance indicators.

Secondly, our data shows that knowledge protection activities are not correlated with any of the HRM practices or any of the performance measures. Conversely, knowledge sharing activities are significantly correlated with all HRM practices except knowledge securing, and they are also associated with both subjective and innovative performance.

Multiple regression analysis with performance measures, taking knowledge sharing and protection activities together, confirmed the bigger weight of the former over the latter, hence confirming H3a and H4a (knowledge sharing activities and subjective performance [$B = 0.159$, t-value $= 2.620$, $p = 0.010$], and innovation performance [$B = 0.177$, $t = 3.023$, $p = 0.003$]), but not H3b and H4b (knowledge protection activities and performance).

These findings suggest that general HRM practices in the respondent organisations seem to be designed towards stimulating sharing of knowledge, rather than promoting its protection. The fact that there is no association between knowledge sharing activities and specific activities designed at managing individuals' knowledge securing suggests that HRM is still pretty much aiming at generic behaviours in the organisation, and do not care for managing the balance between knowledge protection and knowledge sharing. It is like generic HRM practices are operating to send the message "share knowledge in this company...", but are not capable of transmitting its important complement: "... but do not share it with the outside world". In light of this, employees may get a sense that talking about critical knowledge inside or outside the company is not regulated. In sum, these findings indicate that the respondent companies value and respect knowledge

HR Practices, Knowledge Sharing and Protection Activities, and Performance

sharing practices, and see their contribution to performance in the organization; however, they do not have a well-developed policy regarding protecting sensitive knowledge from leaving or leaking to the outside.

The last hypotheses were investigated with hierarchical regression analyses. Control variables were entered first, then independent variables, and finally the moderator effects were examined. Both control and independent variables were mean-centred before running the regressions. Some outliers were identified and removed from all regressions. In total, eight regressions were performed for each dependent variable, 16 in total.

Contrary to expected, only two of these 16 regressions showed significant effects, lending some support to H5b (the different HRM practices moderate the relationship between knowledge protection activities and subjective performance) and H6a: (the different HRM practices moderate the relationship between knowledge sharing activities and innovation performance) — no support was found for H5a or H6b. Due to the considerable amount of information, only these two cases are shown in Tables 2 and 3.

From these two tables, a few points are worth mentioning. Firstly, combining knowledge sharing activity with knowledge securing practices seems to generate positive change in terms of innovation performance. Awareness of the need to secure knowledge assets, and developing the skills to do so limit excessive

Table 2. Hierarchical regression analysis for variables predicting *subjective performance.*

	Model 1			Model 2			Model 3		
Variables	B	SE B	β	B	SE B	β	B	SE B	β
Control									
Share R&D	0.43	0.18	0.23*	0.35	0.19	0.19	0.28	0.19	0.15
Size	0.52	0.34	0.32	0.41	0.35	0.25	0.47	0.34	0.28
Age	−0.16	0.22	−0.07	−0.20	0.22	−0.09	−0.23	0.22	−0.10
Turnover	−0.01	0.28	−0.01	0.03	0.28	0.02	0.02	0.27	0.01
Independent									
K-protection				−0.04	0.08	−0.05	0.03	0.08	0.04
Pers. compensation and appraisal				0.12	0.08	0.16	0.13	0.08	0.17
Moderator									
K-protection × Pers. compensation and appraisal							−0.15	0.06	−0.25*
R^2		0.375*		0.405				0.460*	
F for change in R^2		3.804*		2.984*				3.451*	

Notes: $^*p < 0.05$ $^{**}p < 0.01$.

Table 3. Hierarchical regression analysis for variables predicting *innovation performance*.

	Model 1			Model 2			Model 3		
Variables	B	SE B	β	B	SE B	β	B	SE B	β
Control									
Share R&D	0.53	0.22	0.24*	0.48	0.23	0.21	0.51	0.22	0.23*
Size	0.87	0.40	0.48*	0.87	0.40	0.48*	0.79	0.38	0.44
Age	0.07	0.28	0.02	0.10	0.29	0.03	−0.01	0.28	−0.00
Turnover	−0.30	0.32	−0.20	−0.34	0.33	−0.23	−0.32	0.31	−0.21
Independent									
K-sharing				0.14	0.10	0.14	0.18	0.10	0.18
Knowledge securing practices				−0.01	0.10	−0.01	0.05	0.10	0.05
Moderator									
K-sharing × Knowledge securing practices							0.30	0.10	0.30*
R^2		0.364*			0.386			0.481*	
F for change in R^2		3.511*			2.634			3.837*	

Notes: $*p < 0.05$, $**p < 0.01$.

knowledge transfer. Innovation performance is subsequently affected, as there is more incentive to produce new innovation: others cannot capture the generated outputs as easily.

Secondly, the interaction of knowledge protection activity and the HR practices of personnel compensation and appraisal generates negative outcomes with regard to subjective performance. This finding can be connected to the notions of Bulgurcu *et al.* (2010) on the limited power of rewards used in connection to knowledge protection. Our findings could be interpreted so that personnel compensation and appraisal can yield adverse effects if it strengthens protective approach too much. While Hypotheses 5 and 6 do not receive much support, the data suggests that there might be aspects on the alignment to be revealed.

Conclusions

As a conclusion, we can note that there are HRM practices (development and recruitment, compensation and appraisal, in particular) that relate positively to subjective and innovation performance, and that of these performance indicators, especially innovation performance can be affected. Of knowledge-related activities, knowledge sharing relates positively to both performance types. On the other hand, safeguarding knowledge only emerges as relevant when it is combined with other factors: it seems that knowledge protection as an activity, and knowledge securing as a HR practice work towards better performance when they are

HR Practices, Knowledge Sharing and Protection Activities, and Performance

contained to a suitable level: over-emphasis is harmful, but some practices are inevitably needed. However, more research is needed to confirm these ideas.

By bringing forward these findings, our study contributes to the existing knowledge by bridging two research streams: HRM and innovation. We provide evidence on the nuances regarding the relationships between HRM and performance outcomes, and involve organisation's activities into the discussion. This allows tapping into the 'black box', i.e., in explaining the impact of HRM systems on organizational-level variables such as performance (see Gomes and Sanders, 2012; Boselie *et al.*, 2005). Understanding the limits and 'best uses' of individual HRM practices increases comprehension of when and for which purposes varying HRM mechanisms suit best. Also, this enables evaluation of their interactions in a novel way, and this triggers practical and managerial contributions. It may be, for example, that a specific HR practice is valuable — even necessary — to a certain point, but after that it needs to be replaced with other activities and practices in order to produce the final performance outputs. The earlier findings of Clark and Colling (2005) and Popaitoon and Siengthai (2014) in the context of project management point towards this direction.

Communicating the change in emphases to employees is, of course, a central task of management. In fact, an important managerial implication is that rather than developing more or better HR practices, we argue that managers working especially in companies operating in highly creative and innovative sectors should be focused on developing smarter HR systems that reflect the complex interplay between securing sensitive knowledge, on one hand, and spreading useful knowledge to generate more value, on the other hand. This logic should also be extendable to securing productivity (exploitation and utilisation of existing resources and competitive advantages), and supporting renewal and change (exploration of new opportunities), that is, to balancing and changing between differing goals. Placing managerial attention to the alignment of the activities and goals of the organisation and its HRM practices is highly relevant, and dynamism may be needed so as to ensure that different opportunities and threats can be handled efficiently. Different means indeed lead to different ends. This means that when the emphases placed on specific activities change, HRM has to be responsive and the practices that are employed need to be adapted accordingly. Understanding the applicability of HR practices for different purposes allows firms to build such smart HRM systems that they need in the continuously changing business environments.

This study has several limitations. First of all, the data were collected in one specific geographical area, Finland. The country is known for its viable legal system and high trust business relationships inherent in the relatively small market area. Both of these issues could affect the results: trust in others can make knowledge sharing easier, and strong and efficient legal system enhances the power of legal knowledge protection mechanisms, and therefore makes relationships and behaviour more predictable. The co-existence of trust and small market can actually also lessen the need for formal protection in the first place, which may explain the limited attention paid to knowledge protection. Second, the sample size, while rather sufficient for the analyses in question, could be larger: Bigger datasets could potentially expose some more underlying relationships. Moreover, testing for mediating effects might also reveal important aspects on the alignment of the different factors. One limitation is that the sample concerns companies in technology industries. Technology-intensive companies may face different kinds of challenges from those of other companies. However, the technology-intensiveness makes a fruitful context for examination of developed HRM practices and knowledge sharing and protection activities, as the firms included in the sample are likely paying attention to these issues as the human resources and action of the employees in terms of knowledge sharing are vital part of their innovativeness.

The results and limitations suggest paths for further studies. Firstly, as the data is collected in a single-country setting, we encourage further surveys to be conducted in different countries with different cultures. Surveys conducted in less technology-oriented industries could also be beneficial to explore the differences in knowledge sharing and protection actions of employees from one industry to another. More complicated models are likely needed as well, and for this, some measures may need to be modified. Nevertheless, we hope that the findings of this study can provide ground for such works.

Appendix A. Items and Scales

Personnel Development and Recruitment (Bae and Lawler, 2000; Delery and Doty, 1996)

We use a lot of money on the training and development of our personnel
We provide opportunities for the training and development of personnel
We make different kinds of training available
We utilise a systematically structured training process
We consider the training of our personnel a high priority
We provide extensive training for general skills
Our employees have very little future within this organisation (reverse item)*
Our employees have clear career paths within the organisation
Employees' career aspirations within the company are known by their supervisors
We provide opportunities for job rotation

We put a lot of effort into recruiting the right persons
We spend a lot of money to recruit the right persons
We hire people with general rather than specific skills
We place great importance on the staffing process
We focus on long-run employee potential when selecting staff
We have high/extensive selection criteria in our firm

*Item removed from final scale computation

Personnel Compensation and Appraisal (Wright *et al.*, 1999; Bae and Lawler, 2000; modified)

Our pay is tied to employees' individual performance
There are major differences in the pay of personnel in similar positions
Our employees are also compensated for with other means than money
Employees get feedback for a job well done
Employees are personally acknowledged from a job well done
A lot of effort is put to measuring employee performance
Raises, promotions, etc. are closely tied to performance appraisal
Individual performance is regularly discussed with employees
Many people provide their input to performance evaluation

Employee Commitment and Involvement (Guest, 2003; Ahmad and Schroeder, 2003)

Employees are provided with information on business plans
Employees are provided with information on financial objectives
Employees are provided with information on the firm's performance
Employees are provided with information on important initiatives
Direct feedback from employees is collected regularly
We pursue to gather opinions from many employees through issues discussed in teams
Employee teams are encouraged to try and solve business-related problems
In the past 3 years, many problems have been solved in small groups
We try our best to keep the promises made to our employees
We conduct ourselves ethically towards our employees
We conduct ourselves rightfully towards our employees
We try our best to take the employees' benefit into account

Employee Knowledge Securing Practices (Hurmelinna-Laukkanen, 2012)

Educating personnel on IPR issues
Educating personnel on secrecy with regard to business critical knowledge

Making personnel committed to the firm
Small personnel turnover/minimising it
Increasing the personnel's loyalty to the firm

Efficiency of Knowledge Protection Activities (new measure adapted and extended from Ritala *et al.*, 2015 — small values indicate that protection has been successful)

Our employees accidentally leak business critical knowledge to our partners
Our employees accidentally leak business critical knowledge in other situations
Our employees leak business critical knowledge on purpose to our partners
Our employees leak business critical knowledge on purpose in other situations

Efficiency of Knowledge Sharing Activities (new measure adapted and extended from Ritala *et al.*, 2015)

Our employees share their work reports and official documents with co-workers within the same firm
Our employees share their work reports and official documents with people employed by the firm's partners
Our employees share their manuals and methodologies with co-workers within the same firm
Our employees share their manuals and methodologies with people employed by the firm's partners
Our employees share their experience or know-how with co-workers within the same firm
Our employees share their experience or know-how with people employed by the firm's partners

Subjective Performance (Delaney and Huselid, 1996; Pertusa-Ortega *et al.*, 2009; Alegre and Chiva, 2008)

Growth in sales
Profitability
Market share
Market growth
Employment growth
Cash flow
Returns of investment
Replacement of products being phased out
Replacement of services being phased out
Extension of product/service range within the main market

HR Practices, Knowledge Sharing and Protection Activities, and Performance

Extension of product/services range outside the main market
Development of environmentally friendly products/services
Opening of new markets abroad
Opening of new domestic target groups

Innovation Performance (Weerawardena, 2003)

Products and services to the customers
Production methods and processes
Management practices
Marketing practices

References

Alegre, J and R Chiva (2008). Assessing the impact of organizational learning capability on product innovation performance: An empirical test. *Technovation*, 28, 315–326.

Alegre, J, K Sengupta and R Lapiedra (2013). Knowledge management and innovation performance in a high-tech SMEs industry. *International Small Business Journal*, 31, 454–470.

Bae, J and JJ Lawler (2000). Organizational and HRM strategies in Korea: Impact on firm performance in an emerging economy. *Academy of Management Journal*, 43(3), 502–517.

Baughn, CC, JH Stevens, JG Denekamp and RN Osborn (1997). Protecting intellectual capital in international alliances. *Journal of World Business*, 32(2), 103–117.

Boon, C, DN Den Hartog, P Boselie and J Paauwe (2011). The relationship between perceptions of HR practices and employee outcomes: Examining the role of person–organisation and person-job fit. *The International Journal of Human Resource Management*, 22(1), 138–162.

Boselie, P, G Dietz and C Boon (2005). Commonalities and contradictions in HRM and performance research. *Human Resource Management Journal*, 15(3), 67–94.

Bulgurcu, B, H Cavusoglu and I Benbasat (2010). Information security policy compliance: An empirical study of rationality-based beliefs and information security awareness. *MIS Quarterly*, 34(3), 523–548.

Cabrera, EF and A Cabrera (2005). Fostering knowledge sharing through people management practices. *The International Journal of Human Resource Management*, 16(5), 720–735.

Camelo-Ordaz, C, J Garcia-Cruz, E Sousa-Ginel and R Valle-Cabrera (2011). The influence of human resource management on knowledge sharing and innovation in Spain: The mediating role of affective commitment. *The International Journal of Human Resource Management*, 22, 1442–1463.

Clark, I and T Colling (2005). The management of human resources in project management-led organizations. *Personnel Review*, 34, 178–191.

Delaney, JT and MA Huselid (1996). The impact of human resource management practices on perceptions of organizational performance. *Academy of Management Journal*, 39(4), 949–969.

Delery, JE and DH Doty (1996). Modes of theorizing in strategic human resource management: Tests of universalistic, contingency, and configurational performance predictions. *Academy of management Journal*, 39(4), 802–835.

Donate, MJ and F Guadamillas (2015). An empirical study on the relationships between knowledge management, knowledge-oriented human resource practices and innovation. *Knowledge Management Research & Practice*, 13(2), 134–148.

Ferris, GR, MM Arthur, HM Berkson, DM Kaplan, G Harrell-Cook and DD Frink (1998). Toward a social context theory of the human resource management-organization effectiveness relationship. *Human Resource Management Review*, 8(3), 235–264.

Gomes, JFS and K Sanders (2012). Formal and informal HRM: Implications for the HRM process perspective. *Caucus at the Academy of Management,* Annual Meeting, August 3–7, Boston, MA.

Guest, D (1997). Human resource management and performance: A review and research agenda. *International Journal of Human Resource Management*, 8(3), 263–276.

Guest, D (2011). Human resource management and performance: Still searching for some answers. *Human Resource Management Journal*, 21, 3–13.

Hannah, DR (2005). Should I keep a secret? The effects of trade secret protection procedures on employees' obligations to protect trade secrets. *Organisation Science*, 16(1), 71–84.

Hannah, DR and K Robertson (2016). Why and how do employees break and bend confidential information protection rules? *Journal of Management Studies*, 52, 381–413.

Hurmelinna-Laukkanen, P and K Puumalainen (2007). Nature and dynamics of appropriability: Strategies for appropriating returns on innovation. *R&D Management*, 37, 95–112.

Hurmelinna-Laukkanen, P, JFS Gomes and H Olander (2016). What did you expect to happen? Aligning HR practices with knowledge management outcomes. In *Entrepreneurship, Business and Economics* — Vol. 1, Eurasian Studies on Business and Economics 3/1, MH Bilgin and H Danis (Eds.), pp. 165–182. Switzerland: Springer International Publishing.

Husted, K and S Michailova (2010). Dual allegiance and knowledge sharing in inter-firm R&D collaborations. *Organization Dynamics*, 39(1), 37–47.

Husted, K, S Michailova and H Olander (2013). Dual allegiance, knowledge sharing, and knowledge protection: An empirical examination. *International Journal of Innovation Management*, 17(6), 1340022-1–1340022-33.

Kale, P, H Singh and H Perlmutter. (2000). Learning and protection of proprietary assets in strategic alliances: Building relational capital. *Strategic Management Journal*, 21(3), 217–237.

Kumar, N, L Stern and J Anderson (1993). Conducting interorganizational research using key informants. *Academy of Management Journal*, 36, 1633–1651.

HR Practices, Knowledge Sharing and Protection Activities, and Performance

Miles, RE and CC Snow (1978). *Organizational Strategy, Structure, and Process*. New York: McGraw-Hill Book Co.

Olander, H and P Hurmelinna-Laukkanen (2015). Proactive HRM for reducing knowledge risks — evaluating commitment and trustworthiness. *International Journal of Innovation Management*, 19(6), 1540011.

Olander, H, P Hurmelinna-Laukkanen and M von Zedtwitz (2016). Intentional or not – The nature and dimensions of knowledge mobility. *ISPIM Conference*, 19–22 June, Porto Portugal.

O'Neill, BS and M Adya (2007). Knowledge sharing and the psychological contract. *Journal of Managerial Psychology*, 22(4), 411–436.

Pereira, CMM and JSF Gomes (2012). The strength of human resource practices and transformational leadership: Impact on organisational performance. *The International Journal of HRM*, 23(20), 4301–4318.

Pertusa-Ortega, EM, JF Molina-Azorín and E Claver-Cortés (2009). Competitive strategies and firm performance: A comparative analysis of pure, hybrid and 'stuck-in-the-middle' strategies in Spanish firms. *British Journal of Management*, 20(4), 508–523.

Popaitoon, S and S Siengthai (2014). The moderating effect of human resource management practices on the relationship between knowledge absorptive capacity and project performance in project-oriented companies. *International Journal of Project Management*, 32(6), 908–920.

Porter Liebeskind, J (1996). Knowledge, strategy, and the theory of the firm. *Strategic Management Journal*, 17, 93–107.

Porter Liebeskind, J (1997). Keeping organizational secrets: Protective institutional mechanisms and their costs. *Industrial and Corporate Change*, 6, 623–663.

Ribeiro, T, JP Coelho and JFS Gomes (2011). HR Strength, situation strength and improvisation behavior. *Management Research*, 9(2), 118–136.

Ritala, P, H Olander, S Michailova and K Husted (2015). Knowledge sharing, knowledge leaking and relative innovation performance: An empirical study. *Technovation*, 35, 22–31.

Sanders, K, H Shipton and JFS Gomes (2014). Guest Editors' Introduction: Is the HRM Process important? Past, current, and future challenges. *Human Resource Management*, 53(4), 489–503.

Wright, PM and TM Gardner (2003). The human resource-firm performance relationship: Methodological and theoretical challenges. In *The New Work Place: A Guide to the Human Impact of Modern Working Practices,* D Holman, TD Wall, CW Clegg, P Sparrow and A Howard (Eds). London: John Wiley & Sons.

Wright, PM, B McCormick, WS Sherman and GC McMahan (1999). The role of human resource practices in petro-chemical refinery performance. *International Journal of Human Resource Management*, 10(4), 551–571.

Yang, SM, SC Fang, SR Fang and CH Chou (2014). Knowledge exchange and knowledge protection in interorganizational learning: The ambidexterity perspective. *Industrial Marketing Management*, 43(2), 346–358.

Chapter 15

USING EMPLOYEE CREATIVITY TO UNPACK THE 'BLACK BOX' IN THE HIGH-PERFORMANCE WORK SYSTEM (HPWS)-FIRM PERFORMANCE NEXUS†

ABDUSSALAAM IYANDA ISMAIL*

College of Business Administration
University of Fujairah, Fujairah
United Arab Emirates
iyandaismail@yahoo.com

ABDUL-HALIM ABDUL-MAJID

School of Business Management, College of Business
Universiti Utara Malaysia Sintok, 06010 Kedah, Malaysia

ABDULLATEEF AMEEN

Department of Public Administration
Faculty of Management Sciences, University of Ilorin, Nigeria

SAQLAIN RAZA

School of Business Management, College of Business
Universiti Utara Malaysia, Sintok, 06010 Kedah, Malaysia

IYIOLA TOMILAYO AKINDELE

Department of Public Administration
Faculty of Management Sciences, University of Ilorin, Nigeria

Published 18 September 2019

The extant research findings have identified lacunas (i.e. gaps, unresolved issues, and black box) in the High-Performance Work System (HPWS)-Performance relationship and suggested usage of a mechanism (mediator) that can close up the identified lacunas. Thus, this study investigates whether employee creativity can play a mediating role in the relationship between HPWS and firm non-financial performance. The sample size of the study is 518, and respondents were selected through stratified sampling technique. Data were collected

*Corresponding author.

†This article originally appeared in *International Journal of Innovation Management*, **24** 2050052-1-30 © 2020 World Scientific Publishing Europe Ltd.

from the sampled 518 managers in Nigerian firms. Partial Least Squares (PLS) algorithm and bootstrapping techniques were used for data analysis. The result indicates that employee creativity competitively/partially mediates the relationship between HPWS and non-financial performance. Employee creativity represents an appropriate mechanism to explain the relationship between HPWS and non-financial performance. Hence, the positive indirect effect via the mediator variable (employee creativity) reveals the 'true' relationship between HPWS and non-financial performance. This result implies that HPWS may not necessarily enhance non-financial performance. Ill-configured HPWS could jeopardize non-financial performance, but HPWS that stimulates employee creativity would enhance non-financial performance. Lastly, the implications, limitations and suggestions for future research are discussed.

Keywords: High Work Performance System; HRM; creativity; strategic HRM; non-financial performance.

Introduction

The extant strategic HRM literature indicates that HPWS is crucial to firm performance. HR system that boosts employee competencies, commitment and productivity is frequently referred to as HPWS (Appelbaum *et al.*, 2000; Choi, 2014; Datta *et al.*, 2005). Bundles of HR practices are more influential than individual practices in isolation (Choi, 2014; Chuang and Liao, 2010). In the research by Ismail *et al.* (2018), it is found that HPWS is a strong and positive predictor of firm performance, indicating that HPWS constitutes an indispensable part of the whole of competitive advantage (Ismail *et al.*, 2016, 2017; Kaufman, 2010).

Substantial numbers of studies (see Mihail and Kloutsiniotis, 2016; Muduli *et al.*, 2016; Ogunyomi and Bruning, 2016; Shin and Konrad, 2017) have strongly established that HPWS influences organisational performance. Nevertheless, several other studies have recognised vague process, otherwise known as 'black box' within the HPWS-performance link. These studies recommend usage of a mechanism through which the so called 'black box' could be unpacked (Chadwick and Dabu, 2009; Ismail *et al.*, 2018; Yen, 2015). On this, Boxall (2012) mentioned the absence of issue in the direct HRM-Performance nexus, but there are many vague processes about the chain of nexuses that are persistent inside the 'black box' of HRM.

Moreover, employee creativity is becoming more and more indispensable in the organisation, given the increasingly volatile environments and high levels of competition. Creativity denotes getting out of the comfort zone of individual employee and experimentation of new way or method of doing things with no fear of failure (Ismail *et al.*, 2018). Creativity can be induced via employee-oriented HPWS (Martinaityte, 2014). In addition, employee creative ideas engendered by AMO-enhancing HPWS can engender firms' competitiveness (Baer, 2010) and its consequent firm performance (Choi, 2014; Moulang, 2015; Shalley and Gilson, 2004). HPWS can induce employee's task motivation, domain-relevant skills, and creativity-relevant skills (Chiang *et al.*, 2015; He *et al.*, 2018), produce innovative outcomes which would enhance the organisational chance to remain competitive and perform better (Ismail *et al.*, 2016; Jiang *et al.*, 2012), and in turn metamorphosed to non-financial performance. Summing up the above exposition, this study aims to examine the effect of HPWS on non-financial firm performance and the mediating effect of employee creativity on HPWS-non-financial performance nexus.

Therefore, the following questions were prepared to give direction to the study:

(i) Does HPWS impact non-financial firm performance?
(ii) Does employee creativity mediate the HPWS-non-financial performance nexus?

Literature Review and Hypotheses Development

Firm performance

It has become common knowledge that organisational performance is the most vital issue for every organisation, whether such organisations are profit-making-oriented or otherwise. This has underscored the fact that managers/leaders should be aware of the factors that influence performance of organisations, as this will enable them to take proper steps to initiate them. Nevertheless, due to unanimity among the scholar regarding definition, conceptualisation and measurement of the concept performance, it has become a tedious task to have a unified definition, conceptualisation and measurement of performance. Thus, it remains a contentious issue among organisational researchers (Barney, 1997). The fundamental issue in this regard is connected with the suitability of numerous approaches to the concept utilisation and measurement of organisational performance (Van der Stede, 2001).

The effort by the scholars to assist firms' managers in tackling the problem of shortfalls in the extant performance measurements systems dated back to 1980s. The extant performance measurement systems fall short of abetting managers to identify changes in the business environments and to recognise the factors critical to the success of firms (Ittner and Larcker, 1996). In the present competitive business environment, performance measurement is considered a key management control tool for business firms, and it is directly connected with the design of firm's core competency. Performance measurement significantly and positively predicts the growth and development of organisations.

Moreover, some research, despite the acknowledgement of multi-dimensionality of organisational performance, still adopts one indicator to symbolise the concept of firm performance (Miller *et al.*, 2013). Peloza and Papania (2008) observed that profit and growth should be included in the components of firm performance, given their roles as the pertinent drivers for the existence of firms. Likewise, Maskell (1992) advocates for the adoption of non-financial performance measures. He also recommended change over time, since every firm needs change. Scholars (e.g., Kaplan and Norton, 1996; Neely, 2002; Neely *et al.*, 2002) included customer service and satisfaction, product quality, learning and innovation as qualitative pointers of performance. Interestingly, since over a decade, considerable research (e.g., Gronum *et al.*, 2012; Kaplan and Norton, 1992; Hilman, 2009; MacDoughall and Pike, 2003) have suggested both financial and non-financial performance to form organisational performance measurement.

Therefore, firm performance, in this study, refers to the indicators that appraise how well the enterprise accomplishes its objectives (Ho, 2008), involving financial and non-financial performance (Kaplan and Norton, 2000).

Configuring HPWS in the Current Study

Given the fact that systematic combination and integration of HR architectures will give birth to synergistic human resources management system that works together to get the best results for an organisation (Subramony, 2009), the bundling-up of the HPWS in this study will be drawn upon contingency approach. Selective hiring, training, performance appraisal and pay for performance, non-financial rewards are assumed to be forces driving the knowledge, skills and abilities (KSAs) of the employees, employee motivation and creativity and creative performance, which should be the preoccupation of every firms. Hence, the internal fit (as proposed by contingency approach) is ensured in the configuration.

It can also be asserted that the configuration of HPWS in this study is context-specific, given the fact that the configuration was done by selecting the practices that would enhance the capabilities and motivation of the employees. Since highly committed, well-motivated and qualified employees are crucial to the survival and sustainability of firms, and research evidence has demonstrated heavy reliance of the organisational success on employees' contributions (Behrends, 2007; Ojokuku, 2012). Based on this and underpinned by AMO model and the suggestion of Posthuma *et al.* (2013), the proposed configured HPWS connote selective hiring, training and development, performance appraisal, pay for performance and non-financial rewards.

Furthermore, selective hiring is one of the seven practices which define systems that create wealth through the management of people (Pfeffer, 1998). It is empirically evident that hiring is an essential organisational practice as it can induce higher profitability and greater labour productivity (Michie and Sheehan,

2005). It can also induce increased levels of employee commitment (Fiorito *et al.*, 2007; Taylor *et al.*, 2008) and higher overall performance (Takeuchi *et al.*, 2007). In addition, training and development involves the practices designed to improve worker's skills and competencies required for the performance of present and future tasks (Posthuma *et al.*, 2013). For the optimum performance, training and development should be given due priority in the organisation in which employees would have the opportunity to acquire new skills (Ulrich, 1997). Hence, training becomes an important element in the HPWS system because it has linear effect on the functional capability of the organisation (Truss, 2001). Training and development can be designed to improve domain- and creativity-relevant skills. Training workers can enhance creativity by boosting employees' feeling of competence and consequently give rise to enhanced intrinsic motivation (Ryan and Deci, 2000).

Besides, performance appraisal forms a vital part of performance management in which performance of workers are defined, gauged, stimulated and developed (DeNisi and Pritchard, 2006; Kinicki *et al.*, 2013). Performance appraisal is a crucial practice, given the fact that it can align individual and team performance with organisational strategies (Zhang and Li, 2009). Appraisal practices comprise frequent feedback based on team and organisation goals, managing objectives that are tied to organisational strategies. Performance appraisal stimulates creative behaviours on the part of employee because employee is aware that behaviours are assessed and connected to performance. Feedback on overall performance is useful for assessing worker's performance state as feedback on particular job aspects is helpful for the employee who aims at performance advancement (Pritchard *et al.*, 2002).

With regards to pay for performance, it is a core HPWP that has been empirically studied across clusters of countries and thereby cross-cultural, generalisable and fit to be part of HPWS system. It refers to a technique through which individual or group performance is directly compensated in the form of money (Armstrong, 2005). It is also a scheme designed to reward the workers based on their performance (Boachie-Mensah and Dogbe, 2011). It is also based upon merit as empirically appraised in the firm's performance appraisal program, with a chance to receive above market pay by the employees demonstrating exceptional performance (Matsumura and Shin, 2004). This type of compensation is increasingly being adopted by firms with the aims of transforming their reward system. The basic drive of any performance-based reward system is to relate employees' salaries directly to their performance. Connecting rewards to performance bolsters workers to increase their efficiency. Pay for performance entitles employees to a basic income and the chance to get extra reward if their outputs surpass the set standard (Grobler *et al.*, 2006).

Likewise, non-financial rewards are a broad HPWP that has been widely studied but not up to the level of the core HPWP such as pay for performance.

Non-financial reward has been identified to be understudied and this necessitates more research on its promising effect on the organisational performance. Non-financial reward promotes commitment, motivation and a sense of culture in the organisation (Posthuma *et al.*, 2013). It is a HPWP practice that involves many tools and methods that can be adopted in addition to monetary rewards to induce employee's high productivity.

Non-financial rewards include social recognition, genuine appreciation, certificate and acknowledgement (Neckermann and Kosfeld, 2008), paid vacation, training programmes, praise and promotion (Jeffrey, 2003). Also, non-financial reward should cater for the internal needs of employees. It has been suggested that long-lasting motivation of workers can be achieved through the mix of financial and non-financial rewards (Armstrong, 1993). Employee turnover has been observed to be high in a system devoid of non-financial reward (Mushrush, 2002). Hence, Shields (2007) recommended that it is very imperative for firms to recognise the kind of non-financial rewards that can foster the preferred employee behaviours.

Linking HPWS to Non-Financial Firm Performance

Strategic human resource management is a key foundation of competitive advantage (Bamberger and Meshoulam, 2000), and that will consequently enhance performance (Seidu, 2011). Human resources and its management form an indispensable part of the whole of competitive advantage (Allen and Wright, 2007; Boxall and Purcell, 2003; Pfeffer, 1998). Strategic HR that enhance task, targets and performance are formed through the effective adoption of HPWS. Good strategy gives rise to competitive advantage of an organisation over another, and it is connected with the improvement in industrial competencies, productivity and performances of such organisation. Such feat cannot just come about except through the instrumentality of employees who are equipped with the required skills, knowledge and competencies needed for the execution of organisational strategy and planning (Fu, 2013; Ismail, 2014; Ismail *et al.*, 2015; Mansour *et al.*, 2014). HPWS formed a part of numerous resources which give rise to sustainable competitive advantages for the organisations, and consequently enhance organisational performance (Choi, 2014; Choi and Lee, 2013; Chuang and Liao, 2010; Demirbag *et al.*, 2014; Fan *et al.*, 2014; Fu, 2013; Shin and Konrad, 2014; Seidu, 2011).

The HPWS literature has reported that HPWS has consistently led to higher individual and organisational performance (Werner, 2011) indicating a linear causal relationship between HPWS and performance. Many HRM models were designed to link a firm's organisational strategy to the main personnel operations such as performance appraisal, reward and employee development. HRM is widely seen as a way to maximise organisations' competitiveness (Guest, 1987; Legge, 1995).

Scholars from different disciplines have deployed various theoretical approaches to study the relationships between HPWS and organisational performance. These theoretical approaches include: resource dependency theory, human capital theory, strategic management, expectancy theory, behavioural science, organisational theory, resource-based theory, etc. (Delaney and Huselid, 1996; Guest, 1997; Paauwe and Richardson, 1997). In general, these theories stress the importance of HPWS in improving both employee- and firm-level performances via their impact on employees' skills, knowledge, ability, motivation and flexibility (Arthur, 1994; Gephart and Van Buren, 1996; Guest, 1997; Ichniowski *et al.*, 1997; Paauwe and Richardson, 1997; Vandenberg *et al.*, 1999). Moreover, many authors (e.g., Arthur, 1994; Delaney and Huselid, 1996; Pfeffer, 1998) have explained how well-functioning HPWS are associated with a higher organisational performance. For example, HPWS enhances workers' skills and competence through training and development. Skilled and knowledgeable employees are motivated and empowered the provision of proper rewards.

Based on the above discussion, this study hypothesises thus: HPWS would positively influence non-financial firm performance.

Mediating Role of Employee Creativity in the Relationship Between HPWS and Non-Financial Firm Performance

Research on creativity has been in existence since four decades ago. Creativity has attracted different approaches among which are person, process and product approaches (Runco, 2004). Creativity refers to quality of individual intellectual endowments and personalities (Hennessey and Amabile, 2010; Runco, 2004). Creativity entails creation of original, new and valuable ideas in any sphere (Amabile, 1996). Creativity entails production and development of novel and valuable ideas, processes, or techniques by an individual or by a group of individuals working as a team in an organisation (Amabile, 1988; Madjar *et al.*, 2002; Zhou and Shalley, 2003).

Creativity always goes along with innovation. In some research, both concepts are used interchangeably. Innovation is believed to entail fostering and executing novel ideas (Baer, 2012; Gong *et al.*, 2009). Martinaityte (2014) conceptualised creativity to involve innovation claiming that the line between the two concepts is fuzzy. From the interview she conducted, it was gathered that creativity has to do with offering of solution to the customers' problems. Creativity involves both the generation of ideas only and turning of the idea into new behaviours. In addition, creativity involves offering solution to customer's problems, treating them exclusively, testing new sales technique, suggesting the best way to work better and enhancing job effectiveness. This view is also held by the scholars such as Chen *et al.* (2013) and Yuan and Woodman (2010). Hence, creativity and innovation are considered one and the same in this study. Moreover, research (e.g., Florida, 2002) has demonstrated that creativity is part of the drivers of economic growth in the 21st century. In this exposition, the focus is on individual employee creativity as it is becoming more and more indispensable in the organisation, given the increasingly stormy environments and high levels of competition.

Employee creativity has been suggested to greatly influence organisational innovation (Amabile, 1996; Jiang *et al.*, 2012) and firm performance (Gong *et al.*, 2013). Given the importance of employee creativity, numerous researchers have examined its antecedents such as empowering leadership (Harris *et al.*, 2014), and employee learning orientation (Gong *et al.*, 2009). However, as employees are members of their respective organisations and experience many management practices, it is expected that employees' attitudes and behaviour would depend on management systems (Chiang *et al.*, 2015). Therefore, it is vital to examine the influence of management systems, such as HRM systems, on employee creativity. As systems of work practices that make a great contribution to superior organisational performance (Boxall and Macky, 2009), HPWS have been found to inspire creative ideas (Chiang *et al.*, 2015) and innovation (Messersmith and Guthrie, 2010).

Furthermore, going by the present economic situation, high quality and innovative products and services are regarded crucial (Martinaityte, 2014). Likewise, the current trends in the world of business today underscore the importance of creativity and innovation as a strategic objective of majority of organisations. Thus, research has noted creativity performance nexus (e.g., Coelho *et al.*, 2011; Gilson, 2008). Likewise, studies have established HRM-creativity interconnection (e.g., (Binyamin and Carmeli, 2010; Byron and Khananchi, 2012; Chang *et al.*, 2014; Martinaityte, 2014); HRM-performance connection is pinned down too (e.g., Demirbag *et al.*, 2014; Fan *et al.*, 2014; Shin and Konrad, 2014). However, development and validation of HPWS system in relation to creativity has evaded the concern of scholars in the HPWS research field. Hence, the research on HPWS-creativity nexus is imperative.

In addition, Baron and Kenny's (1986) supposition indicates that creativity is logically and empirically fit to be the mechanism (mediator) through which the identified lacunas is resolved. It is portended that there is possibility of having a particular construct as a mediator, if there is nexus between the construct, independent variable and dependent variable, and there is nexus between the independent variable and dependent variable. Going by this, it can be proposed that creativity can play a role of mediator in the relationship between HPWS and non-financial firm performance.

Based on the above discussion, this study hypothesises thus: Employee creativity would mediate the relationship between HPWS and non-financial financial performance.

Proposed Research Framework

Owing to the discussions in the previous sections, this study projects a model indicating that employee creativity could unpack the 'Black Box' in the HPWS-non-financial performance connection in the HRM research field. The model is underpinned by resource-based view (RBV) which advocates that firm performance is enhanced by its organisational resources and competences. Companies are capable of accomplishing better performance via the effective utilisation of their organisational resources and capabilities that cannot be imitated by the competitors. This is demonstrated in Fig. 1.

Methodology

This study considered the Krejcie and Morgan's (1970) study on sample size determination. The population of the study comprises 11,044 Nigerian firms. Based on Krejcie and Morgan's (1970) study, the sample of the study is 370. Moreover, in order to minimalise and abate sampling error, and to take care of non-response rate issues that may come up, it is suggested by Salkind (1997) that 40% increase should be added to the original sample size. Therefore, the overall

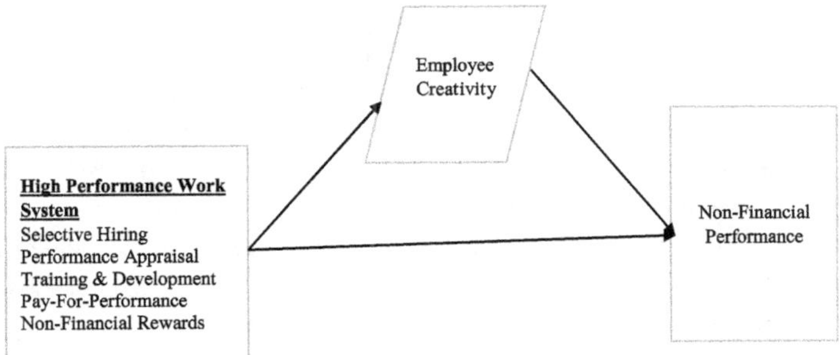

Fig. 1. Research framework.

sample size is 518. This is also consistent with the fact that the higher the sample the more accurate the result will be (Alreck and Settle, 1995). Eventually, this would ensure adequate representation of the population under study.

The data, which were collected from the sampled 518 managers in the Nigerian firms, were analysed via smart PLS 3 software packages. This would guarantee that measurement errors are minimalised and duly taken care of. The respondents were selected through stratified sampling technique. Stratified sampling technique involves definition of population (i.e., 11,044). Then, the determination of the strata, which are 13 industries of the selected firms in Nigeria, and the determination of an average number of population elements per strata. This is done by dividing the population size by the number of strata (850 [i.e., 11,044/13]). To be determined next is the percentage of respondents to be taken from each stratum. This is done by dividing the calculated sample size by the population of the study and then multiplying by 100 (4.70% [i.e., 518/11,044*100] is the percentage of respondents to be taken from each stratum).

The next step is the determination of the number of subjects in the sample. This is achieved by multiplying the total number of each element in the population by the calculated percentage (71 [i.e., 1500*4.70%]). The final step in the selected proportionate stratified sampling technique is systematic sampling which was employed in selecting the sample from the available strata. It started with the determination of the number of subjects/elements in the sample from the total number of firms/elements in the identified thirteen strata. Then, this was followed by random selection of 518 firms from the total 11,044 firms that make up the thirteen strata. This was done by selecting sampled firms from each stratum.

The process of selection started with the estimation of sampling fraction for each stratum, which was estimated by dividing the population size of each stratum (i.e., 1,500 in the case of manufacturing stratum) by the sample in each stratum (i.e., 71 in the case of manufacturing stratum). The estimated sample fraction for the manufacturing stratum is 21. Thus, one firm was selected in every 21 firms of the 1,500 manufacturing firms that make up the stratum. To select the first firm, a random number table was used, and the first firm was 7th. So, every 7th in the list of 1,500 of manufacturing stratum was selected as the respondents. In this way, the sample was composed of 7th, 28th, 49th, 35th, . . . , 1,500th. The selected numbered elements were then approached and given the questionnaire to fill. The process was repeated for other strata.

Data collection was conducted as 518 questionnaires were distributed to the respondents, but 372 completed questionnaires, representing 72% response rate, were returned and usable for further analysis. This response rate is considered adequate and sufficient, given the position of Sekaran (2003) which signifies that a response rate of 30% is sufficient for survey. Moreover, the analysis technique in the current study involved descriptive analysis and inferential analysis. Inferential analysis connotes 2-step approach: measurement and structural models (Chin, 1998; Hair *et al.*, 2011, 2012), as this guarantees valid and reliable results. To guarantee the constructs validity and reliability, which involve internal consistency reliability, convergent validity and reliability and discriminant validity, measurement model evaluation was done. Measurement model represents the relationships between constructs and their corresponding indicator variables (generally called the outer models in PLS-SEM). The basis for determining these relationships is measurement theory. A sound measurement theory is a necessary condition to obtain useful results from PLS-SEM (Hair *et al.*, 2017).

As for the measurements of the constructs of the study, HPWS in the current study involves selective hiring, training & development, performance appraisal, pay for performance and non-financial rewards and the measurements of the construct were adapted from (Martinaityte, 2014). Employee creativity measures were adapted from Wang and Netemeyer (2004) and Martinaityte and Sacramento (2013) while firm performance measures were adapted from Ogunyomi and Bruning (2016). The survey instruments included demographic information of the respondents (six items), instruments of selective hiring (four items); training and development (five items); performance appraisal (three items); pay-for-performance (two items) and non-financial rewards (two items). With regard to the instruments of employee creativity and firm performance, seven items belong to the former while six items belong to the latter (see Appendix A). All the measures of HPWS, employee creativity and firm performance are in reflective form.

The scale for all the constructs, except firm performance, ranged from 1 (strongly disagree) to 5 (strongly agree). Firm performance was scaled using a 5-point interval scale bordering on 1 = Very Weak; 2 = Weak; 3 = Not Sure; 4 = Strong; 5 = Very Strong. However, demographical variable was measured as categorical variable. This kind of interval scale is deemed fit for this study, going by the suggestion of Zikmund and Babin (2010).

Data Analysis

(a) Demographic and Descriptive Analysis

Table 1 depicts that demographic information of the respondents of the current study indicates that 137 (37%) respondents out of 372 respondents are executive directors in their respected firms while 94 (25%) and 44 (12%) are marketing managers and HR manager, respectively. The remaining 97 (26%) respondents are either supervisors or line managers. Forty percent of the sampled firms are in agriculture-related business, as 22% of them are firms dealing on construction,

Table 1. Descriptive analysis of demographic data.

Demography	Indicators	Frequency	Percentage
Position	Executive Director	137	37
	HR Manager	44	12
	Marketing Manager	94	25
	Others (e.g., Supervisor, line manager)	97	26
	Total	372	100
Industry	Agriculture, Food Products, Bus Service	147	40
	Construction, Logistics, Oil Energy	83	22
	Computer, Financial, Manufacturing	46	12
	Information Tech, Mechanical, Medical	39	11
	Others	57	15
	Total	372	100
Operation's Year	1–10 Years	147	40
	11–20 Years	83	22
	21–30 Years	50	13
	31–40 Years	39	11
	41 and above	53	14
	Total	372	100
Ownership	Sole Proprietorship	169	45
	Partnership	70	19
	Private Limited Liability Company	82	22
	Cooperative	19	5
	Faith Based Organisation	20	5
	Others	12	3
	Total	372	100
Staff	<100 Employees	348	94
	101–150 Employees	16	4
	151–200 Employees	8	2
	Total	372	100
Labor Cost	<25%	183	49
	26–50%	129	35
	51–75%	52	14
	>75%	8	2
	Total	372	100

logistics and oil Energy, 46 (12%) and 39 (11%) are workers in the firms transacting in computer, financial, manufacturing and info-tech, mechanical and medical equipment. The remaining firms, which are 57 (15%) in numbers, belong to Arts, Entertainment and Recreation or Water Supply, Sewage, Waste Management industries. In addition, majority of the firms sampled (40%) have been operating for a decade or less while 83 (22%) firms' years of operation ranged between 11 and 20 years and 50 (13%) firms' years of operation ranged between 21 and 30 years. While 39 (11%) firms' years of operation ranged between 21 and 40 years, 53 (14%) firms have been in operation for more than four decades. In addition, the selected firms have different forms of ownership structure, 169 (45%) firms are owned by individual owners (sole proprietors), 70 (19%) firms are owned by two or more people called partners (partnership). A total of 82 (22%) firms among the selected firms are Private Limited Liability Companies, but 19 (5%) firms are cooperative companies. As 20 (5%) firms are faith-based organisations, the remaining 12 (3%) firms are franchise-based business.

Concerning the number of employees in the respondents' firms, 348 (94%) firms have 100 employees or less. While 16 (4%) firms have between 101 and 150 employees, the remaining 8 (2%) firms have between 151 and 200 employees. Moreover, the total annual operating expenses accounted for by labor costs in 183 (49%) respondents' firms are 25% or less, while that of 129 (35%) firms ranged between 26% and 50%. While 52 (14%) firms' total annual operating expenses accounted for by labor costs ranged between 51% and 75%, only 8 (2%) firms have the total annual operating expenses accounted for by labor costs of more than 75%.

Overall, the respondents of this study varied substantially in terms of their backgrounds, and this implies that the data used in the study were from the respondents of diverse demographic backgrounds, and thus enriching generalisability of the result of the research.

As illustrated in Table 2, all variables possessed the mean scores ranging from 3.71 to 6.76, and the standard deviation of all dimensions ranged from 0.72 to 1.06. These values of overall mean and standard deviation for all the variables and their dimensions are quite acceptable. Hence, it can be proven that the responses of the respondents clearly indicate an acceptable and satisfactory level of implementation with regard to the constructs: selective hiring, non-financial reward, pay-for-performance, performance appraisal, training & development, employee creativity and non-financial performance.

Table 2. Descriptive statistics for latent variables.

Latent constructs	No. of Items	Mean	St. Deviation
Selective hiring	4	5.94	0.965
Non-financial reward	2	5.51	1.056
Pay-for-performance	2	6.76	0.724
Performance appraisal	3	5.62	0.984
Training & development	5	5.33	0.831
Employee creativity	7	4.69	0.793
Non-financial performance	6	3.71	0.800

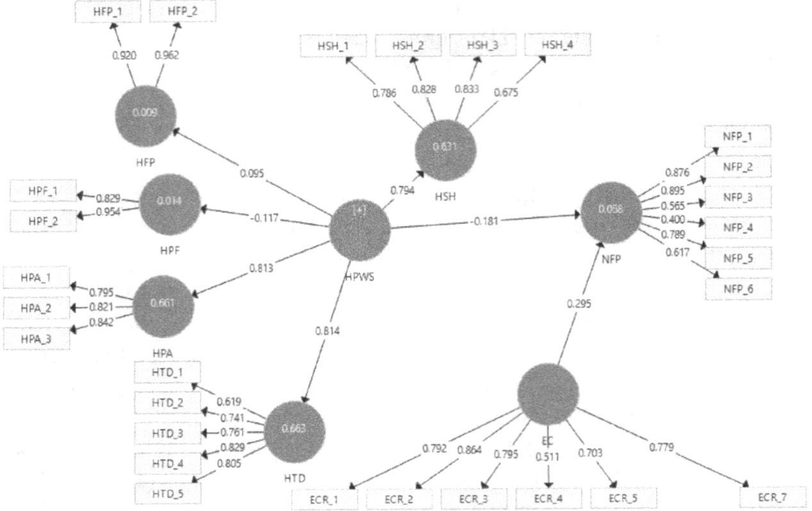

Fig. 2. Measurement model.

a. Measurement Model Evaluation

In this section, internal consistency reliability, convergent validity and reliability and discriminant validity were vetted to satisfy the conditions required for constructs' reliability and validity (Hair *et al.*, 2011, 2014). Figure 2, Tables 1 and 2 below show the outputs from the measurement model evaluation:

Drawn upon Fig. 2 and Table 3, it is crystal clear that each item of the constructs has higher value on their respective constructs, and thus affirming the content validity of the constructs, except that one item from employee creativity, which fell below the threshold of 0.4 (Stevens, 1992), was deleted. Also, the constructs of the study have high levels of internal consistency reliability, as the composite reliability and Cronbach's alpha values of all the constructs are well above the threshold values of 0.7 and 0.6, respectively. The Average Variance Extracted (AVE) values of the reflective scales exceed the minimum requirements of 0.5 (Hair *et al.*, 2011).

As for discriminant validity assessment, the rotrait-monotrait ratio (HTMT) of the correlations was adopted. HTMT is the ratio of the between-trait correlations to the within-trait correlations (Hair *et al.*, 2017). The result in Table 4 confirms the discriminant validity of this study's constructs, as the HTMT values for all pairs of constructs in the matrixes fell below the threshold value of 0.90. In addition to evaluation of the HTMT ratios, the HTMT values were tested via bootstrapping method (see Table 5) and found that they are significantly different

Table 3. Internal consistency and convergent validity.

Constructs	Items	Loadings	CA	CR	AVE
Employee creativity	ECR_1	0.792	0.859	0.882	0.561
	ECR_2	0.864			
	ECR_3	0.795			
	ECR_4	0.511			
	ECR_5	0.703			
	ECR_7	0.779			
Non-financial rewards	HFP_1	0.920	0.875	0.939	0.886
	HFP_2	0.962			
Performance appraisal	HPA_1	0.795	0.755	0.860	0.671
	HPA_2	0.821			
	HPA_3	0.842			
Pay-for-performance	HPF_1	0.829	0.768	0.888	0.799
	HPF_2	0.954			
Selective hiring	HSH_1	0.786	0.787	0.863	0.613
	HSH_2	0.828			
	HSH_3	0.833			
	HSH_4	0.675			
Training and development	HTD_1	0.619	0.814	0.868	0.569
	HTD_2	0.741			
	HTD_3	0.761			
	HTD_4	0.829			
	HTD_5	0.805			
	NFP_1	0.876	0.874	0.853	0.508
	NFP_2	0.895			
	NFP_3	0.565			
	NFP_4	0.400			
	NFP_5	0.789			
	NFP_6	0.617			

Note: AVE: Average Variance Extracted; CR: Composite Reliability; CA: Cronbach Alpha.

from 1, indicating that the constructs of the study have discriminant validity (Henseler *et al.*, 2015).

Overall, having confirmed the content validity, convergent validity and discriminant validity of the constructs of this research, it can then be claimed that the constructs' validity has been established in this study.

b. Structural Model Evaluation

Figure 3 and Table 6 provide the result of the structural model evaluation and mediating effect testing. *R* square value is 0.058 (see Fig. 2), indicating that

Table 4. Discriminant validity (HTMT criterion).

Constructs	EC	HFP	HPA	HPF	HSH	HTD	NFP
EC							
HFP	0.089						
HPA	0.725	0.129					
HPF	0.179	0.062	0.217				
HSH	0.594	0.175	0.751	0.150			
HTD	0.539	0.294	0.705	0.140	0.518		
NFP	0.142	0.073	0.149	0.208	0.181	0.138	

Note: HSH: Selective Hiring; HFP: Non-Financial Reward; HPF: Pay-for-Performance; HPA: Performance Appraisal; HTD: Training and Development; EC: Employee Creativity; NFP: Non-Financial Performance.

Table 5. Confidence intervals.

Relationships	BETA	STDEV	*P* Values	5.0%	95.0%
HPWS -> EC_	0.668	0.046	0.000	0.590	0.739
NFP -> EC_	0.190	0.043	0.000	0.122	0.258
NFP -> HPWS	0.103	0.032	0.001	0.057	0.116

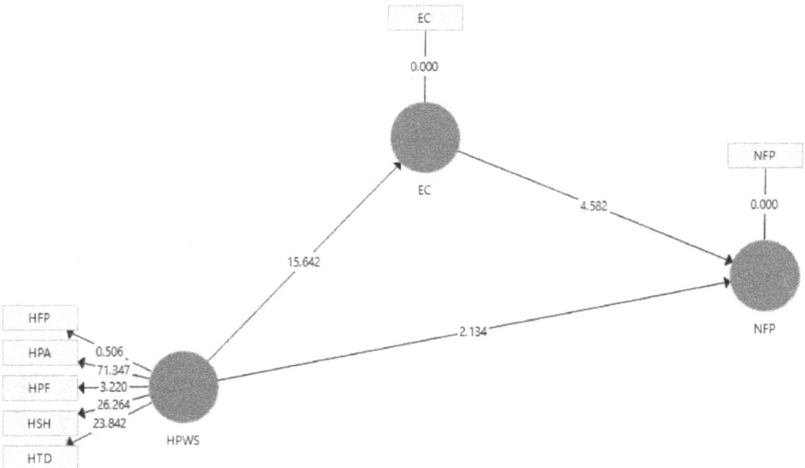

Fig. 3. Structural model.

Table 6. Hypotheses testing.

Hypotheses	Beta	STD	T Stat	*P* Values	5.0%	95.0%	Decision
Direct Path							
EC_ -> NFP	0.270	0.059	4.582	0.000	0.172	0.362	Supported
HPWS -> EC_	0.606	0.039	15.642	0.000	0.548	0.673	Supported
HPWS -> NFP	−0.132	0.062	2.134	0.017	−0.226	−0.034	Not supported
Mediation Effect							
HPWS -> EC_ -> NFP	0.164	0.037	4.472	0.000	0.104	0.223	Competitive mediation

exogenous latent variables (i.e., HPWS and employee creativity) explain 10% of the variance in the endogenous latent variable which is considered to be minimum acceptable level (Falk and Miller, 1992). With regard to testing of the hypotheses, the direct path regarding relationship between HPWS and non-financial performance (HPWS -> NFP) is significant but negative ($\beta = -0.132$, $t = 2.134$, $p < 0.05$). With this result, hypothesis 1 is not supported. However, the direct paths regarding HPWS-employee creativity nexus and employee creativity-performance nexus are significant and positive ($\beta = 0.606$, $t = 15.642$, $p < 0.001$; $\beta = 0.270$, $t = 4.582$, $p < 0.001$) respectively. The indirect effect (HPWS -> EC -> NFP [$\beta = 0.164, t = 4.472, p < 0.001$]) is significant, and the 95% confidence intervals do not include zero. Thus, it can be asserted that employee creativity competitively/partially mediates the relationship between HPWS and non-financial performance. Hence, hypotheses 2 is supported.

In this mediation model, employee creativity represents an appropriate mechanism to explain the relationship between HPWS and non-financial performance. Hence, the positive indirect effect via the mediator variable (employee creativity) reveals the 'true' relationship between HPWS and non-financial performance (Hair *et al.*, 2017), because an estimated cause–effect relationship between HPWS and non-financial performance may not be the 'true' effect, if employee creativity (i.e., mediating variable or suppressor variable) is not accounted for in this research model. Overall, this result implies that HPWS may not necessarily enhance non-financial performance. Ill-configured HPWS could jeopardize non-financial performance, but HPWS that stimulates employee creativity would enhance non-financial performance.

In furtherance of the inferential analysis, the effect size of the exogenous constructs on the endogenous construct, firm performance was examined. The result indicates that firm performance is explained by both HPWS and employee creativity with effect size (f2) of 0.02 (Cohen, 1988; Hair *et al.*, 2016), indicating that HPWS and employee creativity have small effect on non-financial performance.

Discussion

Although the existing literature (see Ogunyomi and Bruning, 2016; Shin and Konrad, 2014), the findings of this study reveal further that the positive effect of HPWS on performance depends on employee creativity which serves as a mechanism that unpacks the vague process between HPWS and firm performance. Moreover, in the strategic HRM literature, it is held that the creativity-inducing HPWS is crucial to organisational effectiveness and performance. Drawing upon RBV, the result of this research indicates that the way in which human resources are managed forms a potential source of sustainable competitive advantage for the firms (Guest, 2011).

The mediating role of employee creativity in HPWS-performance link is consistent with many studies such as Chang *et al.* (2014); Martinaityte (2014); Kehoe and Wright (2013); Messersmith *et al.* (2011). This result indicates that employee-oriented bundles of HR architectures, which enhance employees' KSAs and employees' empowerment via discretionary use of time and talent and employees' motivation, will drive employee creativity by getting employees out of their comfort's zone and make them explore new way or method of doing things with no fear of failure. HPWS can stimulate employees to wield the desired behaviour that is compatible with the organisational strategy.

Moreover, this result complements the componential theory of creativity which postulates that HPWS, which is a macro-level system, can induce a creative situation that will lead to meso-level individual creativity bordering on task motivation, domain-relevant skills and creativity-relevant skills (Amabile, 1983). For example, training can broaden employees' repertoire of domain-relevant knowledge and skills required for being creative (Amabile, 1983). Recurrent performance appraisal for various HR management purposes (Murphy and Cleveland, 1995; Rynes *et al.*, 2005) and associated feedback which has a developmental purpose delivered in an informational manner would improve employee creativity, given the fact that such kind of appraisal avails the employees of areas of improvements in terms of their domain-relevant skills (Shalley and Perry-Smith, 2001; Zhou and Oldham, 2001). Generally, the findings of this research corroborate some of the existing literature such as Ismail *et al.* (2018), Ismail *et al.* (2015); Mansour *et al.* (2014) and Werner (2011). For instance, Ismail *et al.* (2015) study signifies that employee creativity play a mediating role in the relationship between HPWS and performance. This indicates that HPWS enhances performance. Yet, HPWS is not enough to stimulate high performance until it induces employee creativity which will in turn precipitate higher firm performance.

In summary, this study contributes to the present body of knowledge on HPWS-performance link. The findings of the study can be a useful guide for the stakeholders and policy makers in Nigeria on how they can boost the performances of organisations, which will in turn facilitate Nigeria to become one of the top 20 economies in the world by 2020. Nevertheless, given that the data used for this study were collected from Nigerian firms' managers, future research should replicate the research in another context to improve generalisability of the study's findings. Also, data were collected from the organisations' managers and thus indicating organisational unit of analysis but investigating employees' perspective regarding HPWS and firm performance would constitute a viable research direction for the future studies. The reason is that examining employee' perspectives on HPWS-performance nexus would expand the understanding and enrich the body of knowledge in the research field.

Conclusion

This study offers a unique theoretical model and empirical analysis that unearth the 'black box' in the HPWS-Performance nexus. The result proves that employee creativity mediates the relationship between HPWS and non-financial performance, and thus employee creativity represents an appropriate mechanism that explains the relationship between HPWS and non-financial performance. As explicated earlier, the positive indirect effect via the mediator variable (employee creativity) reveals the 'true' relationship between HPWS and non-financial performance (Hair *et al.*, 2017), and an estimated cause–effect relationship between HPWS and non-financial performance may not be the 'true' effect, if employee creativity (i.e., mediating variable or suppressor variable) is not accounted for in this research model. Overall, this result implies that HPWS may not necessarily enhance non-financial performance. Configured HPWS could jeopardize non-financial performance, but HPWS that stimulates employee creativity would enhance non-financial performance.

Appendix A. Demographic Variable

Please tick the option that best describes you and your firm

(1) Which of the following best describes your position in the company? [ ] Executive Director; [ ] HR Manager; [ ] Marketing Manager; [ ] Others (specify):____________________.
(2) Kindly tick the industry to which your firm belongs? [ ] Agriculture; [ ] Food products & Beverages; [ ] Business Services; [ ] Construction & Building

A. I. Ismail et al.

Materials; [ ] Logistics & Packaging; [ ] Oil, Energy, Solar, Greentech; [ ] Computer Software Engineering; [ ] Financial Services; [ ] Manufacturing; [ ] Information Technology, Services, IT, Telecommunications, Wireless & Mobile; [ ] Mechanical & Industrial Engineering; [ ] Medical Practice & Equipment; [ ] Other (Please specify):____________________.

(3) How long has your firm been in operation in Nigeria? [ ] years.

(4) Which of the following describes the type of your company ownership? [ ] Sole proprietorship; [ ] Partnership; [ ] Private Limited Liability Company; [ ] Cooperative; [ ] Faith-Based Organization; [ ] others (specify): ________________.

(5) What is the total number of employees in your company? [ ] 10–100 employees [ ] 101–150 employees [ ] 151–200 employees.

(6) Which category best approximates the percentage of your total annual operating expenses accounted for by labor costs in your firm? (Please circle one category). (a) 5%–25% (b) 26–50% (c) 51–75% (d) >75%.

Please tick one option that best describes HR practices your firm
Options: 1 = Strongly Disagree; 2 = Disagree; 3 = Neutral; 4 = Agree; 5 = Strongly Agree

S/N	Statement	1	2	3	4	5
	Selective Hiring					
1.	Our firm's recruitment emphasises traits and abilities required for creativity.					
2.	Our firm's recruitment emphasises job-specific traits and abilities.					
3.	Our firm gives preference to candidates' potential to learn and develop new skills.					
4.	Our firm selects the best all-around candidates					
	Non-Financial Rewards and Pay-For-Performance					
5.	In our firm, employees are rewarded with non-monetary reward for creative ideas.					
6.	In our firm, employees are rewarded with public recognition for creative ideas.					
7.	In our firm, employees are rewarded partially based on individual merit or performance.					
8.	In our firm, pay for performance is adopted in order to attract and retain employees.					
	Performance Appraisal					
9.	In our firm, employees receive developmental performance appraisal.					
10.	In our firm, performance appraisal is very much focused on the accomplishment of results.					
11.	In our firm, employees receive developmental feedback for their creative ideas.					

Unpacking 'Black Box' in The SHRM Research Field

(Continued)

S/N	Statement	1	2	3	4	5
	Training and Development					
12.	In our firm, employees do receive training on general skills that are not necessarily related directly to their jobs.					
13.	In our firm, employees are trained on a variety of job skills.					
14.	In our firm, employees receive training on problem solving techniques.					
15.	In our firm, employees receive training on creativity.					
16.	During the induction, creative approach to problem-solving is emphasised in our firm.					

Please tick one option that best describes HR practices your firm Options: 1 = Strongly Disagree; 2 = Disagree; 3 = Neutral; 4 = Agree; 5 = Strongly Agree

S/N	Statement	1	2	3	4	5
	Employee Creativity					
1.	Workers in our firm accomplish their works in innovative ways.					
2.	Workers in our firm accomplish their tasks in ways that are resourceful.					
3.	Workers in our firm do come up with new ideas in their work.					
4.	Workers in our firm do generate and evaluate multiple alternatives for novel work-related problems.					
5.	Workers in our firm have fresh perspectives on old problems.					
6.	Workers in our firm do improvise methods for solving a problem when solution is not available yet.					
7.	Workers in our firm do generate creative work-related ideas.					

This section is about the performance of your company. Please circle the most appropriate number for each statement. Relative to the industry average, how do you rate your company's current performance in the following areas?

Options: 1 = Very Weak; 2 = Weak; 3 = Not Sure; 4 = Strong; 5 = Very Strong

S/N	Statement	1	2	3	4	5
	Financial Performance					
1.	In terms of profitability.					
2.	In terms of financial strength.					
3.	In terms of operating efficiency.					
4.	In terms of performance stability.					
5.	In terms of ability to raise capital.					
6.	In terms of level of indebtedness.					
	Non-Financial Performance					
7.	In terms of public image and goodwill.					
8.	In terms of employees' morale.					
9.	In terms of adaptability.					
10.	In terms of innovativeness.					
11.	In terms of customers patronage.					
12.	In terms of growth rate of number of employees.					

References

Allen, MR and PM Wright (2007). Strategic management and HRM. In *The Oxford Handbook of Human Resource Management*, PF Boxall, J Purcell and PM Wright (eds.), pp. 88–107. Oxford, UK: Oxford University Press.

Alreck, PL and RB Settle (1995). *The Survey Research Handbook*, 2nd Ed. Boston: Irwin.

Amabile, TM (1983). Social psychology of creativity: A componential conceptualization. *Journal of Personality and Social Psychology*, 45(2), 997–1013.

Amabile, TM (1988). A model of creativity and innovation in organizations. *Research in Organizational Behavior*, 10(1), 123–167.

Amabile, TM (1996). *Creativity in context: Update to the Social Psychology of Creativity*. Hachette UK: Westview Press.

Amabile, TM, R Conti, H Coon, J Lazenby and M Herron (1996). Assessing the work environment for creativity. *Academy of Management Journal*, 39(5), 1154–1184.

Appelbaum, E, T Bailey, PB Berg, AL Kalleberg and TA Bailey (2000). *Manufacturing advantage: Why High-Performance Work Systems Pay Off*. Cornell University Press.

Armstrong, M (1993). *Managing Reward Systems*. Buckingham: Open University Press.

Armstrong, M (2005). *A Handbook of Human Resource Management Practice*, 5th Ed. Ohio: Kogan Page.

Arthur, JB (1994). Effects of human resource systems on manufacturing performance and turnover. *Academy of Management Journal*, 37(3), 670–687.

Baer, M (2010). The strength-of-weak-ties perspective on creativity: A comprehensive examination and extension. *Journal of Applied Psychology*, 95(3), 592.

Baer, M (2012). Putting creativity to work: The implementation of creative ideas in organizations. *Academy Management Journal*, 55(5), 1102–1119.

Bamberger, P and I Meshoulam (2000). *Advanced Topics in Organizational Behavior: Human Resource Strategy: Formulation, Implementation, and Impact*. Thousand Oaks, CA: SAGE Publications, doi: http://dx.doi.org/10.4135/9781452204680.

Barney, J (1997). *Gaining and Sustaining Competitive Advantage*. New York: Addison Wesley.

Baron, RM and DA Kenny (1986). The moderator–mediator variable distinction in social psychological research: Conceptual, strategic, and statistical considerations. *Journal of Personality and Social Psychology*, 51(6), 1173–1182.

Behrends, T (2007). Recruitment practices in small and medium size enterprises: An empirical study among knowledge-intensive professional service firms. *Management Revue*, 18(1), 55–74.

Binyamin, G and A Carmeli (2010). Does structuring of human resource management processes enhance employee creativity? The mediating role of psychological availability. *Human Resource Management*, 49(6), 999–1024.

Boachie-Mensah, F and OD Dogbe (2011). Performance-based pay as a motivational tool for achieving organizational performance: An exploratory case study. *International Journal of Business and Management*, 6(12), 270–285.

Boxall, P and J Purcell (2003). *Strategy and Human Resource Management*. New York: Palgrave MacMillan.

Boxall, P and K Macky (2009). Research and theory on high-performance work systems: Progressing the high-involvement stream. *Human Resource Management Journal*, 19(1), 3–23.

Boxall, P (2012). High-performance work systems: What, why, how and for whom? *Asia Pacific Journal of Human Resources*, 50(2), 169–186.

Byron, K and S Khananchi (2012). Rewards and creative performance: A meta-analytic test of theoretically derived hypotheses. *Psychological Bulletin*, 138, 809–830.

Chadwick, C and A Dabu (2009). Human resources, human resource management, and the competitive advantage of firms: Toward a more comprehensive model of causal linkages. *Organization Science*, 20(1), 253–272.

Chang, S, L Jia, R Takeuchi and Y Cai (2014). Do high-commitment work systems affect creativity? A multilevel combinational approach to employee creativity. *Journal of Applied Psychology*, 99(4), 665.

Chen, G, JL Farh, EM Campbell-Bush, Z Wu and X Wu (2013). Teams as innovative systems: Multilevel motivational antecedents of innovation in R&D teams. *Journal of Applied Psychology*, 98(6), 1018–1027.

Chiang, Y-H, C-C Hsu and HA Shih (2015). Experienced high-performance work system, extroversion personality, and creativity performance. *Asia Pacific Journal of Management*, 32(2), 531–549.

Chin, WW (1998). The partial least squares approach to structural equation modeling. *Modern Methods for Business Research*, 295(2), 295–336.

Choi, JN (2004). Individual and contextual predictors of creative performance: The mediating role of psychological processes. *Creativity Research Journal*, 16(2–3), 187–199.

Choi, JH (2014a). The HR-performance link using two differently measured HR practices. *Asia Pacific Journal of Human Resources*, 52(3), 370–387.

Choi, JH (2014b). Who should be the respondent? Comparing predictive powers between managers' and employees' responses in measuring high-performance work systems practices. *The International Journal of Human Resource Management*, 25(19), 2667–2680.

Choi, JH and KP Lee (2013). Effects of employees' perceptions on the relationship between HR practices and firm performance for Korean firms. *Personnel Review*, 42(5).

Chuang, CH and HUI Liao (2010). Strategic human resource management in service context: Taking care of business by taking care of employees and customers. *Personnel Psychology*, 63(1), 153–196.

Coelho, F, M Augusto and LF Lages (2011). Contextual factors and the creativity of frontline employees: The mediating effects of role stress and intrinsic motivation. *Journal of Retailing*, 87(1), 31–45.

Cohen, J (1988). *Statistical Power Analysis for the Behavioral Sciences*, 2nd Ed. Hillsdale, NJ: Lawrence Erlbaum.

Datta, DK, JP Guthrie and PM Wright (2005). Human resource management and labor productivity: Does industry matter? *Academy of Management Journal*, 48(1), 135–145.

Delaney, JT and MA Huselid (1996). The impact of human resource management practices on perceptions of organizational performance. *Academy of Management Journal*, 39(4), 949–969.

Demirbag, M, DG Collings, E Tatoglu, K Mellahi and G Wood (2014). High performance work systems and organizational performance in emerging economies: Evidence from MNEs in Turkey. *Management International Review*, 54(3), 325–359.

DeNisi, AS and RD Pritchard (2006). Performance appraisal, performance management and improving individual performance: A motivational framework. *Management and Organization Review*, 2(2), 253–277.

Falk, RF and NB Miller (1992). *A Primer for Soft Modeling*. University of Akron Press.

Fan, D, L Cui, MM Zhang, CJ Zhu, CE Härtel and C Nyland (2014). Influence of high performance work systems on employee subjective well-being and job burnout: Empirical evidence from the Chinese healthcare sector. *The International Journal of Human Resource Management*, 25(7), 931–950.

Fiorito, J, DP Bozeman, A Young and JA Meurs (2007). Organizational commitment, human resource practices, and organizational characteristics. *Journal of Managerial Issues*, 19, 186–207.

Florida, R (2002). *The Rise of the Creative Class*. New York, USA: Basic Books.

Fu, N (2013). Exploring the impact of high performance work systems in professional service firms: A practices-resources-uses performance approach. *Consulting Psychology Journal: Practice and Research*, 65(3), 240–257.

Gephart, MA and ME Van Buren (1996). Building synergy: The power of high-performance work systems. *Training & Development*, 50(10), 21–9.

Gilson, LL (2008). Why be creative: A review of the practical outcomes associated with creativity at the individual, group, and organizational levels. In *Handbook of organizational creativity*, JZACE Shalley (ed.), pp. 303–322. NY: Laurence Erlbaum.

Gong, Y, KS Law, S Chang and KR Xin (2009). Human resource management and firm performance: The differential role of managerial affective and continuance commitment. *Journal of Applied Psychology*, 94, 263–275.

Gong, Y, J Zhou and S Chang (2013). Core knowledge employee creativity and firm performance: The moderating role of riskiness orientation, firm size, and realized absorptive capacity. *Personnel Psychology*, 66, 443–482.

Grobler, P, S Warnich, MR Carell, NF Elbert and RD Hatfield (2006). *Human Resource Management in South Africa*. South Africa: Cengage Learning EMEA.

Gronum, S, ML Verreynne and T Kastelle (2012). The role of networks in small and medium-sized enterprise innovation and firm performance. *Journal of Small Business Management*, 50(2), 257–282.

Guest, D (1997). Human resource management and performance: A review and research agenda. *International Journal of Human Resource Management*, 8(3), 263–276.

Guest, DE (1987). Human resource management and industrial relations. *Journal of Management Studies*, 24(5), 503–521.

Guest, DE (2011). Human resource management and performance: Still searching for some answers. *Human Resource Management Journal*, 21(1), 3–13.

Hair Jr. JF, GTM Hult, C Ringle and M Sarstedt (2016). *A Primer on Partial Least Squares Structural Equation Modeling (PLS-SEM)*. Sage publications.

Hair, JF, GTM Hult, CM Ringle and M Sarstedt (2014). *A Primer on Partial Least Squares Structural Equation Modeling*. Thousand Oaks: Sage.

Hair, JF, GTM Hult, C Ringle and M Sarstedt (2017). *A Primer on Partial Least Squares Structural Equation Modeling (PLS-SEM)*. Sage Publications.

Hair, JF, CM Ringle and M Sarstedt (2011). PLS-SEM: Indeed, a silver bullet. *Journal of Marketing Theory and Practice*, 19(2), 139–152.

Hair, JF, M Sarstedt, CM Ringle and JA Mena (2012). An assessment of the use of partial least squares structural equation modeling in marketing research. *Journal of the Academy of Marketing Science*, 40(3), 414–433.

He, C, J Gu and H Liu (2018). How do department high-performance work systems affect creative performance? A cross-level approach. *Asia Pacific Journal of Human Resources*, 56(3), 402–426.

Hennessey, BA and TM Amabile (2010). *Creativity. Annual Review of Psychology*, 61, 569–598.

Henseler, J, CM Ringle and M Sarstedt (2015). A new criterion for assessing discriminant validity in variance-based structural equation modeling. *Journal of the Academy of Marketing Science*, 43, 115–135.

Hilman, HA (2009). The relationship of competitive strategy, strategic flexibility and sourcing strategy on organizational performances. Unpublished Doctoral dissertation.

Ho, LA (2008). What affects organizational performance? The linking of learning and knowledge management. *Industrial Management & Data Systems*, 108(9), 1234–1254.

Ichniowski, C, K Shaw and G Prennushi (1997). The effects of human resource management practices on productivity: A study of steel finishing lines. *The American Economic Review*, 87(3), 291–313.

Ismail, AI, A Abdul-Halim and M Joarder (2016). High performance work system-SMEs performance Nexus: A conceptual model. *International Journal of Entrepreneurship and Small & Medium Enterprise (IJESME)*, 115–130.

Ismail, A, SE Abdelrahman and A-HA Majid (2018). Closing strategic human resource management research lacunas with mediating role of employee creativity. *Academy of Strategic Management Journal.*

Ismail, A, A-H Abdul-Majid and MHR Joarder (2017). Management philosophy: An internal boundary condition to HPWS-SME performance nexus in Nigeria. *Academy of Strategic Management Journal.*

Ismail, AI (2014). *The mediating role of distributive fairness in the relationship between performance-based pay, career incentives, organizational benefits and employee performance*. Unpublished Master thesis, Universiti Utara Malaysia.

Ismail, AI, AM Abdul-Halim and MHR Joarder (2015). Mediating role of distributive justice in the relationship between career incentives and employee performance. *Journal of Economics, Business and Management*, 3(10), 929–935.

Ittner, CD and DF Larcker (1996). Measuring the impact of quality initiatives on firm financial performance. *Advances in the Management of Organizational Quality*, 1(1), 1–37.

Jeffrey, S (2003). *Non-Monetary Rewards: Employees' Choices and Organizational Practices*. Retrieved on the April, 11th 2015 from: http://www.maritzrewards.com/pdfs/sitebenefits.

Jiang, J, S Wang and S Zhao (2012). Does HRM facilitate employee creativity and organizational innovation? A study of Chinese firms. *The International Journal of Human Resource Management*, 23(19), 4025–4047.

Kaplan, RS and DP Norton (1992). The balanced scorecard: Measures that drive performance. *Harvard Business Review*, 70(1), 71–79.

Kaplan, RS and DP Norton (1996). *The Balanced Scorecard: Translating Strategy into Action*. Harvard Business Press.

Kaplan, RS and DP Norton (2000). *The Strategy Focused Organization: How Balanced Scorecard Companies Thrive in the New Business Environment*. Boston, MA: Harvard Business School Press.

Kaufman, BE (2010). SHRM theory in the post-Huselid era: Why it is fundamentally misspecified. Industrial Relations. *A Journal of Economy and Society*, 49(2), 286–313.

Kehoe, RR and PM Wright (2013). The impact of high-performance human resource practices on employees' attitudes and behaviors. *Journal of Management*, 39(2), 366–391.

Kinicki, AJ, KJ Jacobson, SJ Peterson and GE Prussia (2013). Development and validation of the performance management behavior questionnaire. *Personnel Psychology*, 66(1), 1–45.

Krejcie, RV and DW Morgan (1970). Determining sample size for research activities. *Educational and Psychological Measurement*, 30(3), 607–610.

Legge, K (1995). *Human Resource Management-Rhetorics and Realities*. Basingstoke: MacMillan Press.

MacDoughall, SL and RH Pike (2003). Consider your options: Changes to strategic value during implementation of advanced manufacturing technology. *Omega*, 31(1), 115.

Madjar, N, GR Oldham and MG Pratt (2002). There's no place like home? The contributions of work and non- work creativity support to employees' creative performance. *Academy of Management Journal*, 45(4), 757–767.

Mansour, N, E Gara and C Gaha (2014). Getting inside the black box. *Personnel Review*, 43(4), 490–514.

Martinaityte, I (2014). *Leveraging Employee Creativity Through High Performance Work Systems: A Multilevel Perspective*. Doctoral Dissertation, Aston University.

Martinaityte, I and CA Sacramento (2013). When creativity enhances sales effectiveness: The moderating role of leader–member exchange. *Journal of Organizational Behavior*, 34(7), 974–994.

Maskell, B (1992). *Performance Measurement for World Class Manufacturing*. Corporate Controller, January/February 44–8.

Matsumura, EM and JY Shin (2004). An empirical analysis of a relative performance-based incentive plan: Evidence from a postal service.

Messersmith, JG and JP Guthrie (2010). High performance work systems in emergent organizations: Implications for firm performance. *Human Resource Management*, 49(2), 241–264.

Messersmith, JG, PC Patel, DP Lepak and JS Gould-Williams (2011). Unlocking the black box: Exploring the link between high-performance work systems and performance. *Journal of Applied Psychology*, 96(6), 1105.

Michie, J and M Sheehan (2005). Business strategy, human resources, labour market flexibility and competitive advantage. *The International Journal of Human Resource Management*, 16(3), 445–464.

Mihail, DM and PV Kloutsiniotis (2016). Modeling patient care quality: An empirical high-performance work system approach. *Personnel Review*, 45(6), 1176–1199.

Miller, CC, NT Washburn and WH Glick (2013). Perspective — The myth of firm performance. *Organization Science*, 24(3), 948–964.

Moulang, C (2015). Performance measurement system use in generating psychological empowerment and individual creativity. *Accounting & Finance*, 55(2), 519–544.

Muduli, A, S Verma and SK Datta (2016). High performance work system in India: Examining the role of employee engagement. *Journal of Asia-Pacific Business*, 17(2), 130–150.

Murphy, KR and J Cleveland (1995). *Understanding Performance Appraisal: Social, Organizational, and Goal-based Perspectives*. Sage Publications.

Mushrush, W (2002). Reducing employee turnover. Missouri small business development and technology center.

Neckermann, S and M Kosfeld (2008). *Working for Nothing*? The effect of non-material awards on employee performance, Goethe-University Frankfurt, Germany.

Neely, A (2002). *Business Performance Measurement: Theory and Practice*. Cambridge: Cambridge University Press.

Neely, AD, C Adams and M Kennerley (2002). *The Performance Prism: The Scorecard for Measuring and Managing Business Success*. London: Financial Times/Prentice Hall.

Ogunyomi, P and NS Bruning (2016a). Human resource management and organizational performance of small and medium enterprises (SMEs) in Nigeria. *The International Journal of Human Resource Management*, 27(6), 612–634.

Ogunyomi, P and NS Bruning (2016b). Human resource management and organizational performance of small and medium enterprises (SMEs) in Nigeria. *The International Journal of Human Resource Management*, 27(6), 612–634.

Ojokuku, RM (2012). Human resources management demands and challenges in small and medium scale enterprises. *International Journal of Economic Development Research and Investment*, 3(3), 1–10.

Paauwe, J and R Richardson (1997). Strategic human resource management and performance: Introduction. *International Journal of Human Resource Management*, 8(3), 257–262.

Peloza, J and L Papania (2008). The missing link between corporate social responsibility and financial performance: Stakeholder salience and identification. *Corporate Reputation Review*, 11(2), 169–181.

Pfeffer, J (1998). *The Human Equation: Building Profits by Putting People First*. Boston, MA: Harvard Business School Press.

Posthuma, RA, MC Campion, M Masimova and MA Campion (2013). A high-performance work practices taxonomy: Integrating the literature and directing future research. *Journal of Management*, 39(5), 1184–1220.

Pritchard, RD, H Holling, F Lammers and BD Clark (2002). *Improving Organizational Performance with the Productivity Measurement and Enhancement System: An International Collaboration*. Huntington, NY: Nova Science.

Runco, MA (2004). Creativity. *Annual Review of Psychology*, 55, 657–687.

Ryan, RM and EL Deci (2000). Self-determination theory and the facilitation of intrinsic motivation, social development, and well-being. *American psychologist*, 55(1), 68.

Rynes, SL, B Gerhart and L Parks (2005). Personnel psychology: Performance evaluation and pay for performance. *Annual Review of Psychology*, 56, 571–600.

Salkind, NJ (1997). *Exploring Research*, 3rd edn. New Jersey, Upper Saddle River: Prentice Hall.

Seidu, Y (2011). *Human Resource Management and Organizational Performance: Evidence from the Retail Banking Sector*. Unpublished Doctoral dissertation, Aston University.

Sekaran, U (2003). *Research Methods for Business: A Skill Building Approach*, 4th Ed. New York: John Wiley & Sons.

Shalley, CE and LL Gilson (2004). What leaders need to know: A review of social and contextual factors that can foster or hinder creativity. *The Leadership Quarterly*, 15(1), 33–53.

Shalley, CE and JE Perry-Smith (2001). Effects of social-psychological factors on creative performance: The role of informational and controlling expected evaluation and modeling experience. *Organizational Behavior and Human Decision Processes*, 84(1), 1–22.

Shields, J (2007). *Managing Employee Performance and Reward: Concepts, Practices, Strategies*. Cambridge: Cambridge University Press.

Shin, D and AM Konrad (2014). Causality between high-performance work systems and organizational performance. *Journal of Management*, 43(4), 973–997.

Shin, D and AM Konrad (2017). Causality between high-performance work systems and organizational performance. *Journal of Management*, 43(4), 973–997.

Stevens, J (1992). *Applied Multivariate Statistics for the Social Sciences*, 2nd Ed. Hillsdale, NJ, US: Lawrence Erlbaum Associates.

Subramony, M (2009). A meta-analytic investigation of the relationship between HRM bundles and firm performance. *Human Resource Management*, 48(5), 745–768.

Takeuchi, R, DP Lepak, H Wang and K Takeuchi (2007). An empirical examination of the mechanisms mediating between high-performance work systems and the performance of Japanese organizations. *Journal of Applied Psychology*, 92(4), 1069–1083.

Taylor, S, O Levy, NA Boyacigiller and S Beechler (2008). Employee commitment in MNCs: Impacts of organizational culture, HRM and top management orientations. *The International Journal of Human Resource Management*, 19(4), 501–527.

Truss, C (2001). Complexities and controversies in linking HRM with organizational outcomes. *Journal of Management Studies*, 38(8), 1121–1149.

Ulrich, D (1997). *Human Resource Champions: The Next Agenda for Adding Value and Delivering Results*. Boston: Harvard Business School Press.

Van der Stede, WA (2001). Measuring 'tight budgetary control'. *Management Accounting Research*, 12(1), 119–137.

Vandenberg, RJ, HA Richardson and LJ Eastman (1999). The impact of high involvement work processes on organizational effectiveness. *Group & Organization Management*, 24(3), 300–339.

Wang, G and RG Netemeyer (2004). Salesperson creative performance: Conceptualization, measurement, and nomological validity. *Journal of Business Research*, 57(8), 805–812.

Werner, S (2011). High performance work systems in the global context: A commentary essay. *Journal of Business Research*, 64(8), 919–921, http://doi.org/10.1016/j.jbusres.2010.09.002.

Yen, H-Y (2015). National Central University.

Yuan, F and RW Woodman (2010). Innovative behavior in the workplace: The role of performance and image outcome expectations. *Academy of Management Journal*, 53(2), 323–342.

Zhang, Y and S Li (2009). High performance work practices and firm performance: Evidence from the pharmaceutical industry in China. *International Journal of Human Resource Management*, 20(11), 2331–2348.

Zhou J and CE Shalley (2008). Expanding the scope and impact of organizational creativity research. In *Handbook of Organizational Creativity*, J Zhou, CE Shalley (eds.), pp. 347–368. New York, NY: Erlbaum.

Zhou, J and GR Oldham (2001). Enhancing creative performance: Effects of expected developmental assessment strategies and creative personality. *The Journal of Creative Behavior*, 35(3), 151–167.

Zikmund, WG and BJ Babin (2010). *Essentials of Marketing Research*, 4th Ed. Mason, OH: South-Western, Cengage Learning.

Chapter 16

ABSORBING INTEGRATION: EMPIRICAL EVIDENCE ON THE MEDIATING ROLE OF ABSORPTIVE CAPACITY BETWEEN FUNCTIONAL-/CROSS-FUNCTIONAL INTEGRATION AND INNOVATION PERFORMANCE†

JOHANN PIET HAUSBERG*

Osnabrück University, School of Business Administration and Economics
Rolandstr. 8, 49078 Osnabrück, Germany
piet.hausberg@uni-osnabrueck.de

PETER S. H. LEEFLANG

University of Groningen
Faculty of Economics and Business
Nettelbosje 2 9747 AE Groningen, The Netherlands

Aston Business School
Aston Triangle, Birmingham, B4 7ET, UK
p.s.h.leeflang@rug.nl

Published 16 November 2018

Integration of organisational units has been extensively researched in various streams of management and organization sciences. It is very important whenever knowledge differences have to be overcome due to functional departmentalisation and the ensuing knowledge specialisation. However, extant literature does not yet appreciate the mediating role of absorptive capacity (AC) in this context. We argue that departments use integration mechanisms in order to develop and maintain such an organisational capability to absorb knowledge from other departments, so that integration can succeed to increase innovation performance. Our unique dataset of Italian manufacturing firms from various industries allows us to study this in the context of the integration of research and development (R&D) and marketing and sales (M&S) departments. Thereby, we provide empirical evidence on the mediating role of AC. We find evidence that R&D departments build AC via formal cross-functional integration, while M&S departments do so through informal integration. Moreover, we provide evidence of AC's mediating role for the relationship between cross-functional integration mechanisms and innovation performance. Our findings also reveal significant differences between R&D and M&S functions in terms of effect sizes and

*Corresponding author.

†This article originally appeared in *International Journal of Innovation Management*, **24** 1950056-1-37

significance levels. AC of R&D departments has a significant and substantial effect on innovation performance and thus effectively acts as a mediating variable, while in case of M&S departments we observe a significant direct effect between formal cross-functional integration and innovation performance without any mediation by AC.

Keywords: Innovation performance; cross-functional integration; Absorptive capacity; structural equation modeling.

Introduction

Specialisation offers a substantial efficiency advantage, but also creates silos of specialised knowledge (Lessard and Zaheer, 1996). In order to remain innovative, it is fundamental for firms to successfully integrate these departments without compromising the benefits of specialisation (Burns and Stalker, 1961; Galbraith, 1974; Iansiti and Clark, 1994; Lawrence and Lorsch, 1967; Lee and Kapoor, 2017). Integration is "the process of achieving unity of effort among the various subsystems [functional departments] in the accomplishment of the organization's tasks" (Lawrence and Lorsch, 1967, p. 4). However, knowledge specialisation can lead to conflicting or incompatible thought worlds (Dougherty, 1992), impede effective communication (Bechky, 2003), and raise several barriers for comprehension and cooperation (Carlile, 2004). Therefore, integration mechanisms have to either transcend or traverse these knowledge differences (Majchrzak *et al.*, 2012).

For the scope of our study, we differentiate between corporate functions and departments. Corporate functions are intra-firm systems that are differentiated relative to the requirements of the particular environment with which they deal (Lawrence and Lorsch, 1967). Examples for such corporate functions are research and development (R&D) and marketing and sales (M&S). Departments are subsystems within such functions (Clark and Wheelright, 1992). For example, the "lighting technology R&D" and the "driver assistance systems and automated driving R&D" departments of an automobile manufacturer both are departments belonging to the R&D function. Knowledge differences obviously exist between departments of different corporate functions. However, they also exist between departments of the *same* corporate function. In fact, many studies show that intra- and cross-functional integration increase innovation performance, i.e., the degree to which innovation objectives are met (Atuahene-Gima *et al.*, 2005; Foss *et al.*, 2011).

However, substantial divergence persists in findings regarding the relation between cross-functional integration and new product success, and, ultimately innovation performance (Rubera *et al.*, 2012; Troy *et al.*, 2008). Some argue that higher functional integration is always more beneficial for the firm (e.g., Song and Parry, 1997). Others, by contrast, suggest that the optimal degree of integration is not necessarily its maximum (e.g., Griffin and Hauser, 1996). Several studies have even found negative outcomes of cross-functional integration (Bommer *et al.*, 2002; Hansen, 2009; Hoegl *et al.*, 2004). This divergence might be explained by (a) the different processes or mechanisms used to operationalise integration, as well as (b) the different nature of the organisational units to be integrated.

Indeed, regarding (a), previous research studied several different integration mechanisms, including not only functional and cross-functional but also formal and informal ones (Griffin and Hauser, 1996; Leenders and Wierenga, 2002). Examples of *formal* mechanisms are job rotation, regular meetings, and cross-functional project teams. Examples of *informal* mechanisms are ad hoc lateral communication, bypassing official channels, or the maintenance of open communication channels in the day-to-day operations with other departments. As a result, previous research found different effects for different integration mechanisms. Moenaert *et al.* (1994) report a positive impact of formalisation on communication flows, while Maltz *et al.* (2001) could not find support for their hypothesis of a positive impact of informal integration in form of socialisation opportunities on the conceptual use of marketing information by R&D managers. Other studies are agnostic towards the actual processes and operationalise integration by the level of interaction (Lamore *et al.*, 2013; Li and Calantone, 1998).

Regarding (b), R&D and M&S are two types of corporate functions that seem to offer particularly high returns to integration. This is apparently due to their high complementarity. Griffin and Hauser (1996) state that their "responsibilities in the new product development are neither independent nor static; they cannot be analyzed separately" (p. 192). Consequently, a large number of studies focus on both R&D and M&S, many of which demonstrate that their integration has a positive effect on innovation performance (Galbraith, 1974; Griffin and Hauser, 1996; Gupta *et al.*, 1986; Jansen *et al.*, 2009; Lawrence and Lorsch, 1967; Ruekert and Walker, 1987). Similarly, findings from the literature on market orientation underline the crucial role that marketing plays in increasing performance (Jaworski and Kohli, 1993; Menon and Varadarajan, 1992; Verhoef and Leeflang, 2009). Just as earlier studies mostly focused on R&D-marketing integration, more recent ones likewise suggest that R&D-sales integration is highly relevant for new product development (Homburg *et al.*, 2017). Research also shows the importance of integration of complementary units with similar functions, but covering different product markets, such as in multiproduct firms (Lee and Kapoor, 2017). However, what has been neglected so far is the role of organisational capabilities, such as that the capability to absorb knowledge in case of potentially asymmetric task interdependencies between such complementary departments.

Hence, focusing on formal and informal integration mechanisms in R&D and M&S departments, we address both of these explanations for persistently divergent findings regarding the benefits of functional integration. We explain the effects of different integration mechanisms on innovation performance arguing that organisational units of different functional natures can use these mechanisms to different degrees to build capabilities required for integration. Given the fundamental importance of knowledge for innovation performance, we suggest that the capability to absorb knowledge from other units is particularly important for innovation performance.

Absorptive Capacity (AC) is a firm's ability to recognise the value of external knowledge, assimilate it, and exploit it to commercial ends (Cohen and Levinthal, 1990). We argue that this ability not only exists at a firm's external boundaries where such a capability can foster for example technology transfer (Bauer *et al.*, 2018). It also exists beyond the firm-level at lower organisational levels as well, such as the department-level. Without a sufficiently high degree of AC, the costs of coordination associated with integration can have negative effects on innovation performance that are not outweighed by its benefits, like overspending, project delay, and project termination (Cuijpers *et al.*, 2011). However, while research intensely investigated AC (e.g., Adams *et al.*, 2016; Todorova and Durisin, 2007; Volberda *et al.*, 2010; Zahra and George, 2002), AC literature is limited to analyses at the firm or business unit level. Only recently, research started to investigate the micro-foundations of AC (Distel, 2018). However, the explicit consideration of the nature of the absorbed knowledge as well as the analysis of AC at levels below the business unit are important and yet poorly explored subjects (Volberda *et al.*, 2010). This raises important research questions: *Can the capability of departments to absorb knowledge from other departments improve innovation performance? Which integration mechanisms do actually contribute to the development of such an ability? Is the relevance of AC symmetric or does it follow potential asymmetries in task interdependence?* In this study, we aim to answer these research questions and thus make several important contributions to research on AC as well as to research on functional and cross-functional integration.

Theoretical Framework

Integration mechanisms and innovation performance

In line with previous research, we consider four types of integration mechanisms. First, we distinguish between formal and informal ones (Bauer *et al.*, 2018; Burgers *et al.*, 2009; Moenaert *et al.*, 1994) and, for each, we further distinguish between intra- and cross-functional integration mechanisms (Hoegl *et al.*, 2004; Olson *et al.*, 2001). These integration mechanisms can serve either to coordinate tasks of interdependent functional departments or to transfer knowledge between them. However, also in case of mere coordination, the departments need to exchange information. Hence, the sending and receiving of information and knowledge is at the core of all integration mechanisms. Several studies have shown the positive effects functional integration can have. The literature on team and group behaviour investigates the direct impact of different kinds of integrating processes on performance (Ancona and Caldwell, 1992), such as boundary spanning behaviour (Allen and Cohen, 1969; Tushman, 1977; Zhao and Anand, 2013). Further empirical findings have corroborated the direct effect of integration on innovation in form of corporate entrepreneurship (Burgers and Covin, 2016; Foss *et al.*, 2011).

However, the richness of integration mechanisms, such as their capacity to transfer a high variety and amount of information, comes at the cost of higher complexity (Tushman and Nadler, 1978). Moreover, Sherman and Keller (2011) have shown that managers often misconceive the degree to which their unit's tasks and the tasks of other functional units are interdependent and may, therefore, choose wrong degrees of integration. Ultimately, this can lead to lower performance as is explained in several studies reporting negative effects of integration mechanisms (Troy *et al.*, 2008). The successful exchange of information and knowledge is necessary to carry out the innovation related tasks that drive innovation performance. For this exchange to be successful, receiving departments need to have the capability to absorb the incoming information and knowledge.

Absorptive capacities of functionally specialized departments

Cohen and Levinthal (1990) first conceptualised AC as the ability of firms to *recognise the value* of external knowledge, *assimilate* it, and *exploit* it to commercial ends. Most of the extant research on AC treats prior related knowledge as the most fundamental antecedent of AC (Todorova and Durisin, 2007; Zahra and George, 2002). This is in part because most studies investigate AC at the firm level, for which it had been initially conceptualised. At this level, organisational knowledge is most aggregate and hence analysed in a correspondingly general manner. Despite this high level of analysis, extant studies on AC almost always implicitly focus on technological knowledge.

In fact, Cohen and Levinthal (1990) deemed R&D and manufacturing operations the major sources of AC because these provide "prior related knowledge", which refers to such knowledge present in an organisation prior to absorption and related to the target knowledge. However, while this focus is justified at the organisational boundary, where firms try to absorb external technological knowledge relevant for new innovations, it falls short in explaining the relevance of AC within the firm, where M&S needs feedback on what is technologically feasible in order to make better market predictions and R&D needs updates on how the market conditions and customer expectations have changed. Yet, no study so far has conceptualised AC as a phenomenon on the level of departments of different functional specialisations, limiting the scope to one functional setting or to higher levels, e.g., the transfer of more or less sticky practices among operational units (Szulanski, 1996) or across subsidiaries of multinational corporations (Gupta and Govindarajan, 1991, 2000).

Moreover, different functions have different goals and incentives and are in different degrees senders and receivers of knowledge (Gupta *et al.*, 1986; Song *et al.*, 2001; Troy *et al.*, 2008). The departments are also embedded in completely different communities of practice (Brown and Duguid, 2001) and they may use different narratives and stories to interpret their environment and the knowledge available to them (Beverland *et al.*, 2016; Boland and Tenkasi, 1995; Dougherty, 1992). Hence, barriers[1] to knowledge integration can arise from different vocabulary (syntactic barriers); different meanings (semantic); or different interests (pragmatic) (Carlile, 2002, 2004).

Therefore, the challenges at departmental boundaries *within* corporate functions like the R&D function (e.g., interactions and knowledge integration between two R&D departments) are fundamentally different from the challenges at inter-departmental boundaries *across* corporate functions (Brettel *et al.*, 2011; Gupta *et al.*, 1986), like the boundary between an R&D and an M&S department. As a consequence, the involved unit's capability to absorb knowledge needs to be conceptualised as two distinct abilities in order to explain why the same integration mechanisms may have different effects in different contexts. We thus assert that

> *Functional AC* (*FAC*) and *Cross-Functional AC* (*CFAC*) refer to the ability of a functionally specialised department to value, assimilate and apply the functionally specialised knowledge available from other departments of the SAME or a DIFFERENT corporate function, respectively, in order to fulfil the department's tasks.

Antecedents of functional and cross-functional ACs

In line with Griffin and Hauser (1996), who suggest functions need to integrate in case of environmental uncertainty, Rubera *et al.* (2012) find that integration is particularly useful in case of exploration of new competences. However, AC is

[1]While Carlile uses the term "boundaries," we use "barriers" in order to clearly distinguish these mostly cognitive and communicative barriers to integration from organisational/structural boundaries.

assumed to depend principally on prior related knowledge and absorbing units have qua definition little *prior* knowledge when they explore new fields. Hence, AC is lowest when it is needed most. The degree to which different integration mechanisms are used affects the degree of specific capabilities related therewith. Hence, we argue that the ability to absorb new knowledge not only depends on what the absorbing unit already knows on a topic (*prior related factual knowledge)*, which may be helpful for resourceful sensemaking (Beverland *et al.*, 2016), but it also depends on *prior related procedural knowledge*. This can be knowledge regarding which useful new knowledge resides in which other departments, how to get access to this new knowledge, or how to interact with the source department.

Moreover, since AC depends on prior *related* knowledge it is not generally high or low for a specific organisational unit, but always specific to a particular knowledge domain. That means that, an R&D department can exhibit high AC regarding the knowledge of a fellow R&D department from a different business unit and at the same time exhibit low AC regarding the knowledge of an M&S department, possibly due to potential tensions between the different personalities of marketers and engineers (Shaw and Shaw, 1998). Cohen and Levinthal (1990) focused on R&D and mostly ignored the influence of M&S, leading to AC being studied in relation to technological knowledge only, at least implicitly. While several studies find that innovation and performance are positively affected by AC (Rothaermel and Alexandre, 2009), AC literature lacks empirical studies that explicitly consider the type of knowledge being absorbed, such as technology and market knowledge. Therefore, we theorise and operationalise the concept of AC at the level of functional departments in the form of two distinct abilities — functional and cross-functional AC — and reveal their mediating role in the relationship between integration mechanisms and innovation performance.

Hypotheses

Effects of intra-functional integration mechanisms on departmental ACs

The important ability to integrate knowledge is essentially based on communication capabilities (Daft and Lengel, 1986). Intra-functional communication is regarded as an important element in the R&D process (Allen and Cohen, 1969; Szulanski, 1996) and particularly relevant in the intermediate phase of the innovation process (Tushman, 1977). Organisational units at any level have to develop and improve these capabilities, and there is substantial evidence that organisations learn through experience (Ingram and Baum, 1997); through the repetition of a specific behaviour like integration mechanisms. Both formal and informal integration mechanisms are notable forms of organisational memory (Moorman and

Miner, 1998; Walsh and Ungson, 1991). Consequently, they not only are subject to depreciation but also can be forgotten if not applied continuously. All intra-functional integration mechanisms have in common that they require the absorption of knowledge from functional peers; that is, from departments that are specialised within the same corporate function, such as two R&D departments of different product divisions. The more they interact with each other and exchange knowledge, be it by means of formal or informal integration mechanisms, the more sophisticated they should become in the use of these mechanisms and, hence, the better they will be able to absorb knowledge from their peer departments. Therefore, it has to be assumed that the extensive use of intra-functional integration mechanisms in general entails a higher departmental FAC.

Hypothesis 1: *The more extensively a department uses either (a) INFORMAL or (b) FORMAL intra-functional integration mechanisms, the higher its FAC.*

Effects of cross-functional integration mechanisms on departmental ACs

It has been shown that R&D managers use market information that is perceived as being of high quality both instrumentally, for immediate decisions; and conceptually, to adapt their view of the market environment (Maltz *et al.*, 2001). For example, in the case of a disagreement in the R&D department regarding the potential of a particular technical improvement or development path, integration mechanisms might help to obtain a fast expert opinion on the market potential of technological developments. Informal cross-functional integration mechanisms have the potential to provide departments with feedback on ideas previously out of search scope that might help to reconcile conflicting interests because of their potential to be used ad hoc much more quickly and more spontaneously. Hence, informal cross-functional integration mechanisms also help receiving departments to better understand the value of incoming knowledge from their own functional area, thus supporting the integration with other departments belonging to the same corporate function.

Hypothesis 2: *The more extensively a department uses informal cross-functional integration mechanisms, the higher its FAC.*

In different departments, systematically different personalities exist, such as marketers and engineers (Shaw and Shaw, 1998); differences between them must be considered and understood in order to avoid misunderstandings and conflicts. Moreover, in cross-functional integration, different departmental thought worlds face each other (Dougherty, 1992), so departments must make a greater effort to develop knowledge on how to deal with different types of departments to a greater extent than in intra-functional integration.

In turn, the way in which AC builds through the use of *formal* integration mechanisms differs from that of informal integration mechanisms. Formal mechanisms can enhance, above all, the information flow and knowledge exchange in predetermined directions (Moenaert *et al.*, 1994). An essential part of cross-functional integration is knowledge exchange between functional units that are task interdependent: those units that depend on each other in their task accomplishment (Fry and Slocum, 1984). However, task interdependence is often asymmetric (De Jong *et al.*, 2007), so that the required knowledge flows can be asymmetric, too. This is particularly pronounced in the case of the M&S-R&D interface. Understanding feedback from M&S departments is vital in many stages and types of innovation projects (Wang, 1997). In fact, one important conclusion according to the marketing-R&D interface literature is that "(. . .) it is through the marketing-R&D interface that market knowledge is transferred, to and integrated with technological knowledge" (Li and Calantone, 1998, p. 15). What is more, formal integration mechanisms are an important means to make market knowledge available to the R&D function (Ernst *et al.*, 2010; Li and Calantone, 1998; Song *et al.*, 1998). The direction of knowledge from M&S to R&D is most obvious in the market-pull approach to new product development (Rothwell, 1994). With knowledge flowing primarily from M&S to R&D and much less so vice-versa, strong CFAC is more relevant for R&D than for M&S departments. The very use of integration mechanisms can lead to learning by doing (Ingram and Baum, 1997), thereby increasing departmental AC. Therefore, we expect R&D departments to be more often the absorbing part when using integration mechanisms, thus building CFAC; in contrast, M&S departments use these mechanisms mostly to *provide* knowledge, not build CFAC.

Hypothesis 3(a): *The more formal cross-functional integration mechanisms are used by R&D departments, the higher is their CFAC, while more extensive use of these mechanisms by M&S departments has no impact on CFAC.*

Informal integration mechanisms can positively impact cross-functional integration to the same degree as formal ones (Pinto and Pinto, 1990; Zahra and Nielsen, 2002). In particular, M&S departments that do not improve CFAC through formal cross-functional integration mechanisms have the chance to get more insight into the thought-worlds and practices of R&D departments when they engage informally with them. However, there are at least three reasons why R&D departments might suffer in their development of CFAC when they engage in informal cross-functional integration mechanisms.

The first reason is that the informal nature of a communication channel might provide opportunities and therefore tempt individual employees to advance their personal agendas or even induce them to send more information than through formal communication channels (Johnson *et al.*, 1994). In these cases, informal communication channels can produce an information overload for departments that already receive information through formal mechanisms. Such information is, furthermore, potentially contrasting and confusing as it is conveyed informally in an unstructured form. Altogether, the overload via unstructured information ties all attention and resources of the receiving department, thereby preventing reflection of the knowledge absorption process itself and, ultimately, leading to a collapse of sensemaking (Weick, 1993).

Secondly, a negative impact of informal cross-functional integration mechanisms on CFAC might be the result of the different types of knowledge involved. Technological knowledge is very much path dependent (Dosi, 1982), which explains the focus on prior related knowledge in AC literature as it is concerned principally with technological knowledge. Market demands, however, might change radically over time, thus more frequently creating disruptions (Avagyan *et al.*, 2016; Christensen, 2003). Evidence suggests that companies fail to adapt to radically changing environments, despite having the technological capabilities to do so, because new market knowledge is rejected by key actors or units (Tripsas, 2009). Formal cross-functional integration mechanisms can challenge such outdated market knowledge outright, although not without conflict. Informal communication, however, offers more possibilities to avoid conflict and to communicate only with less challenging sources that, rather, confirm existing convictions. This is consistent with the tendency known as confirmation bias: the "tendency, when testing an existing belief, to search for evidence which could confirm that belief, rather than for evidence which could disconfirm it." (Jones and Sugden, 2001, p. 59).

Thirdly, recent empirical evidence suggests that informal communication might disrupt new product development particularly in cases of complex products (Sosa *et al.*, 2015). This occurs when informal communication provides cyclic exchange across a social network, as often happens when teams responsible for the early stages of the innovation process, such as the development stage, receive informal feedback from teams responsible for the later stages, such as, the commercialisation stage. This continuously interrupts the innovation process rather than creating higher market orientation. Consequently, we expect the effect EYJLEJ of informal cross-functional integration mechanisms on CFAC to be positive only for M&S, while we expect it to be negative in the case of R&D departments.

Hypothesis 3(b): *The more informal cross-functional integration mechanisms are used by R&D departments, the lower their CFAC is, while more extensive use of* *informal cross-functional integration mechanisms by M&S departments positively impacts CFAC.*

Effect of departmental ACs on innovation performance

FAC and CFAC should be closely related. FAC can be considered as a kind of fundamental AC of a functionally specialised department. While FAC enables the absorption of knowledge from other departments of the same functional specialisation, this ability impacts the ability to absorb knowledge from other corporate functions, i.e., CFAC. The understanding of the process of absorption in general without the confounding element of different corporate functions can be regarded as the prior related procedural knowledge with respect to how to recombine, transform, and exploit new extra-departmental knowledge internally. This allows then for the more efficient absorption of complementary, cross-functional knowledge. Therefore, we specify:

Hypothesis 4: *The higher the departments' FAC, the higher their CFAC.*

Once the departments have developed FAC, they can valorise potential synergies and complementarities existing between their own and other departments' corporate function by absorbing their knowledge. Empirical studies of firms' subunit's AC provide evidence that the recipient's AC is a major determinant of the success or failure of intra-organisational knowledge transfer (van Wijk *et al.*, 2008). This finding should be valid for both FAC and CFAC and should also apply to both technological and market knowledge. For example, Luo *et al.* (2006) find that interdepartmental *cooperative ability* regarding market knowledge among departments — defined in terms of AC — positively affects both customer and financial performance.

However, in context of cross-functional integration, M&S and R&D are not equally likely to be recipients of knowledge. While relations have been found between knowledge flows from R&D to M&S and NPD performance (Moenaert *et al.*, 1994), studies analysing the effect at various stages suggest that the role of R&D-M&S integration mainly consists in the provision of market feedback to the R&D department (Brettel *et al.*, 2011; Drechsler *et al.*, 2013; Olson *et al.*, 2001), for example during the stages of market opportunity analysis, development, and pretesting (Song *et al.*, 1998) or, with the goal to improve market orientation (Jaworski and Kohli, 1993) or customer connection (Moorman and Rust, 1999). We may therefore conclude that the knowledge most important to innovation performance flows from M&S to R&D. R&D departments cannot simply participate in integration mechanisms and benefit from these without being able to actually absorb the knowledge in question, which might be possible for the M&S departments providing knowledge instead of absorbing it. We hence hypothesise:

Hypothesis 5a: *FAC of R&D and M&S departments shows a positive direct effect on innovation performance.*
Hypothesis 5b: *CFAC of R&D departments shows a positive direct effect on innovation performance, whereas CFAC of M&S departments shows no direct effect on innovation performance.*

Indirect effects of integration mechanisms

The above discussion implies some potential mediation effects. The consequence of the direct effects from informal cross-functional integration mechanisms on FAC, and from FAC on CFAC is that informal cross-functional integration mechanisms indirectly positively affect cross-functional AC in the case of R&D departments. This means that in turn it could counterbalance the negative direct effect that we predict informal cross-functional integration mechanisms could exert on CFAC of R&D departments. Thus, we put forward the following related hypothesis:

Hypothesis 6: *For R&D departments, there is a positive indirect effect from the use of informal cross-functional integration mechanisms via FAC on CFAC.*

Finally, CFAC of R&D departments mediates the effects of two antecedents of innovation performance: the effects of FAC and formal cross-functional integration mechanisms. Cross-functional integration aims at providing the necessary knowledge directly through lateral relations to those who need it in other functions due to task interdependence. Hence, in order to valorise formal cross-functional integration mechanisms, knowledge must be absorbed successfully. As argued above, the mere collaboration without understanding is not sufficient for a receiving unit. In this case, the receiving unit is hypothesised to be the R&D unit, which heavily relies on market information from M&S departments to direct and orient its work towards current and future market demand. As information providers, the M&S departments, in turn, are less dependent on a precise understanding of technological knowledge. Thus, if the data confirm a direct effect of integration mechanisms for M&S departments — as hypothesised above — while, at the same time, negating such an effect for R&D departments (supporting instead the hypothesis of an indirect effect through CFAC), this would clearly support the thesis that the direction of knowledge flow from M&S to R&D is more important than the reverse.

Hypothesis 7a: *FAC of R&D departments shows a positive indirect effect on innovation performance via CFAC.*
Hypothesis 7b: *There is a positive indirect effect from R&D departments' use of formal cross-functional integration mechanisms via CFAC on innovation performance.*

Direct effects of integration mechanisms on innovation performance

Since our conceptualisation of departmental AC is derived from the firm-level AC, it likewise includes not only the search and evaluation of external knowledge, but also its transfer and exploitation. This would reflect successful integration, which is supposed to improve innovation performance. Therefore, we hypothesised that departmental AC mediates all relevant integration mechanisms. In our model, the mediation should capture the entire effects from integration mechanisms on innovation performance. The presence of direct effects would imply that integration mechanisms achieve more than just (cross-) functional integration.

However, given that M&S departments are usually the party providing access, they are less required to build ability for absorption. In the case of R&D-M&S interfaces, where innovation activities are organised according to the market-pull model, it is particularly clear that there might be a *per se* predominant direction of task dependence and hence knowledge flow (Rothwell, 1994). M&S departments' engagement in integration mechanisms, obviously, can only directly result in higher innovation performance if either (i) the absorbing counterpart knows how to absorb or (ii) the integration mechanism is highly formalised and codified so that no particular prior related procedural knowledge is required. Given that we already expect *informal* cross-functional integration mechanisms to have a negative effect on R&D departments' CFAC, the only direct impact from integration mechanisms on innovation performance can be expected to result from the use of *formal* cross-functional integration mechanisms by M&S departments.

Hypothesis 8: (*a/b/c*) *None of the studied integration mechanisms directly affects innovation performance,* (*d*) *with the exception of M&S department's use of FORMAL cross-functional integration mechanisms, which positively affects innovation performance.*

Methodology

Sampling and data collection

We empirically tested our hypotheses using data from the Italian manufacturing industry. In a first step, we selected all Italian manufacturing firms from the AIDA database of Italian public and private firms. This database has been used in many previous studies (Colombo *et al.*, 2007) and is considered almost exhaustive, as it includes not only publicly listed companies but also privately held SMEs. It includes 3769 firms with at least 200 employees, which was the minimum threshold we had to set since we could include only firms that had at least two departments of each type in focus: R&D and M&S departments. Several firms also had to be removed from this list because they were no longer active. In a second step, an online pool of potential survey participants was accessed, allowing us to select professionals by firm and department. These restrictions reduced our sample to 541 professionals from either R&D or M&S departments. Professionals who had worked less than one year in their current firm were excluded from our study because we could not assume their responses to be sufficiently reliable, as the process of socialisation usually takes some time. The professionals thus matched were then contacted and asked to complete an online questionnaire. The distribution of experience of survey participants is slightly skewed towards shorter professional experience. This is due to an overrepresentation of younger professionals in the database itself. Since this does not relate to our particular research questions we see no reason to suspect any systematic bias.

The questionnaire was hosted on a dedicated server under the official university domain, and it was password protected to signal careful and confidential use of the participants' data. Moreover, in the contact e-mail all participants were not only assured of the confidentiality of their answers, but incentivised also with a personalised benchmark report. There were two rounds of reminder e-mails. The responses received amounted to 140, of which 126 were completed. Of the 126 complete questionnaires, 51 were filled in by M&S professionals while 75 were completed by employees of R&D departments. Thus, we altogether achieved a response rate of over 23%, which is seen also in similar studies using online surveys (e.g., Verhoef and Leeflang, 2009) and generally a good rate for online surveys of managers, given the decline in online survey response rates since the introduction of the Internet (Sheehan, 2001).

The sectors represented in our final sample include automotive and suppliers, food and beverages, consumer electronics, instruments and industrial machinery.[2] The sectoral composition of respondents does not differ much from that of non-respondents. We tested for non-response bias using financial data from the AIDA database, since this data was also available for non-respondents. The variables chosen were major performance indicators such as sales, EBIT, and ROE, but also

[2]The 2-digit ATECO codes of the sectors represented in our sample are the following: 10, 15, 17, 20, 21, 22, 23, 24, 25, 26, 27, 28, 29, 30, 31, 32, 33.

indicators of differences between sectors. This analysis was performed by means of a paired-sample *t*-test on mean differences for each of the selected key variables regarding both the entire sample and the two sub-samples of respondents from R&D and M&S departments. At no point were significant differences found, and we concluded that there is no non-response bias.

In order to avoid any biases related to the sequence of items in a battery, all item batteries used were presented in a random order. Moreover, it was important to avoid the creation of an overly lengthy questionnaire that could have increased the number of response interruptions and, consequently, could have led to a higher number of incomplete responses. The median response time, though, is more informative and was approximately 15 min. Finally, construct validity was assessed in two steps. In a first step, the questionnaire was discussed with senior researchers from both innovation management and marketing. In the second step, a pretest was carried out with several professionals who were afterwards interviewed about the comprehensibility and validity of the constructs. Both researchers and professionals were Italian native speakers with an excellent command of the English language and were also asked to confirm the validity of the translation. However, the questionnaire language could be chosen and changed online by the respondents. Good construct validity can thus be assumed.

Operationalisation

With the exception of the newly established construct of departmental ACs (i.e., FAC and CFAC), all variables have been measured based on previously validated items used in the management literature (see Appendix). The scales for the new concepts FAC and CFAC have been constructed on the basis of items established in the literature measuring AC at the organisational or sub-unit level and adapted slightly to fit the context of the functionally specialised departments chosen: R&D and M&S (Flatten *et al.*, 2011; Hansen and Nohria, 2004; Jansen *et al.*, 2005; Szulanski, 1996).

Innovation performance was assessed by means of a set of items chosen to measure innovation performance, based on instruments that are used in both marketing and management literature (Atuahene-Gima *et al.*, 2005; De Luca and Atuahene-Gima, 2007). It was measured as the degree to which the stated objectives of innovation projects have been reached in the following four dimensions: market share, sales, return on investment, and product performance.

Luo *et al.* (2006, p. 72) conceptualised cross-functional cooperative ability as the "ability to assimilate and deploy market knowledge in lateral interactions among functional areas", a special case of our more general CFAC. However, this definition refers exclusively to market knowledge, so that it is not suited to distinguish between FAC and CFAC. As a consequence, the items used by Luo and colleagues do not distinguish between the department's own and other functional knowledge domains. In contrast, the present study focuses on this distinction, aimed at measuring FAC and CFAC explicitly as two distinct concepts. Particular care was taken to select only reflective items from the previous literature.

Furthermore, we made sure that these items were coherent with the theoretic conceptualisation of the construct as an ability, rather than as a set of specific processes and routines. This means that only those items were included which avoided asking "how extensively do you apply process X (a *process* that *aims* at knowledge absorption)?" but, instead, asked "how successful are you in terms of Y (an *aspect* of knowledge absorption)?"

Formal and informal integration mechanisms can be implemented at both types of interface, thus, requiring four variables: formal and informal intra-functional integration mechanisms, as well as formal and informal cross-functional integration mechanisms. Informal integration was measured by means of four items from previous studies (Zahra and Nielsen, 2002) as a reflective scale, thus, indicating the degree of a latent informal integration. While functional integration has been measured unidimensional in the past, for example, in terms of extensive use of cross-disciplinary teams within the R&D function (Henderson and Clark, 1990), formal integration mechanisms have been adopted from previous literature in terms of a formative, multi-dimensional scale (Gupta and Govindarajan, 2000; Jansen *et al.*, 2005). The formative scale of formal integration mechanisms was also measured by means of an additional item in order to achieve a more complete construct, which is particularly important for formative constructs (Edwards and Bagozzi, 2000).

Our model also includes several control variables. We analyse *industry effects* by means of the variable IND2ROS, that is the industry average return on sales (ROS) calculated based on the two-digit ATECO code (Coombs and Bierly, 2006). Alternatively, common industry dummies based on two-digit ATECO codes have been used in OLS regression analyses as a further robustness check (Cassiman and Veugelers, 2006). We control for *firm size* by applying one of the most common measures: the logarithm of the number of full-time equivalent employees. We control for the *degree of centralisation* applying the measure used by Jaworski and Kohli (1993) and for the degree to which the firm or business unit *directly serves end consumers* (B2C) rather than other businesses (B2B) using the scale applied by (Verhoef and Leeflang, 2009).*Environmental turbulence* is controlled for by means of a formative item battery (Verhoef and Leeflang, 2009). Finally, we control for *market oriented reward mechanisms* using items from Jaworski and Kohli (1993).

Data

The sample in the present study includes responses from 126 professionals in R&D and/or M&S departments from 79 different firms (in 37 cases, we received a response from only one department). Although it has been found that Structural Equation Models (SEM) can perform well, even with sample sizes as low as 50 (Iacobucci, 2010), it is well known that one should aim for sample sizes above 100 (preferably 200) cases (Bagozzi and Yi, 2012). While our sample size is admittedly towards the lower bound of admissible sample sizes, other recent studies have applied SEM on similar topics with similar values (Stock *et al.*, 2014, for example, use a sample size of 125). However, in order to further check the impact of sample size on the robustness of our models in terms of stable parameter estimates, we tested our model initially by means of the first 100 cases and, subsequently, by means of the final set of 126 cases. There was no indication of bias.

Missing data can have serious effects on data quality and the conclusions that can be drawn from empirical data (Byrne, 2010; Schafer and Graham, 2002). The variables with most missing cases showed less than 10% of cases missing, which would still sufficiently limit potential bias (Schafer and Graham, 2002). The two most common imputation techniques have been chosen for the missing data: variable means and maximum likelihood estimation as available in AMOS (cf. Byrne, 2010). Moreover, all analyses of the measurement and structural models were performed based on both types of imputation techniques showing no substantial differences. Since the maximum likelihood estimation of missing observations is generally regarded as robust even in cases where the missing-at-random condition is not exactly met (Byrne, 2010), we report results based on this imputation technique.

Common method bias was checked by means of Harman's single-factor test that is commonly applied in cross-sectional studies (Harman, 1967). Thus, a principal component analysis of all items of the survey extracting factors with eigenvalues above 1 has been performed, which resulted in many factors explaining about 75% of total variance and another principal component analysis constraining the extraction of one single factor of the unrotated solution. This single factor could explain only about 23.8% of total variance. Thus, we found no indication that common method bias is a major problem. To reduce the potential of social desirability bias, particular care was taken to indicate full anonymity of both individuals and firms. In order to avoid biases due to the order of items, the items of all multi-item scales were presented in random order each time the site was accessed.

Model specification

Given the low sample size, we tested the measurement and the structural model separately (Anderson and Gerbing, 1988). First, the pure measurement model of the reflective scales was estimated in a confirmatory factor analysis. In this way, we estimated not only composite reliability (CR), but also convergent and discriminant validities. We subsequently used the derived composite variables for the estimation of the pure structural model in a path analysis. An important criterion is the logic of causal direction theorised, which should be confirmed by high inter-item correlations in case of reflective scales (Edwards and Bagozzi, 2000) since, if there is a common latent factor influencing the items, these will have to be correlated to some degree. In contrast, there is no such constraint if the indicators *form* the latent variable. Indeed, for all scales for which we argue that are formative, the inter-item correlations, although significant, are not as high as one might expect if they were reflective. While commonly formative scales are simple, that is, non-weighted averages of the equally scaled items, formal integration mechanisms have been differently summed in extant literature. The items we use to measure cross-functional integration or interfaces have been combined into a weighted average in previous studies, the weights being 1 for liaison personnel, 2 for temporary task forces, and 3 for permanent teams (Gupta and Govindarajan, 2000; Jansen *et al.*, 2005). The same weights have been applied in this study, while the additional indicator "job rotation" is a weighted one, because by nature it is closest to liaison personnel as it involves only single individuals.

Results

Measurement model results

Items of reflective scales have been found to correlate at least over 0.45 and significantly so, mostly at the 1%-level. This is in line with the pattern of factor loadings identified by the exploratory factor analysis where all items of the reflective scales load together on their respective factors, with the exception of a few items of the FAC and CFAC scales. The confirmatory factor analysis led to the elimination of several items from the original scales because factor loadings were too low (< 0.55). Moreover, a test for metric invariance during confirmatory factor analysis revealed that FAC and CFAC have to be measured by different items. This further corroborates that the two concepts are actually different. Both the Tucker–Lewis-Index (TLI) and the comparative fit index (CFI) are over 0.9 with values of 0.921 and 0.941, respectively, the root mean square error of approximation (RMSEA) at 0.063 being in a well acceptable range (< 0.1 moderate;

< 0.05 good), and chi-square/d.f. at 1.491 being below the conservative threshold of 2. Model fit is at least as good for the solution with variable means imputed data, for which the estimate of SRMR was well below the threshold of 0.08, too (Hu and Bentler, 1999). Moreover, no indication of problems with model fit could be found following a check of the matrix of the standardised residual covariances available for the analysis with mean imputed variable means, since no value is larger than 2.58 (cf. Byrne, 1999, p. 86). The values for CR of all scales were largely above the 0.7 threshold (Bagozzi and Yi, 1988). Moreover, for all variables, convergent and discriminant validity is supported, since average variance extracted (AVE) is always smaller than CR and larger than both maximum shared squared variance (MSV) and average shared squared variance (ASV).

Structural model results

The structural model is based on the specified hypotheses and includes the specified control variables. Table 1 and Fig. 1 summarise our results. In multi-group SEM models, an R-square value is estimated contemporaneously in one model for every endogenous variable for each group. All six of our R-square values are between 0.35 and 0.59 and hence show that our model explains a relatively large percentage of variance of the endogenous variables.

Our first hypotheses could not be confirmed. We found no significant effects of either informal (H1a) or formal (H1b) intra-functional integration mechanisms on FAC. A possible explanation is that, within functional areas, vertical information flows are more important than lateral ones and complementarities are realised directly and exclusively in projects rather than at the level of departments.

Another possible explanation is that FAC depends more on in-depth knowledge since it concerns the absorption of knowledge from the same domain (e.g., a marketing department in the USA absorbing knowledge from a marketing department in Europe). In this case, successful absorption hinges more on the departments' knowledge bases being already very similar rather than their organisational integration. By contrast, where knowledge bases are always relatively distant and little common ground exists, integration mechanisms and higher frequency of exchange substitute for the common ground provided by a similar domain background. In fact, the positive effect of informal integration across functional domains on FAC is found to be highly significant for both R&D and M&S departments, which confirms our Hypothesis 2.

Likewise, we find support for Hypotheses 3a and 3b. We can confirm for R&D departments that formal cross-functional integration mechanisms highly significantly and positively affect CFAC, while informal cross-functional integration mechanisms have a slightly significant negative effect on CFAC. Moreover, we

Table 1. Structural path model results with control variables (ML estimation of missing data).

			R&D			M&S				
DV	Hypothesis	Path	R^2	β	(p-val.)	R^2	β	(p-val.)	Expected	**Confirmed**
FAC			**0.357**			**0.590**				
	H1a:	FAC ← IIM		0.079	(0.362)		−0.098	(0.362)	+	**No**
	H1b:	FAC ← FIM		−0.002	(0.982)		−0.002	(0.982)	+	**No**
	H2:	FAC ← IXM		−0.379***	(0.000)		−0.437***	(0.000)	+	**Yes**
	C1:	FAC ← CNTR		−0.169*	(0.013)		−0.207*	(0.013)	−	**Yes**
	C2:	FAC ← IND2ROS		-0.106^{+}	(0.112)		-0.102^{+}	(0.112)	−	~
	C3:	FAC ← REW		−0.247***	(0.000)		−0.329***	(0.000)	+	**Yes**
CFAC			**0.529**			**0.407**				
	H3a (R&D):	CFAC ← FXM		−0.378***	(0.000)				+	**Yes**
	H3a (M&S):	CFAC ← FXM					0	(n.a.)	**0**	**Yes**
	H3b (R&D):	CFAC ← IXM		-0.185^{+}	(0.108)				−	~
	H3b (M&S):	CFAC ← IXM					-0.209^{++}	(0.073)	+	~
	H4:	CFAC ← FAC		−0.523***	(0.000)		−0.497***	(0.000)	+	**Yes**
	C4 (R&D):	CFAC ← REW		−0.183*	(0.046)				+	**Yes**
	C4 (M&S):	CFAC ← REW					0	(n.a.)	0	**Yes**
IP			**0.372**			**0.356**				
	H5a:	IP ← FAC		−0.020	(0.847)		−0.016	(0.847)	+	**No**
	H5b (R&D):	IP ← CFAC		−0.560***	(0.000)				++	**Yes**
	H5b (M&S):	IP ← CFAC					0	(n.a.)	**0**	**Yes**
	H8a:	IP ← IIM		0	(n.a.)		0	(n.a.)	0	~
	H8b:	IP ← IXM		0	(n.a.)		0	(n.a.)	0	~
	H8c:	IP ← FIM		0	(n.a.)		0	(n.a.)	0	~
	H8d (R&D):	IP ← FXM		0	(n.a.)				0	~
	H8d (M&S):	IP ← FXM					0.227^{++}	(0.061)	+	~

Table 1. (*Continued*)

DV	Hypothesis	Path	R&D			M&S			Expected	Confirmed
			R^2	β	(p-val.)	R^2	β	(p-val.)		
	C5:	IP ← B2C		−0.136$^+$	(0.101)		−0.120$^+$	(0.101)	+	~
	C6:	IP ← ENV		−0.100	(0.255)		−0.068	(0.255)	+	**No**
	C7 (R&D):	IP ← SIZE		−0.077	(0.425)				−	**No**
	C7 (M&S):	IP ← SIZE					−0.364**	(0.002)	−	**Yes**
	C8:	IP ← IND2ROS		−0.102	(0.204)		−0.079	(0.204)	−	**No**
	C9 (R&D):	IP ← REW		−0.084	(0.487)				+	**No**
	C9 (M&S):	IP ← REW					−0.408**	(0.002)	+	**Yes**
Indirect effects of integration mechanisms										
	H6:	CFAC ← FAC ← IXM		−0.198***	(0.000)				+	**Yes**
	H7a:	IP ← CFAC ← FAC		−0.283***	(0.000)				+	**Yes**
	H7b:	IP ← CFAC ← FXM		−0.204**	(0.000)				+	**Yes**

Notes: $n = 126$; $^+ < 0.11$, $^{++} < 0.07$, $^* < 0.05$, $^{**} < 0.01$ $^{***} < 0.001$; $\chi^2 = 30.645$; d.f. = 45; $p = 0.950$; χ^2/d.f. = 0.681; TLI = 1.142; CFI = 1.00; RMSEA = 0.000 (90% confidence interval 0.000 → 0.003); SRMR = not defined for data with missing values. β = standardised parameter estimates. Significance levels of indirect effects based on two-tailed Sobel-test.

Hypotheses regarding zero effects have been tested by constraining the parameters in question to zero and calculate the chi-square difference test statistic to compare it with the unconstrained model. Acceptance based on chi-square difference test always coincided with decision if based on AIC.

Abbreviations: Innovation Performance (IP), Functional AC (FAC), Cross-functional AC (CFAC), Informal (IXM) and formal (FXM) cross-functional integration mechanisms, Informal (IIM) and formal (FIM) intra-functional integration mechanisms, Market oriented reward mechanisms (REW), Centralisation (CNTR), Environmental turbulence (ENV), Industry average of Return on Sales (IND2ROS), Percentage of Business-to-Consumer sales of total sales (B2C).

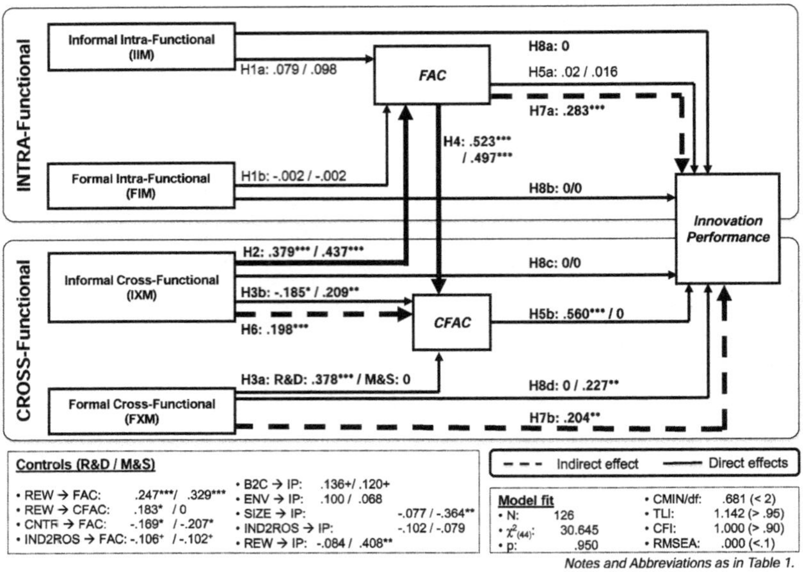

Notes: Abbreviations as in Table 1.

Fig. 1. Overview of structural model results.

find evidence that these effects of formal and informal cross-functional integration mechanisms are, as predicted, partly inversed when considering M&S departments. Constraining the path of formal cross-functional integration mechanisms on CFAC to zero for M&S departments significantly improves model fit, and the effect of informal mechanisms has a positive rather than negative effect that is significant at 7%.

We find support for Hypothesis 4, that is, for the interrelation between FAC and CFAC. FAC has a significant and highly positive impact on CFAC. FAC can thus be regarded as a fundamental capability on which CFAC can build. One may also interpret FAC as an auxiliary capability for successful cross-functional integration. Cross-functional integration processes sometimes require additional information from peer departments, thus making FAC to a certain degree a precondition for CFAC.

We find no support for our Hypothesis 5a, whereby FAC positively affects innovation performance. A possible explanation for the insignificant result regarding Hypothesis 6a is that in most organisations the departmental structure, in particular that of R&D departments, mirrors more or less closely the modular structure of the underlying technology. That means that each of the loosely coupled modules corresponds to an organisational unit to develop it, and that these units are coupled as loosely as the modules (MacCormack *et al.*, 2012). If this is the case, there are fewer interdependencies between peer departments, between, for example an R&D department responsible for innovations and improvements around module A, and another department responsible for module B. The relevance of knowledge absorption depends on these interdependencies; hence, in these cases, FAC should exhibit low to no impact on innovation performance. In contrast to 5a, we can confirm our Hypothesis 5b: in case of R&D departments, CFAC significantly and positively affects innovation performance, as expected. This effect is robust across diverse model specifications.

We find support for Hypothesis 6: there is a significant, positive indirect effect from cross-functional integration mechanisms through FAC on CFAC. In the case of R&D departments, this indirect effect compensates for the negative direct effect of these mechanisms on CFAC, resulting in a total effect close to zero.

The hypothesised indirect effects from FAC (H7a) and formal cross-functional integration mechanisms (H7b) through CFAC on innovation performance are highly significant, too. The significance levels of all indirect effects are based on a two-tailed Sobel-test. Together with the hypothesis of zero effects for direct paths of cross-functional integration mechanisms on innovation performance, as confirmed above, this might explain previous contrasting results that find negative, positive or no effects at all from these mechanisms on innovation performance. In particular, the indirect positive effect of informal cross-functional integration mechanisms via FAC on CFAC of R&D departments does balance out the negative effect that these mechanisms exert directly on CFAC. This could explain why previous studies did not find any significant effect for informal cross-functional integration mechanisms on integration success (Leenders and Wierenga, 2002).

None of the integration mechanisms included in hypotheses 8a-c affects innovation performance directly. These, and all other zero-effect hypotheses, were tested by means of chi-square difference tests of the nested models and can thus be regarded as not rejected. All models specifying a direct effect of integration mechanisms on innovation performance had to be rejected due to bad model fit. Hence, this confirms our Hypotheses 8a-c. We also find that Hypothesis 8d is confirmed; hence, formal cross-functional integration mechanisms have the expected significant, positive direct effect on innovation performance for M&S departments, whereas they do not show such effect in the case of R&D departments, where the direct effect is zero but the indirect effect is highly significant and positive. This can be interpreted as evidence of the direction of knowledge flow between departments and indirectly supports our assumption that M&S departments do not need CFAC to increase innovation performance, since they deliver the required knowledge without the necessity to absorb R&D knowledge in turn. In contrast, R&D departments can use all formal integration mechanisms according to their needs; however, without learning how to use these mechanisms to foster knowledge absorption, there will be no significantly positive effect on innovation performance.

Most control variables load as anticipated. Industry sectors, as measured by average return on sales of the sector, have no effect, as confirmed by mostly insignificant industry dummies in OLS regressions (see section on further robustness checks below).

Further robustness checks

We discuss the outcomes of several competing models that have been tested and compared with the base model. In model (1), we assume that FAC is not a prerequisite causing CFAC as argued above, but rather that both variables independently cause innovation performance. Given the differences of the alternative models, we compare them based on Akaike's Information Criterion (AIC). With an AIC value of 391.685, this model has a fit which is worse compared with the base model, which has an AIC value of 356.645.

In model (2), we assume that not only informal but also formal cross-functional integration mechanisms affect FAC. Knowledge about the formal integration mechanisms used across domain boundaries could also be transferred to improve the implementation of these integration mechanisms with other departments of the own corporate function, thus improving FAC. Not only is the newly introduced effect of formal cross-functional integration mechanisms on FAC itself insignificant (p-level 0.253), but the chi-square difference test also fails to indicate a significant difference (p-level 0.269). Moreover, the AIC of this alternative model is higher than that of the original model. Our original model thus overall outperforms this alternative specification as well.

In model (3), we also tested for reversed causality. In this model, we try to address potential endogeneity as much as possible. We assume in this model that higher innovation performance increases managers' perception of their department's ability to absorb new external knowledge. While model 3 performs better than model 1, it performs worse than the original model, based not only on the comparison of the AIC (360.210) but also on all other model fit indicators, except for CFI, which is equally maximised.

Finally, in model (4), OLS regression was applied to double check the principal hypotheses. This allows us to check for robustness not only in terms of model configuration, but also in terms of an alternative and still more common way to assess industry effects, namely by means of the usual industry dummies. All other controls and composite variables are those used in the structural model. At the same time, OLS also permits a check for multicollinearity issues by means of inspection of the variance inflation factors (VIF). Here, we found all factors ranging between 1 and 3, far below the upper threshold value of 5 (De Vaus, 2002; Kutner *et al.*, 2005). Visual inspection as to heteroskedasticity does not suggest such an issue for any of the OLS models we ran. Generally, the OLS models confirm our principal hypotheses that are also confirmed by the SEM model. Moreover, we cannot exclude firm-specific effects, but since we had only very few cases per firm, we can relatively safely assume unrelated residual errors. However, as a robustness check, we created a dummy variable for those firms from which we had received only one response. It is not possible to include dummies in an ML estimation-based SEM, but we controlled for the influence of this dummy on the main results in the OLS regressions. Our findings were still supported when controlling for number of responses per firm.

Discussion and Conclusion

We argued that a crucial aspect of integration success at inter-departmental boundaries in terms of innovation performance is the capability of the organisational units to absorb each other's knowledge. We hence empirically studied integration within and between the M&S and R&D functions and were able to explain a considerable share of the variance of innovation performance. Previous research on this phenomenon investigated the direct relationship between differently operationalised integration mechanisms and innovation performance without taking into account the nature of the units' corporate function. This led to contrasting empirical results and explanations. Hence, we investigated whether the ability of departments to absorb knowledge from other departments can improve innovation performance, as well as whether such an ability can be built by means of integration mechanisms.

Based on our analysis, however, we found evidence of contrasting direct and indirect effects of some integration mechanisms on CFAC and hence innovation performance. In fact, it is important to note that, in case of R&D departments, the use of informal cross-functional integration mechanisms has a positive indirect effect on CFAC mediated by FAC, while, at the same time, it has a negative direct effect on CFAC. That is, it generally improves the ability to understand what types of external knowledge from within the department's own functional domain are most valuable given the complementarity with other functional domains, but it may likewise provide too much potentially contradictory information that hinders the integration of these other functional domains. Since the indirect effect of informal cross-functional integration via FAC on CFAC is highly significant and positive, while the direct effect is significantly negative, the total effect on CFAC — and thus innovation performance — is close to zero. This is in line with previous findings that did not consider the mediation but only the aggregate effect, and hence did not find a significant relation (Leenders and Wierenga, 2002).

Moreover, the CFAC of R&D departments enables them to improve innovation performance. We found this construct, which we conceptualise for the first time at this level of analysis, to be an important mediating variable. It shows that the mere implementation of integration mechanisms is not a sufficient criterion for improved innovation performance. R&D departments have to learn how to use them and how to absorb knowledge from M&S in order to develop more valuable and better performing innovations. We also show that M&S departments need not be particularly skilled in absorbing knowledge from R&D departments to provide the necessary updated market knowledge to R&D departments. While these findings confirm previous studies on the direction of knowledge flow from M&S to R&D departments in new product development, they also contribute to the clarification of previous contrasting findings regarding the effects of integration mechanisms on innovation performance.

Several limitations have to be mentioned, however. First, the results are limited so far to the Italian context, and a cross-national replication would add to the reliability of the generalisation of the results. Secondly, the fact that the study is based on cross-sectional data makes the causal directions depend fundamentally on the theory developed. A future study based on panel data could add to the strength of the causal inference, as changes over time in terms of departmental FAC and CFAC and their impact on innovation performance could actually then be analysed. This model can be refined using scales that better reflect the theorised multi-dimensionality. However, these simpler preliminary scales could be used already for further inquiries. A third limitation is the relatively small sample size. The statistical power of the model is relatively limited; in particular the hypotheses of zero effects have to be regarded with caution, since, with a comparatively low power, the probability of false negatives increases.

Theoretical implications

We conceptualise Functional and Cross-functional Absorptive Capacity (FAC and CFAC, respectively) and apply technically valid and reliable empirical measurement instruments for these concepts. In doing so, we follow similar considerations expressed in the conceptualisation of relative AC at the firm level (Lane and Lubatkin, 1998) and address highly relevant yet under-researched issues of the AC literature (Volberda *et al.*, 2010). Hence, this study contributes to theory in several important ways. We provide theoretical underpinning for the relevance of AC (in form of FAC and CFAC) for functional integration and innovation performance. Based on an original database from Italian manufacturing firms from a broad range of different sectors, we also provide the first empirical evidence for the role that departmental AC plays in functional integration. Hence, our study also provides quantitative evidence of CFAC's positive mediation of the effect that formal cross-functional integration mechanisms have on innovation performance.

Furthermore, we contribute to the theory of cross-functional integration through analysing the role of AC in this context, thus providing a deeper understanding of the integration process. Our differentiated view, based on the revised conceptualisation of AC helps to explain previously contrasting results in the literature (Troy *et al.*, 2008). Departments' absorptive capacities are specific to the type of intra-organisational boundary; hence, these distinct capabilities mediate differently the effects of different integration mechanisms (i.e., formal and informal) on innovation performance. In particular, with our distinction of two fundamental types of integration mechanisms (formal versus informal) at two different types of organisational boundaries (intra-versus cross-functional), we allow for a nuanced understanding of how departmental ACs affect innovation performance.

Finally, including and comparing R&D and M&S departments in one joint analysis, we can show how these effects differ across different corporate functions. In this way, we contribute to a better understanding of the differences in successful functional integration and to an explanation for the contrasting findings on the role of integration for innovation performance (Troy *et al.*, 2008).

Clearly, there are many new research questions implied by our findings, of which we can only point to some we view as most relevant. Regarding functional and cross-functional integration, the recognition of these mediating effects permits more fine-grained analyses of contingency theories and moderating effects regarding differentiation and reintegration in functionally specialised organisations. Future research hence could, for example, address the issue of intra-firm heterogeneity regarding not only the development, but also the use of these abilities. Furthermore, future research could analyse what this means in the context of multinational corporations and globally dispersed innovation activities as well as in terms of recent contingency views on integration (Burgers and Covin, 2016). Multinational corporations have to differentiate and reintegrate in different environments and different degrees of innovation dynamism. On one hand, departmental ACs could help to explain heterogeneity on the levels of success of integration across countries. A multinational that tries to integrate knowledge inflows from its foreign subsidies should perform better when its receiving home-country departments exhibit high levels of AC. On the other hand, the multinational context could help to explain differences in the way and speed in which geographically dispersed departments develop these ACs. For example, R&D departments of a multinational corporation are necessarily integrated more through formal integration mechanisms, since geographical distance reduces the likelihood of informal exchange, leading thus to higher CFAC.

Regarding AC, this concept is still mostly theorised and observed at the firm-level. While most recent research tries to connect individual employee-level directly to firm-level AC (Distel, 2018; Ebers and Maurer, 2014; Yao and Chang, 2017) in order to establish micro-foundations (Felin *et al.*, 2012) more research is needed to develop sound micro-foundations for AC on the department-level as well, for which we offer a starting point. This means appreciating the fact that, in hierarchical organisations with many levels, the observation and analysis of meso-level phenomena helps one to understand the emergence of more macro-level phenomena.

Managerial implications

Our findings also have several implications for managing departments involved in new product development. In particular, we demonstrate that informal, spontaneous communication might pose serious pitfalls for R&D departments and for the new product development process altogether. This is in line with and adds to rather recent findings (Sosa *et al.*, 2015). We find a positive effect on FAC and a negative one on CFAC. This could be leveraged by focusing on strengthening the positive first effect and avoiding the second negative one. First, firms should focus on the scope of informal communication between M&S and R&D departments on the product development stages in which such communication helps R&D departments understand the markets and, hence, to develop requirements and targets of their peer R&D departments with which they cooperate. The informal communication with M&S could thus complement and integrate the rather technical communication with their R&D peers. On the other hand, to avoid any negative effect on CFAC, continuous interruptions of their own development process through informal feedback at arbitrary development stages should be avoided, because they disrupt the workflow. This is in line with recent findings based on social network analysis in complex new product development (Sosa *et al.*, 2015). Companies can benchmark their departments based on our scales in order to judge the need to pay more attention to the development of departmental absorptive capacities, thereby improving strategic decisions in innovation management. This allows firms to allocate the appropriate level of attention, time, et cetera to build departmental absorptive capacities.

Empirical Evidence of the Mediating Role of AC

Acknowledgements

We thank Francesco Rullani, Sebastian Spaeth, Diego Stea, Kinsuk Mani Sinha, Felice Simonelli, Luca Sabini and Alfredo Valentino for their helpful comments and discussions. We are furthermore very grateful for excellent proofreading by Alexandra Christiansen, Sara Turner, and Sarah McCarthy. This article is based on a part of Piet Hausberg's dissertation.

Appendix

Table A1. Core scales used in the questionnaire.

Cross-/Functional AC (CFAC/FAC) (reflective)	Item based on:	Mean (SD) FAC	Mean (SD) CFAC
Members of our department...			
(5) quickly analyse and interpret changing opportunities of "technologies"/"markets".	Jansen *et al.* (2005)	4.17 (1.55)	4.10 (1.44)
(6) structure and integrate new external knowledge with ease.	Jansen *et al.* (2005)	a	3.94 (1.46)
(9) recognise timely the consequences of new external knowledge to our mode of operation.	(Flatten *et al.* 2011)	4.37 (1.51)	a
(10) are able to apply new external knowledge in their practical work.	Flatten *et al.* (2011)	4.59 (1.51)	a
(11) regularly reconsider their knowledge and adapt it according to new external knowledge.	Jansen *et al.* (2005)	4.52 (1.53)	4.13 (1.46)
(12) know to share and apply new external knowledge with those in our department who is most apt.	Szulanski (1996)	4.19 (1.53)	a

Informal Integration (IIM & IXM Scales) Based on Zahra and Nielsen (2002). (reflective)	Mean (SD) IIM	Mean (SD) IXM
To what extent does your department use ...		
(1) free exchange of operating and financial information, with ...	a	3.06 (1.80)
(2) bypassing of formal communication channels, as needed, with ...	a	3.53 (1.90)
(3) informal relationships for getting things done, with ...	4.71 (1.69)	4.05 (1.84)
(4) maintains open communication channels in its operations with ...	4.61 (1.63)	a
other departments of the (own/other function[a])		

Table A.1. (*Continued*)

Formal Integration (FIM & FXM Scales) Based on Gupta and Govindarajan (2000), Jansen *et al.* (2005). (formative)	Item weights		Mean (SD)	
	Extant	Adj.	FIM	FXM
To what extent does your department use:				
(1) liaison personnel with ...	1	1	3.94 (1.77)	3.52 (1.98)
(2) temporary task forces with ...	2	2	4.01 (1.86)	3.28 (1.94)
(3) permanent teams with ...	3	3	4.32 (1.86)	3.66 (2.03)
(4) job rotation with ... other departments of the (own/other function[b])	N.A.	1	2.98 (1.88)	2.02 (1.37)

Innovation Performance (IP) Based on Atuahene-Gima *et al.* (2005) (reflective)	Mean (SD)
Rate how your business unit is performing on the following new product development objectives relative to your firm's stated objectives:	
(1) Market share	4.37 (1.25)
(3) ROI	4.35 (1.37)
(4) Profitability	4.47 (1.42)

Notes: Scaling for CFAC, FAC, IIM, IXM, FIM, FXM: 1 — "No or very little extent" ... 7 — "Very large extent"

Scaling for IP: 1 — "much worse" ... 7 — "much better".

[a]Item deleted.

[b](own function) replaced with "R&D function" for R&D departments and "M&S function" for M&S departments (FIM); (other function) replaced with "M&S function" for R&D departments and "R&D function" for M&S departments (FXM).

References

Adams, DR, TC Flatten, H Brinkmann and M Brettel (2016). Consequences and antecedents of absorptive capacity in a cross-cultural context. *International Journal of Innovation Management*, 20(1), 1650003.

Allen, TJ and SI Cohen (1969). Information flow in research and development laboratories. *Administrative Science Quarterly*, 14(1), 12–19.

Ancona, DG and DF Caldwell (1992). Bridging the boundary. external activity and performance in organizational teams. *Administrative Science Quarterly*, 37, 634–665.

Anderson, JC and DW Gerbing (1988). Structural equation modeling in practice: A review and recommended two-step approach. *Psychological Bulletin*, 103(3), 411–423.

Atuahene-Gima, K, SF Slater and EM Olson (2005). The contingent value of responsive and proactive market orientations for new product program performance. *Journal of Product Innovation Management*, 22, 464–482.

Avagyan, V, M Esteban-Bravo and JM Vidal-Sanz (2016). Riding successive product diffusion waves. Building a tsunami via upgrade-rebate programs. *International Journal of Research in Marketing*, 33(4), 780–796.

Bagozzi, RP and Y Yi (1988). On the evaluation of structural equation models. *Academy of Marketing Science*, 16(1), 74–94.

Bagozzi, RP and Y Yi (2012). Specification, evaluation, and interpretation of structural equation models. *Journal of the Academy of Marketing Science*, 40(1), 8–34.

Bauer, U, H Endres, M Dowling and R Helm (2018). Organisational capabilities for technology transfer: A study of R&D-intensive firms in Germany. *International Journal of Innovation Management*, 22(4). doi: 10.1142/S136391961850041X.

Bechky, BA (2003). Sharing meaning across occupational communities: The transformation of understanding on a production floor. *Organization Science*, 14(3), 312–330.

Beverland, MB, P Micheli and FJ Farrelly (2016). Resourceful sensemaking: Overcoming barriers between marketing and design in NPD. *Journal of Product Innovation Management*, 33(5), 628–648. doi: 10.1111/jpim.12313.

Boland, RJJ and RV Tenkasi (1995). Perspective making and perspective taking in communities of knowing. *Organization Science*, 6(4), 350–372.

Bommer, M, R De La Porte and J Higgins (2002). Skunkworks approach to project management. *Journal of Management in Engineering*, 18(1), 21–28.

Brettel, M, F Heinemann, A Engelen and S Neubauer (2011). Cross-functional integration of R&D, marketing, and manufacturing in radical and incremental product innovations and its effects on project effectiveness and efficiency. *Journal of Product Innovation Management*, 28, 251–269.

Brown, JS and P Duguid (2001). Knowledge and organization: A social-practice perspective. *Organization Science*, 12(2), 198–213.

Burgers, JH and JG Covin (2016). The contingent effects of differentiation and integration on corporate entrepreneurship. *Strategic Management Journal*, 37(3), 521–540.

Burgers, JH, JJP Jansen, FAJ van den Bosch and HW Volberda (2009). Structural differentiation and corporate venturing: The moderating role of formal and informal integration mechanisms. *Journal of Business Venturing*, 24(3), 206–220.

Burns, T and GM Stalker (1961). *The Management of Innovation*. London: Tavistock Publications.

Byrne, BM (2010). *Structural Equation Modeling with AMOS: Basic Concepts, Applications, and Programming*, 2nd Ed., p. 418. New York, NY: Routledge.

Carlile, PR (2002). A pragmatic view of knowledge and boundaries. Boundary objects in new product development. *Organization Science*, 13(4), 442–455.

Carlile, PR (2004). Transferring, translating, and transforming: An integrative framework for managing knowledge across boundaries. *Organization Science*, 15(5), 555–568.

Cassiman, B and R Veugelers (2006). In search of complementarity in innovation strategy: Internal R&D and external knowledge acquisition. *Management Science*, 52(1), 68–82.

Christensen, CM (2003). *The Innovator's Dilemma: The Revolutionary Book that will Change the Way you do Business.* New York, NY: HarperBusiness Essentials. Available at http://www.loc.gov/catdir/description/hc041/2002027518.html

Clark, KB and SC Wheelwright (1992). Organizing and leading "heavyweight" development teams. *California Management Review*, 34(3), 9–28.

Cohen, WM and DA Levinthal (1990). Absorptive capacity. A new perspective on learning and innovation. *Administrative Science Quarterly*, 35, 128–152.

Colombo, MG, M Delmastro and L Rabbiosi (2007). High performance work practices, decentralization, and profitability: Evidence from panel data. *Industrial and Corporate Change*, 16(6), 1037–1067.

Coombs, JE and PEI Bierly (2006). Measuring technological capability and performance. *R&D Management*, 36, 421–438.

Cuijpers, M, H Guenter and K Hussinger (2011). Costs and benefits of inter-departmental innovation collaboration. *Research policy: Policy and Management Studies of Science, Technology and Innovation*, 40(4), 565–575.

Daft, RL and RH Lengel (1986). Organizational information requirements, media richness and structural design. *Management Science*, 32(5), 554–571.

De Jong, SB, GS Van der Vegt and E Molleman (2007). The relationships among asymmetry in task dependence, perceived helping behavior, and trust. *Journal of Applied Psychology*, 92(6), 1625–1637.

De Luca, LM and K Atuahene-Gima (2007). Market knowledge dimensions and cross-functional collaboration: Examining the different routes to product innovation performance. *Journal of Marketing*, 71, 95–112.

De Vaus, DA (2002). *Surveys in Social Research*, 5th ed. London: Routledge.

Distel, AP (2018). Unveiling the microfoundations of absorptive capacity: A study of Coleman's Bathtub model. *Journal of Management*. doi: 10.1177/0149206317741963.

Dosi, G (1982). Technological paradigms and technological trajectories: A suggested interpretation of the determinants and directions of technical change. *Research Policy: A Journal Devoted to Research Policy, Research Management and Planning*, 11(3), 147–162.

Dougherty, D (1992). Interpretive barriers to successful product innovation in large firms. *Organization science*, 3(2), 179–202.

Drechsler, W, M Natter and PSH Leeflang (2013). Improving marketing's contribution to new product development. *Journal of Product Innovation Management*, 30(2), 298–315.

Ebers, M and I Maurer (2014). Connections count: How relational embeddedness and relational empowerment foster absorptive capacity. *Research Policy*, 43(2), 318–332.

Edwards, JR and RP Bagozzi (2000). On the nature and direction of relationships between constructs and measures. *Psychological Methods*, 5(2), 155–174.

Ernst, H, WD Hoyer and C Rübsaamen (2010). Sales, marketing, and research-and-development cooperation across new product development stages: Implications for success. *Journal of Marketing*, 74(5), 80–92.

Felin, T, NJ Foss, KH Heimeriks and TL Madsen (2012). Microfoundations of routines and capabilities: Individuals, processes, and structure. *Journal of Management Studies*, 49(8), 1351–1374.

Flatten, TC, A Engelen, SA Zahra and M Brettel (2011). A measure of absorptive capacity: Scale development and validation. *European Management Journal*, 29(2), 98–116.

Foss, NJ, K Laursen and T Pedersen (2011). Linking customer interaction and innovation: The mediating role of new organizational practices. *Organization Science*, 22(4), 980–999.

Fry, LW and JW Slocum (1984). Technology, structure, and workgroup effectiveness: A test of a contingency model. *Academy of Management Journal*, 27(2), 221–246.

Galbraith, JR (1974). Organization design: An information processing view. *Interfaces: An International Journal of the Institute for Operations Research and the Management Sciences*, 4(3), 28–36.

Griffin, A and JR Hauser (1996). Integrating R&D and marketing. A review and analysis of the literature. *Journal of Product Innovation Management*, 13, 191–215.

Gupta, Anil K and V Govindarajan (1991). Knowledge flows and the structure of control within multinational corporations. *Academy of Management Review*, 16(4), 768–792.

Gupta, Anil K and V Govindarajan (2000). Knowledge flows within multinational corporations. *Strategic Management Journal*, 21(4), 473–496.

Gupta, Ashok K, SP Raj and D Wilemon (1986). A model for studying R&D-marketing interface in the product innovation process. *Journal of Marketing*, 50(April), 7–17.

Hansen, MT (2009). When internal collaboration is bad for your company. *Harvard Business Review*, 87(4), 82–88.

Hansen, MT and N Nohria (2004). How to build collaborative advantage. *MIT Sloan Management Review*, 46(1), 21–30.

Harman, HH (1967). *Modern Factor Analysis*, 2nd Ed. Chicago: University of Chicago Press.

Henderson, RM and KB Clark (1990). Architectural innovation: The reconfiguration of existing product technologies and the failure of established firms. *Administrative Science Quarterly*, 35(1), 9–30.

Hoegl, M, K Weinkauf and HG Gemuenden (2004). Interteam coordination, project commitment, and teamwork in multiteam R&D projects: A longitudinal study. *Organization Science*, 15(1), 38–55.

Homburg, C, S Alavi, T Rajab and J Wieseke (2017). The contingent roles of R&D–sales versus R&D–marketing cooperation in new-product development of business-to-business firms. *International Journal of Research in Marketing*, 34(1), 212–230. doi: 10.1016/j.ijresmar.2016.05.008.

Hu, L and PM Bentler (1999). Cutoff criteria for fit indexes in covariance structure analysis: Conventional criteria versus new alternatives. *Structural Equation Modeling: A Multidisciplinary Journal*, 6(1), 1–55.

Iacobucci, D (2010). Structural equations modeling: Fit Indices, sample size, and advanced topics. *Journal of Consumer Psychology*, 20, 90–98.

Iansiti, M and KB Clark (1994). Integration and dynamic capability: Evidence from product development in automobiles and mainframe computers. *Industrial and Corporate Change*, 3(3), 557–605.

Ingram, P and JAC Baum (1997). Opportunity and constraint: Organizations' learning from the operating and competitive experience of industries. *Strategic Management Journal*, 18(Summer Special Issue), 75–98.

Jansen, JJP, MP Tempelaar, FAJ van den Bosch and HW Volberda (2009). Structural differentiation and ambidexterity: The mediating role of integration mechanisms. *Organization Science*, 20(4), 797–811.

Jansen, JJP, FAJ van den Bosch and HW Volberda (2005). Managing potential and realized absorptive capacity: How do organizational antecedents matter? *Academy of Management Journal*, 48(6), 999–1015. doi: 10.5465/AMJ.2005.19573106.

Jaworski, BJ and AK Kohli (1993). Market orientation. Antecedents and consequences. *Journal of Marketing*, 57(July), 53–70.

Johnson, JD, WA Donohue, CK Atkin and S Johnson (1994). Differences between formal and informal communication channels. *Journal of Business Communication*, 31(2), 111–122.

Jones, M and R Sugden (2001). Positive confirmation bias in the acquisition of information. *Theory and Decision: An International Journal for Multidisciplinary Advances in Decision Science*, 50(1), 59–99.

Kutner, MH, CJ Nachtsheim, J Neter and W Li (2005). *Applied Linear Statistical Models*, 5. Ed., internat. ed. Boston, Mass.: McGraw-Hill.

Lamore, PR, D Berkowitz and PA Farrington (2013). Proactive/responsive market orientation and marketing — Research and development integration. *Journal of Product Innovation Management*, 30(4), 695–711.

Lane, PJ and M Lubatkin (1998). Relative absorptive capacity and interorganizational learning. *Strategic Management Journal*, 19, 461–477.

Lawrence, PR and JW Lorsch (1967). Differentiation and integration in complex organizations. *Administrative Science Quarterly*, 12(1), 1–47.

Lee, JM and R Kapoor (2017). Complementarities and coordination: Implications for governance mode and performance of multiproduct firms. *Organization Science, Articles in Advance*, 28(5), 931–946.

Leenders, MA and B Wierenga (2002). The effectiveness of different mechanisms for integrating marketing and R&D. *Journal of Product Innovation Management*, 19, 305–317.

Lessard, DR and S Zaheer (1996). Breaking the silos: Distributed knowledge and strategic responses to volatile exchange rates. *Strategic Management Journal*, 17(7), 513–533.

Li, T and RJ Calantone (1998). The impact of market knowledge competence on new product advantage: Conceptualization and empirical examination. *Journal of Marketing*, 62(4), 13–29. doi: 10.2307/1252284.

Luo, X, RJ Slotegraaf and X Pan (2006). Cross-functional coopetition: The simultaneous role of cooperation and competition within firms. *Journal of Marketing*, 70(April), 67–80.

MacCormack, A, C Baldwin and J Rusnak (2012). Exploring the duality between product and organizational architectures: A test of the \d qmirroring\d q hypothesis. *Research Policy: Policy And Management Studies of Science, Technology and Innovation*, 41(8), 1309–1324.

Majchrzak, A, PH More and S Faraj (2012). Transcending knowledge differences in cross-functional teams. *Organization Science*, 23(4), 951–970.

Maltz, E, WE Souder and A Kumar (2001). Influencing R&D/marketing integration and the use of market information by R&D managers: Intended and unintended effects of managerial actions. *Journal of Business Research*, 52(1), 69–82.

Menon, A and R Varadarajan (1992). A model of marketing knowledge use within firms. *Journal of Marketing*, 52(4), 53–71.

Moenaert, RK, WE Souder, A de Meyer and D Deschoolmeester (1994). R&D-marketing integration mechanisms, communication flows, and innovation success. *Journal of Product Innovation Management*, 11(1), 31–45.

Moorman, C and AS Miner (1998). Organizational improvisation and organizational memory. *Academy of Management Review*, 23(4), 698–723.

Moorman, C and RT Rust (1999). The role of marketing. *Journal of Marketing*, 63(SI), 180–197.

Olson, EM, OC Walker, RW Ruekert and JM Bonner (2001). Patterns of cooperation during new product development among marketing, operations and R&D. Implications for project performance. *Journal of Product Innovation Management*, 18, 258–271.

Pinto, MB and JK Pinto (1990). Project team communication and cross-functional co-operation in new program development. *Journal of Product Innovation Management*, 7(3), 200–212.

Rothaermel, FT and MT Alexandre (2009). Ambidexterity in technology sourcing: The moderating role of absorptive capacity. *Organization Science*, 20(4), 759–780.

Rothwell, R (1994). Towards the fifth-generation innovation process. *International Marketing Review*, 11(1), 7–31.

Rubera, G, A Ordanini and R Calantone (2012). Whether to integrate R&D and marketing: The effect of firm competence. *Journal of Product Innovation Management*, 29(5), 766–783.

Ruekert, RW and OC Walker (1987). Marketings's interaction with other functional units: A conceptual framework and empirical evidence. *Journal of Marketing*, 51(1), 1–19.

Schafer, JL and JW Graham (2002). Missing data: Our view of the state of the art. *Psychological Methods*, 7(2), 147–177.

Shaw, V and CT Shaw (1998). Conflict between engineers and marketers. *Industrial Marketing Management*, 27(4), 279–291.

Sheehan, KB (2001). E-mail survey response rates: A review. *Journal of Computer-Mediated Communication*, 6(2). https://doi.org/10.1111/j.1083-6101.2001.tb00117.x.

Sherman, JD and RT Keller (2011). Suboptimal assessment of interunit task interdependence: Modes of integration and information processing for coordination performance. *Organization Science*, 22(1), 245–261.

Song, XM and ME Parry (1997). Teamwork barriers in Japanese high technology firms: The sociocultural differences between R&D and marketing managers. *Journal of Product Innovation Management*, 14, 356–367.

Song, XM, RJ Thieme and J Xie (1998). The impact of cross-functional joint involvement across product development stages. An exploratory study. *Journal of Product Innovation Management*, 15, 289–303.

Song, XM, J Xie and CA Di Benedetto (2001). Message and source factors, market uncertainty, and extrafunctional information processing. Hypotheses and empirical evidence. *IEEE Transaction on Engineering Management*, 48(2), 223–238.

Sosa, ME, M Gargiulo and C Rowles (2015). Can informal communication networks disrupt coordination in new product development projects? *Organization Science*, 26(4), 1059–1078.

Stock, RM, F Totzauer and NA Zacharias (2014). A closer look at cross-functional R&D cooperation for innovativeness: Innovation-oriented leadership and human resource practices as driving forces. *Journal of Product Innovation Management*, 31(5), 924–938. doi: 10.1111/jpim.12132.

Szulanski, G (1996). Exploring internal stickiness: Impediments to the transfer of best practice within the firm. *Strategic Management Journal*, 17(Special Issue (Winter): Knowledge and the Firm), 27–43.

Todorova, G and B Durisin (2007). Absorptive capacity: Valuing a reconceptualization. *Academy of Management Review*, 32(3), 774–786.

Tripsas, M (2009). Technology, identity, and inertia through the lens of \dq the digital photography company \d q. *Organization Science*, 20(2), 441–460.

Troy, LC, T Hirunyawipada and AK Paswan (2008). Cross-functional integration and new product success. An empirical investigation of the findings. *Journal of Marketing*, 72(Nov), 132–146.

Tushman, ML (1977). Special boundary roles in the innovation process. *Administrative Science Quarterly*, 22(4), 587–605.

Tushman, ML and DA Nadler (1978). Information processing as an integrating concept in organizational design. *Academy of Management Review*, 3(3), 613–624.

Van Wijk, R, JJP Jansen and MA Lyles (2008). Inter- and intra-organizational knowledge transfer: A meta-analytic review and assessment of its antecedents and consequences. *Journal of Management Studies*, 45(4), 830–853. doi: 10.1111/j.1467-6486.2008.00771.x.

Verhoef, PC and PSH Leeflang (2009). Understanding the marketing department's influence within the firm. *Journal of Marketing*, 73, 1–42.

Volberda, HW, NJ Foss and MA Lyles (2010). Absorbing the concept of absorptive capacity: How to realize its potential in the organization field. *Organization Science*, 21(4), 931–951.

Walsh, JP and GR Ungson (1991). Organizational memory. *Administrative Science Quarterly*, 16(1), 57–91.

Wang, Q (1997). R&D/Marketing Interface in a firm's capability-building process: Evidence from pharmaceutical firms. *International Journal of Innovation Management*, 1(1), 23–52. doi: 10.1142/S1363919697000036.

Weick, K (1993). The collapse of sensemaking in organizations: The Mann Gulch Disaster. *Administrative Science Quarterly*, 38(4), 628–652.

Yao, FK and S Chang (2017). Do individual employees' learning goal orientation and civic virtue matter? A micro-foundations perspective on firm absorptive capacity. *Strategic Management Journal*. Available at http://onlinelibrary.wiley.com/doi/10.1002/smj.2636/full.

Zahra, SA and G George (2002). Absorptive capacity. A review, reconceptualization, and extension. *Academy of Management Review*, 27(2), 185–203.

Zahra, SA and AP Nielsen (2002). Sources of capabilities, integration and technology commercialization. *Strategic Management Journal*, 23(5), 377–398. doi: 10.1002/smj.229.

Zhao, ZJ and J Anand (2013). Beyond boundary spanners: The \ dq collective bridge \ dq as an efficient interunit structure for transferring collective knowledge. *Strategic Management Journal*, 34(13), 1513–1530.

Chapter 17

KNOWLEDGE ABSORPTIVE CAPACITY, INNOVATION, AND FIRM'S PERFORMANCE: INSIGHTS FROM THE SOUTH OF BRAZIL[†]

GUILLERMO ANTONIO DÁVILA*

Department of Knowledge Engineering and Management
Federal University of Santa Catarina
Campus Universitario Trindade, Florianópolis/SC, 88040-900, Brazil
guillermo.davila@posgrad.ufsc.br

SUSANNE DURST

School of Business, University of Skövde
Högskolevägen, 541 28 Skövde, Sweden
susanne.durst@his.se

GREGORIO VARVAKIS

Department of Knowledge Engineering and Management
Federal University of Santa Catarina
Campus Universitario Trindade, Florianópolis/SC, 88040-900, Brazil
g.varvakis@ufsc.br

Published 16 June 2017

This paper aims to verify the relationships that may exist between knowledge absorptive capacity (ACAP), innovation performance, and organisational performance in Brazilian firms. A sample of 111 firms from Southern Brazil was surveyed and PLSSEM was used to test the theoretical hypotheses. The relevance of ACAP for innovation and organisational performance is supported. The research also shows that realised ACAP has more influence on innovation performance compared with potential ACAP. Some guidelines for furthering ACAP models suitable for developing countries are provided as well. The findings are a good reference for practitioners as they identify possible actions which can enhance ACAP and thereby contribute to improving innovativeness and performance. This research complements earlier studies which called for the exploration of the role of ACAP on

*Corresponding author.

[†]This article originally appeared in *International Journal of Innovation Management*, **24** 1850013-1-34

innovation performance and firm's competitiveness in developing countries, and it opens new avenues for multidisciplinary research.

Keywords: Knowledge absorptive capacity; innovation; firm's performance; knowledge management.

Introduction

Brazilian firms also seem to acknowledge knowledge as a key resource that needs to be managed for continuously improving outcomes, such as innovative capabilities and performance, in order to remain competitive. In the Brazilian business context, knowledge exists independently from human beings, it can be transferred and is usually related to technology (Paiva *et al.*, 2008; Ferraresi *et al.*, 2012; Dominguez Gonzalez *et al.*, 2014). These characteristics are in line with the knowledge-based view (KBV) of the firm, in which knowledge is the key resource for competitiveness. Thus, the main role of firms is to transform knowledge from its specialists into goods and services by deploying efficient knowledge creation and application processes (Grant, 1996).

In fact, some relevant studies around the world treat knowledge as a source and a product of innovation (e.g., Scarbrough, 2003; Fosfuri and Tribó, 2008), which in turn is essential for firm's survival and competitiveness (Schumpeter, 1927; Teece, 2010). Interest in innovation, its processes, and management has increased over the years, because firms need to innovate in response to changing customer demands and to take advantage of the opportunities offered by new technologies and/or new marketplaces (Baregheh *et al.*, 2009; Teece, 2010; Vargo *et al.*, 2015). One ability that helps dealing with these challenges is absorptive capacity (ACAP), which can be defined as a set of routines and organisational processes for acquiring, assimilating, transforming, and exploring knowledge to improve organisational skills, and consequently, to sustain and increase its competitive advantage (Zahra and George, 2002). This definition of Zahra and George integrates different ACAP definitions from related research streams, such as knowledge creation (Nonaka and Takeuchi, 1995), knowledge integration (Grant, 1996), organisational learning (Cohen and Levinthal, 1989, 1990; Edmondson and Moingeon, 1998), and others. For instance, Grant (1996) stated that ACAP depends on the capacity of aggregation, which is one of the KBV foundations, defined as the firm's ability to put new knowledge into previously existing knowledge, which in turn can be facilitated by the existence of common knowledge. Based on Zahra and George's (2002) definition and considering related research streams, Flatten *et al.* (2011a) developed a measure for ACAP and its dimensions. In contrast to ACAP measures that are based on R&D proxies and treating ACAP as a static resource (Lane *et al.*, 2006), Flatten *et al.*'s (2011a) measure treats ACAP as a capability. This is also done in the present study. Doing so facilitates a more systematic analysis such as assessing the intensity of each ACAP dimension and its degree of contribution to firm outcomes (Flatten *et al.*, 2011a).

A wide range of empirical studies point out that ACAP is closely related to innovation performance (IP) (Becheikh, 2013; Tidd and Bessant, 2009; Flatten *et al.*, 2011b; Gray, 2006; Petraite, 2010; Wuryaningrat, 2013). Innovating, however, is a real challenge for several firms, because of the existence of some barriers related — for instance — to organisational size, economic context, or culture. Leadership issues, lack of empowerment, limited capacity to access and share knowledge, to finance operations and new initiatives, to attract and retain qualified professionals, or to capture ideas from employees have been identified as other barriers in peripheral regions (McAdam *et al.*, 2004) and in developing countries (North *et al.*, 2013).

Both the unique knowledge characteristics and innovation barriers in developing countries have led to recognise a particular need for studies about the role of ACAP for innovation and firm's performance in these contexts. Although there is some research about ACAP and innovation in developed economies (e.g., Ben Zaied and Affes, 2015; Darroch, 2005; Jansen *et al.*, 2006; Roxas *et al.*, 2014), there are only a few studies that have investigated the effects of internal firm elements, such as ACAP, on innovation and competitiveness in developing economies such as Brazil (Nagano *et al.*, 2014). In fact, recent research has shown the need for studying the relationships between knowledge-related capabilities, such as ACAP, and innovation in developing countries (Inkinen *et al.*, 2015).

Against this background, the purpose of this paper is to answer the following questions: (1) Which guidelines could future research follow in order to develop suitable models for studying ACAP and innovation in developing countries such as Brazil? and (2) What is the relationship between ACAP, innovation performance, and organisational performance (OP) in Brazilian firms? By answering these questions, this study aims to advance our understanding of ACAP's contribution to innovation and firm's performance in developing countries.

The paper addresses these issues from a positivist point of view, as used in most KBV studies (Nonaka and Peltokorpi, 2006). Positivism is in line with previous studies about knowledge management (KM) and innovation conducted in the Brazilian business context (e.g., Paiva *et al.*, 2008; Ferraresi *et al.*, 2012; Davila, 2016) and other contexts (e.g., Moos *et al.*, 2013; Adams *et al.*, 2015). By choosing positivism, aligned with a Brazilian perspective, the authors of this study assume that knowledge is objective and can thus be transferred as it exists separately from human beings (Grant, 1996; Nonaka and Peltokorpi, 2006).

This paper is structured as follows: first, innovation and ACAP are theoretically discussed by (1) defining them as KM-based constructs and (2) by exploring the relationship among them and how they could affect the organisational performance. Then, the relationships between ACAP, innovation performance, and organisational performance are empirically examined, using data collected from 111 southern Brazilian firms with at least 20 employees. Finally, the findings are discussed, and some implications for new ACAP models in developing countries and for enhancing firm's competitiveness are presented.

Theoretical Background

Analysing the contribution of ACAP on innovative and organisational performance in emerging countries like Brazil requires two things that are presented next. First, the involved constructs, such as ACAP, innovation performance, and organisational performance, should be properly defined (it means according to the Brazilian context) and their relations discussed theoretically in a suitable form. Second, it is necessary to have an understanding of specific key contextual factors that can influence KM initiatives in Brazilian firms. Thereby, we classify these factors into three groups: national culture, political and economical level, and firm level. In addition, this study uses the positivist point of view. Following positivism, Zins (2007, p. 487) defines knowledge as "a set of signs that represent the meaning (or the content) of thoughts that the individual justifiably believes that are true." As knowledge exists outside the individual world, it can be transferred. As Ritala *et al.* (2015) stress, the objective nature of knowledge does not imply that it is independent of meaning, but it rather indicates that meanings exist separately from the individual who perceives it. Positivism has strong limitations when used to explain a non-static phenomenon (Nonaka and Peltokorpi, 2006) such as knowledge creation, which, however, is not the goal of the study. We chose a positivist point of view for two reasons: firstly, positivism is being used in other relevant studies about knowledge and innovation (Gloet and Terziovski, 2004; Gray, 2006; Fosfuri and Tribó, 2008; Flatten *et al.*, 2011b; Kianto and Andreeva, 2014; Roxas *et al.*, 2014; Inkinen *et al.*, 2015). Secondly, we believe that a positivist approach is more appropriate for managing studies in Brazilian business context, in which knowledge appears to be considered as a transferable object that is linked to technology and managed to obtain competitive advantages (Paiva *et al.*, 2008; Ferraresi *et al.*, 2012; Dominguez Gonzalez *et al.*, 2014).

Innovation

Academics have studied innovation from different disciplines such as business administration, economic sciences, technology, engineering, and others (Baregheh *et al.*, 2009). It has been treated as a process, as an outcome, or both; but mostly the view of innovation as an adoption of a new idea or behaviour is shared (Jimenez-Jimenez and Sanz-Valle, 2011). Schumpeter (1927) in his seminal work defines innovation as being one or many of the following: the introduction of a new good or the introduction of an improvement to an existing one, the introduction of a new production method, and the opening of a new market; all of which leads to a new economic condition.

Innovation can occur in many ways, with different intensity and over different organisational elements. For example, recent approaches based on the research of Schumpeter (1927) classify innovations into four types: product, process, marketing, and organisational innovation (Damanpour, 1991; Sawhney *et al.*, 2006). Marketing innovations are related to customer experience and market solutions, whereas organisational innovation occurs when the organisational model is improved or changed.

Much of the current literature supports the hypothesis that innovation usually involves the dealing with diversity of technologies and markets, thus, with a set of knowledge elements that are put together into a new configuration (Díaz-Díaz and de Saá Pérez, 2014; Figueiredo, 2013; Leonard-Barton, 1995). Similarly, empirical studies have demonstrated that an important part of this knowledge comes from external sources (Fosfuri and Tribó, 2008), and this external know-how can significantly increase innovation performance (Cassiman and Veugelers, 2006). Tidd and Bessant (2009) also stated that managing innovation is about having a clear strategy, providing a supportive organisational climate, and managing external links and learning.

For Tidd and Bessant (2009), the ability to manage innovation is positively related to a firm's sustaining competitiveness. The authors point out that this ability can be improved by learning in two aspects (p. 591):

- Acquisition of new knowledge (for example about technology, market, and legislation) to expand the firm's knowledge base for timely use in new/improved products and processes [this is what research means with ACAP; see, e.g., Cohen and Levinthal (1990), Grant (1996), and Zahra and George (2002)].
- Knowledge of the innovation process itself, or the ability to develop and operate the set of routines needed for managing (planning and executing) innovation. This is also defined by Wang *et al.* (2013) as a meta-knowledge which is used for producing new knowledge.

Consequently, KM can be seen as a critical approach for helping organisations to better understand and improve the management of both the specified knowledge involved in the innovation process and the 'meta-knowledge' about the process itself.

Knowledge management and its importance for innovation management

An interesting feature of KBV approach is that it provides the basis for understanding organisational innovations, by considering the renovation of traditional organisational structures (e.g., empowerment, team-based structures, or strategic alliances), the importance of knowledge-based competences, and the existence of knowledge creation and application processes that leads to value creation. According to KBV, the main role of the firm is to integrate specialised knowledge resident in humans into goods and services. Consequently, the KBV approach suggests that firm's innovation is an outcome of knowledge integration (Grant, 1996).

In this line, many scholars stress the strong relationship between knowledge and innovation. For example, Scarbrough (2003) defines innovation as an interactive process that integrates knowledge and action of creating value, and consequently, knowledge management exists as a medium and outcome in this process. Since knowledge is both a key resource for and outcome of the innovation process, it needs to be managed. Evidence confirms that KM research had increased dramatically during the recent years, but there is still no a consensual definition of KM (Edvardsson and Durst, 2013). In the present study, based on Dalkir (2005) and Wiig (1993), KM is understood as a set of intentional processes and routines, performed by people, usually supported by technology, and aligned with organisational strategic goals, which aim to maximise the contribution of the resource knowledge.

Empirical studies have demonstrated the relationship between knowledge management and innovative performance as a key driver for organisational competitiveness. For example, Gloet and Terziovski (2004) who studied manufacturing companies from Australia and New Zealand, concluded that KM practices make a significant contribution to innovation performance, especially the ones which are oriented to human resource management and which are supported by information technology (IT). Other studies conducted in New Zealand have shown that a firm with knowledge management capabilities tends to be more innovative and has better performance (Darroch, 2005; Zack *et al.*, 2009; Roxas *et al.*, 2014). In their research with Taiwanese firms, Chen and Huang (2009) identified a positive mediating role of knowledge management capacity between strategic human resources practices and innovation performance. More recently, Inkinen *et al.* (2015) had similar results in Finnish firms, as they showed that innovation performance is supported by some KM practices related to strategy, compensation, and IT.

Knowledge management systems and organisational knowledge are positively linked to innovation success in the research of Moos *et al.* (2013). On the other hand, a study of French biotechnological SMEs conducted by Alegre *et al.* (2013) demonstrated an indirect and positive impact of KM practices on innovation performance, through the existence of dynamic capabilities.

Theoretical and empirical researches show that innovation and sustainable competitiveness depend on how firms execute KM processes, but they also depend on how firms expand and reconfigure their knowledge base by adding new knowledge (Alegre *et al.*, 2013; Darroch, 2005; Inkinen *et al.*, 2015; Forés and Camisón, 2016). Therefore, a firm that improves its ACAP (by investing in R&D, training, and others) would be likely to succeed on innovation (Tidd and Bessant, 2009).

Absorptive capacity and its dimensions

ACAP is a multidisciplinary construct, which has been analysed from many research streams (Flatten *et al.*, 2011a). Initially, ACAP was defined as the firm's ability to take advantage of external knowledge, in a process that includes the use of basic skills for recognising the value of the new information, assimilating, and applying this information for commercial purposes (Cohen and Levinthal, 1990), and even for predicting the nature of future technological advances (Cohen and Levinthal, 1994). For Cohen and Levinthal (1990), ACAP is one of the firm's learning capabilities, which is supported by Lane *et al.* (2006) who stress that organisational learning enhances the firm's knowledge base, which further increases ACAP, and facilitates even more learning.

In their seminal work, Cohen and Levinthal (1990) used R&D function for analysing and describing ACAP, and following this, many scholars analysed ACAP based on R&D proxies, mostly using the view (RBV) perspective. For example, Liu and White (1997, p. 119) found "most innovative industries couple investments in both R&D personnel and technology imports rather than relying on either input alone," and Tsai (2001) showed the relationship between R&D investments and innovation. Later, scholars criticized the use of R&D proxies for analysing ACAP, arguing that they consider ACAP as a static resource, limit ACAP to technology-intensive firms, have resulted in very divergent results, and are unable to analyse ACAP as a capability (Lane *et al.*, 2006; Flatten *et al.*, 2011a).

ACAP has also been studied from the KBV perspective, which has helped to understand how firms transfer knowledge, by adding new knowledge to previously existing one (Grant, 1996). In another study, Van den Bosch *et al.* (1999) presented a framework for improving the understanding of ACAP as a facilitator for organisational flexibility. In line with Cohen and Levinthal (1990), the framework stresses the importance of 'prior knowledge' element as a determinant of ACAP.

The term 'prior knowledge' refers to the knowledge previously accumulated by the organisation intended to enhance future learning processes. The works of Grant (1996) and Van den Bosch *et al.* (1999) referred to ACAP as a capability, and not as a resource.

Also, based on Cohen and Levinthal (1990), Zahra and George (2002) proposed a multidimensional definition of ACAP. According to them, ACAP is a dynamic capability composed of a set of routines and organisational processes by which firms acquire, assimilate, transform, and explore knowledge to improve organisational skills, and consequently, to sustain and increase competitive advantage. In the present study, ACAP is addressed as a capability, which includes "in addition to knowledge content, organisational routines and processes" (Lane *et al.*, 2006, p. 844).

Following the processual nature of ACAP, Zahra and George (2002) emphasise the existence of four dimensions — acquisition, assimilation, transformation, and exploitation. Acquisition refers to the ability of the organisation to identify and acquire knowledge generated externally and critical to its operation. Knowledge assimilation routines allow the firm to analyse, interpret, and understand process information captured from external sources. The factor that promotes the assimilation of knowledge is understanding. The transformation ability facilitates the identification of opportunities by developing and refining the routines and practices that allow you to combine new knowledge with prior knowledge base through the addition of knowledge, knowledge elimination or 'bissociation,' which occurs when the same idea is perceived by two self-consistent but incompatible backgrounds. Finally, exploitation is the ability to refine, develop, and/or change existing skills for new ones, by incorporating in the operational routines the new knowledge previously acquired, assimilated, and processed.

In addition, Zahra and George (2002) highlight two roles. Potential ACAP is a role which includes capabilities of acquisition and assimilation of knowledge whereas realised ACAP refers to the transformation and exploitation of knowledge. In comparison with realised ACAP, Zahra and George (2002) found that a low and disproportionate number of studies referred to potential ACAP, characterized by such authors as the dimension that provides organisations with the strategic flexibility to adapt and evolve in contexts of high speed.

The model developed by Zahra and George (2002) has formed the basis for further studies on ACAP, and most of them have also suggested that potential ACAP has a positive influence on realised ACAP (e.g., Cepeda-Carrion *et al.*, 2012; Chang *et al.*, 2013; Leal-Rodriguez *et al.*, 2014; Lev *et al.*, 2009; Santos, 2013; Xia and Roper, 2016). Based on these studies, the following hypothesis was posed:

H_1. *Potential ACAP positively influences realised ACAP.*

It is important to observe that while the ACAP definition of Cohen and Levinthal (1990) uses the term 'new information,' the majority of following definitions, including the one by Zahra and George (2002), use the term 'knowledge.' In the universal domain, which is used in positivism and thus in the present study, both information and knowledge are human artefacts. "Information is a set of signs, which represent empirical knowledge, and knowledge is a set of signs that represent the meaning (or the content) of thoughts that the individual justifiably believes that they are true" (Zins, 2007, p. 487).

The link between absorptive capacity and innovation performance

Zahra and George (2002) pointed to a significant relationship between ACAP, especially realised ACAP, and innovative output. The authors define potential ACAP as a creator of flexibility for adapting and evolving in high-velocity environments and realised ACAP as a capability which produces competitive advantages by the consistent creation of new goods, procedures, systems, knowledge, or new organisational forms. This view is supported by subsequent studies which define ACAP as a source of innovation, by aiming to reconfigure the firm's knowledge base which is used to innovate (Leonard-Barton, 1995; Figueiredo, 2013; Díaz-Díaz and de Saá Pérez, 2014), allowing firms to 'repeat the trick' Tidd and Bessant (2009, p. 259).

ACAP is a key capability for organisational innovation, considering that innovation can be seen as a process where new knowledge is produced (Wang *et al.*, 2013), and an important part of this knowledge comes from external sources (Popadiuk and Choo, 2006; Fosfuri and Tribó, 2008).

Recently, some empirical works have examined the influence of ACAP on innovation performance (Tsai, 2001; Lund Vinding, 2006; Chen *et al.*, 2009; Tseng *et al.*, 2011; Kostopoulos *et al.*, 2011; Cepeda-Carrion *et al.*, 2012; Wuryaningrat, 2013; Tortoriello, 2014; Huang *et al.*, 2015; Lau and Lo, 2015). For example, in their research in Spanish firms, Fosfuri and Tribó (2008) found that organisations with higher levels of potential ACAP systematically achieve better performance through new or improved products. According to Zahra and George (2002), realised ACAP is a necessary condition for achieving innovation performance through potential ACAP. The study of Kostopoulos *et al.* (2011) concluded that external knowledge inflows and ACAP are positively related to innovation performance. In a same line of thinking, the study of Cepeda-Carrion *et al.* (2012) shows a positive influence of realised ACAP, together with information system capabilities, on firm's innovativeness. Inside organisations, a research in business units has also demonstrated the positive effect of ACAP in innovation performance (Tsai, 2001). Corral de Zubielqui *et al.* (2016) conclude that ACAP has a positive direct influence on innovation outcomes and an indirect effect on firm's performance through innovation. Thus, the study of Corral de Zubielqui *et al.* (2016) set up the basis for discussing individual effects of potential ACAP and realised ACAP. Based on those studies, this work tests the following hypotheses:

$H_{2.1}$. *Potential ACAP positively influences innovation performance.*
$H_{2.2}$. *Realised ACAP positively influences innovation performance.*

Innovation performance and organisational performance

Analysing the effects of innovation on organisational performance has typically been a challenge because of some difficulties, such as the weakness between inputs and outputs at the firm level, the number and complexity of other internal and external variables that affect organisational behaviour, and because firm's indicators directed to financial markets are more focussed on management and technological efficiency rather than innovation indexes. Due to these aspects, it is also necessary to look for correlations between key indicators such as new products launch, patents, R&D expenditures, productivity growth, profitability, or market values of firms (Tidd and Bessant, 2009). Other classic (Dess and Robinson, 1984; Romijn and Albaladejo, 2002) and recent (Huang *et al.*, 2016; Lau and Lo, 2015; Inkinen *et al.*, 2015; Roxas *et al.*, 2014) studies in management have demonstrated that subjective indicators also are usable for analysing the concepts of innovation and organisational performance.

Thus, the relationship between innovation performance and organisational performance has been explored in many studies, and most of them identified positive links between these constructs. For example, the study of (Damanpour *et al.*, 1989) highlights the importance and significance of technical innovations for organisational performance and states that administrative innovations are necessary for facilitating technical innovations over time. In a similar way, the empirical study of Jimenez-Jimenez and Sanz-Valle (2011) verified that innovation performance influences directly and positively organisational performance.

Akgun *et al.* (2009) explored the impact of some innovation types over organisational performance, concluding that product innovations and process innovations have a strong and significant influence on organisational performance. Jansen *et al.* (2006) found that exploratory innovations are likely to increase financial performance when organisational units operate in more dynamic environments. On the other hand, organisations in competitive environments improve their performance by pursuing exploitative innovations.

Based on these studies and other recent empirical studies (e.g., Huang *et al.*, 2016; Jurksiene and Giniuniene, 2015; Luis Leal-Rodriguez *et al.*, 2015), this study is going to test the following hypotheses:

H_3. *Innovation performance has a positive influence on organisational performance.*

Key contextual factors for KM in Brazilian firms

The importance of ACAP for innovation performance and sustainable competitiveness has been demonstrated in several studies. However, most of these studies are based on samples from developed and Western countries (e.g., Flatten *et al.*, 2011b). How would the concept work in different contexts? Which guidelines could future research follow in order to develop suitable models and frameworks for studying ACAP and innovation in developing countries such as Brazil? The answer to both questions will depend on some contextual factors, which influence the utilisation and efficiency of KM in each context. Table 1 presents these factors for Brazil with a particular focus on KM.

Table 1. Key contextual factors for KM usage and efficiency in Brazilian firms.

Environmental factors
National Culture
Collectivism. Brazilians have a lower practice of institutional collectivism. Nevertheless, Brazilians have high in-group collectivism, in terms of values and practice. They tend to express pride, loyalty, and cohesiveness in their social groups or families (House *et al.*, 2004).
Power distance. In Brazil, there is a higher power distance when compared with other nations (House *et al.*, 2004). For Strese *et al.* (2016, p. 1164), employees in environments of "high power distance might lose their personal, intrinsic commitment to strive for an efficient transformation and exploitation of knowledge since they might only act based on orders from distant supervisors". Organisational competencies such as ACAP, are even better supported by adhocracy culture in countries with a high level of power distance.
Risk avoidance. Brazilian national culture is risk-averse, even when this uncertainty avoidance tends to decrease in practice (House *et al.*, 2004), maybe because frequently people need to take their daily decisions facing some turbulent events. "The risk-taking adhocracy culture is even more effective in fostering knowledge management processes in a risk-averse national culture such as that of Brazil" (Strese *et al.*, 2016, p. 1165).
Leadership. Brazilian leaders are on average more charismatic, more team-oriented, more participative, and less autonomous when compared with leaders from other countries (House *et al.*, 2004). Negotiations are slower and are based much more on personal contact, and consequently, conducting business first and the rest later (like Americans) would be found rude by Brazilians. "Their relationships with other business people are interpersonal in nature, and they place a high value on human relations" (Turner and Kleiner, 2001, p. 62).
From tacit to explicit knowledge. Klafke *et al.* (2016, p. 812) point that "Brazil, Russia, and India have an easier way of converting tacit knowledge into explicit knowledge compared to China,

Table 1. (*Continued*)

Environmental factors
where informal relationships of trust and friendship play a special role within organisations." In Brazil, idiosyncratic characteristic of the professionals being open to colleagues, a personalisation-orientated knowledge management strategy, and a flexible organisational structure contributes with the willingness of the professionals to transfer tacit knowledge (Joia and Lemos, 2010).
Multiculturalism. "People living in one section of Brazil perceive themselves as separate and distinct from those residing elsewhere in the country" (Turner and Kleiner, 1996, p. 59). Even when Brazilians value their diversified origin and imagine themselves as a society without prejudices; in Brazil, opportunities in the education system and labour market are usually defined by the economic and racial origin. The challenge for organisations is to learn how to manage multicultural teams to take the best advantages in terms of competitiveness and differentiation (Fleury, 1999).
Politics and Economy
Instability. Economic and market conditions in Brazil are unstable when compared with other markets such as Europe or the USA. This instability complicates firms' operation management and creates a need for innovation (Alves Filho *et al.*, 2015). In addition, workers are "willing to adapt to new working methods in order to keep their jobs" (Strategic Direction, 2005, p. 28). Governmental and corporate education play an important role in transforming this flexibility in improved competitiveness (Strategic Direction, 2005; Klafke *et al.*, 2016).
R & D & I. "Brazil appears to be going in the right direction in terms of policy supporting the development of technology, skilled workers and the promotion of innovation" (Sparkman, 2015, p. 676). From 2004, "an increased focus on technology has resulted in the development of several policies designed to encourage to promote research, innovation, and development — RDI" (Sparkman, 2015). These policies aimed to overcome important barriers to economic growth (Nogueira *et al.*, 2014). Thus, Brazil has shown modest progress in its Technology Achievement Index (TAI) score, from 0.311 in 2002 to 0.335 in 2009 (Sparkman, 2015).
Complex demand. "Customers not only demand innovative products/services and high quality, they also demand both reasonable lead times and prices. Thus, rather than focusing on one competitive priority, companies must find ways of competing on a blend of outcomes." Innovativeness has emerged as a new key priority (Thürer *et al.*, 2013, p. 872).
Opportunities for KM. Firms' R&D initiatives used to involve clients and the drivers have been local market demands and particularities (Bagno and Cheng, 2007). "Brazil's embrace of technology creates research opportunities in the areas of knowledge management and e-learning" (Sparkman, 2015, p. 677).
Role of people. "In Brazil, the main KM practices are closely connected to the people and intellectual capital development, in which human resource departments play a special role. Human capital management is essential in a knowledge society, where people look for recognition and continuous refinement of their abilities and skills" (Klafke *et al.*, 2016, p. 823).
Firm-Level Factors
Strategic alliances. The importance of networks and alliances is growing. It is important to know that knowledge is the resource interchanged inside networks, and the expected result is collective learning (Fleury and Fleury, 1997). For example, in the food industry, external integration with

Table 1. (*Continued*)

Firm-Level Factors
suppliers and customers is positively related to innovation outcomes, and radical innovation is directly related to large companies rather than non-large ones (Nogueira *et al.*, 2014).
Inter-firm information. There is a higher influence of customers' information than suppliers' information, which may indicate issues such as a possible lack of trust between suppliers and companies. Firms need real-time information for quick decisions, this promotes an increasing adoption of computer-based systems for manufacturing management (Paiva *et al.*, 2012).
Incentives. "The generation of more incentives for people to interact, to use creativity and to work in teams' will generate new flexible and adaptable procedures, which will transform the organisational climate of trust and cooperation." (De Guimarães *et al.*, 2016, p. 144). Also, in Brazilian firms, monetary incentives are less used than in countries such as Japan or Korea, because firms try to avoid "habitually", which means incentives are automatically incorporated to the salary. Even though, a growing number of companies are considering to adopt monetary incentives (Fleury and Fleury, 1997).
Knowledge sharing. Knowledge sharing is related to organisational performance, and this relationship is mediated by the absorptive capacity of the organisation (Nodari *et al.*, 2016). "Brazil, Russia, and India practice similar KM mechanisms such as the use of technology, process standardization, and electronic data management. They also model the positive experiences of Western companies" (Klafke *et al.*, 2016, p. 812).
External knowledge. Research showed that in developed countries such as Spain, external knowledge is important for firms to have a resource-based orientation (e.g., being sensitive to client demands), while it is not significant for Brazilian firms (Paiva *et al.*, 2012).
Barriers. The "five main barriers to KM in large Brazilian companies are a lack of interest from employee, inefficient communication, lack of culture in sharing, lack of competence of staff and lack of incentive" (Oliva, 2014, p. 1071). Firms' response to people development has taken the form of corporate education. An increasing number of firms offer technical training, management and leadership development (Sparkman, 2015).

Some of these factors are supposed to influence the efficiency of activities related to ACAP, and oriented to improve firm's competitiveness. They will be discussed together with the results of the study.

Research Methodology

This paper addresses its research aim using a positivistic point of view. An analysis of the relationships between ACAP, innovation performance, and organisational performance in Brazilian firms implies a definition of a set of causal relationships that can be examined using a quantitative approach. In research this is considered as useful for obtaining evidence to verify the veracity of expected relationships between constructs (Nonaka and Peltokorpi, 2006; Schwab, 2013).

This study adopts the criteria for methodological fit in management studies presented by Edmondson and McManus (2007) because (i) the constructs involved such as ACAP, innovation performance, and organisational performance have reached a mature state in the literature with extensive knowledge about them. (ii) This state of the art is aligned with the research purpose that aims at identifying guidelines to develop suitable models for analysing the relationship between ACAP, innovation performance, and organisational performance in developing countries such as Brazil. (iii) The previous state of the art and the study's purpose are consistent with the quantitative approach used for testing the hypotheses of the present study.

Sample and data collection

The sample population consisted of 1,548 cross-industry firms in Santa Catarina, one of the prosperous Brazilian states located in the South region. Santa Catarina is responsible for 4.8% of gross domestic product (GDP), has the fourth highest GDP per capita, and employ 7.8% of Brazilian workforce (IBGE, 2014). In their study with Brazilian entrepreneurs and business executives, Hofstede *et al.* (2010, p. 347) wrote about the South of Brazil as "European and prosperous, is more hierarchical, less formal, more individualist, and more masculine (achievement-oriented)."

The target enterprises were selected from a database of Federation of Industries of Santa Catarina State (FIESC/SC). Data collection was carried out between November 2015 and March 2016, using an online cross-sectional survey. In total, 146 responses were received, representing a response rate of 9.3%.

Because ACAP and innovation are KM-related concepts, this study focuses on firms which practice KM in an intentional and systematical way. Jennings and Beaver (1997) state that in firms with 20 or more employees, the owner starts sharing responsibility with a more professional management. Thus, and in line with other KM research (Jensen *et al.*, 2007), this study selected firms with 20 or more employees. Consequently, 35 responses were excluded which means 111 responses remained for further analysis.

The most well-represented industries were food and beverages (35.6%), textile (9%), metallurgy (8%), and IT services (7%). The majority of enterprises employ between 20 and 50 employees (42.6%) and 25% of the enterprises have more than 500 employees.

Most respondents belonged to the top management (39%), another significant group holds middle-management positions (27%). The remaining respondents, with minor exceptions, hold supervisory or specialist positions in key business units.

Measures

Organisational ACAP was measured using the scale developed in the research of Flatten *et al.* (2011a) and used in recent studies (Herath and Mahmood, 2014; Adams *et al.*, 2015). The scale has in total 14 items that are oriented to measure the four ACAP processes: acquisition (three items), assimilation (four items), transformation (four items), and exploitation (three items).

The innovation performance scale used was presented in the work of Inkinen *et al.* (2015). It consists of five items in which respondents are requested to compare their performance to the competitors in terms of product, service, managerial, marketing, and business model innovations.

The scale developed by Darroch (2005) was used for organisational performance. It uses seven items oriented to measure performance-related elements such as profit, market, growth, goal achievement, and internal performance.

All items used in the survey have a five-point Likert scale with values ranging from 1: strongly disagree to 5: strongly agree.

Methods of analysis

Hypotheses were tested using structural equation modelling (SEM), which supports analysis of "causal paths and the identification of the collective strength of multiple variables" (Creswell, 2010, p. 13). SmartPLS was the partial least squares (PLS) software used for the analysis of data. According to Henseler *et al.* (2016), PLS path models have two types of linear equations: The measurement model (outer model), which "specifies the relations between a construct and its observed indicators" (p. 4), and the structural model (inner model), composed of the endogenous and exogenous constructs, and the relationships between them.

First, a measurement model analysis was conducted to assure construct reliability, convergent validity, and discriminant validity. Construct reliability verifies that the amount of random error in construct scores is acceptable (Henseler *et al.*, 2016), even when, typically, Cronbach's alpha is used for measuring the construct reliability. Recently, the composite reliability test [also known as Jöreskog's Rho (ρc)] and the Rho A test proposed by Dijkstra and Henseler (2015) are widely used (Henseler *et al.*, 2016). Usually each construct is expected to have a value above 0.7 for both tests (Nunnally and Bernstein, 1994). Following Fornell and Larcker (1981), the convergent validity of indicators representing the same construct was assessed, checking that the average variance extracted (AVE) is above 0.5 for each construct. Complementarily, indicator loadings of each construct were also checked to assure they are above the recommended threshold of 0.65 as proposed by Hair *et al.* (2006), or the more conservative threshold of 0.7 (Bagozzi and Yi,

1991). Finally, each pair of constructs derived from theoretically different concepts should be also statistically different, in other words they must have discriminant validity. Discriminant validity was assessed by verifying that the AVE of each individual construct is higher than the shared variance between the given construct and others (Henseler *et al.*, 2016).

After validating the measurement model, elements in the structural model were evaluated. A good model fit assessment criterion is the Standardised Root Mean Square Residual (SRMR), which, according to Henseler *et al.* (2016), is defined as the difference between observed correlation and the predicted correlation. An adequate SRMR value is expected to be lower than 0.10, but a more conservative approach (see Hu and Bentler, 1998) proposes a threshold of 0.08. In addition, the adjusted R^2 value was calculated to identify the amount of variance of organisational performance and innovation performance explained by organisational ACAP. After this, the statistical significance and the strength of path estimate between constructs were evaluated to test the research hypotheses. Even more, a bootstrapping procedure was performed (with 5000 bootstrap samples) to obtain and present confidence intervals about each construct and path in the model. Then, according to Cohen (2013), the effect size (f^2) was evaluated to quantify how substantial the significant effects are. Large, medium, and small f^2 are represented by values above 0.35, 0.15, and 0.02, respectively. In order to verify the predictive relevance of each construct in the model, Stone-Geisser's Q^2 values were calculated using a blindfolding procedure (Stone, 1974; Geisser, 1975). Q^2 values above 0 means a good predictive relevance.

Results

Based on the theoretical premises, a model was developed to test the hypotheses proposed in this study. The model has eight latent constructs: Potential ACAP, a second-order construct formed by acquisition and assimilation constructs; and realised ACAP, another second-order construct, composed by transformation and exploitation constructs. Innovation performance and organisational performance are the other two constructs in the model.

The following subsection presents the results of the analysis done over measurement model and structural model, supported by SmartPLS software.

Measurement model

The first measurement model test gave unsuccessful results for the assimilation and organisational performance constructs. Three indicators had loadings below the recommendable thresholds (AS4 = 0.610, OP1 = 0.569, and OP2 = 0.605) which produced reliability issues and, in the case of assimilation construct, derived in a lack of discriminant validity. These three indicators were removed.

As shown in Table 2, adequate scores for Cronbach's alpha, composite reliability, and Rho A tests assured a good reliability. In the same way, all AVE scores are above 0.5, and all indicators have loadings above accepted thresholds, providing evidence of an adequate convergent validity.

Discriminant validity was assessed by comparing the AVE for each construct with the shared variance between the given construct and others. Table 3 shows that in all cases, AVE is higher than the shared variance, providing evidence about an adequate discriminant validity. The measurement model assessments provided good evidence about reliability and validity for representing the concepts discussed in this study. Next, the structural model is going to be assessed.

Structural model

The model developed in this study is shown in Fig. 1. The results evidence a good SRMR index (0.051), below the maximum thresholds of 0.10 (or 0.08 in the more conservative approach).

In accordance with the adequate SRMR index, and as shown in Table 4, the model explains 45.2% of realised ACAP, 38.8% of innovation performance, and 34.7% of organisational performance. This conclusion is based on the resultant R^2 values (see Table 4), which indicate the percentage of variability accounted for by the predictive constructs in the model. The adjusted R^2 values "take into account model complexity and sample size, and are thus to compare different models or the explanatory power of a model across different data sets" (Henseler *et al.*, 2016).

After running the bootstrapping procedure, the empirical evidence supports the four hypotheses (H_1, $H_{2.1}$, $H_{2.2}$ and H_3). The results obtained suggested the existence of statistically significant paths between potential ACAP and realised ACAP (0.676, $p < 0.01$), potential ACAP and innovation performance (0.245, $p < 0.05$), realised ACAP and innovation performance (0.439, $p < 0.01$), and innovation performance with organisational performance (0.594, $p < 0.01$) as shown in Table 5.

Additionally, based on the effect size (f^2) classification proposed by Cohen (2013), the model presents large f^2 in relationships tested in H_1 and H_4, a medium f^2 in $H_{2.2}$, and a small f^2 for $H_{2.1}$. Finally, the blindfolding procedure calculated Q^2 values > 0 for all exogenous constructs (see Table 4), which provided good evidence about the predictability of the model.

Table 2. Measurement test results for final indicators.

Construct		Indicators	Mean	Loadings	Cronbach's alpha	Composite reliability	Rho A	AVE
Potential ACAP (Flatten *et al.*, 2011a)								
Acquisition	AQ1	The search for relevant information concerning our industry is everyday business in our company	4.00	0.769				
	AQ2	Our management motivates the employees to use information sources within our industry	3.96	0.839	0.699	0.833	0.705	0.625
	AQ3	Our management expects that the employees deal with information beyond our industry	3.98	0.763				
Assimilation	AS1	In our company ideas and concepts are communicated cross-departmental	3.81	0.809				
	AS2	Our management emphasises cross-departmental support to solve problems	4.14	0.843	0.709	0.838	0.716	0.634
	AS3	In our company there is a quick information flow, e.g., if a business unit obtains important information it communicates this information promptly to all other business units or departments	3.83	0.732				
Realised ACAP (Flatten *et al.*, 2011a)								
Transformation	TR1	Our employees have the ability to structure and to use collected knowledge	3.67	0.865				
	TR2	Our employees are used to absorbing new knowledge as well as to prepare it for further purposes and to make it available	3.43	0.903	0.895	0.895	0.896	0.761
	TR3	Our employees successfully link existing knowledge with new insights	3.50	0.868				
	TR4	Our employees are able to apply new knowledge in their practical work	3.67	0.852				

Table 2. (*Continued*)

Construct		Indicators	Mean	Loadings	Cronbach's alpha	Composite reliability	Rho A	AVE
Exploitation	EX1	Our management supports the development of prototypes	4.02	0.734				
	EX2	Our company regularly reconsiders technologies and adapts them in accordance to new knowledge	4.00	0.911	0.777	0.870	0.811	0.692
	EX3	Our company has the ability to work more effectively by adopting new technologies	4.05	0.840				
Innovation Performance (Inkinen *et al.*, 2015)								
	IP1	Compared to its competitors, during the last year our company successfully managed to create innovations in new products or services for customers	3.69	0.895				
	IP2	Compared to its competitors, during the last year our company successfully managed to create innovations in new production methods and processes	3.75	0.790	0.872	0.907	0.875	0.663
	IP3	Compared to its competitors, during the last year our company successfully managed to create innovations in new management practices	3.73	0.841				
	IP4	Compared to its competitors, during the last year our company successfully managed to create innovations in new marketing practices	3.23	0.738				
	IP5	Compared to its competitors, during the last year our company successfully managed to create innovations in new business models	3.61	0.798				

Table 2. (*Continued*)

Construct		Indicators	Mean	Loadings	Cronbach's alpha	Composite reliability	Rho A	AVE
Organisational Performance (Darroch, 2005)								
	OP3	Compared with the industry average, we are growing more rapidly	3.55	0.684				
	OP4	In general, our organisation is performing better than it did 12 months ago	4.01	0.650	0.802	0.863	0.822	0.560
	OP5	In general, our organisation is performing better than it did five years ago	4.19	0.715				
	OP6	Over the past 12 months, our organisation has met its performance objectives	3.71	0.838				
	OP7	Over the past five years, our organisation has met its performance objectives	3.81	0.835				

Table 3. Correlations between constructs (square root of AVE in diagonal).

			1	2	3	4	5	6
1	Potential ACAP	Acquisition	**0.791**					
2		Assimilation	0.606	**0.796**				
3	Realised ACAP	Transformation	0.434	0.558	**0.873**			
4		Exploitation	0.465	0.479	0.418	**0.832**		
5	Innovation performance		0.470	0.509	0.519	0.512	**0.814**	
6	Organisational performance		0.308	0.379	0.432	0.391	0.593	**0.748**

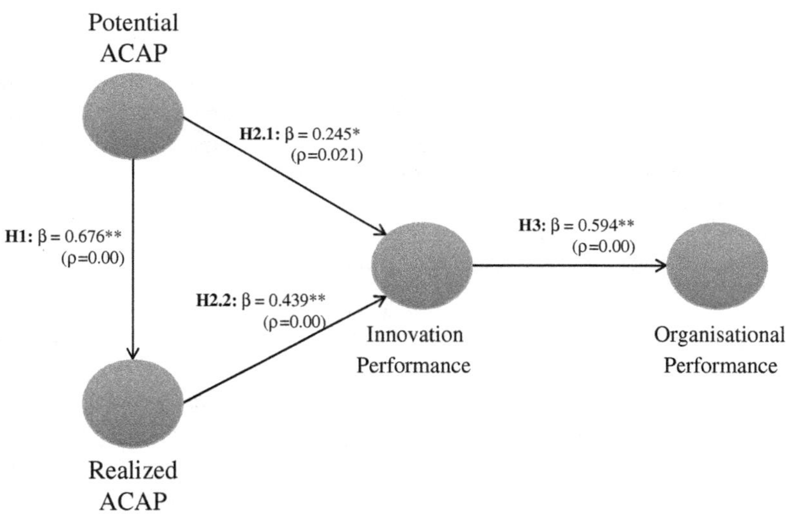

Fig. 1. Structural model for ACAP and innovation performance.

Table 4. The R^2 and Q^2 values.

	R^2	Adjusted-R^2	Q^2
Realised ACAP	0.457	0.452	0.457
Innovation performance	0.399	0.388	0.257
Organisational performance	0.353	0.347	0.183

Table 5. Path estimates, p-values, and Cohen's f^2-values.

	Hypothesis	β	Standard deviation (STDEV)	T-statistics (|O/STDEV|)	p-values	Cohen's f^2
H_1	Potential ACAP → Realised ACAP	0.676	0.057	11.967	0.000	0.843
H_2.1	Potential ACAP → Innovation performance	0.245	0.106	2.318	0.021	0.054
H_2.2	Realised ACAP → Innovation performance	0.439	0.096	4.557	0.000	0.174
H_3	Innovation performance → Organisational performance	0.594	0.067	8.812	0.000	0.545

Discussion

This research improves the understanding of how ACAP needs to be addressed and managed in order to improve innovation and firm's performance. Specifically, the hypotheses tested are discussed and subsequently, some guidelines for new ACAP suitable models for developing countries are discussed.

Potential ACAP and innovation performance

The present study identifies a significant and positive influence of potential ACAP on innovation performance (see Table 5). Zahra and George (2002) stated that potential ACAP helps firms to sustain competitiveness by providing strategic flexibility that allows them to change and reconfigure their operations. In this research, the results demonstrate that during acquisition and assimilation dimensions, Brazilian firms are using daily routines for searching relevant information about the firm's industry. Also, managers, who are charismatic and participative (House *et al.*, 2004), are encouraging cross-departmental support for problem-solving (see mean values in Table 2). However, results suggest that Brazilian firms need to improve "the speed of information flow between business units or departments for communicating ideas and concepts," which has a low mean but a high importance for knowledge assimilation (see loadings in Table 2). Lack of speed of information flow between units can be explained by the low institutional collectivism in the Brazilian society (House *et al.*, 2004). This represents an opportunity for improvement because recent research has suggested that the effect of potential ACAP on innovation performance is stronger when internal information flows are more consistent. Because, the density of connections improves the socialization capabilities which in turn support external knowledge assimilation (Fosfuri and Tribó, 2008). When potential ACAP capability is structured together with other organisational elements or capabilities, it is possible to innovate without significant and explicit transformation and exploitation efforts. For example, a firm's quality committee could identify a problem pattern which is affecting the service, and immediate actions such as a simple training could be initiated to improve the service process for achieving better organisational performance. Viewing innovation as a process, Tidd and Bessant (2009) identified four phases: search, select, implement, and capture. Thus, the positive impact of potential ACAP on innovation performance found in this study could be explained by more insights during the two earlier innovation phases (search and select), merging firm's strategy and external opportunities, and derived from the reconfiguration of the firm's knowledge base with external knowledge flows. Fosfuri and Tribó (2008) argument showed that the larger the potential ACAP, the larger the amount of external information that reaches the implementing stage of the innovation process, supports this finding.

Realised ACAP and innovation performance

The results derived from this research (as shown in Table 5) are in line with most empirical studies which have shown the relationship between realised ACAP and innovative outputs (Cepeda-Carrion *et al.*, 2012; Wang and Han, 2011; Zahra and George, 2002). Firms need to have the ability to transform and exploit combined (new and existing) knowledge (Fosfuri and Tribó, 2008) because it is essential to transform opportunities derived from this combined knowledge into innovations (Leal-Rodriguez *et al.*, 2014). The present study shows that Brazilian firms seem to have a constant interest in identifying new technologies to incorporate them into their operation's processes and products, an activity that is highly correlated with the transformation dimension (see Table 2). Brazilian workers have become used to deal with technology because of political efforts in recent years oriented at promoting the development of technology (Nogueira *et al.*, 2014; Sparkman, 2015). In fact, previous evidence in Brazilian manufacturing firms highlight that technology acquisition (mainly embodied in machinery and equipment) and/or internal technology development increase product and process innovations (Goedhuys and Veugelers, 2012). When process innovation is the goal, specialised suppliers are the best source of knowledge (Reichstein and Salter, 2006), and technology acquisition is through technological convergence, for example, in production-intensive firms (Pavitt, 1984). When it happens, the firm provides operating experience and test facilities, and suppliers provide specialised knowledge and experience embodied in machinery and equipment (Pavitt, 1984); thus external knowledge flows are generated which could be better exploited by enhanced ACAP. Other aspects shown in the present study, which are highly correlated with realised ACAP, but which need to be improved in Brazilian firms, are the capacity of developing links between existing knowledge and new insights, and the ability to use new knowledge, to prepare it for further purposes and to make it available. Brazilian firms seem to be focussed on acquiring and managing technology rather than knowledge. They are managing what Nonaka and Peltokorpi (2006) called 'objectified' knowledge. These results suggest that there is an opportunity for implementing widely-used KM practices and tools, mainly focussed on tacit knowledge, which supports KM processes involved in the transition from realised ACAP to innovations. Recent evidence concluded that firms which combine their knowledge base with external knowledge flows can improve their radical innovation capabilities (Forés and Camisón, 2016). From a process perspective, innovation activities inside the implement and capture phases, which are related to putting new ideas in the market and taking advantages of them (Tidd and Bessant, 2009), are most likely to be improved by enhanced realised ACAP capability. Fosfuri and Tribó (2008) explained this by arguing that the exploitation of knowledge, which incorporates new knowledge into operations, is crucial for later stages in the innovation process.

Innovation performance and organisational performance

In Brazilian firms there is a positive and direct relationship between innovation performance and organisational performance (see Table 5). This result is in line with recent studies that show that innovation plays an important role in firm's performance and competitiveness (Chen *et al.*, 2009; Darroch, 2005; Huang *et al.*, 2016). In Brazilian firms operating in the food sector, for example, the added value grows faster than that of the entire economy (Wijnands *et al.*, 2007). One interesting finding is that Brazilian firms are more likely to innovate in processes, managerial practices, and products (see mean values in Table 2) than marketing processes or business model. This correlation between product and process innovations in Brazilian firms could be explained by an increased effect of combined process and product innovations on sales growth (Goedhuys and Veugelers, 2012). Typically, process innovations are triggered by the need to operate to full capacity, and they are most likely to happen in production-intensive firms (Pavitt, 1984) by identifying bottlenecks which, once corrected, increase firm's performance. Moreover, in line with Pavitt (1984), this study showed that internal performance is the indicator with the highest load on the firm's performance construct (see Table 2). Another important finding was that the product innovation indicator has the highest loading over the innovation performance construct (see Table 2). An explanation for this might be found in the work of Pietrobelli and Rabellotti (2011), which studied Brazilian shoe firms, that showed that these firms are constantly adapting their product designs to local environments (phenomenon known as *tropicalização*) instead of starting projects intended to develop completely new products which would in turn also require big changes (innovations) in processes, marketing, and business model.

Guidelines for new ACAP suitable models for Brazilian firms

The evidence presented in this paper might lead to a modification of the ACAP model of Zahra and George (2002) for developing economies where an emphasis on the acquisition and exploitation dimensions is found. This is due to the situation that Brazilian firms are used to manage 'objectified' knowledge, which is embedded mainly in technology, rather than know-how or tacit knowledge. In other words, improved models should be able to make possible a deeper analysis of activities such as information gathering, technology acquisition and transfer capabilities, process technology, and prototyping and their contribution to firm's innovation and competitiveness.

In addition, related studies suggest that cross-cultural variables such as easiness for converting tacit knowledge into explicit knowledge (Klafke *et al.*, 2016), leadership or group/institutional collectivism (House *et al.*, 2004) should be considered in improved ACAP models. Even though these factors were not empirically tested in this paper, they helped to explain relevant findings, and deserve more attention in further research on ACAP.

Moreover, Brazilian firms have the potential for developing competitive advantages, if they improve the way they manage information and knowledge. Specifically, improving internal information flows is going to improve assimilation processes (potential ACAP), and a better management of tacit knowledge is going to facilitate transformation processes (realised ACAP) (see loadings in Table 2). Unfortunately, the successful public policies and incentives for developing research and technology were not replicated to the area of knowledge management. In fact, the "National Education Basis and Principles Law,"[1] a guideline for primary and higher education in Brazil, does not consider the need for developing knowledge creation and knowledge application abilities. This impacts directly firm's performance, assuming that firms are entities, which take advantage of the knowledge of their specialists for achieving both efficient knowledge creation and knowledge application processes (Grant, 1996). In the short term, corporate education can be a good response for technical training in knowledge management and for leadership development necessary to improve cross-unit information flow (Sparkman, 2015). In the long term, a mindset change will be needed.

[1]For more information, visit: https://www2.senado.leg.br/bdsf/bitstream/handle/id/70320/65.pdf.

Conclusion

The purpose of the study was to explore ACAP and its role in improving innovation performance and organisational performance taking a Brazilian business context. The relevance of ACAP for innovation and organisational performance is clearly supported by the findings. The findings also clearly show that realised ACAP has more influence on innovation performance than potential ACAP does. This study contributes to KBV of the firm because it analyses a firm's capability such as ACAP, and it helps to improve our understanding about which knowledge-related factors make some firms take competitive advantages in Brazilian business context.

Considering ACAP as a KM-based competence, this research extends our knowledge about the importance of KM activities for the innovation value chain in firms. Additionally, it responded to earlier discussion that highlighted the need for exploring the role of KM on firm's competitiveness in developing countries (Inkinen *et al.*, 2015). Taken together, the presented findings support the idea that widely-used KM practices need to be incorporated in firms and must be managed by them to enhance innovation and organisational performance.

Besides, the findings also suggest a number of possible actions for practitioners. By identifying the influence of each absorptive capacity dimension on firms' innovation performance, Brazilian managers and entrepreneurs will be able to manage their knowledge resources more efficiently and effectively, which, in turn, can make the firms more competitive in the long run. The findings can support awareness creation for Brazilian managers and managers who are operating in similar business environments. The findings highlight the different dimensions of ACAP, what are its means, management, knowledge competences, technological competences, and others. Therefore, they can improve the efficiency of KM practices in these firms. Specifically, this study suggests some KM practices which could be prioritised considering their contribution to innovation and firm's performance. Further, dedicated KM strategies should be initiated to support knowledge flows inside the innovation process. This would also involve the implementation of appropriate systems for tracking improvements in ACAP necessary for improving innovativeness and performance in a sustainable way.

Further research opportunities can be derived from the limitations of this research, going back to its design or the chosen context. Firstly, the research has examined the relationship between ACAP, innovation, and organisational performance in a developing country such as Brazil. For this reason, results cannot be transferred to other geographical or cultural contexts without further studies with different samples. Secondly, each firm had a single respondent who evaluated the constructs involved in this research at a specified point in time. In future studies, several participants from individual firms should be involved and the constructs should be studied with a longitudinal research design. In addition, even when subjective measures for assessing innovation and organisational performance are reliable (Moorman and Rust, 1999), objective measures could provide more precision in the results. Thirdly, further studies could aim to identify which innovation types are likely to be derived from potential ACAP and realised ACAP, and to which extent these capabilities influence the different phases of the innovation process. As constructs such as ACAP and innovation performance may differ between industries, cross-sector studies should be conducted to analyse these possible differences. Finally, the selection of a positivist position is also up for discussion since knowledge is also considered as a process rather than a commodity as assumed in this paper.

Acknowledgements

The authors wish to thank the anonymous reviewers that gave us useful suggestions for improving this paper, and the Industry Federation of Santa Catarina (FIESC) for supporting data collection.

References

Adams, DR, T Flatten, H Brinkmann and M Brettel (2015). Consequences and antecedents of absorptive capacity in a cross-cultural context. *International Journal of Innovation Management*, 20, 1650003.

Akgun, AE, H Keskin and J Byrne (2009). Organizational emotional capability, product and process innovation, and firm performance: An empirical analysis. *Journal of Engineering and Technology Management*, 26, 103–130.

Alegre, J, K Sengupta and R Lapiedra (2013). Knowledge management and innovation performance in a high-tech SMEs industry. *International Small Business Journal*, 31, 454–470.

Alves Filho, AG, E Nogueira and PEG Bento (2015). Operations strategies of engine assembly plants in the Brazilian automotive industry. *International Journal of Operations & Production Management*, 35(5), 817–838.

Bagno, RB and LC Cheng (2007). In search of the elements of an intra-organizational innovation system for Brazilian automotive subsidiaries. In *Complex Systems Concurrent Engineering*, pp. 693–700. London: Springer.

Bagozzi, RP and Y Yi (1991). Multitrait-multimethod matrices in consumer research. *Journal of Consumer Research*, 17(4), 426–439.

Baregheh, A, J Rowley and S Sambrook (2009). Towards a multidisciplinary definition of innovation. *Management Decision*, 47, 1323–1339.

Becheikh, N (2013). The impact of knowledge acquisition and absorptive capacity on technological innovations in developing countries: Evidence from Egyptian small and medium-sized enterprises. *Journal of African Business*, 14, 127–140.

Ben Zaied, RM and H Affes (2015). The relationship between the sources of knowledge management, organizational innovation and organizational performance. *International Journal of Information, Business and Management*, 8(3), 185–206.

Cassiman, B and R Veugelers (2006). In search of complementarity in innovation strategy: Internal R&D and external knowledge acquisition. *Management Science*, 52, 68–82.

Cepeda-Carrion, G, JG Cegarra-Navarro and D Jimenez-Jimenez (2012). The effect of absorptive capacity on innovativeness: Context and information systems capability as catalysts. *British Journal of Management*, 23, 110–129.

Cohen, J (2013). *Statistical Power Analysis for the Behavioral Sciences*. Hoboken: Taylor & Francis.

Cohen, WM and Levinthal, DA (1989). Innovation and learning: The two faces of R&D. *The Economic Journal*, 99(397), 569–596.

Cohen, WM and DA Levinthal (1990). Absorptive capacity: A new perspective on learning and innovation. *Administrative Science Quarterly*, 35(1), 128–152.

Cohen, WM and DA Levinthal (1994). Fortune favors the prepared firm. *Management Science*, 40, 227–251.

Corral de Zubielqui, G, J Jones and L Lester (2016). Knowledge inflows from market- and science-based actors, absorptive capacity, innovation and performance: A study of SMEs. *International Journal of Innovation Management*, 20, 1650055.

Creswell, JW (2010). Projeto de pesquisa: métodos qualitativo, quantitativo e misto. Porto Alegre: Artmed.

Chang, S, Y Gong, SA Way and L Jia (2013). Flexibility-oriented HRM systems, absorptive capacity, and market responsiveness and firm innovativeness. *Journal of Management*, 39, 1924–1951.

Chen, C-J and J-W Huang (2009). Strategic human resource practices and innovation performance — The mediating role of knowledge management capacity. *Journal of Business Research*, 62, 104–114.

Chen, Y-S, M-JJ Lin and C-H Chang (2009). The positive effects of relationship learning and absorptive capacity on innovation performance and competitive advantage in industrial markets. *Industrial Marketing Management*, 38, 152–158.

Dalkir, K (2005). *Knowledge Management in Theory and Practice*. Abingdon: Routledge.

Damanpour, F (1991). Organizational innovation: A meta-analysis of effects of determinants and moderators. *Academy of Management Journal*, 34, 555–590.

Damanpour, F, KA Szabat and WM Evan (1989). The relationship between types of innovation and organizational performance. *Journal of Management Studies*, 26, 587–601.

Darroch, J (2005). Knowledge management, innovation and firm performance. *Journal of Knowledge Management*, 9, 101–115.

Davila, GA (2016). Relationships between knowledge management practices, absorptive capacity and performance: Evidence of southern Brazil. Unpublished doctoral dissertation, Federal University of Santa Catarina. Available at: http://btd.egc.ufsc.br/wp-content/uploads/2016/09/Guillermo-Antonio-Davila.pdf [accessed].

De Guimarães, JCF, EA Severo, ECH Dorion, F Coallier and PM Olea (2016). The use of organizational resources for product innovation and organizational performance: A survey of the Brazilian furniture industry. *International Journal of Production Economics*, 180, 135–147.

Dess, GG and RB Robinson (1984). Measuring organizational performance in the absence of objective measures: The case of the privately-held firm and conglomerate business unit. *Strategic Management Journal*, 5, 265–273.

Díaz-Díaz, NL and P de Saá Pérez (2014). The interaction between external and internal knowledge sources: An open innovation view. *Journal of Knowledge Management*, 18, 430–446.

Dijkstra, TK and J Henseler (2015). Consistent partial least squares path modeling. *Management Information Systems Quarterly*, 39, 297–316.

Dominguez Gonzalez, RV, F Martins and JC Toledo (2014). Managing knowledge in a service provider: A network structure-based model. *Journal of Knowledge Management*, 18, 611–630.

Edmondson, AC and SE McManus (2007). Methodological fit in management field research. *Academy of Management Review*, 32(4), 1246–1264.

Edmondson, A and B Moingeon (1998). From organizational learning to the learning organization. *Management Learning*, 29(1), 5–20.

Edvardsson, IR and S Durst (2013). Does knowledge management deliver the goods in SMEs? *Business and Management Research*, 2, 1–9.

Ferraresi, AA, CO Quandt, SA Dos Santos and JR Frega (2012). Knowledge management and strategic orientation: Leveraging innovativeness and performance. *Journal of Knowledge Management*, 16, 688–701.

Figueiredo, PN (2013). Embedding with multiple knowledge sources to improve innovation performance: The learning experience of Motorola in Brazil. *Knowledge Management Research & Practice*, 11, 361–373.

Flatten, T, A Engelen, S Zahra and M Brettel (2011a). A measure of absorptive capacity: Scale development and validation. *European Management Journal*, 29, 98–116.

Flatten, TC, GI Greve and M Brettel (2011b). Absorptive capacity and firm performance in SMEs: The mediating influence of strategic alliances. *European Management Review*, 8, 137–152.

Fleury, T (1999). The management of culture diversity: Lessons from Brazilian companies. *Industrial Management & Data Systems*, 99(3), 109–114.

Fleury A, Fleury MTL (1997). Aprendizagem e inovação organizacional: as experiências de Japão, Coréia e Brasil. 2 Edition. São Paulo: Atlas, 237pp.

Forés, B and C Camisón (2016). Does incremental and radical innovation performance depend on different types of knowledge accumulation capabilities and organizational size? *Journal of Business Research*, 69, 831–848.

Fornell, C and DF Larcker (1981). Evaluating structural equation models with unobservable variables and measurement error. *Journal of Marketing Research*, 18(1), 39–50.

Fosfuri, A and JA Tribó (2008). Exploring the antecedents of potential absorptive capacity and its impact on innovation performance. *Omega — International Journal of Management Science*, 36, 173–187.

Geisser, S (1975). The predictive sample reuse method with applications. *Journal of the American Statistical Association*, 70, 320–328.

Gloet, M and M Terziovski (2004). Exploring the relationship between knowledge management practices and innovation performance. *Journal of Manufacturing Technology Management*, 15, 402–409.

Goedhuys, M and R Veugelers (2012). Innovation strategies, process and product innovations and growth: Firm-level evidence from Brazil. *Structural Change and Economic Dynamics*, 23, 516–529.

Grant, RM (1996). Toward a knowledge-based theory of the firm. *Strategic Management Journal*, 17(S2), 109–122.

Gray, C (2006). Absorptive capacity, knowledge management and innovation in entrepreneurial small firms. *International Journal of Entrepreneurial Behaviour and Research*, 12, 345–360.

Hair, JF, WC Black, BJ Babin, RE Anderson and RL Tatham (2006). *Multivariate Data Analysis*. Upper Saddle River, NJ: Pearson Prentice Hall.

Henseler, J, G Hubona and PA Ray (2016). Using PLS path modeling in new technology research: Updated guidelines. *Industrial Management & Data Systems*, 116, 2–20.

Herath, HMA and R Mahmood (2014). Strategic orientations and SME performance: Moderating effect of absorptive capacity of the firm. *Asian Social Science*, 10, 95–107.

Hofstede, G, AVG de Hilal, S Malvezzi, B Tanure and H Vinken (2010). Comparing regional cultures within a country: Lessons from Brazil. *Journal of Cross-Cultural Psychology*, 41, 336–352.

House, RJ, PJ Hanges, M Javidan, PW Dorfman and V Gupta (Eds.) (2004). *Culture, Leadership and Organizations: The GLOBE Study of 62 Societies*. USA: Sage publications.

Hu, L-T and PM Bentler (1998). Fit indices in covariance structure modeling: Sensitivity to underparameterized model misspecification. *Psychological Methods*, 3, 424.

Huang, K-E, J-H Wu, S-Y Lu and Y-C Lin (2016). Innovation and technology creation effects on organizational performance. *Journal of Business Research*, 69, 2187–2192.

Huang, KF, KH Lin, LY Wu and PH Yu (2015). Absorptive capacity and autonomous R&D climate roles in firm innovation. *Journal of Business Research*, 68, 87–94.

IBGE (2014). *Brazil in Figures*. Brazil: IBGE.

Inkinen, HT, A Kianto and M Vanhala (2015). Knowledge management practices and innovation performance in Finland. *Baltic Journal of Management*, 10, 432–455.

Jansen, JJP, FAJ Van Den Bosch and HW Volberda (2006). Exploratory innovation, exploitative innovation, and performance: Effects of organizational antecedents and environmental moderators. *Management Science*, 52(11), 1661–1674.

Jennings, P and G Beaver (1997). The performance and competitive advantage of small firms: A management perspective. *International Small Business Journal*, 15, 63–75.

Jensen, MB, B Johnson, E Lorenz and BÅ Lundvall (2007). Forms of knowledge and modes of innovation. *Research Policy*, 36, 680–693.

Jimenez-Jimenez, D and R Sanz-Valle (2011). Innovation, organizational learning, and performance. *Journal of Business Research*, 64, 408–417.

Joia, LA and B Lemos (2010). Relevant factors for tacit knowledge transfer within organizations. *Journal of Knowledge Management*, 14(3), 410–427.

Jurksiene, L and J Giniuniene (2015). Interorganizational networks and firm performance: The mediating role of organizational learning and innovation. In *Proc. 10th European Conf. Innovation and Entrepreneurship*, RP Dameri, R Garelli, M Resta and L Beltrametti (Eds.), pp. 341–348.

Kianto, A and T Andreeva (2014). Knowledge management practices and results in service-oriented versus product-oriented companies. *Knowledge and Process Management*, 21(4), 221–230.

Klafke, RV, C Lievore, C Picinin, AC Francisco and LA Pilatti (2016). Primary knowledge management practices applied in Brazil, Russia, India and China (BRIC) industries from 2001–2010. *Journal of Knowledge Management*, 20(4), 812–828.

Kostopoulos, K, A Papalexandris, M Papachroni and G Ioannou (2011). Absorptive capacity, innovation, and financial performance. *Journal of Business Research*, 64, 1335–1343.

Lane, P, B Koka and S Pathak (2006). The reification of absorptive capacity: A critical review and rejuvenation of the construct. *Academy of Management Review*, 31(4), 833–863.

Lau, AKW and W Lo (2015). Regional innovation system, absorptive capacity and innovation performance: An empirical study. *Technological Forecasting and Social Change*, 92, 99–114.

Leal-Rodriguez, AL, JL Roldan, JA Ariza-Montes and A Leal-Millan (2014). From potential absorptive capacity to innovation outcomes in project teams: The conditional mediating role of the realized absorptive capacity in a relational learning context. *International Journal of Project Management*, 32, 894–907.

Leonard-Barton, D (1995). *Wellsprings of Knowledge: Building and Sustaining the Sources of Innovation*. Harvard: Harvard Business School Press.

Lev, S, A Fiegenbaum and A Shoham (2009). Managing absorptive capacity stocks to improve performance: Empirical evidence from the turbulent environment of Israeli hospitals. *European Management Journal*, 27, 13–25.

Liu, X and RS White (1997). The relative contributions of foreign technology and domestic inputs to innovation in Chinese manufacturing industries. *Technovation*, 17(3), 119–125.

Luis Leal-Rodriguez, A, S Eldridge, J Luis Roldan, A Genaro Leal-Millan and J Ortega-Gutierrez (2015). Organizational unlearning, innovation outcomes, and performance: The moderating effect of firm size. *Journal of Business Research*, 68, 803–809.

Lund Vinding, A (2006). Absorptive capacity and innovative performance: A human capital approach. *Economics of Innovation and New Technology*, 15, 507–517.

McAdam, R, T Mcconvery and G Armstrong (2004). Barriers to innovation within small firms in a peripheral location. *International Journal of Entrepreneurial Behavior & Research*, 10, 206–221.

Moorman, C and RT Rust (1999). The role of marketing. *The Journal of Marketing*, 63, 180–197.

Moos, B, D Beimborn, H-T Wagner and T Weitzel (2013). The role of knowledge management systems for innovation: An absorptive capacity perspective. *International Journal of Innovation Management*, 17, 1350019.

Nagano, MS, JP Stefanovitz and TE Vick (2014). Innovation management processes, their internal organizational elements and contextual factors: An investigation in Brazil. *Journal of Engineering and Technology Management*, 33, 63–92.

Nodari, F, M Oliveira and ACG Maçada (2016). Organizational performance through the Donation and Collection of Interorganizational Knowledge. *VINE Journal of Information and Knowledge Management Systems*, 46(1), 85–103.

Nogueira, T, F Rosales, M Batalha and R Alcantara (2014). Analyzing effects of external integration on innovations outcomes in large and non-large Brazilian food companies. *British Food Journal*, 116(6), 984–999.

Nonaka, I and H Takeuchi (1995). *The Knowledge Creating Company*. New York: Oxford University Press.

Nonaka, I and V Peltokorpi (2006). Objectivity and subjectivity in knowledge management: A review of 20 top articles. *Knowledge and Process Management*, 13, 73–82.

North, K, E Da Silva Neto and GA Dávila (2013). Vencendo os desafios do crescimento: O método "aprender a crescer" para pequenas e médias empresas brasileiras. *Navus-Revista de Gestão e Tecnologia*, 3, 06–19.

Nunnally, JC and IH Bernstein (1994). *Psychometric Theory*. New York, NY: McGraw-Hill.

Oliva, FL (2014). Knowledge management barriers, practices and maturity model. *Journal of Knowledge Management*, 18(6), 1053–1074.

Paiva, EL, AV Roth and JE Fensterseifer (2008). Organizational knowledge and the manufacturing strategy process: A resource-based view analysis. *Journal of Operations Management*, 26, 115–132.

Paiva, EL, E Revilla Gutierrez and AV Roth (2012). Manufacturing strategy process and organizational knowledge: A cross-country analysis. *Journal of Knowledge Management*, 16(2), 302–328.

Pavitt, K (1984). Sectoral patterns of technical change: Towards a taxonomy and a theory. *Research Policy*, 13, 343–373.

Petraite, M (2010). Knowledge absorption for innovation in new technology based firms: Lithuanian case. In *Proc. European Conf. Knowledge Management (ECKM)*, pp. 767–773. Academic Publishing Limited. Reading, UK.

Pietrobelli, C and R Rabellotti (2011). Global value chains meet innovation systems: Are there learning opportunities for developing countries? *World Development*, 39, 1261–1269.

Popadiuk, S and CW Choo (2006). Innovation and knowledge creation: How are these concepts related? *International Journal of Information Management*, 26(4), 302–312.

Reichstein, T and A Salter (2006). Investigating the sources of process innovation among UK manufacturing firms. *Industrial and Corporate Change*, 15, 653–682.

Ritala, P, H Olander, S Michailova and K Husted (2015). Knowledge sharing, knowledge leaking and relative innovation performance: An empirical study. *Technovation*, 35, 22–31.

Romijn, H and M Albaladejo (2002). Determinants of innovation capability in small electronics and software firms in southeast England. *Research Policy*, 31, 1053–1067.

Roxas, B, M Battisti and D Deakins (2014). Learning, innovation and firm performance: Knowledge management in small firms. *Knowledge Management Research and Practice*, 12, 443–453.

Santos, JLS (2013). *Relações entre capacidade de absorção de conhecimento, sistemas de memória organizacional e desempenho financeiro*. Unpublished doctoral dissertation, Federal University of Santa Catarina.

Sawhney, M, RC Wolcott and I Arroniz (2006). The 12 different ways for companies to innovate. *MIT Sloan Management Review*, 47, 75.

Scarbrough, H (2003). Knowledge management, HRM and the innovation process. *International Journal of Manpower*, 24, 501–516.

Schumpeter, J (1927). The explanation of the business cycle. *Economica*, 21, 286–311.

Schwab, DP (2013). *Research Methods for Organizational Studies*. UK: Psychology Press.

Sparkman, TE (2015). The factors and conditions for national human resource development in Brazil. *European Journal of Training and Development*, 39(8), 666–680.

Stone, M (1974). Cross-validatory choice and assessment of statistical predictions. *Journal of the Royal Statistical Society, Series B (Methodological)*, 36(2), 111–147.

Strategic Direction (2005). Volvo's Latin American style: Lean production in Swedish truck giant's Brazilian plants shows how to combine best practice and local culture. *Strategic Direction*, 21(1), 28–29.

Strese, S, DR Adams, TC Flatten and M Brettel (2016). Corporate culture and absorptive capacity: The moderating role of national culture dimensions on innovation management. *International Business Review*, 25(5), 1149–1168.

Teece, DJ (2010). Business models, business strategy and innovation. *Long Range Planning*, 43, 172–194.

Thürer, M, M Godinho Filho, M Stevenson and LD Fredendall (2013). Competitive priorities of small manufacturers in Brazil. *Industrial Management & Data Systems*, 113(6), 856–874.

Tidd, J and J Bessant (2009). *Managing Innovation: Integrating Technological, Market and Organizational Change*. USA: Wiley.

Tortoriello, M (2014). The social underpinnings of absorptive capacity: The moderating effects of structural holes on innovation generation based on external knowledge. *Strategic Management Journal*, 36(4), 586–597.

Tsai, W (2001). Knowledge transfer in intraorganizational networks: Effects of network position and absorptive capacity on business unit innovation and performance. *Academy of Management Journal*, 44, 996–1004.

Tseng, CY, DC Pai and CH Hung (2011). Knowledge absorptive capacity and innovation performance in KIBS. *Journal of Knowledge Management*, 15, 971–983.

Turner, W and BH Kleiner (2001). What managers must know to conduct business in Brazil. *Management Research Review*, 24(3–4), 72.

Van den Bosch, FAJ, HW Volberda and M de Boer (1999). Coevolution of firm absorptive capacity and knowledge environment: Organizational forms and combinative capabilities. *Organization Science*, 10, 551–568.

Vargo, SL, H Wieland and MA Akaka (2015). Innovation through institutionalization: A service ecosystems perspective. *Industrial Marketing Management*, 44, 63–72.

Wang, C and Y Han (2011). Linking properties of knowledge with innovation performance: The moderate role of absorptive capacity. *Journal of Knowledge Management*, 15, 802–819.

Wang, GF, XT Tian, JH Geng and B Guo (2013). A process innovation knowledge management framework and its application. *Advanced Materials Research*, 655, 655–657.

Wiig, KM (1993). *Knowledge Management Foundations: Thinking about Thinking — How People and Organizations Represent, Create, and Use Knowledge*. USA: Schema Press.

Wijnands, J, B Van Der Meulen and K Poppe (2007). *Competitiveness of the European Food Industry. An Economic and Legal Assessment. Luxemburg: Office for Official Publications of the European Communities.*

Wuryaningrat, NF (2013). Knowledge sharing, absorptive capacity and innovation capabilities: An empirical study on small and medium enterprises in North Sulawesi, Indonesia. *Gadjah Mada International Journal of Business*, 15, 61–78.

Xia, T and S Roper (2016). Unpacking open innovation: Absorptive capacity, exploratory and exploitative openness, and the growth of entrepreneurial biopharmaceutical firms. *Journal of Small Business Management*, 54(3), 931–952. doi: 10.1111/jsbm.12220.

Zack, M, J Mckeen and S Singh (2009). Knowledge management and organizational performance: An exploratory analysis. *Journal of Knowledge Management*, 13, 392–409.

Zahra, SA and G George (2002). Absorptive capacity: A review, reconceptualization, and extension. *Academy of Management Review*, 27, 185–203.

Zins, C (2007). Conceptual approaches for defining data, information, and knowledge: Research articles. *Journal of the American Society for Information Science and Technology*, 58, 479–493.

Chapter 18

INTANGIBLE RESOURCES AND INSTITUTION PERFORMANCE: THE CONCERN OF INTELLECTUAL CAPITAL, EMPLOYEE PERFORMANCE, JOB SATISFACTION, AND ITS IMPACT ON ORGANIZATION PERFORMANCE§

DIDI MUWARDI*, SAIDE SAIDE†,‡,||, RICHARDUS EKO INDRAJIT§, MOHAMMAD IQBAL¶, ENDANG SITI ASTUTI¶ and HERZAVINA HERZAVINA†,‡

*Department of Agribusiness, Universitas Riau, Indonesia

†Department of Information System (Pro-Knowledge Research Group) Faculty of Science and Technology State Islamic University of Sultan Syarif Kasim Riau (UIN SUSKA Riau), Indonesia

‡Department of Information Management National Taiwan University of Science and Technology (NTUST), Taiwan

§ABFI Institute of Perbanas, South Jakarta, Indonesia

¶Faculty of Administrative Science Brawijaya University, Malang, Indonesia

||saide@uin-suska.ac.id/saidefc@gmail.com

Published 14 April 2020

Purpose: The aim of this research paper is to examine the relationships between intangible assets, employee's performance, and job satisfaction (JS) with structural model. The research explores both the practical and theoretical basis of these paradigms on organisation performance. This research also aims to identify whether a relation can be established between these aspects in the context of non-profit organisation performance in Indonesia. Design/methodology/approach: Reviewing the literature explores a theoretical existence of related context preceding the organisational performance. The authors used structural equation modelling to check the research prototype with a sample of 121 respondents. The respondents were heads of departments and general employees. In addition, SPSS was used to measure demographic, non-response bias, and generate descriptive statistics. Findings: Overall, the results demonstrate that organisation with a higher level of intellectual capital (IC), employee performance (EP), and job performance (JP) are important

||Corresponding author.

§This article originally appeared in *International Journal of Innovation Management*, **24** 2150009-1-21

predictors of organisational performance in this sample. Similarly, JS and IC predicted EP. It is acknowledged that emotional intelligence such as satisfaction and dissatisfaction are important incentives to necessitate action tendencies. Research limitations/implications: This research is focused on organisations. Further research may extend the focus to different types of organisations and countries. Practical implications: The findings of this study may help institutions and HR departments to initiate new strategies such as integrating the traditional company performance measurement systems based on various indicators of this study. These factors succeed in providing an effective representation of a set of intangible assets that are developed by the company and that contribute to the improvement of company's performance. Additionally, to maximise IC assets, the company can implement knowledge sharing practices among employees and experts as well. Original value/knowledge contribution: This research is useful for organisations and academics as a reference of the comparative and intersecting explanation of enhancing organisational performance. Moreover, various main concepts/theories are combined, namely, IC, JS, and employee's performance to solve the obstacles of organisation performance.

Keywords: Intellectual capital; organisation performance; employee performance; job satisfaction; knowledge management; intangible asset.

Introduction

In achieving business goals, a company is required to improve related aspects of performance in their firm. The potential success of a company depends on the company's performance, which means its ability to effectively implement strategies to achieve institutional objectives (Almatrooshi *et al.*, 2016). In addition, by measuring organisation performance, it allows the management to identify best practices in every single level (down-top level) in an organisation and expand their usage elsewhere. Prior studies found that several segments affect firm performance, namely, intellectual capital (IC) (Sumedrea, 2013), job satisfaction (JS) (Smith *et al.*, 1969; Bakotić, 2016), and employee performance (EP) (Sadikoglu, 2010). Previous studies indicate the existence of links between business performance and workplace, especially high-performance workplace practices such as employee involvement and profit. Since performance is a function of ability and motivation, leaders can influence performance through policies and practices that have the potential to increase employee motivation. Company performance is influenced by various segments, both internal and external factors that influence the company. Studies focusing on the relationship between related factors and firm performance is much smaller in relation to the number of studies.

EP plays an important role in improving firm performance. Basically, performance is level of work success in executing a job, whereby a degree of willingness and a certain level of ability is vital in completing a given task. Employees' willingness and skills are ineffective when a task is conducted without a clear understanding and direction. Current problems regarding EP includes misunderstanding with the management of the company. Thus, it is necessary to identify the factors that affect employee's performance in order to create new strategy or policy. Besides, the company also needs to maintain pleasant feelings in the workplace by gaining praises for work, placement, treatment, equipment, and a good working environment for the employees, these environments can affect an employee's emotional intelligent. Moreover, emotional intelligent increases individual competencies that are essential for organisational performance and has been equated with a pleasurable emotional state (Dormann and Zapf, 2001). Cherniss and Goleman (2001) found that emotional intelligent influences an individual's success in an organisation; meanwhile, Latif *et al.* (2013) found a positive correlation between JS and company performance.

In the era of knowledge resources-based business, IC is considered as a critical strategy for firms to create and sustain their competitive performance (Kamukama *et al.*, 2011; Jardon and Martos, 2012). IC as a resource of intangible assets (knowledge, skill, and experience) contribute to value-creating that can provide a competitive advantage for the company (Bontis *et al.*, 1999; Serenko and Bontis, 2013). Moreover, the organisational development and success can be achieved based on available human resources and the development of human capital. Since businesses environments are becoming more complex, dynamic and globally competitive, knowledge and intelligent workers (who know how to use and develop a knowledge) are valuable intangible assets (part of IC in an organisation), which increase the capacity of creating value for its members (Sumedrea, 2013). While empirical literature has discussed the direct effect of IC on performance, several studies have also explored factors relationship. For example, using knowledge management (KM) approach, researcherS found that the fit between IC and KM strategies (one of the tools to maximise intangible assets such as knowledge and skills), both operational and financial performance (Ling, 2013; Wang *et al.*, 2016). Similarly, several IC studies have considered management accounting system as an important mechanism within knowledge-based organisations that can increase the importance of IC for business performance (Jordão and Novas, 2017).

Hence, it is crucial to understand how different dimensions of IC, EP, and JS may affect the process of non-profit organisation's performance. Although substantial theoretical and empirical literature have discussed the impacts of IC, EP, JS on performance, a consensus on how the components (simultaneously) are related to firm performance has yet to be ascertained. In addition, many elements may influence the organisational outcomes; little is known about these factors in the context of non-profit institutions, especially in a developing country. Finally, this research addresses these limitations by studying the main elements and the support to organisation performance. The following describes the concept in detail and clarifies the aspects related to the basic content if the studied variables and processes.

Literature Review

IC is the collection of intangible resources and their flows, where intangible resources contribute to the value-creating process of the company and controlled by the company (Bontis, 2001). Lynn (1998) explains that IC is the wealth of ideas and the ability to innovate, both being factors (the raw of intelligence, skills, and expertise of human actors) that determine the future goals of organisation. Guthrie *et al.* (2005) infer that IC is an inseparable part of the firm's value, despite appraising its actual value as a crucial intangible asset. Principally, the components of IC is divided into human capital, structural capital, and customer capital (Bontis, 1998). Human capital such as a talent, creativity, skills, and capabilities in workforce, are seen in innovative strategies, plans, and processes that are developed and within the spirit of achieving success in the company. Structural capital is the accumulation of knowledge and experience owned by a company. Several segments in this capital include process, software, patents, and most importantly, knowledge and experience of people in organisation. Bontis (1998) stated that structural capital provides mechanisms and structures of organisation that support employee's performance, including overall business performance.

Aside from IC, JS is one of the most researched variables in the organisation. The definition of JS within the occupational and organisation performance context differs from study to study. However, the two most common definitions describe JS as: "the pleasurable emotional state resulting from the appraisal of one's job as achieving or facilitating the achievement of one's job values"; and "the extent to which people like (satisfaction) or dislike (dissatisfaction) their jobs" (Maslow, 1954; Zerzberg, 1984). Particularly, JS is a component of organisational members' attitude, which is a description of degree of personal feeling in an organisation. JS has attracted extensive research because it is widely acknowledged that JS is crucial for institutions to provide effective and efficient services (Miller *et al.*, 2009). Likewise, Hong *et al.* (2016) explained that JS can be considered as a component related to job quality.

The other instrument to enhance firm performance is worker's performance. Performance is an important criterion for company's outcomes and success. Job performance (JP) is attributed as an individual-level variable. Campbell *et al.* (1990) define performance as individual observable behaviours, which conform to the goals of the organisation. In addition, this differentiates from more encompassing constructs such as organisational performance, which are higher-level variables (Campbell, 1994). Moreover, Locke (1970) found that the effect of performance on satisfaction is viewed as a function of the degree to which performance entails or leads to the attainment of the individual's important job values. It is acknowledged that emotions such as satisfaction and dissatisfaction are -important incentives to action in that they entail action tendencies. Performance is complex and attempts to model the complexity that have taken many forms. The term *active performance* describes employees' capabilities for going beyond the organisation's prescribed requirements and taking additional actions that will result in achieving valued outcomes (Frese, 2008). Active performance means initiating in a useful way in response to the organisation's goals.

Lastly, measuring firm's performance is a vital part of monitoring a firm's progress. It comprises measuring the actual performance outcomes or results of an organisation towards its intended goals. Performance is a subjective perception of reality, which explains the multitude of critical reflections on the concept and its measuring instruments (Richard *et al.*, 2009). This requires a top-down approach to setting performance criteria rather than a bottom-up approach that often occur in many organisations. The strategic plan provides performance targets for the firm; it sets the corporate direction. Yet, how often does the strategic plan set performance measurement target for all levels of the organisation. Firm performance can be measured in three dimensions, namely, IC (Sumedrea, 2013), JS (Bakotić, 2016), and EP (Sadikoglu, 2010).

Hypothesis Development

The business environment rapidly has been changed to a new economic era, which is the pattern of business based on intangible assets (Moeller, 2009), which is argued to be one possible contributor to the disparity between company value as per their accounting records, and company value as per their market capitalisation (Lev and Daum, 2004). Intangible assets include land, vehicles, equipment, and inventory. Additionally, financial assets such as stocks and bonds, which derive their value from contractual claims, are considered tangible assets. Formerly, in contrast, tangible assets such as physical form, machines, and various other facilities are the key resources in the economic and production era; nowadays, the modern business view has included tangible knowledge asset and a tangible asset (Guthrie, 2001).

Meanwhile, IC is the intangible value of a business, comprising human capital, relational capital, and structural capital (Nahapiet and Ghoshal, 1998). Youndt *et al.* (2004) state that IC has been interpreted as the knowledge for company competitive advantage including human capital (knowledge, skills, abilities), structural capital (routines, processes, databases), and relational capital (individuals interactions and their networks). IC can produce competitive advantage and superior performance I within employees of an organisation (Barney, 1991). Thus, the role of IC is a crucial element in EP and at the same time will affect company's performance. Thus, the company can enhance employee's ability by evaluating EP.

Nowadays, knowledge and experience resources refer to capabilities to increase employees and organisations goals. Many researchers argue that knowledge is power and a major asset of modern business (Nonaka, 1994; Nonaka and Konno, 1998; Saide *et al.*, 2017; Saide and Mahendrawathi, 2015). Helmiatin and Idrus (2016) in their study obtained the role of IC on employees' performance in higher education. By using several independent latent variables (exogenous), namely, human capital, structural capital, and customer capital as well a latent variable or dependent (endogenous) of EP, the study reveals that human capital does not affect the performance of employees significantly, while customer capital and structural capital significantly influence EP. Wang *et al.* (2015) examined relationships between IC and performance in a multi-level perspective. They argued that individual performance is affected by IC, and in addition, job autonomy and team interdependence as a mediator is influenced by performance. Therefore, in today's global business environment, IC is seen as a crucial subject for a company to support their business goals in short and long term. Accordingly, IC is presumed to be positively related to EP.

Hypothesis 1: *Intellectual capital has a positive effect on employee performance.*

Several researchers and practitioners have provided their own definitions of JS. However, the two most common definitions describe JS as: "the pleasurable emotional state resulting from the appraisal of one's job as achieving or facilitating the achievement of one's job values and "the extent to which people like (satisfaction) or dislike (dissatisfaction) their jobs (Locke, 1976). In addition, JS can be considered related to work or attitudes about various aspects of the workplace (Lu *et al.*, 2016). Likewise, JS is a pre-condition for competitive levels and organisational success (García-Bernal *et al.*, 2005). Thus, JS is necessary for an employee to affect their emotional intelligence that increases individual competencies and organisational performance (Cherniss and Goleman, 2001; Lam and Kirby, 2002). Dormann and Zapf (2001) state that employees' emotion is related to personality because JS has been equated with a pleasurable emotional feeling. Moreover, previous study Hoboubi *et al.* (2017) and Petty *et al.* (1984) found positive correlation between JS and workforce productivity. Accordingly, JS is presumed to be positively related to EP.

Hypothesis 2: *Job satisfaction has a positive effect on employee performance.*

IC is also known as the new invisible asset, and the most widely used definition of IC is "knowledge that is of value to an organization." In addition, Bayburina and Golovko (2009) explain that IC includes human capital, process, innovation capital, and network capital. IC can increase competitive advantage and superior performance (Barney, 1991; Yıldız *et al.*, 2014). Other researchers stated that IC is one of the basic factors of firm performance (Serenko and Bontis, 2013). In Thailand, the study by Phusavat *et al.* (2011) found that IC significantly affects a manufacturing firm's performance. The findings highlight the role of IC in reinforcing a manufacturing firm's competitive advantage in long-term. The complexity of these characteristics represents the competitive advantage that is originated within the company. Thus, competitive success of a firm depends highly on IC as compared to other resources. IC is the most necessary strategic assets in assessing the performance of an organisation in the developing and underdeveloped countries (Khalique *et al.*, 2011) so that organisational performance will increase if the company can manage IC in their company. Accordingly, IC is presumed as positively related to firm performance.

Hypothesis 3: *Intellectual capital has a positive effect on firm performance.*

Company performance is influenced by several factors, both internal, which the company can influence, and external, which are beyond the company's influence (Bakotić, 2016). Attitudes in general and especially JS affect organisational behaviour in a number of cases, but not always. Since satisfaction feeling is a psychological process (García-Bernal *et al.*, 2005), it will help workers to explore their ideas and develop their potential. Thus, the quality of employees' work for a company, also provide benefits to their personal life. Other researchers found that employee satisfaction influences firm performance through direct association (Santiago, 2005). Hence, company performance cannot be viewed as a simple sum of individual performances. Studies of many studies suggest the existence of positive correlation between JS and individual performances (Judge *et al.*, 2001; Harter *et al.*, 2003). In specific, once an employee feels comfortable with workplace environment, then work satisfaction will be achieved. This condition will generate a good, concentration mood, and positive thinking of employees. Accordingly, JS is presumed to be positively related to firm performance.

Hypothesis 4: *Job satisfaction has a positive effect on firm performance.*

Another aspect of a company is EP. This element is the related expected result of workers and how well those activities were executed. Organisation assesses the employee's performance on an annual or quarterly basis in order to help them identify suggested areas for improvement. An effective performance usually focuses on work outcomes that is directly related to the organisation's goals and support business strategy implementation. To realise these goals, employees need to understand that EP dimension is a factor that will be evaluated by an organisation. An employee's performance is divided into several activities such as improvement, learning, and development in order to achieve the overall business strategy and to create high performance of employee.

Darline Vandaele (2000) indicates that high performance depends on company capability to create an innovation, protecting and using intangible knowledge assets. Usually, performance focuses on organisation's ways regarding constraints pertaining to the objectives and without forces their members (Martz, 2013). In addition, organisations are required to be more responsive in a challenging environment (Kennerley and Neely, 2003). Study by Masa'deh *et al.* (2016) found a significant relationship between JP and firm performance. Similar results were obtained by Darline Vandaele (2000) who discovered that firm performance outcome, which include quality and productivity are influenced by extra-role JP. Therefore, performance of an employee has critical importance and value in achieving organisational goals and performance. Accordingly, EP is presumed to be positively related to firm performance.

Hypothesis 5: *Employee performance has a positive effect on firm performance.*

Methodology

This study proposes a correlation among IC, JS, EP, and firm performance. The IC is composed by five items based on the study by Bontis (1998) and Stewart (1998). This section mainly describes the resources of organisations such as human capital, organisation capital, and relationship capital with six items question. On the other hand, JS is described as co-workers, promotion, responsibility, salary, and supervisor with 10 items question in total (Smith *et al.*, 1969). Another construct is EP. This variable is described as quality, quantity, timeliness, cost-effectiveness, supervision, and interpersonal impact with 12 items question in total (Bernardin and Russell, 1993). In the last construct, firm performance is measured with six items adopted from Dwiyanto (2006); Hansen and Wernerfelt (1989); Ramanujam (1986); Anderson and Reeb (2003). These questions are related to company performance such as organisational support, management ability and effectivity, and performance of the company's members.

Instrument scheme

In the questionnaire form, the first part is a brief introduction about the research. The second part is about demographic information of the respondents, which included seven items (i.e., position in company, working period, gender, and educational level). The third part contains questionnaire measured based on the constructs under study. The last part of the questionnaire is a comment section by the respondents. SPSS was used to measure demographic scales and generate descriptive statistics. Firstly, data of sample target was established through SPSS, and the narrative statistical analysis and non-response bias of the samples was tested prior and after the research. Then, factors verification was completed through SmartPLS 2.0 for research model and path analysis. These items were scored using a five-point Likert scale, with 1 corresponding to "strongly disagree" and 5 to "strongly agree".

Sampling, non-response bias, and common method variation

A survey method using questionnaires was used to collect the data. A total of 127 employees in PT. Permodalan Ekonomi Rakyat (Riau Province, Indonesia) participated in the survey. The respondents profile were classified into working time (in details: 1–5 years with 51 employees or 40.2%, 6–10 years with 27 employees or 21.3%, 11–15 years with 49 employees or 38.6%, educational level (senior high school with 68 employees or 53.5%, undergraduate with 58 employees or 45.7%, graduate with 1 employee or 0.8%), age (17–30 years with 19 employees or 15%, 31–40 years with 47 employees or 37%, 41–50 years with 53 employees or 41.7%), and gender (104 males or 81.9% and 23 females or 18.1%). In addition, to stimulate the respondent's responses, in the questionnaire form that we wrote "when each questionnaire is completed and sent back to us, it will randomly select winner respondents to get a coupon/gift.

Employees examined the test of non-response bias sample of this study. In the process of distributing samples, 50 valid samples were collected for the first time, and 30 valid samples for the second time. Therefore, the T-test was used to verify the questionnaires for the first and second time. The test results showed that the p-values were all greater than 0.05 at a significant level of 0.05, indicating that there was no significant difference in the questionnaires observed before and after survey, so it can be seen that the questionnaires observed before and after the study was homogenous.

Moreover, the common method variation (CMV) will inappropriately expand the relationship among variables. Also, statistically, the result will significant increase or decrease, which in turn influences the establishment hypothesis test. Therefore, the variables of this study were analysed before testing for CMVs. This study uses Harman's single factor test to determine whether there are CMVs in research variables (Podsakoff *et al.*, 2003). In the Harman's single factor test method, the main treatment method is to analyse all items in the non-rotating factor, and the value is greater than 1 as criterion. Therefore, this standard can be used to determine the conceptual model.

Analysis and Hypothesis Results

This section of the study explains the data analysis techniques and the conceptual result. A detailed description of the dataset's validity, including validity assessment, and construct validity tests are indicated in the tables below. The measurement model was further assessed for reliability and validity of construct. Computing composite reliability assessed construct reliability. The composite reliability for each construct of this study is presented in Table 1. Prior scholars found that all indicators factor loading should be significant and exceed 0.6, and composite reliability should exceed 0.7 (Chin, 2010). Data quality test consists of testing validity and reliability. Validity testing uses correlation techniques, namely correlating scores on each item with a total score. Therefore, regarding Tables 1 and 2, all conditions for convergent validity were met. Cronbach alpha values in Table 2 indicate all constructs are reliable for this research. The composite reliability values were used to examine reliability as shown in Table 1, all composite reliability exceeded the recommended cutoff that indicate a commonly acceptable level for confirmatory research.

Based on the results of the validity and reliability test, it can be concluded that the data shows a fairly good level of consistency and accuracy. Reliability test results are carried out with requirement number of Cronbach's alpha. On the other

Table 1. Hypothesis results.

Influential variables	Variables influenced	Estimated value	C.R	P	Status
IC	EP	0.443	4.373	0.000	Approved
	Firm Performance	0.289	2.405	0.016	Approved
JS	EP	0.440	3.874	0.000	Approved
	Firm Performance	0.249	2.033	0.042	Approved
EP	Firm Performance	0.320	2.170	0.030	Approved

Table 2. Validity and reliability analysis.

Variable	Correlation range	Cronbach alpha	Status
IC (X1)	0.755–0.817	0.926	Valid
JS (X2)	0.521–0.731	0.898	Valid
EP (Y1)	0.523–0.653	0.889	Valid
Firm Performance (Y2)	0.667–0.722	0.883	Valid

hand, the testing of the hypothesis proposed in this study was carried out based on the critical ratio (CR) value of the causality relationship between variables. Table 1 showed direct effect of each variable between exogenous variable and endogenous variable. The value of estimated path coefficient was presented based on standardised regression weights, while significance of effect based on value number of C.R or probability value (p).

As it can be seen in Table 1 and Fig. 1, the finding supports Hypothesis 1 with a positive relationship between IC and EP (CR = 4.373, $p = 0.000 < 0.05$). Likewise, the findings provided support for Hypothesis 2, showing IC has a positive impact on firm performance (CR = 2.405, $p = 0.016 < 0.05$). Similarly, Hypothesis 3 showed that relationship between JS and EP was positive (CR = 3.874, $p = 0.000 < 0.05$). Besides, Hypothesis 4 showed positive correlation between JS on firm performance (CR = 2.033, p = 0.042 < 0.05). Lastly, the findings provided supported Hypothesis 5, showing that EP has a positive relation with firm performance (CR = 2.170, $p = 0.030 < 0.05$). An in-depth discussion among all correlation factors are discussed in section below.

Moreover, the overall fit of the model (GFI, NFI, CFI, AGFI, and RMSEA) is measured. In the conceptual model, this study found GFI with number 0.896, indicating a fairly good fit to accept the model. In addition to the above indices, a stringent goodness-of-fit adjusts the measure of fit to provide comparisons between models with differing number of coefficients. The indicator is the comparative fit

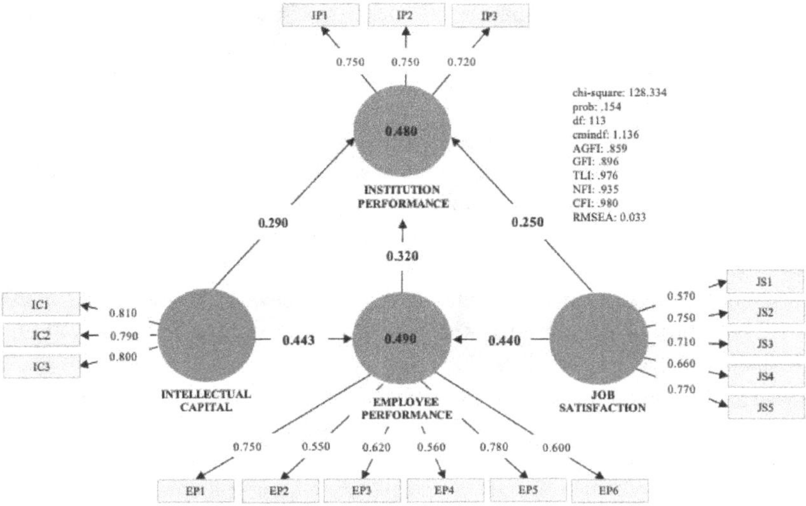

Fig. 1. Full model result.

index (CFI) with the recommended value greater than 0.90 and our result model showed CFI is 0.980. Additionally, the root means square error of approximation (RMSEA) takes into consideration the sample size and parsimony. RMSEA result showed 0.033. The recommended RMSEA is the value less than 0.08. Figure 1 indicates the RMSEA and PCLOSE fit measures of this study.

Discussion

The research combined several issues such as IC, JS, EP, and firm performance. The results indicate that IC has positive effect on EP. The IC resources of employees in this case has a good condition. Employees were given a creative innovation to increase company performance. In addition, the employees also obtained support from leadership to improve their work. The results of this study are similar with prior research (Carson *et al.*, 2004; Kamukama *et al.*, 2010; Tastan and Davoudi, 2015), whereby IC has a significant effect on EP. Moreover, EP can be increased if support is provided from co-workers in the organisation. Similarly, Boekestein (2006) and Joia (2000), stated that IC is an intangible asset that contains knowledge, which can affect the company's performance for decision making and in future targets. Thus, each employee is expected to be able to continue exploring their knowledge and not be dependent on the company's system. Additionally, since IC as knowledge assets is different from stakeholder's resources (networking and human resources) and structural resources (physical and virtual infrastructure), the employees with high IC would contribute in increasing work-competition in organisational environment. In other words, higher the IC of a company, higher the outcome of employee's performance.

On the other hand, based on conceptual results, JS has a significant effect on EP. JS of employees is a crucial condition that a company should consider, as JS is an aspect that improves EP. In addition, through JS, organisation knows the level of employee's feelings of their workers. once the company knows their employee's feelings, the company can offer a strategy on increasing positivity of the workers, as reward is important once a target is achieved. Therefore, JS involves the psychology of an individual, which increases their spirit in work environment. In addition, according to Elloy (2005) and Scott-Ladd *et al.* (2006), JS reflects a feeling of pride, happiness, and satisfaction as an effective response to the behaviour of leaders, job, and work environment situations that fulfill the aspirations, desires, needs, and expected values. Thus, if JS is high, the productivity of employees will be increased. Another reason is that if employees feel happy, they will do the best for their company. In addition, improving EP will benefit in the progress of the company to survive in a competitive business environment; thus, JS is one of the factors that can affect EP. This research was in line with research conducted by Indarti *et al.* (2017) and Matthews *et al.* (2018), whose results showed that there was a positive and significant relationship between satisfaction and performance improvement.

Besides, the company has successfully increased firm performance through IC. In the last few decades, IC has become a very interesting issue for an in-depth research. Due to it being a part of the business foundation that resource to create and maintain a competitive advantage with companies' partners and competitors. In general, human capital or IC is the most important capital to drive the growth of firm performance. In the context of economy analysis, the importance of human sustainability in production process led to the term "human capital" is more appropriate than workers (Arshad and Munir, 2018; Mthanti and Ojah, 2018). Now, companies are more interested in paying attention to IC in their companies, because IC as an intangible asset is one of the factors the effect the company's performance. In line with this, study by Joia (2000) showed that IC has significant effect on the existing and future of the company's performance. Thus, as the IC of the company increases, performance of the company will increase too.

Based on Fig. 1, JS also supports firm performance. In this case, employee satisfaction is a measure of employee's contentedness with their job, whether they are in favour of the job or individual aspects or facets of works, such is the nature of work or supervision. In this relationship, JS is a pleasant emotion or vice versa of employees pertaining to their work. For the employees who have a high level of JS usually love their job, feel justice in work environment, and feel positive features such as challenge, autonomy, and pleasant co-workers. Moreover, employees who are happy at work will even devote private time to their work activities; thus, they will be creative and committed, and assist their colleagues and superiors. Employees are an important resource and not just a homogeneous cost of production. Therefore, JS is measured as an effective construct that encompasses overall satisfaction. It has also been measured as a cognitive concept that refers to various aspects of a job. Affective or global JS is usually theorised as a unitary concept that represents an overall positive emotional response to a job as a whole. Meanwhile, cognitive is based on a more rational evaluation of different job conditions. Regarding the specific facets of JS, most of the extant instruments include similar components.

EP is a crucial aspect that needs to consider continuation by the management. The simple reason is that employee's performance will automatically affect the level of company's performance as well. Currently, companies that know how to use and invest in their resources can sustain by devising a business strategy based on the emerging markets. This is mainly considered a managerial responsibility and the results depend not only on management's capabilities, but also on employee's performance. In general, to complete a task or job, employees should have a degree of willingness and ability. A person's willingness and skills are not effective enough to complete the job without a clear understanding on the relevant method of the task. In addition, Schweitzer and Lyons (2008) highlight the importance of a high value relationship creation between the employees and employers. For this to be possible, those types of potential employees must be identified, and recruitment of these persons in an employment relationship, will benefit both the employer and employee, a fact that will inevitably lead to the increase of the performance.

As the company's performance is directly influenced by employee's ability, the leaders should try increasing performance and retain performance of the employees. Hence, all the respondents agreed that encouraging personal development, initiative, appropriate environment, and opportunities are methods that can increase the level of performance. Moreover, creating a competitive environment and a positive image of the company on the market, employees are stimulated to perform better and to stay with the company. Managers mostly choose methods such as promotion or salary increase as well as training sessions and human development programs, as special requirements in retaining the employees.

Conclusions and Implications

The results framework (Fig. 1) explains how the variables are influenced, respectively. Management level can maximise resources in their organisation. Essentially, this research proposed four main variables, namely, JS, IC, EP, and organisation performance. The result of this research offers a new framework for performance measurement as a tool to guide them in implementing a strategy. While a number of researches has been proposed to develop the relationships between IC, EP, and firm performance, and though there have been much theorising in this area, few validated instruments have been developed for empirical testing of these theories, especially for the perspective of fit in non-profit organisation.

Due to the importance of strategic alignment, these factors are acknowledged and regarded as having a significant positive direct effect upon business performance (Nonaka, 1994; Stewart, 1998; Camuffo and Comacchio, 2005; Kamukama *et al.*, 2010; Bakotić, 2016; Mthanti and Ojah, 2018), several factors must consider the realities of strategic alignment in the performance field. Moreover, maximising intangible asset through IC theory or KM approach is one of the key factors of organisation performance practices and can be added to the proposed model in future studies (Allameh, 2018; Indrajit *et al.*, 2018).

The results of this study are also relevant for managerial perspective. These findings suggest to HR managers that one of the key drivers of company attractiveness is maximising intangible assets (knowledge, experience, skills, etc.) of their members. This means that managers should push for investing in collaborative and long-term learning collaboration if they want to conquer the attention of potential valuable by employees' performance. In addition, managers can use the theoretical/conceptual model periodically to assess where their firm stands in the firm performance indicators (IC, JS, and EP). Managers can also measure the effects of these considerations on various performance measures in order to evaluate the effectiveness of firm performance. It can motivate the management of the firm to commit and improve the employees' (internal resource) satisfaction, motivation, commitment, and effort in order to achieve their goals through innovation, potential employee, and competitiveness. Besides, willingness of managers to manage a collaborative relationship and to share information is required for sustainability. When these factors are not present, pushing collaborative initiatives can result in a failure of the business project. In a more specific approach, managers should also consider KM strategy in obtaining knowledge and competencies to increase knowledge cycle in a company, which have an impact on employees and firm's performance as well (Saide *et al.*, 2019).

Further research could be identified either specific organisation or specific countries could be performed to address whether significant differences would appear in different areas of investigation. This can be explored in future study on the subject, through a qualitative or quantitative data collection approach to complement the reliability of research findings. A further study can also use multiple methods and multiple informants to eliminate potential common method bias and improve the ability of the findings to be generalised. In addition, the moderating control of contextual factors such as firm size, type, operations, competition level, managerial knowledge, and leadership style can be studied to evaluate complex relationships among these variables as well.

References

Allameh, SM (2018). Antecedents and consequences of intellectual capital: The role of social capital, knowledge sharing and innovation. *Journal of Intellectual Capital*, 19(5), 858–874.

Almatrooshi, B, SK Singh and S Farouk (2016). Determinants of organizational performance: A proposed framework. *International Journal of Productivity and Performance Management*, 65(6), 844–859.

Anderson, RC and DM Reeb (2003). Founding-family ownership and firm performance: Evidence from the S&P 500. *The Journal of Finance*, LVIII(3), 1301–1328.

Arshad, S and K Munir (2018). Factor accumulation and economic growth in Pakistan: Incorporating human capital. *International Journal of Social Economics*, 45(3), 480–491.

Bakotić, D (2016). Relationship between job satisfaction and organisational performance. *Economic Research-Ekonomska Istrazivanja*, 29(1), 118–130.

Barney, JB (1991). Firm resources and sustained competitive advantage. *Journal of Management*, 17(1), 99–120.

Bayburina, E and T Golovko (2009). Design of sustainable development: Intellectual value of large BRIC companies and factors of their growth. *Electronic Journal of Knowledge Management*, 7(5), 535–558.

Boekestein, B (2006). The relation between intellectual capital and intangible assets of pharmaceutical companies. *Journal of Intellectual Capital*, 7(2), 241–253.

Bontis, N (1998). Intellectual capital: An exploratory study that develops measure and models. *Management Decision*, 36(2), 63–76.

Bontis, N (2001). Assessing knowledge assets: A review of the models used to measure intellectual capital. *International Journal of Management Reviews*, 3(1), 41–60.

Bontis, N, NC Dragonetti, K Jacobsen and G Roos (1999). The knowledge toolbox: A review of the tools available to measure and manage intangible resources. *European Management Journal*, 17(4), 391–402.

Campbell, JP (1994). *Behavior, Performance, and Effectiveness — In the 21st Century*. New York: Oxford Press.

Campbell, JP, JJ McHenry and LL Wise (1990). Modeling job performance in a populations of jobs. *Personnel Psychology*, 43(2), 313–333.

Camuffo, A and A Comacchio (2005). Linking intellectual capital and competitive advantage: A cross-firm competence model for north-east Italian SMEs in the manufacturing industry. *Human Resource Development International*, 8(3), 361–377.

Carson, E, R Ranzijn, A Winefield and H Marsden (2004). Intellectual capital: Mapping employee and work group attributes. *Journal of Intellectual Capital*, 5(3), 443–463.

Cherniss, C and D Goleman (2001). The emotionally intelligent workplace: How to select for, measure, and improve emotional intelligence in individuals, groups, and organizations. *Jossey-Bass*, Available at https://doi.org/10.1017/CBO9781107415324.004.

Chin, WW (2010). How to write up and report PLS analyses. In *Handbook of Partial Least Squares*, Springer Handbooks, pp. 655–690.

Darline Vandaele, PG (2000). Strategies for managing knowledge assets: The role of firm structure and industrial context. *Long Range Planning*, 33(1), 35–54.

Dormann, C and D Zapf (2001). Job satisfaction: A meta-analysis of stabilities. *Journal of Organization Behavior*, 22(5), 483–504.

Elloy, DF (2005). The influence of superleader behaviors on organization commitment, job satisfaction and organization self-esteem in a self-managed work team. *Leadership and Organization Development Journal*, 26(2), 120–127.

Fornell, C and DF Larcker (1981). Structural equation models with unobservable variables and measurement error: Algebra and statistics. *Journal of Marketing Research*, 18(3), 382.

Frese, M (2008). The word is out: We need an active performance concept for modern work places. *Industrial and Organizational Psychology: Perspectives on Science and Practice*, 1–7.

García-Bernal, J, A Gargallo-Castel, M Marzo-Navarro and P Rivera-Torres (2005). Job satisfaction: Empirical evidence of gender differences. *Women in Management Review*, 20(4), 279–288.

Guthrie, J (2001). The management, measurement and the reporting of intellectual capital. *Intellectual Capital*, 2(1), 27–41.

Guthrie, J, R Petty and F Ricceri (2006). The voluntary reporting of intellectual capital comparing evidence from Hong Kong and Australia. *Journal of Intellectual Capital*, 7(2), 254–271.

Hansen, GS and B Wernerfelt (1989). Determinants of firm performance: The relative importance of economic and organizational factors. *Strategic Management Journal*, 10(1), 399–411.

Harter, JK, FL Schmidt and CLM Keyes (2003). Well-being in the workplace and its relationship to business outcomes: A review of the gallup studies. *American Psychological Association*, 205–224.

Helmiatin and O Idrus (2016). Proceeding of the First American Academic Research Conference on Global Business, Economics, Finance and Social Sciences. In *Proceeding of the First American Academic Research Conference on Global Business, Economics, Finance and Social Sciences*, New York, USA, pp. 1–10.

Hoboubi, N, AR Choobineh, FK Ghanavati, S Keshavarzi and AA Hosseini (2017). The impact of job stress and job satisfaction on workforce productivity in an Iranian petrochemical industry. *Safety and Health at Work*, 8(1).

Hong, L, E Alison and KLB While (2016). The relationships between structural and psychological empowerment and job satisfaction among nurses. *Journal of Hayat*, 22(3), 201–215.

Hulland, J (1999). Use of partial least squares (PLS) in strategic management research: A review of four recent studies. *Strate*, 20(2), 195–204.

Indarti, S, S Solimun, AAR Fernandes and W Hakim (2017). The effect of OCB in relationship between personality, organizational commitment and job satisfaction to performance. *Journal of Management Development*.

Indrajit, RE, S Saide, R Trialih, H Wei and H Herzavina (2018). A brief review: The roles in triggering knowledge management scheme adoption to increase enterprise performance. *The 9th International Conference on ICT Convergence*, pp. 79–84.

Jardon, CM and MS Martos (2012). Intellectual capital as competitive advantage in emerging clusters in Latin America. *Journal of Intellectual Capital*, 13(4), 462–481.

Joia, LA (2000). Linking business strategy with intellectual capital. *Journal of Intellectual Capital*, 1(1), 68–84.

Jordão, RVD and JC Novas (2017). Knowledge management and intellectual capital in networks of small- and medium-sized enterprises. *Journal of Intellectual Capital*, 18(3), 667–692.

Judge, TA, CJ Thoresen, JE Bono and GK Patton (2001). The job satisfaction-job performance relationship: A qualitative and quantitative review. *Psychological Bulletin*, 127(3), 376–407.

Kamukama, N, A Ahiauzu and JM Ntayi (2010). Intellectual capital and performance: Testing interaction effects. *Journal of Intellectual Capital*, 11(4), 554–574.

Kamukama, N, A Ahiauzu and JM Ntayi (2011). Competitive advantage: Mediator of intellectual capital and performance. *Journal of Intellectual Capital*, 12(1), 152–164.

Kennerley, M and A Neely (2003). Measuring performance in a changing business environment performance. *International Journal of Operations & Production Management*, 23(2), 213–229.

Khalique, M, J Abdul Nassir Shaari, AH Md. Isa and A Ageel (2011). Role of intellectual capital on the organizational performance of electrical and electronic SMEs in Pakistan. *International Journal of Business and Management*, 6(9), 253–257.

Lam, LT and SL Kirby (2002). Is emotional intelligence an advantage? an exploration of the impact of emotional and general intelligence on individual performance. *The Journal of Social Psychology*, 142(1), 133–143.

Latif, MS, M Ahmad, Q Muhammad, A Ferdoos and H Naeem (2013). Impact of employee's job satisfaction on organizational performance. *European Journal of Business and Management*, 5(5), 166–171.

Lev, B and JH Daum (2004). The dominance of intangible assets: Consequences for enterprise management and corporate reporting. *Measuring Business Excellence*, 8(1), 6–17.

Ling, YH (2013). The influence of intellectual capital on organizational performance-Knowledge management as moderator. *Asia Pacific Journal of Management*, 30(3), 937–964.

Locke, EA (1970). Job satisfaction and job performance: A theoretical analysis. *Organizational Behavior and Human Performance*, 5(5), 484–500.

Locke, EA (1976). The nature and causes of job satisfaction. In *Handbook of Industrial and Organizational Psychology*, pp. 1297–1343.

Lynn, BE (1998). Performance evaluation in the new economy: Bringing the measurement and evaluation of intellectual capital into the management planning and control system. *International Journal of Technology Management*, 16(1/2/3), 162.

Martz, W (2013). Evaluating organizational performance: Rational, natural, and open system models. *American Journal of Evaluation*, 34(3), 385–401.

Masa'deh, R, BY Obeidat and A Tarhini (2016). A Jordanian empirical study of the associations among transformational leadership, transactional leadership, knowledge sharing, job performance, and firm performance: A structural equation modelling approach. *Journal of Management Development*, 35(5), 681–705.

Maslow, AH (1954). *Motivation and Personality*, Harper & Row Publishers, Available at https://doi.org/10.1098/rstb.2010.0126.

Matthews, B, J Daigle and M Houston (2018). A dyadic of employee readiness and job satisfaction: Does there exist a theoretical precursor to the satisfaction-performance paradigm?. *International Journal of Organizational Analysis*, 26(5), 842–857.

Melián-González, S, J Bulchand-Gidumal and BG López-Valcárcel (2015). New evidence of the relationship between employee satisfaction and firm economic performance. *Personnel Review*, 44(6), 906–929.

Miller, HA, S Mire and B Kim (2009). Predictors of job satisfaction among police officers: Does personality matter? *Journal of Criminal Justice*, 37(5), 419–426.

Moeller, K (2009). Intangible and financial performance: Causes and effects. *Intellectual Capital*, 10(2), 224–245.

Mthanti, T and K Ojah (2018). Institutions, human capital and entrepreneurial orientation: Implications for growth policy. *Journal of Entrepreneurship and Public Policy*, 7(2), 135–160.

Nahapiet, J and S Ghoshal (1998). Social capital, intellectual capital, and the organizational advantage. *The Academy of Management Review*, 23(2), 242.

Nonaka, I (1994). A dynamic theory of organizational knowledge creation. *Organization Science*, 5(1), 14–37.

Nonaka, I and N Konno (1998). The concept of 'Ba': Building a foundation for knowledge creation. *California Management Review*.

Onofrei, M, J Hunt, J Siemienczuk, DR Touchette and B Middleton (2004). A first step towards translating evidence into practice: Heart failure in a community practice-based research network. *Informatics in Primary Care*, 12(3), 139–145.

Osinski, M, PM Selig, F Matos and Darlan José Roman (2017). Methods of evaluation of intangible assets and intellectual capital. *Journal of Intellectual Capital*, 18(3), 470–485.

Petty, AMM, GW Mcgee, JW Cavender, GW Mcgee and JW Cavender (1984). Meta-analysis of between individual and individual the relationships job satisfaction. 9(4), 712–721.

Phusavat, K, N Comepa, A Sitko-Lutek and K Ooi (2011). Interrelationships between intellectual capital and performance. *Industrial Management & Data Systems*, 111(6), 810–829.

Podsakoff, PM, SB MacKenzie, JY Lee and NP Podsakoff (2003). Common method biases in behavioral research: A critical review of the literature and recommended remedies. *Journal of Applied Psychology*, 88(5), 879–903.

Ramanujam, V (1986). Measurement of business performance in strategy research: A comparison of approaches massachusetts institute of technology. *Academy of Management Review*, 11(4), 801–814.

Richard, PJ, TM Devinney, GS Yip and G Johnson (2009). Measuring organizational performance: Towards methodological best practice. *Journal of Management*, 35(3), 718–804.

Bontis, N, NC Dragonetti, K Jacobsen and G Roos (1999). The knowledge toolbox: A review of the tools available to measure and manage intangible resources. *European Management Journal*, 17(4), 391–402.

Sadikoglu (2010). Investigating the effects of innovation and employee performance on the relationship between total quality management practices and firm performance:

An empirical study of Turkish firms. *International Journal of Production Economics*, 127(1), 13–26.

Saide and ER Mahendrawathi (2015). Knowledge management support for enterprise resource planning implementation. *Procedia Computer Science*, 72, 613–621.

Saide, TR, HL Wei, Okfalisa and W Anugrah (2017). Knowledge sharing behavior and quality among workers of academic institutions in Indonesia. *International Journal of Business and Society*, 18(S2), 353–368.

Saide, S, RE Indrajit, R Trialih, S Ramadhani and N Najamuddin (2019a). A theoretical and empirical validation of information technology and path-goal leadership on knowledge creation in university. *Journal of Science and Technology Policy Management*, 1–19. doi: https://doi.org/10.1108/JSTPM-06-2018-0067.

Saide, S., Astuti, E., Indrajit, R., Trialih, R., Diniaty, A., Dewi, F. and Herzavina, H. (2019b). What we give, we get back: Investigating the dimensions that influence knowledge sharing on profit enterprise in Indonesia, *Journal of Science and Technology Policy Management*, 10(5), 1047–1062. https://doi.org/10.1108/JSTPM-06-2018-0056.

Schweitzer, L and S Lyons (2008). The market within: A marketing approach to creating and developing high-value employment relationships. *Business Horizons*, 51(6), 555–565.

Scott-Ladd, B, A Travaglione and V Marshall (2006). Causal inferences between participation in decision making, task attributes, work effort, rewards, job satisfaction and commitment. *Leadership and Organization Development Journal*, 27(5), 399–414.

Serenko, A and N Bontis (2013). Investigating the current state and impact of the intellectual capital academic discipline. *Journal of Intellectual Capital*, 14(4), 476–500.

Smith, PC, LM Kendall and CL Hulin (1969). *The Measurement of Satisfaction in Work and Retirement: A Strategy for the Study of Attitudes, Chicago, Ill., Rand McNally*, Chicago, Ill., Rand McNally.

Stewart, T (1998). *Intellectual Capital: The New Wealth of Organizations, Information Doubleday/Currency*, Available at https://doi.org/10.1002/pfi.4140370713.

Sumedrea, S (2013). Intellectual capital and firm performance: A dynamic relationship in crisis time. *Procedia Economics and Finance*, 6(13), 137–144.

Tastan, S and SM Mousavi Davoudi (2015). A research on the relevance of intellectual capital and employee job performance as measured with distinct constructs of in-role and extra-role behaviors. *Indian Journal of Science and Technology*, 8, 724–734.

Wang, CH, CD Yen and GHW Liu (2015). How intellectual capital influences individual performance: A multi-level perspective. *Computers in Human Behavior*, 51, 930–937.

Wang, Z, N Wang, J Cao and X Ye (2016). The impact of intellectual capital — knowledge management strategy fit on firm performance. *Management Decision*, 54(8), 1861–1885.

Yıldız, S, C Meydan and M Güner (2014). Measurement of intellectual capital components through activity reports of companies. *Procedia — Social and Behavioral Sciences*, 109, 614–621.

Youndt, MA, M Subramaniam and SA Snell (2004). Intellectual capital profiles: An examination of investments and returns. *Journal of Management Studies*, 41(2), 335–361.

Zerzberg (1984). *Materiality in Children's Meaning-Making Practices*, p. 19. New York: Wiley.

Series on Technology Management

(Continuation of series card page)

Vol. 29 *Exploiting Intellectual Property to Promote Innovation and Create Value*
edited by Joseph Tidd (University of Sussex, UK)

Vol. 28 *Promoting Innovation in New Ventures and Small- and Medium-Sized Enterprises*
edited by Joseph Tidd (University of Sussex, UK)

Vol. 27 *The Role of Creativity in the Management of Innovation: State of the Art and Future Research Outlook*
edited by Alexander Brem (University of Southern Denmark, Denmark),
Rogelio Puente-Diaz (University Anáhuac, Mexico) &
Marine Agogué (HEC Montréal, Canada)

Vol. 26 *Total Value Development: How to Drive Service Innovation*
by Frank M. Hull (Cass Business School and Fordham University Graduate School of Business-Executive Education, USA) &
Christopher David Storey (University of Sussex, UK)

Vol. 25 *Small Firms as Innovators: From Innovation to Sustainable Growth*
by Helena Forsman (University of Tampere, Finland)

Vol. 24 *The Knowledge Enterprise: Innovation Lessons from Industry Leaders (Second Edition)*
by E. Huizenga (University of Amsterdam, The Netherlands)

Vol. 23 *Open Innovation Research, Management and Practice*
edited by J. Tidd (University of Sussex, UK)

Vol. 22 *Discontinuous Innovation: Learning to Manage the Unexpected*
by P. Augsdörfer (Technische Hochschule Ingolstadt, Germany),
J. Bessant (University of Exeter, UK),
K. Möslein (Universität Erlangen-Nürnberg, Germany),
B. von Stamm (Innovation Leadership Forum, UK) &
F. Piller (RWTH Aachen University, Germany)

Vol. 21 *Workbook for Opening Innovation: Bridging Networked Business, Intellectual Property and Contracting*
by Jaakko Paasi (VTT Technical Research Centre of Finland, Finland),
Katri Valkokari (VTT Technical Research Centre of Finland, Finland),
Henri Hytönen (VTT Technical Research Centre of Finland, Finland),
Laura Huhtilainen (University of Eastern Finland, Finland) &
Soili Nystén-Haarala (University of Eastern Finland, Finland)

Vol. 20 *Bazaar of Opportunities for New Business Development: Bridging Networked Innovation, Intellectual Property and Business*
by Jaakko Paasi (VTT Technical Research Centre of Finland, Finland),
Katri Valkokari (VTT Technical Research Centre of Finland, Finland),
Tuija Rantala (VTT Technical Research Centre of Finland, Finland),
Soili Nystén-Haarala (University of Eastern Finland, Finland),
Nari Lee (University of Eastern Finland, Finland) &
Laura Huhtilainen (University of Eastern Finland, Finland)

Vol. 19 *From Knowledge Management to Strategic Competence: Assessing Technological, Market and Organisational Innovation (Third Edition)*
edited by Joe Tidd (University of Sussex, UK)

Vol. 18 *Perspectives on Supplier Innovation: Theories, Concepts and Empirical Insights on Open Innovation and the Integration of Suppliers*
edited by Alexander Brem (University of Erlangen-Nuremberg, Germany) &
Joe Tidd (University of Sussex, UK)

Vol. 17 *Managing Process Innovation: From Idea Generation to Implementation*
by Thomas Lager (Grenoble Ecole de Management, France)

Vol. 16 *Perspectives on User Innovation*
edited by Stephen Flowers (University of Brighton, UK) &
Flis Henwood (University of Brighton, UK)

Vol. 15 *Gaining Momentum: Managing the Diffusion of Innovations*
edited by Joe Tidd (SPRU, University of Sussex, UK)

Vol. 14 *Innovation and Strategy of Online Games*
by Jong H. Wi (Chung-Ang University, South Korea)

Vol. 13 *Building Innovation Capability in Organizations: An International Cross-Case Perspective*
by Milé Terziovski (University of Melbourne, Australia)

Vol. 12 *Project-Based Organization in the Knowledge-Based Society*
by Mitsuru Kodama (Nihon University, Japan)

Vol. 11 *Involving Customers in New Service Development*
edited by Bo Edvardsson (Karlstad University, Sweden),
Anders Gustafsson (Karlstad University, Sweden),
Per Kristensson (Karlstad University, Sweden),
Peter Magnusson (Karlstad University, Sweden) &
Jonas Matthing (Karlstad University, Sweden)

Vol. 10 *Open Source: A Multidisciplinary Approach*
by Moreno Muffatto (University of Padua, Italy)

Vol. 9 *Service Innovation: Organizational Responses to Technological Opportunities & Market Imperatives*
edited by Joe Tidd (University of Sussex, UK) &
Frank M. Hull (Fordham University, USA)

Vol. 8 *Digital Innovation: Innovation Processes in Virtual Clusters and Digital Regions*
edited by Giuseppina Passiante (University of Lecce, Italy),
Valerio Elia (University of Lecce, Italy) &
Tommaso Massari (University of Lecce, Italy)

Vol. 7 *Innovation Management in the Knowledge Economy*
edited by Ben Dankbaar (University of Nijmegen, The Netherlands)

Vol. 6 *Social Interaction and Organisational Change: Aston Perspectives on Innovation Networks*
edited by Oswald Jones (Aston University, UK),
Steve Conway (Aston University, UK) & Fred Steward (Aston University, UK)

Vol. 5 *R&D Strategy and Organisation: Managing Technical Change in Dynamic Contexts*
by Vittorio Chiesa (Università degli Studi di Milano-Bicocca, Milan, Italy)

Vol. 4 *Japanese Cost Management*
by Yasuhiro Monden (University of Tsukuba, Japan)

Vol. 3 *From Knowledge Management to Strategic Competence: Measuring Technological, Market and Organizational Innovation*
edited by Joe Tidd (SPRU, University of Sussex, UK)

Vol. 2 *The Knowledge Enterprise: Implementation of Intelligent Business Strategies*
by J. Friso den Hertog (MERIT, Maastricht University & Altuïtion bv, 's Hertogenbosch, The Netherlands) &
Edward Huizenga (Altuïtion bv, 's Hertogenbosch, The Netherlands)

Vol. 1 *Engines of Prosperity: Templates for the Information Age*
by Gerardo R. Ungson (University of Oregon, USA) &
John D. Trudel (The Trudel Group, USA)

CPSIA information can be obtained
at www.ICGtesting.com
Printed in the USA
JSHW021342270421
14030JS00001B/4

9 781800 610309